CW01648100

THE LETTERS OF SAINT JEROME

SAINT JEROME

AETERNA PRESS

COPYRIGHT © 2016 BY AETERNA PRESS.
ALL RIGHTS RESERVED.

PUBLISHED BY AETERNA PRESS.
COVER DESIGN BY AETERNA PRESS.

TRANSLATED BY THE HON. W. H. FREMANTLE, M.A., CANON OF CANTERBURY CATHEDRAL AND FELLOW AND TUTOR OF BALLIOL COLLEGE, OXFORD, WITH THE ASSISTANCE OF THE REV. G. LEWIS, M.A., OF BALLIOL COLLEGE, OXFORD, VICAR OF DODDERHILL NEAR DROITWICK, AND THE REV. W. G. MARTLEY, M.A., OF BALLIOL COLLEGE, OXFORD.

JEROME: THE PRINCIPAL WORKS OF ST. JEROME CREATOR(S): JEROME, ST. SCHAFF, PHILIP (1819–1893) (EDITOR) FREEMANTLE, M.A., THE HON. W.H. (TRANSLATOR) PRINT BASIS: NEW YORK: CHRISTIAN LITERATURE PUBLISHING CO., 1892.

ISBN-13: 978-1-78516-899-4

AVAILABLE AS AN E-BOOK:
WWW.AETERNAPRESS.COM

CONTENTS

LETTER I. TO INNOCENT

Not only the first of the letters but probably the earliest extant composition of Jerome (c. 370 a.d.). Innocent, to whom it is addressed, was one of the little band of enthusiasts whom Jerome gathered round him in Aquileia. He followed his friend to Syria, where he died in 374 a.d. (See Letter III., 3.)

1. You have frequently asked me, dearest Innocent, not to pass over in silence the marvellous event which has happened in our own day. I have declined the task from modesty and, as I now feel, with justice, believing myself to be incapable of it, at once because human language is inadequate to the divine praise, and because inactivity, acting like rust upon the intellect, has dried up any little power of expression that I have ever had. You in reply urge that in the things of God we must look not at the work which we are able to accomplish, but at the spirit in which it is undertaken, and that he can never be at a loss for words who has believed on the Word.

2. What, then, must I do? The task is beyond me, and yet I dare not decline it. I am a mere unskilled passenger, and I find myself placed in charge of a freighted ship. I have not so much as handled a rowboat on a lake, and now I have to trust myself to the noise and turmoil of the Euxine. I see the shores sinking beneath the horizon, "sky and sea on every side"; darkness lowers over the water, the clouds are black as night, the waves only are white with foam. You urge me to hoist the swelling sails, to loosen the sheets, and to take the helm. At last I obey your commands, and as charity can do all things, I will trust in the Holy Ghost to guide my course, and I shall console myself, whatever the event. For, if our ship is wafted by the surf into the wished-for haven, I shall be content to be told that the pilotage was poor. But, if through my unpolished diction we run aground amid the rough cross-currents of language, you may blame my lack of power, but you will at least recognize my good intentions.

3. To begin, then: Vercellae is a Ligurian town, situated not far from the base of the Alps, once important, but now sparsely peopled and fallen into decay. When the consular was holding his visitation there, a poor woman and her paramour were brought before him—the charge of adultery had been fastened upon them by the husband—and were both consigned to the penal horrors of a prison. Shortly after an attempt was made to elicit the truth by

torture, and when the blood-stained hook smote the young man's livid flesh and tore furrows in his side, the unhappy wretch sought to avoid prolonged pain by a speedy death. Falsely accusing his own passions, he involved another in the charge; and it appeared that he was of all men the most miserable, and that his execution was just inasmuch as he had left to an innocent woman no means of self-defence. But the woman, stronger in virtue if weaker in sex, though her frame was stretched upon the rack, and though her hands, stained with the filth of the prison, were tied behind her, looked up to heaven with her eyes, which alone the torturer had been unable to bind, and while the tears rolled down her face, said: "Thou art witness, Lord Jesus, to whom nothing is hid, who triest the reins and the heart. Thou art witness that it is not to save my life that I deny this charge. I refuse to lie because to lie is sin. And as for you, unhappy man, if you are bent on hastening your death, why must you destroy not one innocent person, but two? I also, myself, desire to die. I desire to put off this hated body, but not as an adulteress. I offer my neck; I welcome the shining sword without fear; yet I will take my innocence with me. He does not die who is slain while purposing so to live."

4. The consular, who had been feasting his eyes upon the bloody spectacle, now, like a wild beast, which after once tasting blood always thirsts for it, ordered the torture to be doubled, and cruelly gnashing his teeth, threatened the executioner with like punishment if he failed to extort from the weaker sex a confession which a man's strength had not been able to keep back.

5. Send help, Lord Jesus. For this one creature of Thine every species of torture is devised. She is bound by the hair to a stake, her whole body is fixed more firmly than ever on the rack; fire is brought and applied to her feet; her sides quiver beneath the executioner's probe; even her breasts do not escape. Still the woman remains unshaken; and, triumphing in spirit over the pain of the body, enjoys the happiness of a good conscience, round which the tortures rage in vain. The cruel judge rises, overcome with passion. She still prays to God. Her limbs are wrenched from their sockets; she only turns her eyes to heaven. Another confesses what is thought their common guilt. She, for the confessor's sake, denies the confession, and, in peril of her own life, clears one who is in peril of his.

6. Meantime she has but one thing to say: "Beat me, burn me, tear me, if you will; I have not done it. If you will not believe my words, a day will come when this charge shall be carefully sifted. I have One who will judge me." Wearied out at last, the torturer sighed in response to her groans; nor could he find a spot on which to inflict a fresh wound. His cruelty overcome, he shuddered to see the body he had torn. Immediately the consular cried, in a fit of

passion, "Why does it surprise you, bystanders, that a woman prefers torture to death? It takes two people, most assuredly, to commit adultery; and I think it more credible that a guilty woman should deny a sin than that an innocent young man should confess one."

7. Like sentence, accordingly, was passed on both, and the condemned pair were dragged to execution. The entire people poured out to see the sight; indeed, so closely were the gates thronged by the out-rushing crowd, that you might have fancied the city itself to be migrating. At the very first stroke of the sword the head of the hapless youth was cut off, and the headless trunk rolled over in its blood. Then came the woman's turn. She knelt down upon the ground, and the shining sword was lifted over her quivering neck. But though the headsman summoned all his strength into his bared arm, the moment it touched her flesh the fatal blade stopped short, and, lightly glancing over the skin, merely grazed it sufficiently to draw blood. The striker saw, with terror, his hand unnerved, and, amazed at his defeated skill and at his drooping sword, he whirled it aloft for another stroke. Again the blade fell forceless on the woman, sinking harmlessly on her neck, as though the steel feared to touch her. The enraged and panting officer, who had thrown open his cloak at the neck to give his full strength to the blow, shook to the ground the brooch which clasped the edges of his mantle, and not noticing this, began to poise his sword for a fresh stroke. "See," cried the woman, "a jewel has fallen from your shoulder. Pick up what you have earned by hard toil, that you may not lose it."

8. What, I ask, is the secret of such confidence as this? Death draws near, but it has no terrors for her. When smitten she exults, and the executioner turns pale. Her eyes see the brooch, they fail to see the sword. And, as if intrepidity in the presence of death were not enough, she confers a favor upon her cruel foe. And now the mysterious Power of the Trinity rendered even a third blow vain. The terrified soldier, no longer trusting the blade, proceeded to apply the point to her throat, in the idea that though it might not cut, the pressure of his hand might plunge it into her flesh. Marvel unheard of through all the ages! The sword bent back to the hilt, and in its defeat looked to its master, as if confessing its inability to slay.

9. Let me call to my aid the example of the three children, who, amid the cool, encircling fire, sang hymns, instead of weeping, and around whose turbans and holy hair the flames played harmlessly. Let me recall, too, the story of the blessed Daniel, in whose presence, though he was their natural prey, the lions crouched, with fawning tails and frightened mouths. Let Susannah also rise in the nobility of her faith before the thoughts of all; who, after she had been condemned by an unjust sentence, was saved through a youth inspired by

the Holy Ghost. In both cases the Lord's mercy was alike shewn; for while Susannah was set free by the judge, so as not to die by the sword, this woman, though condemned by the judge, was acquitted by the sword.

10. Now at length the populace rise in arms to defend the woman. Men and women of every age join in driving away the executioner, shouting round him in a surging crowd. Hardly a man dares trust his own eyes. The disquieting news reaches the city close at hand, and the entire force of constables is mustered. The officer who is responsible for the execution of criminals bursts from among his men, and

Staining his hoary hair with soiling dust,

exclaims: "What! citizens, do you mean to seek my life? Do you intend to make me a substitute for her? However much your minds are set on mercy, and however much you wish to save a condemned woman, yet assuredly I—I who am innocent—ought not to perish." His tearful appeal tells upon the crowd, they are all benumbed by the influence of sorrow, and an extraordinary change of feeling is manifested. Before it had seemed a duty to plead for the woman's life, now it seemed a duty to allow her to be executed.

11. Accordingly a new sword is fetched, a new headsman appointed. The victim takes her place, once more strengthened only with the favor of Christ. The first blow makes her quiver, beneath the second she sways to and fro, by the third she falls wounded to the ground. Oh, majesty of the divine power highly to be extolled! She who previously had received four strokes without injury, now, a few moments later, seems to die that an innocent man may not perish in her stead.

12. Those of the clergy whose duty it is to wrap the blood-stained corpse in a winding-sheet, dig out the earth and, heaping together stones, form the customary tomb. The sunset comes on quickly, and by God's mercy the night of nature arrives more swiftly than is its wont. Suddenly the woman's bosom heaves, her eyes seek the light, her body is quickened into new life. A moment after she sighs, she looks round, she gets up and speaks. At last she is able to cry: "The Lord is on my side; I will not fear. What can man do unto me?"

13. Meantime an aged woman, supported out of the funds of the church, gave back her spirit to heaven from which it came. It seemed as if the course of events had been thus purposely ordered, for her body took the place of the other beneath the mound. In the gray dawn the devil comes on the scene in the form of a constable, asks for the corpse of her who had been slain, and desires to have her grave pointed out to him. Surprised that she could have died, he fancies her to be still alive. The clergy show him the fresh turf, and meet his demands by pointing to the earth lately heaped up, taunting him with

such words as these: "Yes, of course, tear up the bones which have been buried! Declare war anew against the tomb, and if even that does not satisfy you, pluck her limb from limb for birds and beasts to mangle! Mere dying is too good for one whom it took seven strokes to kill."

14. Before such opprobrious words the executioner retires in confusion, while the woman is secretly revived at home. Then, lest the frequency of the doctor's visits to the church might give occasion for suspicion, they cut her hair short and send her in the company of some virgins to a sequestered country house. There she changes her dress for that of a man, and scars form over her wounds. Yet even after the great miracles worked on her behalf, the laws still rage against her. So true is it that, where there is most law, there, there is also most injustice.

15. But now see whither the progress of my story has brought me; we come upon the name of our friend Evagrius. So great have his exertions been in the cause of Christ that, were I to suppose it possible adequately to describe them, I should only show my own folly; and were I minded deliberately to pass them by, I still could not prevent my voice from breaking out into cries of joy. Who can fittingly praise the vigilance which enabled him to bury, if I may so say, before his death Auxentius of Milan, that curse brooding over the church? Or who can sufficiently extol the discretion with which he rescued the Roman bishop from the toils of the net in which he was fairly entangled, and showed him the means at once of overcoming his opponents and of sparing them in their discomfiture? But

Such topics I must leave to other bards,
Shut out by envious straits of time and space.

I am satisfied now to record the conclusion of my tale. Evagrius seeks a special audience of the Emperor; importunes him with his entreaties, wins his favor by his services, and finally gains his cause through his earnestness. The Emperor restored to liberty the woman whom God had restored to life.

LETTER II. TO THEODOSIUS AND THE REST OF THE ANCHORITES

Written from Antioch, 374 a.d., while Jerome was still in doubt as to his future course. Theodosius appears to have been the head of the solitaries in the Syrian Desert.

How I long to be a member of your company, and with uplifting of all my powers to embrace your admirable community! Though, indeed, these poor eyes are not worthy to look upon it. Oh! that I could behold the desert, lovelier to me than any city! Oh! that I could see those lonely spots made into a paradise by the saints that throng them! But since my sins prevent me from thrusting into your blessed company a head laden with every transgression, I adjure you (and I know that you can do it) by your prayers to deliver me from the darkness of this world. I spoke of this when I was with you, and now in writing to you I repeat anew the same request; for all the energy of my mind is devoted to this one object. It rests with you to give effect to my resolve. I have the will but not the power; this last can only come in answer to your prayers. For my part, I am like a sick sheep astray from the flock. Unless the good Shepherd shall place me on his shoulders and carry me back to the fold, my steps will totter, and in the very effort of rising I shall find my feet give way. I am the prodigal son who although I have squandered all the portion entrusted to me by my father, have not yet bowed the knee in submission to him; not yet have I commenced to put away from me the allurements of my former excesses. And because it is only a little while since I have begun not so much to abandon my vices as to desire to abandon them, the devil now ensnares me in new toils, he puts new stumbling-blocks in my path, he encompasses me on every side.

The seas around, and all around the main.

I find myself in mid-ocean, unwilling to retreat and unable to advance. It only remains that your prayers should win for me the gale of the Holy Spirit to waft me to the haven upon the desired shore.

LETTER III. TO RUFINUS THE MONK

Written from Antioch, 374 a.d., to Rufinus in Egypt. Jerome narrates his travels and the events which have taken place since his arrival in Syria, particularly the deaths of Innocent and Hylas (S:3). He also describes the life of Bonosus, who was now a hermit on an island in the Adriatic (S:4). The main object of the letter is to induce Rufinus to come to Syria.

1. That God gives more than we ask Him for, and that He often grants us things which "eye hath not seen nor ear heard, neither have they entered into the heart of man," I knew indeed before from the mystic declaration of the sacred volumes; but now, dearest Rufinus, I have had proof of it in my own case. For I who fancied it too bold a wish to be allowed by an exchange of letters to counterfeit to myself your presence in the flesh, hear that you are penetrating the remotest parts of Egypt, visiting the monks and going round God's family upon earth. Oh, if only the Lord Jesus Christ would suddenly

transport me to you as Philip was transported to the eunuch, and Habakkuk to Daniel, with what a close embrace would I clasp your neck, how fondly would I press kisses upon that mouth which has so often joined with me of old in error or in wisdom. But as I am unworthy (not that you should so come to me but) that I should so come to you, and because my poor body, weak even when well, has been shattered by frequent illnesses; I send this letter to meet you instead of coming myself, in the hope that it may bring you hither to me caught in the meshes of love's net.

2. My first joy at such unexpected good tidings was due to our brother, Heliodorus. I desired to be sure of it, but did not dare to feel sure, especially as he told me that he had only heard it from some one else, and as the strangeness of the news impaired the credit of the story. Once more my wishes hovered in uncertainty and my mind wavered, till an Alexandrian monk who had some time previously been sent over by the dutiful zeal of the people to the Egyptian confessors (in will already martyrs), impelled me by his presence to believe the tidings. Even then, I must admit I still hesitated. For on the one hand he knew nothing either of your name or country: yet on the other what he said seemed likely to be true, agreeing as it did with the hint which had already reached me. At last the truth broke upon me in all its fulness, for a constant stream of persons passing through brought the report: "Rufinus is at Nitria, and has reached the abode of the blessed Macarius." At this point I cast away all that restrained my belief, and then first really grieved to find myself ill. Had it not been that my wasted and enfeebled frame fettered my movements, neither the summer heat nor the dangerous voyage should have had power to retard the rapid steps of affection. Believe me, brother, I look forward to seeing you more than the storm-tossed mariner looks for his haven, more than the thirsty fields long for the showers, more than the anxious mother sitting on the curving shore expects her son.

3. After that sudden whirlwind dragged me from your side, severing with its impious wrench the bonds of affection in which we were knit together,

The dark blue raincloud lowered o'er my head:
On all sides were the seas, on all the sky.

I wandered about, uncertain where to go. Thrace, Pontus, Bithynia, the whole of Galatia and Cappadocia, Cilicia also with its burning heat, one after another shattered my energies. At last Syria presented itself to me as a most secure harbor to a shipwrecked man. Here, after undergoing every possible kind of sickness, I lost one of my two eyes; for Innocent, the half of my soul, was taken away from me by a sudden attack of fever. The one eye which I now enjoy, and which is all in all to me, is our Evagrius, upon whom I with my constant infirmities have come as an additional burden. We had with us also Hylas, the servant of the holy Melanium, who by his stainless conduct had wiped out the taint of his previous servitude. His death opened afresh the wound which had not yet healed. But as the apostle's words forbid us to mourn for those who sleep, and as my excess of grief has been tempered by the joyful news that has since come to me, I recount this last, that, if you have not heard it, you may learn it; and that, if you know it already, you may rejoice over it with me.

4. Bonosus, your friend, or, to speak more truly, mine as well as yours, is now climbing the ladder foreshown in Jacob's dream. He is bearing his cross, neither taking thought for the morrow nor looking back at what he has left. He is sowing in tears that he may reap in joy. As Moses in a type so he in reality is lifting up the serpent in the wilderness. This is a true story, and it may well put to shame the lying marvels described by Greek and Roman pens. For here you have a youth educated with us in the refining accomplishments of the world, with abundance of wealth, and in rank inferior to none of his associates; yet he forsakes his mother, his sisters, and his dearly loved brother, and settles like a new tiller of Eden on a dangerous island, with the sea roaring round its reefs; while its rough crags, bare rocks, and desolate aspect make it more terrible still. No peasant or monk is to be found there. Even the little Onesimus you know of, in whose kisses he used to rejoice as in those of a brother, in this tremendous solitude no longer remains at his side. Alone upon the island—or rather not alone, for Christ is with him—he sees the glory of God, which even the apostles saw not save in the desert. He beholds, it is true, no embattled towns, but he has enrolled his name in the new city. Garments of sackcloth disfigure his limbs, yet so clad he will be the sooner caught up to meet Christ in the clouds. No watercourse pleasant to the view supplies his wants, but from the Lord's side he drinks the water of life. Place all this before your eyes, dear friend, and with all the faculties of your mind picture to yourself the scene. When you realize the effort of the fighter then you will be able to praise his victory. Round the entire island roars the frenzied sea, while the beetling crags along its winding shores resound as the billows beat against them. No grass makes the ground green; there are no shady copses and no fertile fields. Precipitous cliffs surround his dreadful abode as if it were a prison. But he, careless, fearless, and armed from head to foot with the apostle's armor, now listens to God by reading the Scriptures, now speaks to God as he prays to the Lord; and it may be that, while he lingers in the island, he sees some vision such as that once seen by John.

5. What snares, think you, is the devil now weaving? What stratagems is he preparing? Perchance, mindful of his old trick, he will try to tempt Bonosus with hunger. But he has been answered already: "Man shall not live by bread alone." Perchance he will lay before him wealth and fame. But it shall be said to him: "They that desire to be rich fall into a trap and temptations," and "For me all glorying is in Christ." He will come, it may be, when the limbs are weary with fasting, and rack them with the pangs of disease; but the cry of the apostle will repel him: "When I am weak, then am I strong," and "My strength is made perfect in weakness." He will hold out threats of death; but the reply will be: "I desire to depart and to be with Christ." He will brandish his fiery darts, but they will be received on the shield of faith. In a word, Satan will assail him, but Christ will defend. Thanks be to Thee, Lord Jesus, that in Thy day I have one able to pray to Thee for me. To Thee all hearts are open, Thou searchest the secrets of the heart, Thou seest the prophet shut up in the fish's belly in the midst of the sea. Thou knowest then how he and I grew up together from tender infancy to vigorous manhood, how we were fostered in the bosoms of the same nurses, and carried in the arms of the same bearers; and how after studying together at Rome we lodged in the same house and shared the same food by the half savage banks of the Rhine. Thou knowest, too, that it was I who first began to seek to serve Thee. Remember, I beseech Thee, that this warrior of Thine was once a raw recruit with me. I have before me the declaration of Thy majesty: "Whosoever shall teach and not do shall be called least in the kingdom of heaven." May he enjoy the crown of virtue, and in return for his daily martyrdoms may he follow the Lamb robed in white raiment! For "in my Father's house are many mansions," and "one star differeth from another star in glory." Give me strength to raise my head to a level with the saints' heels! I willed, but he performed. Do Thou therefore pardon me that I failed to keep my resolve, and reward him with the guerdon of his deserts.

I may perhaps have been tedious, and have said more than the short compass of a letter usually allows; but this, I find, is always the case with me when I have to say anything in praise of our dear Bonosus.

6. However, to return to the point from which I set out, I beseech you do not let me pass wholly out of sight and out of mind. A friend is long sought, hardly found, and with difficulty kept. Let those who will, allow gold to dazzle them and be borne along in splendor, their very baggage glittering with gold and silver. Love is not to be purchased, and affection has no price. The friendship which can cease has never been real. Farewell in Christ.

LETTER IV. TO FLORENTIUS

Sent to Florentius along with the preceding letter, which Jerome requests him to deliver to Rufinus. This Florentius was a rich Italian who had retired to Jerusalem to pursue the monastic life. Jerome subsequently speaks of him as "a distinguished monk so pitiful to the needy that he was generally known as the father of the poor." (Chron. ad a.d. 381.)

1. How much your name and sanctity are on the lips of the most different peoples you may gather from the fact that I commence to love you before I know you. For as, according to the apostle, "Some men's sins are evident going before unto judgment," so contrariwise the report of your charity is so widespread that it is considered not so much praiseworthy to love you as criminal to refuse to do so. I pass over the countless instances in which you have supported Christ, fed, clothed, and visited Him. The aid you rendered to our brother Heliodorus in his need may well loose the utterance of the dumb. With what gratitude, with what commendation, does he speak of the kindness with which you smoothed a pilgrim's path. I am, it is true, the most sluggish of men, consumed by an unendurable sickness; yet keen affection and desire have winged my feet, and I have come forward to salute and embrace you. I wish you every good thing, and pray that the Lord may establish our nascent friendship.

2. Our brother, Rufinus, is said to have come from Egypt to Jerusalem with the devout lady, Melanium. He is inseparably bound to me in brotherly love; and I beg you to oblige me by delivering to him the annexed letter. You must not, however, judge of me by the virtues that you find in him. For in him you will see the clearest tokens of holiness, whilst I am but dust and vile dirt, and even now, while still living, nothing but ashes. It is enough for me if my weak eyes can bear the brightness of his excellence. He has but now washed himself and is clean, yea, is made white as snow; whilst I, stained with every sin, wait day and night with trembling to pay the uttermost farthing. But since "the Lord looseth the prisoners," and resteth upon him who is of a contrite spirit, and that trembleth at His words, perchance he may say even to me who lie in the grave of sin: "Jerome, come forth."

The reverend presbyter, Evagrius, warmly salutes you. We both with united respect salute the brother, Martinianus. I desire much to see him, but I am impeded by the chain of sickness. Farewell in Christ.

LETTER V. TO FLORENTIUS

Written a few months after the preceding (about the end of 374 a.d.) from the Syrian Desert. After dilating on his friendship for Florentius, and making a passing allusion to Rufinus, Jerome mentions certain books, copies of which he desires to be sent to him. He also speaks of a runaway slave about whom Florentius had written to him.

1. Your letter, dear friend, finds me dwelling in that quarter of the desert which is nearest to Syria and the Saracens. And the reading of it rekindles in my mind so keen a desire to set out for Jerusalem that I am almost ready to violate my monastic vow in order to gratify my affection. Wishing to do the best I can, as I cannot come in person I send you a letter instead; and thus, though absent in the body, I come to you in love and in spirit. For my earnest prayer is that our infant friendship, firmly cemented as it is in Christ, may never be rent asunder by time or distance. We ought rather to strengthen the bond by an interchange of letters. Let these pass between us, meet each other on the way, and converse with us. Affection will not lose much if it keeps up an intercourse of this kind.

2. You write that our brother, Rufinus, has not yet come to you. Even if he does come it will do little to satisfy my longing, for I shall not now be able to see him. He is too far away to come hither, and the conditions of the lonely life that I have adopted forbid me to go to him. For I am no longer free to follow my own wishes. I entreat you, therefore, to ask him to allow you to have the commentaries of the reverend Rhetitius, bishop of Augustodunum, copied, in which he has so eloquently explained the Song of Songs. A countryman of the aforesaid brother Rufinus, the old man Paul, writes that Rufinus has his copy of Tertullian, and urgently requests that this may be returned. Next I have to ask you to get written on paper by a copyist certain books which the subjoined list will show you that I do not possess. I beg also that you will send me the explanation of the Psalms of David, and the copious work on Synods of the reverend Hilary, which I copied for him at Treves with my own hand. Such books, you know, must be the food of the Christian soul if it is to meditate in the law of the Lord day and night.

Others you welcome beneath your roof, you cherish and comfort, you help out of your own purse; but so far as I am concerned, you have given me everything when once you have granted my request. And since, through the Lord's bounty, I am rich in volumes of the sacred library, you may command me in turn. I will send you what you please; and do not suppose that an order from you will give me trouble. I have pupils devoted to the art of copying. Nor do I merely promise a favor because I am asking one. Our brother, Heliodorus, tells me that there are many parts of the Scriptures which you seek and cannot find. But even if you have them all, affection is sure to assert its rights and to seek for itself more than it already has.

3. As regards the present master of your slave—of whom you have done me the honor to write—I have no doubt but that he is his kidnapper. While I was still at Antioch the presbyter, Evagrius, often reproved him in my presence. To whom he made this answer: "I have nothing to fear." He declares that his master has dismissed him. If you both want him, he is here; send him whither you will. I think I am not wrong in refusing to allow a runaway to stray farther. Here in the wilderness I cannot myself execute your orders; and therefore I have asked my dear friend Evagrius to push the affair vigorously, both for your sake and for mine. I desire your welfare in Christ.

LETTER VI. TO JULIAN, A DEACON OF ANTIOCH

This letter, written in 374 a.d., is chiefly interesting for its mention of Jerome's sister. It would seem that she had fallen into sin and had been restored to a life of virtue by the deacon, Julian. Jerome speaks of her again in the next letter (S:4).

It is an old saying, "Liars are disbelieved even when they speak the truth." And from the way in which you reproach me for not having written, I perceive that this has been my lot with you. Shall I say, "I wrote often, but the bearers of my letters were negligent"? You will reply, "Your excuse is the old one of all who fail to write." Shall I say, "I could not find any one to take my letters"? You will say that numbers of persons have gone from my part of the world to yours. Shall I contend that I have actually given them letters? They not having delivered them, will deny that they have received them. Moreover, so great a distance separates us that it will be hard to come at the truth. What shall I do then? Though really not to blame, I ask your forgiveness, for I think it better to fall back and make overtures for peace than to keep my ground and offer battle. The truth is that constant sickness of body and vexation of mind have so weakened me that with death so close at hand I have not been as collected as usual. And lest you should account this plea a false one, now that I have stated my case, I shall, like a pleader, call witnesses to prove it. Our reverend brother, Heliodorus, has been here; but in spite of his wish to dwell in the desert with me, he has been frightened away by my crimes. But my present wordiness will atone for my past remissness; for, as Horace says in his satire:

All singers have one fault among their friends:
They never sing when asked, unasked they never cease.

Henceforth I shall overwhelm you with such bundles of letters that you will take the opposite line and beg me not to write.

I rejoice that my sister—to you a daughter in Christ—remains steadfast in her purpose, a piece of news which I owe in the first instance to you. For here where I now am I am ignorant not only as to what goes on in my native land, but even as to its continued existence. Even though the Iberian viper shall rend me with his baneful fangs, I will not fear men's judgment, seeing that I shall have God to judge me. As one puts it:

Shatter the world to fragments if you will:
'Twill fall upon a head which knows not fear.

Bear in mind, then, I pray you, the apostle's precept that we should make our work abiding; prepare for yourself a reward from the Lord in my sister's salvation; and by frequent letters increase my joy in that glory in Christ which we share together.

LETTER VII. TO CHROMATIUS, JOVINUS, AND EUSEBIUS

This letter (written like the preceding in 374 a.d.) is addressed by Jerome to three of his former companions in the religious life. It commends Bonosus (S:3), asks guidance for the writer's sister (S:4), and attacks the conduct of Lupicinus, Bishop of Stridon (S:5).

1. Those whom mutual affection has joined together, a written page ought not to sunder. I must not, therefore, distribute my words some to one and some to another. For so strong is the love that binds you together that affection unites all three of you in a bond no less close than that which naturally connects two of your number. Indeed, if the conditions of writing would only admit of it, I should amalgamate your names and express them under a single symbol. The very letter which I have received from you challenges me in each of you to see all three, and in all three to recognize each. When the reverend Evagrius transmitted it to me in the corner of the desert which stretches between the Syrians and the Saracens, my joy was intense. It wholly surpassed the rejoicings felt at Rome when the defeat of Cannae was retrieved, and Marcellus at Nola cut to pieces the forces of Hannibal. Evagrius frequently comes to see me, and cherishes me in Christ as his own bowels. Yet as he is separated from me by a long distance, his departure has generally left me as much regret as his arrival has brought me joy.

2. I converse with your letter, I embrace it, it talks to me; it alone of those here speaks Latin. For hereabout you must either learn a barbarous jargon or else hold your tongue. As often as the lines—traced in a well-known hand—bring back to me the faces which I hold so dear, either I am no longer here, or else you are here with me. If you will credit the sincerity of affection, I seem to see you all as I write this.

Now at the outset I should like to ask you one petulant question. Why is it that, when we are separated by so great an interval of land and sea, you have sent me so short a letter? Is it that I have deserved no better treatment, not having first written to you? I cannot believe that paper can have failed you while Egypt continues to supply its wares. Even if a Ptolemy had closed the seas, King Attalus would still have sent you parchments from Pergamum, and so by his skins you could have made up for the want of paper. The very name parchment is derived from a historical incident of the kind which occurred generations ago. What then? Am I to suppose the messenger to have been in haste? No matter how long a letter may be, it can be written in the course of a night. Or had you some business to attend to which prevented you from writing? No claim is prior to that of affection. Two suppositions remain, either that you felt disinclined to write or else that I did not deserve a letter. Of the two I prefer to charge you with sloth than to condemn myself as undeserving. For it is easier to mend neglect than to quicken love.

3. You tell me that Bonosus, like a true son of the Fish, has taken to the water. As for me who am still foul with my old stains, like the basilisk and the scorpion I haunt the dry places. Bonosus has his heel already on the serpent's head, whilst I am still as food to the same serpent which by divine appointment devours the earth. He can scale already that ladder of which the psalms of degrees are a type; whilst I, still weeping on its first step, hardly know whether I shall ever be able to say: "I will lift up mine eyes unto the hills, from whence cometh my help." Amid the threatening billows of the world he is sitting in the safe shelter of his island, that is, of the church's pale, and it may be that even now, like John, he is being called to eat God's book; whilst I, still lying in the sepulchre of my sins and bound with the chains of my iniquities, wait for the Lord's command in the Gospel: "Jerome, come forth." But Bonosus has done more than this. Like the prophet he has carried his girdle across the Euphrates (for all the devil's strength is in the loins), and has hidden it there in a hole of the rock. Then, afterwards finding it rent, he has sung: "O Lord, thou hast possessed my reins. Thou hast broken my bonds in sunder. I will offer to thee the sacrifice of thanksgiving." But as for me, Nebuchadnezzar has brought me in chains to Babylon, to the babel that is of a distracted mind.

There he has laid upon me the yoke of captivity; there inserting in my nostrils a ring of iron, he has commanded me to sing one of the songs of Zion. To whom I have said, "The Lord looseth the prisoners; the Lord openeth the eyes of the blind." To complete my contrast in a single sentence, whilst I pray for mercy Bonosus looks for a crown.

4. My sister's conversion is the fruit of the efforts of the saintly Julian. He has planted, it is for you to water, and the Lord will give the increase. Jesus Christ has given her to me to console me for the wound which the devil has inflicted on her. He has restored her from death to life. But in the words of the pagan poet, for her

There is no safety that I do not fear.

You know yourselves how slippery is the path of youth—a path on which I have myself fallen, and which you are now traversing not without fear. She, as she enters upon it, must have the advice and the encouragement of all, she must be aided by frequent letters from you, my reverend brothers. And—for "charity endureth all things,"—I beg you to get from Pope Valerian a letter to confirm her resolution. A girl's courage, as you know, is strengthened when she realizes that persons in high place are interested in her.

5. The fact is that my native land is a prey to barbarism, that in it men's only God is their belly, that they live only for the present, and that the richer a man is the holier he is held to be. Moreover, to use a well-worn proverb, the dish has a cover worthy of it; for Lupicinus is their priest. Like lips like lettuce, as the saying goes—the only one, as Lucilius tells us, at which Crassus ever laughed—the reference being to a donkey eating thistles. What I mean is that an unstable pilot steers a leaking ship, and that the blind is leading the blind straight to the pit. The ruler is like the ruled.

6. I salute your mother and mine with the respect which, as you know, I feel towards her. Associated with you as she is in a holy life, she has the start of you, her holy children, in that she is your mother. Her womb may thus be truly called golden. With her I salute your sisters, who ought all to be welcomed wherever they go, for they have triumphed over their sex and the world, and await the Bridegroom's coming, their lamps replenished with oil. O happy the house which is a home of a widowed Anna, of virgins that are prophetesses, and of twin Samuels bred in the Temple! Fortunate the roof which shelters the martyr-mother of the Maccabees, with her sons around her, each and all wearing the martyr's crown! For although you confess Christ every day by keeping His commandments, yet to this private glory you have added the public one of an open confession; for it was through you that the poison of the Arian heresy was formerly banished from your city.

You are surprised perhaps at my thus making a fresh beginning quite at the close of my letter. But what am I to do? I cannot refuse expression to my feelings. The brief limits of a letter compel me to be silent; my affection for you urges me to speak. I write in haste, my language is confused and ill-arranged; but love knows nothing of order.

LETTER VIII. TO NICEAS, SUB-DEACON OF AQUILEIA

Niceas, the sub-deacon, had accompanied Jerome to the East but had now returned home. In after-years he became bishop of Aquileia in succession to Chromatius. The date of the letter is 374 a.d.

The comic poet Turpilius says of the exchange of letters that it alone makes the absent present. The remark, though occurring in a work of fiction, is not untrue. For what more real presence—if I may so speak—can there be between absent friends than speaking to those whom they love in letters, and in letters hearing their reply? Even those Italian savages, the Cascans of Ennius, who—as Cicero tells us in his books on rhetoric—hunted their food like beasts of prey, were wont, before paper and parchment came into use, to exchange letters written on tablets of wood roughly planed, or on strips of bark torn from the trees. For this reason men called letter-carriers tablet-bearers, and letter-writers bark-users, because they used the bark of trees. How much more then are we, who live in a civilized age, bound not to omit a social duty performed by men who lived in a state of gross savagery, and were in some respects entirely ignorant of the refinements of life. The saintly Chromatius, look you, and the reverend Eusebius, brothers as much by compatibility of disposition as by the ties of nature, have challenged me to diligence by the letters which they have showered upon me. You, however, who have but just left me, have not merely unknit our new-made friendship; you have torn it asunder—a process which Laelius, in Cicero's treatise, wisely forbids. Can it be that the East is so hateful to you that you dread the thought of even your letters coming hither? Wake up, wake up, arouse yourself from sleep, give to affection at least one sheet of paper. Amid the pleasures of life at home sometimes heave a sigh over the journeys which we have made together. If you love me, write in answer to my prayer. If you are angry with me, though angry still write. I find my longing soul much comforted when I receive a letter from a friend, even though that friend be out of temper with me.

LETTER IX. TO CHRYSOGONUS, A MONK OF AQUILEIA

A bantering letter to an indifferent correspondent. Of the same date as the preceding.

Heliodorus, who is so dear to us both, and who loves you with an affection no less deep than my own, may have given you a faithful account of my feelings towards you; how your name is always on my lips, and how in every conversation which I have with him I begin by recalling my pleasant intercourse with you, and go on to marvel at your lowliness, to extol your virtue, and to proclaim your holy love.

Lynxes, they say, when they look behind them, forget what they have just seen, and lose all thought of what their eyes have ceased to behold. And so it seems to be with you. For so entirely have you forgotten our joint attachment that you have not merely blurred but erased the writing of that epistle which, as the apostle tells us, is written in the hearts of Christians. The creatures that I have mentioned lurk on branches of leafy trees and pounce on fleet roes or frightened stags. In vain their victims fly, for they carry their tormentors with them, and these rend their flesh as they run. Lynxes, however, only hunt when an empty belly makes their mouths dry. When they have satisfied their thirst for blood, and have filled their stomachs with food, satiety induces forgetfulness, and they bestow no thought on future prey till hunger recalls them to a sense of their need.

Now in your case it cannot be that you have already had enough of me. Why then do you bring to a premature close a friendship which is but just begun? Why do you let slip what you have hardly as yet fully grasped? But as such remissness as yours is never at a loss for an excuse, you will perhaps declare that you had nothing to write. Had this been so, you should still have written to inform me of the fact.

LETTER X. TO PAUL, AN OLD MAN OF CONCORDIA

Jerome writes to Paul of Concordia, a centenarian (S:2), and the owner of a good theological library (S:3), to lend him some commentaries. In return he sends him his life (newly written) of Paul the hermit. The date of the letter is 374 a.d.

1. The shortness of man's life is the punishment for man's sin; and the fact that even on the very threshold of the light death constantly overtakes the newborn child proves that the times are continually sinking into deeper depravity.

For when the first tiller of paradise had been entangled by the serpent in his snaky coils, and had been forced in consequence to migrate earthwards, although his deathless state was changed for a mortal one, yet the sentence of man's curse was put off for nine hundred years, or even more, a period so long that it may be called a second immortality. Afterwards sin gradually grew more and more virulent, till the ungodliness of the giants brought in its train the shipwreck of the whole world. Then when the world had been cleansed by the baptism—if I may so call it—of the deluge, human life was contracted to a short span. Yet even this we have almost altogether wasted, so continually do our iniquities fight against the divine purposes. For how few there are, either who go beyond their hundredth year, or who, going beyond it, do not regret that they have done so; according to that which the Scripture witnesses in the book of Psalms: "the days of our years are threescore years and ten; and if by reason of strength they be fourscore years, yet is their strength labor and sorrow."

2. Why, say you, these opening reflections so remote and so far fetched that one might use against them the Horatian witticism:

Back to the eggs which Leda laid for Zeus,
The bard is fain to trace the war of Troy?

Simply that I may describe in fitting terms your great age and hoary head as white as Christ's. For see, the hundredth circling year is already passing over you, and yet, always keeping the commandments of the Lord, amid the circumstances of your present life you think over the blessedness of that which is to come. Your eyes are bright and keen, your steps steady, your hearing good, your teeth are white, your voice musical, your flesh firm and full of sap; your ruddy cheeks belie your white hairs, your strength is not that of your age. Advancing years have not, as we too often see them do, impaired the tenacity of your memory; the coldness of your blood has not blunted an intellect at once warm and wary. Your face is not wrinkled nor your brow furrowed. Lastly, no tremors palsy your hand or cause it to travel in crooked pathways over the wax on which you write. The Lord shows us in you the bloom of the resurrection that is to be ours; so that whereas in others who die by inches whilst yet living, we recognize the results of sin, in your case we ascribe it to righteousness that you still simulate youth at an age to which it is foreign. And although we see the like haleness of body in many even of those who are sinners, in their case it is a grant of the devil to lead them into sin, whilst in yours it is a gift of God to make you rejoice.

3. Tully in his brilliant speech on behalf of Flaccus describes the learning of the Greeks as "innate frivolity and accomplished vanity."

Certainly their ablest literary men used to receive money for pronouncing eulogies upon their kings or princes. Following their example, I set a price upon my praise. Nor must you suppose my demand a small one. You are asked to give me the pearl of the Gospel, "the words of the Lord," "pure words, even as the silver which from the earth is tried, and purified seven times in the fire," I mean the commentaries of Fortunatian and—for its account of the persecutors—the History of Aurelius Victor, and with these the Letters of Novatian; so that, learning the poison set forth by this schismatic, we may the more gladly drink of the antidote supplied by the holy martyr Cyprian. In the mean time I have sent to you, that is to say, to Paul the aged, a Paul that is older still. I have taken great pains to bring my language down to the level of the simpler sort. But, somehow or other, though you fill it with water, the jar retains the odor which it acquired when first used. If my little gift should please you, I have others also in store which (if the Holy Spirit shall breathe favorably), shall sail across the sea to you with all kinds of eastern merchandise.

LETTER XI. TO THE VIRGINS OF AEMONA

AEmona was a Roman colony not far from Stridon, Jerome's birthplace. The virgins to whom the note is addressed had omitted to answer his letters, and he now writes to upbraid them for their remissness. The date of the letter is 374 a.d.

This scanty sheet of paper shows in what a wilderness I live, and because of it I have to say much in few words. For, desirous though I am to speak to you more fully, this miserable scrap compels me to leave much unsaid. Still ingenuity makes up for lack of means, and by writing small I can say a great deal. Observe, I beseech you, how I love you, even in the midst of my difficulties, since even the want of materials does not stop me from writing to you.

Pardon, I beseech you, an aggrieved man: if I speak in tears and in anger it is because I have been injured. For in return for my regular letters you have not sent me a single syllable. Light, I know, has no communion with darkness, and God's handmaidens no fellowship with a sinner, yet a harlot was allowed to wash the Lord's feet with her tears, and dogs are permitted to eat of their masters' crumbs. It was the Saviour's mission to call sinners and not the righteous; for, as He said Himself, "they that be whole need not a physician." He wills the repentance of a sinner rather than his death, and carries home the poor stray sheep on His own shoulders. So, too, when the prodigal son returns, his father receives him with joy. Nay more, the apostle says: "Judge nothing before the time." For "who art thou that judgest another man's servant? To his own master he standeth or falleth." And "let him that standeth take heed lest he fall." "Bear ye one another's burdens."

Dear sisters, man's envy judges in one way, Christ in another; and the whisper of a corner is not the same as the sentence of His tribunal. Many ways seem right to men which are afterwards found to be wrong. And a treasure is often stowed in earthen vessels. Peter thrice denied his Lord, yet his bitter tears restored him to his place. "To whom much is forgiven, the same loveth much." No word is said of the flock as a whole, yet the angels joy in heaven over the safety of one sick ewe. And if any one demurs to this reasoning, the Lord Himself has said: "Friend, is thine eye evil because I am good?"

LETTER XII. TO ANTONY, MONK

The subject of this letter is similar to that of the preceding. Of Antony nothing is known except that some mss. describe him as "of AEmona." The date of the letter is 374 a.d.

While the disciples were disputing concerning precedence our Lord, the teacher of humility, took a little child and said: "Except ye be converted and become as little children ye cannot enter the kingdom of heaven." And lest He should seem to preach more than he practised, He fulfilled His own precept in His life. For He washed His disciples' feet, he received the traitor with a kiss, He conversed with the woman of Samaria, He spoke of the kingdom of heaven with Mary at His feet, and when He rose again from the dead He showed Himself first to some poor women. Pride is opposed to humility, and through it Satan lost his eminence as an archangel. The Jewish people perished in their pride, for while they claimed the chief seats and salutations in the market place, they were superseded by the Gentiles, who had before been counted as "a drop of a bucket." Two poor fishermen, Peter and James, were sent to confute the sophists and the wise men of the world. As the Scripture says: "God resisteth the proud and giveth grace to the humble." Think, brother, what a sin it must be which has God for its opponent. In the Gospel the Pharisee is rejected because of his pride, and the publican is accepted because of his humility.

Now, unless I am mistaken, I have already sent you ten letters, affectionate and earnest, whilst you have not deigned to give me even a single line. The Lord speaks to His servants, but you, my brother servant, refuse to speak to me. Believe me, if reserve did not check my pen, I could show my annoyance in such invective that you would have to reply—even though it might be in anger. But since anger is human, and a Christian must not act injuriously, I fall back once more on entreaty, and beg you to love one who loves you, and to write to him as a servant should to his fellow-servant. Farewell in the Lord.

LETTER XIII. TO CASTORINA, HIS MATERNAL AUNT

An interesting letter, as throwing some light on Jerome's family relations. Castorina, his maternal aunt, had, for some reason, become estranged from him, and he now writes to her to effect a reconciliation. Whether he succeeded in doing so, we do not know. The date of the letter is 374 a.d.

The apostle and evangelist John rightly says, in his first epistle, that "whosoever hateth his brother is a murderer." For, since murder often springs from hate, the hater, even though he has not yet slain his victim, is at heart a murderer. Why, you ask, do I begin in this style? Simply that you and I may both lay aside past ill feeling and cleanse our hearts to be a habitation for God. "Be ye angry," David says, "and sin not," or, as the apostle more fully expresses it, "let not the sun go down upon your wrath." What then shall we do in the day of judgment, upon whose wrath the sun has gone down not one day but many years? The Lord says in the Gospel: "If thou bring thy gift to the altar, and there rememberest that thy brother hath aught against thee; leave there thy gift before the altar, and go thy way; first be reconciled to thy brother, and then come and offer thy gift." Woe to me, wretch that I am; woe, I had almost said, to you also. This long time past we have either offered no gift at the altar or have offered it whilst cherishing anger "without a cause." How have we been able in our daily prayers to say "Forgive us our debts as we forgive our debtors," whilst our feelings have been at variance with our words, and our petition inconsistent with our conduct? Therefore I renew the prayer which I made a year ago in a previous letter, that the Lord's legacy of peace may be indeed ours, and that my desires and your feelings may find favor in His sight. Soon we shall stand before His judgment seat to receive the reward of harmony restored or to pay the penalty for harmony broken. In case you shall prove unwilling—I hope that it may not be so—to accept my advances, I for my part shall be free. For this letter, when it is read, will insure my acquittal.

LETTER XIV. TO HELIODORUS, MONK

Heliodorus, originally a soldier, but now a presbyter of the Church, had accompanied Jerome to the East, but, not feeling called to the solitary life of the desert, had returned to Aquileia. Here he resumed his clerical duties, and in course of time was raised to the episcopate as bishop of Altinum.

The letter was written in the first bitterness of separation and reproaches Heliodorus for having gone back from the perfect way of the ascetic life. The description given of this is highly colored and seems to have produced a great impression in the West. Fabiola was so much enchanted by it that she learned the letter by heart. The date is 373 or 374 a.d.

1. So conscious are you of the affection which exists between us that you cannot but recognize the love and passion with which I strove to prolong our common sojourn in the desert. This very letter—blotted, as you see, with tears—gives evidence of the lamentation and weeping with which I accompanied your departure. With the pretty ways of a child you then softened your refusal by soothing words, and I, being off my guard, knew not what to do. Was I to hold my peace? I could not conceal my eagerness by a show of indifference. Or was I to entreat you yet more earnestly? You would have refused to listen, for your love was not like mine. Despised affection has taken the one course open to it. Unable to keep you when present, it goes in search of you when absent. You asked me yourself, when you were going away, to invite you to the desert when I took up my quarters there, and I for my part promised to do so. Accordingly I invite you now; come, and come quickly. Do not call to mind old ties; the desert is for those who have left all. Nor let the hardships of our former travels deter you. You believe in Christ, believe also in His words: "Seek ye first the kingdom of God and all these things shall be added unto you." Take neither scrip nor staff. He is rich enough who is poor—with Christ.

2. But what is this, and why do I foolishly importune you again? Away with entreaties, an end to coaxing words. Offended love does well to be angry. You have spurned my petition; perhaps you will listen to my remonstrance. What keeps you, effeminate soldier, in your father's house? Where are your ramparts and trenches? When have you spent a winter in the field? Lo, the trumpet sounds from heaven! Lo, the Leader comes with clouds! He is armed to subdue the world, and out of His mouth proceeds a two-edged sword to mow down all that encounters it. But as for you, what will you do? Pass straight from your chamber to the battle-field, and from the cool shade into the burning sun? Nay, a body used to a tunic cannot endure a buckler; a head that has worn a

cap refuses a helmet; a hand made tender by disuse is galled by a sword-hilt. Hear the proclamation of your King: "He that is not with me is against me, and he that gathereth not with me scattereth." Remember the day on which you enlisted, when, buried with Christ in baptism, you swore fealty to Him, declaring that for His sake you would spare neither father nor mother. Lo, the enemy is striving to slay Christ in your breast. Lo, the ranks of the foe sigh over that bounty which you received when you entered His service. Should your little nephew hang on your neck, pay no regard to him; should your mother with ashes on her hair and garments rent show you the breasts at which she nursed you, heed her not; should your father prostrate himself on the threshold, trample him under foot and go your way. With dry eyes fly to the standard of the cross. In such cases cruelty is the only true affection.

3. Hereafter there shall come—yes, there shall come—a day when you will return a victor to your true country, and will walk through the heavenly Jerusalem crowned with the crown of valor. Then will you receive the citizenship thereof with Paul. Then will you seek the like privilege for your parents. Then will you intercede for me who have urged you forward on the path of victory.

I am not ignorant of the fetters which you may plead as hindrances. My breast is not of iron nor my heart of stone. I was not born of flint or suckled by a tigress. I have passed through troubles like yours myself. Now it is a widowed sister who throws her caressing arms around you. Now it is the slaves, your foster-brothers, who cry, "To what master are you leaving us?" Now it is a nurse bowed with age, and a body-servant loved only less than a father, who exclaim: "Only wait till we die and follow us to our graves." Perhaps, too, an aged mother, with sunken bosom and furrowed brow, recalling the lullaby with which she once soothed you, adds her entreaties to theirs. The learned may call you, if they please,

The sole support and pillar of your house.

The love of God and the fear of hell will easily break such bonds.

Scripture, you will argue, bids us obey our parents. Yes, but whoso loves them more than Christ loses his own soul. The enemy takes sword in hand to slay me, and shall I think of a mother's tears? Or shall I desert the service of Christ for the sake of a father to whom, if I am Christ's servant, I owe no rites of burial, albeit if I am Christ's true servant I owe these to all? Peter with his cowardly advice was an offence to the Lord on the eve of His passion; and to the brethren who strove to restrain him from going up to Jerusalem, Paul's one answer was: "What mean ye to weep and to break my heart? For I am ready not to be bound only, but also to die at Jerusalem for the name of the Lord Jesus." The battering-ram of natural affection which so often shatters faith must recoil powerless from the wall of the Gospel. "My mother and my brethren are these whosoever do the will of my Father which is in heaven." If they believe in Christ let them bid me God-speed, for I go to fight in His name. And if they do not believe, "let the dead bury their dead."

4. But all this, you argue, only touches the case of martyrs. Ah! my brother, you are mistaken, you are mistaken, if you suppose that there is ever a time when the Christian does not suffer persecution. Then are you most hardly beset when you know not that you are beset at all. "Our adversary as a roaring lion walketh about seeking whom he may devour," and do you think of peace? "He sitteth in the lurking-places of the villages: in the secret places doth he murder the innocent; his eyes are privily set against the poor. He lieth in wait secretly as a lion in his den; he lieth in wait to catch the poor;" and do you slumber under a shady tree, so as to fall an easy prey? On one side self-indulgence presses me hard; on another covetousness strives to make an inroad; my belly wishes to be a God to me, in place of Christ, and lust would fain drive away the Holy Spirit that dwells in me and defile His temple. I am pursued, I say, by an enemy

Whose name is Legion and his wiles untold;

and, hapless wretch that I am, how shall I hold myself a victor when I am being led away a captive?

5. My dear brother, weigh well the various forms of transgression, and think not that the sins which I have mentioned are less flagrant than that of idolatry. Nay, hear the apostle's view of the matter. "For this ye know," he writes, "that no whore-monger or unclean person, nor covetous man, who is an idolater, hath any inheritance in the kingdom of Christ and of God." In a general way all that is of the devil savors of enmity to God, and what is of the devil is idolatry, since all idols are subject to him. Yet Paul elsewhere lays down the law in express and unmistakable terms, saying: "Mortify your members, which are upon the earth, laying aside fornication, uncleanness, evil concupiscence and covetousness, which are idolatry, for which things' sake the wrath of God cometh."

Idolatry is not confined to casting incense upon an altar with finger and thumb, or to pouring libations of wine out of a cup into a bowl. Covetousness is idolatry, or else the selling of the Lord for thirty pieces of silver was a righteous act. Lust involves profanation, or else men may defile with common harlots those members of Christ which should be "a living sacrifice acceptable to God." Fraud is idolatry, or else they are worthy of imitation who, in the Acts of the Apostles, sold their inheritance, and because they kept back part of the price, perished by an instant doom. Consider well, my brother; nothing is yours to keep. "Whosoever he be of you," the Lord says, "that forsaketh not all that he hath, he cannot be my disciple." Why are you such a half-hearted Christian?

6. See how Peter left his net; see how the publican rose from the receipt of custom. In a moment he became an apostle. "The Son of man hath not where to lay his head," and do you plan wide porticos and spacious halls? If you look to inherit the good things of the world you can no longer be a joint-heir with Christ. You are called a monk, and has the name no meaning? What brings you, a solitary, into the throng of men? The advice that I give is that of no inexperienced mariner who has never lost either ship or cargo, and has never known a gale. Lately shipwrecked as I have been myself, my warnings to other voyagers spring from my own fears. On one side, like Charybdis, self-indulgence sucks into its vortex the soul's salvation. On the other, like Scylla, lust, with a smile on her girl's face, lures it on to wreck its chastity. The coast is savage, and the devil with a crew of pirates carries irons to fetter his captives. Be not credulous, be not over-confident. The sea may be as smooth and smiling as a pond, its quiet surface may be scarcely ruffled by a breath of air, yet sometimes its waves are as high as mountains. There is danger in its depths, the foe is lurking there. Ease your sheets, spread your sails, fasten the cross as an ensign on your prow. The calm that you speak of is itself a tempest. "Why so?" you will perhaps argue; "are not all my fellow-townsmen Christians?" Your case, I reply, is not that of others. Listen to the words of the Lord: "If thou wilt be perfect go and sell that thou hast, and give to the poor, and come and follow me." You have already promised to be perfect. For when you forsook the army and made yourself an eunuch for the kingdom of heaven's sake, you did so that you might follow the perfect life. Now the perfect servant of Christ has nothing beside Christ. Or if he have anything beside Christ he is not perfect. And if he be not perfect when he has promised God to be so, his profession is a lie. But "the mouth that lieth slayeth the soul." To conclude, then, if you are perfect you will not set your heart on your father's goods; and if you are not perfect you have deceived the Lord. The Gospel thunders forth its divine warning: "Ye cannot serve two masters," and does any one dare to make Christ a liar by serving at once both God and Mammon? Repeatedly does He proclaim, "If any one will come after me let him deny himself and take up his cross and follow me." If I load myself with gold can I think that I am following Christ? Surely not. "He that saith he abideth in Him ought himself also so to walk even as He walked."

7. I know you will rejoin that you possess nothing. Why, then, if you are so well prepared for battle, do you not take the field? Perhaps you think that you

can wage war in your own country, although the Lord could do no signs in His? Why not? you ask. Take the answer which comes to you with his authority: "No prophet is accepted in his own country." But, you will say, I do not seek honor; the approval of my conscience is enough for me. Neither did the Lord seek it; for when the multitudes would have made Him a king he fled from them. But where there is no honor there is contempt; and where there is contempt there is frequent rudeness; and where there is rudeness there is vexation; and where there is vexation there is no rest; and where there is no rest the mind is apt to be diverted from its purpose. Again, where, through restlessness, earnestness loses any of its force, it is lessened by what it loses, and that which is lessened cannot be called perfect. The upshot of all which is that a monk cannot be perfect in his own country. Now, not to aim at perfection is itself a sin.

8. Driven from this line of defence you will appeal to the example of the clergy. These, you will say, remain in their cities, and yet they are surely above criticism. Far be it from me to censure the successors of the apostles, who with holy words consecrate the body of Christ, and who make us Christians. Having the keys of the kingdom of heaven, they judge men to some extent before the day of judgment, and guard the chastity of the bride of Christ. But, as I have before hinted, the case of monks is different from that of the clergy. The clergy feed Christ's sheep; I as a monk am fed by them. They live of the altar: I, if I bring no gift to it, have the axe laid to my root as to that of a barren tree. Nor can I plead poverty as an excuse, for the Lord in the gospel has praised an aged widow for casting into the treasury the last two coins that she had. I may not sit in the presence of a presbyter; he, if I sin, may deliver me to Satan, "for the destruction of the flesh that the spirit may be saved." Under the old law he who disobeyed the priests was put outside the camp and stoned by the people, or else he was beheaded and expiated his contempt with his blood. But now the disobedient person is cut down with the spiritual sword, or he is expelled from the church and torn to pieces by ravening demons. Should the entreaties of your brethren induce you to take orders, I shall rejoice that you are lifted up, and fear lest you may be cast down. You will say: "If a man desire the office of a bishop, he desireth a good work." I know that; but you should add what follows: such an one "must be blameless, the husband of one wife, vigilant, sober, chaste, of good behavior, given to hospitality, apt to teach, not given to wine, no striker but patient." After fully explaining the qualifications of a bishop the apostle speaks of ministers of the third degree with equal care. "Likewise must the deacons be grave," he writes, "not double-tongued, not given to much wine, not greedy of filthy lucre, holding the mystery of the faith

in a pure conscience. And let these also first be proved; then, let them minister, being found blameless." Woe to the man who goes in to the supper without a wedding garment. Nothing remains for him but the stern question, "Friend, how camest thou in hither?" And when he is speechless the order will be given, "Bind him hand and foot, and take him away, and cast him into outer darkness; there shall be weeping and gnashing of teeth." Woe to him who, when he has received a talent, has bound it in a napkin; and, whilst others make profits, only preserves what he has received. His angry lord shall rebuke him in a moment. "Thou wicked servant," he will say, "wherefore gavest thou not my money into the bank that at my coming I might have required mine own with usury?" That is to say, you should have laid before the altar what you were not able to bear. For whilst you, a slothful trader, keep a penny in your hands, you occupy the place of another who might double the money. Wherefore, as he who ministers well purchases to himself a good degree, so he who approaches the cup of the Lord unworthily shall be guilty of the body and blood of the Lord.

9. Not all bishops are bishops indeed. You consider Peter; mark Judas as well. You notice Stephen; look also on Nicolas, sentenced in the Apocalypse by the Lord's own lips, whose shameful imaginations gave rise to the heresy of the Nicolaitans. "Let a man examine himself and so let him come." For it is not ecclesiastical rank that makes a man a Christian. The centurion Cornelius was still a heathen when he was cleansed by the gift of the Holy Spirit. Daniel was but a child when he judged the elders. Amos was stripping mulberry bushes when, in a moment, he was made a prophet. David was only a shepherd when he was chosen to be king. And the least of His disciples was the one whom Jesus loved the most. My brother, sit down in the lower room, that when one less honorable comes you may be bidden to go up higher. Upon whom does the Lord rest but upon him that is lowly and of a contrite spirit, and that trembleth at His word? To whom God has committed much, of him He will ask the more. "Mighty men shall be mightily tormented." No man need pride himself in the day of judgment on merely physical chastity, for then shall men give account for every idle word, and the reviling of a brother shall be counted as the sin of murder. Paul and Peter now reign with Christ, and it is not easy to take the place of the one or to hold the office of the other. There may come an angel to rend the veil of your temple, and to remove your candlestick out of its place. If you intend to build the tower, first count the cost. Salt that has lost its savor is good for nothing but to be cast out and to be trodden under foot of swine. If a monk fall, a priest shall intercede for him; but who shall intercede for a fallen priest?

10. At last my discourse is clear of the reefs: at last this frail bark has passed from the breakers into deep water. I may now spread my sails to the breeze; and, as I leave the rocks of controversy astern, my epilogue will be like the joyful shout of mariners. O desert, bright with the flowers of Christ! O solitude whence come the stones of which, in the Apocalypse, the city of the great king is built! O wilderness, gladdened with God's especial presence! What keeps you in the world, my brother, you who are above the world? How long shall gloomy roofs oppress you? How long shall smoky cities immure you? Believe me, I have more light than you. Sweet it is to lay aside the weight of the body and to soar into the pure bright ether. Do you dread poverty? Christ calls the poor blessed. Does toil frighten you? No athlete is crowned but in the sweat of his brow. Are you anxious as regards food? Faith fears no famine. Do you dread the bare ground for limbs wasted with fasting? The Lord lies there beside you. Do you recoil from an unwashed head and uncombed hair? Christ is your true head. Does the boundless solitude of the desert terrify you? In the spirit you may walk always in paradise. Do but turn your thoughts thither and you will be no more in the desert. Is your skin rough and scaly because you no longer bathe? He that is once washed in Christ needeth not to wash again. To all your objections the apostle gives this one brief answer: "The sufferings of this present time are not worthy to be compared with the glory" which shall come after them, "which shall be revealed in us." You are too greedy of enjoyment, my brother, if you wish to rejoice with the world here, and to reign with Christ hereafter.

11. It shall come, it shall come, that day when this corruptible shall put on incorruption, and this mortal shall put on immortality. Then shall that servant be blessed whom the Lord shall find watching. Then at the sound of the trumpet the earth and its peoples shall tremble, but you shall rejoice. The world shall howl at the Lord who comes to judge it, and the tribes of the earth shall smite the breast. Once mighty kings shall tremble in their nakedness. Venus shall be exposed, and her son too. Jupiter with his fiery bolts will be brought to trial; and Plato, with his disciples, will be but a fool. Aristotle's arguments shall be of no avail. You may seem a poor man and country bred, but then you shall exult and laugh, and say: Behold my crucified Lord, behold my judge. This is He who was once an infant wrapped in swaddling clothes and crying in a manger. This is He whose parents were a workingman and a working-woman. This is He, who, carried into Egypt in His mother's bosom, though He was God, fled before the face of man. This is He who was clothed in a scarlet robe and crowned with thorns. This is He who was called a sorcerer and a man with a devil and a Samaritan. Jew, behold the hands which you

nailed to the cross. Roman, behold the side which you pierced with the spear. See both of you whether it was this body that the disciples stole secretly and by night. For this you profess to believe.

My brother, it is affection which has urged me to speak thus; that you who now find the Christian life so hard may have your reward in that day.

LETTER XV. TO POPE DAMASUS

This letter, written in 376 or 377 a.d., illustrates Jerome's attitude towards the see of Rome at this time held by Damasus, afterwards his warm friend and admirer. Referring to Rome as the scene of his own baptism and as a church where the true faith has remained unimpaired (S:1), and laying down the strict doctrine of salvation only within the pale of the church (S:2), Jerome asks "the successor of the fisherman" two questions, viz.: (1) who is the true bishop of the three claimants of the see of Antioch, and (2) which is the correct terminology, to speak of three "hypostases" in the Godhead, or of one? On the latter question he expresses fully his own opinion.

1. Since the East, shattered as it is by the long-standing feuds, subsisting between its peoples, is bit by bit tearing into shreds the seamless vest of the Lord, "woven from the top throughout," since the foxes are destroying the vineyard of Christ, and since among the broken cisterns that hold no water it is hard to discover "the sealed fountain" and "the garden inclosed," I think it my duty to consult the chair of Peter, and to turn to a church whose faith has been praised by Paul. I appeal for spiritual food to the church whence I have received the garb of Christ. The wide space of sea and land that lies between us cannot deter me from searching for "the pearl of great price." "Wheresoever the body is, there will the eagles be gathered together." Evil children have squandered their patrimony; you alone keep your heritage intact. The fruitful soil of Rome, when it receives the pure seed of the Lord, bears fruit an hundredfold; but here the seed corn is choked in the furrows and nothing grows but darnel or oats. In the West the Sun of righteousness is even now rising; in the East, Lucifer, who fell from heaven, has once more set his throne above the stars. "Ye are the light of the world," "ye are the salt of the earth," ye are "vessels of gold and of silver." Here are vessels of wood or of earth, which wait for the rod of iron, and eternal fire.

2. Yet, though your greatness terrifies me, your kindness attracts me. From the priest I demand the safe-keeping of the victim, from the shepherd the protection due to the sheep. Away with all that is overweening; let the state of

Roman majesty withdraw. My words are spoken to the successor of the fisherman, to the disciple of the cross. As I follow no leader save Christ, so I communicate with none but your blessedness, that is with the chair of Peter. For this, I know, is the rock on which the church is built! This is the house where alone the paschal lamb can be rightly eaten. This is the ark of Noah, and he who is not found in it shall perish when the flood prevails. But since by reason of my sins I have betaken myself to this desert which lies between Syria and the uncivilized waste, I cannot, owing to the great distance between us, always ask of your sanctity the holy thing of the Lord. Consequently I here follow the Egyptian confessors who share your faith, and anchor my frail craft under the shadow of their great argosies. I know nothing of Vitalis; I reject Meletius; I have nothing to do with Paulinus. He that gathers not with you scatters; he that is not of Christ is of Antichrist.

3. Just now, I am sorry to say, those Arians, the Campenses, are trying to extort from me, a Roman Christian, their unheard-of formula of three hypostases. And this, too, after the definition of Nicaea and the decree of Alexandria, in which the West has joined. Where, I should like to know, are the apostles of these doctrines? Where is their Paul, their new doctor of the Gentiles? I ask them what three hypostases are supposed to mean. They reply three persons subsisting. I rejoin that this is my belief. They are not satisfied with the meaning, they demand the term. Surely some secret venom lurks in the words. "If any man refuse," I cry, "to acknowledge three hypostases in the sense of three things hypostatized, that is three persons subsisting, let him be anathema." Yet, because I do not learn their words, I am counted a heretic. "But, if any one, understanding by hypostasis essence, deny that in the three persons there is one hypostasis, he has no part in Christ." Because this is my confession I, like you, am branded with the stigma of Sabellianism.

4. If you think fit enact a decree; and then I shall not hesitate to speak of three hypostases. Order a new creed to supersede the Nicene; and then, whether we are Arians or orthodox, one confession will do for us all. In the whole range of secular learning hypostasis never means anything but essence. And can any one, I ask, be so profane as to speak of three essences or substances in the Godhead? There is one nature of God and one only; and this, and this alone, truly is. For absolute being is derived from no other source but is all its own. All things besides, that is all things created, although they appear to be, are not. For there was a time when they were not, and that which once was not may again cease to be. God alone who is eternal, that is to say, who has no beginning, really deserves to be called an essence. Therefore also He says to Moses from the bush, "I am that I am," and Moses says of Him, "I am hath

sent me." As the angels, the sky, the earth, the seas, all existed at the time, it must have been as the absolute being that God claimed for himself that name of essence, which apparently was common to all. But because His nature alone is perfect, and because in the three persons there subsists but one Godhead, which truly is and is one nature; whosoever in the name of religion declares that there are in the Godhead three elements, three hypostases, that is, or essences, is striving really to predicate three natures of God. And if this is true, why are we severed by walls from Arius, when in dishonesty we are one with him? Let Ursicinus be made the colleague of your blessedness; let Auxentius be associated with Ambrose. But may the faith of Rome never come to such a pass! May the devout hearts of your people never be infected with such unholy doctrines! Let us be satisfied to speak of one substance and of three subsisting persons—perfect, equal, coeternal. Let us keep to one hypostasis, if such be your pleasure, and say nothing of three. It is a bad sign when those who mean the same thing use different words. Let us be satisfied with the form of creed which we have hitherto used. Or, if you think it right that I should speak of three hypostases, explaining what I mean by them, I am ready to submit. But, believe me, there is poison hidden under their honey; the angel of Satan has transformed himself into an angel of light. They give a plausible explanation of the term hypostasis; yet when I profess to hold it in the same sense they count me a heretic. Why are they so tenacious of a word? Why do they shelter themselves under ambiguous language? If their belief corresponds to their explanation of it, I do not condemn them for keeping it. On the other hand, if my belief corresponds to their expressed opinions, they should allow me to set forth their meaning in my own words.

5. I implore your blessedness, therefore, by the crucified Saviour of the world, and by the consubstantial trinity, to authorize me by letter either to use or to refuse this formula of three hypostases. And lest the obscurity of my present abode may baffle the bearers of your letter, I pray you to address it to Evagrius, the presbyter, with whom you are well acquainted. I beg you also to signify with whom I am to communicate at Antioch. Not, I hope, with the Campenses; for they—with their allies the heretics of Tarsus—only desire communion with you to preach with greater authority their traditional doctrine of three hypostases.

LETTER XVI. TO POPE DAMASUS

This letter, written a few months after the preceding, is another appeal to Damasus to solve the writer's doubts. Jerome once more refers to his baptism at Rome, and declares that his one answer to the factions at Antioch is, "He who clings to the chair of Peter is accepted by me." Written from the desert in the year 377 or 378.

1. By her importunity the widow in the gospel at last gained a hearing, and by the same means one friend induced another to give him bread at midnight, when his door was shut and his servants were in bed. The publican's prayers overcame God, although God is invincible. Nineveh was saved by its tears from the impending ruin caused by its sin. To what end, you ask, these far-fetched references? To this end, I make answer; that you in your greatness should look upon me in my littleness; that you, the rich shepherd, should not despise me, the ailing sheep. Christ Himself brought the robber from the cross to paradise, and, to show that repentance is never too late, He turned a murderer's death into a martyrdom. Gladly does Christ embrace the prodigal son when he returns to Him; and, leaving the ninety and nine, the good shepherd carries home on His shoulders the one poor sheep that is left. From a persecutor Paul becomes a preacher. His bodily eyes are blinded to clear the eyes of his soul, and he who once haled Christ's servants in chains before the council of the Jews, lives afterwards to glory in the bonds of Christ.

2. As I have already written to you, I, who have received Christ's garb in Rome, am now detained in the waste that borders Syria. No sentence of banishment, however, has been passed upon me; the punishment which I am undergoing is self-inflicted. But, as the heathen poet says:

They change not mind but sky who cross the sea.

The untiring foe follows me closely, and the assaults that I suffer in the desert are severer than ever. For the Arian frenzy raves, and the powers of the world support it. The church is rent into three factions, and each of these is eager to seize me for its own. The influence of the monks is of long standing, and it is directed against me. I meantime keep crying: "He who clings to the chair of Peter is accepted by me." Meletius, Vitalis, and Paulinus all profess to cleave to you, and I could believe the assertion if it were made by one of them only. As it is, either two of them or else all three are guilty of falsehood. Therefore I implore your blessedness, by our Lord's cross and passion, those necessary glories of our faith, as you hold an apostolic office, to give an apostolic decision. Only tell me by letter with whom I am to communicate in Syria, and I will pray for you that you may sit in judgment enthroned with the twelve;

that when you grow old, like Peter, you may be girded not by yourself but by another, and that, like Paul, you may be made a citizen of the heavenly kingdom. Do not despise a soul for which Christ died.

LETTER XVII. TO THE PRESBYTER MARCUS

In this letter, addressed to one who seems to have had some pre-eminence among the monks of the Chalcidian desert, Jerome complains of the hard treatment meted out to him because of his refusal to take any part in the great theological dispute then raging in Syria. He protests his own orthodoxy, and begs permission to remain where he is until the return of spring, when he will retire from "the inhospitable desert." Written in a.d. 378 or 379.

1. I had made up my mind to use the words of the psalmist: "While the wicked was before me I was dumb with silence; I was humbled, and I held my peace even from good" and "I, as a deaf man, heard not; and I was as a dumb man that openeth not his mouth. Thus I was as a man that heareth not." But charity overcomes all things, and my regard for you defeats my determination. I am, indeed, less careful to retaliate upon my assailants than to comply with your request. For among Christians, as one has said, not he who endures an outrage is unhappy, but he who commits it.

2. And first, before I speak to you of my belief (which you know full well), I am forced to cry out against the inhumanity of this country. A hackneyed quotation best expresses my meaning:

What savages are these who will not grant
A rest to strangers, even on their sands!
They threaten war and drive us from their coasts.

I take this from a Gentile poet that one who disregards the peace of Christ may at least learn its meaning from a heathen. I am called a heretic, although I preach the consubstantial trinity. I am accused of the Sabellian impiety although I proclaim with unwearied voice that in the Godhead there are three distinct, real, whole, and perfect persons. The Arians do right to accuse me, but the orthodox forfeit their orthodoxy when they assail a faith like mine. They may, if they like, condemn me as a heretic; but if they do they must also condemn Egypt and the West, Damasus and Peter. Why do they fasten the guilt on one and leave his companions uncensured? If there is but little water in the stream, it is the fault, not of the channel, but of the source. I blush to say it, but from the caves which serve us for cells we monks of the desert condemn the world. Rolling in sack-cloth and ashes, we pass sentence on bishops. What use is the robe of a penitent if it covers the pride of a king? Chains, squalor, and long hair are by right tokens of sorrow, and not ensigns of royalty. I merely ask leave to remain silent. Why do they torment a man who does not deserve their ill-will? I am a heretic, you say. What is it to you if I am? Stay quiet, and all is said. You are afraid, I suppose, that, with my fluent knowledge of Syriac and Greek, I shall make a tour of the churches, lead the people into error, and form a schism! I have robbed no man of anything; neither have I taken what I have not earned. With my own hand daily and in the sweat of my brow I labor for my food, knowing that it is written by the apostle: "If any will not work, neither shall he eat."

3. Reverend and holy father, Jesus is my witness with what groans and tears I have written all this. "I have kept silence, saith the Lord, but shall I always keep silence? Surely not." I cannot have so much as a corner of the desert. Every day I am asked for my confession of faith; as though when I was regenerated in baptism I had made none. I accept their formulas, but they are still dissatisfied. I sign my name to them, but they still refuse to believe me. One thing only will content them, that I should leave the country. I am on the point of departure. They have already torn away from me my dear brothers, who are a part of my very life. They are, as you see, anxious to depart—nay, they are actually departing; it is preferable, they say, to live among wild beasts rather than with Christians such as these. I myself, too, would be at this moment a fugitive were I not withheld by physical infirmity and by the severity of the winter. I ask to be allowed the shelter of the desert for a few months till spring returns; or if this seems too long a delay, I am ready to depart now. "The earth is the Lord's and the fulness thereof." Let them climb up to heaven alone; for them alone Christ died; they possess all things and glory in all. Be it so. "But God forbid that I should glory save in the cross of our Lord Jesus Christ, by whom the world is crucified unto me and I unto the world."

4. As regards the questions which you have thought fit to put to me concerning the faith, I have given to the reverend Cyril a written confession which sufficiently answers them. He who does not so believe has no part in Christ. My faith is attested both by your ears and by those of your blessed brother, Zenobius, to whom, as well as to yourself, we all of us here send our best greeting.

LETTER XVIII. TO POPE DAMASUS

This (written from Constantinople in a.d. 381) is the earliest of Jerome's expository letters. In it he explains at length the vision recorded in the sixth chapter of Isaiah, and enlarges upon its mystical meaning. "Some of my predecessors," he writes, "make the Lord sitting upon a throne' God the Father, and suppose the seraphim to represent the Son and the Holy Spirit. I do not agree with them, for John expressly tells us that it was Christ and not the Father whom the prophet saw." And again, "The word seraphim means either glow' or beginning of speech,' and the two seraphim thus stand for the Old and New Testaments. Did not our heart burn within us,' said the disciples, while he opened to us the Scriptures?' Moreover, the Old Testament is written in Hebrew, and this unquestionably was man's original language." Jerome then speaks of the unity of the sacred books. "Whatever," he asserts, "we read in the Old Testament we find also in the Gospel; and what we read in the Gospel is deduced from the Old Testament. There is no discord between them, no disagreement. In both Testaments the Trinity is preached."

The letter is noticeable for the evidence it affords of the thoroughness of Jerome's studies. Not only does he cite the several Greek versions of Isaiah in support of his argument, but he also reverts to the Hebrew original. So far as the West was concerned he may be said to have discovered this anew. Even educated men like Augustine had ceased to look beyond the LXX., and were more or less aghast at the boldness with which Jerome rejected its time-honored but inaccurate renderings.

The letter also shows that independence of judgment which always marked Jerome's work. At the time when he wrote it he was much under the sway of Origen. But great as was his admiration for the master, he was not afraid to discard his exegesis when, as in the case of the seraphim, he believed it to be erroneous.

LETTER XIX. FROM POPE DAMASUS

A letter from Damasus to Jerome, in which he asks for an explanation of the word "Hosanna" (a.d. 383).

LETTER XX. TO POPE DAMASUS

Jerome's reply to the foregoing. Exposing the error of Hilary of Poitiers, who supposed the expression to signify "redemption of the house of David," he goes on to show that in the gospels it is a quotation from Psa. cxviii. 25 and that its true meaning is "save now" (so A.V.). "Let us," he writes, "leave the streamlets of conjecture and return to the fountain-head. It is from the Hebrew writings that the truth is to be drawn." Written at Rome a.d. 383.

LETTER XXI. TO DAMASUS

In this letter Jerome, at the request of Damasus, gives a minutely detailed explanation of the parable of the prodigal son.

LETTER XXII. TO EUSTOCHIUM

Perhaps the most famous of all the letters. In it Jerome lays down at great length (1) the motives which ought to actuate those who devote themselves to a life of virginity, and (2) the rules by which they ought to regulate their daily conduct. The letter contains a vivid picture of Roman society as it then was—the luxury, profligacy, and hypocrisy prevalent among both men and women, besides some graphic autobiographical details (S:S:7, 30), and concludes with a full account of the three kinds of monasticism then practised in Egypt (S:S:34–36). Thirty years later Jerome wrote a similar letter to Demetrias (CXXX.), with which this ought to be compared. Written at Rome 384 a.d.

1. "Hear, O daughter, and consider, and incline thine ear; forget also thine own people and thy father's house, and the king shall desire thy beauty." In this forty-fourth psalm God speaks to the human soul that, following the example of Abraham, it should go out from its own land and from its kindred, and should leave the Chaldeans, that is the demons, and should dwell in the country of the living, for which elsewhere the prophet sighs: "I think to see the good things of the Lord in the land of the living." But it is not enough for you to go out from your own land unless you forget your people and your father's house; unless you scorn the flesh and cling to the bridegroom in a close embrace. "Look not behind thee," he says, "neither stay thou in all the plain; escape to the mountain lest thou be consumed." He who has grasped the plough must not look behind him or return home from the field, or having

Christ's garment, descend from the roof to fetch other raiment. Truly a marvellous thing, a father charges his daughter not to remember her father. "Ye are of your father the devil, and the lusts of your father it is your will to do." So it was said to the Jews. And in another place, "He that committeth sin is of the devil." Born, in the first instance, of such parentage we are naturally black, and even when we have repented, so long as we have not scaled the heights of virtue, we may still say: "I am black but comely, O ye daughters of Jerusalem." But you will say to me, "I have left the home of my childhood; I have forgotten my father, I am born anew in Christ. What reward do I receive for this?" The context shows—"The king shall desire thy beauty." This, then, is the great mystery. "For this cause shall a man leave his father and his mother and shall be joined unto his wife, and they two shall be" not as is there said, "of one flesh," but "of one spirit." Your bridegroom is not haughty or disdainful; He has "married an Ethiopian woman." When once you desire the wisdom of the true Solomon and come to Him, He will avow all His knowledge to you; He will lead you into His chamber with His royal hand; He will miraculously change your complexion so that it shall be said of you, "Who is this that goeth up and hath been made white?"

2. I write to you thus, Lady Eustochium (I am bound to call my Lord's bride "lady"), to show you by my opening words that my object is not to praise the virginity which you follow, and of which you have proved the value, or yet to recount the drawbacks of marriage, such as pregnancy, the crying of infants, the torture caused by a rival, the cares of household management, and all those fancied blessings which death at last cuts short. Not that married women are as such outside the pale; they have their own place, the marriage that is honorable and the bed undefiled. My purpose is to show you that you are fleeing from Sodom and should take warning by Lot's wife. There is no flattery, I can tell you, in these pages. A flatterer's words are fair, but for all that he is an enemy. You need expect no rhetorical flourishes setting you among the angels, and while they extol virginity as blessed, putting the world at your feet.

3. I would have you draw from your monastic vow not pride but fear. You walk laden with gold; you must keep out of the robber's way. To us men this life is a race-course: we contend here, we are crowned elsewhere. No man can lay aside fear while serpents and scorpions beset his path. The Lord says: "My sword hath drunk its fill in heaven," and do you expect to find peace on the earth? No, the earth yields only thorns and thistles, and its dust is food for the serpent. "For our wrestling is not against flesh and blood, but against the principalities, against the powers, against the world-rulers of this darkness, against the spiritual hosts of wickedness in the heavenly places." We are

hemmed in by hosts of foes, our enemies are upon every side. The weak flesh will soon be ashes: one against many, it fights against tremendous odds. Not till it has been dissolved, not till the Prince of this world has come and found no sin therein, not till then may you safely listen to the prophet's words: "Thou shalt not be afraid for the terror by night nor for the arrow that flieth by day; nor for the trouble which haunteth thee in darkness; nor for the demon and his attacks at noonday. A thousand shall fall at thy side and ten thousand at thy right hand; but it shall not come nigh thee." When the hosts of the enemy distress you, when your frame is fevered and your passions roused, when you say in your heart, "What shall I do?" Elisha's words shall give you your answer, "Fear not, for they that be with us are more than they that be with them." He shall pray, "Lord, open the eyes of thine handmaid that she may see." And then when your eyes have been opened you shall see a fiery chariot like Elijah's waiting to carry you to heaven, and shall joyfully sing: "Our soul is escaped as a bird out of the snare of the fowlers: the snare is broken and we are escaped."

4. So long as we are held down by this frail body, so long as we have our treasure in earthen vessels; so long as the flesh lusteth against the spirit and the spirit against the flesh, there can be no sure victory. "Our adversary the devil goeth about as a roaring lion seeking whom he may devour." "Thou makest darkness," David says, "and it is night: wherein all the beasts of the forest do creep forth. The young lions roar after their prey and seek their meat from God." The devil looks not for unbelievers, for those who are without, whose flesh the Assyrian king roasted in the furnace. It is the church of Christ that he "makes haste to spoil." According to Habakkuk, "His food is of the choicest." A Job is the victim of his machinations, and after devouring Judas he seeks power to sift the [other] apostles. The Saviour came not to send peace upon the earth but a sword. Lucifer fell, Lucifer who used to rise at dawn; and he who was bred up in a paradise of delight had the well-earned sentence passed upon him, "Though thou exalt thyself as the eagle, and though thou set thy nest among the stars, thence will I bring thee down, saith the Lord." For he had said in his heart, "I will exalt my throne above the stars of God," and "I will be like the Most High." Wherefore God says every day to the angels, as they descend the ladder that Jacob saw in his dream, "I have said ye are Gods and all of you are children of the Most High. But ye shall die like men and fall like one of the princes." The devil fell first, and since "God standeth in the congregation of the Gods and judgeth among the Gods," the apostle writes to those who are ceasing to be Gods—"Whereas there is among you envying and strife, are ye not carnal and walk as men?"

5. If, then, the apostle, who was a chosen vessel separated unto the gospel of Christ, by reason of the pricks of the flesh and the allurements of vice keeps under his body and brings it into subjection, lest when he has preached to others he may himself be a castaway; and yet, for all that, sees another law in his members warring against the law of his mind, and bringing him into captivity to the law of sin; if after nakedness, fasting, hunger, imprisonment, scourging and other torments, he turns back to himself and cries "Oh, wretched man that I am, who shall deliver me from the body of this death?" do you fancy that you ought to lay aside apprehension? See to it that God say not some day of you: "The virgin of Israel is fallen and there is none to raise her up." I will say it boldly, though God can do all things He cannot raise up a virgin when once she has fallen. He may indeed relieve one who is defiled from the penalty of her sin, but He will not give her a crown. Let us fear lest in us also the prophecy be fulfilled, "Good virgins shall faint." Notice that it is good virgins who are spoken of, for there are bad ones as well. "Whosoever looketh on a woman," the Lord says, "to lust after her hath committed adultery with her already in his heart." So that virginity may be lost even by a thought. Such are evil virgins, virgins in the flesh, not in the spirit; foolish virgins, who, having no oil, are shut out by the Bridegroom.

6. But if even real virgins, when they have other failings, are not saved by their physical virginity, what shall become of those who have prostituted the members of Christ, and have changed the temple of the Holy Ghost into a brothel? Straightway shall they hear the words: "Come down and sit in the dust, O virgin daughter of Babylon, sit on the ground; there is no throne, O daughter of the Chaldaeans: for thou shalt no more be called tender and delicate. Take the millstone and grind meal; uncover thy locks, make bare the legs, pass over the rivers; thy nakedness shall be uncovered, yea, thy shame shall be seen." And shall she come to this after the bridal-chamber of God the Son, after the kisses of Him who is to her both kinsman and spouse? Yes, she of whom the prophetic utterance once sang, "Upon thy right hand did stand the queen in a vesture of gold wrought about with divers colours," shall be made naked, and her skirts shall be discovered upon her face. She shall sit by the waters of loneliness, her pitcher laid aside; and shall open her feet to every one that passeth by, and shall be polluted to the crown of her head. Better had it been for her to have submitted to the yoke of marriage, to have walked in level places, than thus, aspiring to loftier heights, to fall into the deep of hell. I pray you, let not Zion the faithful city become a harlot: let it not be that where the Trinity has been entertained, there demons shall dance and owls make their nests, and jackals build. Let us not loose the belt that binds the breast. When

lust tickles the sense and the soft fire of sensual pleasure sheds over us its pleasing glow, let us immediately break forth and cry: "The Lord is on my side: I will not fear what the flesh can do unto me." When the inner man shows signs for a time of wavering between vice and virtue, say: "Why art thou cast down, O my soul, and why art thou disquieted within me? Hope thou in God, for I shall yet praise Him who is the health of my countenance and my God." You must never let suggestions of evil grow on you, or a babel of disorder win strength in your breast. Slay the enemy while he is small; and, that you may not have a crop of tares, nip the evil in the bud. Bear in mind the warning words of the Psalmist: "Hapless daughter of Babylon, happy shall he be that rewardeth thee as thou hast served us. Happy shall he be that taketh and dasheth thy little ones against the stones." Because natural heat inevitably kindles in a man sensual passion, he is praised and accounted happy who, when foul suggestions arise in his mind, gives them no quarter, but dashes them instantly against the rock. "Now the Rock is Christ."

7. How often, when I was living in the desert, in the vast solitude which gives to hermits a savage dwelling-place, parched by a burning sun, how often did I fancy myself among the pleasures of Rome! I used to sit alone because I was filled with bitterness. Sackcloth disfigured my unshapely limbs and my skin from long neglect had become as black as an Ethiopian's. Tears and groans were every day my portion; and if drowsiness chanced to overcome my struggles against it, my bare bones, which hardly held together, clashed against the ground. Of my food and drink I say nothing: for, even in sickness, the solitaries have nothing but cold water, and to eat one's food cooked is looked upon as self-indulgence. Now, although in my fear of hell I had consigned myself to this prison, where I had no companions but scorpions and wild beasts, I often found myself amid bevies of girls. My face was pale and my frame chilled with fasting; yet my mind was burning with desire, and the fires of lust kept bubbling up before me when my flesh was as good as dead. Helpless, I cast myself at the feet of Jesus, I watered them with my tears, I wiped them with my hair: and then I subdued my rebellious body with weeks of abstinence. I do not blush to avow my abject misery; rather I lament that I am not now what once I was. I remember how I often cried aloud all night till the break of day and ceased not from beating my breast till tranquillity returned at the chiding of the Lord. I used to dread my very cell as though it knew my thoughts; and, stern and angry with myself, I used to make my way alone into the desert. Wherever I saw hollow valleys, craggy mountains, steep cliffs, there I made my oratory, there the house of correction for my unhappy flesh. There, also—the Lord Himself is my witness—when I had shed copious tears and had

strained my eyes towards heaven, I sometimes felt myself among angelic hosts, and for joy and gladness sang: "because of the savour of thy good ointments we will run after thee."

8. Now, if such are the temptations of men who, since their bodies are emaciated with fasting, have only evil thoughts to fear, how must it fare with a girl whose surroundings are those of luxury and ease? Surely, to use the apostle's words, "She is dead while she liveth." Therefore, if experience gives me a right to advise, or clothes my words with credit, I would begin by urging you and warning you as Christ's spouse to avoid wine as you would avoid poison. For wine is the first weapon used by demons against the young. Greed does not shake, nor pride puff up, nor ambition infatuate so much as this. Other vices we easily escape, but this enemy is shut up within us, and wherever we go we carry him with us. Wine and youth between them kindle the fire of sensual pleasure. Why do we throw oil on the flame—why do we add fresh fuel to a miserable body which is already ablaze. Paul, it is true, says to Timothy "drink no longer water, but use a little wine for thy stomach's sake, and for thine often infirmities." But notice the reasons for which the permission is given, to cure an aching stomach and a frequent infirmity. And lest we should indulge ourselves too much on the score of our ailments, he commands that but little shall be taken; advising rather as a physician than as an apostle (though, indeed, an apostle is a spiritual physician). He evidently feared that Timothy might succumb to weakness, and might prove unequal to the constant moving to and fro involved in preaching the Gospel. Besides, he remembered that he had spoken of "wine wherein is excess," and had said, "it is good neither to eat flesh nor to drink wine." Noah drank wine and became intoxicated; but living as he did in the rude age after the flood, when the vine was first planted, perhaps he did not know its power of inebriation. And to let you see the hidden meaning of Scripture in all its fulness (for the word of God is a pearl and may be pierced on every side) after his drunkenness came the uncovering of his body; self-indulgence culminated in lust. First the belly is crammed; then the other members are roused. Similarly, at a later period, "The people sat down to eat and to drink and rose up to play." Lot also, God's friend, whom He saved upon the mountain, who was the only one found righteous out of so many thousands, was intoxicated by his daughters. And, although they may have acted as they did more from a desire of offspring than from love of sinful pleasure—for the human race seemed in danger of extinction—yet they were well aware that the righteous man would not abet their design unless intoxicated. In fact he did not know what he was doing, and his sin was not wilful. Still his error was a grave one, for it made him the father of Moab and Ammon,

Israel's enemies, of whom it is said: "Even to the fourteenth generation they shall not enter into the congregation of the Lord forever."

9. When Elijah, in his flight from Jezebel, lay weary and desolate beneath the oak, there came an angel who raised him up and said, "Arise and eat." And he looked, and behold there was a cake and a cruse of water at his head. Had God willed it, might He not have sent His prophet spiced wines and dainty dishes and flesh basted into tenderness? When Elisha invited the sons of the prophets to dinner, he only gave them field-herbs to eat; and when all cried out with one voice: "There is death in the pot," the man of God did not storm at the cooks (for he was not used to very sumptuous fare), but caused meal to be brought, and casting it in, sweetened the bitter mess with spiritual strength as Moses had once sweetened the waters of Mara. Again, when men were sent to arrest the prophet, and were smitten with physical and mental blindness, that he might bring them without their own knowledge to Samaria, notice the food with which Elisha ordered them to be refreshed. "Set bread and water," he said, "before them, that they may eat and drink and go to their master." And Daniel, who might have had rich food from the king's table, preferred the mower's breakfast, brought to him by Habakkuk, which must have been but country fare. He was called "a man of desires," because he would not eat the bread of desire or drink the wine of concupiscence.

10. There are, in the Scriptures, countless divine answers condemning gluttony and approving simple food. But as fasting is not my present theme and an adequate discussion of it would require a treatise to itself, these few observations must suffice of the many which the subject suggests. By them you will understand why the first man, obeying his belly and not God, was cast down from paradise into this vale of tears; and why Satan used hunger to tempt the Lord Himself in the wilderness; and why the apostle cries: "Meats for the belly and the belly for meats, but God shall destroy both it and them;" and why he speaks of the self-indulgent as men "whose God is their belly." For men invariably worship what they like best. Care must be taken, therefore, that abstinence may bring back to Paradise those whom satiety once drove out.

11. You will tell me, perhaps, that, high-born as you are, reared in luxury and used to lie softly, you cannot do without wine and dainties, and would find a stricter rule of life unendurable. If so, I can only say: "Live, then, by your own rule, since God's rule is too hard for you." Not that the Creator and Lord of all takes pleasure in a rumbling and empty stomach, or in fevered lungs; but that these are indispensable as means to the preservation of chastity. Job was dear to God, perfect and upright before Him; yet hear what he says of the devil: "His strength is in the loins, and his force is in the navel."

The terms are chosen for decency's sake, but the reproductive organs of the two sexes are meant. Thus, the descendant of David, who, according to the promise is to sit upon his throne, is said to come from his loins. And the seventy-five souls descended from Jacob who entered Egypt are said to come out of his thigh. So, also, when his thigh shrank after the Lord had wrestled with him, he ceased to beget children. The Israelites, again, are told to celebrate the passover with loins girded and mortified. God says to Job: "Gird up thy loins as a man." John wears a leathern girdle. The apostles must gird their loins to carry the lamps of the Gospel. When Ezekiel tells us how Jerusalem is found in the plain of wandering, covered with blood, he uses the words: "Thy navel has not been cut." In his assaults on men, therefore, the devil's strength is in the loins; in his attacks on women his force is in the navel.

12. Do you wish for proof of my assertions? Take examples. Sampson was braver than a lion and tougher than a rock; alone and unprotected he pursued a thousand armed men; and yet, in Delilah's embrace, his resolution melted away. David was a man after God's own heart, and his lips had often sung of the Holy One, the future Christ; and yet as he walked upon his housetop he was fascinated by Bathsheba's nudity, and added murder to adultery. Notice here how, even in his own house, a man cannot use his eyes without danger. Then repenting, he says to the Lord: "Against thee, thee only, have I sinned and done this evil in Thy sight." Being a king he feared no one else. So, too, with Solomon. Wisdom used him to sing her praise, and he treated of all plants "from the cedar tree that is in Lebanon even unto the hyssop that springeth out of the wall;" and yet he went back from God because he was a lover of women. And, as if to show that near relationship is no safeguard, Amnon burned with illicit passion for his sister Tamar.

13. I cannot bring myself to speak of the many virgins who daily fall and are lost to the bosom of the church, their mother: stars over which the proud foe sets up his throne, and rocks hollowed by the serpent that he may dwell in their fissures. You may see many women widows before wedded, who try to conceal their miserable fall by a lying garb. Unless they are betrayed by swelling wombs or by the crying of their infants, they walk abroad with tripping feet and heads in the air. Some go so far as to take potions, that they may insure barrenness, and thus murder human beings almost before their conception. Some, when they find themselves with child through their sin, use drugs to procure abortion, and when (as often happens) they die with their offspring, they enter the lower world laden with the guilt not only of adultery against Christ but also of suicide and child murder. Yet it is these who say: "Unto the pure all things are pure;' my conscience is sufficient guide for me. A pure heart

is what God looks for. Why should I abstain from meats which God has created to be received with thanksgiving?" And when they wish to appear agreeable and entertaining they first drench themselves with wine, and then joining the grossest profanity to intoxication, they say "Far be it from me to abstain from the blood of Christ." And when they see another pale or sad they call her "wretch" or "manichaean;" quite logically, indeed, for on their principles fasting involves heresy. When they go out they do their best to attract notice, and with nods and winks encourage troops of young fellows to follow them. Of each and all of these the prophet's words are true: "Thou hast a whore's forehead; thou refusest to be ashamed." Their robes have but a narrow purple stripe, it is true; and their head-dress is somewhat loose, so as to leave the hair free. From their shoulders flutters the lilac mantle which they call "ma-forte;" they have their feet in cheap slippers and their arms tucked up tight-fitting sleeves. Add to these marks of their profession an easy gait, and you have all the virginity that they possess. Such may have eulogizers of their own, and may fetch a higher price in the market of perdition, merely because they are called virgins. But to such virgins as these I prefer to be displeasing.

14. I blush to speak of it, it is so shocking; yet though sad, it is true. How comes this plague of the agapetae to be in the church? Whence come these unwedded wives, these novel concubines, these harlots, so I will call them, though they cling to a single partner? One house holds them and one chamber. They often occupy the same bed, and yet they call us suspicious if we fancy anything amiss. A brother leaves his virgin sister; a virgin, slighting her unmarried brother, seeks a brother in a stranger. Both alike profess to have but one object, to find spiritual consolation from those not of their kin; but their real aim is to indulge in sexual intercourse. It is on such that Solomon in the book of proverbs heaps his scorn. "Can a man take fire in his bosom," he says, "and his clothes not be burned? Can one go upon hot coals and his feet not be burned?"

15. We cast out, then, and banish from our sight those who only wish to seem and not to be virgins. Henceforward I may bring all my speech to bear upon you who, as it is your lot to be the first virgin of noble birth in Rome, have to labor the more diligently not to lose good things to come, as well as those that are present. You have at least learned from a case in your own family the troubles of wedded life and the uncertainties of marriage. Your sister, Blaesilla, before you in age but behind you in declining the vow of virginity, has become a widow but seven months after she has taken a husband. Hapless plight of us mortals who know not what is before us! She has lost, at once, the crown of virginity and the pleasures of wedlock. And, although, as a widow,

the second degree of chastity is hers, still can you not imagine the continual crosses which she has to bear, daily seeing in her sister what she has lost herself; and, while she finds it hard to go without the pleasures of wedlock, having a less reward for her present continence? Still she, too, may take heart and rejoice. The fruit which is an hundredfold and that which is sixtyfold both spring from one seed, and that seed is chastity.

16. Do not court the company of married ladies or visit the houses of the high-born. Do not look too often on the life which you despised to become a virgin. Women of the world, you know, plume themselves because their husbands are on the bench or in other high positions. And the wife of the emperor always has an eager throng of visitors at her door. Why do you, then, wrong your husband? Why do you, God's bride, hasten to visit the wife of a mere man? Learn in this respect a holy pride; know that you are better than they. And not only must you avoid intercourse with those who are puffed up by their husbands' honors, who are hedged in with troops of eunuchs, and who wear robes inwrought with threads of gold. You must also shun those who are widows from necessity and not from choice. Not that they ought to have desired the death of their husbands; but that they have not welcomed the opportunity of continence when it has come. As it is, they only change their garb; their old self-seeking remains unchanged. To see them in their capacious litters, with red cloaks and plump bodies, a row of eunuchs walking in front of them, you would fancy them not to have lost husbands but to be seeking them. Their houses are filled with flatterers and with guests. The very clergy, who ought to inspire them with respect by their teaching and authority, kiss these ladies on the forehead, and putting forth their hands (so that, if you knew no better, you might suppose them in the act of blessing), take wages for their visits. They, meanwhile, seeing that priests cannot do without them, are lifted up into pride; and as, having had experience of both, they prefer the license of widowhood to the restraints of marriage, they call themselves chaste livers and nuns. After an immoderate supper they retire to rest to dream of the apostles.

17. Let your companions be women pale and thin with fasting, and approved by their years and conduct; such as daily sing in their hearts: "Tell me where thou feedest thy flock, where thou makest it to rest at noon," and say, with true earnestness, "I have a desire to depart and to be with Christ." Be subject to your parents, imitating the example of your spouse. Rarely go abroad, and if you wish to seek the aid of the martyrs seek it in your own chamber. For you will never need a pretext for going out if you always go out when there is need. Take food in moderation, and never overload your stom-

ach. For many women, while temperate as regards wine, are intemperate in the use of food. When you rise at night to pray, let your breath be that of an empty and not that of an overfull stomach. Read often, learn all that you can. Let sleep overcome you, the roll still in your hands; when your head falls, let it be on the sacred page. Let your fasts be of daily occurrence and your refreshment such as avoids satiety. It is idle to carry an empty stomach if, in two or three days' time, the fast is to be made up for by repletion. When cloyed the mind immediately grows sluggish, and when the ground is watered it puts forth the thorns of lust. If ever you feel the outward man sighing for the flower of youth, and if, as you lie on your couch after a meal, you are excited by the alluring train of sensual desires; then seize the shield of faith, for it alone can quench the fiery darts of the devil. "They are all adulterers," says the prophet; "they have made ready their heart like an oven." But do you keep close to the footsteps of Christ, and, intent upon His words, say: "Did not our heart burn within us by the way while Jesus opened to us the Scriptures?" and again: "Thy word is tried to the uttermost, and thy servant loveth it." It is hard for the human soul to avoid loving something, and our mind must of necessity give way to affection of one kind or another. The love of the flesh is overcome by the love of the spirit. Desire is quenched by desire. What is taken from the one increases the other. Therefore, as you lie on your couch, say again and again: "By night have I sought Him whom my soul loveth." "Mortify, therefore," says the apostle, "your members which are upon the earth." Because he himself did so, he could afterwards say with confidence: "I live, yet not I, but Christ, liveth in me." He who mortifies his members, and feels that he is walking in a vain show, is not afraid to say: "I am become like a bottle in the frost. Whatever there was in me of the moisture of lust has been dried out of me." And again: "My knees are weak through fasting; I forget to eat my bread. By reason of the voice of my groaning my bones cleave to my skin."

18. Be like the grasshopper and make night musical. Nightly wash your bed and water your couch with your tears. Watch and be like the sparrow alone upon the housetop. Sing with the spirit, but sing with the understanding also. And let your song be that of the psalmist: "Bless the Lord, O my soul; and forget not all his benefits; who forgiveth all thine iniquities; who healeth all thy diseases; who redeemeth thy life from destruction." Can we, any of us, honestly make his words our own: "I have eaten ashes like bread and mingled my drink with weeping?" Yet, should we not weep and groan when the serpent invites us, as he invited our first parents, to eat forbidden fruit, and when after expelling us from the paradise of virginity he desires to clothe us with mantles of skins such as that which Elijah, on his return to paradise, left behind him on

earth? Say to yourself: "What have I to do with the pleasures of sense that so soon come to an end? What have I to do with the song of the sirens so sweet and so fatal to those who hear it?" I would not have you subject to that sentence whereby condemnation has been passed upon mankind. When God says to Eve, "In pain and in sorrow thou shalt bring forth children," say to yourself, "That is a law for a married woman, not for me." And when He continues, "Thy desire shall be to thy husband," say again: "Let her desire be to her husband who has not Christ for her spouse." And when, last of all, He says, "Thou shalt surely die," once more, say, "Marriage indeed must end in death; but the life on which I have resolved is independent of sex. Let those who are wives keep the place and the time that properly belong to them. For me, virginity is consecrated in the persons of Mary and of Christ."

19. Some one may say, "Do you dare detract from wedlock, which is a state blessed by God?" I do not detract from wedlock when I set virginity before it. No one compares a bad thing with a good. Wedded women may congratulate themselves that they come next to virgins. "Be fruitful," God says, "and multiply, and replenish the earth." He who desires to replenish the earth may increase and multiply if he will. But the train to which you belong is not on earth, but in heaven. The command to increase and multiply first finds fulfilment after the expulsion from paradise, after the nakedness and the fig-leaves which speak of sexual passion. Let them marry and be given in marriage who eat their bread in the sweat of their brow; whose land brings forth to them thorns and thistles, and whose crops are choked with briars. My seed produces fruit a hundredfold. "All men cannot receive God's saying, but they to whom it is given."

Some people may be eunuchs from necessity; I am one of free will. "There is a time to embrace and a time to refrain from embracing. There is a time to cast away stones, and a time to gather stones together." Now that out of the hard stones of the Gentiles God has raised up children unto Abraham, they begin to be "holy stones rolling upon the earth." They pass through the whirlwinds of the world, and roll on in God's chariot on rapid wheels. Let those stitch coats to themselves who have lost the coat woven from the top throughout; who delight in the cries of infants which, as soon as they see the light, lament that they are born. In paradise Eve was a virgin, and it was only after the coats of skins that she began her married life. Now paradise is your home too. Keep therefore your birthright and say: "Return unto thy rest, O my soul." To show that virginity is natural while wedlock only follows guilt, what is born of wedlock is virgin flesh, and it gives back in fruit what in root it has lost. "There shall come forth a rod out of the stem of Jesse, and a flower shall grow out of his roots." The rod is the mother of the Lord—simple, pure, unsullied; drawing no germ of life from without but fruitful in singleness like God Himself. The flower of the rod is Christ, who says of Himself: "I am the rose of Sharon and the lily of the valleys." In another place He is foretold to be "a stone cut out of the mountain without hands," a figure by which the prophet signifies that He is to be born a virgin of a virgin. For the hands are here a figure of wedlock as in the passage: "His left hand is under my head and his right hand doth embrace me." It agrees, also, with this interpretation that the unclean animals are led into Noah's ark in pairs, while of the clean an uneven number is taken. Similarly, when Moses and Joshua were bidden to remove their shoes because the ground on which they stood was holy, the command had a mystical meaning. So, too, when the disciples were appointed to preach the gospel they were told to take with them neither shoe nor shoe-latchet; and when the soldiers came to cast lots for the garments of Jesus they found no boots that they could take away. For the Lord could not Himself possess what He had forbidden to His servants.

20. I praise wedlock, I praise marriage, but it is because they give me virgins. I gather the rose from the thorns, the gold from the earth, the pearl from the shell. "Doth the plowman plow all day to sow?" Shall he not also enjoy the fruit of his labor? Wedlock is the more honored, the more what is born of it is loved. Why, mother, do you grudge your daughter her virginity? She has been reared on your milk, she has come from your womb, she has grown up in your bosom. Your watchful affection has kept her a virgin. Are you angry with her because she chooses to be a king's wife and not a soldier's? She has conferred on you a high privilege; you are now the mother-in-law of God. "Concerning virgins," says the apostle, "I have no commandment of the Lord." Why was this? Because his own virginity was due, not to a command, but to his free choice. For they are not to be heard who feign him to have had a wife; for, when he is discussing continence and commending perpetual chastity, he uses the words, "I would that all men were even as I myself." And farther on, "I say, therefore, to the unmarried and widows, it is good for them if they abide even as I." And in another place, "have we not power to lead about wives even as the rest of the apostles?" Why then has he no commandment from the Lord concerning virginity? Because what is freely offered is worth more than what is extorted by force, and to command virginity would have been to abrogate wedlock. It would have been a hard enactment to compel opposition to nature and to extort from men the angelic life; and not only so, it would have been to condemn what is a divine ordinance.

21. The old law had a different ideal of blessedness, for therein it is said: "Blessed is he who hath seed in Zion and a family in Jerusalem:" and "Cursed is the barren who beareth not:" and "Thy children shall be like olive-plants round about thy table." Riches too are promised to the faithful and we are told that "there was not one feeble person among their tribes." But now even to eunuchs it is said, "Say not, behold I am a dry tree," for instead of sons and daughters you have a place forever in heaven. Now the poor are blessed, now Lazarus is set before Dives in his purple. Now he who is weak is counted strong. But in those days the world was still unpeopled: accordingly, to pass over instances of childlessness meant only to serve as types, those only were considered happy who could boast of children. It was for this reason that Abraham in his old age married Keturah; that Leah hired Jacob with her son's mandrakes, and that fair Rachel—a type of the church—complained of the closing of her womb. But gradually the crop grew up and then the reaper was sent forth with his sickle. Elijah lived a virgin life, so also did Elisha and many of the sons of the prophets. To Jeremiah the command came: "Thou shalt not take thee a wife." He had been sanctified in his mother's womb, and now he was forbidden to take a wife because the captivity was near. The apostle gives the same counsel in different words. "I think, therefore, that this is good by reason of the present distress, namely that it is good for a man to be as he is." What is this distress which does away with the joys of wedlock? The apostle tells us, in a later verse: "The time is short: it remaineth that those who have wives be as though they had none." Nebuchadnezzar is hard at hand. The lion is bestirring himself from his lair. What good will marriage be to me if it is to end in slavery to the haughtiest of kings? What good will little ones be to me if their lot is to be that which the prophet sadly describes: "The tongue of the sucking child cleaveth to the roof of his mouth for thirst; the young children ask for bread and no man breaketh it unto them"? In those days, as I have said, the virtue of continence was found only in men: Eve still continued to travail with children. But now that a virgin has conceived in the womb and has borne to us a child of which the prophet says that "Government shall be upon his shoulder, and his name shall be called the mighty God, the everlasting Father," now the chain of the curse is broken. Death came through Eve, but life has come through Mary. And thus the gift of virginity has been bestowed most richly upon women, seeing that it has had its beginning from a woman. As soon as the Son of God set foot upon the earth, He formed for Himself a new household there; that, as He was adored by angels in heaven, angels might serve Him also on earth. Then chaste Judith once more cut off the head of Holofernes. Then Haman—whose name means iniquity—was once more

burned in fire of his own kindling. Then James and John forsook father and net and ship and followed the Saviour: neither kinship nor the world's ties, nor the care of their home could hold them back. Then were the words heard: "Whosoever will come after me, let him deny himself and take up his cross and follow me." For no soldier goes with a wife to battle. Even when a disciple would have buried his father, the Lord forbade him, and said: "Foxes have holes and the birds of the air have nests, but the Son of Man hath not where to lay His head." So you must not complain if you have but scanty house-room. In the same strain, the apostle writes: "He that is unmarried careth for the things that belong to the Lord, how he may please the Lord: but he that is married careth for the things that are of the world how he may please his wife. There is difference also between a wife and a virgin. The unmarried woman careth for the things of the Lord that she may be holy both in body and in spirit. But she that is married careth for the things of the world how she may please her husband."

22. How great inconveniences are involved in wedlock and how many anxieties encompass it I have, I think, described shortly in my treatise—published against Helvidius—on the perpetual virginity of the blessed Mary. It would be tedious to go over the same ground now; and any one who pleases may draw from that fountain. But lest I should seem wholly to have passed over the matter, I will just say now that the apostle bids us pray without ceasing, and that he who in the married state renders his wife her due cannot so pray. Either we pray always and are virgins, or we cease to pray that we may fulfil the claims of marriage. Still he says: "If a virgin marry she hath not sinned. Nevertheless such shall have trouble in the flesh." At the outset I promised that I should say little or nothing of the embarrassments of wedlock, and now I give you notice to the same effect. If you want to know from how many vexations a virgin is free and by how many a wife is fettered you should read Tertullian "to a philosophic friend," and his other treatises on virginity, the blessed Cyprian's noble volume, the writings of Pope Damasus in prose and verse, and the treatises recently written for his sister by our own Ambrose. In these he has poured forth his soul with such a flood of eloquence that he has sought out, set forth, and put in order all that bears on the praise of virgins.

23. We must proceed by a different path, for our purpose is not the praise of virginity but its preservation. To know that it is a good thing is not enough: when we have chosen it we must guard it with jealous care. The first only requires judgment, and we share it with many; the second calls for toil, and few compete with us in it. "He that shall endure unto the end," the Lord says, "the same shall be saved," and "many are called but few are chosen." Therefore

I conjure you before God and Jesus Christ and His elect angels to guard that which you have received, not readily exposing to the public gaze the vessels of the Lord's temple (which only the priests are by right allowed to see), that no profane person may look upon God's sanctuary. Uzzah, when he touched the ark which it was not lawful to touch, was struck down suddenly by death. And assuredly no gold or silver vessel was ever so dear to God as is the temple of a virgin's body. The shadow went before, but now the reality is come. You indeed may speak in all simplicity, and from motives of amiability may treat with courtesy the veriest strangers, but unchaste eyes see nothing aright. They fail to appreciate the beauty of the soul, and only value that of the body. Hezekiah showed God's treasure to the Assyrians, who ought never to have seen what they were sure to covet. The consequence was that Judaea was torn by continual wars, and that the very first things carried away to Babylon were these vessels of the Lord. We find Belshazzar at his feast and among his concubines (vice always glories in defiling what is noble) drinking out of these sacred cups.

24. Never incline your ear to words of mischief. For men often say an improper word to make trial of a virgin's steadfastness, to see if she hears it with pleasure, and if she is ready to unbend at every silly jest. Such persons applaud whatever you affirm and deny whatever you deny; they speak of you as not only holy but accomplished, and say that in you there is no guile. "Behold," say they, "a true hand-maid of Christ; behold entire singleness of heart. How different from that rough, unsightly, countrified fright, who most likely never married because she could never find a husband." Our natural weakness induces us readily to listen to such flatterers; but, though we may blush and reply that such praise is more than our due, the soul within us rejoices to hear itself praised.

Like the ark of the covenant Christ's spouse should be overlaid with gold within and without; she should be the guardian of the law of the Lord. Just as the ark contained nothing but the tables of the covenant, so in you there should be no thought of anything that is outside. For it pleases the Lord to sit in your mind as He once sat on the mercy-seat and the cherubims. As He sent His disciples to loose Him the foal of an ass that he might ride on it, so He sends them to release you from the cares of the world, that leaving the bricks and straw of Egypt, you may follow Him, the true Moses, through the wilderness and may enter the land of promise. Let no one dare to forbid you, neither mother nor sister nor kinswoman nor brother: "The Lord hath need of you." Should they seek to hinder you, let them fear the scourges that fell on Pharaoh, who, because he would not let God's people go that they might serve Him, suffered the plagues described in Scripture. Jesus entering into the temple cast out those things which belonged not to the temple. For God is jealous and will not allow the father's house to be made a den of robbers. Where money is counted, where doves are sold, where simplicity is stifled where, that is, a virgin's breast glows with cares of this world; straightway the veil of the temple is rent, the bridegroom rises in anger, he says: "Your house is left unto you desolate." Read the gospel and see how Mary sitting at the feet of the Lord is set before the zealous Martha. In her anxiety to be hospitable Martha was preparing a meal for the Lord and His disciples; yet Jesus said to her: "Martha, Martha, thou art careful and troubled about many things. But few things are needful or one. And Mary hath chosen that good part which shall not be taken away from her." Be then like Mary; prefer the food of the soul to that of the body. Leave it to your sisters to run to and fro and to seek how they may fitly welcome Christ. But do you, having once for all cast away the burden of the world, sit at the Lord's feet and say: "I have found him whom my soul loveth; I will hold him, I will not let him go." And He will answer: "My dove, my undefiled is but one; she is the only one of her mother, she is the choice one of her that bare her." Now the mother of whom this is said is the heavenly Jerusalem.

25. Ever let the privacy of your chamber guard you; ever let the Bridegroom sport with you within. Do you pray? You speak to the Bridegroom. Do you read? He speaks to you. When sleep overtakes you He will come behind and put His hand through the hole of the door, and your heart shall be moved for Him; and you will awake and rise up and say: "I am sick of love." Then He will reply: "A garden inclosed is my sister, my spouse; a spring shut up, a fountain sealed."

Go not from home nor visit the daughters of a strange land, though you have patriarchs for brothers and Israel for a father. Dinah went out and was seduced. Do not seek the Bridegroom in the streets; do not go round the corners of the city. For though you may say: "I will rise now and go about the city: in the streets and in the broad ways I will seek Him whom my soul loveth," and though you may ask the watchmen: "Saw ye Him whom my soul loveth?" no one will deign to answer you. The Bridegroom cannot be found in the streets: "Strait and narrow is the way which leadeth unto life." So the Song goes on: "I sought him but I could not find him: I called him but he gave me no answer." And would that failure to find Him were all. You will be wounded and stripped, you will lament and say: "The watchmen that went about the city found me: they smote me, they wounded me, they took away my veil from me." Now if one who could say: "I sleep but my heart waketh," and "A bundle of myrrh is my well beloved unto me; he shall lie all night betwixt my breasts"; if one who could speak thus suffered so much because she went abroad, what shall become of us who are but young girls; of us who, when the bride goes in with the Bridegroom, still remain without? Jesus is jealous. He does not choose that your face should be seen of others. You may excuse yourself and say: "I have drawn close my veil, I have covered my face and I have sought Thee there and have said: Tell me, O Thou whom my soul loveth, where Thou feedest Thy flock, where Thou makest it to rest at noon. For why should I be as one that is veiled beside the flocks of Thy companions?'" Yet in spite of your excuses He will be wroth, He will swell with anger and say: "If thou know not thyself, O thou fairest among women, go thy way forth by the footsteps of the flock and feed thy goats beside the shepherd's tents." You may be fair, and of all faces yours may be the dearest to the Bridegroom; yet, unless you know yourself, and keep your heart with all diligence, unless also you avoid the eyes of the young men, you will be turned out of My bride-chamber to feed the goats, which shall be set on the left hand.

26. These things being so, my Eustochium, daughter, lady, fellow-servant, sister—these names refer the first to your age, the second to your rank, the third to your religious vocation, the last to the place which you hold in my affection—hear the words of Isaiah: "Come, my people, enter thou into thy chambers, and shut thy doors about thee: hide thyself as it were for a little moment, until the indignation" of the Lord "be overpast." Let foolish virgins stray abroad, but for your part stay at home with the Bridegroom; for if you shut your door, and, according to the precept of the Gospel, pray to your Father in secret, He will come and knock, saying: "Behold, I stand at the door and knock; if any man . . . open the door, I will come in to him, and will sup with him, and he with me." Then straightway you will eagerly reply: "It is the voice of my beloved that knocketh, saying, Open to me, my sister, my love, my dove, my undefiled." It is impossible that you should refuse, and say: "I have put off my coat; how shall I put it on? I have washed my feet; how shall I defile them?" Arise forthwith and open. Otherwise while you linger He may pass on and you may have mournfully to say: "I opened to my beloved, but my beloved was gone." Why need the doors of your heart be closed to the Bridegroom? Let them be open to Christ but closed to the devil according to the saying: "If the spirit of him who hath power rise up against thee, leave not thy place." Daniel, in that upper story to which he withdrew when he could no longer continue below, had his windows open toward Jerusalem. Do you too keep your windows open, but only on the side where light may enter and

whence you may see the eye of the Lord. Open not those other windows of which the prophet says: "Death is come up into our windows."

27. You must also be careful to avoid the snare of a passion for vainglory. "How," Jesus says, "can ye believe which receive glory one from another?" What an evil that must be the victim of which cannot believe! Let us rather say: "Thou art my glorying," and "He that glorieth, let him glory in the Lord," and "If I yet pleased men I should not be the servant of Christ," and "Far be it from me to glory save in the cross of our Lord Jesus Christ, through whom the world hath been crucified unto me and I unto the world;" and once more: "In God we boast all the day long; my soul shall make her boast in the Lord." When you do alms, let God alone see you. When you fast, be of a cheerful countenance. Let your dress be neither too neat nor too slovenly; neither let it be so remarkable as to draw the attention of passers-by, and to make men point their fingers at you. Is a brother dead? Has the body of a sister to be carried to its burial? Take care lest in too often performing such offices you die yourself. Do not wish to seem very devout nor more humble than need be, lest you seek glory by shunning it. For many, who screen from all men's sight their poverty, charity, and fasting, desire to excite admiration by their very disdain of it, and strangely seek for praise while they profess to keep out of its way. From the other disturbing influences which make men rejoice, despond, hope, and fear I find many free; but this is a defect which few are without, and he is best whose character, like a fair skin, is disfigured by the fewest blemishes. I do not think it necessary to warn you against boasting of your riches, or against priding yourself on your birth, or against setting yourself up as superior to others. I know your humility; I know that you can say with sincerity: "Lord, my heart is not haughty nor mine eyes lofty;" I know that in your breast as in that of your mother the pride through which the devil fell has no place. It would be time wasted to write to you about it; for there is no greater folly than to teach a pupil what he knows already. But now that you have despised the boastfulness of the world, do not let the fact inspire you with new boastfulness. Harbor not the secret thought that having ceased to court attention in garments of gold you may begin to do so in mean attire. And when you come into a room full of brothers and sisters, do not sit in too low a place or plead that you are unworthy of a footstool. Do not deliberately lower your voice as though worn out with fasting; nor, leaning on the shoulder of another, mimic the tottering gait of one who is faint. Some women, it is true, disfigure their faces, that they may appear unto men to fast. As soon as they catch sight of any one they groan, they look down; they cover up their faces, all but one eye, which they keep free to see with. Their dress is sombre, their girdles are of

sackcloth, their hands and feet are dirty; only their stomachs—which cannot be seen—are hot with food. Of these the psalm is sung daily: "The Lord will scatter the bones of them that please themselves." Others change their garb and assume the mien of men, being ashamed of being what they were born to be—women. They cut off their hair and are not ashamed to look like eunuchs. Some clothe themselves in goat's hair, and, putting on hoods, think to become children again by making themselves look like so many owls.

28. But I will not speak only of women. Avoid men, also, when you see them loaded with chains and wearing their hair long like women, contrary to the apostle's precept, not to speak of beards like those of goats, black cloaks, and bare feet braving the cold. All these things are tokens of the devil. Such an one Rome groaned over some time back in Antimus; and Sophronius is a still more recent instance. Such persons, when they have once gained admission to the houses of the high-born, and have deceived "silly women laden with sins, ever learning and never able to come to the knowledge of the truth," feign a sad mien and pretend to make long fasts while at night they feast in secret. Shame forbids me to say more, for my language might appear more like invective than admonition. There are others—I speak of those of my own order—who seek the presbyterate and the diaconate simply that they may be able to see women with less restraint. Such men think of nothing but their dress; they use perfumes freely, and see that there are no creases in their leather shoes. Their curling hair shows traces of the tongs; their fingers glisten with rings; they walk on tiptoe across a damp road, not to splash their feet. When you see men acting in this way, think of them rather as bridegrooms than as clergymen. Certain persons have devoted the whole of their energies and life to the single object of knowing the names, houses, and characters of married ladies. I will here briefly describe the head of the profession, that from the master's likeness you may recognize the disciples. He rises and goes forth with the sun; he has the order of his visits duly arranged; he takes the shortest road; and, troublesome old man that he is, forces his way almost into the bedchambers of ladies yet asleep. If he sees a pillow that takes his fancy or an elegant table-cover—or indeed any article of household furniture—he praises it, looks admiringly at it, takes it into his hand, and, complaining that he has nothing of the kind, begs or rather extorts it from the owner. All the women, in fact, fear to cross the news-carrier of the town. Chastity and fasting are alike distasteful to him. What he likes is a savory breakfast—say off a plump young crane such as is commonly called a cheeper. In speech he is rude and forward, and is always ready to bandy reproaches. Wherever you turn he is the first man that you see before you. Whatever news is noised abroad he is either the origi-

nator of the rumor or its magnifier. He changes his horses every hour; and they are so sleek and spirited that you would take him for a brother of the Thracian king.

29. Many are the stratagems which the wily enemy employs against us. "The serpent," we are told, "was more subtile than any beast of the field which the Lord God had made." And the apostle says: "We are not ignorant of his devices." Neither an affected shabbiness nor a stylish smartness becomes a Christian. If there is anything of which you are ignorant, if you have any doubt about Scripture, ask one whose life commends him, whose age puts him above suspicion, whose reputation does not belie him; one who may be able to say: "I have espoused you to one husband that I may present you as a chaste virgin to Christ." Or if there should be none such able to explain, it is better to avoid danger at the price of ignorance than to court it for the sake of learning. Remember that you walk in the midst of snares, and that many veteran virgins, of a chastity never called in question, have, on the very threshold of death, let their crowns fall from their hands.

If any of your handmaids share your vocation, do not lift up yourself against them or pride yourself because you are their mistress. You have all chosen one Bridegroom; you all sing the same psalms; together you receive the Body of Christ. Why then should your thoughts be different? You must try to win others, and that you may attract the more readily you must treat the virgins in your train with the greatest respect. If you find one of them weak in the faith, be attentive to her, comfort her, caress her, and make her chastity your treasure. But if a girl pretends to have a vocation simply because she desires to escape from service, read aloud to her the words of the apostle: "It is better to marry than to burn."

Idle persons and busybodies, whether virgins or widows; such as go from house to house calling on married women and displaying an unblushing effrontery greater than that of a stage parasite, cast from you as you would the plague. For "evil communications corrupt good manners," and women like these care for nothing but their lowest appetites. They will often urge you, saying, "My dear creature, make the best of your advantages, and live while life is yours," and "Surely you are not laying up money for your children." Given to wine and wantonness, they instill all manner of mischief into people's minds, and induce even the most austere to indulge in enervating pleasures. And "when they have begun to wax wanton against Christ they will marry, having condemnation because they have rejected their first faith."

Do not seek to appear over-eloquent, nor trifle with verse, nor make yourself gay with lyric songs. And do not, out of affectation, follow the sickly taste of married ladies who, now pressing their teeth together, now keeping their lips wide apart, speak with a lisp, and purposely clip their words, because they fancy that to pronounce them naturally is a mark of country breeding. Accordingly they find pleasure in what I may call an adultery of the tongue. For "what communion hath light with darkness? And what concord hath Christ with Belial?" How can Horace go with the psalter, Virgil with the gospels, Cicero with the apostle? Is not a brother made to stumble if he sees you sitting at meat in an idol's temple? Although "unto the pure all things are pure," and "nothing is to be refused if it be received with thanksgiving," still we ought not to drink the cup of Christ, and, at the same time, the cup of devils. Let me relate to you the story of my own miserable experience.

30. Many years ago, when for the kingdom of heaven's sake I had cut myself off from home, parents, sister, relations, and—harder still—from the dainty food to which I had been accustomed; and when I was on my way to Jerusalem to wage my warfare, I still could not bring myself to forego the library which I had formed for myself at Rome with great care and toil. And so, miserable man that I was, I would fast only that I might afterwards read Cicero. After many nights spent in vigil, after floods of tears called from my inmost heart, after the recollection of my past sins, I would once more take up Plautus. And when at times I returned to my right mind, and began to read the prophets, their style seemed rude and repellent. I failed to see the light with my blinded eyes; but I attributed the fault not to them, but to the sun. While the old serpent was thus making me his plaything, about the middle of Lent a deep-seated fever fell upon my weakened body, and while it destroyed my rest completely—the story seems hardly credible—it so wasted my unhappy frame that scarcely anything was left of me but skin and bone. Meantime preparations for my funeral went on; my body grew gradually colder, and the warmth of life lingered only in my throbbing breast. Suddenly I was caught up in the spirit and dragged before the judgment seat of the Judge; and here the light was so bright, and those who stood around were so radiant, that I cast myself upon the ground and did not dare to look up. Asked who and what I was I replied: "I am a Christian." But He who presided said: "Thou liest, thou art a follower of Cicero and not of Christ. For where thy treasure is, there will thy heart be also.'" Instantly I became dumb, and amid the strokes of the lash—for He had ordered me to be scourged—I was tortured more severely still by the fire of conscience, considering with myself that verse, "In the grave who shall give thee thanks?" Yet for all that I began to cry and to bewail myself, saying: "Have mercy upon me, O Lord: have mercy upon me." Amid the sound of the scourges this cry still made itself heard. At last the bystanders, falling down

before the knees of Him who presided, prayed that He would have pity on my youth, and that He would give me space to repent of my error. He might still, they urged, inflict torture on me, should I ever again read the works of the Gentiles. Under the stress of that awful moment I should have been ready to make even still larger promises than these. Accordingly I made oath and called upon His name, saying: "Lord, if ever again I possess worldly books, or if ever again I read such, I have denied Thee." Dismissed, then, on taking this oath, I returned to the upper world, and, to the surprise of all, I opened upon them eyes so drenched with tears that my distress served to convince even the incredulous. And that this was no sleep nor idle dream, such as those by which we are often mocked, I call to witness the tribunal before which I lay, and the terrible judgment which I feared. May it never, hereafter, be my lot to fall under such an inquisition! I profess that my shoulders were black and blue, that I felt the bruises long after I awoke from my sleep, and that thenceforth I read the books of God with a zeal greater than I had previously given to the books of men.

31. You must also avoid the sin of covetousness, and this not merely by refusing to seize upon what belongs to others, for that is punished by the laws of the state, but also by not keeping your own property, which has now become no longer yours. "If have not been faithful," the Lord says, "in that which is another man's, who shall give you that which is your own?" "That which is another man's" is a quantity of gold or of silver, while "that which is our own" is the spiritual heritage of which it is elsewhere said: "The ransom of a man's life is his riches." "No man can serve two masters, for either he will hate the one and love the other; or else he will hold to the one and despise the other. Ye cannot serve God and Mammon." Riches, that is; for in the heathen tongue of the Syrians riches are called mammon. The "thorns" which choke our faith are the taking thought for our life. Care for the things which the Gentiles seek after is the root of covetousness.

But you will say: "I am a girl delicately reared, and I cannot labor with my hands. Suppose that I live to old age and then fall sick, who will take pity on me?" Hear Jesus speaking to the apostles: "Take no thought what ye shall eat; nor yet for your body what ye shall put on. Is not the life more than meat, and the body than raiment? Behold the fowls of the air: for they sow not, neither do they reap nor gather into barns; yet your heavenly Father feedeth them." Should clothing fail you, set the lilies before your eyes. Should hunger seize you, think of the words in which the poor and hungry are blessed. Should pain afflict you, read "Therefore I take pleasure in infirmities," and "There was given to me a thorn in the flesh, the messenger of Satan to buffet me, lest I should be exalted above measure." Rejoice in all God's judgments; for does not the psalmist say: "The daughters of Judah rejoiced because of thy judgments, O Lord"? Let the words be ever on your lips: "Naked came I out of my mother's womb, and naked shall I return thither;" and "We brought nothing into this world, and it is certain we can carry nothing out."

32. To-day you may see women cramming their wardrobes with dresses, changing their gowns from day to day, and for all that unable to vanquish the moths. Now and then one more scrupulous wears out a single dress; yet, while she appears in rags, her boxes are full. Parchments are dyed purple, gold is melted into lettering, manuscripts are decked with jewels, while Christ lies at the door naked and dying. When they hold out a hand to the needy they sound a trumpet; when they invite to a love-feast they engage a crier. I lately saw the noblest lady in Rome—I suppress her name, for I am no satirist—with a band of eunuchs before her in the basilica of the blessed Peter. She was giving money to the poor, a coin apiece; and this with her own hand, that she might be accounted more religious. Hereupon a by no means uncommon incident occurred. An old woman, "full of years and rags," ran forward to get a second coin, but when her turn came she received not a penny but a blow hard enough to draw blood from her guilty veins.

"The love of money is the root of all evil," and the apostle speaks of covetousness as being idolatry. "Seek ye first the kingdom of God and all these things shall be added unto you." The Lord will never allow a righteous soul to perish of hunger. "I have been young," the psalmist says, "and now am old, yet have I not seen the righteous forsaken nor his seed begging bread." Elijah is fed by ministering ravens. The widow of Zarephath, who with her sons expected to die the same night, went without food herself that she might feed the prophet. He who had come to be fed then turned feeder, for, by a miracle, he filled the empty barrel. The apostle Peter says: "Silver and gold have I none, but such as I have give I thee. In the name of Jesus Christ rise up and walk." But now many, while they do not say it in words, by their deeds declare: "Faith and pity have I none; but such as I have, silver and gold, these I will not give thee." "Having food and raiment let us be therewith content." Hear the prayer of Jacob: "If God will be with me and will keep me in this way that I go, and will give me bread to eat and raiment to put on, then shall the Lord be my God." He prayed only for things necessary; yet, twenty years afterwards, he returned to the land of Canaan rich in substance and richer still in children. Numberless are the instances in Scripture which teach men to "Beware of covetousness."

33. As I have been led to touch to the subject—it shall have a treatise to itself if Christ permit—I will relate what took place not very many years ago at Nitria. A brother, more thrifty than covetous, and ignorant that the Lord had been sold for thirty pieces of silver, left behind him at his death a hundred pieces of money which he had earned by weaving linen. As there were about five thousand monks in the neighborhood, living in as many separate cells, a council was held as to what should be done. Some said that the coins should be distributed among the poor; others that they should be given to the church, while others were for sending them back to the relatives of the deceased. However, Macarius, Pambo, Isidore and the rest of those called fathers, speaking by the Spirit, decided that they should be interred with their owner, with the words: "Thy money perish with thee." Nor was this too harsh a decision; for so great fear has fallen upon all throughout Egypt, that it is now a crime to leave after one a single shilling.

34. As I have mentioned the monks, and know that you like to hear about holy things, lend an ear to me for a few moments. There are in Egypt three classes of monks. First, there are the coenobites, called in their Gentile language Sauses, or, as we should say, men living in a community. Secondly, there are the anchorites, who live in the desert, each man by himself, and are so called because they have withdrawn from human society. Thirdly, there is the class called Remoboth, a very inferior and little regarded type, peculiar to my own province, or, at least, originating there. These live together in twos and threes, but seldom in larger numbers, and are bound by no rule; but do exactly as they choose. A portion of their earnings they contribute to a common fund, out of which food is provided for all. In most cases they reside in cities and strongholds; and, as though it were their workmanship which is holy, and not their life, all that they sell is extremely dear. They often quarrel because they are unwilling, while supplying their own food, to be subordinate to others. It is true that they compete with each other in fasting; they make what should be a private concern an occasion for a triumph. In everything they study effect: their sleeves are loose, their boots bulge, their garb is of the coarsest. They are always sighing, or visiting virgins, or sneering at the clergy; yet when a holiday comes, they make themselves sick—they eat so much.

35. Having then rid ourselves of these as of so many plagues, let us come to that more numerous class who live together, and who are, as we have said, called Coenobites. Among these the first principle of union is to obey superiors and to do whatever they command. They are divided into bodies of ten and of a hundred, so that each tenth man has authority over nine others, while the hundredth has ten of these officers under him. They live apart from each

other, in separate cells. According to their rule, no monk may visit another before the ninth hour; except the deans above mentioned, whose office is to comfort, with soothing words, those whose thoughts disquiet them. After the ninth hour they meet together to sing psalms and read the Scriptures according to usage. Then when the prayers have ended and all have sat down, one called the father stands up among them and begins to expound the portion of the day. While he is speaking the silence is profound; no man ventures to look at his neighbor or to clear his throat. The speaker's praise is in the weeping of his hearers. Silent tears roll down their cheeks, but not a sob escapes from their lips. Yet when he begins to speak of Christ's kingdom, and of future bliss, and of the glory which is to come, every one may be noticed saying to himself, with a gentle sigh and uplifted eyes: "Oh, that I had wings like a dove! For then would I fly away and be at rest." After this the meeting breaks up and each company of ten goes with its father to its own table. This they take in turns to serve each for a week at a time. No noise is made over the food; no one talks while eating. Bread, pulse and greens form their fare, and the only seasoning that they use is salt. Wine is given only to the old, who with the children often have a special meal prepared for them to repair the ravages of age and to save the young from premature decay. When the meal is over they all rise together, and, after singing a hymn, return to their dwellings. There each one talks till evening with his comrade thus: "Have you noticed so-and-so? What grace he has! How silent he is! How soberly he walks!" If any one is weak they comfort him; or if he is fervent in love to God, they encourage him to fresh earnestness. And because at night, besides the public prayers, each man keeps vigil in his own chamber, they go round all the cells one by one, and putting their ears to the doors, carefully ascertain what their occupants are doing. If they find a monk slothful, they do not scold him; but, dissembling what they know, they visit him more frequently, and at first exhort rather than compel him to pray more. Each day has its allotted task, and this being given in to the dean, is by him brought to the steward. This latter, once a month, gives a scrupulous account to their common father. He also tastes the dishes when they are cooked, and, as no one is allowed to say, "I am without a tunic or a cloak or a couch of rushes," he so arranges that no one need ask for or go without what he wants. In case a monk falls ill, he is moved to a more spacious chamber, and there so attentively nursed by the old men, that he misses neither the luxury of cities nor a mother's kindness. Every Lord's day they spend their whole time in prayer and reading; indeed, when they have finished their tasks, these are their usual occupations. Every day they learn by heart a portion of Scripture. They keep the same fasts all the year round, but in Lent they are allowed to live more strictly. After Whitsuntide they exchange their evening meal for a mid-day one; both to satisfy the tradition of the church and to avoid overloading their stomachs with a double supply of food.

A similar description is given of the Essenes by Philo, Plato's imitator; also by Josephus, the Greek Livy, in his narrative of the Jewish captivity.

36. As my present subject is virgins, I have said rather too much about monks. I will pass on, therefore, to the third class, called anchorites, who go from the monasteries into the deserts, with nothing but bread and salt. Paul introduced this way of life; Antony made it famous, and—to go farther back still—John the Baptist set the first example of it. The prophet Jeremiah describes one such in the words: "It is good for a man that he bear the yoke in his youth. He sitteth alone and keepeth silence, because he hath borne it upon him. He giveth his cheek to him that smiteth him, he is filled full with reproach. For the Lord will not cast off forever." The struggle of the anchorites and their life—in the flesh, yet not of the flesh—I will, if you wish, explain to you at some other time. I must now return to the subject of covetousness, which I left to speak of the monks. With them before your eyes you will despise, not only gold and silver in general, but earth itself and heaven. United to Christ, you will sing, "The Lord is my portion."

37. Farther, although the apostle bids us to "pray without ceasing," and although to the saints their very sleep is a supplication, we ought to have fixed hours of prayer, that if we are detained by work, the time may remind us of our duty. Prayers, as every one knows, ought to be said at the third, sixth and ninth hours, at dawn and at evening. No meal should be begun without prayer, and before leaving table thanks should be returned to the Creator. We should rise two or three times in the night, and go over the parts of Scripture which we know by heart. When we leave the roof which shelters us, prayer should be our armor; and when we return from the street we should pray before we sit down, and not give the frail body rest until the soul is fed. In every act we do, in every step we take, let our hand trace the Lord's cross. Speak against nobody, and do not slander your mother's son. "Who art thou that judgest the servant of another? To his own lord he standeth or falleth; yea, he shall be made to stand, for the Lord hath power to make him stand." If you have fasted two or three days, do not think yourself better than others who do not fast. You fast and are angry; another eats and wears a smiling face. You work off your irritation and hunger in quarrels. He uses food in moderation and gives God thanks. Daily Isaiah cries: "Is it such a fast that I have chosen, saith the Lord?" and again: "In the day of your fast ye find your own pleasure, and oppress all your laborers. Behold ye fast for strife and contention, and to

smite with the fist of wickedness. How fast ye unto me?" What kind of fast can his be whose wrath is such that not only does the night go down upon it, but that even the moon's changes leave it unchanged?

38. Look to yourself and glory in your own success and not in others' failure. Some women care for the flesh and reckon up their income and daily expenditure: such are no fit models for you. Judas was a traitor, but the eleven apostles did not waver. Phygellus and Alexander made shipwreck; but the rest continued to run the race of faith. Say not: "So-and-so enjoys her own property, she is honored of men, her brothers and sisters come to see her. Has she then ceased to be a virgin?" In the first place, it is doubtful if she is a virgin. For "the Lord seeth not as man seeth; for man looketh upon the outward appearance, but the Lord looketh on the heart." Again, she may be a virgin in body and not in spirit. According to the apostle, a true virgin is "holy both in body and in spirit." Lastly, let her glory in her own way. Let her override Paul's opinion and live in the enjoyment of her good things. But you and I must follow better examples.

Set before you the blessed Mary, whose surpassing purity made her meet to be the mother of the Lord. When the angel Gabriel came down to her, in the form of a man, and said: "Hail, thou that art highly favored; the Lord is with thee," she was terror-stricken and unable to reply, for she had never been saluted by a man before. But, on learning who he was, she spoke, and one who had been afraid of a man conversed fearlessly with an angel. Now you, too, may be the Lord's mother. "Take thee a great roll and write in it with a man's pen Maher-shalal-hash-baz." And when you have gone to the prophetess, and have conceived in the womb, and have brought forth a son, say: "Lord, we have been with child by thy fear, we have been in pain, we have brought forth the spirit of thy salvation, which we have wrought upon the earth." Then shall your Son reply: "Behold my mother and my brethren." And He whose name you have so recently inscribed upon the table of your heart, and have written with a pen upon its renewed surface—He, after He has recovered the spoil from the enemy, and has spoiled principalities and powers, nailing them to His cross—having been miraculously conceived, grows up to manhood; and, as He becomes older, regards you no longer as His mother, but as His bride. To be as the martyrs, or as the apostles, or as Christ, involves a hard struggle, but brings with it a great reward.

All such efforts are only of use when they are made within the church's pale; we must celebrate the passover in the one house, we must enter the ark with Noah, we must take refuge from the fall of Jericho with the justified harlot, Rahab. Such virgins as there are said to be among the heretics and among the followers of the infamous Manes must be considered, not virgins, but prostitutes. For if—as they allege—the devil is the author of the body, how can they honor that which is fashioned by their foe? No; it is because they know that the name virgin brings glory with it, that they go about as wolves in sheep's clothing. As antichrist pretends to be Christ, such virgins assume an honorable name, that they may the better cloak a discreditable life. Rejoice, my sister; rejoice, my daughter; rejoice, my virgin; for you have resolved to be, in reality, that which others insincerely feign.

39. The things that I have here set forth will seem hard to her who loves not Christ. But one who has come to regard all the splendor of the world as off-scourings, and to hold all things under the sun as vain, that he may win Christ; one who has died with his Lord and risen again, and has crucified the flesh with its affections and lusts; he will boldly cry out: "Who shall separate us from the love of Christ? Shall tribulation, or distress, or persecution, or famine, or nakedness, or peril, or sword?" and again: "I am persuaded that neither death nor life, nor angels, nor principalities nor powers, nor things present, nor things to come, nor height, nor depth, nor any other creature shall be able to separate us from the love of God which is in Christ Jesus, our Lord."

For our salvation the Son of God is made the Son of Man. Nine months He awaits His birth in the womb, undergoes the most revolting conditions, and comes forth covered with blood, to be swathed in rags and covered with caresses. He who shuts up the world in His fist is contained in the narrow limits of a manger. I say nothing of the thirty years during which he lives in obscurity, satisfied with the poverty of his parents. When He is scourged He holds His peace; when He is crucified, He prays for His crucifiers. "What shall I render unto the Lord for all His benefits towards me? I will take the cup of salvation and call upon the name of the Lord. Precious in the sight of the Lord is the death of His saints." The only fitting return that we can make to Him is to give blood for blood; and, as we are redeemed by the blood of Christ, gladly to lay down our lives for our Redeemer. What saint has ever won his crown without first contending for it? Righteous Abel is murdered. Abraham is in danger of losing his wife. And, as I must not enlarge my book unduly, seek for yourself: you will find that all holy men have suffered adversity. Solomon alone lived in luxury and perhaps it was for this reason that he fell. For "whom the Lord loveth, He chasteneth, and scourgeth every son whom He receiveth." Which is best—for a short time to do battle, to carry stakes for the palisades, to bear arms, to faint under heavy bucklers, that ever afterwards we may rejoice as victors? or to become slaves forever, just because we cannot endure for a single hour?

40. Love finds nothing hard; no task is difficult to the eager. Think of all that Jacob bore for Rachel, the wife who had been promised to him. "Jacob," the Scripture says, "served seven years for Rachel. And they seemed unto him but a few days for the love he had to her." Afterwards he himself tells us what he had to undergo. "In the day the drought consumed me and the frost by night." So we must love Christ and always seek His embraces. Then everything difficult will seem easy; all things long we shall account short; and smitten with His arrows, we shall say every moment: "Woe is me that I have prolonged my pilgrimage." For "the sufferings of this present time are not worthy to be compared with the glory which shall be revealed in us." For "tribulation worketh patience, and patience experience, and experience hope; and hope maketh not ashamed." When your lot seems hard to bear read Paul's second epistle to the Corinthians: "In labors more abundant; in stripes above measure; in prisons more frequent; in deaths oft. Of the Jews five times received I forty stripes save one; thrice was I beaten with rods; once was I stoned; thrice I suffered shipwreck; a night and a day I have been in the deep; in journeyings often, in perils of waters, in perils of robbers, in perils by mine own countrymen, in perils by the heathen, in perils in the city, in perils in the wilderness, in perils in the sea, in perils among false brethren, in weariness and painfulness, in watchings often, in hunger and thirst, in fastings often, in cold and nakedness." Which of us can claim the veriest fraction of the virtues here enumerated? Yet it was these which afterwards made him bold to say: "I have finished my course, I have kept the faith. Henceforth there is laid up for me a crown of righteousness which the Lord, the righteous Judge, shall give me at that day."

But we, if our food is less appetizing than usual, get sullen, and fancy that we do God a favor by drinking watered wine. And if the water brought to us is a trifle too warm, we break the cup and overturn the table and scourge the servant in fault until blood comes. "The kingdom of heaven suffereth violence and the violent take it by force." Still, unless you use force you will never seize the kingdom of heaven. Unless you knock importunately you will never receive the sacramental bread. Is it not truly violence, think you, when the flesh desires to be as God and ascends to the place whence angels have fallen to judge angels?

41. Emerge, I pray you, for a while from your prison-house, and paint before your eyes the reward of your present toil, a reward which "eye hath not seen, nor ear heard, neither hath it entered into the heart of man." What will be the glory of that day when Mary, the mother of the Lord, shall come to meet you, accompanied by her virgin choirs! When, the Red Sea past and Pharaoh drowned with his host, Miriam, Aaron's sister, her timbrel in her

hand, shall chant to the answering women: "Sing ye unto the Lord, for he hath triumphed gloriously; the horse and his rider hath he thrown into the sea." Then shall Thecla fly with joy to embrace you. Then shall your Spouse himself come forward and say: "Rise up, my love, my fair one, and come away, for lo! the winter is past, the rain is over and gone." Then shall the angels say with wonder: "Who is she that looketh forth as the morning, fair as the moon, clear as the sun?" "The daughters shall see you and bless you; yea, the queens shall proclaim and the concubines shall praise you." And, after these, yet another company of chaste women will meet you. Sarah will come with the wedded; Anna, the daughter of Phanuel, with the widows. In the one band you will find your natural mother and in the other your spiritual. The one will rejoice in having borne, the other will exult in having taught you. Then truly will the Lord ride upon his ass, and thus enter the heavenly Jerusalem. Then the little ones (of whom, in Isaiah, the Saviour says: "Behold, I and the children whom the Lord hath given me") shall lift up palms of victory and shall sing with one voice: "Hosanna in the highest, blessed is he that cometh in the name of the Lord, hosanna in the highest." Then shall the "hundred and forty and four thousand" hold their harps before the throne and before the elders and shall sing the new song. And no man shall have power to learn that song save those for whom it is appointed. "These are they which were not defiled with women; for they are virgins. These are they which follow the Lamb whithersoever he goeth." As often as this life's idle show tries to charm you; as often as you see in the world some vain pomp, transport yourself in mind to Paradise, essay to be now what you will be hereafter, and you will hear your Spouse say: "Set me as a sunshade in thine heart and as a seal upon thine arm." And then, strengthened in body as well as in mind, you, too, will cry aloud and say: "Many waters cannot quench love, neither can the floods drown it."

LETTER XXIII. TO MARCELLA

Jerome writes to Marcella to console her for the loss of a friend who, like herself, was the head of a religious society at Rome. The news of Lea's death had first reached Marcella when she was engaged with Jerome in the study of the 73d psalm. Later in the day he writes this letter in which, after extolling Lea, he contrasts her end with that of the consul-elect, Vettius Agorius Praetextatus, a man of great ability and integrity, whom he declares to be now "in Tartarus." Written at Rome in 384 a.d.

1. To-day, about the third hour, just as I was beginning to read with you the seventy-second psalm—the first, that is, of the third book—and to explain that its title belonged partly to the second book and partly to the third—the previous book, I mean, concluding with the words "the prayers of David the son of Jesse are ended," and the next commencing with the words "a psalm of Asaph"—and just as I had come on the passage in which the righteous man declares: "If I say, I will speak thus; behold I should offend against the generation of thy children," a verse which is differently rendered in our Latin version:—suddenly the news came that our most saintly friend Lea had departed from the body. As was only natural, you turned deadly pale; for there are few persons, if any, who do not burst into tears when the earthen vessel breaks. But if you wept it was not from doubt as to her future lot, but only because you had not rendered to her the last sad offices which are due to the dead. Finally, as we were still conversing together, a second message informed us that her remains had been already conveyed to Ostia.

2. You may ask what is the use of repeating all this. I will reply in the apostle's words, "much every way." First, it shows that all must hail with joy the release of a soul which has trampled Satan under foot, and won for itself, at last, a crown of tranquillity. Secondly, it gives me an opportunity of briefly describing her life. Thirdly, it enables me to assure you that the consul-elect, that detractor of his age, is now in Tartarus.

Who can sufficiently eulogize our dear Lea's mode of living? So complete was her conversion to the Lord that, becoming the head of a monastery, she showed herself a true mother to the virgins in it, wore coarse sackcloth instead of soft raiment, passed sleepless nights in prayer, and instructed her companions even more by example than by precept. So great was her humility that she, who had once been the mistress of many, was accounted the servant of all; and certainly, the less she was reckoned an earthly mistress the more she became a servant of Christ. She was careless of her dress, neglected her hair, and ate only the coarsest food. Still, in all that she did, she avoided ostentation that she might not have her reward in this world.

3. Now, therefore, in return for her short toil, Lea enjoys everlasting felicity; she is welcomed into the choirs of the angels; she is comforted in Abraham's bosom. And, as once the beggar Lazarus saw the rich man, for all his purple, lying in torment, so does Lea see the consul, not now in his triumphal robe but clothed in mourning, and asking for a drop of water from her little finger. How great a change have we here! A few days ago the highest dignitaries of the city walked before him as he ascended the ramparts of the capitol like a general celebrating a triumph; the Roman people leapt up to welcome and

applaud him, and at the news of his death the whole city was moved. Now he is desolate and naked, a prisoner in the foulest darkness, and not, as his unhappy wife falsely asserts, set in the royal abode of the milky way. On the other hand Lea, who was always shut up in her one closet, who seemed poor and of little worth, and whose life was accounted madness, now follows Christ and sings, "Like as we have heard, so have we seen in the city of our God."

4. And now for the moral of all this, which, with tears and groans, I conjure you to remember. While we run the way of this world, we must not clothe ourselves with two coats, that is, with a twofold faith, or burthen ourselves with leathern shoes, that is, with dead works; we must not allow scrips filled with money to weigh us down, or lean upon the staff of worldly power. We must not seek to possess both Christ and the world. No; things eternal must take the place of things transitory; and since, physically speaking, we daily anticipate death, if we wish for immortality we must realize that we are but mortal.

LETTER XXIV. TO MARCELLA

Concerning the virgin Asella. Dedicated to God before her birth, Marcella's sister had been made a church-virgin at the age of ten. From that time she had lived a life of the severest asceticism, first as a member and then as the head of Marcella's community upon the Aventine. Jerome, who subsequently wrote her a letter (XLV) on his departure from Rome, now holds her up as a model to be admired and imitated. Written at Rome a.d. 384.

1. Let no one blame my letters for the eulogies and censures which are contained in them. To arraign sinners is to admonish those in like case, and to praise the virtuous is to quicken the zeal of those who wish to do right. The day before yesterday I spoke to you concerning Lea of blessed memory, and I had hardly done so, when I was pricked in my conscience. It would be wrong for me, I thought, to ignore a virgin after speaking of one who, as a widow, held a lower place. Accordingly, in my present letter, I mean to give you a brief sketch of the life of our dear Asella. Please do not read it to her; for she is sure to be displeased with eulogies of which she is herself the object. Show it rather to the young girls of your acquaintance, that they may guide themselves by her example, and may take her behavior as the pattern of a perfect life.

2. I pass over the facts that, before her birth, she was blessed while still in her mother's womb, and that, virgin-like, she was delivered to her father in a dream in a bowl of shining glass brighter than a mirror. And I say nothing of

her consecration to the blessed life of virginity, a ceremony which took place when she was hardly more than ten years old, a mere babe still wrapped in swaddling clothes. For all that comes before works should be counted of grace; although, doubtless, God foreknew the future when He sanctified Jeremiah as yet unborn, when He made John to leap in his mother's womb, and when, before the foundation of the world, He set apart Paul to preach the gospel of His son.

3. I come now to the life which after her twelfth year she, by her own exertion, chose, laid hold of, held fast to, entered upon, and fulfilled. Shut up in her narrow cell she roamed through paradise. Fasting was her recreation and hunger her refreshment. If she took food it was not from love of eating, but because of bodily exhaustion; and the bread and salt and cold water to which she restricted herself sharpened her appetite more than they appeased it.

But I have almost forgotten to mention that of which I should have spoken first. When her resolution was still fresh she took her gold necklace made in the lamprey pattern (so called because bars of metal are linked together so as to form a flexible chain), and sold it without her parents' knowledge. Then putting on a dark dress such as her mother had never been willing that she should wear, she concluded her pious enterprise by consecrating herself forthwith to the Lord. She thus showed her relatives that they need hope to wring no farther concessions from one who, by her very dress, had condemned the world.

4. To go on with my story, her ways were quiet and she lived in great privacy. In fact, she rarely went abroad or spoke to a man. More wonderful still, much as she loved her virgin sister, she did not care to see her. She worked with her own hands, for she knew that it was written: "If any will not work neither shall he eat." To the Bridegroom she spoke constantly in prayer and psalmody. She hurried to the martyrs' shrines unnoticed. Such visits gave her pleasure, and the more so because she was never recognized. All the year round she observed a continual fast, remaining without food for two or three days at a time; but when Lent came she hoisted—if I may so speak—every stitch of canvas and fasted well-nigh from week's end to week's end with "a cheerful countenance." What would perhaps be incredible, were it not that "with God all things are possible," is that she lived this life until her fiftieth year without weakening her digestion or bringing on herself the pain of colic. Lying on the dry ground did not affect her limbs, and the rough sackcloth that she wore failed to make her skin either foul or rough. With a sound body and a still sounder soul she sought all her delight in solitude, and found for herself a monkish hermitage in the centre of busy Rome.

5. You are better acquainted with all this than I am, and the few details that I have given I have learned from you. So intimate are you with Asella that you have seen, with your own eyes, her holy knees hardened like those of a camel from the frequency of her prayers. I merely set forth what I can glean from you. She is alike pleasant in her serious moods and serious in her pleasant ones: her manner, while winning, is always grave, and while grave is always winning. Her pale face indicates continence but does not betoken ostentation. Her speech is silent and her silence is speech. Her pace is neither too fast nor too slow. Her demeanor is always the same. She disregards refinement and is careless about her dress. When she does attend to it it is without attending. So entirely consistent has her life been that here in Rome, the centre of vain shows, wanton license, and idle pleasure, where to be humble is to be held spiritless, the good praise her conduct and the bad do not venture to impugn it. Let widows and virgins imitate her, let wedded wives make much of her, let sinful women fear her, and let bishops look up to her.

LETTER XXV. TO MARCELLA

An explanation of the ten names given to God in the Hebrew Scriptures. The ten names are El, Elohim, Sabaoth, Elion, Asher yeheyeh (Ex. iii. 14), Adonai, Jah, the tetragram JHVH, and Shaddai. Written at Rome 384 a.d.

LETTER XXVI. TO MARCELLA

An explanation of certain Hebrew words which have been left untranslated in the versions. The words are Alleluia, Amen, Maran atha. Written at Rome 384 a.d.

LETTER XXVII. TO MARCELLA

In this letter Jerome defends himself against the charge of having altered the text of Scripture, and shows that he has merely brought the Latin Version of the N.T. into agreement with the Greek original. Written at Rome 384 a.d.

1. After I had written my former letter, containing a few remarks on some Hebrew words, a report suddenly reached me that certain contemptible creatures were deliberately assailing me with the charge that I had endeavored to correct passages in the gospels, against the authority of the ancients and the

opinion of the whole world. Now, though I might—as far as strict right goes—treat these persons with contempt (it is idle to play the lyre for an ass), yet, lest they should follow their usual habit and reproach me with superciliousness, let them take my answer as follows: I am not so dull-wilted nor so coarsely ignorant (qualities which they take for holiness, calling themselves the disciples of fishermen as if men were made holy by knowing nothing)—I am not, I repeat, so ignorant as to suppose that any of the Lord's words is either in need of correction or is not divinely inspired; but the Latin manuscripts of the Scriptures are proved to be faulty by the variations which all of them exhibit, and my object has been to restore them to the form of the Greek original, from which my detractors do not deny that they have been translated. If they dislike water drawn from the clear spring, let them drink of the muddy streamlet, and when they come to read the Scriptures, let them lay aside the keen eye which they turn on woods frequented by game-birds and waters abounding in shellfish. Easily satisfied in this instance alone, let them, if they will, regard the words of Christ as rude sayings, albeit that over these so many great intellects have labored for so many ages rather to divine than to expound the meaning of each single word. Let them charge the great apostle with want of literary skill, although it is said of him that much learning made him mad.

2. I know that as you read these words you will knit your brows, and fear that my freedom of speech is sowing the seeds of fresh quarrels; and that, if you could, you would gladly put your finger on my mouth to prevent me from even speaking of things which others do not blush to do. But, I ask you, wherein have I used too great license? Have I ever embellished my dinner plates with engravings of idols? Have I ever, at a Christian banquet, set before the eyes of virgins the polluting spectacle of Satyrs embracing bacchanals? or have I ever assailed any one in too bitter terms? Have I ever complained of beggars turned millionaires? Have I ever censured heirs for the funerals which they have given to their benefactors? The one thing that I have unfortunately said has been that virgins ought to live more in the company of women than of men, and by this I have made the whole city look scandalized and caused every one to point at me the finger of scorn. "They that hate me without a cause are more than the hairs of mine head," and I am become "a proverb to them." Do you suppose after this that I will now say anything rash?

3. But "when I set the wheel rolling I began to form a wine flagon; how comes it that a waterpot is the result?" Lest Horace laugh at me I come back to my two-legged asses, and din into their ears, not the music of the lute, but the blare of the trumpet. They may say if they will, "rejoicing in hope; serving the time," but we will say "rejoicing in hope; serving the Lord." They may see fit

to receive an accusation against a presbyter unconditionally; but we will say in the words of Scripture, "Against an elder receive not an accusation, but before two or three witnesses. Them that sin rebuke before all." They may choose to read, "It is a man's saying, and worthy of all acceptation;" we are content to err with the Greeks, that is to say with the apostle himself, who spoke Greek. Our version, therefore, is, it is "a faithful saying, and worthy of all acceptation." Lastly, let them take as much pleasure as they please in their Gallican "geldings;" we will be satisfied with the simple "ass" of Zechariah, loosed from its halter and made ready for the Saviour's service, which received the Lord on its back, and so fulfilled Isaiah's prediction: "Blessed is he that soweth beside all waters, where the ox and the ass tread under foot."

LETTER XXVIII. TO MARCELLA

An explanation of the Hebrew word Selah. This word, rendered by the LXX. diapsalma and by Aquila aei, was as much a crux in Jerome's day as it is in ours. "Some," he writes, "make it a change of metre,' others a pause for breath,' others the beginning of a new subject.' According to yet others it has something to do with rhythm or marks a burst of instrumental music." Jerome himself inclines to follow Aquila and Origen, who make the word mean "forever," and suggests that it betokens completion, like the "explicit" or "feliciter" in contemporary Latin mss. Written at Rome a.d. 384.

LETTER XXIX. TO MARCELLA

An explanation of the Hebrew words Ephod bad (1 Sam. ii. 18) and Teraphim (Judges xvii. 5). Written at Rome to Marcella, also at Rome a.d. 384.

LETTER XXX. TO PAULA

Some account of the so-called alphabetical psalms (XXXVII., CXI., CXII., CXIX., CXLV.). After explaining the mystical meaning of the alphabet, Jerome goes on thus: "What honey is sweeter than to know the wisdom of God? others, if they will, may possess riches, drink from a jewelled cup, shine in silks, and try in vain to exhaust their wealth in the most varied pleasures. Our riches are to meditate in the law of the Lord day and night, to knock at the closed door, to receive the three loaves' of the Trinity, and, when the Lord goes before us, to walk upon the water of the world." Written at Rome a.d. 384.

LETTER XXXI. TO EUSTOCHIUM

Jerome writes to thank Eustochium for some presents sent to him by her on the festival of St. Peter. He also moralizes on the mystical meaning of the articles sent. The letter should be compared with Letter XLIV., of which the theme is similar. Written at Rome in 384 a.d. (on St. Peter's Day).

1. Doves, bracelets, and a letter are outwardly but small gifts to receive from a virgin, but the action which has prompted them enhances their value. And since honey may not be offered in sacrifice to God, you have shown skill in taking off their overmuch sweetness and making them pungent—if I may so say—with a dash of pepper. For nothing that is simply pleasurable or merely sweet can please God. Everything must have in it a sharp seasoning of truth. Christ's passover must be eaten with bitter herbs.

2. It is true that a festival such as the birthday of Saint Peter should be seasoned with more gladness than usual; still our merriment must not forget the limit set by Scripture, and we must not stray too far from the boundary of our wrestling-ground. Your presents, indeed, remind me of the sacred volume, for in it Ezekiel decks Jerusalem with bracelets, Baruch receives letters from Jeremiah, and the Holy Spirit descends in the form of a dove at the baptism of Christ. But to give you, too, a sprinkling of pepper and to remind you of my former letter, I send you to-day this three-fold warning. Cease not to adorn yourself with good works—the true bracelets of a Christian woman. Rend not the letter written on your heart as the profane king cut with his penknife that delivered to him by Baruch. Let not Hosea say to you as to Ephraim, "Thou art like a silly dove."

My words are too harsh, you will say, and hardly suitable to a festival like the present. If so, you have provoked me to it by the nature of your own gifts. So long as you put bitter with sweet, you must expect the same from me, sharp words that is, as well as praise.

3. However, I do not wish to make light of your gifts, least of all the basket of fine cherries, blushing with such a virgin modesty that I can fancy them freshly gathered by Lucullus himself. For it was he who first introduced the fruit at Rome after his conquest of Pontus and Armenia; and the cherry tree is so called because he brought it from Cerasus. Now as the Scriptures do not mention cherries, but do speak of a basket of figs, I will use these instead to

point my moral. May you be made of fruits such as those which grow before God's temple and of which He says, "Behold they are good, very good." The Saviour likes nothing that is half and half, and, while he welcomes the hot and does not shun the cold, he tells us in the Apocalypse that he will spew the lukewarm out of his mouth. Wherefore we must be careful to celebrate our holy day not so much with abundance of food as with exultation of spirit. For it is altogether unreasonable to wish to honor a martyr by excess who himself, as you know, pleased God by fasting. When you take food always recollect that eating should be followed by reading, and also by prayer. And if, by taking this course, you displease some, repeat to yourself the words of the Apostle: "If I yet pleased men I should not be the servant of Christ"

LETTER XXXII. TO MARCELLA

Jerome writes that he is busy collating Aquila's Greek version of the Old Testament with the Hebrew, inquires after Marcella's mother, and forwards the two preceding letters (XXX., XXXI.). Written at Rome in 384 a.d.

1. There are two reasons for the shortness of this letter, one that its bearer is impatient to start, and the other that I am too busy to waste time on trifles. You ask what business can be so urgent as to stop me from a chat on paper. Let me tell you, then, that for some time past I have been comparing Aquila's version of the Old Testament with the scrolls of the Hebrew, to see if from hatred to Christ the synagogue has changed the text; and—to speak frankly to a friend—I have found several variations which confirm our faith. After having exactly revised the prophets, Solomon, the psalter, and the books of Kings, I am now engaged on Exodus (called by the Jews, from its opening words, Eleh shemoth), and when I have finished this I shall go on to Leviticus. Now you see why I can let no claim for a letter withdraw me from my work. However, as I do not wish my friend Currentius to run altogether in vain, I have tacked on to this little talk two letters which I am sending to your sister Paula, and to her dear child Eustochium. Read these, and if you find them instructive or pleasant, take what I have said to them as meant for you also.

2. I hope that Albina, your mother and mine, is well. In bodily health, I mean, for I doubt not of her spiritual welfare. Pray salute her for me, and cherish her with double affection, both as a Christian and as a mother.

LETTER XXXIII. TO PAULA

A fragment of a letter in which Jerome institutes a comparison between the industry as writers of M. T. Varro and Origen. It is noteworthy as passing an unqualified eulogium upon Origen, which contrasts strongly with the tone adopted by the writer in subsequent years (see, e.g., Letter LXXXIV.). Its date is probably 384 a.d.

1. Antiquity marvels at Marcus Terentius Varro, because of the countless books which he wrote for Latin readers; and Greek writers are extravagant in their praise of their man of brass, because he has written more works than one of us could so much as copy. But since Latin ears would find a list of Greek writings tiresome, I shall confine myself to the Latin Varro. I shall try to show that we of to-day are sleeping the sleep of Epimenides, and devoting to the amassing of riches the energy which our predecessors gave to sound, if secular, learning.

2. Varro's writings include forty-five books of antiquities, four concerning the life of the Roman people.

3. But why, you ask me, have I thus mentioned Varro and the man of brass? Simply to bring to your notice our Christian man of brass, or, rather, man of adamant—Origen, I mean—whose zeal for the study of Scripture has fairly earned for him this latter name. Would you learn what monuments of his genius he has left us? The following list exhibits them. His writings comprise thirteen books on Genesis, two books of Mystical Homilies, notes on Exodus, notes on Leviticus, * * * * also single books, four books on First Principles, two books on the Resurrection, two dialogues on the same subject.

* * * * * * * * * * *

4. So, you see, the labors of this one man have surpassed those of all previous writers, Greek and Latin. Who has ever managed to read all that he has written? Yet what reward have his exertions brought him? He stands condemned by his bishop, Demetrius, only the bishops of Palestine, Arabia, Phenicia, and Achaia dissenting. Imperial Rome consents to his condemnation, and even convenes a senate to censure him, not—as the rabid hounds who now pursue him cry—because of the novelty or heterodoxy of his doctrines, but because men could not tolerate the incomparable eloquence and knowledge which, when once he opened his lips, made others seem dumb.

5. I have written the above quickly and incautiously, by the light of a poor lantern. You will see why, if you think of those who to-day represent Epicurus and Aristippus.

LETTER XXXIV. TO MARCELLA

In reply to a request from Marcella for information concerning two phrases in Ps. cxxvii. ("bread of sorrow," v. 2, and "children of the shaken off," A.V. "of the youth," v. 4). Jerome, after lamenting that Origen's notes on the psalm are no longer extant, gives the following explanations:

The Hebrew phrase "bread of sorrow" is rendered by the LXX. "bread of idols"; by Aquila, "bread of troubles"; by Symmachus, "bread of misery." Theodotion follows the LXX. So does Origen's Fifth Version. The Sixth renders "bread of error." In support of the LXX. the word used here is in Ps. cxv. 4, translated "idols." Either the troubles of life are meant or else the tenets of heresy.

With the second phrase he deals at greater length. After showing that Hilary of Poitiers's view (viz. that the persons meant are the apostles, who were told to shake the dust off their feet, Matt. x. 14) is untenable and would require "shakers off" to be substituted for "shaken off," Jerome reverts to the Hebrew as before and declares that the true rendering is that of Symmachus and Theodotion, viz. "children of youth." He points out that the LXX. (by whom the Latin translators had been misled) fall into the same mistake at Neh. iv. 16. Finally he corrects a slip of Hilary as to Ps. cxxviii. 2, where, through a misunderstanding of the LXX., the latter had substituted "the labors of thy fruits" for "the labors of thy hands." He speaks throughout with high respect of Hilary, and says that it was not the bishop's fault that he was ignorant of Hebrew. The date of the letter is probably a.d. 384.

LETTER XXXV. FROM POPE DAMASUS

Damasus addresses five questions to Jerome with a request for information concerning them. They are:

1. What is the meaning of the words "Whosoever slayeth Cain vengeance shall be taken on him sevenfold"? (Gen. iv. 5.)

2. If God has made all things good, how comes it that He gives charge to Noah concerning unclean animals, and says to Peter, "What God hath cleansed that call not thou common"? (Acts x. 15.)

3. How is Gen. xv. 16, "in the fourth generation they shall come hither again," to be reconciled with Ex. xiii. 18, LXX, "in the fifth generation the children of Israel went up out of the land of Egypt"?

4. Why did Abraham receive circumcision as a seal of his faith? (Rom. iv. 11.)

5. Why was Isaac, a righteous man and dear to God, allowed by God to become the dupe of Jacob? (Gen. xxvii.) Written at Rome 384 a.d.

LETTER XXXVI. TO POPE DAMASUS

Jerome's reply to the foregoing. For the second and fourth questions he refers Damasus to the writings of Tertullian, Novatian, and Origen. The remaining three he deals with in detail.

Gen. iv. 15, he understands to mean "the slayer of Cain shall complete the sevenfold vengeance which is to be wreaked upon him."

Exodus xiii. 18, he proposes to reconcile with Gen. xv. 16, by supposing that in the one place the tribe of Levi is referred to, in the other the tribe of Judah. He suggests, however, that the words rendered by the LXX. "in the fifth generation" more probably mean "harnessed" (so A.V.) or "laden." In reply to the question about Isaac he says: "No man save Him who for our salvation has deigned to put on flesh has full knowledge and a complete grasp of the truth. Paul, Samuel, David, Elisha, all make mistakes, and holy men only know what God reveals to them." He then goes on to give a mystical interpretation of the passage suggested by the martyr Hippolytus. Written the day after the previous letter.

LETTER XXXVII. TO MARCELLA

Marcella had asked Jerome to lend her a copy of a commentary by Rhetitius, bishop of Augustodunum (Autun), on the Song of Songs. He now refuses to do so on the ground that the work abounds with errors, of which the two following are samples: (1) Rhetitius identifies Tharshish with Tarsus, and (2) he supposes that Uphaz (in the phrase "gold of Uphaz") is the same as Cephas. Written at Rome a.d. 384.

LETTER XXXVIII. TO MARCELLA

Blaesilla, the daughter of Paula and sister of Eustochium, had lost her husband seven months after her marriage. A dangerous illness had then led to her conversion, and she was now famous throughout Rome for the length to which she carried her austerities. Many censured her for what they deemed her fanaticism, and Jerome, as her spiritual adviser, came in for some of the blame. In the present letter he defends her conduct, and declares that persons who cavil at lives like hers have no claim to be considered Christians. Written at Rome in 385 a.d.

1. When Abraham is tempted to slay his son the trial only serves to strengthen his faith. When Joseph is sold into Egypt, his sojourn there enables him to support his father and his brothers. When Hezekiah is panic-stricken at the near approach of death, his tears and prayers obtain for him a respite of fifteen years. If the faith of the apostle, Peter, is shaken by his Lord's passion, it is that, weeping bitterly, he may hear the soothing words: "Feed my sheep." If Paul, that ravening wolf, that little Benjamin, is blinded in a trance, it is that he may receive his sight, and may be led, by the sudden horror of surrounding darkness, to call Him Lord Whom before he persecuted as man.

2. So is it now, my dear Marcella, with our beloved Blaesilla. The burning fever from which we have seen her suffering unceasingly for nearly thirty days has been sent to teach her to renounce her over-great attention to that body which the worms must shortly devour. The Lord Jesus has come to her in her sickness, and has taken her by the hand, and behold, she arises and ministers unto Him. Formerly her life savored somewhat of carelessness; and, fast bound in the bands of wealth, she lay as one dead in the tomb of the world. But Jesus was moved with indignation, and was troubled in spirit, and cried aloud and said, Blaesilla, come forth. She, at His call, has arisen and has come forth, and sits at meat with the Lord. The Jews, if they will, may threaten her in their wrath; they may seek to slay her, because Christ has raised her up. It is enough that the apostles give God the glory. Blaesilla knows that her life is due to Him who has given it back to her. She knows that now she can clasp the feet of Him whom but a little while ago she dreaded as her judge. Then life had all but forsaken her body, and the approach of death made her gasp and shiver. What succour did she obtain in that hour from her kinsfolk? What comfort was there in their words lighter than smoke? She owes no debt to you, ye unkindly kindred, now that she is dead to the world and alive unto Christ. The Christian must rejoice that it is so, and he that is vexed must admit that he has no claim to be called a Christian.

3. A widow who is "loosed from the law of her husband" has, for her one duty, to continue a widow. But, you will say, a sombre dress vexes the world. In that case, John the Baptist would vex it, too; and yet, among those that are born of women, there has not been a greater than he. He was called an angel; he baptized the Lord Himself, and yet he was clothed in raiment of camel's

hair, and girded with a leathern girdle. Is the world displeased because a widow's food is coarse? Nothing can be coarser than locusts, and yet these were the food of John. The women who ought to scandalize Christians are those who paint their eyes and lips with rouge and cosmetics; whose chalked faces, unnaturally white, are like those of idols; upon whose cheeks every chance tear leaves a furrow; who fail to realize that years make them old; who heap their heads with hair not their own; who smooth their faces, and rub out the wrinkles of age; and who, in the presence of their grandsons, behave like trembling school-girls. A Christian woman should blush to do violence to nature, or to stimulate desire by bestowing care upon the flesh. "They that are in the flesh," the apostle tells us, "cannot please God."

4. In days gone by our dear widow was extremely fastidious in her dress, and spent whole days before her mirror to correct its deficiencies. Now she boldly says: "We all with unveiled face, beholding as in a glass the glory of the Lord, are changed into the same image, from glory to glory, even as by the spirit of the Lord." In those days maids arranged her hair, and her head, which had done no harm, was forced into a waving head-dress. Now she leaves her hair alone, and her only head-dress is a veil. In those days the softest featherbed seemed hard to her, and she could scarcely find rest on a pile of mattresses. Now she rises eager for prayer, her shrill voice cries Alleluia before every other, she is the first to praise her Lord. She kneels upon the bare ground, and with frequent tears cleanses a face once defiled with white lead. After prayer comes the singing of psalms, and it is only when her neck aches and her knees totter, and her eyes begin to close with weariness, that she gives them leave reluctantly to rest. As her dress is dark, lying on the ground does not soil it. Cheap shoes permit her to give to the poor the price of gilded ones. No gold and jewels adorn her girdle; it is made of wool, plain and scrupulously clean. It is intended to keep her clothes right, and not to cut her waist in two. Therefore, if the scorpion looks askance upon her purpose, and with alluring words tempts her once more to eat of the forbidden tree, she must crush him beneath her feet with a curse, and say, as he lies dying in his allotted dust: "Get thee behind me, Satan." Satan means adversary, and one who dislikes Christ's commandments, is more than Christ's adversary; he is anti-christ.

5. But what, I ask you, have we ever done that men should be offended at us? Have we ever imitated the apostles? We are told of the first disciples that they forsook their boat and their nets, and even their aged father. The publican stood up from the receipt of custom and followed the Saviour once for all. And when a disciple wished to return home, that he might take leave of his kinsfolk, the Master's voice refused consent. A son was even forbidden to bury his

father, as if to show that it is sometimes a religious duty to be undutiful for the Lord's sake. With us it is different. We are held to be monks if we refuse to dress in silk. We are called sour and severe if we keep sober and refrain from excessive laughter. The mob salutes us as Greeks and impostors if our tunics are fresh and clean. They may deal in still severer witticisms if they please; they may parade every fat paunch they can lay hold of, to turn us into ridicule. Our Blaesilla will laugh at their efforts, and will bear with patience the taunts of all such croaking frogs, for she will remember that men called her Lord, Beelzebub.

LETTER XXXIX. TO PAULA

Blaesilla died within three months of her conversion, and Jerome now writes to Paula to offer her his sympathy and, if possible, to moderate her grief. He asks her to remember that Blaesilla is now in paradise, and so far to control herself as to prevent enemies of the faith from cavilling at her conduct. Then he concludes with the prophecy (since more than fulfilled) that in his writings Blaesilla's name shall never die. Written at Rome in 389 a.d.

1. "Oh that my head were waters and mine eyes a fountain of tears: that I might weep," not as Jeremiah says, "For the slain of my people," nor as Jesus, for the miserable fate of Jerusalem, but for holiness, mercy, innocence, chastity, and all the virtues, for all are gone now that Blaesilla is dead. For her sake I do not grieve, but for myself I must; my loss is too great to be borne with resignation. Who can recall with dry eyes the glowing faith which induced a girl of twenty to raise the standard of the Cross, and to mourn the loss of her virginity more than the death of her husband? Who can recall without a sigh the earnestness of her prayers, the brilliancy of her conversation, the tenacity of her memory, and the quickness of her intellect? Had you heard her speak Greek you would have deemed her ignorant of Latin; yet when she used the tongue of Rome her words were free from a foreign accent. She even rivalled the great Origen in those acquirements which won for him the admiration of Greece. For in a few months, or rather days, she so completely mastered the difficulties of Hebrew as to emulate her mother's zeal in learning and singing the psalms. Her attire was plain, but this plainness was not, as it often is, a mark of pride. Indeed, her self-abasement was so perfect that she dressed no better than her maids, and was only distinguished from them by the greater ease of her walk. Her steps tottered with weakness, her face was pale and quivering, her slender neck scarcely upheld her head. Still she always had in her

hand a prophet or a gospel. As I think of her my eyes fill with tears, sobs impede my voice, and such is my emotion that my tongue cleaves to the roof of my mouth. As she lay there dying, her poor frame parched with burning fever, and her relatives gathered round her bed, her last words were: "Pray to the Lord Jesus, that He may pardon me, because what I would have done I have not been able to do." Be at peace, dear Blaesilla, in full assurance that your garments are always white. For yours is the purity of an everlasting virginity. I feel confident that my words are true: conversion can never be too late. The words to the dying robber are a pledge of this: "Verily I say unto thee, today shalt thou be with me in paradise." When at last her spirit was delivered from the burden of the flesh, and had returned to Him who gave it; when, too, after her long pilgrimage, she had ascended up into her ancient heritage, her obsequies were celebrated with customary splendor. People of rank headed the procession, a pall made of cloth of gold covered her bier. But I seemed to hear a voice from heaven, saying: "I do not recognize these trappings; such is not the garb I used to wear; this magnificence is strange to me."

2. But what is this? I wish to check a mother's weeping, and I groan myself. I make no secret of my feelings; this entire letter is written in tears. Even Jesus wept for Lazarus because He loved him. But he is a poor comforter who is overcome by his own sighs, and from whose afflicted heart tears are wrung as well as words. Dear Paula, my agony is as great as yours. Jesus knows it, whom Blaesilla now follows; the holy angels know it, whose company she now enjoys. I was her father in the spirit, her foster-father in affection. Sometimes I say: "Let the day perish wherein I was born," and again, "Woe is me, my mother, that thou hast borne me a man of strife and a man of contention to the whole earth." I cry: "Righteous art thou, O Lord . . . yet let me talk with thee of thy judgments. Wherefore doth the way of the wicked prosper?" and "as for me, my feet were almost gone, my steps had well-nigh slipped. For I was envious at the foolish when I saw the prosperity of the wicked, and I said: How doth God know? and is there knowledge in the most high? Behold these are the ungodly who prosper in the world; they increase in riches." But again I recall other words, "If I say I will speak thus, behold I should offend against the generation of thy children." Do not great waves of doubt surge up over my soul as over yours? How comes it, I ask, that godless men live to old age in the enjoyment of this world's riches? How comes it that untutored youth and innocent childhood are cut down while still in the bud? Why is it that children three years old or two, and even unweaned infants, are possessed with devils, covered with leprosy, and eaten up with jaundice, while godless men and profane, adulterers and murderers, have health and strength to blaspheme God? Are we not told

that the unrighteousness of the father does not fall upon the son, and that "the soul that sinneth it shall die?" Or if the old doctrine holds good that the sins of the fathers must be visited upon the children, an old man's countless sins cannot fairly be avenged upon a harmless infant. And I have said: "Verily, I have cleansed my heart in vain, and washed my hands in innocency. For all the day long have I been plagued." Yet when I have thought of these things, like the prophet I have learned to say: "When I thought to know this, it was too painful for me; until I went into the sanctuary of God; then understood I their end." Truly the judgments of the Lord are a great deep. "O the depth of the riches both of the wisdom and knowledge of God! How unsearchable are His judgments, and His ways past finding out!" God is good, and all that He does must be good also. Does He decree that I must lose my husband? I mourn my loss, but because it is His will I bear it with resignation. Is an only son snatched from me? The blow is hard, yet it can be borne, for He who has taken away is He who gave. If I become blind a friend's reading will console me. If I become deaf I shall escape from sinful words, and my thoughts shall be of God alone. And if, besides such trials as these, poverty, cold, sickness, and nakedness oppress me, I shall wait for death, and regard them as passing evils, soon to give way to a better issue. Let us reflect on the words of the sapiential psalm: "Righteous art thou, O Lord, and upright are thy judgments." Only he can speak thus who in all his troubles magnifies the Lord, and, putting down his sufferings to his sins, thanks God for his clemency.

The daughters of Judah, we are told, rejoiced, because of all the judgments of the Lord. Therefore, since Judah means confession, and since every believing soul confesses its faith, he who claims to believe in Christ must rejoice in all Christ's judgments. Am I in health? I thank my Creator. Am I sick? In this case, too, I praise God's will. For "when I am weak, then am I strong;" and the strength of the spirit is made perfect in the weakness of the flesh. Even an apostle must bear what he dislikes, that ailment for the removal of which he besought the Lord thrice. God's reply was: "My grace is sufficient for thee; for my strength is made perfect in weakness." Lest he should be unduly elated by his revelations, a reminder of his human weakness was given to him, just as in the triumphal car of the victorious general there was always a slave to whisper constantly, amid the cheerings of the multitude, "Remember that thou art but man."

3. But why should that be hard to bear which we must one day ourselves endure? And why do we grieve for the dead? We are not born to live forever. Abraham, Moses, and Isaiah, Peter, James, and John, Paul, the "chosen vessel," and even the Son of God Himself have all died; and are we vexed when a soul

leaves its earthly tenement? Perhaps he is taken away, "lest that wickedness should alter his understanding . . . for his soul pleased the Lord: therefore hasted he to take him away from the people"—lest in life's long journey he should lose his way in some trackless maze. We should indeed mourn for the dead, but only for him whom Gehenna receives, whom Tartarus devours, and for whose punishment the eternal fire burns. But we who, in departing, are accompanied by an escort of angels, and met by Christ Himself, should rather grieve that we have to tarry yet longer in this tabernacle of death. For "whilst we are at home in the body, we are absent from the Lord." Our one longing should be that expressed by the psalmist: "Woe is me that my pilgrimage is prolonged, that I have dwelt with them that dwell in Kedar, that my soul hath made a far pilgrimage." Kedar means darkness, and darkness stands for this present world (for, we are told, "the light shineth in darkness; and the darkness comprehendeth it not"). Therefore we should congratulate our dear Blaesilla that she has passed from darkness to light, and has in the first flush of her dawning faith received the crown of her completed work. Had she been cut off (as I pray that none may be) while her thoughts were full of worldly desires and passing pleasures, then mourning would indeed have been her due, and no tears shed for her would have been too many. As it is, by the mercy of Christ she, four months ago, renewed her baptism in her vow of widowhood, and for the rest of her days spurned the world, and thought only of the religious life. Have you no fear, then, lest the Saviour may say to you: "Are you angry, Paula, that your daughter has become my daughter? Are you vexed at my decree, and do you, with rebellious tears, grudge me the possession of Blaesilla? You ought to know what my purpose is both for you and for yours. You deny yourself food, not to fast but to gratify your grief; and such abstinence is displeasing to me. Such fasts are my enemies. I receive no soul which forsakes the body against my will. A foolish philosophy may boast of martyrs of this kind; it may boast of a Zeno a Cleombrotus, or a Cato. My spirit rests only upon him "that is poor and of a contrite spirit, and that trembleth at my word. Is this the meaning of your vow to me that you would lead a religious life? Is it for this that you dress yourself differently from other matrons, and array yourself in the garb of a nun? Mourning is for those who wear silk dresses. In the midst of your tears the call will come, and you, too, must die; yet you flee from me as from a cruel judge, and fancy that you can avoid falling into my hands. Jonah, that headstrong prophet, once fled from me, yet in the depths of the sea he was still mine. If you really believed your daughter to be alive, you would not grieve that she had passed to a better world. This is the commandment that I have given you through my apostle, that you sorrow not for them that sleep, even as the Gentiles, which have no hope. Blush, for you are put to shame by the example of a heathen. The devil's handmaid is better than mine. For, while she imagines that her unbelieving husband has been translated to heaven, you either do not or will not believe that your daughter is at rest with me."

4. Why should I not mourn, you say? Jacob put on sackcloth for Joseph, and when all his family gathered round him, refused to be comforted. "I will go down," he said, "into the grave unto my son mourning." David also mourned for Absalom, covering his face, and crying: "O my son, Absalom . . . my son, Absalom! Would God I had died for thee, O Absalom, my son!" Moses, too, and Aaron, and the rest of the saints were mourned for with a solemn mourning. The answer to your reasoning is simple. Jacob, it is true, mourned for Joseph, whom he fancied slain, and thought to meet only in the grave (his words were: "I will go down into the grave unto my son mourning"), but he only did so because Christ had not yet broken open the door of paradise, nor quenched with his blood the flaming sword and the whirling of the guardian cherubim. (Hence in the story of Dives and Lazarus, Abraham and the beggar, though really in a place of refreshment, are described as being in hell.) And David, who, after interceding in vain for the life of his infant child, refused to weep for it, knowing that it had not sinned, did well to weep for a son who had been a parricide—in will, if not in deed. And when we read that, for Moses and Aaron, lamentation was made after ancient custom, this ought not to surprise us, for even in the Acts of the Apostles, in the full blaze of the gospel, we see that the brethren at Jerusalem made great lamentation for Stephen. This great lamentation, however, refers not to the mourners, but to the funeral procession and to the crowds which accompanied it. This is what the Scripture says of Jacob: "Joseph went up to bury his father: and with him went up all the servants of Pharaoh, the elders of his house, and all the elders of the land of Egypt, and all the house of Joseph and his brethren"; and a few lines farther on: "And there went up with him both chariots and horsemen: and it was a great company." Finally, "they mourned with a great and very sore lamentation." This solemn lamentation does not impose prolonged weeping upon the Egyptians, but simply describes the funeral ceremony. In like manner, when we read of weeping made for Moses and Aaron, this is all that is meant.

I cannot adequately extol the mysteries of Scripture, nor sufficiently admire the spiritual meaning conveyed in its most simple words. We are told, for instance, that lamentation was made for Moses; yet when the funeral of Joshua is described no mention at all is made of weeping. The reason, of course, is that under Moses—that is under the old Law—all men were bound by the sentence passed on Adam's sin, and when they descended into hell were rightly accompanied with tears. For, as the apostle says, "death reigned from Adam to Moses, even over them that had not sinned." But under Jesus, that is, under the Gospel of Christ, who has unlocked for us the gate of paradise, death is accompanied, not with sorrow, but with joy. The Jews go on weeping to this day; they make bare their feet, they crouch in sackcloth, they roll in ashes. And to make their superstition complete, they follow a foolish custom of the Pharisees, and eat lentils, to show, it would seem, for what poor fare they have lost their birthright. Of course they are right to weep, for as they do not believe in the Lord's resurrection they are being made ready for the advent of antichrist. But we who have put on Christ and according to the apostle are a royal and priestly race, we ought not to grieve for the dead. "Moses," the Scripture tells us, "said unto Aaron and unto Eleazar, and unto Ithamar, his sons that were left: Uncover not your heads, neither rend your clothes; lest ye die, and lest wrath come upon all the people." Rend not your clothes, he says, neither mourn as pagans, lest you die. For, for us sin is death. In this same book, Leviticus, there is a provision which may perhaps strike some as cruel, yet is necessary to faith: the high priest is forbidden to approach the dead bodies of his father and mother, of his brothers and of his children; to the end, that no grief may distract a soul engaged in offering sacrifice to God, and wholly devoted to the Divine mysteries. Are we not taught the same lesson in the Gospel in other words? Is not the disciple forbidden to say farewell to his home or to bury his dead father? Of the high priest, again, it is said: "He shall not go out of the sanctuary, and the sanctification of his God shall not be contaminated, for the anointing oil of his God is upon him." Certainly, now that we have believed in Christ, and bear Him within us, by reason of the oil of His anointing which we have received, we ought not to depart from His temple—that is, from our Christian profession—we ought not to go forth to mingle with the unbelieving Gentiles, but always to remain within, as servants obedient to the will of the Lord.

5. I have spoken plainly, lest you might ignorantly suppose that Scripture sanctions your grief; and that, if you err, you have reason on your side. And, so far, my words have been addressed to the average Christian woman. But now it will not be so. For in your case, as I well know, renunciation of the world has been complete; you have rejected and trampled on the delights of life, and you give yourself daily to fasting, to reading, and to prayer. Like Abraham, you desire to leave your country and kindred, to forsake Mesopotamia and the Chaldaeans, to enter into the promised land. Dead to the world before your death, you have spent all your mere worldly substance upon the poor, or have

bestowed it upon your children. I am the more surprised, therefore, that you should act in a manner which in others would justly call for reprehension. You call to mind Blaesilla's companionship, her conversation, and her endearing ways; and you cannot endure the thought that you have lost them all. I pardon you the tears of a mother, but I ask you to restrain your grief. When I think of the parent I cannot blame you for weeping: but when I think of the Christian and the recluse, the mother disappears from my view. Your wound is still fresh, and any touch of mine, however gentle, is more likely to inflame than to heal it. Yet why do you not try to overcome by reason a grief which time must inevitably assuage? Naomi, fleeing because of famine to the land of Moab, there lost her husband and her sons. Yet when she was thus deprived of her natural protectors, Ruth, a stranger, never left her side. And see what a great thing it is to comfort a lonely woman! Ruth, for her reward, is made an ancestress of Christ. Consider the great trials which Job endured, and you will see that you are over-delicate. Amid the ruins of his house, the pains of his sores, his countless bereavements, and, last of all, the snares laid for him by his wife, he still lifted up his eyes to heaven, and maintained his patience unbroken. I know what you are going to say: "All this befell him as a righteous man, to try his righteousness." Well, choose which alternative you please. Either you are holy, in which case God is putting your holiness to the proof; or else you are a sinner, in which case you have no right to complain. For if so, you endure far less than your deserts.

Why should I repeat old stories? Listen to a modern instance. The holy Melanium, eminent among Christians for her true nobility (may the Lord grant that you and I may have part with her in His day!), while the dead body of her husband was still unburied, still warm, had the misfortune to lose at one stroke two of her sons. The sequel seems incredible, but Christ is my witness that my words are true. Would you not suppose that in her frenzy she would have unbound her hair, and rent her clothes, and torn her breast? Yet not a tear fell from her eyes. Motionless she stood there; then casting herself at the feet of Christ, she smiled, as though she held Him with her hands. "Henceforth, Lord," she said, "I will serve Thee more readily, for Thou hast freed me from a great burden." But perhaps her remaining children overcame her determination. No, indeed; she set so little store by them that she gave up all that she had to her only son, and then, in spite of the approaching winter, took ship for Jerusalem.

6. Spare yourself, I beseech you, spare Blaesilla, who now reigns with Christ; at least spare Eustochium, whose tender years and inexperience depend on you for guidance and instruction. Now does the devil rage and complain

that he is set at naught, because he sees one of your children exalted in triumph. The victory which he failed to win over her that is gone he hopes to obtain over her who still remains. Too great affection towards one's children is disaffection towards God. Abraham gladly prepares to slay his only son, and do you complain if one child out of several has received her crown? I cannot say what I am going to say without a groan. When you were carried fainting out of the funeral procession, whispers such as these were audible in the crowd. "Is not this what we have often said. She weeps for her daughter, killed with fasting. She wanted her to marry again, that she might have grandchildren. How long must we refrain from driving these detestable monks out of Rome? Why do we not stone them or hurl them into the Tiber? They have misled this unhappy lady; that she is not a nun from choice is clear. No heathen mother ever wept for her children as she does for Blaesilla." What sorrow, think you, must not Christ have endured when He listened to such words as these! And how triumphantly must Satan have exulted, eager as he is to snatch your soul! Luring you with the claims of a grief which seems natural and right, and always keeping before you the image of Blaesilla, his aim is to slay the mother of the victress, and then to fall upon her forsaken sister. I do not speak thus to terrify you. The Lord is my witness that I address you now as though I were standing at His judgment seat. Tears which have no meaning are an object of abhorrence. Yours are detestable tears, sacrilegious tears, unbelieving tears; for they know no limits, and bring you to the verge of death. You shriek and cry out as though on fire within, and do your best to put an end to yourself. But to you and others like you Jesus comes in His mercy and says: "Why weepest thou? the damsel is not dead but sleepeth." The bystanders may laugh him to scorn; such unbelief is worthy of the Jews. If you prostrate yourself in grief at your daughter's tomb you too will hear the chiding of the angel, "Why seek ye the living among the dead?" It was because Mary Magdalene had done this that when she recognized the Lord's voice calling her and fell at His feet, He said to her: "Touch me not, for I am not yet ascended to my Father;" that is to say, you are not worthy to touch, as risen, one whom you suppose still in the tomb.

7. What crosses and tortures, think you, must not our Blaesilla endure to see Christ angry with you, though it be but a little! At this moment she cries to you as you weep: "If ever you loved me, mother, if I was nourished at your breast, if I was taught by your precepts, do not grudge me my exaltation, do not so act that we shall be separated forever. Do you fancy that I am alone? In place of you I now have Mary the mother of the Lord. Here I see many whom before I have not known. My companions are infinitely better than any that I

had on earth. Here I have the company of Anna, the prophetess of the Gospel; and—what should kindle in you more fervent joy—I have gained in three short months what cost her the labor of many years to win. Both of us widows indeed, we have been both rewarded with the palm of chastity. Do you pity me because I have left the world behind me? It is I who should, and do, pity you who, still immured in its prison, daily fight with anger, with covetousness, with lust, with this or that temptation leading the soul to ruin. If you wish to be indeed my mother, you must please Christ. She is not my mother who displeases my Lord." Many other things does she say which here I pass over; she prays also to God for you. For me, too, I feel sure, she makes intercession and asks God to pardon my sins in return for the warnings and advice that I bestowed on her, when to secure her salvation I braved the ill will of her family.

8. Therefore, so long as breath animates my body, so long as I continue in the enjoyment of life, I engage, declare, and promise that Blaesilla's name shall be forever on my tongue, that my labors shall be dedicated to her honor, and that my talents shall be devoted to her praise. No page will I write in which Blaesilla's name shall not occur. Wherever the records of my utterance shall find their way, thither she, too, will travel with my poor writings. Virgins, widows, monks and priests, as they read, will see how deeply her image is impressed upon my mind. Everlasting remembrance will make up for the shortness of her life. Living as she does with Christ in heaven, she will live also on the lips of men. The present will soon pass away and give place to the future, and that future will judge her without partiality and without prejudice. As a childless widow she will occupy a middle place between Paula, the mother of children, and Eustochium the virgin. In my writings she will never die. She will hear me conversing of her always, either with her sister or with her mother.

LETTER XL. TO MARCELLA

Onasus, of Segesta, the subject of this letter, was among Jerome's Roman opponents. He is here held up to ridicule in a manner which reflects little credit on the writer's urbanity. The date of the letter is 385 a.d.

1. The medical men called surgeons pass for being cruel, but really deserve pity. For is it not pitiful to cut away the dead flesh of another man with merciless knives without being moved by his pangs? Is it not pitiful that the man who is curing the patient is callous to his sufferings, and has to appear as his

enemy? Yet such is the order of nature. While truth is always bitter, pleasantness waits upon evil-doing. Isaiah goes naked without blushing as a type of captivity to come. Jeremiah is sent from Jerusalem to the Euphrates (a river in Mesopotamia), and leaves his girdle to be marred in the Chaldaean camp, among the Assyrians hostile to his people. Ezekiel is told to eat bread made of mingled seeds and sprinkled with the dung of men and cattle. He has to see his wife die without shedding a tear. Amos is driven from Samaria. Why is he driven from it? Surely in this case as in the others, because he was a spiritual surgeon, who cut away the parts diseased by sin and urged men to repentance. The apostle Paul says: "Am I therefore become your enemy because I tell you the truth?" And so the Saviour Himself found it, from whom many of the disciples went back because His sayings seemed hard.

2. It is not surprising, then, that by exposing their faults I have offended many. I have arranged to operate on a cancerous nose; let him who suffers from wens tremble. I wish to rebuke a chattering daw; let the crow realize that she is offensive. Yet, after all, is there but one person in Rome

"Whose nostrils are disfigured by a scar?"

Is Onasus of Segesta alone in puffing out his cheeks like bladders and balancing hollow phrases on his tongue?

I say that certain persons have, by crime, perjury, and false pretences, attained to this or that high position. How does it hurt you who know that the charge does not touch you? I laugh at a pleader who has no clients, and sneer at a penny-a-liner's eloquence. What does it matter to you who are such a refined speaker? It is my whim to inveigh against mercenary priests. You are rich already, why should you be angry? I wish to shut up Vulcan and burn him in his own flames. Are you his guest or his neighbor that you try to save an idol's shrine from the fire? I choose to make merry over ghosts and owls and monsters of the Nile; and whatever I say, you take it as aimed at you. At whatever fault I point my pen, you cry out that you are meant. You collar me and drag me into court and absurdly charge me with writing satires when I only write plain prose!

So you really think yourself a pretty fellow just because you have a lucky name! Why it does not follow at all. A brake is called a brake just because the light does not break through it. The Fates are called "sparers," just because they never spare. The Furies are spoken of as gracious, because they show no grace. And in common speech Ethiopians go by the name of silverlings. Still, if the showing up of faults always angers you, I will soothe you now with the words of Persius: "May you be a catch for my lord and lady's daughter! May the pretty ladies scramble for you! May the ground you walk on turn to a rose-bed!"

3. All the same, I will give you a hint what features to hide if you want to look your best. Show no nose upon your face and keep your mouth shut. You will then stand some chance of being counted both handsome and eloquent.

LETTER XLI. TO MARCELLA

An effort having been made to convert Marcella to Montanism, Jerome here summarizes for her its leading doctrines, which he contrasts with those of the Church. Written at Rome in 385 a.d.

1. As regards the passages brought together from the gospel of John with which a certain votary of Montanus has assailed you, passages in which our Saviour promises that He will go to the Father, and that He will send the Paraclete—as regards these, the Acts of the Apostles inform us both for what time the promises were made, and at what time they were actually fulfilled. Ten days had elapsed, we are told, from the Lord's ascension and fifty from His resurrection, when the Holy Spirit came down, and the tongues of the believers were cloven, so that each spoke every language. Then it was that, when certain persons of those who as yet believed not declared that the disciples were drunk with new wine, Peter standing in the midst of the apostles, and of all the concourse said: "Ye men of Judaea and all ye that dwell at Jerusalem, be this known unto you and hearken to my words: for these are not drunken as ye suppose, seeing it is but the third hour of the day. But this is that which was spoken of by the prophet Joel. And it shall come to pass in the last days, saith God, I will pour out of my spirit upon all flesh: and your sons and daughters shall prophesy, and your young men shall see visions, and your old men shall dream dreams: and on my servants, and on my handmaidens I will pour out . . . of my spirit."

2. If, then, the apostle Peter, upon whom the Lord has founded the Church, has expressly said that the prophecy and promise of the Lord were then and there fulfilled, how can we claim another fulfilment for ourselves? if the Montanists reply that Philip's four daughters prophesied at a later date, and that a prophet is mentioned named Agabus, and that in the partition of the spirit, prophets are spoken of as well as apostles, teachers and others, and that Paul himself prophesied many things concerning heresies still future, and the end of the world; we tell them that we do not so much reject prophecy—

for this is attested by the passion of the Lord—as refuse to receive prophets whose utterances fail to accord with the Scriptures old and new.

3. In the first place we differ from the Montanists regarding the rule of faith. We distinguish the Father, the Son, and the Holy Spirit as three persons, but unite them as one substance. They, on the other hand, following the doctrine of Sabellius, force the Trinity into the narrow limits of a single personality. We, while we do not encourage them, yet allow second marriages, since Paul bids the younger widows to marry. They suppose a repetition of marriage a sin so awful that he who has committed it is to be regarded as an adulterer. We, according to the apostolic tradition (in which the whole world is at one with us), fast through one Lent yearly; whereas they keep three in the year as though three saviours had suffered. I do not mean, of course, that it is unlawful to fast at other times through the year—always excepting Pentecost—only that while in Lent it is a duty of obligation, at other seasons it is a matter of choice. With us, again, the bishops occupy the place of the apostles, but with them a bishop ranks not first but third. For while they put first the patriarchs of Pepusa in Phrygia, and place next to these the ministers called stewards, the bishops are relegated to the third or almost the lowest rank. No doubt their object is to make their religion more pretentious by putting that last which we put first. Again they close the doors of the Church to almost every fault, whilst we read daily, "I desire the repentance of a sinner rather than his death," and "Shall they fall and not arise, saith the Lord," and once more "Return ye backsliding children and I will heal your backslidings." Their strictness does not prevent them from themselves committing grave sins, far from it; but there is this difference between us and them, that, whereas they in their self-righteousness blush to confess their faults, we do penance for ours, and so more readily gain pardon for them.

4. I pass over their sacraments of sin, made up as they are said to be, of sucking children subjected to a triumphant martyrdom. I prefer, I say, not to credit these; accusations of blood-shedding may well be false. But I must confute the open blasphemy of men who say that God first determined in the Old Testament to save the world by Moses and the prophets, but that finding Himself unable to fulfil His purpose He took to Himself a body of the Virgin, and preaching under the form of the Son in Christ, underwent death for our salvation. Moreover that, when by these two steps He was unable to save the world, He last of all descended by the Holy Spirit upon Montanus and those demented women Prisca and Maximilia; and that thus the mutilated and emasculate Montanus possessed a fulness of knowledge such as was never

claimed by Paul; for he was content to say, "We know in part, and we prophesy in part," and again, "Now we see through a glass darkly."

These are statements which require no refutation. To expose the infidelity of the Montanists is to triumph over it. Nor is it necessary that in so short a letter as this I should overthrow the several absurdities which they bring forward. You are well acquainted with the Scriptures; and, as I take it, you have written, not because you have been disturbed by their cavils, but only to learn my opinion about them.

LETTER XLII. TO MARCELLA

At Marcella's request Jerome explains to her what is "the sin against the Holy Ghost" spoken of by Christ, and shows Novatian's explanation of it to be untenable. Written at Rome in 385 a.d.

1. The question you send is short and the answer is clear. There is this passage in the gospel: "Whosoever speaketh a word against the Son of Man, it shall be forgiven him; but whosoever speaketh against the Holy Ghost, it shall not be forgiven him neither in this world nor in the world to come." Now if Novatian affirms that none but Christian renegades can sin against the Holy Ghost, it is plain that the Jews who blasphemed Christ were not guilty of this sin. Yet they were wicked husbandmen, they had slain the prophets, they were then compassing the death of the Lord; and so utterly lost were they that the Son of God told them that it was they whom he had come to save. It must be proved to Novatian, therefore, that the sin which shall never be forgiven is not the blasphemy of men disembowelled by torture who in their agony deny their Lord, but is the captious clamor of those who, while they see that God's works are the fruit of virtue, ascribe the virtue to a demon and declare the signs wrought to belong not to the divine excellence but to the devil. And this is the whole gist of our Saviour's argument, when He teaches that Satan cannot be cast out by Satan, and that his kingdom is not divided against itself. If it is the devil's object to injure God's creation, how can he wish to cure the sick and to expel himself from the bodies possessed by him? Let Novatian prove that of those who have been compelled to sacrifice before a judge's tribunal any has declared of the things written in the gospel that they were wrought not by the Son of God but by Beelzebub, the prince of the devils; and then he will be able to make good his contention that this is the blasphemy against the Holy Ghost which shall never be forgiven.

2. But to put a more searching question still: let Novatian tell us how he distinguishes speaking against the Son of Man from blasphemy against the Holy Ghost. For I maintain that on his principles men who have denied Christ under persecution have only spoken against the Son of Man, and have not blasphemed the Holy Ghost. For when a man is asked if he is a Christian, and declares that he is not; obviously in denying Christ, that is the Son of Man, he does no despite to the Holy Ghost. But if his denial of Christ involves a denial of the Holy Ghost, this heretic can perhaps tell us how the Son of Man can be denied without sinning against the Holy Ghost. If he thinks that we are here intended by the term Holy Ghost to understand the Father, no mention at all of the Father is made by the denier in his denial. When the apostle Peter, taken aback by a maid's question, denied the Lord, did he sin against the Son of Man or against the Holy Ghost? If Novatian absurdly twists Peter's words, "I know not the man," to mean a denial not of Christ's Messiahship but of His humanity, he will make the Saviour a liar, for He foretold that He Himself, that is His divine Sonship, must be denied. Now, when Peter denied the Son of God, he wept bitterly and effaced his threefold denial by a threefold confession. His sin, therefore, was not the sin against the Holy Ghost which can never be forgiven. It is obvious, then, that this sin involves blasphemy, calling one Beelzebub for his actions, whose virtues prove him to be God. If Novatian can bring an instance of a renegade who has called Christ Beelzebub, I will at once give up my position and admit that after such a fall the denier can win no forgiveness. To give way under torture and to deny oneself to be a Christian is one thing, to say that Christ is the devil is another. And this you will yourself see if you read the passage attentively.

3. I ought to have discussed the matter more fully, but some friends have visited my humble abode, and I cannot refuse to give myself up to them. Still, as it might seem arrogant not to answer you at once, I have compressed a wide subject into a few words, and have sent you not a letter but an explanatory note.

LETTER XLIII. TO MARCELLA

Jerome draws a contrast between his daily life and that of Origen, and sorrowfully admits his own shortcomings. He then suggests to Marcella the advantages which life in the country offers over life in town, and hints that he is himself disposed to make trial of it. Written at Rome in 385 a.d.

1. Ambrose who supplied Origen, true man of adamant and of brass, with money, materials and amanuenses to bring out his countless books—Ambrose, in a letter to his friend from Athens, states that they never took a meal together without something being read, and never went to bed till some portion of Scripture had been brought home to them by a brother's voice. Night and day, in fact, were so ordered that prayer only gave place to reading and reading to prayer.

2. Have we, brute beasts that we are, ever done the like? Why, we yawn if we read for over an hour; we rub our foreheads and vainly try to suppress our languor. And then, after this great feat, we plunge for relief into worldly business once more.

I say nothing of the meals with which we dull our faculties, and I would rather not estimate the time that we spend in paying and receiving visits. Next we fall into conversation; we waste our words, we attack people behind their backs, we detail their way of living, we carp at them and are carped at by them in turn. Such is the fare that engages our attention at dinner and afterwards. Then, when our guests have retired, we make up our accounts, and these are sure to cause us either anger or anxiety. The first makes us like raging lions, and the second seeks vainly to make provision for years to come. We do not recollect the words of the Gospel: "Thou fool, this night thy soul shall be required of thee: then whose shall those things be which thou hast provided?" The clothing which we buy is designed not merely for use but for display. Where there is a chance of saving money we quicken our pace, speak promptly, and keep our ears open. If we hear of household losses—such as often occur—our looks become dejected and gloomy. The gain of a penny fills us with joy; the loss of a half-penny plunges us into sorrow. One man is of so many minds that the prophet's prayer is: "Lord, in thy city scatter their image." For created as we are in the image of God and after His likeness, it is our own wickedness which makes us assume masks. Just as on the stage the same actor now figures as a brawny Hercules, now softens into a tender Venus, now shivers in the role of Cybele; so we—who, if we were not of the world, would be hated by the world—for every sin that we commit have a corresponding mask.

3. Wherefore, seeing that we have journeyed for much of our life through a troubled sea, and that our vessel has been in turn shaken by raging blasts and shattered upon treacherous reefs, let us, as soon as may be, make for the haven of rural quietude. There such country dainties as milk and household bread, and greens watered by our own hands, will supply us with coarse but harmless fare. So living, sleep will not call us away from prayer, nor satiety from reading.

In summer the shade of a tree will afford us privacy. In autumn the quality of the air and the leaves strewn under foot will invite us to stop and rest. In springtime the fields will be bright with flowers, and our psalms will sound the sweeter for the twittering of the birds. When winter comes with its frost and snow, I shall not have to buy fuel, and, whether I sleep or keep vigil, shall be warmer than in town. At least, so far as I know, I shall keep off the cold at less expense. Let Rome keep to itself its noise and bustle, let the cruel shows of the arena go on, let the crowd rave at the circus, let the playgoers revel in the theatres and—for I must not altogether pass over our Christian friends—let the House of Ladies hold its daily sittings. It is good for us to cleave to the Lord, and to put our hope in the Lord God, so that when we have exchanged our present poverty for the kingdom of heaven, we may be able to exclaim: "Whom have I in heaven but thee? and there is none upon earth that I desire beside thee." Surely if we can find such blessedness in heaven we may well grieve to have sought after pleasures poor and passing here upon earth. Farewell.

LETTER XLIV. TO MARCELLA

Marcella had sent some small articles as a present (probably to Paula and Eustochium) and Jerome now writes in their name to thank her for them. He notices the appropriateness of the gifts, not only to the ladies, but also to himself. Written at Rome in 385 a.d.

When absent in body we are wont to converse together in spirit. Each of us does what he or she can. You send us gifts, we send you back letters of thanks. And as we are virgins who have taken the veil, it is our duty to show that hidden meanings lurk under your nice presents. Sackcloth, then, is a token of prayer and fasting, the chairs remind us that a virgin should never stir abroad, and the wax tapers that we should look for the bridegroom's coming with our lights burning. The cups also warn us to mortify the flesh and always to be ready for martyrdom. "How bright," says the psalmist, "is the cup of the Lord, intoxicating them that drink it!" Moreover, when you offer to matrons little fly-flaps to brush away mosquitoes, it is a charming way of hinting that they should at once check voluptuous feelings, for "dying flies," we are told, "spoil sweet ointment." In such presents, then, as these, virgins can find a model, and matrons a pattern. To me, too, your gifts convey a lesson, although one of an opposite kind. For chairs suit idlers, sackcloth does for penitents, and cups are wanted for the thirsty. And I shall be glad to light your tapers, if only to banish the terrors of the night and the fears of an evil conscience.

LETTER XLV. TO ASELLA

After leaving Rome for the East, Jerome writes to Asella to refute the calumnies by which he had been assailed, especially as regards his intimacy with Paula and Eustochium. Written on board ship at Ostia, in August, 385 a.d.

1. Were I to think myself able to requite your kindness I should be foolish. God is able in my stead to reward a soul which is consecrated to Him. So unworthy, indeed, am I of your regard that I have never ventured to estimate its value or even to wish that it might be given me for Christ's sake. Some consider me a wicked man, laden with iniquity; and such language is more than justified by my actual sins. Yet in dealing with the bad you do well to account them good. It is dangerous to judge another man's servant; and to speak evil of the righteous is a sin not easily pardoned. The day will surely come when you and I shall mourn for others; for not a few will be in the flames.

2. I am said to be an infamous turncoat, a slippery knave, one who lies and deceives others by Satanic arts. Which is the safer course, I should like to know, to invent or credit these charges against innocent persons, or to refuse to believe them, even of the guilty? Some kissed my hands, yet attacked me with the tongues of vipers; sympathy was on their lips, but malignant joy in their hearts. The Lord saw them and had them in derision, reserving my poor self and them for judgment to come. One would attack my gait or my way of laughing; another would find something amiss in my looks; another would suspect the simplicity of my manner. Such is the company in which I have lived for almost three years.

It often happened that I found myself surrounded with virgins, and to some of these I expounded the divine books as best I could. Our studies brought about constant intercourse, this soon ripened into intimacy, and this, in turn, produced mutual confidence. If they have ever seen anything in my conduct unbecoming a Christian let them say so. Have I taken any one's money? Have I not disdained all gifts, whether small or great? Has the chink of any one's coin been heard in my hand? Has my language been equivocal, or my eye wanton? No; my sex is my one crime, and even on this score I am not assailed, save when there is a talk of Paula going to Jerusalem. Very well, then. They believed my accuser when he lied; why do they not believe him when he retracts? He is the same man now that he was then, and yet he who before declared me guilty now confesses that I am innocent. Surely a man's words under torture are more trustworthy than in moments of gayety, except, indeed, that people are prone to believe falsehoods designed to gratify their ears, or, worse still, stories which, till then uninvented, they have urged others to invent.

3. Before I became acquainted with the family of the saintly Paula, all Rome resounded with my praises. Almost every one concurred in judging me worthy of the episcopate. Damasus, of blessed memory, spoke no words but mine. Men called me holy, humble, eloquent.

Did I ever cross the threshold of a light woman? Was I ever fascinated by silk dresses, or glowing gems, or rouged faces, or display of gold? Of all the ladies in Rome but one had power to subdue me, and that one was Paula. She mourned and fasted, she was squalid with dirt, her eyes were dim from weeping. For whole nights she would pray to the Lord for mercy, and often the rising sun found her still at her prayers. The psalms were her only songs, the Gospel her whole speech, continence her one indulgence, fasting the staple of her life. The only woman who took my fancy was one whom I had not so much as seen at table. But when I began to revere, respect, and venerate her as her conspicuous chastity deserved, all my former virtues forsook me on the spot.

4. Oh! envy, that dost begin by tearing thyself! Oh! cunning malignity of Satan, that dost always persecute things holy! Of all the ladies in Rome, the only ones that caused scandal were Paula and Melanium, who, despising their wealth and deserting their children, uplifted the cross of the Lord as a standard of religion. Had they frequented the baths, or chosen to use perfumes, or taken advantage of their wealth and position as widows to enjoy life and to be independent, they would have been saluted as ladies of high rank and saintliness. As it is, of course, it is in order to appear beautiful that they put on sackcloth and ashes, and they endure fasting and filth merely to go down into the Gehenna of fire! As if they could not perish with the crowd whom the mob applauds! If it were Gentiles or Jews who thus assailed their mode of life, they would at least have the consolation of failing to please only those whom Christ Himself has failed to please. But, shameful to say, it is Christians who thus neglect the care of their own households, and, disregarding the beams in their own eyes, look for motes in those of their neighbors. They pull to pieces every profession of religion, and think that they have found a remedy for their own doom, if they can disprove the holiness of others, if they can detract from every

one, if they can show that those who perish are many, and sinners, a great multitude.

5. You bathe daily; another regards such over-niceness as defilement. You surfeit yourself on wild fowl and pride yourself on eating sturgeon; I, on the contrary, fill my belly with beans. You find pleasure in troops of laughing girls; I prefer Paula and Melanium who weep. You covet what belongs to others; they disdain what is their own. You like wines flavored with honey; they drink cold water, more delicious still. You count as lost what you cannot have, eat up, and devour on the moment; they believe in the Scriptures, and look for good things to come. And if they are wrong, and if the resurrection of the body on which they rely is a foolish delusion, what does it matter to you? We, on our side, look with disfavor on such a life as yours. You can fatten yourself on your good things as much as you please; I for my part prefer paleness and emaciation. You suppose that men like me are unhappy; we regard you as more unhappy still. Thus we reciprocate each other's thoughts, and appear to each other mutually insane.

6. I write this in haste, dear Lady Asella, as I go on board, overwhelmed with grief and tears; yet I thank my God that I am counted worthy of the world's hatred. Pray for me that, after Babylon, I may see Jerusalem once more; that Joshua, the son of Josedech, may have dominion over me, and not Nebuchadnezzar, that Ezra, whose name means helper, may come and restore me to my own country. I was a fool in wishing to sing the Lord's song in a strange land, and in leaving Mount Sinai, to seek the help of Egypt. I forgot that the Gospel warns us that he who goes down from Jerusalem immediately falls among robbers, is spoiled, is wounded, is left for dead. But, although priest and Levite may disregard me, there is still the good Samaritan who, when men said to him, "Thou art a Samaritan and hast a devil," disclaimed having a devil, but did not disclaim being a Samaritan, this being the Hebrew equivalent for our word guardian. Men call me a mischief-maker, and I take the title as a recognition of my faith. For I am but a servant, and the Jews still call my master a magician. The apostle, likewise, is spoken of as a deceiver. There hath no temptation taken me but such as is common to man. How few distresses have I endured, I who am yet a soldier of the cross! Men have laid to my charge a crime of which I am not guilty; but I know that I must enter the kingdom of heaven through evil report as well as through good.

7. Salute Paula and Eustochium, who, whatever the world may think, are always mine in Christ. Salute Albina, your mother, and Marcella, your sister; Marcellina also, and the holy Felicitas; and say to them all: "We must all stand

before the judgment seat of Christ, and there shall be revealed the principle by which each has lived."

And now, illustrious model of chastity and virginity, remember me, I beseech you, in your prayers, and by your intercessions calm the waves of the sea.

LETTER XLVI. PAULA AND EUSTOCHIUM TO MARCELLA

Jerome writes to Marcella in the name of Paula and Eustochium, describing the charms of the Holy Land, and urging her to leave Rome and to join her old companions at Bethlehem. Much of the letter is devoted to disposing of the objection that since the Passion of Christ the Holy Land has been under a curse. The date of the letter is a.d. 386. It is written from Bethlehem, which now becomes Jerome's home for the remainder of his life.

1. Love cannot be measured, impatience knows no bounds, and eagerness can brook no delay. Wherefore we, oblivious of our weakness, and relying more on our will than our capacity, desire—pupils though we be—to instruct our mistress. We are like the sow in the proverb, which sets up to teach the goddess of invention. You were the first to set our tinder alight; the first, by precept and example, to urge us to adopt our present life. As a hen gathers her chickens, so did you take us under your wing. And will you now let us fly about at random with no mother near us? Will you leave us to dread the swoop of the hawk and the shadow of each passing bird of prey? Separated from you, we do what we can: we utter our mournful plaint, and more by sobs than by tears we adjure you to give back to us the Marcella whom we love. She is mild, she is suave, she is sweeter than the sweetest honey. She must not, therefore, be stern and morose to us, whom her winning ways have roused to adopt a life like her own.

2. Assuming that what we ask is for the best, our eagerness to obtain it is nothing to be ashamed of. And if all the Scriptures agree with our view, we are not too bold in urging you to a course to which you have yourself often urged us.

What are God's first words to Abraham? "Get thee out of thy country and from thy kindred unto a land that I will show thee." The patriarch—the first to receive a promise of Christ—is here told to leave the Chaldees, to leave the city of confusion and its rehoboth or broad places; to leave also the plain of Shinar, where the tower of pride had been raised to heaven. He has to pass through the waves of this world, and to ford its rivers; those by which the saints sat down and wept when they remembered Zion, and Chebar's flood, whence Ezekiel was carried to Jerusalem by the hair of his head. All this Abraham undergoes that he may dwell in a land of promise watered from above, and not like Egypt, from below, no producer of herbs for the weak and ailing, but a land that looks for the early and the latter rain from heaven. It is a land of hills and valleys, and stands high above the sea. The attractions of the world it entirely wants, but its spiritual attractions are for this all the greater. Mary, the mother of the Lord, left the lowlands and made her way to the hill country, when, after receiving the angel's message, she realized that she bore within her womb the Son of God. When of old the Philistines had been overcome, when their devilish audacity had been smitten, when their champion had fallen on his face to the earth, it was from this city that there went forth a procession of jubilant souls, a harmonious choir to sing our David's victory over tens of thousands. Here, too, it was that the angel grasped his sword, and while he laid waste the whole of the ungodly city, marked out the temple of the Lord in the threshing floor of Ornan, king of the Jebusites. Thus early was it made plain that Christ's church would grow up, not in Israel, but among the Gentiles. Turn back to Genesis, and you will find that this was the city over which Melchizedek held sway, that king of Salem who, as a type of Christ, offered to Abraham bread and wine, and even then consecrated the mystery which Christians consecrate in the body and blood of the Saviour.

3. Perhaps you will tacitly reprove us for deserting the order of Scripture, and letting our confused account ramble this way and that, as one thing or another strikes us. If so, we say once more what we said at the outset: love has no logic, and impatience knows no rule. In the Song of Songs the precept is given as a hard one: "Regulate your love towards me." And so we plead that, if we err, we do so not from ignorance but from feeling.

Well, then, to bring forward something still more out of place, we must go back to yet remoter times. Tradition has it that in this city, nay, more, on this very spot, Adam lived and died. The place where our Lord was crucified is called Calvary, because the skull of the primitive man was buried there. So it came to pass that the second Adam, that is the blood of Christ, as it dropped from the cross, washed away the sins of the buried protoplast, the first Adam, and thus the words of the apostle were fulfilled: "Awake, thou that sleepest, and arise from the dead, and Christ shall give thee light."

It would be tedious to enumerate all the prophets and holy men who have been sent forth from this place. All that is strange and mysterious to us is familiar and natural to this city and country. By its very names, three in number, it proves the doctrine of the trinity. For it is called first Jebus, then Salem, then Jerusalem: names of which the first means "down-trodden," the second "peace," and the third "vision of peace." For it is only by slow stages that we reach our goal; it is only after we have been trodden down that we are lifted up to see the vision of peace. Because of this peace Solomon, the man of peace, was born there, and "in peace was his place made." King of kings, and lord of lords, his name and that of the city show him to be a type of Christ. Need we speak of David and his descendants, all of whom reigned here? As Judaea is exalted above all other provinces, so is this city exalted above all Judaea. To speak more tersely, the glory of the province is derived from its capital; and whatever fame the members possess is in every case due to the head.

4. You have long been anxious to break forth into speech; the very letters we have formed perceive it, and our paper already understands the question you are going to put. You will reply to us by saying: it was so of old, when "the Lord loved the gates of Zion more than all the dwellings of Jacob," and when her foundations were in the holy mountains. Even these verses, however, are susceptible of a deeper interpretation. But things are changed since then. The risen Lord has proclaimed in tones of thunder: "Your house is left unto you desolate." With tears He has prophesied its downfall: "O Jerusalem, Jerusalem, thou that killest the prophets, and stonest them which are sent unto thee; how often would I have gathered thy children together even as a hen gathereth her chickens under her wings, and ye would not. Behold your house is left unto you desolate." The veil of the temple has been rent; an army has encompassed Jerusalem, it has been stained by the blood of the Lord. Now, therefore, its guardian angels have forsaken it and the grace of Christ has been withdrawn. Josephus, himself a Jewish writer, asserts that at the Lord's crucifixion there broke from the temple voices of heavenly powers, saying: "Let us depart hence." These and other considerations show that where grace abounded there did sin much more abound. Again, when the apostles received the command: "Go ye and teach all nations," and when they said themselves: "It was necessary that the word of God should first have been spoken to you, but seeing ye put it from you . . . lo we turn to the Gentiles," then all the spiritual importance of Judaea and its old intimacy with God were transferred by the apostles to the nations.

5. The difficulty is strongly stated, and may well puzzle even those proficient in Scripture; but for all that, it admits of an easy solution. The Lord wept for the fall of Jerusalem, and He would not have done so if He did not love it. He wept for Lazarus because He loved him. The truth is that it was the people who sinned and not the place. The capture of a city is involved in the slaying of its inhabitants. If Jerusalem was destroyed, it was that its people might be punished; if the temple was overthrown, it was that its figurative sacrifices

might be abolished. As regards its site, lapse of time has but invested it with fresh grandeur. The Jews of old reverenced the Holy of Holies, because of the things contained in it—the cherubim, the mercy-seat, the ark of the covenant, the manna, Aaron's rod, and the golden altar. Does the Lord's sepulchre seem less worthy of veneration? As often as we enter it we see the Saviour in His grave clothes, and if we linger we see again the angel sitting at His feet, and the napkin folded at His head. Long before this sepulchre was hewn out by Joseph, its glory was foretold in Isaiah's prediction, "his rest shall be glorious," meaning that the place of the Lord's burial should be held in universal honor.

6. How, then, you will say, do we read in the apocalypse written by John: "The beast that ascendeth out of the bottomless pit shall . . . kill them [that is, obviously, the prophets], and their dead bodies shall lie in the street of the great city which spiritually is called Sodom and Egypt, where also their Lord was crucified?" If the great city where the Lord was crucified is Jerusalem, and if the place of His crucifixion is spiritually called Sodom and Egypt; then as the Lord was crucified at Jerusalem, Jerusalem must be Sodom and Egypt. Holy Scripture, I reply first of all, cannot contradict itself. One book cannot invalidate the drift of the whole. A single verse cannot annul the meaning of a book. Ten lines earlier in the apocalypse it is written: "Rise and measure the temple of God, and the altar, and them that worship therein. But the court which is without the temple leave out and measure it not; for it is given unto the Gentiles; and the holy city shall they tread under foot forty and two months." The apocalypse was written by John long after the Lord's passion, yet in it he speaks of Jerusalem as the holy city. But if so, how can he spiritually call it Sodom and Egypt? It is no answer to say that the Jerusalem which is called holy is the heavenly one which is to be, while that which is called Sodom is the earthly one tottering to its downfall. For it is the Jerusalem to come that is referred to in the description of the beast, "which shall ascend out of the bottomless pit, and shall make war against the two prophets, and shall overcome them and kill them, and their dead bodies shall lie in the street of the great city." At the close of the book it is farther described thus: "And the city lieth four-square, and the length of it and the breadth are the same as the height; and he measured the city with the golden reed twelve thousand furlongs. The length and the breadth and the height of it are equal. And he measured the walls thereof, an hundred and forty and four cubits, according to the measure of a man, that is, of the angel. And the building of the wall of it was of jasper; and the city was pure gold"—and so on. Now where there is a square there can be neither length nor breadth. And what kind of measurement is that which makes length and breadth equal to height? And how can

there be walls of jasper, or a whole city of pure gold; its foundations and its streets of precious stones, and its twelve gates each glowing with pearls?

7. Evidently this description cannot be taken literally (in fact, it is absurd to suppose a city the length, breadth and height of which are all twelve thousand furlongs), and therefore the details of it must be mystically understood. The great city which Cain first built and called after his son must be taken to represent this world, which the devil, that accuser of his brethren, that fratricide who is doomed to perish, has built of vice cemented with crime, and filled with iniquity. Therefore it is spiritually called Sodom and Egypt. Thus it is written, "Sodom shall return to her former estate," that is to say, the world must be restored as it has been before. For we cannot believe that Sodom and Gomorrah, Admah and Zeboim are to be built again: they must be left to lie in ashes forever. We never read of Egypt as put for Jerusalem: it always stands for this world. To collect from Scripture the countless proofs of this would be tedious: I shall adduce but one passage, a passage in which this world is most clearly called Egypt. The apostle Jude, the brother of James, writes thus in his catholic epistle: "I will, therefore, put you in remembrance, though ye once knew this how that Jesus, having saved the people out of the land of Egypt, afterward destroyed them that believed not." And, lest you should fancy Joshua the son of Nun to be meant, the passage goes on thus: "And the angels which kept not their first estate, but left their own habitation, he hath reserved in everlasting chains, under darkness, unto the judgment of the great day." Moreover, to convince you that in every place where Egypt, Sodom and Gomorrah are named together it is not these spots, but the present world, which is meant, he mentions them immediately in this sense. "Even as Sodom and Gomorrah," he writes, "and the cities about them, in like manner giving themselves over to fornication and going after strange flesh, are set forth for an example, suffering the vengeance of eternal fire." But what need is there to collect more proofs when, after the passion and the resurrection of the Lord, the evangelist Matthew tells us: "The rocks rent, and the graves were opened; and many bodies of the saints which slept arose and came out of the graves after his resurrection, and went into the holy city and appeared unto many"? We must not interpret this passage straight off, as many people absurdly do, of the heavenly Jerusalem: the apparition there of the bodies of the saints could be no sign to men of the Lord's rising. Since, therefore, the evangelists and all the Scriptures speak of Jerusalem as the holy city, and since the psalmist commands us to worship the Lord "at his footstool;" allow no one to call it Sodom and Egypt, for by it the Lord forbids men to swear because "it is the city of the great king."

8. The land is accursed, you say, because it has drunk in the blood of the Lord. On what grounds, then, do men regard as blessed those spots where Peter and Paul, the leaders of the Christian host, have shed their blood for Christ? If the confession of men and servants is glorious, must there not be glory likewise in the confession of their Lord and God? Everywhere we venerate the tombs of the martyrs; we apply their holy ashes to our eyes; we even touch them, if we may, with our lips. And yet some think that we should neglect the tomb in which the Lord Himself is buried. If we refuse to believe human testimony, let us at least credit the devil and his angels. For when in front of the Holy Sepulchre they are driven out of those bodies which they have possessed, they moan and tremble as if they stood before Christ's judgment-seat, and grieve, too late that they have crucified Him in whose presence they now cower. If—as a wicked theory maintains—this holy place has, since the Lord's passion, become an abomination, why was Paul in such haste to reach Jerusalem to keep Pentecost in it? Yet to those who held him back he said: "What mean ye to weep and to break my heart? For I am ready not to be bound only, but also to die at Jerusalem, for the name of the Lord Jesus." Need I speak of those other holy and illustrious men who, after the preaching of Christ, brought their votive gifts and offerings to the brethren who were at Jerusalem?

9. Time forbids me to survey the period which has passed since the Lord's ascension, or to recount the bishops, the martyrs, the divines, who have come to Jerusalem from a feeling that their devotion and knowledge would be incomplete and their virtue without the finishing touch, unless they adored Christ in the very spot where the gospel first flashed from the gibbet. If a famous orator blames a man for having learned Greek at Lilybaeum instead of at Athens, and Latin in Sicily instead of at Rome (on the ground, obviously, that each province has its own characteristics), can we suppose a Christian's education complete who has not visited the Christian Athens?

10. In speaking thus we do not mean to deny that the kingdom of God is within us, or to say that there are no holy men elsewhere; we merely assert in the strongest manner that those who stand first throughout the world are here gathered side by side. We ourselves are among the last, not the first; yet we have come hither to see the first of all nations. Of all the ornaments of the Church our company of monks and virgins is one of the finest; it is like a fair flower or a priceless gem. Every man of note in Gaul hastens hither. The Briton, "sundered from our world," no sooner makes progress in religion than he leaves the setting sun in quest of a spot of which he knows only through Scripture and common report. Need we recall the Armenians, the Persians, the

peoples of India and Arabia? Or those of our neighbor, Egypt, so rich in monks; of Pontus and Cappadocia; of Caele-Syria and Mesopotamia and the teeming east? In fulfilment of the Saviour's words, "Wherever the body is, thither will the eagles be gathered together," they all assemble here and exhibit in this one city the most varied virtues. Differing in speech, they are one in religion, and almost every nation has a choir of its own. Yet amid this great concourse there is no arrogance, no disdain of self-restraint; all strive after humility, that greatest of Christian virtues. Whosoever is last is here regarded as first. Their dress neither provokes remark nor calls for admiration. In whatever guise a man shows himself he is neither censured nor flattered. Long fasts help no one here. Starvation wins no deference, and the taking of food in moderation is not condemned. "To his own master" each one "standeth or falleth." No man judges another lest he be judged of the Lord. Backbiting, so common in other parts, is wholly unknown here. Sensuality and excess are far removed from us. And in the city there are so many places of prayer that a day would not be sufficient to go round them all.

11. But, as every one praises most what is within his reach, let us pass now to the cottage-inn which sheltered Christ and Mary. With what expressions and what language can we set before you the cave of the Saviour? The stall where he cried as a babe can be best honored by silence; for words are inadequate to speak its praise. Where are the spacious porticoes? Where are the gilded ceilings? Where are the mansions furnished by the miserable toil of doomed wretches? Where are the costly halls raised by untitled opulence for man's vile body to walk in? Where are the roofs that intercept the sky, as if anything could be finer than the expanse of heaven? Behold, in this poor crevice of the earth the Creator of the heavens was born; here He was wrapped in swaddling clothes; here He was seen by the shepherds; here He was pointed out by the star; here He was adored by the wise men. This spot is holier, methinks, than that Tarpeian rock which has shown itself displeasing to God by the frequency with which it has been struck by lightning.

12. Read the apocalypse of John, and consider what is sung therein of the woman arrayed in purple, and of the blasphemy written upon her brow, of the seven mountains, of the many waters, and of the end of Babylon. "Come out of her, my people," so the Lord says, "that ye be not partakers of her sins, and that ye receive not of her plagues." Turn back also to Jeremiah and pay heed to what he has written of like import: "Flee out of the midst of Babylon, and deliver every man his soul." For "Babylon the great is fallen, is fallen, and is become the habitation of devils, and the hold of every foul spirit." It is true that Rome has a holy church, trophies of apostles and martyrs, a true confes-

sion of Christ. The faith has been preached there by an apostle, heathenism has been trodden down, the name of Christian is daily exalted higher and higher. But the display, power, and size of the city, the seeing and the being seen, the paying and the receiving of visits, the alternate flattery and detraction, talking and listening, as well as the necessity of facing so great a throng even when one is least in the mood to do so—all these things are alike foreign to the principles and fatal to the repose of the monastic life. For when people come in our way we either see them coming and are compelled to speak, or we do not see them and lay ourselves open to the charge of haughtiness. Sometimes, also, in returning visits we are obliged to pass through proud portals and gilded doors and to face the clamor of carping lackeys. But, as we have said above, in the cottage of Christ all is simple and rustic: and except for the chanting of psalms there is complete silence. Wherever one turns the laborer at his plough sings alleluia, the toiling mower cheers himself with psalms, and the vine-dresser while he prunes his vine sings one of the lays of David. These are the songs of the country; these, in popular phrase, its love ditties: these the shepherd whistles; these the tiller uses to aid his toil.

13. But what are we doing? Forgetting what is required of us, we are taken up with what we wish. Will the time never come when a breathless messenger shall bring the news that our dear Marcella has reached the shores of Palestine, and when every band of monks and every troop of virgins shall unite in a song of welcome? In our excitement we are already hurrying to meet you: without waiting for a vehicle, we hasten off at once on foot. We shall clasp you by the hand, we shall look upon your face; and when, after long waiting, we at last embrace you, we shall find it hard to tear ourselves away. Will the day never come when we shall together enter the Saviour's cave, and together weep in the sepulchre of the Lord with His sister and with His mother? Then shall we touch with our lips the wood of the cross, and rise in prayer and resolve upon the Mount of Olives with the ascending Lord. We shall see Lazarus come forth bound with grave clothes, we shall look upon the waters of Jordan purified for the washing of the Lord. Thence we shall pass to the folds of the shepherds, we shall pray together in the mausoleum of David. We shall see the prophet, Amos, upon his crag blowing his shepherd's horn. We shall hasten, if not to the tents, to the monuments of Abraham, Isaac and Jacob, and of their three illustrious wives. We shall see the fountain in which the eunuch was immersed by Philip. We shall make a pilgrimage to Samaria, and side by side venerate the ashes of John the Baptist, of Elisha, and of Obadiah. We shall enter the very caves where in the time of persecution and famine the companies of the prophets were fed. If only you will come, we shall go to see Nazareth, as its

name denotes, the flower of Galilee. Not far off Cana will be visible, where the water was turned into wine. We shall make our way to Tabor, and see the tabernacles there which the Saviour shares, not, as Peter once wished, with Moses and Elijah, but with the Father and with the Holy Ghost. Thence we shall come to the Sea of Gennesaret, and when there we shall see the spots where the five thousand were filled with five loaves, and the four thousand with seven. The town of Nain will meet our eyes, at the gate of which the widow's son was raised to life. Hermon too will be visible, and the torrent of Endor, at which Sisera was vanquished. Our eyes will look also on Capernaum, the scene of so many of our Lord's signs—yes, and on all Galilee besides. And when, accompanied by Christ, we shall have made our way back to our cave through Shiloh and Bethel, and those other places where churches are set up like standards to commemorate the Lord's victories, then we shall sing heartily, we shall weep copiously, we shall pray unceasingly. Wounded with the Saviour's shaft, we shall say one to another: "I have found Him whom my soul loveth; I will hold Him and will not let Him go."

LETTER XLVII. TO DESIDERIUS

Jerome invites two of his old friends at Rome, Desiderius and his sister (or wife) Serenilla, to join him at Bethlehem. It is possible but not probable that this Desiderius is the same with Desiderius of Aquitaine, who afterwards induced Jerome to write against Vigilantius.

An interval of seven years separates this letter (of which the date is 393 a.d.) from the preceding, and all the letters written during this period have wholly perished.

1. Surprised as I have been, my excellent friend, to read the language which your kindness has prompted you to hold concerning me, I have rejoiced that I possess the testimony of one both eloquent and sincere; but when I turn from you to myself I feel vexed that, owing to my unworthiness, your words of praise and eulogy rather weigh me down than lift me up. You know, of course, that I make it a principle to raise the standard of humility, and to prepare for scaling the heights by walking for the present in the lowest places. For what am I or what is my significance that I should have the voice of learning raised to bear witness of me, or that the palm of eloquence should be laid at my feet by one whose style is so charming that it has almost deterred me from writing a letter at all? I must, however, make the attempt in order that charity which

seeks not her own but always her neighbor's good, may at least return a compliment, since it cannot convey a lesson.

2. I offer my congratulations to you and to your holy and revered sister, Serenilla, who, true to her name, has trodden down the troubled waves of the world, and has passed to Christ's calm haven: a happiness which—if we may trust the augury of your name—is in store for you also. For we read that the holy Daniel was called "a man of desires," and the friend of God, because he desired to know His mysteries. Therefore, I do with pleasure what the revered Paula has asked of me. I urge and implore you both by the charity of the Lord that you will give your presence to us, and that a visit to the holy places may induce you to enrich us with this great gift. Even supposing that you do not care for our society, it is still your duty as believers to worship on the spot where the Lord's feet once stood and to see for yourselves the still fresh traces of His birth, His cross, and His passion.

3. Several of my little pieces have flown away out of their nest, and have rashly sought for themselves the honor of publication. I have not sent you any lest I should send works which you already have. But if you care to borrow copies of them, you can do so either from our holy sister, Marcella, who has her abode upon the Aventine, or from that holy man, Domnio, who is the Lot of our times. Meantime, I look for your arrival, and will give you all I have when you once come; or, if any hindrances prevent you from joining us, I will gladly send you such treatises as you shall desire. Following the example of Tranquillus and of Apollonius the Greek, I have written a book concerning illustrious men from the apostles' time to our own; and after enumerating a great number I have put myself down on the last page as one born out of due time, and the least of all Christians. Here I have found it necessary to give a short account of my writings down to the fourteenth year of the Emperor Theodosius. If you find, on procuring this treatise from the persons mentioned above, that there are any pieces mentioned which you have not already got, I will have them copied for you by degrees, if you wish it.

LETTER XLVIII. TO PAMMACHIUS

An "apology" for the two books "against Jovinian" which Jerome had written a short time previously, and of which he had sent copies to Rome. These Pammachius and his other friends had withheld from publication, thinking that Jerome had unduly exalted virginity at the expense of marriage. He now writes to make good his position, and to do this makes copious extracts from the obnoxious treatise. The date of the letter is 393 or 394 a.d.

1. Your own silence is my reason for not having written hitherto. For I feared that, if I were to write to you without first hearing from you, you would consider me not so much a conscientious as a troublesome correspondent. But, now that I have been challenged by your most delightful letter, a letter which calls upon me to defend my views by an appeal to first principles, I receive my old fellow-learner, companion, and friend with open arms, as the saying goes; and I look forward to having in you a champion of my poor writings; if, that is to say, I can first conciliate your judgment to give sentence in my favor, and can instruct my advocate in all those points on which I am assailed. For both your favorite, Cicero, and before him—in his one short treatise—Antonius, write to this effect, that the chief requisite for victory is to acquaint one's self carefully with the case which one has to plead.

2. Certain persons find fault with me because in the books which I have written against Jovinian I have been excessive (so they say) in praise of virginity and in depreciation of marriage; and they affirm that to preach up chastity till no comparison is left between a wife and a virgin is equivalent to a condemnation of matrimony. If I remember aright the point of the dispute, the question at issue between myself and Jovinian is that he puts marriage on a level with virginity, while I make it inferior; he declares that there is little or no difference between the two states, I assert that there is a great deal. Finally—a result due under God to your agency—he has been condemned because he has dared to set matrimony on an equality with perpetual chastity. Or, if a virgin and a wife are to be looked on as the same, how comes it that Rome has refused to listen to this impious doctrine? A virgin owes her being to a man, but a man does not owe his to a virgin. There can be no middle course. Either my view of the matter must be embraced, or else that of Jovinian. If I am blamed for putting wedlock below virginity, he must be praised for putting the two states on a level. If, on the other hand, he is condemned for supposing them equal, his condemnation must be taken as testimony in favor of my treatise. If men of the world chafe under the notion that they occupy a position inferior to that of virgins, I wonder that clergymen and monks—who both live celibate lives—refrain from praising what they consistently practise. They cut themselves off from their wives to imitate the chastity of virgins, and yet they will have it that married women are as good as these. They should either be joined again to their wives whom they have renounced, or, if they persist in living apart from them, they will have to confess—by their lives if not by their words—that, in preferring virginity to marriage, they have chosen the better course. Am I then

a mere novice in the Scriptures, reading the sacred volumes for the first time? And is the line there drawn between virginity and marriage so fine that I have been unable to observe it? I could know nothing, forsooth, of the saying, "Be not righteous overmuch!" Thus, while I try to protect myself on one side, I am wounded on the other; to speak more plainly still, while I close with Jovinian in hand-to-hand combat, Manichaeus stabs me in the back. Have I not, I would ask, in the very forefront of my work set the following preface: "We are no disciples of Marcion or of Manichaeus, to detract from marriage. Nor are we deceived by the error of Tatian, the chief of the Encratites, into supposing all cohabitation unclean. For he condemns and reprobates not marriage only, but foods also which God has created for us to enjoy. We know that in a large house there are vessels not only of silver and of gold, but of wood also and of earth. We know, too, that on the foundation of Christ which Paul the master builder has laid, some build up gold, silver, and precious stones; others, on the contrary, hay, wood, and stubble. We are not ignorant that marriage is honorable . . . and the bed undefiled.' We have read the first decree of God: Be fruitful and multiply and replenish the earth.' But while we allow marriage, we prefer the virginity which springs from it. Gold is more precious than silver, but is silver on that account the less silver? Is it an insult to a tree to prefer its apples to its roots or its leaves? Is it an injury to corn to put the ear before the stalk and the blade? As apples come from the tree and grain from the straw, so virginity comes from wedlock. Yields of one hundredfold, of sixtyfold, and of thirtyfold may all come from one soil and from one sowing, yet they will differ widely in quantity. The yield thirtyfold signifies wedlock, for the joining together of the fingers to express that number, suggestive as it is of a loving gentle kiss or embracing, aptly represents the relation of husband and wife. The yield sixtyfold refers to widows who are placed in a position of distress and tribulation. Accordingly, they are typified by that finger which is placed under the other to express the number sixty; for, as it is extremely trying when one has once tasted pleasure to abstain from its enticements, so the reward of doing this is proportionately great. Moreover, a hundred—I ask the reader to give me his best attention—necessitates a change from the left hand to the right; but while the hand is different the fingers are the same as those which on the left hand signify married women and widows; only in this instance the circle formed by them indicates the crown of virginity."

3. Does a man who speaks thus, I would ask you, condemn marriage? If I have called virginity gold, I have spoken of marriage as silver. I have set forth that the yields an hundredfold, sixtyfold, and thirtyfold—all spring from one soil and from one sowing, although in amount they differ widely. Will any of

my readers be so unfair as to judge me, not by my words, but by his own opinion? At any rate, I have dealt much more gently with marriage than most Latin and Greek writers; who, by referring the hundredfold yield to martyrs, the sixtyfold to virgins, and the thirtyfold to widows, show that in their opinion married persons are excluded from the good ground and from the seed of the great Father. But, lest it might be supposed that, though cautious at the outset, I was imprudent in the remainder of my work, have I not, after marking out the divisions of it, on coming to the actual questions immediately introduced the following: "I ask all of you of both sexes, at once those who are virgins and continent and those who are married or twice married, to aid my efforts with your prayers." Jovinian is the foe of all indiscriminately, but can I condemn as Manichaean heretics persons whose prayers I need and whose assistance I entreat to help me in my work?

4. As the brief compass of a letter does not suffer us to delay too long on a single point, let us now pass to those which remain. In explaining the testimony of the apostle, "The wife hath not power of her own body, but the husband; and likewise, also, the husband hath not power of his own body, but the wife," we have subjoined the following: "The entire question relates to those who are living in wedlock, whether it is lawful for them to put away their wives, a thing which the Lord also has forbidden in the Gospel. Hence, also, the apostle says: It is good for a man not to touch' a wife or a woman,' as if there were danger in the contact which he who should so touch one could not escape. Accordingly, when the Egyptian woman desired to touch Joseph he flung away his cloak and fled from her hands. But as he who has once married a wife cannot, except by consent, abstain from intercourse with her or repudiate her, so long as she does not sin, he must render unto his wife her due, because he has of his own free will bound himself to render it under compulsion." Can one who declares that it is a precept of the Lord that wives should not be put away, and that what God has joined together man must not, without consent, put asunder—can such an one be said to condemn marriage? Again, in the verses which follow, the apostle says: "But every man hath his proper gift of God, one after this manner, and another after that." In explanation of this saying we made the following remarks: "What I myself would wish, he says, is clear. But since there are diversities of gifts in the church, I allow marriage as well, that I may not appear to condemn nature. Reflect, too, that the gift of virginity is one thing, that of marriage another. For had there been one reward for married women and for virgins he would never, after giving the counsel of continence, have gone on to say: But every man hath his proper gift of God, one after this manner and another after that.' Where each class has its

proper gift, there must be some distinction between the classes. I allow that marriage, as well as virginity, is the gift of God, but there is a great difference between gift and gift. Finally, the apostle himself says of one who had lived in incest and afterwards repented: Contrariwise ye ought rather to forgive him and comfort him,' and To whom ye forgive anything, I forgive also.' And, lest we might suppose a man's gift to be but a small thing, he has added: For if I forgave anything, to whom I forgave it, for your sakes forgave I it in the sight of Christ.' The gifts of Christ are different. Hence Joseph as a type of Him had a coat of many colors. So in the forty-fourth psalm we read of the Church: Upon thy right hand did stand the queen in a vesture of gold, wrought about with divers colors.' The apostle Peter, too, speaks (of husbands and wives) as being heirs together of the manifold grace of God.' In Greek the expression is still more striking, the word used being poikile, that is, many-colored.'"

5. I ask, then, what is the meaning of men's obstinate determination to shut their eyes and to refuse to look on what is as clear as day? I have said that there are diversities of gifts in the Church, and that virginity is one gift and wedlock another. And shortly after I have used the words: "I allow marriage also to be a gift of God, but there is a great difference between gift and gift." Can it be said that I condemn that which in the clearest terms I declare to be the gift of God? Moreover, if Joseph is taken as a type of the Lord, his coat of many colors is a type of virgins and widows, celibates and wedded. Can any one who has any part in Christ's tunic be regarded as an alien? Have we not spoken of the very queen herself—that is, the Church of the Saviour—as wearing a vesture of gold wrought about with divers colors? Moreover, when I came to discuss marriage in connection with the following verses, I still adhered to the same view. "This passage," I said, "has indeed no relation to the present controversy; for, following the decision of the Lord, the apostle teaches that a wife must not be put away saving for fornication, and that, if she has been put away, she cannot during the lifetime of her husband marry another man, or, at any rate, that she ought, if possible, to be reconciled to her husband. In another verse he speaks to the same effect: The wife is bound . . . as long as her husband liveth; but if her husband be dead, she is loosed from the law of her husband; she is at liberty to be married to whom she will; only in the Lord,' that is to a Christian. Thus the apostle, while he allows a second or a third marriage in the Lord, forbids even a first with a heathen."

6. I ask my detractors to open their ears and to realize the fact that I have allowed second and third marriages "in the Lord." If, then, I have not condemned second and third marriages, how can I have proscribed a first? Moreover, in the passage where I interpret the words of the apostle, "Is any man

called being circumcised? Let him not become uncircumcised. Is any called in uncircumcision? let him not be circumcised" (a passage, it is true, which some most careful interpreters of Scripture refer to the circumcision and slavery of the Law), do I not in the clearest terms stand up for the marriage-tie? My words are these: "If any man is called in uncircumcision, let him not be circumcised.' You had a wife, the apostle says, when you believed. Do not fancy your faith in Christ to be a reason for parting from her. For God hath called us in peace.' Circumcision is nothing and uncircumcision is nothing but the keeping of the commandments of God.' Neither celibacy nor wedlock is of the slightest use without works, since even faith, the distinguishing mark of Christians, if it have not works, is said to be dead, and on such terms as these the virgins of Vesta or of Juno, who was constant to one husband, might claim to be numbered among the saints. And a little further on he says: Art thou called being a servant, care not for it; but, if thou mayest be made free, use it rather;' that is to say, if you have a wife, and are bound to her, and render her her due, and have not power of your own body—or, to speak yet more plainly—if you are the slave of a wife, do not allow this to cause you sorrow, do not sigh over the loss of your virginity. Even if you can find pretexts for parting from her to enjoy the freedom of chastity, do not seek your own welfare at the price of another's ruin. Keep your wife for a little, and do not try too hastily to overcome her reluctance. Wait till she follows your example. If you only have patience, your wife will some day become your sister."

7. In another passage we have discussed the reasons which led Paul to say: "Now concerning virgins, I have no commandment of the Lord: yet I give my judgment, as one that hath obtained mercy of the Lord to be faithful." Here also, while we have extolled virginity, we have been careful to give marriage its due. "Had the Lord commanded virginity," we said, "He would have seemed to condemn marriage and to do away with that seed-plot of humanity from which virginity itself springs. Had He cut away the root how could He have looked for fruit? Unless He had first laid the foundations, how could He have built the edifice or crowned it with a roof made to cover its whole extent?" If we have spoken of marriage as the root whose fruit is virginity, and if we have made wedlock the foundation on which the building or the roof of perpetual chastity is raised, which of my detractors can be so captious or so blind as to ignore the foundation on which the fabric and its roof are built, while he has before his eyes both the fabric and the roof themselves? Once more, in another place, we have brought forward the testimony of the apostle to this effect: "Art thou bound unto a wife? Seek not to be loosed. Art thou loosed from a wife? Seek not a wife." To this we have appended the following remarks: "Each of us

has his own sphere allotted to him. Let me have mine, and do you keep yours. If you are bound to a wife, do not put her away. If I am loosed from a wife, let me not seek a wife. Just as I do not loose marriage-ties when they are once made, so do you refrain from binding together what at present is loosed from such ties." Yet another passage bears unmistakable testimony to the view which we have taken of virginity and of wedlock: "The apostle casts no snare upon us, nor does he compel us to be what we do not wish. He only urges us to what is honorable and seemly, inciting us earnestly to serve the Lord, to be anxious always to please Him, and to look for His will which He has prepared for us to do. We are to be like alert and armed soldiers, who immediately execute the orders given to them and perform them without that travail of mind which, according to the preacher, is given to the men of this world to be exercised therewith.'" At the end, also, of our comparison of virgins and married women we have summed up the discussion thus: "When one thing is good and another thing is better; when that which is good has a different reward from that which is better; and when there are more rewards than one, then, obviously, there exists a diversity of gifts. The difference between marriage and virginity is as great as that between not doing evil and doing good—or, to speak more favorably still, as that between what is good and what is still better."

8. In the sequel we go on to speak thus: "The apostle, in concluding his discussion of marriage and of virginity, is careful to observe a mean course in discriminating between them, and, turning neither to the right hand nor to the left, he keeps to the King's highway, and thus fulfils the injunction, Be not righteous overmuch.' Moreover, when he goes on to compare monogamy with digamy, he puts digamy after monogamy, just as before he subordinated marriage to virginity." Do we not clearly show by this language what is typified in the Holy Scriptures by the terms right and left, and also what we take to be the meaning of the words "Be not righteous overmuch"? We turn to the left if, following the lust of Jews and Gentiles, we burn for sexual intercourse; we turn to the right if, following the error of the Manichaeans, we under a pretence of chastity entangle ourselves in the meshes of unchastity. But we keep to the King's highway if we aspire to virginity yet refrain from condemning marriage. Can any one, moreover, be so unfair in his criticism of my poor treatise as to allege that I condemn first marriages, when he reads my opinion on second ones as follows: "The apostle, it is true, allows second marriages, but only to such women as are bent upon them, to such as cannot contain, lest when they have begun to wax wanton against Christ they marry, having condemnation because they have rejected their first faith,' and he makes this concession because many are turned aside after Satan.' But they will be happier if they

abide as widows. To this he immediately adds his apostolical authority, after my judgment.' Moreover, lest any should consider that authority, being human, to be of small weight, he goes on to say, and I think also that I have the spirit of God.' Thus, where he urges men to continence he appeals not to human authority, but to the Spirit of God; but when he gives them permission to marry he does not mention the Spirit of God, but allows prudential considerations to turn the balance, relaxing the strictness of his code in favor of individuals according to their several needs." Having thus brought forward proofs that second marriages are allowed by the apostle, we at once added the remarks which follow: "As marriage is permitted to virgins by reason of the danger of fornication, and as what in itself is not desirable is thus made excusable, so by reason of the same danger widows are permitted to marry a second time. For it is better that a woman should know one man (though he should be a second husband or a third) than that she should know several. In other words, it is preferable that she should prostitute herself to one rather than to many." Calumny may do its worst. We have spoken here not of a first marriage, but of a second, of a third, or (if you like) of a fourth. But lest any one should apply my words (that it is better for a woman to prostitute herself to one man than to several) to a first marriage when my whole argument dealt with digamy and trigamy, I marked my own view of these practices with the words: "All things are lawful, but all things are not expedient.' I do not condemn digamists nor yet trigamists, nor even, to put an extreme, case, octogamists. I will make a still greater concession: I am ready to receive even a whoremonger, if penitent. In every case where fairness is possible, fair consideration must be shown."

9. My calumniator should blush at his assertion that I condemn first marriages when he reads my words just now quoted: "I do not condemn digamists or trigamists, or even, to put an extreme case, octogamists." Not to condemn is one thing, to commend is another. I may concede a practice as allowable and yet not praise it as meritorious. But if I seem severe in saying, "In every case where fairness is possible, fair consideration must be shown," no one, I fancy, will judge me either cruel or stern who reads that the places prepared for virgins and for wedded persons are different from those prepared for trigamists, octogamists, and penitents. That Christ Himself, although in the flesh a virgin, was in the spirit a monogamist, having one wife, even the Church, I have shown in the latter part of my argument. And yet I am supposed to condemn marriage! I am said to condemn it, although I use such words as these: "It is an undoubted fact that the levitical priests were descended from the stock of Aaron, Eleazar, and Phinehas; and, as all these were married men, we might

well be confronted with them if, led away by the error of the Encratites, we were to contend that marriage is in itself deserving of condemnation." Here I blame Tatian, the chief of the Encratites, for his rejection of marriage, and yet I myself am said to condemn it! Once more, when I contrast virgins with widows, my own words show what my view is concerning wedlock, and set forth the threefold gradation which I propose of virgins, widows—whether in practice or in fact—and wedded wives. "I do not deny"—these are my words—"the blessedness of widows who continue such after their baptism, nor do I undervalue the merit of wives who live in chastity with their husbands; but, just as widows receive a greater reward from God than wives obedient to their husbands, they, too, must be content to see virgins preferred before themselves."

10. Again, when explaining the witness of the apostle to the Galatians, "By the works of the law shall no flesh be justified," I have spoken to the following effect: "Marriages also are works of the law. And for this reason there is a curse upon such as do not produce offspring. They are permitted, it is true, even under the Gospel; but it is one thing to concede an indulgence to what is a weakness and quite another to promise a reward to what is a virtue." See my express declaration that marriage is allowed in the Gospel, yet that those who are married cannot receive the rewards of chastity so long as they render their due one to another. If married men feel indignant at this statement, let them vent their anger not on me but on the Holy Scriptures; nay, more, upon all bishops, presbyters, and deacons, and the whole company of priests and levites, who know that they cannot offer sacrifices if they fulfil the obligations of marriage. Again, when I adduce evidence from the Apocalypse, is it not clear what view I take concerning virgins, widows, and wives? "These are they who sing a new song which no man can sing except he be a virgin. These are the first fruits unto God and unto the Lamb,' and they are without spot. If virgins are the first fruits unto God, then widows and wives who live in continence must come after the first fruits—that is to say, in the second place and in the third." We place widows, then, and wives in the second place and in the third, and for this we are charged by the frenzy of a heretic with condemning marriage altogether.

11. Throughout the book I have made many remarks in a tone of great moderation on virginity, widowhood, and marriage. But for the sake of brevity, I will here adduce but one passage, and that of such a kind that no one, I think, will be found to gainsay it save some one who wishes to prove himself malicious or mad. In describing our Lord's visit to the marriage at Cana in Galilee, after some other remarks I have added these: "He who went but once

to a marriage has taught us that a woman should marry but once; and this fact might tell against virginity if we failed to give marriage its due place—after virginity that is, and chaste widowhood. But, as it is only heretics who condemn marriage and tread under foot the ordinance of God, we listen with gladness to every word said by our Lord in praise of marriage. For the Church does not condemn marriage, but only subordinates it. It does not reject it altogether, but regulates it, knowing (as I have said above) that in a great house there are not only vessels of gold and of silver, but also of wood and of earth; and some to honor and some to dishonor. If a man, therefore, purge himself. . . he shall be a vessel unto honor meet . . . and prepared unto every good work.'" I listen with gladness, I say here, to every word said by the apostle in praise of marriage. Do I listen with gladness to the praise of marriage, and do I yet condemn marriage? The Church, I say, does not condemn wedlock, but subordinates it. Whether you like it or not, marriage is subordinated to virginity and widowhood. Even when marriage continues to fulfil its function, the Church does not condemn it, but only subordinates it; it does not reject it, but only regulates it. It is in your power, if you will, to mount the second step of chastity. Why are you angry if, standing on the third and lowest step, you will not make haste to go up higher?

12. Since, then, I have so often reminded my reader of my views; and since I have picked my way like a prudent traveller over every inch of the road, stating repeatedly that, while I receive marriage as a thing in itself admissible, I yet prefer continence, widowhood, and virginity, the wise and generous reader ought to have judged what seemed hard sayings by my general drift, and not to have charged me with putting forward inconsistent opinions in one and the same book. For who is so dull or so inexperienced in writing as to praise and to condemn one and the same object, as to destroy what he has built up, and to build up what he has destroyed; and when he has vanquished his opponent, to turn his sword, last of all against himself? Were my detractors country bred or unacquainted with the arts of rhetoric or of logic, I should pardon their want of insight; nor should I censure them for accusing me if I saw that their ignorance was in fault and not their will. As it is men of intellect who have enjoyed a liberal education make it their object less to understand me than to wound me, and for such I have this short answer, that they should correct my faults and not merely censure me for them. The lists are open, I cry; your enemy has marshalled his forces, his position is plain, and (if I may quote Virgil)—

The foeman calls you: meet him face to face.

Such men should answer their opponent. They ought to keep within the limits of debate, and not to wield the schoolmaster's rod. Their books should aim at showing in what my statements have fallen short of the truth, and in what they have exceeded it. For, although I will not listen to fault-finders, I will follow the advice of teachers. To direct the fighter how to fight when you yourself occupy a post of vantage on the wall is a kind of teaching that does not commend itself; and when you are yourself bathed in perfumes, it is unworthy to charge a bleeding soldier with cowardice. Nor in saying this do I lay myself open to a charge of boasting that while others have slept I only have entered the lists. My meaning simply is that men who have seen me wounded in this warfare may possibly be a little too cautious in their methods of fighting. I would not have you engage in an encounter in which you will have nothing to do but to protect yourself, your right hand remaining motionless while your left manages your shield. You must either strike or fall. I cannot account you a victor unless I see your opponent put to the sword.

13. You are, no doubt, men of vast acquirements; but we too have studied in the schools, and, like you, we have learned from the precepts of Aristotle—or, rather, from those which he has derived from Gorgias—that there are different ways of speaking; and we know, among other things, that he who writes for display uses one style, and he who writes to convince, another. In the former case the debate is desultory; to confute the opposer, now this argument is adduced and now that. One argues as one pleases, saying one thing while one means another. To quote the proverb, "With one hand one offers bread, in the other one holds a stone." In the latter case a certain frankness and openness of countenance are necessary. For it is one thing to start a problem and another to expound what is already proved. The first calls for a disputant, the second for a teacher. I stand in the thick of the fray, my life in constant danger: you who profess to teach me are a man of books. "Do not," you say, "attack unexpectedly or wound by a side-thrust. Strike straight at your opponent. You should be ashamed to resort to feints instead of force." As if it were not the perfection of fighting to menace one part and to strike another. Read, I beg of you, Demosthenes or Cicero, or (if you do not care for pleaders whose aim is to speak plausibly rather than truly) read Plato, Theophrastus, Xenophon, Aristotle, and the rest of those who draw their respective rills of wisdom from the Socratic fountain-head. Do they show any openness? Are they devoid of artifice? Is not every word they say filled with meaning? And does not this meaning always make for victory? Origen, Methodius, Eusebius, and Apollinaris write at great length against Celsus and Porphyry. Consider how subtle are the arguments, how insidious the engines with which they overthrow what the spirit of the devil has wrought. Sometimes, it is true, they are compelled to say not what they think but what is needful; and for this reason they employ

against their opponents the assertions of the Gentiles themselves. I say nothing of the Latin authors, of Tertullian, Cyprian, Minutius, Victorinus, Lactantius, Hilary, lest I should appear not so much to be defending myself as to be assailing others. I will only mention the Apostle Paul, whose words seem to me, as often as I hear them, to be not words, but peals of thunder. Read his epistles, and especially those addressed to the Romans, to the Galatians, and to the Ephesians, in all of which he stands in the thick of the battle, and you will see how skilful and how careful he is in the proofs which he draws from the Old Testament, and how warily he cloaks the object which he has in view. His words seem simplicity itself: the expressions of a guileless and unsophisticated person—one who has no skill either to plan a dilemma or to avoid it. Still, whichever way you look, they are thunderbolts. His pleading halts, yet he carries every point which he takes up. He turns his back upon his foe only to overcome him; he simulates flight, but only that he may slay. He, then, if any one, ought to be calumniated; we should speak thus to him: "The proofs which you have used against the Jews or against other heretics bear a different meaning in their own contexts to that which they bear in your epistles. We see passages taken captive by your pen and pressed into service to win you a victory which in the volumes from which they are taken have no controversial bearing at all." May he not reply to us in the words of the Saviour: "I have one mode of speech for those that are without and another for those that are within; the crowds hear my parables, but their interpretation is for my disciples alone"? The Lord puts questions to the Pharisees, but does not elucidate them. To teach a disciple is one thing; to vanquish an opponent, another. "My mystery is for me," says the prophet; "my mystery is for me and for them that are mine."

14. You are indignant with me because I have merely silenced Jovinian and not instructed him. You, do I say? Nay, rather, they who grieve to hear him anathematized, and who impeach their own pretended orthodoxy by eulogizing in another the heresy which they hold themselves. I should have asked him, forsooth, to surrender peaceably! I had no right to disregard his struggles and to drag him against his will into the bonds of truth! I might use such language had the desire of victory induced me to say anything counter to the rule laid down in Scripture, and had I taken the line—so often adopted by strong men in controversy—of justifying the means by the result. As it is, however, I have been an exponent of the apostle rather than a dogmatist on my own account; and my function has been simply that of a commentator. Anything, therefore, which seems a hard saying should be imputed to the writer expounded by me rather than to me the expounder; unless, indeed, he spoke otherwise than he is

represented to have done, and I have by an unfair interpretation wrested the plain meaning of his words. If any one charges me with this disingenuousness let him prove his charge from the Scriptures themselves.

I have said in my book, "If it is good for a man not to touch a woman,' then it is bad for him to touch one, for bad, and bad only, is the opposite of good. But, if though bad it is made venial, then it is allowed to prevent something which would be worse than bad," and so on down to the commencement of the next chapter. The above is my comment upon the apostle's words: "It is good for a man not to touch a woman. Nevertheless, to avoid fornication, let every man have his own wife, and let every woman have her own husband." In what way does my meaning differ from that intended by the apostle? Except that where he speaks decidedly I do so with hesitation. He defines a dogma, I hazard an inquiry. He openly says: "It is good for a man not to touch a woman." I timidly ask if it is good for a man not to touch one. If I thus waver, I cannot be said to speak positively. He says: "It is good not to touch." I add what is a possible antithesis to "good." And immediately afterwards I speak thus: "Notice the apostle's carefulness. He does not say: It is good for a man not to have a wife,' but, It is good for a man not to touch a woman'; as if there is danger in the very touching of one—danger which he who touches cannot escape." You see, therefore, that I am not expounding the law as to husbands and wives, but simply discussing the general question of sexual intercourse—how in comparison with chastity and virginity, the life of angels, "It is good for a man not to touch a woman."

"Vanity of vanities," says the Preacher, "all is vanity." But if all created things are good, as being the handiwork of a good Creator, how comes it that all things are vanity? If the earth is vanity, are the heavens vanity too?—and the angels, the thrones, the dominations, the powers, and the rest of the virtues? No; if things which are good in themselves as being the handiwork of a good Creator are called vanity, it is because they are compared with things which are better still. For example, compared with a lamp, a lantern is good for nothing; compared with a star, a lamp does not shine at all; the brightest star pales before the moon; put the moon beside the sun, and it no longer looks bright; compare the sun with Christ, and it is darkness. "I am that I am," God says; and if you compare all created things with Him they have no existence. "Give not thy sceptre," says Esther, "unto them that be nothing"—that is to say, to idols and demons. And certainly they were idols and demons to whom she prayed that she and hers might not be given over. In Job also we read how Bildad says of the wicked man: "His confidence shall be rooted out of his tabernacle, and destruction as a king shall trample upon him. The companions also of him who is not shall abide in his tabernacle." This evidently relates to the devil, who must be in existence, otherwise he could not be said to have companions. Still, because he is lost to God, he is said not to be.

Now it was in a similar sense that I declared it to be a bad thing to touch a woman—I did not say a wife—because it is a good thing not to touch one. And I added: "I call virginity fine corn, wedlock barley, and fornication cow-dung." Surely both corn and barley are creatures of God. But of the two multitudes miraculously supplied in the Gospel the larger was fed upon barley loaves, and the smaller on corn bread. "Thou, Lord," says the psalmist, "shalt save both man and beast." I have myself said the same thing in other words, when I have spoken of virginity as gold and of wedlock as silver. Again, in discussing the one hundred and forty-four thousand sealed virgins who were not defiled with women, I have tried to show that all who have not remained virgins are reckoned as defiled when compared with the perfect chastity of the angels and of our Lord Jesus Christ. But if any one thinks it hard or reprehensible that I have placed the same interval between virginity and wedlock as there is between fine corn and barley, let him read the book of the holy Ambrose "On Widows," and he will find, among other statements concerning virginity and marriage, the following: "The apostle has not expressed his preference for marriage so unreservedly as to quench in men the aspiration after virginity; he commences with a recommendation of continence, and it is only subsequently that he stoops to mention the remedies for its opposite. And although to the strong he has pointed out the prize of their high calling, yet he suffers none to faint by the way; whilst he applauds those who lead the van, he does not despise those who bring up the rear. For he had himself learned that the Lord Jesus gave to some barley bread, lest they should faint by the way, but offered to others His own body, that they should strive to attain His kingdom;" and immediately afterwards: "The nuptial tie, then, is not to be avoided as a crime, but to be refused as a hard burden. For the law binds the wife to bring forth children in labor and in sorrow. Her desire is to be to her husband that he should rule over her. It is not the widow, then, but the bride, who is handed over to labor and sorrow in childbearing. It is not the virgin, but the married woman, who is subjected to the sway of a husband." And in another place, "Ye are bought," says the apostle, "with a price; be not therefore the servants of men." You see how clearly he defines the servitude which attends the married state. And a little farther on: "If, then, even a good marriage is servitude, what must a bad one be, in which husband and wife cannot sanctify, but only mutually destroy each other?" What I have said about virginity and marriage diffusely, Ambrose has stated tersely and pointedly, compressing much meaning into a few words. Virginity is described by him as a means of recommending continence, marriage as a remedy for incontinence. And when he descends from broad principles to particular details, he significantly holds out to virgins the prize of the high calling, yet comforts the married, that they may not faint by the way. While eulogizing the one class, he does not despise the other. Marriage he compares to the barley bread set before the multitude, virginity to the body of Christ given to the disciples. There is much less difference, it seems to me, between barley and fine corn than between barley and the body of Christ. Finally, he speaks of marriage as a hard burden, to be avoided if possible, and as a badge of the most unmistakable servitude. He makes, also, many other statements, which he has followed up at length in his three books "On Virgins."

15. From all which considerations it is clear that I have said nothing at all new concerning virginity and marriage, but have followed in all respects the judgment of older writers—of Ambrose, that is to say, and others who have discussed the doctrines of the Church. "And I would sooner follow them in their faults than copy the dull pedantry of the writers of to-day." Let married men, if they please, swell with rage because I have said, "I ask you, what kind of good thing is that which forbids a man to pray, and which prevents him from receiving the body of Christ?" When I do my duty as a husband, I cannot fulfil the requirements of continence. The same apostle, in another place, commands us to pray always. "But if we are always to pray we must never yield to the claims of wedlock for, as often as I render her due to my wife, I incapacitate myself for prayer." When I spoke thus it is clear that I relied on the words of the apostle: "Defraud ye not one the other, except it be with consent for a time, that ye may give yourselves to . . . prayer." The Apostle Paul tells us that when we have intercourse with our wives we cannot pray. If, then, sexual intercourse prevents what is less important—that is, prayer—how much more does it prevent what is more important—that is, the reception of the body of Christ? Peter, too, exhorts us to continence, that our "prayers be not hindered." How, I should like to know, have I sinned in all this? What have I done? How have I been in fault? If the waters of a stream are thick and muddy, it is not the river-bed which is to blame, but the source. Am I attacked because I have ventured to add to the words of the apostle these words of my own: "What kind of good thing is that which prevents a man from receiving the body of Christ?" If so, I will make answer briefly thus: Which is the more important, to pray or to receive Christ's body? Surely to receive Christ's body. If, then, sexual intercourse hinders the less important thing, much more does it hinder that which is the more important.

I have said in the same treatise that David and they that were with him could not have lawfully eaten the shew-bread had they not made answer that for three days they had not been defiled with women—not, of course, with harlots, intercourse with whom was forbidden by the law, but with their own wives, to whom they were lawfully united. Moreover, when the people were about to receive the law on Mount Sinai they were commanded to keep away from their wives for three days. I know that at Rome it is customary for the faithful always to receive the body of Christ, a custom which I neither censure nor indorse. "Let every man be fully persuaded in his own mind." But I appeal to the consciences of those persons who after indulging in sexual intercourse on the same day receive the communion—having first, as Persius puts it, "washed off the night in a flowing stream," and I ask such why they do not presume to approach the martyrs or to enter the churches. Is Christ of one mind abroad and of another at home? What is unlawful in church cannot be lawful at home. Nothing is hidden from God. "The night shineth as the day" before Him. Let each man examine himself, and so let him approach the body of Christ. Not, of course, that the deferring of communion for one day or for two makes a Christian any the holier or that what I have not deserved to-day I shall deserve to-morrow or the day after. But if I grieve that I have not shared in Christ's body it does help me to avoid for a little while my wife's embraces, and to prefer to wedded love the love of Christ. A hard discipline, you will say, and one not to be borne. What man of the world could bear it? He that can bear it, I reply, let him bear it; he that cannot must look to himself. It is my business to say, not what each man can do or will do, but what the Scriptures inculcate.

16. Again, objection has been taken to my comments on the apostle in the following passage: "But lest any should suppose from the context of the words before quoted (namely, that ye may give yourselves . . . to prayer and come together again') that the apostle desires this consummation, and does not merely concede it to obviate a worse downfall, he immediately adds, that Satan tempt you not for your incontinency.' And come together again.' What a noble indulgence the words convey! One which he blushes to speak of in plainer words, which he prefers only to Satan's temptation, and which has its root in incontinence. Do we labor to expound this as a dark saying when the writer has himself explained his meaning? "I speak this," he says, by way of permission, and not as a command.' Do we still hesitate to speak of wedlock as a thing permitted instead of as a thing enjoined? or are we afraid that such permission will exclude second or third marriages or some other case?" What have I said here which the apostle has not said? The phrase, I suppose, "which

he blushes to speak of in plainer words." I imagine that when he says "come together," and does not mention for what, he takes a modest way of indicating what he does not like to name openly—that is, sexual intercourse. Or is the objection to the words which follow—"which he prefers only to Satan's temptation, and which has its root in incontinence"? Are they not the very words of the apostle, only differently arranged—"that Satan tempt you not for your incontinency"? Or do people cavil because I said, "Do we still hesitate to speak of wedlock as a thing permitted instead of as a thing enjoined?" If this seems a hard saying, it should be ascribed to the apostle, who says, "But I speak this by way of permission, and not as a command," and not to me, who, except that I have rearranged their order, have changed neither the words nor their meaning.

17. The shortness of a letter compels me to hasten on. I pass, accordingly, to the points which remain. "I say," remarks the apostle, "to the unmarried and widows, It is good for them if they abide even as I. But if they cannot contain, let them marry; for it is better to marry than to burn." This section I have interpreted thus: "When he has granted to those who are married the use of wedlock, and has made clear his own wishes and concessions, he passes on to those who are unmarried or widows, and sets before them his own example. He calls them happy if they abide even as he, but he goes on, if they cannot contain, let them marry.' He thus repeats his former language, but only to avoid fornication,' and that Satan tempt you not for your incontinence.' And when he says, If they cannot contain, let them marry,' he gives as a reason for his words that it is better to marry than to burn.' It is only good to marry, because it is bad to burn. But take away the fire of lust, and he will not say it is better to marry.' For a thing is said to be better in antithesis to something which is worse, and not simply in contrast with what is admittedly good. It is as though he said, It is better to have one eye than none.'" Shortly afterwards, apostrophizing the apostle, I spoke thus: "If marriage is good in itself, do not compare it with a conflagration, but simply say, It is good to marry.' I must suspect the goodness of a thing which only becomes a lesser evil in the presence of a greater one. I, for my part, would have it not a lighter evil but a downright good." The apostle wishes unmarried women and widows to abstain from sexual intercourse, incites them to follow his own example, and calls them happy if they abide even as he. But if they cannot contain, and are tempted to quench the fire of lust by fornication rather than by continence, it is better, he tells them, to marry than to burn. Upon which precept I have made this comment: "It is good to marry, simply because it is bad to burn," not putting forward a view of my own, but only explaining the apostle's precept, "It is

better to marry than to burn;" that is, it is better to take a husband than to commit fornication. If, then, you teach that burning or fornication is good, the good will still be surpassed by what is still better. But if marriage is only a degree better than the evil to which it is preferred, it cannot be of that unblemished perfection and blessedness which suggest a comparison with the life of angels. Suppose I say, "It is better to be a virgin than a married woman;" in this case I have preferred to what is good what is still better. But suppose I go a step further and say, "It is better to marry than to commit fornication;" in that case I have preferred, not a better thing to a good thing, but a good thing to a bad one. There is a wide difference between the two cases; for, while virginity is related to marriage as better is to good, marriage is related to fornication as good is to bad. How, I should like to know, have I sinned in this explanation? My fixed purpose was not to bend the Scriptures to my own wishes, but simply to say what I took to be their meaning. A commentator has no business to dilate on his own views; his duty is to make plain the meaning of the author whom he professes to interpret. For, if he contradicts the writer whom he is trying to expound, he will prove to be his opponent rather than his interpreter. When I am freely expressing my own opinion, and not commenting upon the Scriptures, then any one that pleases may charge me with having spoken hardly of marriage. But if he can find no ground for such a charge, he should attribute such passages in my commentaries as appear severe or harsh to the author commented on, and not to me, who am only his interpreter.

18. Another charge brought against me is simply intolerable! It is urged that in explaining the apostle's words concerning husbands and wives, "Such shall have trouble in the flesh," I have said: "We in our ignorance had supposed that in the flesh at least wedlock would have rejoicing. But if married persons are to have trouble in the flesh, the only thing in which they seemed likely to have pleasure, what motive will be left to make women marry? for, besides having trouble in spirit and soul, they will also have it even in the flesh." Do I condemn marriage if I enumerate its troubles, such as the crying of infants, the death of children, the chance of abortion, domestic losses, and so forth? Whilst Damasus of holy memory was still living, I wrote a book against Helvidius "On the Perpetual Virginity of the Blessed Mary," in which, duly to extol the bliss of virginity, I was forced to say much of the troubles of marriage. Did that excellent man—versed in Scripture as he was, and a virgin doctor of the virgin Church—find anything to censure in my discourse? Moreover, in the treatise which I addressed to Eustochium I used much harsher language regarding marriage, and yet no one was offended at it. Nay, every lover of chastity strained his ears to catch my eulogy of continence. Read Tertullian, read

Cyprian, read Ambrose, and either accuse me with them or acquit me with them. My critics resemble the characters of Plautus. Their only wit lies in detraction; and they try to make themselves out men of learning by assailing all parties in turn. Thus they bestow their censure impartially upon myself and upon my opponent, and maintain that we are both beaten, although one or other of us must have succeeded.

Moreover, when in discussing digamy and trigamy I have said, "It is better for a woman to know one man, even though he be a second husband or a third, than several; it is more tolerable for her to prostitute herself to one man than to many," have I not immediately subjoined my reason for so saying? "The Samaritan woman in the Gospel, when she declares that her present husband is her sixth, is rebuked by the Lord on the ground that he is not her husband." For my own part, I now once more freely proclaim that digamy is not condemned in the Church—no, nor yet trigamy—and that a woman may marry a fifth husband, or a sixth, or a greater number still just as lawfully as she may marry a second; but that, while such marriages are not condemned, neither are they commended. They are meant as alleviations of an unhappy lot, and in no way redound to the glory of continence. I have spoken to the same effect elsewhere. "When a woman marries more than once—whether she does so twice or three times matters little—she ceases to be a monogamist. All things are lawful . . . but all things are not expedient.' I do not condemn digamists or trigamists, or even, to put an impossible case, octogamists. Let a woman have an eighth husband if she must; only let her cease to prostitute herself."

19. I will come now to the passage in which I am accused of saying that—at least according to the true Hebrew text—the words "God saw that it was good" are not inserted after the second day of the creation, as they are after the first, third, and remaining ones, and of adding immediately the following comment: "We are meant to understand that there is something not good in the number two, separating us as it does from unity, and prefiguring the marriage-tie. Just as in the account of Noah's ark all the animals that enter by twos are unclean, but those of which an uneven number is taken are clean." In this statement a passing objection is made to what I have said concerning the second day, whether on the ground that the words mentioned really occur in the passage, although I say that they do not occur, or because, assuming them to occur, I have understood them in a sense different from that which the context evidently requires. As regards the non-occurrence of the words in question (viz., "God saw that it was good"), let them take not my evidence, but that of all the Jewish and other translators—Aquila namely, Symmachus, and

Theodotion. But if the words, although occurring in the account of the other days, do not occur in the account of this, either let them give a more plausible reason than I have done for their non-occurrence, or, failing such, let them, whether they like it or not, accept the suggestion which I have made. Furthermore, if in Noah's ark all the animals that enter by twos are unclean, whilst those of which an uneven number is taken are clean, and if there is no dispute about the accuracy of the text, let them explain if they can why it is so written. But if they cannot explain it, then, whether they will or not, they must embrace my explanation of the matter. Either produce better fare and ask me to be your guest, or else rest content with the meal that I offer you, however poor it may be.

I must now mention the ecclesiastical writers who have dealt with this question of the odd number. They are, among the Greeks, Clement, Hippolytus, Origen, Dionysius, Eusebius, Didymus; and, among ourselves, Tertullian, Cyprian, Victorinus, Lactantius, Hilary. What Cyprian said to Fortunatus about the number seven is clear from the letter which he sent to him. Or perhaps I ought to bring forward the reasonings of Pythagoras, Archytas of Tarentum, and Publius Scipio in (Cicero's) sixth book "Concerning the Common Weal." If my detractors will not listen to any of these I will make the grammar schools shout in their ears the words of Virgil:

Uneven numbers are the joy of God.

20. To say, as I have done, that virginity is cleaner than wedlock, that the even numbers must give way to the odd, that the types of the Old Testament establish the truth of the Gospel: this, it appears, is a great sin subversive of the churches and intolerable to the world. The remaining points which are censured in my treatise are, I take it, of less importance, or else resolve themselves into this. I have, therefore, refrained from answering them, both that I may not exceed the limit at my disposal, and that I may not seem to distrust your intelligence, knowing as I do that you are ready to be my champion even before I ask you. With my last breath, then, I protest that neither now nor at any former time have I condemned marriage. I have merely answered an opponent without any fear that they of my own party would lay snares for me. I extol virginity to the skies, not because I myself possess it, but because, not possessing it, I admire it all the more. Surely it is a modest and ingenuous confession to praise in others that which you lack yourself. The weight of my body keeps me fixed to the ground, but do I fail to admire the flying birds or to praise the dove because, in the words of Virgil, it

Glides on its liquid path with motionless swift wings?

Let no man deceive himself, let no man, giving ear to the voice of flattery, rush upon ruin. The first virginity man derives from his birth, the second from his second birth. The words are not mine; it is an old saying, "No man can serve two masters;" that is, the flesh and the spirit. For "the flesh lusteth against the spirit, and the spirit against the flesh; and these are contrary the one to the other," so that we cannot do the things that we would. When, then, anything in my little work seems to you harsh, have regard not to my words, but to the Scripture, whence they are taken.

21. Christ Himself is a virgin; and His mother is also a virgin; yea, though she is His mother, she is a virgin still. For Jesus has entered in through the closed doors, and in His sepulchre—a new one hewn out of the hardest rock—no man is laid either before Him or after Him. Mary is "a garden enclosed . . . a fountain sealed," and from that fountain flows, according to Joel, the river which waters the torrent bed either of cords or of thorns; of cords being those of the sins by which we were beforetime bound, the thorns those which choked the seed the goodman of the house had sown. She is the east gate, spoken of by the prophet Ezekiel, always shut and always shining, and either concealing or revealing the Holy of Holies; and through her "the Sun of Righteousness," our "high priest after the order of Melchizedek," goes in and out. Let my critics explain to me how Jesus can have entered in through closed doors when He allowed His hands and His side to be handled, and showed that He had bones and flesh, thus proving that His was a true body and no mere phantom of one, and I will explain how the holy Mary can be at once a mother and a virgin. A mother before she was wedded, she remained a virgin after bearing her son. Therefore, as I was going to say, the virgin Christ and the virgin Mary have dedicated in themselves the first fruits of virginity for both sexes. The apostles have either been virgins or, though married, have lived celibate lives. Those persons who are chosen to be bishops, priests, and deacons are either virgins or widowers; or at least when once they have received the priesthood, are vowed to perpetual chastity. Why do we delude ourselves and feel vexed if while we are continually straining after sexual indulgence, we find the palm of chastity denied to us? We wish to fare sumptuously, and to enjoy the embraces of our wives, yet at the same time we desire to reign with Christ among virgins and widows. Shall there be but one reward, then, for hunger and for excess, for filth and for finery, for sackcloth and for silk? Lazarus, in his lifetime, received evil things, and the rich man, clothed in purple, fat and sleek, while he lived enjoyed the good things of the flesh but, now that they are dead, they occupy different positions. Misery has given place to satisfaction, and

satisfaction to misery. And it rests with us whether we will follow Lazarus or the rich man.

LETTER XLIX. TO PAMMACHIUS

Jerome encloses the preceding letter, thanks Pammachius for his efforts to suppress his treatise "against Jovinian," but declares these to be useless, and exhorts him, if he still has any hesitation in his mind, to turn to the Scriptures and the commentaries made upon them by Origen and others. Written at the same time as the preceding letter.

1. Christian modesty sometimes requires us to be silent even to our friends, and to nurse our humility in peace, where the renewal of an old friendship would expose us to the charge of self-seeking. Thus, when you have kept silence I have kept silence too, and have not cared to remonstrate with you, lest I should be thought more anxious to conciliate a person of influence than to cultivate a friend. But, now that it has become a duty to reply to your letter, I will endeavor always to be beforehand with you, and not so much to answer your queries as to write independently of them. Thus, if I have shown my modesty hitherto by silence, I will henceforth show it still more by coming forward to speak.

2. I quite recognize the kindness and forethought which have induced you to withdraw from circulation some copies of my work against Jovinian. Your diligence, however, has been of no avail, for several people coming from the city have repeatedly read aloud to me passages which they have come across in Rome. In this province, also, the books have already been circulated; and, as you have read yourself in Horace, "Words once uttered cannot be recalled." I am not so fortunate as are most of the writers of the day—able, that is, to correct my trifles whenever I like. When once I have written anything, either my admirers or my ill-wishers—from different motives, but with equal zeal—sow my work broadcast among the public; and their language, whether it is that of eulogy or of criticism, is apt to run to excess. They are guided not by the merits of the piece, but by their own angry feelings. Accordingly, I have done what I could. I have dedicated to you a defence of the work in question, feeling sure that when you have read it you will yourself satisfy the doubts of others on my behalf; or else, if you too turn up your nose at the task, you will have to explain in some new manner that section of the apostle in which he discusses virginity and marriage.

3. I do not speak thus that I may provoke you to write on the subject yourself—although I know your zeal in the study of the sacred writings to be greater than my own—but that you may compel my tormentors to do so. They are educated; in their own eyes no mean scholars; competent not merely to censure but to instruct me. If they write on the subject, my view will be the sooner neglected when it is compared with theirs. Read, I pray you, and diligently consider the words of the apostle, and you will then see that—with a view to avoid misrepresentation—I have been much more gentle towards married persons than he was disposed to be. Origen, Dionysius, Pierius, Eusebius of Caesarea, Didymus, Apollinaris, have used great latitude in the interpretation of this epistle. When Pierius, sifting and expounding the apostle's meaning, comes to the words, "I would that all men were even as I myself," he makes this comment upon them: "In saying this Paul plainly preaches abstinence from marriage." Is the fault here mine, or am I responsible for harshness? Compared with this sentence of Pierius, all that I have ever written is mild indeed. Consult the commentaries of the above-named writers and take advantage of the Church libraries; you will then more speedily finish as you would wish the enterprise which you have so happily begun.

4. I hear that the hopes of the entire city are centred in you, and that bishop and people are agreed in wishing for your exaltation. To be a bishop is much, to deserve to be one is more.

If you read the books of the sixteen prophets which I have rendered into Latin from the Hebrew; and if, when you have done so, you express satisfaction with my labors, the news will encourage me to take out of my desk some other works now shut up in it. I have lately translated Job into our mother tongue: you will be able to borrow a copy of it from your cousin, the saintly Marcella. Read it both in Greek and in Latin, and compare the old version with my rendering. You will then clearly see that the difference between them is that between truth and falsehood. Some of my commentaries upon the twelve prophets I have sent to the reverend father Domnio, also the four books of Kings—that is, the two called Samuel and the two called Malachim. If you care to read these you will learn for yourself how difficult it is to understand the Holy Scriptures, and particularly the prophets; and how through the fault of the translators passages which for the Jews flow clearly on for us abound with mistakes. Once more, you must not in my small writings look for any such eloquence as that which for Christ's sake you disregard in Cicero. A version made for the use of the Church, even though it may possess a literary charm, ought to disguise and avoid it as far as possible; in order that it may not speak to the idle schools and few disciples of the philosophers, but may address itself rather to the entire human race.

LETTER L. TO DOMNIO

Domnio, a Roman (called in Letter XLV. "the Lot of our time"), had written to Jerome to tell him that an ignorant monk had been traducing his books "against Jovinian." Jerome, in reply, sharply rebukes the folly of his critic and comments on the want of straightforwardness in his conduct. He concludes the letter with an emphatic restatement of his original position. Written in 394 a.d.

1. Your letter is full at once of affection and of complaining. The affection is your own, which prompts you unceasingly to warn me of impending danger, and which makes you on my behalf

Of safest things distrustful and afraid.

The complaining is of those who have no love for me, and seek an occasion against me in my sins. They speak against their brother, they slander their own mother's son. You write to me of these—nay, of one in particular—a lounger who is to be seen in the streets, at crossings, and in public places; a monk who is a noisy news-monger, clever only in detraction, and eager, in spite of the beam in his own eye, to remove the mote in his neighbor's. And you tell me that he preaches publicly against me, gnawing, rending, and tearing asunder with his fangs the books that I have written against Jovinian. You inform me, moreover, that this home-grown dialectician, this mainstay of the Plautine company, has read neither the "Categories" of Aristotle nor his treatise "On Interpretation," nor his "Analytics," nor yet the "Topics" of Cicero, but that, moving as he does only in uneducated circles, and frequenting no society but that of weak women, he ventures to construct illogical syllogisms and to unravel by subtle arguments what he is pleased to call my sophisms. How foolish I have been to suppose that without philosophy there can be no knowledge of these subjects; and to account it a more important part of composition to erase than to write! In vain have I perused the commentaries of Alexander; to no purpose has a skilled teacher used the "Introduction" of Porphyry to instruct me in logic; and—to make light of human learning—I have gained nothing at all by having Gregory of Nazianzum and Didymus as my catechists in the Holy Scriptures. My acquisition of Hebrew has been wasted labor; and so also has been the daily study which from my youth I have bestowed upon the Law and the Prophets, the Gospels and the Apostles.

2. Here we have a man who has reached perfection without a teacher, so as to be a vehicle of the spirit and a self-taught genius. He surpasses Cicero in eloquence, Aristotle in argument, Plato in discretion, Aristarchus in learning, Didymus, that man of brass, in the number of his books; and not only Didymus, but all the writers of his time in his knowledge of the Scriptures. It is reported that you have only to give him a theme and he is always ready—like Carneades—to argue on this side or on that, for justice or against it. The world escaped a great danger, and civil actions and suits concerning succession were saved from a yawning gulf on the day when, despising the bar, he transferred himself to the Church. For, had he been unwilling, who could ever have been proved innocent? And, if he once began to reckon the points of the case upon his fingers, and to spread his syllogistic nets, what criminal would his pleading have failed to save? Had he but stamped his foot, or fixed his eyes, or knitted his brow, or moved his hand, or twirled his beard, he would at once have thrown dust in the eyes of the jury. No wonder that such a complete Latinist and so profound a master of eloquence overcomes poor me, who—as I have been some time away (from Rome), and without opportunities for speaking Latin—am half a Greek if not altogether a barbarian. No wonder, I say, that he overcomes me when his eloquence has crushed Jovinian in person. Good Jesus! what! even Jovinian that great and clever man! So clever, indeed, that no one can understand his writings, and that when he sings it is only for himself—and for the muses!

3. Pray, my dear father, warn this man not to hold language contrary to his profession, and not to undo with his words the chastity which he professes by his garb. Whether he elects to be a virgin or a married celibate—and the choice must rest with himself—he must not compare wives with virgins, for that would be to have striven in vain against Jovinian's eloquence. He likes, I am told, to visit the cells of widows and virgins, and to lecture them with his brows knit on sacred literature. What is it that he teaches these poor women in the privacy of their own chambers? Is it to feel assured that virgins are no better than wives? Is it to make the most of the flower of their age, to eat and drink, to frequent the baths, to live in luxury, and not to disdain the use of perfumes? Or does he preach to them chastity, fasting, and neglect of their persons? No doubt the precepts that he inculcates are full of virtue. But if so, let him admit publicly what he says privately. Or, if his private teaching is the same as his public, he should keep aloof altogether from the society of girls. He is a young man—a monk, and in his own eyes an eloquent one (do not pearls fall from his lips, and are not his elegant phrases sprinkled with comic salt and humor?)—I am surprised, therefore, that he can without a blush frequent

noblemen's houses, pay constant visits to married ladies, make our religion a subject of contention, distort the faith of Christ by misapplying words, and—in addition to all this—detract from one who is his brother in the Lord. He may, however, have supposed me to be in error (for "in many things we offend all," and "if any man offend not in word he is a perfect man"). In that case he should have written to convict me or to question me, the course taken by Pammachius, a man of high attainments and position. To this latter I defended myself as best I could, and in a lengthy letter explained the exact sense of my words. He might at least have copied the diffidence which led you to extract and arrange such passages as seemed to give offence; asking me for corrections or explanations, and not supposing me so mad that in one and the same book I should write for marriage and against it.

4. Let him spare himself, let him spare me, let him spare the Christian name. Let him realize his position as a monk, not by talking and arguing, but by holding his peace and sitting still. Let him read the words of Jeremiah: "It is good for a man that he bear the yoke in his youth. He sitteth alone and keepeth silence, because he hath borne it upon him." Or if he has really the right to apply the censor's rod to all writers, and fancies himself a man of learning because he alone understands Jovinian (you know the proverb: Balbus best knows what Balbus means); yet, as Atilius reminds us, "we are not all writers." Jovinian himself—an unlettered man of letters if ever there was one—will with most justice proclaim the fact to him. "That the bishops condemn me," he says, "is not reason but treason. I want no answers from nobodies, who, while they have authority to put me down, have not the wit to teach me. Let one write against me who has a tongue that I can understand, and whom to vanquish will be to vanquish all.

"I know full well: believe me, I have felt
The hero's force when rising o'er his shield
He hurls his whizzing spear.'

He is strong in argument, intricate and tenacious, one to fight with his head down. Often has he cried out against me in the streets from late one night till early the next. He is a well-built man, and his thews are those of an athlete. Secretly I believe him to be a follower of my teaching. He never blushes or stops to weigh his words: his only aim is to speak as loud as possible. So famous is he for his eloquence that his sayings are held up as models to our curly-headed youngsters. How often, when I have met him at meetings, has he aroused my wrath and put me into a passion! How often has he spat upon me, and then departed spat upon! But these are vulgar methods, and any of my followers can use them. I appeal to books, to those memorials which must be handed down to posterity. Let us speak by our writings, that the silent reader may judge between us; and that, as I have a flock of disciples, he may have one also—flatterers and parasites worthy of the Gnatho and Phormio who is their master."

5. It is no difficult matter, my dear Domnio, to chatter at street corners or in apothecaries' shops and to pass judgment on the world. "So-and-so has made a good speech, so-and-so a bad one; this man knows the Scriptures, that one is crazy; this man talks glibly, that never says a word at all." But who considers him worthy thus to judge every one? To make an outcry against a man in every street, and to heap, not definite charges, but vague imputations, on his head, is nothing. Any buffoon or litigiously disposed person can do as much. Let him put forth his hand, put pen to paper, and bestir himself; let him write books and prove in them all he can. Let him give me a chance of replying to his eloquence. I can return bite for bite, if I like; when hurt myself, I can fix my teeth in my opponent. I too have had a liberal education. As Juvenal says, "I also have often withdrawn my hand from the ferule." Of me, too, it may be said in the words of Horace, "Flee from him; he has hay on his horn." But I prefer to be a disciple of Him who says, "I gave my back to the smiters . . . I hid not my face from shame and spitting." When He was reviled He reviled not again. After the buffeting, the cross, the scourge, the blasphemies, at the very last He prayed for His crucifiers, saying, "Father, forgive them, for they know not what they do." I, too, pardon the error of a brother. He has been deceived, I feel sure, by the art of the devil. Among the women he was held clever and eloquent; but, when my poor writings reached Rome, dreading me as a rival, he tried to rob me of my laurels. No man on earth, he resolved, should please his eloquent self, unless such as commanded respect rather than sought it, and showed themselves men to be feared more than favored. A man of consummate address, he desired, like an old soldier, with one stroke of the sword to strike down both his enemies, and to make clear to every one that, whatever view he might take, Scripture was always with him. Well, he must condescend to send me his account of the matter, and to correct my indiscreet language, not by censure but by instruction. If he tries to do this, he will find that what seems forcible on a lounge is not equally forcible in court; and that it is one thing to discuss the doctrines of the divine law amid the spindles and work-baskets of girls and another to argue concerning them among men of education. As it is, without hesitation or shame, he raises again and again the noisy shout, "Jerome condemns marriage," and, whilst he constantly moves among women with child, crying infants, and marriage-beds, he suppresses the words of the apostle just to cover me—poor me—with odium.

However, when he comes by and by to write books and to grapple with me at close quarters, then he will feel it, then he will stick fast; Epicurus and Aristippus will not be near him then; the swineherds will not come to his aid; the prolific sow will not so much as grunt. For I also may say, with Turnus:

Father, I too can launch a forceful spear,
And when I strike blood follows from the wound.

But if he refuses to write, and fancies that abuse is as effective as criticism, then, in spite of all the lands and seas and peoples which lie between us, he must hear at least the echo of my cry, "I do not condemn marriage," "I do not condemn wedlock." Indeed—and this I say to make my meaning quite clear to him—I should like every one to take a wife who, because they get frightened in the night, cannot manage to sleep alone.

LETTER LI. FROM EPIPHANIUS, BISHOP OF SALAMIS, IN CYPRUS, TO JOHN, BISHOP OF JERUSALEM

A coolness had arisen between these two bishops in connection with the Origenistic controversy, which at this time was at its height. Epiphanius had openly charged John with being an Origenist, and had also uncanonically conferred priests' orders on Jerome's brother Paulinian, in order that the monastery at Bethlehem might henceforth be entirely independent of John. Naturally, John resented this conduct and showed his resentment. The present letter is a kind of half-apology made by Epiphanius for what he had done, and like all such, it only seems to have made matters worse. The controversy is fully detailed in the treatise "Against John of Jerusalem" in this volume, esp. S:11–14.

An interesting paragraph (S:9) narrates how Epiphanius destroyed at Anablatha a church-curtain on which was depicted "a likeness of Christ or of some saint"—an early instance of the iconoclastic spirit.

Originally written in Greek, the letter was (by the writer's request) rendered into Latin by Jerome. Its date is 394 a.d.

To the lord bishop and dearly beloved brother, John, Epiphanius sends greeting.

1. It surely becomes us, dearly beloved, not to abuse our rank as clergy, so as to make it an occasion of pride, but by diligently keeping and observing God's commandments, to be in reality what in name we profess to be. For, if the Holy Scriptures say, "Their lots shall not profit them," what pride in our clerical position will be able to avail us who sin not only in thought and feel-

ing, but in speech? I have heard, of course, that you are incensed against me, that you are angry, and that you threaten to write about me—not merely to particular places and provinces, but to the uttermost ends of the earth. Where is that fear of God which should make us tremble with the trembling spoken of by the Lord—"Whosoever is angry with his brother without a cause shall be in danger of the judgment"? Not that I greatly care for your writing what you please. For Isaiah tells us of letters written on papyrus and cast upon the waters—missives soon carried away by time and tide. I have done you no harm, I have inflicted no injury upon you, I have extorted nothing from you by violence. My action concerned a monastery whose inmates were foreigners in no way subject to your provincial jurisdiction. Moreover their regard for my insignificance and for the letters which I frequently addressed to them had commenced to produce a feeling of dislike to communion with you. Feeling, therefore, that too great strictness or scrupulosity on my part might have the effect of alienating them from the Church with its ancient faith, I ordained one of the brothers deacon, and after he had ministered as such, admitted him to the priesthood. You should, I think, have been grateful to me for this, knowing, as you surely must, that it is the fear of God which has compelled me to act in this way, and particularly when you recollect that God's priesthood is everywhere the same, and that I have simply made provision for the wants of the Church. For, although each individual bishop of the Church has under him churches which are placed in his charge, and although no man may stretch himself beyond his measure, yet the love of Christ, which is without dissimulation, is set up as an example to us all; and we must consider not so much the thing done as the time and place, the mode and motive, of doing it. I saw that the monastery contained a large number of reverend brothers, and that the reverend presbyters, Jerome and Vincent, through modesty and humility, were unwilling to offer the sacrifices permitted to their rank, and to labor in that part of their calling which ministers more than any other to the salvation of Christians. I knew, moreover, that you could not find or lay hands on this servant of God who had several times fled from you simply because he was reluctant to undertake the onerous duties of the priesthood, and that no other bishop could easily find him. Accordingly, I was a good deal surprised when, by the ordering of God, he came to me with the deacons of the monastery and others of the brethren, to make satisfaction to me for some grievance or other which I had against them. While, therefore, the Collect was being celebrated in the church of the villa which adjoins our monastery—he being quite ignorant and wholly unsuspicious of my purpose—I gave orders to a number of deacons to seize him and to stop his mouth, lest in his eagerness to free himself he might adjure me in the name of Christ. First of all, then, I ordained him deacon, setting before him the fear of God, and forcing him to minister; for he made a hard struggle against it, crying out that he was unworthy, and protesting that this heavy burden was beyond his strength. It was with difficulty, then, that I overcame his reluctance, persuading him as well as I could with passages from Scripture, and setting before him the commandments of God. And when he had ministered in the offering of the holy sacrifices, once more with great difficulty I closed his mouth and ordained him presbyter. Then, using the same arguments as before, I induced him to sit in the place set apart for the presbyters. After this I wrote to the reverend presbyters and other brothers of the monastery, chiding them for not having written to me about him. For a year before I had heard many of them complain that they had no one to celebrate for them the sacraments of the Lord. All then agreed in asking him to undertake the duty, pointing out how great his usefulness would be to the community of the monastery. I blamed them for omitting to write to me and to propose that I should ordain him, when the opportunity was given to them to do so.

2. All this I have done, as I said just now, relying on that Christian love which you, I feel sure, cherish towards my insignificance; not to mention the fact that I held the ordination in a monastery, and not within the limits of your jurisdiction. How truly blessed is the mildness and complacency of the bishops of (my own) Cyprus, as well as their simplicity, though to your refinement and discrimination it appears deserving only of God's pity! For many bishops in communion with me have ordained presbyters in my province whom I had been unable to capture, and have sent to me deacons and subdeacons whom I have been glad to receive. I myself, too, have urged the bishop Philo of blessed memory, and the reverend Theoprepus, to make provision for the Church of Christ by ordaining presbyters in those churches of Cyprus which, although they were accounted to belong to my see, happened to be close to them, and this for the reason that my province was large and straggling. But for my part I have never ordained deaconesses nor sent them into the provinces of others, nor have I done anything to rend the Church. Why, then, have you thought fit to be so angry and indignant with me for that work of God which I have wrought for the edification of the brethren, and not for their destruction? Moreover, I have been much surprised at the assertion which you have made to my clergy, that you sent me a message by that reverend presbyter, the abbot Gregory, that I was to ordain no one, and that I promised to comply, saying, "Am I a stripling, or do I not know the canons?" By God's word I am telling you the truth when I say that I know and have heard noth-

ing of all this, and that I have not the slightest recollection of using any language of the sort. As, however, I have had misgivings, lest possibly, being only a man, I may have forgotten this among so many other matters, I have made inquiry of the reverend Gregory, and of the presbyter Zeno, who is with him. Of these, the abbot Gregory replies that he knows nothing whatever about the matter, while Zeno says that the presbyter Rufinus, in the course of some desultory remarks, spoke these words. "Will the reverend bishop, think you, venture to ordain any persons?" but that the conversation went no further. I, Epiphanius, however, have never either received the message or answered it. Do not, then, dearly beloved, allow your anger to overcome you or your indignation to get the better of you, lest you should disquiet yourself in vain; and lest you should be thought to be putting forward this grievance only to get scope for tendencies of another kind, and thus to have sought out an occasion of sinning. It is to avoid this that the prophet prays to the Lord, saying: "Turn not aside my heart to words of wickedness, to making excuses for my sins."

3. This also I have been surprised to hear, that certain persons who are in the habit of carrying tales backwards and forwards, and of always adding something fresh to what they have heard, to stir up grievances and disputes between brothers, have succeeded in disquieting you by saying that, when I offer sacrifices to God, I am wont to say this prayer on your behalf: "Grant, O Lord, to John grace to believe aright." Do not suppose me so untutored as to be capable of saying this so openly. To tell you the simple truth, my dearest brother, although I continually use this prayer mentally, I have never confided it to the ears of others, lest I should seem to dishonor you. But when I repeat the prayers required by the ritual of the mysteries, then I say on behalf of all and of you as well as others, "Guard him, that he may preach the truth," or at least this, "Do Thou, O Lord, grant him Thine aid, and guard him, that he may preach the word of truth," as occasion offers itself for the words, and as the turn comes for the particular prayer. Wherefore I beseech you, dearly beloved, and, casting myself down at your feet, I entreat you to grant to me and to yourself this one prayer, that you would save yourself, as it is written, "from an untoward generation." Withdraw, dearly beloved, from the heresy of Origen and from all heresies. For I see that all your indignation has been roused against me simply because I have told you that you ought not to eulogize one who is the spiritual father of Arius, and the root and parent of all heresies. And when I appealed to you not to go astray, and warned you of the consequences, you traversed my words, and reduced me to tears and sadness; and not me only, but many other Catholics who were present. This I take to be the origin of your indignation and of your passion on the present occasion.

On this account you threaten to send out letters against me, and to circulate your version of the matter in all directions; and thus, while with a view to defending your heresy you kindle men's passions against me, you break through the charity which I have shown towards you, and act with so little discretion that you make me regret that I have held communion with you, and that I have by so doing upheld the erroneous opinions of Origen.

4. I speak plainly. To use the language of Scripture, I do not spare to pluck out my own eye if it cause me to offend, nor to cut off my hand and my foot if they cause me to do so. And you must be treated in the same way whether you are my eyes, or my hands, or my feet. For what Catholic, what Christian who adorns his faith with good works, can hear with calmness Origen's teaching and counsel, or believe in his extraordinary preaching? "The Son," he tells us, "cannot see the Father, and the Holy Spirit cannot see the Son." These words occur in his book "On First Principles;" thus we read, and thus Origen has spoken. "For as it is unsuitable to say that the Son can see the Father, it is consequently unsuitable to suppose that the Spirit can see the Son." Can any one, moreover, brook Origen's assertion that men's souls were once angels in heaven, and that having sinned in the upper world, they have been cast down into this, and have been confined in bodies as in barrows or tombs, to pay the penalty for their former sins; and that the bodies of believers are not temples of Christ, but prisons of the condemned? Again, he tampers with the true meaning of the narrative by a false use of allegory, multiplying words without limit; and undermines the faith of the simple by the most varied arguments. Now he maintains that souls, in Greek the "cool things," from a word meaning to be cool, are so called because in coming down from the heavenly places to the lower world they have lost their former heat; and now, that our bodies are called by the Greeks chains, from a word meaning chain, or else (on the analogy of our own Latin word) "things fallen," because our souls have fallen from heaven; and that the other word for body which the abundance of the Greek idiom supplies is by many taken to mean a funeral monument, because the soul is shut up within it in the same way as the corpses of the dead are shut up in tombs and barrows. If this doctrine is true what becomes of our faith? Where is the preaching of the resurrection? Where is the teaching of the apostles, which lasts on to this day in the churches of Christ? Where is the blessing to Adam, and to his seed, and to Noah and his sons? "Be fruitful, and multiply, and replenish the earth." According to Origen, these words must be a curse and not a blessing; for he turns angels into human souls, compelling them to leave the place of highest rank and to come down lower, as though God were unable through the action of His blessing to grant souls to the

human race, had the angels not sinned, and as though for every birth on earth there must be a fall in heaven. We are to give up, then, the teaching of apostles and prophets, of the law, and of our Lord and Saviour Himself, in spite of His language loud as thunder in the gospel. Origen, on the other hand, commands and urges—not to say binds—his disciples not to pray to ascend into heaven, lest sinning once more worse than they had sinned on earth they should be hurled down into the world again. Such foolish and insane notions he generally confirms by distorting the sense of the Scriptures and making them mean what they do not mean at all. He quotes this passage from the Psalms: "Before thou didst humble me by reason of my wickedness, I went wrong;" and this, "Return unto thy rest, O my soul;" this also, "Bring my soul out of prison;" and this, "I will make confession unto the Lord in the land of the living," although there can be no doubt that the meaning of the divine Scripture is different from the interpretation by which he unfairly wrests it to the support of his own heresy. This way of acting is common to the Manichaeans, the Gnostics, the Ebionites, the Marcionites, and the votaries of the other eighty heresies, all of whom draw their proofs from the pure well of the Scriptures, not, however, interpreting it in the sense in which it is written, but trying to make the simple language of the Church's writers accord with their own wishes.

5. Of one position which he strives to maintain I hardly know whether it calls for my tears or my laughter. This wonderful doctor presumes to teach that the devil will once more be what he at one time was, that he will return to his former dignity and rise again to the kingdom of heaven. Oh horror! that a man should be so frantic and foolish as to hold that John the Baptist, Peter, the apostle and evangelist John, Isaiah, Jeremiah, and the rest of the prophets, are made co-heirs of the devil in the kingdom of heaven! I pass over his idle explanation of the coats of skins, and say nothing of the efforts and arguments he has used to induce us to believe that these coats of skins represent human bodies. Among many other things, he says this: "Was God a tanner or a saddler, that He should prepare the hides of animals, and should stitch from them coats of skins for Adam and Eve?" "It is clear," he goes on, "that he is speaking of human bodies." If this is so, how is it that before the coats of skins, and the disobedience, and the fall from paradise, Adam speaks not in an allegory, but literally, thus: "This is now bone of my bones and flesh of my flesh;" or what is the ground of the divine narrative, "And the Lord God caused a deep sleep to fall upon Adam, and he slept; and he took one of his ribs, and closed up the flesh instead thereof; and the rib which the Lord God had taken from man, made He a woman" for him? Or what bodies can Adam and Eve have covered

with fig-leaves after eating of the forbidden tree? Who can patiently listen to the perilous arguments of Origen when he denies the resurrection of this flesh, as he most clearly does in his book of explanations of the first psalm and in many other places? Or who can tolerate him when he gives us a paradise in the third heaven, and transfers that which the Scripture mentions from earth to the heavenly places, and when he explains allegorically all the trees which are mentioned in Genesis, saying in effect that the trees are angelic potencies, a sense which the true drift of the passage does not admit? For the divine Scripture has not said, "God put down Adam and Eve upon the earth," but "He drove them out of the paradise, and made them dwell over against the paradise." He does not say "under the paradise." "He placed . . . cherubims and a flaming sword . . . to keep the way of the tree of life." He says nothing about an ascent to it. "And a river went out of Eden." He does not say "went down from Eden." "It was parted and became into four heads. The name of the first is Pison . . . and the name of the second is Gihon." I myself have seen the waters of Gihon, have seen them with my bodily eyes. It is this Gihon to which Jeremiah points when he says, "What hast thou to do in the way of Egypt to drink the muddy water of Gihon?" I have drunk also from the great river Euphrates, not spiritual but actual water, such as you can touch with your hand and imbibe with your mouth. But where there are rivers which admit of being seen and of being drunk, it follows that there also there will be fig-trees and other trees; and it is of these that the Lord says, "Of every tree of the garden thou mayest freely eat." They are like other trees and timber, just as the rivers are like other rivers and waters. But if the water is visible and real, then the fig-tree and the rest of the timber must be real also, and Adam and Eve must have been originally formed with real and not phantasmal bodies, and not, as Origen would have us believe, have afterwards received them on account of their sin. But, you say, "we read that Saint Paul was caught up to the third heaven, into paradise." You explain the words rightly: "When he mentions the third heaven, and then adds the word paradise, he shows that heaven is in one place and paradise in another." Must not every one reject and despise such special pleading as that by which Origen says of the waters that are above the firmament that they are not waters, but heroic beings of angelic power, and again of the waters that are over the earth—that is, below the firmament—that they are potencies of the contrary sort—that is, demons? If so, why do we read in the account of the deluge that the windows of heaven were opened, and that the waters of the deluge prevailed? in consequence of which the fountains of the deep were opened, and the whole earth was covered with the waters.

6. Oh! the madness and folly of those who have forsaken the teaching of the book of Proverbs, "My son, keep thy father's commandment, and forsake not the law of thy mother," and have turned to error, and say to the fool that he shall be their leader, and do not despise the foolish things which are said by the foolish man, even as the scripture bears witness, "The foolish man speaketh foolishly, and his heart understandeth vanity." I beseech you, dearly beloved, and by the love which I feel towards you, I implore you—as though it were my own members on which I would have pity—by word and letter to fulfil that which is written, "Do not I hate them, O Lord, that hate thee? and am not I grieved with those that rise up against thee?" Origen's words are the words of an enemy, hateful and repugnant to God and to His saints; and not only those which I have quoted, but countless others. For it is not now my intention to argue against all his opinions. Origen has not lived in my day, nor has he robbed me. I have not conceived a dislike to him nor quarrelled with him because of an inheritance or of any worldly matter; but—to speak plainly—I grieve, and grieve bitterly, to see numbers of my brothers, and of those in particular who show the most promise, and have reached the highest rank in the sacred ministry, deceived by his persuasive arguments, and made by his most perverse teaching the food of the devil, whereby the saying is fulfilled: "He derides every stronghold, and his fare is choice, and he hath gathered captives as the sand." But may God free you, my brother, and the holy people of Christ which is intrusted to you, and all the brothers who are with you, and especially the presbyter Rufinus, from the heresy of Origen, and other heresies, and from the perdition to which they lead. For, if for one word or for two opposed to the faith many heresies have been rejected by the Church, how much more shall he be held a heretic who has contrived such perverse interpretations and such mischievous doctrines to destroy the faith, and has in fact declared himself the enemy of the Church! For, among other wicked things, he has presumed to say this, too, that Adam lost the image of God, although Scripture nowhere declares that he did. Were it so, never would all the creatures in the world be subject to Adam's seed—that is, to the entire human race; yet, in the words of the apostle, everything "is tamed and hath been tamed of mankind." For never would all things be subjected to men if men had not—together with their authority over all—the image of God. But the divine Scripture conjoins and associates with this the grace of the blessing which was conferred upon Adam and upon the generations which descended from him. No one can by twisting the meaning of words presume to say that this grace of God was given to one only, and that he alone was made in the image of God (he and his wife, that is, for while he was formed of clay she was

made of one of his ribs), but that those who were subsequently conceived in the womb and not born as was Adam did not possess God's image, for the Scripture immediately subjoins the following statement: "And Adam lived two hundred and thirty years, and knew Eve his wife, and she bare him a son in his image and after his likeness, and called his name Seth." And again, in the tenth generation, two thousand two hundred and forty-two years afterwards, God, to vindicate His own image and to show that the grace which He had given to men still continued in them, gives the following commandment: "Flesh . . . with the blood thereof shall ye not eat. And surely your blood will I require at the hand of every man that sheddeth it; for in the image of God have I made man." From Noah to Abraham ten generations passed away, and from Abraham's time to David's, fourteen more, and these twenty-four generations make up, taken together, two thousand one hundred and seventeen years. Yet the Holy Spirit in the thirty-ninth psalm, while lamenting that all men walk in a vain show, and that they are subject to sins, speaks thus: "For all that every man walketh in the image." Also after David's time, in the reign of Solomon his son, we read a somewhat similar reference to the divine likeness. For in the book of Wisdom, which is inscribed with his name, Solomon says: "God created man to be immortal, and made him to be an image of His own eternity." And again, about eleven hundred and eleven years afterwards, we read in the New Testament that men have not lost the image of God. For James, an apostle and brother of the Lord, whom I have mentioned above—that we may not be entangled in the snares of Origen—teaches us that man does possess God's image and likeness. For, after a somewhat discursive account of the human tongue, he has gone on to say of it: "It is an unruly evil . . . therewith bless we God, even the Father and therewith curse we men, which are made after the similitude of God." Paul, too, the "chosen vessel," who in his preaching has fully maintained the doctrine of the gospel, instructs us that man is made in the image and after the likeness of God. "A man," he says, "ought not to wear long hair, forasmuch as he is the image and glory of God." He speaks of "the image" simply, but explains the nature of the likeness by the word "glory."

7. Instead of the three proofs from Holy Scripture which you said would satisfy you if I could produce them, behold I have given you seven. Who, then, will put up with the follies of Origen? I will not use a severer word and so make myself like him or his followers, who presume at the peril of their soul to assert dogmatically whatever first comes into their head, and to dictate to God, whereas they ought either to pray to Him or to learn the truth from Him. For some of them say that the image of God which Adam had previously received

was lost when he sinned. Others surmise that the body which the Son of God was destined to take of Mary was the image of the Creator. Some identify this image with the soul, others with sensation, others with virtue. These make it baptism, those assert that it is in virtue of God's image that man exercises universal sway. Like drunkards in their cups, they ejaculate now this, now that, when they ought rather to have avoided so serious a risk, and to have obtained salvation by simple faith, not denying the words of God. To God they ought to have left the sure and exact knowledge of His own gift, and of the particular way in which He has created men in His image and after His likeness. Forsaking this course, they have involved themselves in many subtle questions, and through these they have been plunged into the mire of sin. But we, dearly beloved, believe the words of the Lord, and know that God's image remains in all men, and we leave it to Him to know in what respect man is created in His image. And let no one be deceived by that passage in the epistle of John, which some readers fail to understand, where he says: "Now are we the sons of God, and it doth not yet appear what we shall be: but we know that, when He shall appear, we shall be like Him; for we shall see Him as He is." For this refers to the glory which is then to be revealed to His saints; just as also in another place we read the words "from glory to glory," of which glory the saints have even in this world received an earnest and a small portion. At their head stands Moses, whose face shone exceedingly, and was bright with the brightness of the sun. Next to him comes Elijah, who was caught up into heaven in a chariot of fire, and did not feel the effects of the flame. Stephen, too, when he was being stoned, had the face of an angel visible to all. And this which we have verified in a few cases is to be understood of all, that what is written may be fulfilled. "Every one that sanctifieth himself shall be numbered among the blessed." For, "blessed are the pure in heart, for they shall see God."

8. These things being so, dearly beloved, keep watch over your own soul and cease to murmur against me. For the divine Scripture says: "Neither murmur ye [one against another] as some of them also murmured, and were destroyed of serpents." Rather give way to the truth and love me who love both you and the truth. And may the God of peace, according to His mercy, grant to us that Satan may be bruised under the feet of Christians, and that every occasion of evil may be shunned, so that the bond of love and peace may not be rent asunder between us, or the preaching of the right faith be anywise hindered.

9. Moreover, I have heard that certain persons have this grievance against me: When I accompanied you to the holy place called Bethel, there to join you in celebrating the Collect, after the use of the Church, I came to a villa called

Anablatha and, as I was passing, saw a lamp burning there. Asking what place it was, and learning it to be a church, I went in to pray, and found there a curtain hanging on the doors of the said church, dyed and embroidered. It bore an image either of Christ or of one of the saints; I do not rightly remember whose the image was. Seeing this, and being loth that an image of a man should be hung up in Christ's church contrary to the teaching of the Scriptures, I tore it asunder and advised the custodians of the place to use it as a winding sheet for some poor person. They, however, murmured, and said that if I made up my mind to tear it, it was only fair that I should give them another curtain in its place. As soon as I heard this, I promised that I would give one, and said that I would send it at once. Since then there has been some little delay, due to the fact that I have been seeking a curtain of the best quality to give to them instead of the former one, and thought it right to send to Cyprus for one. I have now sent the best that I could find, and I beg that you will order the presbyter of the place to take the curtain which I have sent from the hands of the Reader, and that you will afterwards give directions that curtains of the other sort—opposed as they are to our religion—shall not be hung up in any church of Christ. A man of your uprightness should be careful to remove an occasion of offence unworthy alike of the Church of Christ and of those Christians who are committed to your charge. Beware of Palladius of Galatia—a man once dear to me, but who now sorely needs God's pity—for he preaches and teaches the heresy of Origen; and see to it that he does not seduce any of those who are intrusted to your keeping into the perverse ways of his erroneous doctrine. I pray that you may fare well in the Lord.

LETTER LII. TO NEPOTIAN

Nepotian, the nephew of Heliodorus (for whom see Letter XIV.), had, like his uncle, abandoned the military for the clerical calling, and was now a presbyter at Altinum, where Heliodorus was bishop. The letter is a systematic treatise on the duties of the clergy and on the rule of life which they ought to adopt. It had a great vogue, and called forth much indignation against Jerome. Its date is 394 a.d.

1. Again and again you ask me, my dear Nepotian, in your letters from over the sea, to draw for you a few rules of life, showing how one who has renounced the service of the world to become a monk or a clergyman may keep the straight path of Christ, and not be drawn aside into the haunts of vice. As a young man, or rather as a boy, and while I was curbing by the hard life of the

desert the first onslaughts of youthful passion, I sent a letter of remonstrance to your reverend uncle, Heliodorus, which, by the tears and complainings with which it was filled, showed him the feelings of the friend whom he had deserted. In it I acted the part suited to my age, and as I was still aglow with the methods and maxims of the rhetoricians, I decked it out a good deal with the flourishes of the schools. Now, however, my head is gray, my brow is furrowed, a dewlap like that of an ox hangs from my chin, and, as Virgil says,

The chilly blood stands still around my heart.

Elsewhere he sings:

Old age bears all, even the mind, away.

And a little further on:

So many of my songs are gone from me,
And even my very voice has left me now.

2. But that I may not seem to quote only profane literature, listen to the mystical teaching of the sacred writings. Once David had been a man of war, but at seventy age had chilled him so that nothing would make him warm. A girl is accordingly sought from the coasts of Israel—Abishag the Shunamite—to sleep with the king and warm his aged frame. Does it not seem to you—if you keep to the letter that killeth—like some farcical story or some broad jest from an Atellan play? A chilly old man is wrapped up in blankets, and only grows warm in a girl's embrace. Bathsheba was still living, Abigail was still left, and the remainder of those wives and concubines whose names the Scripture mentions. Yet they are all rejected as cold, and only in the one young girl's embrace does the old man become warm. Abraham was far older than David; still, so long as Sarah lived he sought no other wife. Isaac counted twice the years of David, yet never felt cold with Rebekah, old though she was. I say nothing of the antediluvians, who, although after nine hundred years their limbs must have been not old merely, but decayed with age, had no recourse to girls' embraces. Moses, the leader of the Israelites, counted one hundred and twenty years, yet sought no change from Zipporah.

3. Who, then, is this Shunamite, this wife and maid, so glowing as to warm the cold, yet so holy as not to arouse passion in him whom she warmed? Let Solomon, wisest of men, tell us of his father's favorite; let the man of peace recount to us the embraces of the man of war. "Get wisdom," he writes, "get understanding: forget it not; neither decline from the words of my mouth. Forsake her not and she shall preserve thee: love her and she shall keep thee. Wisdom is the principal thing, therefore get wisdom, and with all thy getting get understanding. Exalt her and she shall promote thee. She shall bring thee

to honor when thou dost embrace her. She shall give to thine head an ornament of grace: a crown of glory shall she deliver to thee."

Almost all bodily excellences alter with age, and while wisdom alone increases all things else decay. Fasts and vigils and almsdeeds become harder. So also do sleeping on the ground, moving from place to place, hospitality to travellers, pleading for the poor, earnestness and steadfastness in prayer, the visitation of the sick, manual labor to supply money for alms-giving. All acts, in short, of which the body is the medium decrease with its decay.

Now, there are young men still full of life and vigor who, by toil and burning zeal, as well as by holiness of life and constant prayer to the Lord Jesus, have obtained knowledge. I do not speak of these, or say that in them the love of wisdom is cold, for this withers in many of the old by reason of age. What I mean is that youth, as such, has to cope with the assaults of passion, and amid the allurements of vice and the tinglings of the flesh is stifled like a fire among green boughs, and cannot develop its proper brightness. But when men have employed their youth in commendable pursuits and have meditated on the law of the Lord day and night, they learn with the lapse of time, fresh experience and wisdom come as the years go by, and so from the pursuits of the past their old age reaps a harvest of delight. Hence that wise man of Greece, Themistocles, perceiving, after the expiration of one hundred and seven years, that he was on the verge of the grave, is reported to have said that he regretted extremely having to leave life just when he was beginning to grow wise. Plato died in his eighty-first year, his pen still in his hand. Isocrates completed ninety years and nine in the midst of literary and scholastic work. I say nothing of other philosophers, such as Pythagoras, Democritus, Xenocrates, Zeno, and Cleanthes, who in extreme old age displayed the vigor of youth in the pursuit of wisdom. I pass on to the poets, Homer, Hesiod, Simonides, Stesichorus, who all lived to a great age, yet at the approach of death sang each of them a swan song sweeter than their wont. Sophocles, when charged by his sons with dotage on account of his advanced years and his neglect of his property, read out to his judges his recently composed play of OEdipus, and made so great a display of wisdom—in spite of the inroads of time—that he changed the decorous silence of the law court into the applause of the theatre. And no wonder, when Cato the censor, that most eloquent of Romans, in his old age neither blushed at the thought of learning Greek nor despaired of succeeding. Homer, for his part, relates that from the tongue of Nestor, even when quite aged and helpless, there flowed speech sweeter than honey.

Even the very name Abishag in its mystic meaning points to the greater wisdom of old men. For the translation of it is, "My father is over and above," or "my father's roaring." The term "over and above" is obscure, but in this passage is indicative of excellence, and implies that the old have a larger stock of wisdom, and that it even overflows by reason of its abundance. In another passage "over and above" forms an antithesis to "necessary." Moreover, Abishag, that is, "roaring," is properly used of the sound which the waves make, and of the murmur which we hear coming from the sea. From which it is plain that the thunder of the divine voice dwells in old men's ears with a volume of sound beyond the voices of men. Again, in our tongue Shunamite means "scarlet," a hint that the love of wisdom becomes warm and glowing through religious study. For though the color may point to the mystery of the Lord's blood, it also sets forth the warm glow of wisdom. Hence it is a scarlet thread that in Genesis the midwife binds upon the hand of Pharez—Pharez "the divider," so called because he divided the partition which had before separated two peoples. So, too, with a mystic reference to the shedding of blood, it was a scarlet cord which the harlot Rahab (a type of the church) hung in her window to preserve her house in the destruction of Jericho. Hence, in another place Scripture says of holy men: "These are they which came from the warmth of the house of the father of Rechab." And in the gospel the Lord says: "I am come to cast fire upon the earth, and fain am I to see it kindled." This was the fire which, when it was kindled in the disciples' hearts, constrained them to say: "Did not our heart burn within us while He talked with us by the way, and while He opened to us the Scriptures?"

4. To what end, you ask, these recondite references? To show that you need not expect from me boyish declamation, flowery sentiments, a meretricious style, and at the close of every paragraph the terse and pointed aphorisms which call forth approving shouts from those who hear them. Let Wisdom alone embrace me; let her nestle in my bosom, my Abishag who grows not old. Undefiled truly is she, and a virgin forever for although she daily conceives and unceasingly brings to the birth, like Mary she remains undeflowered. When the apostle says "be fervent in spirit," he means "be true to wisdom." And when our Lord in the gospel declares that in the end of the world—when the shepherd shall grow foolish, according to the prophecy of Zechariah—"the love of many shall wax cold," He means that wisdom shall decay. Hear, therefore—to quote the sainted Cyprian—"words forcible rather than elegant." Hear one who, though he is your brother in orders, is in years your father; who can conduct you from the cradle of faith to spiritual manhood; and who, while he builds up stage by stage the rules of holy living, can instruct others in instructing you. I know, of course, that from your reverend uncle, Heliodorus, now a bishop of Christ, you have learned and are daily learning all that is holy;

and that in him you have before you a rule of life and a pattern of virtue. Take, then, my suggestions for what they are worth, and compare my precepts with his. He will teach you the perfection of a monk, and I shall show you the whole duty of a clergyman.

5. A clergyman, then, as he serves Christ's church, must first understand what his name means; and then, when he realizes this, must endeavor to be that which he is called. For since the Greek word kleros means "lot," or "inheritance," the clergy are so called either because they are the lot of the Lord, or else because the Lord Himself is their lot and portion. Now, he who in his own person is the Lord's portion, or has the Lord for his portion, must so bear himself as to possess the Lord and to be possessed by Him. He who possesses the Lord, and who says with the prophet, "The Lord is my portion," can hold to nothing beside the Lord. For if he hold to something beside the Lord, the Lord will not be his portion. Suppose, for instance, that he holds to gold or silver, or possessions or inlaid furniture; with such portions as these the Lord will not deign to be his portion. I, if I am the portion of the Lord, and the line of His heritage, receive no portion among the remaining tribes; but, like the Priest and the Levite, I live on the tithe, and serving the altar, am supported by its offerings. Having food and raiment, I shall be content with these, and as a disciple of the Cross shall share its poverty. I beseech you, therefore, and

Again and yet again admonish you;

do not look to your military experience for a standard of clerical obligation. Under Christ's banner seek for no worldly gain, lest having more than when you first became a clergyman, you hear men say, to your shame, "Their portion shall not profit them." Welcome poor men and strangers to your homely board, that with them Christ may be your guest. A clergyman who engages in business, and who rises from poverty to wealth, and from obscurity to a high position, avoid as you would the plague. For "evil communications corrupt good manners." You despise gold; he loves it. You spurn wealth; he eagerly pursues it. You love silence, meekness, privacy; he takes delight in talking and effrontery, in squares, and streets, and apothecaries' shops. What unity of feeling can there be where there is so wide a divergency of manners?

A woman's foot should seldom, if ever, cross the threshold of your home. To all who are Christ's virgins show the same regard or the same disregard. Do not linger under the same roof with them, and do not rely on your past continence. You cannot be holier than David or wiser than Solomon. Always bear in mind that it was a woman who expelled the tiller of paradise from his heritage. In case you are sick one of the brethren may attend you; your sister also or your mother or some woman whose faith is approved with all. But if you have no persons so connected with you or so marked out by chaste behaviour, the Church maintains many elderly women who by their ministrations may oblige you and benefit themselves so that even your sickness may bear fruit in the shape of almsdeeds. I know of cases where the recovery of the body has but preluded the sickness of the soul. There is danger for you in the service of one for whose face you constantly watch. If in the course of your clerical duty you have to visit a widow or a virgin, never enter the house alone. Let your companions be persons association with whom will not disgrace you. If you take a reader with you or an acolyte or a psalm-singer, let their character not their garb be their adornment; let them use no tongs to curl their hair; rather let their mien be an index of their chastity. You must not sit alone with a woman or see one without witnesses. If she has anything confidential to disclose, she is sure to have some nurse or housekeeper, some virgin, some widow, some married woman. She cannot be so friendless as to have none save you to whom she can venture to confide her secret. Beware of all that gives occasion for suspicion; and, to avoid scandal, shun every act that may give colour to it. Frequent gifts of handkerchiefs and garters, of face-cloths and dishes first tasted by the giver—to say nothing of notes full of fond expressions—of such things as these a holy love knows nothing. Such endearing and alluring expressions as my honey' and my darling,' you who are all my charm and my delight' the ridiculous courtesies of lovers and their foolish doings, we blush for on the stage and abhor in men of the world. How much more do we loathe them in monks and clergymen who adorn the priesthood by their vows while their vows are adorned by the priesthood. I speak thus not because I dread such evils for you or for men of saintly life, but because in all ranks and callings and among both men and women there are found both good and bad and in condemning the bad I commend the good.

6. Shameful to say, idol-priests, play-actors, jockeys, and prostitutes can inherit property: clergymen and monks alone lie under a legal disability, a disability enacted not by persecutors but by Christian emperors. I do not complain of the law, but I grieve that we have deserved a statute so harsh. Cauterizing is a good thing, no doubt; but how is it that I have a wound which makes me need it? The law is strict and far-seeing, yet even so rapacity goes on unchecked. By a fiction of trusteeship we set the statute at defiance; and, as if imperial decrees outweigh the mandates of Christ, we fear the laws and despise the Gospels. If heir there must be, the mother has first claim upon her children, the Church upon her flock—the members of which she has borne and reared and nourished. Why do we thrust ourselves in between mother and children?

It is the glory of a bishop to make provision for the wants of the poor; but it is the shame of all priests to amass private fortunes. I who was born (suppose) in a poor man's house, in a country cottage, and who could scarcely get of common millet and household bread enough to fill an empty stomach, am now come to disdain the finest wheat flour and honey. I know the several kinds of fish by name. I can tell unerringly on what coast a mussel has been picked. I can distinguish by the flavour the province from which a bird comes. Dainty dishes delight me because their ingredients are scarce and I end by finding pleasure in their ruinous cost.

I hear also of servile attention shewn by some towards old men and women when these are childless. They fetch the basin, beset the bed and perform with their own hands the most revolting offices. They anxiously await the advent of the doctor and with trembling lips they ask whether the patient is better. If for a little while the old fellow shews signs of returning vigour, they are in agonies. They pretend to be delighted, but their covetous hearts undergo secret torture. For they are afraid that their labours may go for nothing and compare an old man with a clinging to life to the patriarch Methuselah. How great a reward might they have with God if their hearts were not set on a temporal prize! With what great exertions do they pursue an empty heritage! Less labour might have purchased for them the pearl of Christ.

7. Read the divine scriptures constantly; never, indeed, let the sacred volume be out of your hand. Learn what you have to teach. "Hold fast the faithful word as you have been taught that you may be able by sound doctrine to exhort and convince the gainsayers. Continue thou in the things that thou hast learned and hast been assured of, knowing of whom thou hast learned them;" and "be ready always to give an answer to every man that asketh you a reason of the hope and faith that are in you." Do not let your deeds belie your words; lest when you speak in church someone may mentally reply "Why do you not practise what you profess? Here is a lover of dainties turned censor! his stomach is full and he reads us a homily on fasting. As well might a robber accuse others of covetousness." In a priest of Christ mouth, mind, and hand should be at one.

Be obedient to your bishop and welcome him as the parent of your soul. Sons love their fathers and slaves fear their masters. "If I be a father," He says, "where is mine honour? And if I am a master where is my fear?" In your case the bishop combines in himself many titles to your respect. He is at once a monk, a prelate, and an uncle who has before now instructed you in all holy things. This also I say that the bishops should know themselves to be priests not lords. Let them render to the clergy the honour which is their due that the clergy may offer to them the respect which belongs to bishops. There is a witty saying of the orator Domitius which is here to the point: "Why am I to recognize you as leader of the Senate when you will not recognize my rights as a private member?" We should realize that a bishop and his presbyters are like Aaron and his sons. As there is but one Lord and one Temple; so also should there be but one ministry. Let us ever bear in mind the charge which the apostle Peter gives to priests: "feed the flock of God which is among you, taking the oversight thereof not by constraint but willingly as God would have you; not for filthy lucre but of a ready mind; neither as being lords over God's heritage but being ensamples to the flock," and that gladly; that "when the chief-shepherd shall appear ye may receive a crown of glory that fadeth not away." It is a bad custom which prevails in certain churches for presbyters to be silent when bishops are present on the ground that they would be jealous or impatient hearers. "If anything," writes the apostle Paul, "be revealed to another that sitteth by, let the first hold his peace. For ye may all prophesy one by one that all may learn and all may be comforted; and the spirits of the prophets are subject to the prophets. For God is not the author of confusion but of peace." "A wise son maketh a glad father;" and a bishop should rejoice in the discrimination which has led him to choose such for the priests of Christ.

8. When teaching in church seek to call forth not plaudits but groans. Let the tears of your hearers be your glory. A presbyter's words ought to be seasoned by his reading of scripture. Be not a declaimer or a ranter, one who gabbles without rhyme or reason; but shew yourself skilled in the deep things and versed in the mysteries of God. To mouth your words and by your quickness of utterance astonish the unlettered crowd is a mark of ignorance. Assurance often explains that of which it knows nothing; and when it has convinced others imposes on itself. My teacher, Gregory of Nazianzus, when I once asked him to explain Luke's phrase sabbaton deuteroproton , that is "the second-first Sabbath," playfully evaded my request saying: "I will tell you about it in church, and there, when all the people applaud me, you will be forced against your will to know what you do not know at all. For, if you alone remain silent, every one will put you down for a fool." There is nothing so easy as by sheer volubility to deceive a common crowd or an uneducated congregation: such most admire what they fail to understand. Hear Marcus Tullius, the subject of that noble eulogy: "You would have been the first of orators but for Demosthenes: he would have been the only one but for you." Hear what in his speech for Quintus Gallius he has to say about unskilled speakers and popular applause and then you will not be the sport of such illusions. "What I am telling you," said he, "is a recent experience of my own. One who has the name of a

poet and a man of culture has written a book entitled Conversations of Poets and Philosophers. In this he represents Euripides as conversing with Menander and Socrates with Epicurus—men whose lives we know to be separated not by years but by centuries. Nevertheless he calls forth limitless applause and endless acclamations. For the theatre contains many who belong to the same school as he: like him they have never learned letters."

9. In dress avoid sombre colours as much as bright ones. Showiness and slovenliness are alike to be shunned; for the one savours of vanity and the other of pride. To go about without a linen scarf on is nothing: what is praiseworthy is to be without money to buy one. It is disgraceful and absurd to boast of having neither napkin nor handkerchief and yet to carry a well-filled purse.

Some bestow a trifle on the poor to receive a larger sum themselves and under the cloak of almsgiving do but seek for riches. Such are almshunters rather than almsgivers. Their methods are those by which birds, beasts, and fishes are taken. A morsel of bait is put on the hook—to land a married lady's purse! The church is committed to the bishop; let him take heed whom he appoints to be his almoner. It is better for me to have no money to give away than shamelessly to beg what I mean to hoard. It is arrogance too to wish to seem more liberal than he who is Christ's bishop. "All things are not open to us all." In the church one is the eye, another is the tongue, another the hand, another the foot, others ears, belly, and so on. Read Paul's epistle to the Corinthians and learn how the one body is made up of different members. The rude and simple brother must not suppose himself a saint just because he knows nothing; and he who is educated and eloquent must not measure his saintliness merely by his fluency. Of two imperfect things holy rusticity is better than sinful eloquence.

10. Many build churches nowadays; their walls and pillars of glowing marble, their ceilings glittering with gold, their altars studded with jewels. Yet to the choice of Christ's ministers no heed is paid. And let no one allege against me the wealth of the temple in Judaea, its table, its lamps, its censers, its dishes, its cups, its spoons, and the rest of its golden vessels. If these were approved by the Lord it was at a time when the priests had to offer victims and when the blood of sheep was the redemption of sins. They were figures typifying things still future and were "written for our admonition upon whom the ends of the world are come." But now our Lord by His poverty has consecrated the poverty of His house. Let us, therefore, think of His cross and count riches to be but dirt. Why do we admire what Christ calls "the mammon of unrighteousness"? Why do we cherish and love what it is Peter's boast not to possess? Or if we insist on keeping to the letter and find the mention of gold

and wealth so pleasing, let us keep to everything else as well as the gold. Let the bishops of Christ be bound to marry wives, who must be virgins. Let the best-intentioned priest be deprived of his office if he bear a scar and be disfigured. Let bodily leprosy be counted worse than spots upon the soul. Let us be fruitful and multiply and replenish the earth, but let us slay no lamb and celebrate no mystic passover, for where there is no temple, the law forbids these acts. Let us pitch tents in the seventh month and noise abroad a solemn fast with the sound of a horn. But if we compare all these things as spiritual with things which are spiritual; and if we allow with Paul that "the Law is spiritual" and call to mind David's words: "open thou mine eyes that I may behold wondrous things out of thy law;" and if on these grounds we interpret it as our Lord interprets it—He has explained the Sabbath in this way: then, rejecting the superstitions of the Jews, we must also reject the gold; or, approving the gold, we must approve the Jews as well. For we must either accept them with the gold or condemn them with it.

11. Avoid entertaining men of the world, especially those whose honours make them swell with pride. You are the priest of Christ—one poor and crucified who lived on the bread of strangers. It is a disgrace to you if the consul's lictors or soldiers keep watch before your door, and if the Judge of the province has a better dinner with you than in his own palace. If you plead as an excuse your wish to intercede for the unhappy and the oppressed, I reply that a worldly judge will defer more to a clergyman who is self-denying than to one who is rich; he will pay more regard to your holiness than to your wealth. Or if he is a man who will not hear the clergy on behalf of the distressed except over the bowl, I will readily forego his aid and will appeal to Christ who can help more effectively and speedily than any judge. Truly "it is better to trust in the Lord than to put confidence in man. It is better to trust in the Lord than to put confidence in princes."

Let your breath never smell of wine lest the philosopher's words be said to you: "instead of offering me a kiss you are giving me a taste of wine." Priests given to wine are both condemned by the apostle and forbidden by the old Law. Those who serve the altar, we are told, must drink neither wine nor shechar. Now every intoxicating drink is in Hebrew called shechar whether it is made of corn or of the juice of apples, whether you distil from the honeycomb a rude kind of mead or make a liquor by squeezing dates or strain a thick syrup from a decoction of corn. Whatever intoxicates and disturbs the balance of the mind avoid as you would wine. I do not say that we are to condemn what is a creature of God. The Lord Himself was called a "wine-bibber" and wine in moderation was allowed to Timothy because of his weak stomach. I only require that drinkers should observe that limit which their age, their health, or their constitution requires. But if without drinking wine at all I am aglow with youth and am inflamed by the heat of my blood and am of a strong and lusty habit of body, I will readily forego the cup in which I cannot but suspect poison. The Greeks have an excellent saying which will perhaps bear translation,

Fat bellies have no sentiments refined.

12. Lay upon yourself only as much fasting as you can bear, and let your fasts be pure, chaste, simple, moderate, and not superstitious. What good is it to use no oil if you seek after the most troublesome and out-of-the-way kinds of food, dried figs, pepper, nuts, dates, fine flour, honey, pistachios? All the resources of gardening are strained to save us from eating household bread; and to pursue dainties we turn our backs on the kingdom of heaven. There are some, I am told, who reverse the laws of nature and the race; for they neither eat bread nor drink water but imbibe thin decoctions of crushed herbs and beet-juice—not from a cup but from a shell. Shame on us that we have no blushes for such follies and that we feel no disgust at such superstition! To crown all, in the midst of our dainties we seek a reputation for abstinence. The strictest fast is bread and water. But because it brings with it no glory and because we all of us live on bread and water, it is reckoned no fast at all but an ordinary and common matter.

13. Do not angle for compliments, lest, while you win the popular applause, you do despite to God. "If I yet pleased men," says the apostle, "I should not be the servant of Christ." He ceased to please men when he became Christ's servant. Christ's soldier marches on through good report and evil report, the one on the right hand and the other on the left. No praise elates him, no reproaches crush him. He is not puffed up by riches, nor does he shrink into himself because of poverty. Joy and sorrow he alike despises. The sun does not burn him by day nor the moon by night. Do not pray at the corners of the streets, lest the applause of men interrupt the straight course of your prayers. Do not broaden your fringes and for show wear phylacteries, or, despite of conscience, wrap yourself in the self-seeking of the Pharisee. Would you know what mode of apparel the Lord requires? Have prudence, justice, temperance, fortitude. Let these be the four quarters of your horizon, let them be a four-horse team to bear you, Christ's charioteer, at full speed to your goal. No necklace can be more precious than these; no gems can form a brighter galaxy. By them you are decorated, you are girt about, you are protected on every side. They are your defence as well as your glory; for every gem is turned into a shield.

14. Beware also of a blabbing tongue and of itching ears. Neither detract from others nor listen to detractors. "Thou sittest," says the psalmist, "and speakest against thy brother; thou slanderest thine own mother's son. These things hast thou done and I kept silence; thou thoughtest wickedly that I was such an one as thyself, but I will reprove thee and set them in order before thine eyes." Keep your tongue from cavilling and watch over your words. Know that in judging others you are passing sentence on yourself and that you are yourself guilty of the faults which you blame in them. It is no excuse to say: "if others tell me things I cannot be rude to them." No one cares to speak to an unwilling listener. An arrow never lodges in a stone: often it recoils upon the shooter of it. Let the detractor learn from your unwillingness to listen not to be so ready to detract. Solomon says:—"meddle not with them that are given to detraction: for their calamity shall rise suddenly; and who knoweth the destruction of them both?"—of the detractor, that is, and of the person who lends an ear to his detraction.

15. It is your duty to visit the sick, to know the homes and children of ladies who are married, and to guard the secrets of noblemen. Make it your object, therefore, to keep your tongue chaste as well as your eyes. Never discuss a woman's figure nor let one house know what is going on in another. Hippocrates, before he will teach his pupils, makes them take an oath and compels them to swear fealty to him. He binds them over to silence, and prescribes for them their language, their gait, their dress, their manners. How much more reason have we to whom the medicine of the soul has been committed to love the houses of all Christians as our own homes. Let them know us as comforters in sorrow rather than as guests in time of mirth. That clergyman soon becomes an object of contempt who being often asked out to dinner never refuses to go.

16. Let us never seek for presents and rarely accept them when we are asked to do so. For "it is more blessed to give than to receive." Somehow or other the very man who begs leave to offer you a gift holds you the cheaper for your acceptance of it; while, if you refuse it, it is wonderful how much more he will come to respect you. The preacher of continence must not be a maker of marriages. Why does he who reads the apostle's words "it remaineth that they that have wives be as though they had none"—why does he press a virgin to marry? Why does a priest, who must be a monogamist, urge a widow to marry again? How can the clergy be managers and stewards of other men's households, when they are bidden to disregard even their own interests? To wrest a thing from a friend is theft but to cheat the Church is sacrilege. When you have received money to be doled out to the poor, to be cautious or to hesitate while crowds are starving is to be worse than a robber; and to subtract a por-

tion for yourself is to commit a crime of the deepest dye. I am tortured with hunger and are you to judge what will satisfy my cravings? Either divide immediately what you have received, or, if you are a timid almoner, send the donor to distribute his own gifts. Your purse ought not to remain full while I am in need. No one can look after what is mine better than I can. He is the best almoner who keeps nothing for himself.

17. You have compelled me, my dear Nepotian, in spite of the castigation which my treatise on Virginity has had to endure—the one which I wrote for the saintly Eustochium at Rome:—you have compelled me after ten years have passed once more to open my mouth at Bethlehem and to expose myself to the stabs of every tongue. For I could only escape from criticism by writing nothing—a course made impossible by your request; and I knew when I took up my pen that the shafts of all gainsayers would be launched against me. I beg such to hold their peace and to desist from gainsaying: for I have written to them not as to opponents but as to friends. I have not inveighed against those who sin: I have but warned them to sin no more. My judgment of myself has been as strict as my judgment of them. When I have wished to remove the mote from my neighbour's eye, I have first cast out the beam in my own. I have calumniated no one. Not a name has been hinted at. My words have not been aimed at individuals and my criticism of shortcomings has been quite general. If any one wishes to be angry with me he will have first to own that he himself suits my description.

LETTER LIII. TO PAULINUS

Jerome urges Paulinus, bishop of Nola, (for whom see Letter LVIII.) to make a diligent study of the Scriptures and to this end reminds him of the zeal for learning displayed not only by the wisest of the pagans but also by the apostle Paul. Then going through the two Testaments in detail he describes the contents of the several books and the lessons which may be learned from them. He concludes with an appeal to Paulinus to divest himself wholly of his earthly wealth and to devote himself altogether to God. Written in 394 a.d.

1. Our brother Ambrose along with your little gifts has delivered to me a most charming letter which, though it comes at the beginning of our friendship, gives assurance of tried fidelity and of long continued attachment. A true intimacy cemented by Christ Himself is not one which depends upon material considerations, or upon the presence of the persons, or upon an insincere and

exaggerated flattery; but one such as ours, wrought by a common fear of God and a joint study of the divine scriptures.

We read in old tales that men traversed provinces, crossed seas, and visited strange peoples, simply to see face to face persons whom they only knew from books. Thus Pythagoras visited the prophets of Memphis; and Plato, besides visiting Egypt and Archytas of Tarentum, most carefully explored that part of the coast of Italy which was formerly called Great Greece. In this way the influential Athenian master with whose lessons the schools of the Academy resounded became at once a pilgrim and a pupil choosing modestly to learn what others had to teach rather than over confidently to propound views of his own. Indeed his pursuit of learning—which seemed to fly before him all the world over—finally led to his capture by pirates who sold him into slavery to a cruel tyrant. Thus he became a prisoner, a bond-man, and a slave; yet, as he was always a philosopher, he was greater still than the man who purchased him. Again we read that certain noblemen journeyed from the most remote parts of Spain and Gaul to visit Titus Livius, and listen to his eloquence which flowed like a fountain of milk. Thus the fame of an individual had more power to draw men to Rome than the attractions of the city itself; and the age displayed an unheard of and noteworthy portent in the shape of men who, entering the great city, bestowed their attention not upon it but upon something else. Apollonius too was a traveller—the one I mean who is called the sorcerer by ordinary people and the philosopher by such as follow Pythagoras. He entered Persia, traversed the Caucasus and made his way through the Albanians, the Scythians, the Massagetae, and the richest districts of India. At last, after crossing that wide river the Pison, he came to the Brahmans. There he saw Hiarcas sitting upon his golden throne and drinking from his Tantalus-fountain, and heard him instructing a few disciples upon the nature, motions, and orbits of the heavenly bodies. After this he travelled among the Elamites, the Babylonians, the Chaldeans, the Medes, the Assyrians, the Parthians, the Syrians, the Phenicians, the Arabians, and the Philistines. Then returning to Alexandria he made his way to Ethiopia to see the gymnosophists and the famous table of the sun spread in the sands of the desert. Everywhere he found something to learn, and as he was always going to new places, he became constantly wiser and better. Philostratus has written the story of his life at length in eight books.

2. But why should I confine my allusions to the men of this world, when the Apostle Paul, the chosen vessel the doctor of the Gentiles, who could boldly say: "Do ye seek a proof of Christ speaking in me?" knowing that he really had within him that greatest of guests—when even he after visiting

Damascus and Arabia "went up to Jerusalem to see Peter and abode with him fifteen days." For he who was to be a preacher to the Gentiles had to be instructed in the mystical numbers seven and eight. And again fourteen years after he took Barnabas and Titus and communicated his gospel to the apostles lest by any means he should have run or had run in vain. Spoken words possess an indefinable hidden power, and teaching that passed directly from the mouth of the speaker into the ears of the disciples is more impressive than any other. When the speech of Demosthenes against AEschines was recited before the latter during his exile at Rhodes, amid all the admiration and applause he sighed "if you could but have heard the brute deliver his own periods!"

3. I do not adduce these instances because I have anything in me from which you either can or will learn a lesson, but to show you that your zeal and eagerness to learn—even though you cannot rely on help from me—are in themselves worthy of praise. A mind willing to learn deserves commendation even when it has no teacher. What is of importance to me is not what you find but what you seek to find. Wax is soft and easy to mould even where the hands of craftsman and modeller are wanting to work it. It is already potentially all that it can be made. The apostle Paul learned the Law of Moses and the prophets at the feet of Gamaliel and was glad that he had done so, for armed with this spiritual armour, he was able to say boldly "the weapons of our warfare are not carnal, but mighty through God to the pulling down of strongholds;" armed with these we war "casting down imaginations and every high thing that exalteth itself against the knowledge of God, and bringing into captivity every thought to the obedience of Christ; and being in a readiness to revenge all disobedience." He writes to Timothy who had been trained in the holy writings from a child exhorting him to study them diligently and not to neglect the gift which was given him with the laying on of the hands of the presbytery. To Titus he gives commandment that among a bishop's other virtues (which he briefly describes) he should be careful to seek a knowledge of the scriptures: A bishop, he says, must hold fast "the faithful word as he hath been taught that he may be able by sound doctrine both to exhort and to convince the gainsayers." In fact want of education in a clergyman prevents him from doing good to any one but himself and much as the virtue of his life may build up Christ's church, he does it an injury as great by failing to resist those who are trying to pull it down. The prophet Haggai says—or rather the Lord says it by the mouth of Haggai—"Ask now the priests concerning the law." For such is the important function of the priesthood to give answers to those who question them concerning the law. And in Deuteronomy we read "Ask thy father and he will shew thee; thy elders and they will tell thee." Also

in the one hundred and nineteenth psalm "thy statutes have been my songs in the house of my pilgrimage." David too, in the description of the righteous man whom he compares to the tree of life in paradise, amongst his other excellences speaks of this, "His delight is in the law of the Lord; and in his law doth he meditate day and night." In the close of his most solemn vision Daniel declares that "the righteous shall shine as the stars; and the wise, that is the learned, as the firmament." You can see, therefore, how great is the difference between righteous ignorance and instructed righteousness. Those who have the first are compared with the stars, those who have the second with the heavens. Yet, according to the exact sense of the Hebrew, both statements may be understood of the learned, for it is to be read in this way:—"They that be wise shall shine as the brightness of the firmament; and they that turn many to righteousness as the stars forever and ever." Why is the apostle Paul called a chosen vessel? Assuredly because he is a repertory of the Law and of the holy scriptures. The learned teaching of our Lord strikes the Pharisees dumb with amazement, and they are filled with astonishment to find that Peter and John know the Law although they have not learned letters. For to these the Holy Ghost immediately suggested what comes to others by daily study and meditation; and, as it is written, they were "taught of God." The Saviour had only accomplished his twelfth year when the scene in the temple took place; but when he interrogated the elders concerning the Law His wise questions conveyed rather than sought information.

4. But perhaps we ought to call Peter and John ignorant, both of whom could say of themselves, "though I be rude in speech, yet not in knowledge." Was John a mere fisherman, rude and untaught? If so, whence did he get the words "In the beginning was the word, and the word was with God and the word was God." Logos in Greek has many meanings. It signifies word and reason and reckoning and the cause of individual things by which those which are subsist. All of which things we rightly predicate of Christ. This truth Plato with all his learning did not know, of this Demosthenes with all his eloquence was ignorant. "I will destroy," it is said, "the wisdom of the wise, and will bring to nothing the understanding of the prudent." The true wisdom must destroy the false, and, although the foolishness of preaching is inseparable from the Cross, Paul speaks "wisdom among them that are perfect, yet not the wisdom of this world, nor of the princes of this world that come to nought," but he speaks "the wisdom of God in a mystery, even the hidden wisdom, which God ordained before the world." God's wisdom is Christ, for Christ, we are told, is "the power of God and the wisdom of God." He is the wisdom which is hidden in a mystery, of which also we read in the heading of the ninth

psalm "for the hidden things of the son." In Him are hidden all the treasures of wisdom and knowledge. He also who was hidden in a mystery is the same that was foreordained before the world. Now it was in the Law and in the Prophets that he was foreordained and prefigured. For this reason too the prophets were called seers, because they saw Him whom others did not see. Abraham saw His day and was glad. The heavens which were sealed to a rebellious people were opened to Ezekiel. "Open thou mine eyes," saith David, "that I may behold wonderful things out of thy Law." For "the law is spiritual" and a revelation is needed to enable us to comprehend it and, when God uncovers His face, to behold His glory.

5. In the apocalypse a book is shewn sealed with seven seals, which if you deliver to one that is learned saying, Read this, he will answer you, I cannot, for it is sealed. How many there are to-day who fancy themselves learned, yet the scriptures are a sealed book to them, and one which they cannot open save through Him who has the key of David, "he that openeth and no man shutteth; and shutteth and no man openeth." In the Acts of the Apostles the holy eunuch (or rather "man" for so the scripture calls him) when reading Isaiah he is asked by Philip "Understandest thou what thou readest?," makes answer:—"How can I except some man should guide me?" To digress for a moment to myself, I am neither holier nor more diligent than this eunuch, who came from Ethiopia, that is from the ends of the world, to the Temple leaving behind him a queen's palace, and was so great a lover of the Law and of divine knowledge that he read the holy scriptures even in his chariot. Yet although he had the book in his hand and took into his mind the words of the Lord, nay even had them on his tongue and uttered them with his lips, he still knew not Him, whom—not knowing—he worshipped in the book. Then Philip came and shewed him Jesus, who was concealed beneath the letter. Wondrous excellence of the teacher! In the same hour the eunuch believed and was baptized; he became one of the faithful and a saint. He was no longer a pupil but a master; and he found more in the church's font there in the wilderness than he had ever done in the gilded temple of the synagogue.

6. These instances have been just touched upon by me (the limits of a letter forbid a more discursive treatment of them) to convince you that in the holy scriptures you can make no progress unless you have a guide to shew you the way. I say nothing of the knowledge of grammarians, rhetoricians, philosophers, geometers, logicians, musicians, astronomers, astrologers, physicians, whose several kinds of skill are most useful to mankind, and may be ranged under the three heads of teaching, method, and proficiency. I will pass to the less important crafts which require manual dexterity more than mental ability.

Husbandmen, masons, carpenters, workers in wood and metal, wool-dressers and fullers, as well as those artisans who make furniture and cheap utensils, cannot attain the ends they seek without instruction from qualified persons. As Horace says

Doctors alone profess the healing art
And none but joiners ever try to join.

7. The art of interpreting the scriptures is the only one of which all men everywhere claim to be masters. To quote Horace again

Taught or untaught we all write poetry.

The chatty old woman, the doting old man, and the wordy sophist, one and all take in hand the Scriptures, rend them in pieces and teach them before they have learned them. Some with brows knit and bombastic words, balanced one against the other philosophize concerning the sacred writings among weak women. Others—I blush to say it—learn of women what they are to teach men; and as if even this were not enough, they boldly explain to others what they themselves by no means understand. I say nothing of persons who, like myself have been familiar with secular literature before they have come to the study of the holy scriptures. Such men when they charm the popular ear by the finish of their style suppose every word they say to be a law of God. They do not deign to notice what Prophets and apostles have intended but they adapt conflicting passages to suit their own meaning, as if it were a grand way of teaching—and not rather the faultiest of all—to misrepresent a writer's views and to force the scriptures reluctantly to do their will. They forget that we have read centos from Homer and Virgil; but we never think of calling the Christless Maro a Christian because of his lines:—

Now comes the Virgin back and Saturn's reign,
Now from high heaven comes a Child newborn.

Another line might be addressed by the Father to the Son:—

Hail, only Son, my Might and Majesty.

And yet another might follow the Saviour's words on the cross:—

Such words he spake and there transfixed remained.

But all this is puerile, and resembles the sleight-of-hand of a mountebank. It is idle to try to teach what you do not know, and—if I may speak with some warmth—is worse still to be ignorant of your ignorance.

8. Genesis, we shall be told, needs no explanation; its topics are too simple—the birth of the world, the origin of the human race, the division of the earth, the confusion of tongues, and the descent of the Hebrews into Egypt! Exodus, no doubt, is equally plain, containing as it does merely an account of the ten plagues, the decalogue, and sundry mysterious and divine precepts! The

meaning of Leviticus is of course self-evident, although every sacrifice that it describes, nay more every word that it contains, the description of Aaron's vestments, and all the regulations connected with the Levites are symbols of things heavenly! The book of Numbers too—are not its very figures, and Balaam's prophecy, and the forty-two camping places in the wilderness so many mysteries? Deuteronomy also, that is the second law or the foreshadowing of the law of the gospel,—does it not, while exhibiting things known before, put old truths in a new light? So far the five words' of the Pentateuch, with which the apostle boasts his wish to speak in the Church. Then, as for Job, that pattern of patience, what mysteries are there not contained in his discourses? Commencing in prose the book soon glides into verse and at the end once more reverts to prose. By the way in which it lays down propositions, assumes postulates, adduces proofs, and draws inferences, it illustrates all the laws of logic. Single words occurring in the book are full of meaning. To say nothing of other topics, it prophesies the resurrection of men's bodies at once with more clearness and with more caution than any one has yet shewn. "I know," Job says, "that my redeemer liveth, and that at the last day I shall rise again from the earth; and I shall be clothed again with my skin, and in my flesh shall I see God. Whom I shall see for myself, and mine eyes shall behold, and not another. This my hope is stored up in my own bosom." I will pass on to Jesus the son of Nave—a type of the Lord in name as well as in deed—who crossed over Jordan, subdued hostile kingdoms, divided the land among the conquering people and who, in every city, village, mountain, river, hill-torrent, and boundary which he dealt with, marked out the spiritual realms of the heavenly Jerusalem, that is, of the church. In the book of Judges every one of the popular leaders is a type. Ruth the Moabitess fulfils the prophecy of Isaiah:—"Send thou a lamb, O Lord, as ruler of the land from the rock of the wilderness to the mount of the daughter of Zion." Under the figures of Eli's death and the slaying of Saul Samuel shews the abolition of the old law. Again in Zadok and in David he bears witness to the mysteries of the new priesthood and of the new royalty. The third and fourth books of Kings called in Hebrew Malachim give the history of the kingdom of Judah from Solomon to Jeconiah, and of that of Israel from Jeroboam the son of Nebat to Hoshea who was carried away into Assyria. If you merely regard the narrative, the words are simple enough, but if you look beneath the surface at the hidden meaning of it, you find a description of the small numbers of the church and of the wars which the heretics wage against it. The twelve prophets whose writings are compressed within the narrow limits of a single volume, have typical meanings far different from their literal ones. Hosea speaks many times of Ephraim, of

Samaria, of Joseph, of Jezreel, of a wife of whoredoms and of children of whoredoms, of an adulteress shut up within the chamber of her husband, sitting for a long time in widowhood and in the garb of mourning, awaiting the time when her husband will return to her. Joel the son of Pethuel describes the land of the twelve tribes as spoiled and devastated by the palmerworm, the canker-worm, the locust, and the blight, and predicts that after the overthrow of the former people the Holy Spirit shall be poured out upon God's servants and handmaids; the same spirit, that is, which was to be poured out in the upper chamber at Zion upon the one hundred and twenty believers. These believers rising by gradual and regular gradations from one to fifteen form the steps to which there is a mystical allusion in the "psalms of degrees." Amos, although he is only "an herdman" from the country, "a gatherer of sycomore fruit," cannot be explained in a few words. For who can adequately speak of the three transgressions and the four of Damascus, of Gaza, of Tyre, of Idumaea, of Moab, of the children of Ammon, and in the seventh and eighth place of Judah and of Israel? He speaks to the fat kine that are in the mountain of Samaria, and bears witness that the great house and the little house shall fall. He sees now the maker of the grasshopper, now the Lord, standing upon a wall daubed or made of adamant, now a basket of apples that brings doom to the transgressors, and now a famine upon the earth "not a famine of bread, nor a thirst for water, but of hearing the words of the Lord." Obadiah, whose name means the servant of God, thunders against Edom red with blood and against the creature born of earth. He smites him with the spear of the spirit because of his continual rivalry with his brother Jacob. Jonah, fairest of doves, whose shipwreck shews in a figure the passion of the Lord, recalls the world to penitence, and while he preaches to Nineveh, announces salvation to all the heathen. Micah the Morasthite a joint heir with Christ announces the spoiling of the daughter of the robber and lays siege against her, because she has smitten the jawbone of the judge of Israel. Nahum, the consoler of the world, rebukes "the bloody city" and when it is overthrown cries:—"Behold upon the mountains the feet of him that bringeth good tidings." Habakkuk, like a strong and unyielding wrestler, stands upon his watch and sets his foot upon the tower that he may contemplate Christ upon the cross and say "His glory covered the heavens and the earth was full of his praise. And his brightness was as the light; he had horns coming out of his hand: and there was the hiding of his power." Zephaniah, that is the bodyguard and knower of the secrets of the Lord, hears "a cry from the fishgate, and an howling from the second, and a great crashing from the hills." He proclaims "howling to the inhabitants of the mortar; for all the people of Canaan are undone; all they that were laden with silver are cut off." Haggai, that is he who is glad or joyful, who has sown in tears to reap in joy, is occupied with the rebuilding of the temple. He represents the Lord (the Father, that is) as saying "Yet once, it is a little while, and I will shake the heavens, and the earth, and the sea, and the dry land; and I will shake all nations and he who is desired of all nations shall come." Zechariah, he that is mindful of his Lord, gives us many prophecies. He sees Jesus, "clothed with filthy garments," a stone with seven eyes, a candle-stick all of gold with lamps as many as the eyes, and two olive trees on the right side of the bowl and on the left. After he has described the horses, red, black, white, and grisled, and the cutting off of the chariot from Ephraim and of the horse from Jerusalem he goes on to prophesy and predict a king who shall be a poor man and who shall sit "upon a colt the foal of an ass." Malachi, the last of all the prophets, speaks openly of the rejection of Israel and the calling of the nations. "I have no pleasure in you, saith the Lord of hosts, neither will I accept an offering at your hand. For from the rising of the sun even unto the going down of the same, my name is great among the Gentiles: and in every place incense is offered unto my name, and a pure offering." As for Isaiah, Jeremiah, Ezekiel, and Daniel, who can fully understand or adequately explain them? The first of them seems to compose not a prophecy but a gospel. The second speaks of a rod of an almond tree and of a seething pot with its face toward the north, and of a leopard which has changed its spots. He also goes four times through the alphabet in different metres. The beginning and ending of Ezekiel, the third of the four, are involved in so great obscurity that like the commencement of Genesis they are not studied by the Hebrews until they are thirty years old. Daniel, the fourth and last of the four prophets, having knowledge of the times and being interested in the whole world, in clear language proclaims the stone cut out of the mountain without hands that overthrows all kingdoms. David, who is our Simonides, Pindar, and Alcaeus, our Horace, our Catullus, and our Serenus all in one, sings of Christ to his lyre; and on a psaltery with ten strings calls him from the lower world to rise again. Solomon, a lover of peace and of the Lord, corrects morals, teaches nature, unites Christ and the church, and sings a sweet marriage song to celebrate that holy bridal. Esther, a type of the church, frees her people from danger and, after having slain Haman whose name means iniquity, hands down to posterity a memorable day and a great feast. The book of things omitted or epitome of the old dispensation is of such importance and value that without it any one who should claim to himself a knowledge of the scriptures would make himself a laughing stock in his own eyes. Every name used in it, nay even the conjunction of the words, serves to throw light on narratives passed over in the books of Kings and upon questions suggested by the gospel. Ezra and Nehemiah, that is the Lord's helper and His consoler, are united in a single book. They restore the Temple and build up the walls of the city. In their pages we see the throng of the Israelites returning to their native land, we read of priests and Levites, of Israel proper and of proselytes; and we are even told the several families to which the task of building the walls and towers was assigned. These references convey one meaning upon the surface, but another below it.

9. [In Migne, 8.] You see how, carried away by my love of the scriptures, I have exceeded the limits of a letter yet have not fully accomplished my object. We have heard only what it is that we ought to know and to desire, so that we too may be able to say with the psalmist:—"My soul breaketh out for the very fervent desire that it hath alway unto thy judgments." But the saying of Socrates about himself—"this only I know that I know nothing"—is fulfilled in our case also. The New Testament I will briefly deal with. Matthew, Mark, Luke and John are the Lord's team of four, the true cherubim or store of knowledge. With them the whole body is full of eyes, they glitter as sparks, they run and return like lightning, their feet are straight feet, and lifted up, their backs also are winged, ready to fly in all directions. They hold together each by each and are interwoven one with another: like wheels within wheels they roll along and go whithersoever the breath of the Holy Spirit wafts them. The apostle Paul writes to seven churches (for the eighth epistle—that to the Hebrews—is not generally counted in with the others). He instructs Timothy and Titus; he intercedes with Philemon for his runaway slave. Of him I think it better to say nothing than to write inadequately. The Acts of the Apostles seem to relate a mere unvarnished narrative descriptive of the infancy of the newly born church; but when once we realize that their author is Luke the physician whose praise is in the gospel, we shall see that all his words are medicine for the sick soul. The apostles James, Peter, John, and Jude, have published seven epistles at once spiritual and to the point, short and long, short that is in words but lengthy in substance so that there are few indeed who do not find themselves in the dark when they read them. The apocalypse of John has as many mysteries as words. In saying this I have said less than the book deserves. All praise of it is inadequate; manifold meanings lie hid in its every word.

10. [In Migne, 9.] I beg of you, my dear brother, to live among these books, to meditate upon them, to know nothing else, to seek nothing else. Does not such a life seem to you a foretaste of heaven here on earth? Let not the simplicity of the scripture or the poorness of its vocabulary offend you; for these are due either to the faults of translators or else to deliberate purpose: for in this way it is better fitted for the instruction of an unlettered congregation as

the educated person can take one meaning and the uneducated another from one and the same sentence. I am not so dull or so forward as to profess that I myself know it, or that I can pluck upon the earth the fruit which has its root in heaven, but I confess that I should like to do so. I put myself before the man who sits idle and, while I lay no claim to be a master, I readily pledge myself to be a fellow-student. "Every one that asketh receiveth; and he that seeketh findeth; and to him that knocketh it shall be opened." Let us learn upon earth that knowledge which will continue with us in heaven.

11. [In Migne, 10.] I will receive you with open hands and—if I may boast and speak foolishly like Hermagoras—I will strive to learn with you whatever you desire to study. Eusebius who is here regards you with the affection of a brother; he has made your letter twice as precious by telling me of your sincerity of character, your contempt for the world, your constancy in friendship, and your love to Christ. The letter bears on its face (without any aid from him) your prudence and the charm of your style. Make haste then, I beseech you, and cut instead of loosing the hawser which prevents your vessel from moving in the sea. The man who sells his goods because he despises them and means to renounce the world can have no desire to sell them dear. Count as money gained the sum that you must expend upon your outfit. There is an old saying that a miser lacks as much what he has as what he has not. The believer has a whole world of wealth; the unbeliever has not a single farthing. Let us always live "as having nothing and yet possessing all things." Food and raiment, these are the Christian's wealth. If your property is in your own power, sell it: if not, cast it from you. "If any man . . . will take away thy coat, let him have thy cloke also." You are all for delay, you wish to defer action: unless—so you argue—unless I sell my goods piecemeal and with caution, Christ will be at a loss to feed his poor. Nay, he who has offered himself to God, has given Him everything once for all. The apostles did but forsake ships and nets. The widow cast but two brass coins into the treasury and yet she shall be preferred before Croesus with all his wealth. He readily despises all things who reflects always that he must die.

LETTER LIV. TO FURIA

A letter of guidance to a widow on the best means of preserving her widowhood (according to Jerome the second of the three degrees of chastity'). Furia had at one time thought of marrying again but eventually abandoned her intention and devoted herself to the care of her young children and her aged father. Jerome draws a vivid picture of the dangers to which she is exposed at Rome, lays down rules of conduct for her guidance, and commends her to the care of the presbyter Exuperius (afterwards bishop of Toulouse). The date of the letter is 394 a.d.

1. You beg and implore me in your letter to write to you—or rather write back to you—what mode of life you ought to adopt to preserve the crown of widowhood and to keep your reputation for chastity unsullied. My mind rejoices, my reins exult, and my heart is glad that you desire to be after marriage what your mother Titiana of holy memory was for a long time in marriage. Her prayers and supplications are heard. She has succeeded in winning afresh in her only daughter that which she herself when living possessed. It is a high privilege of your family that from the time of Camillus few or none of your house are described as contracting second marriages. Therefore it will not redound so much to your praise if you continue a widow as to your shame if being a Christian you fail to keep what heathen women have jealously guarded for so many centuries.

2. I say nothing of Paula and Eustochium, the fairest flowers of your stock; for, as my object is to exhort you, I do not wish it to appear that I am praising them. Blaesilla too I pass over who following her husband—your brother—to the grave, fulfilled in a short time of life a long time of virtue. Would that men would imitate the laudable examples of women, and that wrinkled old age would pay at last what youth gladly offers at first! In saying this I am putting my hand into the fire deliberately and with my eyes open. Men will knit their brows and shake their clenched fists at me;

In swelling tones will angry Chremes rave.

The leaders will rise as one man against my epistle; the mob of patricians will thunder at me. They will cry out that I am a sorcerer and a seducer; and that I should be transported to the ends of the earth. They may add, if they will, the title of Samaritan; for in it I shall but recognize a name given to my Lord. But one thing is certain. I do not sever the daughter from the mother, I do not use the words of the gospel: "let the dead bury their dead." For whosoever believes in Christ is alive; and he who believes in Him "ought himself also so to walk even as He walked."

3. A truce to the calumnies which the malice of backbiters continually fastens upon all who call themselves Christians to keep them through fear of shame from aspiring to virtue. Except by letter we have no knowledge of each other; and where there is no knowledge after the flesh, there can be no motive for intercourse save a religious one. "Honour thy father," the commandment says, but only if he does not separate you from your true Father. Recognize the

tie of blood but only so long as your parent recognizes his Creator. Should he fail to do so, David will sing to you: "hearken, O daughter, and consider, and incline thine ear; forget also thine own people and thy father's house. So shall the king greatly desire thy beauty, for he is thy Lord." Great is the prize offered for the forgetting of a parent, "the king shall desire thy beauty." You have heard, you have considered, you have inclined your ear, you have forgotten your people and your father's house; therefore the king shall desire your beauty and shall say to you:—"thou art all fair, my love; there is no spot in thee." What can be fairer than a soul which is called the daughter of God, and which seeks for herself no outward adorning. She believes in Christ, and, dowered with this hope of greatness makes her way to her spouse; for Christ is at once her bridegroom and her Lord.

4. What troubles matrimony involves you have learned in the marriage state itself; you have been surfeited with quails' flesh even to loathing; your mouth has been filled with the gall of bitterness; you have expelled the indigestible and unwholesome food; you have relieved a heaving stomach. Why will you again swallow what has disagreed with you? "The dog is turned to his own vomit again and the sow that was washed to her wallowing in the mire." Even brute beasts and flying birds do not fall into the same snares twice. Do you fear extinction for the line of Camillus if you do not present your father with some little fellow to crawl upon his breast and slobber his neck? As if all who marry have children! and as if when they do come, they always resemble their forefathers! Did Cicero's son exhibit his father's eloquence? Had your own Cornelia, pattern at once of chastity and of fruitfulness, cause to rejoice that she was mother of her Gracchi? It is ridiculous to expect as certain the offspring which many, as you can see, have not got, while others who have had it have lost it again. To whom then are you to leave your great riches? To Christ who cannot die. Whom shall you make your heir? The same who is already your Lord. Your father will be sorry but Christ will be glad; your family will grieve but the angels will rejoice with you. Let your father do what he likes with what is his own. You are not his to whom you have been born, but His to whom you have been born again, and who has purchased you at a great price with His own blood.

5. Beware of nurses and waiting maids and similar venomous creatures who try to satisfy their greed by sucking your blood. They advise you to do not what is best for you but what is best for them. They are for ever dinning into your ears Virgil's lines:—

Will you waste all your youth in lonely grief
And children sweet, the gifts of love, forswear?

Wherever there is holy chastity, there is also frugal living; and wherever there is frugal living, servants lose by it. What they do not get is in their minds so much taken from them. The actual sum received is what they look to, and not its relative amount. The moment they see a Christian they at once repeat the hackneyed saying:—"The Greek! The impostor!" They spread the most scandalous reports and, when any such emanates from themselves, they pretend that they have heard it from others, managing thus at once to originate the story and to exaggerate it. A lying rumour goes forth; and this, when it has reached the married ladies and has been fanned by their tongues, spreads through the provinces. You may see numbers of these—their faces painted, their eyes like those of vipers, their teeth rubbed with pumice-stone—raving and carping at Christians with insane fury. One of these ladies,

A violet mantle round her shoulders thrown,
Drawls out some mawkish stuff, speaks through her nose,
And minces half her words with tripping tongue.

Hereupon the rest chime in and every bench expresses hoarse approval. They are backed up by men of my own order who, finding themselves assailed, assail others. Always fluent in attacking me, they are dumb in their own defence; just as though they were not monks themselves, and as though every word said against monks did not tell also against their spiritual progenitors the clergy. Harm done to the flock brings discredit on the shepherd. On the other hand we cannot but praise the life of a monk who holds up to veneration the priests of Christ and refuses to detract from that order to which he owes it that he is a Christian.

6. I have spoken thus, my daughter in Christ, not because I doubt that you will be faithful to your vows, (you would never have asked for a letter of advice had you been uncertain as to the blessedness of monogamy): but that you may realize the wickedness of servants who merely wish to sell you for their own advantage, the snares which relations may set for you and the well meant but mistaken suggestions of a father. While I allow that this latter feels love toward you, I cannot admit that it is love according to knowledge. I must say with the apostle: "I bear them record that they have a zeal of God, but not according to knowledge." Imitate rather—I cannot say it too often—your holy mother whose zeal for Christ comes into my mind as often as I remember her, and not her zeal only but the paleness induced in her by fasting, the alms given by her to the poor, the courtesy shewn by her to the servants of God, the lowliness of her garb and heart, and the constant moderation of her language. Of your father too I speak with respect, not because he is a patrician and of consular rank but because he is a Christian. Let him be true to his profession as such.

Let him rejoice that he has begotten a daughter for Christ and not for the world. Nay rather let him grieve that you have in vain lost your virginity as the fruits of matrimony have not been yours. Where is the husband whom he gave to you? Even had he been lovable and good, death would still have snatched all away, and his decease would have terminated the fleshly bond between you. Seize the opportunity, I beg of you, and make a virtue of necessity. In the lives of Christians we look not to the beginnings but to the endings. Paul began badly but ended well. The start of Judas wins praise; his end is condemned because of his treachery. Read Ezekiel, "The righteousness of the righteous shall not deliver him in the day of his transgression; as for the wickedness of the wicked he shall not fall thereby in the day that he turneth from his wickedness." The Christian life is the true Jacob's ladder on which the angels ascend and descend, while the Lord stands above it holding out His hand to those who slip and sustaining by the vision of Himself the weary steps of those who ascend. But while He does not wish the death of a sinner, but only that he should be converted and live, He hates the lukewarm and they quickly cause him loathing. To whom much is forgiven, the same loveth much.

7. In the gospel a harlot wins salvation. How? She is baptized in her tears and wipes the Lord's feet with that same hair with which she had before deceived many. She does not wear a waving headdress or creaking boots, she does not darken her eyes with antimony. Yet in her squalor she is lovelier than ever. What place have rouge and white lead on the face of a Christian woman? The one simulates the natural red of the cheeks and of the lips; the other the whiteness of the face and of the neck. They serve only to inflame young men's passions, to stimulate lust, and to indicate an unchaste mind. How can a woman weep for her sins whose tears lay bare her true complexion and mark furrows on her cheeks? Such adorning is not of the Lord; a mask of this kind belongs to Antichrist. With what confidence can a woman raise features to heaven which her Creator must fail to recognize? It is idle to allege in excuse for such practices girlishness and youthful vanity. A widow who has ceased to have a husband to please, and who in the apostle's language is a widow indeed, needs nothing more but perseverance only. She is mindful of past enjoyments, she knows what gave her pleasure and what she has now lost. By rigid fast and vigil she must quench the fiery darts of the devil. If we are widows, we must either speak as we are dressed, or else dress as we speak. Why do we profess one thing, and practise another? The tongue talks of chastity, but the rest of the body reveals incontinence.

8. So much for dress and adornment. But a widow "that liveth in pleasure"—the words are not mine but those of the apostle—"is dead while she

liveth." What does that mean—"is dead while she liveth"? To those who know no better she seems to be alive and not, as she is, dead in sin; yes, and in another sense dead to Christ, from whom no secrets are hid. "The soul that sinneth it shall die." "Some men's sins are open . . . going before to judgment: and some they follow after. Likewise also good works are manifest, and they that are otherwise cannot be hid. The words mean this:—Certain persons sin so deliberately and flagrantly that you no sooner see them than you know them at once to be sinners. But the defects of others are so cunningly concealed that we only learn them from subsequent information. Similarly the good deeds of some people are public property, while those of others we come to know only through long intimacy with them. Why then must we needs boast of our chastity, a thing which cannot prove itself to be genuine without its companions and attendants, continence and plain living? The apostle macerates his body and brings it into subjection to the soul lest what he has preached to others he should himself fail to keep; and can a mere girl whose passions are kindled by abundance of food, can a mere girl afford to be confident of her own chastity?

9. In saying this, I do not of course condemn food which God created to be enjoyed with thanksgiving, but I seek to remove from youths and girls what are incentives to sensual pleasure. Neither the fiery Etna nor the country of Vulcan, nor Vesuvius, nor Olympus, burns with such violent heat as the youthful marrow of those who are flushed with wine and filled with food. Many trample covetousness under foot, and lay it down as readily as they lay down their purse. An enforced silence serves to make amends for a railing tongue. The outward appearance and the mode of dress can be changed in a single hour. All other sins are external, and what is external can easily be cast away. Desire alone, implanted in men by God to lead them to procreate children, is internal; and this, if it once oversteps its own bounds, becomes a sin, and by a law of nature cries out for sexual intercourse. It is therefore a work of great merit, and one which requires unremitting diligence to overcome that which is innate in you; while living in the flesh not to live after the flesh; to strive with yourself day by day and to watch the foe shut up within you with the hundred eyes of the fabled Argus. This is what the apostle says in other words: "Every sin that a man doeth is without the body; but he that committeth fornication sinneth against his own body." Physicians and others who have written on the nature of the human body, and particularly Galen in his books entitled On matters of health, say that the bodies of boys and of young men and of full grown men and women glow with an interior heat and consequently that for persons of these ages all food is injurious which tends to promote this heat: while on the

other hand it is highly conducive to health in eating and in drinking to take things cold and cooling. Contrariwise they tell us that warm food and old wine are good for the old who suffer from humours and from chilliness. Hence it is that the Saviour says "Take heed to yourselves lest at any time your hearts be overcharged with surfeiting and drunkenness, and cares of this life." So too speaks the apostle: "Be not drunk with wine, wherein is excess." No wonder that the potter spoke thus of the vessel which He had made when even the comic poet whose only object is to know and to describe the ways of men tells us that

Where Ceres fails and Liber, Venus droops.

10. In the first place then, till you have passed the years of early womanhood, take only water to drink, for this is by nature of all drinks the most cooling. This, if your stomach is strong enough to bear it; but if your digestion is weak, hear what the apostle says to Timothy: "use a little wine for thy stomach's sake and thine often infirmities." Then as regards your food you must avoid all heating dishes. I do not speak of flesh dishes only (although of these the chosen vessel declares his mind thus: "it is good neither to eat flesh nor to drink wine") but of vegetables as well. Everything provocative or indigestible is to be refused. Be assured that nothing is so good for young Christians as the eating of herbs. Accordingly in another place he says: "another who is weak eateth herbs." Thus the heat of the body must be tempered with cold food. Daniel and the three children lived on pulse. They were still boys and had not come yet to that frying-pan on which the King of Babylon fried the elders who were judges. Moreover, by an express privilege of God's own giving their bodily condition was improved by their regimen. We do not expect that it will be so with us, but we look for increased vigour of soul which becomes stronger as the flesh grows weaker. Some persons who aspire to the life of chastity fall midway in their journey from supposing that they need only abstain from flesh. They load their stomachs with vegetables which are only harmless when taken sparingly and in moderation. If I am to say what I think, there is nothing which so much heats the body and inflames the passions as undigested food and breathing broken with hiccoughs. As for you, my daughter, I would rather wound your modesty than endanger my case by understatement. Regard everything as poison which bears within it the seeds of sensual pleasure. A meagre diet which leaves the appetite always unsatisfied is to be preferred to fasts three days long. It is much better to take a little every day than some days to abstain wholly and on others to surfeit oneself. That rain is best which falls slowly to the ground. Showers that come down suddenly and with violence wash away the soil.

11. When you eat your meals, reflect that you must immediately afterwards pray and read. Have a fixed number of lines of holy scripture, and render it as your task to your Lord. On no account resign yourself to sleep until you have filled the basket of your breast with a woof of this weaving. After the holy scriptures you should read the writings of learned men; of those at any rate whose faith is well known. You need not go into the mire to seek for gold; you have many pearls, buy the one pearl with these. Stand, as Jeremiah says, in more ways than one that so you may come on the true way that leads to the Father. Exchange your love of necklaces and of gems and of silk dresses for earnestness in studying the scriptures. Enter the land of promise that flows with milk and honey. Eat fine flour and oil. Let your clothing be, like Joseph's, of many colors. Let your ears like those of Jerusalem be pierced by the word of God that the precious grains of new corn may hang from them. In that reverend man Exuperius you have a man of tried years and faith ready to give you constant support with his advice.

12. Make to yourself friends of the mammon of unrighteousness that they may receive you into everlasting habitations. Give your riches not to those who feed on pheasants but to those who have none but common bread to eat, such as stays hunger while it does not stimulate lust. Consider the poor and needy. Give to everyone that asks of you, but especially unto them who are of the household of faith. Clothe the naked, feed the hungry, visit the sick. Every time that you hold out your hand, think of Christ. See to it that you do not, when the Lord your God asks an alms of you, increase riches which are none of His.

13. Avoid the company of young men. Let long baited youths dandified and wanton never be seen under your roof. Repel a singer as you would some bane. Hurry from your house women who live by playing and singing, the devil's choir whose songs are the fatal ones of sirens. Do not arrogate to yourself a widow's license and appear in public preceded by a host of eunuchs. It is a most mischievous thing for those who are weak owing to their sex and youth to misuse their own discretion and to suppose that things are lawful because they are pleasant. "All things are lawful, but all things are not expedient." No frizzled steward nor shapely foster brother nor fair and ruddy footman must dangle at your heels. Sometimes the tone of the mistress is inferred from the dress of the maid. Seek the society of holy virgins and widows; and, if need arises for holding converse with men, do not shun having witnesses, and let your conversation be marked with such confidence that the entry of a third person shall neither startle you nor make you blush. The face is the mirror of the mind and a woman's eyes without a word betray the secrets of her heart. I

have lately seen a most miserable scandal traverse the entire East. The lady's age and style, her dress and mien, the indiscriminate company she kept, her dainty table and her regal appointments bespoke her the bride of a Nero or of a Sardanapallus. The scars of others should teach us caution. When he that causeth trouble is scourged the fool will be wiser.' A holy love knows no impatience. A false rumor is quickly crushed and the after life passes judgment on that which has gone before. It is not indeed possible that any one should come to the end of life's race without suffering from calumny; the wicked find it a consolation to carp at the good, supposing the guilt of sin to be less, in proportion as the number of those who commit it is greater. Still a fire of straw quickly dies out and a spreading flame soon expires if fuel to it be wanting. Whether the report which prevailed a year ago was true or false, when once the sin ceases, the scandal also will cease. I do not say this because I fear anything wrong in your case but because, owing to my deep affection for you, there is no safety that I do not fear. Oh! that you could see your sister and that it might be yours to hear the eloquence of her holy lips and to behold the mighty spirit which animates her diminutive frame. You might hear the whole contents of the old and new testaments come bubbling up out of her heart. Fasting is her sport, and prayer she makes her pastime. Like Miriam after the drowning Pharaoh she takes up her timbrel and sings to the virgin choir, "Let us sing to the Lord for He hath triumphed gloriously; the horse and his rider hath he thrown into the sea." She teaches her companions to be music girls but music girls for Christ, to be luteplayers but luteplayers for the Saviour. In this occupation she passes both day and night and with oil ready to put in the lamps she waits the coming of the Bridegroom. Do you therefore imitate your kinswoman. Let Rome have in you what a grander city than Rome, I mean Bethlehem, has in her.

14. You have wealth and can easily therefore supply food to those who want it. Let virtue consume what was provided for self-indulgence; one who means to despise matrimony need fear no degree of want. Have about you troops of virgins whom you may lead into the king's chamber. Support widows that you may mingle them as a kind of violets with the virgins' lilies and the martyrs' roses. Such are the garlands you must weave for Christ in place of that crown of thorns in which he bore the sins of the world. Let your most noble father thus find in you his joy and support, let him learn from his daughter the lessons he used to learn from his wife. His hair is already gray, his knees tremble, his teeth fall out, his brow is furrowed through years, death is nigh even at the doors, the pyre is all but laid out hard by. Whether we like it or not, we grow old. Let him provide for himself the provision which is needful for his

long journey. Let him take with him what otherwise he must unwillingly leave behind, nay let him send before him to heaven what if he declines it, will be appropriated by earth.

15. Young widows, of whom some "are already turned aside after Satan, when they have begun to wax wanton against Christ " and wish to marry, generally make such excuses as these. "My little patrimony is daily decreasing, the property which I have inherited is being squandered, a servant has spoken insultingly to me, a maid has neglected my orders. Who will appear for me before the authorities? Who will be responsible for the rents of my estates? Who will see to the education of my children, and to the bringing up of my slaves?" Thus, shameful to say, they put that forward as a reason for marrying again, which alone should deter them from doing so. For by marrying again a mother places over her sons not a guardian but a foe, not a father but a tyrant. Inflamed by her passions she forgets the fruit of her womb, and among the children who know nothing of their sad fate the lately weeping widow dresses herself once more as a bride. Why these excuses about your property and the insolence of slaves? Confess the shameful truth. No woman marries to avoid cohabiting with a husband. At least, if passion is not your motive, it is mere madness to play the harlot just to increase wealth. You do but purchase a paltry and passing gain at the price of a grace which is precious and eternal! If you have children already, why do you want to marry? If you have none, why do you not fear a recurrence of your former sterility? Why do you put an uncertain gain before a certain loss of self-respect?

A marriage-settlement is made in your favour to-day but in a short time you will be constrained to make your will. Your husband will feign sickness and will do for you what he wants you to do for him. Yet he is sure to live and you are sure to die. Or if it happens that you have sons by the second husband, domestic strife is certain to result and intestine disputes. You will not be allowed to love your first children, nor to look kindly on those to whom you have yourself given birth. You will have to give them their food secretly; yet even so your present husband will bear a grudge against your previous one and, unless you hate your sons, he will think that you still love their father. But your husband may have issue by a former wife. If so when he takes you to his home, though you should be the kindest person in the world, all the commonplaces of rhetoricians and declamations of comic poets and writers of mimes will be hurled at you as a cruel stepmother. If your stepson fall sick or have a headache you will be calumniated as a poisoner. If you refuse him food, you will be cruel, while if you give it, you will be held to have bewitched him. I ask you what benefit has a second marriage to confer great enough to compensate for these evils?

16. Do we wish to know what widows ought to be? Let us read the gospel according to Luke. "There was one Anna," he says, "a prophetess, the daughter of Phanuel of the tribe of Aser." The meaning of the name Anna is grace. Phanuel is in our tongue the face of God. Aser may be translated either as blessedness or as wealth. From her youth up to the age of fourscore and four years she had borne the burden of widowhood, not departing from the temple and giving herself to fastings and prayers night and day; therefore she earned spiritual grace, received the title daughter of the face of God,' and obtained a share in the blessedness and wealth' which belonged to her ancestry. Let us recall to mind the widow of Zarephath who thought more of satisfying Elijah's hunger than of preserving her own life and that of her son. Though she believed that she and he must die that very night unless they had food, she determined that her guest should survive. She preferred to sacrifice her life rather than to neglect the duty of almsgiving. In her handful of meal she found the seed from which she was to reap a harvest sent her by the Lord. She sows her meal and lo! a cruse of oil comes from it. In the land of Judah grain was scarce for the corn of wheat had died there; but in the house of a heathen widow oil flowed in streams. In the book of Judith—if any one is of opinion that it should be received as canonical—we read of a widow wasted with fasting and wearing the sombre garb of a mourner, whose outward squalor indicated not so much the regret which she felt for her dead husband as the temper in which she looked forward to the coming of the Bridegroom. I see her hand armed with the sword and stained with blood. I recognize the head of Holofernes which she has carried away from the camp of the enemy. Here a woman vanquishes men, and chastity beheads lust. Quickly changing her garb, she puts on once more in the hour of victory her own mean dress finer than all the splendours of the world.

17. Some from a misapprehension number Deborah among the widows, and suppose that Barak the leader of the army is her son, though the scripture tells a different story. I will mention her here because she was a prophetess and is reckoned among the judges, and again because she might have said with the psalmist:—"How sweet are thy words unto my taste! yea sweeter than honey to my mouth." Well was she called the bee for she fed on the flowers of scripture, was enveloped with the fragrance of the Holy Spirit, and gathered into one with prophetic lips the sweet juices of the nectar. Then there is Naomi, in Greek parakeklemene or she who is consoled, who, when her husband and her children died abroad, carried her chastity back home and, being supported on

the road by its aid, kept with her her Moabitish daughter-in-law, that in her the prophecy of Isaiah might find a fulfilment. "Send out the lamb, O Lord, to rule over the land from the rock of the desert to the mount of the daughter of Zion." I pass on to the widow in the gospel who, though she was but a poor widow was yet richer than all the people of Israel. She had but a grain of mustard seed, but she put her leaven in three measures of flour; and, combining her confession of the Father and of the Son with the grace of the Holy Spirit, she cast her two mites into the treasury. All the substance that she had, her entire possessions, she offered in the two testaments of her faith. These are the two seraphim which glorify the Trinity with threefold song and are stored among the treasures of the church. They also form the legs of the tongs by which the live coal is caught up to purge the sinner's lips.

18. But why should I recall instances from history and bring from books types of saintly women, when in your own city you have many before your eyes whose example you may well imitate? I shall not recount their merits here lest I should seem to flatter them. It will suffice to mention the saintly Marcella who, while she is true to the claims of her birth and station, has set before us a life which is worthy of the gospel. Anna "lived with an husband seven years from her virginity"; Marcella lived with one for seven months. Anna looked for the coming of Christ; Marcella holds fast the Lord whom Anna received in her arms. Anna sang His praise when He was still a wailing infant; Marcella proclaims His glory now that He has won His triumph. Anna spoke of Him to all those who waited for the redemption of Israel; Marcella cries out with the nations of the redeemed: "A brother redeemeth not, yet a man shall redeem," and from another psalm: "A man was born in her, and the Highest Himself hath established her."

About two years ago, as I well remember, I published a book against Jovinian in which by the authority of scripture I crushed the objections raised on the other side on account of the apostle's concession of second marriages. It is unnecessary that I should repeat my arguments afresh here, as you can find them all in this treatise. That I may not exceed the limits of a letter, I will only give you this one last piece of advice. Think every day that you must die, and you will then never think of marrying again.

LETTER LV. TO AMANDUS

A very interesting letter. Amandus a presbyter of Burdigala (Bourdeaux) had written to Jerome for an explanation of three passages of scripture, viz. Matt.

vi. 34, 1 Cor. vi. 18, 1 Cor. xv. 25, 26, and had in the same letter on behalf of a sister' (supposed by Thierry to have been Fabiola) put the following question: Can a woman who has divorced her first husband on account of his vices and who has during his lifetime under compulsion married again, communicate with the Church without first doing penance?' Jerome in his reply gives the explanations asked for but answers the farther question, that concerning the sister,' with an emphatic negative. Written about the year 394 a.d.

1. A short letter does not admit of long explanations; compressing much matter into a small space it can only give a few words to topics which suggest many thoughts. You ask me what is the meaning of the passage in the gospel according to Matthew, "take no thought for the morrow. Sufficient unto the day is the evil thereof." In the holy scriptures "the morrow" signifies the time to come. Thus in Genesis Jacob says: "So shall my righteousness answer for me to-morrow." Again when the two tribes of Reuben and Gad and the half tribe of Manasseh had built an altar and when all Israel had sent to them an embassy, they made answer to Phinehas the high priest that they had built the altar lest "to-morrow" it might be said to their children, "ye have no part in the Lord." You may find many similar passages in the old instrument. While then Christ forbids us to take thought for things future, He has allowed us to do so for things present, knowing as He does the frailty of our mortal condition. His remaining words "sufficient unto the day is the evil thereof" are to be understood as meaning that it is sufficient for us to think of the present troubles of this life. Why need we extend our thoughts to contingencies, to objects which we either cannot obtain or else having obtained must soon relinquish? The Greek word kakia rendered in the Latin version "wickedness" has two distinct meanings, wickedness and tribulation, which latter the Greek call kakosin and in this passage "tribulation" would be a better rendering than "wickedness." But if any one demurs to this and insists that the word kakia must mean "wickedness" and not "tribulation" or "trouble," the meaning must be the same as in the words "the whole world lieth in wickedness" and as in the Lord's prayer in the clause, "deliver us from evil:" the purport of the passage will then be that our present conflict with the wickedness of this world should be enough for us.

2. Secondly, you ask me concerning the passage in the first epistle of the blessed apostle Paul to the Corinthians where he says: "every sin that a man doeth is without the body; but he that committeth fornication sinneth against his own body." Let us go back a little farther and read on until we come to these words, for we must not seek to learn the whole meaning of the section, from the concluding parts of it, or, if I may so say, from the tail of the chapter.

"The body is not for fornication but for the Lord; and the Lord for the body. And God hath both raised up the Lord and will also raise up us [with Him] by his own power. Know ye not that your bodies are the members of Christ? Shall I then take the members of Christ, and make them the members of an harlot? God forbid. What! Know ye not that he which is joined to an harlot is one body? For two, saith he, shall be one flesh. But he that is joined unto the Lord is one spirit. Flee fornication. Every sin that a man doeth is without the body; but he that committeth fornication sinneth against his own body," and so on. The holy apostle has been arguing against excess and has just before said "meats for the belly and the belly for meats: but God shall destroy both it and them." Now he comes to treat of fornication. For excess in eating is the mother of lust; a belly that is distended with food and saturated with draughts of wine is sure to lead to sensual passion. As has been elsewhere said "the arrangement of man's organs suggests the course of his vices." Accordingly all such sins as theft, manslaughter, pillage, perjury, and the like can be repented of after they have been committed; and, however much interest may tempt him, conscience always smites the offender. It is only lust and sensual pleasure that in the very hour of penitence undergo once more the temptations of the past, the itch of the flesh, and the allurements of sin; so that the very thought which we bestow on the correction of such transgressions becomes in itself a new source of sin. Or to put the matter in a different light: other sins are outside of us; and whatever we do we do against others. But fornication defiles the fornicator both in conscience and body; and in accordance with the words of the Lord, "for this cause shall a man leave father and mother, and shall cleave to his wife; and they twain shall be one flesh," he too becomes one body with a harlot and sins against his own body by making what is the temple of Christ the body of a harlot. Not to pass over any suggestion of the Greek commentators, I shall give you one more explanation. It is one thing, they say, to sin with the body, and another to sin in the body. Theft, manslaughter, and all other sins except fornication we commit with our hands outside ourselves. Fornication alone we commit inside ourselves in our bodies and not with our bodies upon others. The preposition with' denotes the instrument used in sinning, while the preposition in' signifies the sphere of the passion is ourselves. Some again give this explanation that according to the scripture a man's body is his wife and that when a man commits fornication he is said to sin against his own body that is against his wife inasmuch as he defiles her by his own fornication and causes her though herself free from sin to become a sinner through her intercourse with him.

3. I find joined to your letter of inquiries a short paper containing the following words: "ask him, (that is me,) whether a woman who has left her husband on the ground that he is an adulterer and sodomite and has found herself compelled to take another may in the lifetime of him whom she first left be in communion with the church without doing penance for her fault." As I read the case put I recall the verse "they make excuses for their sins." We are all human and all indulgent to our own faults; and what our own will leads us to do we attribute to a necessity of nature. It is as though a young man were to say, "I am over-borne by my body, the glow of nature kindles my passions, the structure of my frame and its reproductive organs call for sexual intercourse." Or again a murderer might say, "I was in want, I stood in need of food, I had nothing to cover me. If I shed the blood of another, it was to save myself from dying of cold and hunger." Tell the sister, therefore, who thus enquires of me concerning her condition, not my sentence but that of the apostle. "Know ye not, brethren (for I speak to them that know the law,) how that the law hath dominion over a man as long as he liveth? For the woman which hath an husband is bound by the law to her husband, so long as he liveth; but if the husband be dead, she is loosed from the law of her husband. So then, if, while her husband liveth, she be married to another man, she shall be called an adulteress." And in another place: "the wife is bound by the law as long as her husband liveth; but if her husband be dead, she is at liberty to be married to whom she will; only in the Lord." The apostle has thus cut away every plea and has clearly declared that, if a woman marries again while her husband is living, she is an adulteress. You must not speak to me of the violence of a ravisher, a mother's pleading, a father's bidding, the influence of relatives, the insolence and the intrigues of servants, household losses. A husband may be an adulterer or a sodomite, he may be stained with every crime and may have been left by his wife because of his sins; yet he is still her husband and, so long as he lives, she may not marry another. The apostle does not promulgate this decree on his own authority but on that of Christ who speaks in him. For he has followed the words of Christ in the gospel: "whosoever shall put away his wife, saving for the cause of fornication, causeth her to commit adultery: and whosoever shall marry her that is divorced, committeth adultery." Mark what he says: "whosoever shall marry her that is divorced committeth adultery." Whether she has put away her husband or her husband her, the man who marries her is still an adulterer. Wherefore the apostles seeing how heavy the yoke of marriage was thus made said to Him: "if the case of the man be so with his wife, it is not good to marry," and the Lord replied, "he that is able to receive it, let him receive it." And immediately by the instance of

the three eunuchs he shows the blessedness of virginity which is bound by no carnal tie.

4. I have not been able quite to determine what it is that she means by the words "has found herself compelled" to marry again. What is this compulsion of which she speaks? Was she overborne by a crowd and ravished against her will? If so, why has she not, thus victimized, subsequently put away her ravisher? Let her read the books of Moses and she will find that if violence is offered to a betrothed virgin in a city and she does not cry out, she is punished as an adulteress: but if she is forced in the field, she is innocent of sin and her ravisher alone is amenable to the laws. Therefore if your sister, who, as she says, has been forced into a second union, wishes to receive the body of Christ and not to be accounted an adulteress, let her do penance; so far at least as from the time she begins to repent to have no farther intercourse with that second husband who ought to be called not a husband but an adulterer. If this seems hard to her and if she cannot leave one whom she has once loved and will not prefer the Lord to sensual pleasure, let her hear the declaration of the apostle: "ye cannot drink the cup of the Lord and the cup of devils: ye cannot be partakers of the Lord's table and of the table of devils," and in another place: "what communion hath light with darkness? and what concord hath Christ with Belial?" What I am about to say may sound novel but after all it is not new but old for it is supported by the witness of the old testament. If she leaves her second husband and desires to be reconciled with her first, she cannot be so now; for it is written in Deuteronomy: "When a man hath taken a wife, and married her, and it come to pass that she find no favour in his eyes, because he hath found some uncleanness in her; then let him write her a bill of divorcement, and give it in her hand, and send her out of his house. And when she is departed out of his house, she may go and be another man's wife. And if the latter husband hate her, and write her a bill of divorcement and giveth it in her hand, and sendeth her out of his house; or if the latter husband die which took her to be his wife; her former husband, which sent her away may not take her again to be his wife, after that she is defiled; for that is abomination before the Lord: and thou shalt not cause the land to sin, which the Lord thy God giveth thee for an inheritance." Wherefore, I beseech you, do your best to comfort her and to urge her to seek salvation. Diseased flesh calls for the knife and the searing-iron. The wound is to blame and not the healing art, if with a cruelty that is really kindness a physician to spare does not spare, and to be merciful is cruel.

5. Your third and last question relates to the passage in the same epistle where the apostle in discussing the resurrection, comes to the words: "for he

must reign, till he hath put all things under his feet. The last enemy that shall be destroyed is death. For he hath put all things under his feet. But when he saith, all things are put under him, it is manifest that he is excepted, which did put all things under him. And when all things shall be subdued unto him, then shall the Son also himself be subject unto him that put all things under him that God may be all in all." I am surprised that you have resolved to question me about this passage when that reverend man, Hilary, bishop of Poictiers, has occupied the eleventh book of his treatise against the Arians with a full examination and explanation of it. Yet I may at least say a few words. The chief stumbling-block in the passage is that the Son is said to be subject to the Father. Now which is the more shameful and humiliating, to be subject to the Father (often a mark of loving devotion as in the psalm "truly my soul is subject unto God") or to be crucified and made the curse of the cross? For "cursed is everyone that hangeth on a tree." If Christ then for our sakes was made a curse that He might deliver us from the curse of the law, are you surprised that He is also for our sakes subject to the Father to make us too subject to Him as He says in the gospel: "No man cometh unto the Father but by me," and "I, if I be lifted up from the earth, will draw all men unto me." Christ then is subject to the Father in the faithful; for all believers, nay the whole human race, are accounted members of His body. But in unbelievers, that is in Jews, heathens, and heretics, He is said to be not subject; for these members of His body are not subject to the faith. But in the end of the world when all His members shall see Christ, that is their own body, reigning, they also shall be made subject to Christ, that is to their own body, that the whole of Christ's body may be subject unto God and the Father, and that God may be all in all. He does not say "that the Father may be all in all" but that "God" may be, a title which properly belongs to the Trinity and may be referred not only to the Father but also to the Son and to the Holy Ghost. His meaning therefore is "that humanity may be subject to the Godhead." By humanity we here intend not that gentleness and kindness which the Greeks call philanthropy but the whole human race. Moreover when he says "that God may be all in all," it is to be taken in this sense. At present our Lord and Saviour is not all in all, but only a part in each of us. For instance He is wisdom in Solomon, generosity in David, patience in Job, knowledge of things to come in Daniel, faith in Peter, zeal in Phinehas and Paul, virginity in John, and other virtues in others. But when the end of all things shall come, then shall He be all in all, for then the saints shall severally possess all the virtues and all will possess Christ in His entirety.

LETTER LVI. FROM AUGUSTINE

Augustine's first letter to Jerome (printed in his correspondence in this Library as Letter XXVIII.): through a series of accidents it was not delivered until nine years after it had been written. In it Augustine comments on Jerome's new Latin version of the O.T. and advises him in his future labours to adhere more closely to the text of the LXX. He also discusses Jerome's account (in his commentary on the epistle to the Galatians) of the quarrel between Paul and Peter at Antioch. This according to Jerome was not a real misunderstanding but only one artificially got up' to put clearly before the Church the mischief of Christians conforming to the now obsolete Mosaic Law. Augustine strongly controverts this view and maintains that it is fatal to the veracity and authority claimed for scripture. Written from Hippo about the year 394 a.d.

LETTER LVII. TO PAMMACHIUS ON THE BEST METHOD OF TRANSLATING

Written to Pammachius (for whom see Letter LXVI.) in a.d. 395. In the previous year Jerome had rendered into Latin Letter LI. (from Epiphanius to John of Jerusalem) under circumstances which he here describes (S:2). His version soon became public and incurred severe criticism from some person not named by Jerome but supposed by him to have been instigated by Rufinus (S:12). Charged with having falsified his original he now repudiates the charge and defends his method of translation ("to give sense for sense and not word for word" S:5) by an appeal to the practice of classical (S:5), ecclesiastical (S:6), and N.T. (S:S:7–10) writers.

When at a subsequent period Rufinus gave to the world what was in Jerome's opinion a misleading version of Origen's First Principles, he appealed to this letter as giving him ample warranty for what he had done. See Letters LXXX, and LXXXI, and Rufinus' Preface to the peri 'Aechon in Vol. iii. of this series.

1. The apostle Paul when he appeared before King Agrippa to answer the charges which were brought against him, wishing to use language intelligible to his hearers and confident of the success of his cause, began by congratulating himself in these words: "I think myself happy, King Agrippa, because I shall answer for myself this day before thee touching all the things whereof I am accused by the Jews: especially because thou art expert in all customs and questions which are among the Jews." He had read the saying of Jesus: "Well is

him that speaketh in the ears of them that will hear;" and he knew that a pleader only succeeds in proportion as he impresses his judge. On this occasion I too think myself happy that learned ears will hear my defence. For a rash tongue charges me with ignorance or falsehood; it alleges that in translating another man's letter I have made mistakes through incapacity or carelessness; it convicts me of either an involuntary error or a deliberate offence. And lest it should happen that my accuser—encouraged by a volubility which stops at nothing and by an impunity which arrogates to itself an unlimited license—should accuse me as he has already done our father (Pope) Epiphanius; I send this letter to inform you—and through you others who think me worthy of their regard—of the true order of the facts.

2. About two years ago the aforesaid Pope Epiphanius sent a letter to Bishop John, first finding fault with him as regarded some of his opinions and then mildly calling him to penitence. Such was the repute of the writer or else the elegance of the letter that all Palestine fought for copies of it. Now there was in our monastery a man of no small estimation in his country, Eusebius of Cremona, who, when he found that this letter was in everybody's mouth and that the ignorant and the educated alike admired it for its teaching and for the purity of its style, set to work to beg me to translate it for him into Latin and at the same time to simplify the argument so that he might more readily understand it; for he was himself altogether unacquainted with the Greek language. I consented to his request and calling to my aid a secretary speedily dictated my version, briefly marking on the side of the page the contents of the several chapters. The fact is that he asked me to do this merely for himself, and I requested of him in return to keep his copy private and not too readily to circulate it. A year and six months went by, and then the aforesaid translation found its way by a novel stratagem from his desk to Jerusalem. For a pretended monk—either bribed as there is much reason to believe or actuated by malice of his own as his tempter vainly tries to convince us—shewed himself a second Judas by robbing Eusebius of his literary property and gave to the adversary an occasion of railing against me. They tell the unlearned that I have falsified the original, that I have not rendered word for word, that I have put dear friend' in place of honourable sir,' and more shameful still! that I have cut down my translation by omitting the words aidesimotate Pappa. These and similar trifles form the substance of the charges brought against me.

3. At the outset before I defend my version I wish to ask those persons who confound wisdom with cunning, some few questions. Where did you get your copy of the letter? Who gave it to you? How have you the effrontery to bring forward what you have procured by fraud? What place of safety will be left us

if we cannot conceal our secrets even within our own walls and our own writing-desks? Were I to press such a charge against you before a legal tribunal, I could make you amenable to the laws which even in fiscal cases appoint penalties for meddlesome informers and condemn the traitor even while they accept his treachery. For though they welcome the profit which the information gives them, they disapprove the motive which actuates the informer. A little while ago a man of consular rank named Hesychius (against whom the patriarch Gamaliel waged an implacable war) was condemned to death by the emperor Theodosius simply because he had laid hold of imperial papers through a secretary whom he had tempted. We read also in old histories that the schoolmaster who betrayed the children of the Faliscans was sent back to his boys and handed over to them in bonds, the Roman people refusing to accept a dishonourable victory. When Pyrrhus king of Epirus was lying in his camp ill from the effects of a wound, his physician offered to poison him, but Fabricius thinking it shame that the king should die by treachery sent the traitor back in chains to his master, refusing to sanction crime even when its victim was an enemy. A principle which the laws uphold, which is maintained by enemies, which warfare and the sword fail to violate, has hitherto been held unquestioned among the monks and priests of Christ. And can any one of them presume now, knitting his brow and snapping his fingers, to spend his breath in saying: "What if he did use bribes or other inducements! he did what suited his purpose." A strange plea truly to defend a fraud as though robbers, thieves, and pirates did not do the same. Certainly, when Annas and Caiaphas led hapless Judas astray, they only did what they believed to be expedient for themselves.

4. Suppose that I wish to write down in my note books this or that silly trifle, or to make comments upon the scriptures, to retort upon my calumniators, to digest my wrath, to practise myself in the use of commonplaces and to stow away sharp shafts for the day of battle. So long as I do not publish my thoughts, they are only unkind words not matter for a charge of libel; in fact they are not even unkind words for the public ear never hears them. You may bribe my slaves and tamper with my clients. You may, as the fable has it, penetrate by means of your gold to the chamber of Danae; and then, dissembling what you have done, you may call me a falsifier; but, if you do so, you will have to plead guilty yourself to a worse charge than any that you can bring against me. One man inveighs against you as a heretic, another as a perverter of doctrine. You are silent yourself; you do not venture to answer; you assail the translator; you cavil about syllables and you fancy your defence complete if your calumnies provoke no reply. Suppose that I have made a mistake or an

omission in my rendering. Your whole case turns upon this; this is the defence which you offer to your accusers. Are you no heretic because I am a bad translator? Mind, I do not say that I know you to be a heretic; I leave such knowledge to your accuser, to him who wrote the letter: what I do say is that it is the height of folly for you when you are accused by one man to attack another, and when you are covered with wounds yourself to seek comfort by wounding one who is still quiescent and unaggressive.

5. In the above remarks I have assumed that I have made alterations in the letter and that a simple translation may contain errors though not wilful ones. As, however the letter itself shews that no changes have been made in the sense, that nothing has been added, and that no doctrine has been foisted into it, "obviously their object is understanding to understand nothing;" and while they desire to arraign another's want of skill, they betray their own. For I myself not only admit but freely proclaim that in translating from the Greek (except in the case of the holy scriptures where even the order of the words is a mystery) I render sense for sense and not word for word. For this course I have the authority of Tully who has so translated the Protagoras of Plato, the OEconomicus of Xenophon, and the two beautiful orations which AEschines and Demosthenes delivered one against the other. What omissions, additions, and alterations he has made substituting the idioms of his own for those of another tongue, this is not the time to say. I am satisfied to quote the authority of the translator who has spoken as follows in a prologue prefixed to the orations. "I have thought it right to embrace a labour which though not necessary for myself will prove useful to those who study. I have translated the noblest speeches of the two most eloquent of the Attic orators, the speeches which AEschines and Demosthenes delivered one against the other; but I have rendered them not as a translator but as an orator, keeping the sense but altering the form by adapting both the metaphors and the words to suit our own idiom. I have not deemed it necessary to render word for word but I have reproduced the general style and emphasis. I have not supposed myself bound to pay the words out one by one to the reader but only to give him an equivalent in value." Again at the close of his task he says, "I shall be well satisfied if my rendering is found, as I trust it will be, true to this standard. In making it I have utilized all the excellences of the originals, I mean the sentiments, the forms of expression and the arrangement of the topics, while I have followed the actual wording only so far as I could do so without offending our notions of taste. If all that I have written is not to be found in the Greek, I have at any rate striven to make it correspond with it." Horace too, an acute and learned writer, in his Art of Poetry gives the same advice to the skilled translator:—

And care not thou with over anxious thought
To render word for word.

Terence has translated Menander; Plautus and Caecilius the old comic poets. Do they ever stick at words? Do they not rather in their versions think first of preserving the beauty and charm of their originals? What men like you call fidelity in transcription, the learned term pestilent minuteness. Such were my teachers about twenty years ago; and even then I was the victim of a similar error to that which is now imputed to me, though indeed I never imagined that you would charge me with it. In translating the Chronicle of Eusebius of Caesarea into Latin, I made among others the following prefatory observations: "It is difficult in following lines laid down by others not sometimes to diverge from them, and it is hard to preserve in a translation the charm of expressions which in another language are most felicitous. Each particular word conveys a meaning of its own, and possibly I have no equivalent by which to render it, and if I make a circuit to reach my goal, I have to go many miles to cover a short distance. To these difficulties must be added the windings of hyperbata, differences in the use of cases, divergencies of metaphor; and last of all the peculiar and if I may so call it, inbred character of the language. If I render word for word, the result will sound uncouth, and if compelled by necessity I alter anything in the order or wording, I shall seem to have departed from the function of a translator." And after a long discussion which it would be tedious to follow out here, I added what follows:—"If any one imagines that translation does not impair the charm of style, let him render Homer word for word into Latin, nay I will go farther still and say, let him render it into Latin prose, and the result will be that the order of the words will seem ridiculous and the most eloquent of poets scarcely articulate."

6. In quoting my own writings my only object has been to prove that from my youth up I at least have always aimed at rendering sense not words, but if such authority as they supply is deemed insufficient, read and consider the short preface dealing with this matter which occurs in a book narrating the life of the blessed Antony. "A literal translation from one language into another obscures the sense; the exuberance of the growth lessens the yield. For while one's diction is enslaved to cases and metaphors, it has to explain by tedious circumlocutions what a few words would otherwise have sufficed to make plain. I have tried to avoid this error in the translation which at your request I have made of the story of the blessed Antony. My version always preserves the sense although it does not invariably keep the words of the original. Leave others to catch at syllables and letters, do you for your part look for the meaning." Time would fail me were I to unfold the testimonies of all who have

translated only according to the sense. It is sufficient for the present to name Hilary the confessor who has turned some homilies on Job and several treatises on the Psalms from Greek into Latin; yet has not bound himself to the drowsiness of the letter or fettered himself by the stale literalism of inadequate culture. Like a conqueror he has led away captive into his own tongue the meaning of his originals.

7. That secular and church writers should have adopted this line need not surprise us when we consider that the translators of the Septuagint, the evangelists, and the apostles, have done the same in dealing with the sacred writings. We read in Mark of the Lord saying Talitha cumi and it is immediately added "which is interpreted, Damsel, I say unto thee, arise." The evangelist may be charged with falsehood for having added the words "I say unto thee" for the Hebrew is only "Damsel arise." To emphasize this and to give the impression of one calling and commanding he has added "I say unto thee." Again in Matthew when the thirty pieces of silver are returned by the traitor Judas and the potter's field is purchased with them, it is written:—"Then was fulfilled that which was spoken of by Jeremy the prophet, saying, And they took the thirty pieces of silver the price of him that was valued which they of the children of Israel did value, and gave them for the potter's field, as the Lord appointed me.'" This passage is not found in Jeremiah at all but in Zechariah, in quite different words and an altogether different order. In fact the Vulgate renders it as follows:—"And I will say unto them, If it is good in your sight, give ye me a price or refuse it: So they weighed for my price thirty pieces of silver. And the Lord said unto me, Put them into the melting furnace and consider if it is tried as I have been tried by them. And I took the thirty pieces of silver and cast them into the house of the Lord." It is evident that the rendering of the Septuagint differs widely from the quotation of the evangelist. In the Hebrew also, though the sense is the same, the words are quite different and differently arranged. It says: "And I said unto them, If ye think good, give me my price; and, if not, forbear. So they weighed for my price thirty pieces of silver. And the Lord said unto me, Cast it unto the potter; a goodly price that I was priced at of them. And I took the thirty pieces of silver and cast them to the potter in the house of the Lord." They may accuse the apostle of falsifying his version seeing that it agrees neither with the Hebrew nor with the translators of the Septuagint: and worse than this, they may say that he has mistaken the author's name putting down Jeremiah when it should be Zechariah. Far be it from us to speak thus of a follower of Christ, who made it his care to formulate dogmas rather than to hunt for words and syllables. To take another instance from Zechariah, the evangelist John quotes from the Hebrew, "They

shall look on him whom they pierced," for which we read in the Septuagint, "And they shall look upon me because they have mocked me," and in the Latin version, "And they shall look upon me for the things which they have mocked or insulted." Here the evangelist, the Septuagint, and our own version all differ; yet the divergence of language is atoned by oneness of spirit. In Matthew again we read of the Lord preaching flight to the apostles and confirming His counsel with a passage from Zechariah. "It is written," he says, "I will smite the shepherd, and the sheep of the flock shall be scattered abroad." But in the Septuagint and in the Hebrew it reads differently, for it is not God who speaks, as the evangelist makes out, but the prophet who appeals to God the Father saying:—"Smite the shepherd, and the sheep shall be scattered." In this instance according to my judgment—and I have some careful critics with me—the evangelist is guilty of a fault in presuming to ascribe to God what are the words of the prophet. Again the same evangelist writes that at the warning of an angel Joseph took the young child and his mother and went into Egypt and remained there till the death of Herod; "that it might be fulfilled which was spoken of the Lord by the prophet saying, Out of Egypt have I called my son." The Latin manuscripts do not so give the passage, but in Hosea the true Hebrew text has the following:—"When Israel was a child then I loved him, and called my son out of Egypt." Which the Septuagint renders thus:—"When Israel was a child then I loved him, and called his sons out of Egypt." Are they altogether to be rejected because they have given another turn to a passage which refers primarily to the mystery of Christ? Or should we not rather pardon the shortcomings of the translators on the score of their human frailty according to the saying of James, "In many things we offend all. If any man offend not in word the same is a perfect man and able also to bridle the whole body." Once more it is written in the pages of the same evangelist, "And he came and dwelt in a city called Nazareth: that it might be fulfilled which was spoken by the prophets, He shall be called a Nazarene." Let these word fanciers and nice critics of all composition tell us where they have read the words; and if they cannot, let me tell them that they are in Isaiah. For in the place where we read and translate, "There shall come forth a rod out of the stem of Jesse, and a branch shall grow out of his roots," in the Hebrew idiom it is written thus, "There shall come forth a rod out of the root of Jesse and a Nazarene shall grow from his root." How can the Septuagint leave out the word Nazarene,' if it is unlawful to substitute one word for another? It is sacrilege either to conceal or to set at naught a mystery.

8. Let us pass on to other passages, for the brief limits of a letter do not suffer us to dwell too long on any one point. The same Matthew says:—"Now all

this was done that it might be fulfilled which was spoken of the Lord by the prophet saying, Behold a virgin shall be with child and shall bring forth a son and they shall call his name Emmanuel." The rendering of the Septuagint is, "Behold a virgin shall receive seed and shall bring forth a son, and ye shall call his name Emmanuel." If people cavil at words, obviously to receive seed' is not the exact equivalent of to be with child,' and ye shall call' differs from they shall call.' Moreover in the Hebrew we read thus, "Behold a virgin shall conceive and bear a son and shall call his name Immanuel." Ahaz shall not call him so for he was convicted of want of faith, nor the Jews for they were destined to deny him, but she who is to conceive him, and bear him, the virgin herself. In the same evangelist we read that Herod was troubled at the coming of the Magi and that gathering together the scribes and the priests he demanded of them where Christ should be born and that they answered him, "In Bethlehem of Judaea: for thus it is written by the prophet; And thou Bethlehem in the land of Judah art not the least among the princes of Judah, for out of thee shall come a governour that shall rule my people Israel." In the Vulgate this passage appears as follows:—"And thou Bethlehem, the house of Ephratah, art small to be among the thousands of Judah, yet one shall come out of thee for me to be a prince in Israel." You will be more surprised still at the difference in words and order between Matthew and the Septuagint if you look at the Hebrew which runs thus:—"But thou Bethlehem Ephratah, though thou be little among the thousands of Judah, yet out of thee shall he come forth unto me that is to be ruler in Israel." Consider one by one the words of the evangelist:—"And thou Bethlehem in the land of Judah." For "the land of Judah" the Hebrew has "Ephratah" while the Septuagint gives "the house of Ephratah." The evangelist writes, "art not the least among the princes of Judah." In the Septuagint this is, "art small to be among the thousands of Judah," while the Hebrew gives, "though thou be little among the thousands of Judah." There is a contradiction here—and that not merely verbal—between the evangelist and the prophet; for in this place at any rate both Septuagint and Hebrew agree. The evangelist says that he is not little among the princes of Judah, while the passage from which he queries says exactly the opposite of this, "Thou art small indeed and little; but yet out of thee, small and little as thou art, there shall come forth for me a leader in Israel," a sentiment in harmony with that of the apostle, "God hath chosen the weak things of the world to confound the things which are mighty." Moreover the last clause "to rule" or "to feed my people Israel" clearly runs differently in the original.

9. I refer to these passages, not to convict the evangelists of falsification—a charge worthy only of impious men like Celsus, Porphyry, and Julian—but to bring home to my critics their own want of knowledge, and to gain from them such consideration that they may concede to me in the case of a simple letter what, whether they like it or not, they will have to concede to the Apostles in the Holy Scriptures. Mark, the disciple of Peter, begins his gospel thus:—"The beginning of the gospel of Jesus Christ, as it is written in the prophet Isaiah: Behold I send my messenger before thy face which shall prepare thy way before thee. The voice of one crying in the wilderness, Prepare ye the way of the Lord, make his paths straight." This quotation is made up from two prophets, Malachi that is to say and Isaiah. For the first part: "Behold I send my messenger before thy face which shall prepare thy way before thee," occurs at the close of Malachi. But the second part: "The voice of one crying, etc.," we read in Isaiah. On what grounds then has Mark in the very beginning of his book set the words: "As it is written in the prophet Isaiah, Behold I send my messenger," when, as we have said, it is not written in Isaiah at all, but in Malachi the last of the twelve prophets? Let ignorant presumption solve this nice question if it can, and I will ask pardon for being in the wrong. The same Mark brings before us the Saviour thus addressing the Pharisees: "Have ye never read what David did when he had need and was an hungred, he and they that were with him, how he went into the house of God in the days of Abiathar the highpriest, and did eat the shew-bread which is not lawful to eat but for the priests?" Now let us turn to the books of Samuel, or, as they are commonly called, of Kings, and we shall find there that the highpriest's name was not Abiathar but Ahimelech, the same that was afterwards put to death with the rest of the priests by Doeg at the command of Saul. Let us pass on now to the apostle Paul who writes thus to the Corinthians: "For had they known it, they would not have crucified the Lord of glory. But, as it is written, Eye hath not seen nor ear heard, neither have entered into the heart of man, the things which God hath prepared for them that love Him." Some writers on this passage betake themselves to the ravings of the apocryphal books and assert that the quotation comes from the Revelation of Elijah; whereas the truth is that it is found in Isaiah according to the Hebrew text: "Since the beginning of the world men have not heard nor perceived by the ear, neither hath the eye seen, O God, beside thee what thou hast prepared for them that wait for thee." The Septuagint has rendered the words quite differently: "Since the beginning of the world we have not heard, neither have our eyes seen any God beside thee and thy true works, and thou wilt shew mercy to them that wait for thee." We see then from what place the quotation is taken and yet the apostle has not

rendered his original word for word, but, using a paraphrase, he has given the sense in different terms. In his epistle to the Romans the same apostle quotes these words from Isaiah: "Behold I lay in Sion a stumbling-stone and rock of offence," a rendering which is at variance with the Greek version yet agrees with the original Hebrew. The Septuagint gives an opposite meaning, "that you fall not on a stumblingstone nor on a rock of offence." The apostle Peter agrees with Paul and the Hebrew, writing: "but to them that do not believe, a stone of stumbling and a rock of offence." From all these passages it is clear that the apostles and evangelists in translating the old testament scriptures have sought to give the meaning rather than the words, and that they have not greatly cared to preserve forms or constructions, so long as they could make clear the subject to the understanding.

10. Luke the evangelist and companion of apostles describes Christ's first martyr Stephen as relating what follows in a Jewish assembly. "With threescore and fifteen souls Jacob went down into Egypt, and died himself, and our fathers were carried over into Sychem, and laid in the sepulchre that Abraham bought for a sum of money of the sons of Emmor the father of Sychem." In Genesis this passage is quite differently given, for it is Abraham that buys of Ephron the Hittite, the son of Zohar, near Hebron, for four hundred shekels of silver, a double cave, and the field that is about it, and that buries in it Sarah his wife. And in the same book we read that, after his return from Mesopotamia with his wives and his sons, Jacob pitched his tent before Salem, a city of Shechem which is in the land of Canaan, and that he dwelt there and "bought a parcel of a field where he had spread his tent at the hand of Hamor, the father of Sychem, for an hundred lambs," and that "he erected there an altar and called there upon the God of Israel." Abraham does not buy the cave from Hamor the father of Sychem, but from Ephron the son of Zohar, and he is not buried in Sychem but in Hebron which is corruptly called Arboch. Whereas the twelve patriarchs are not buried in Arboch but in Sychem, in the field purchased not by Abraham but by Jacob. I postpone the solution of this delicate problem to enable those who cavil at me to search and see that in dealing with the scriptures it is the sense we have to look to and not the words. In the Hebrew the twenty-second psalm begins with the exact words which the Lord uttered on the cross: Eli Eli lama azabthani, which means, "My God, my God, why hast thou forsaken me?" Let my critics tell me why the Septuagint introduces here the words "look thou upon me." For its rendering is as follows: "My God, my God, look thou upon me, why hast thou forsaken me?" They will answer no doubt that no harm is done to the sense by the addition of a couple of words. Let them acknowledge then that, if in the haste of dictation I

have omitted a few, I have not by so doing endangered the position of the churches.

11. It would be tedious now to enumerate, what great additions and omissions the Septuagint has made, and all the passages which in church-copies are marked with daggers and asterisks. The Jews generally laugh when they hear our version of this passage of Isaiah, "Blessed is he that hath seed in Zion and servants in Jerusalem." In Amos also after a description of self-indulgence there come these words: "They have thought of these things as halting and not likely to fly," a very rhetorical sentence quite worthy of Tully. But how shall we deal with the Hebrew originals in which these passages and others like them are omitted, passages so numerous that to reproduce them all would require books without number? The number of the omissions is shown alike by the asterisks mentioned above and by my own version when compared by a careful reader with the old translation. Yet the Septuagint has rightly kept its place in the churches, either because it is the first of all the versions in time, made before the coming of Christ, or else because it has been used by the apostles (only however in places where it does not disagree with the Hebrew). On the other hand we do right to reject Aquila, the proselyte and controversial translator, who has striven to translate not words only but their etymologies as well. Who could accept as renderings of "corn and wine and oil" such words as cheima oporismos stilpnotes , or, as we might say, pouring,' and fruitgathering,' and shining'? or, because Hebrew has in addition to the article other prefixes as well, he must with an unhappy pedantry translate syllable by syllable and letter by letter thus: sun ton ouranon kai sun ten gen, a construction which neither Greek nor Latin admits of, as many passages in our own writers shew. How many are the phrases charming in Greek which, if rendered word for word, do not sound well in Latin, and again how many there are that are pleasing to us in Latin, but which—assuming the order of the words not to be altered—would not please in Greek.

12. But to pass by this limitless field of discussion and to shew you, most Christian of nobles, and most noble of Christians, what is the kind of falsification which is censured in my translation, I will set before you the opening words of the letter in the Greek original and as rendered by me, that from one count in the indictment you may form an opinion of all. The letter begins Edei hemas, agapete, me te oi& 208;sei ton kleron pheresthai which I remember to have rendered as follows: "Dearly beloved, we ought not to misuse our position as ministers to gratify our pride." See there, they cry, what a number of falsehoods in a single line! In the first place agapetos means loved,' not dearly beloved.' Then oiesis means estimate,' not pride,' for this and not

oidema is the word used. Oidema signifies a swelling' but oi& 208;sis means judgment.' All the rest, say they: "not to misuse our position to gratify our pride" is your own. What is this you are saying, O pillar of learning and latter day Aristarchus, who are so ready to pass judgment upon all writers? It is all for nothing then that I have studied so long; that, as Juvenal says, "I have so often withdrawn my hand from the ferule." The moment I leave the harbour I run aground. Well, to err is human and to confess one's error wise. Do you therefore, who are so ready to criticise and to instruct me, set me right and give me a word for word rendering of the passage. You tell me I should have said: "Beloved, we ought not to be carried away by the estimation of the clergy." Here, indeed we have eloquence worthy of Plautus, here we have Attic grace, the true style of the Muses. The common proverb is true of me: "He who trains an ox for athletics loses both oil and money." Still he is not to blame who merely puts on the mask and plays the tragedy for another: his teachers are the real culprits; since they for a great price have taught him—to know nothing. I do not think the worse of any Christian because he lacks skill to express himself; and I heartily wish that we could all say with Socrates "I know that I know nothing;" and carry out the precept of another wise man, "Know thyself." I have always held in esteem a holy simplicity but not a wordy rudeness. He who declares that he imitates the style of apostles should first imitate the virtue of their lives; the great holiness of which made up for much plainness of speech. They confuted the syllogisms of Aristotle and the perverse ingenuities of Chrysippus by raising the dead. Still it would be absurd for one of us—living as we do amid the riches of Croesus and the luxuries of Sardanapalus—to make his boast of mere ignorance. We might as well say that all robbers and criminals would be men of culture if they were to hide their blood-stained swords in books of philosophy and not in trunks of trees.

13. I have exceeded the limits of a letter, but I have not exceeded in the expression of my chagrin. For, though I am called a falsifier, and have my reputation torn to shreds, wherever there are shuttles and looms and women to work them; I am content to repudiate the charge without retaliating in kind. I leave everything to your discretion. You can read the letter of Epiphanius both in Greek and in Latin; and, if you do so, you will see at once the value of my accusers' lamentations and insulting complaints. For the rest, I am satisfied to have instructed one of my dearest friends and am content simply to stay quiet in my cell and to wait for the day of judgment. If it may be so, and if my enemies allow it, I hope to write for you, not philippics like those of Demosthenes or Tully, but commentaries upon the scriptures.

LETTER LVIII. TO PAULINUS

In this his second letter to Paulinus of Nola Jerome dissuades him from making a pilgrimage to the Holy Places, and describes Jerusalem not as it ought to be but as it is. He then gives his friend counsels for his life similar to those which he has previously addressed to Nepotian, praises Paulinus for his Panegyric (now no longer extant) on the Emperor Theodosius, compares his style with those of the great writers of the Latin Church, and concludes with a commendation of his messenger, that Vigilantius who was soon to become the object of his bitterest contempt. Written about the year 395 a.d.

1. "A good man out of the good treasure of the heart bringeth forth good things," and "every tree is known by his fruit." You measure me by the scale of your own virtues and because of your own greatness magnify my littleness. You take the lowest room at the banquet that the goodman of the house may bid you to go up higher. For what is there in me or what qualities do I possess that I should merit praise from a man of learning? that I, small and lowly as I am, should be eulogized by lips which have pleaded on behalf of our most religious sovereign? Do not, my dearest brother, estimate my worth by the number of my years. Gray hairs are not wisdom; it is wisdom which is as good as gray hairs. At least that is what Solomon says: "wisdom is the gray hair unto men." Moses too in choosing the seventy elders is told to take those whom he knows to be elders indeed, and to select them not for their years but for their discretion. And, as a boy, Daniel judges old men and in the flower of youth condemns the incontinence of age. Do not, I repeat, weigh faith by years, nor suppose me better than yourself merely because I have enlisted under Christ's banner earlier than you. The apostle Paul, that chosen vessel framed out of a persecutor, though last in the apostolic order is first in merit. For though last he has laboured more than they all. To Judas it was once said: thou art a man who didst take sweet food with me, my guide and mine acquaintance; we walked in the house of God with company:" yet the Saviour accuses him of betraying his friend and master. A line of Virgil well describes his end:

From a high beam he knots a hideous death.

The dying robber, on the contrary, exchanges the cross for paradise and turns to martyrdom the penalty of murder. How many there are nowadays who have lived so long that they bear corpses rather than bodies and are like whited sepulchres filled with dead men's bones! A newly kindled heat is more effective than a long continued lukewarmness.

2. As for you, when you hear the Saviour's counsel: "if thou wilt be perfect, go and sell that thou hast, and give to the poor, and come follow me," you

translate his words into action; and baring yourself to follow the bare cross you mount Jacob's ladder the easier for carrying nothing. Your dress changes with the change in your convictions, and you aim at no showy shabbiness which leaves your purse as full as before. No, with pure hands and a clear conscience you make it your glory that you are poor both in spirit and in deed. There is nothing great in wearing a sad or a disfigured face, in simulating and in showing off fasts, or in wearing a cheap cloak while you retain a large income. When Crates the Theban—a millionaire of days gone by—was on his way to Athens to study philosophy, he cast away untold gold in the belief that wealth could not be compatible with virtue. What a contrast he offers to us, the disciples of a poor Christ, who cram our pockets with gold and cling under pretext of almsgiving to our old riches. How can we faithfully distribute what belongs to another when we thus timidly keep back what is our own? When the stomach is full, it is easy to talk of fasting. What is praiseworthy is not to have been at Jerusalem but to have lived a good life while there. The city which we are to praise and to seek is not that which has slain the prophets and shed the blood of Christ, but that which is made glad by the streams of the river, which is set upon a mountain and so cannot be hid, which the apostle declares to be a mother of the saints, and in which he rejoices to have his citizenship with the righteous.

3. In speaking thus I am not laying myself open to a charge of inconsistency or condemning the course which I have myself taken. It is not, I believe, for nothing that I, like Abraham, have left my home and people. But I do not presume to limit God's omnipotence or to restrict to a narrow strip of earth Him whom the heaven cannot contain. Each believer is judged not by his residence in this place or in that but according to the deserts of his faith. The true worshippers worship the Father neither at Jerusalem nor on mount Gerizim; for "God is a spirit, and they that worship Him must worship Him in spirit and in truth." "Now the spirit bloweth where it listeth," and "the earth is the Lord's and the fulness thereof." When the fleece of Judaea was made dry although the whole world was wet with the dew of heaven, and when many came from the East and from the West and sat in Abraham's bosom: then God ceased to be known in Judah only and His name to be great in Israel alone; the sound of the apostles went out into all the earth and their words into the ends of the world. The Saviour Himself speaking to His disciples in the temple said: "arise, let us go hence," and to the Jews: "your house is left unto you desolate." If heaven and earth must pass away, obviously all things that are earthly must pass away also. Therefore the spots which witnessed the crucifixion and the resurrection profit those only who bear their several crosses, who day by day

rise again with Christ, and who thus shew themselves worthy of an abode so holy. Those who say "the temple of the Lord, the temple of the Lord," should give ear to the words of the apostle: "ye are the temple of the Lord," and the Holy Ghost "dwelleth in you." Access to the courts of heaven is as easy from Britain as it is from Jerusalem; for "the kingdom of God is within you." Antony and the hosts of monks who are in Egypt, Mesopotamia, Pontus, Cappadocia, and Armenia, have never seen Jerusalem: and the door of Paradise is opened for them at a distance from it. The blessed Hilarion, though a native of and a dweller in Palestine, only set eyes on Jerusalem for a single day, not wishing on the one hand when he was so near to neglect the holy places, nor yet on the other to appear to confine God within local limits. From the time of Hadrian to the reign of Constantine—a period of about one hundred and eighty years—the spot which had witnessed the resurrection was occupied by a figure of Jupiter; while on the rock where the cross had stood, a marble statue of Venus was set up by the heathen and became an object of worship. The original persecutors, indeed, supposed that by polluting our holy places they would deprive us of our faith in the passion and in the resurrection. Even my own Bethlehem, as it now is, that most venerable spot in the whole world of which the psalmist sings: "the truth hath sprung out of the earth," was overshadowed by a grove of Tammuz, that is of Adonis; and in the very cave where the infant Christ had uttered His earliest cry lamentation was made for the paramour of Venus.

4. Why, you will say, do I make these remote allusions? To assure you that nothing is lacking to your faith although you have not seen Jerusalem and that I am none the better for living where I do. Be assured that, whether you dwell here or elsewhere, a like recompense is in store for your good works with our Lord. Indeed, if I am frankly to express my own feelings, when I take into consideration your vows and the earnestness with which you have renounced the world, I hold that as long as you live in the country one place is as good as another. Forsake cities and their crowds, live on a small patch of ground, seek Christ in solitude, pray on the mount alone with Jesus, keep near to holy places: keep out of cities, I say, and you will never lose your vocation. My advice concerns not bishops, presbyters, or the clergy, for these have a different duty. I am speaking only to a monk who having been a man of note in the world has laid the price of his possessions at the apostles' feet, to shew men that they must trample on their money, and has resolved to live a life of loneliness and seclusion and always to continue to reject what he has once rejected. Had the scenes of the Passion and of the Resurrection been elsewhere than in a populous city with court and garrison, with prostitutes, playactors, and buf-

foons, and with the medley of persons usually found in such centres; or had the crowds which thronged it been composed of monks; then a city would be a desirable abode for those who have embraced the monastic life. But, as things are, it would be the height of folly first to renounce the world, to forswear one's country, to forsake cities, to profess one's self a monk; and then to live among still greater numbers the same kind of life that you would have lived in your own country. Men rush here from all quarters of the world, the city is filled with people of every race, and so great is the throng of men and women that here you will have to tolerate in its full dimensions an evil from which you desired to flee when you found it partially developed elsewhere.

5. Since you ask me as a brother in what path you should walk, I will be open with you. If you wish to take duty as a presbyter, and are attracted by the work or dignity which falls to the lot of a bishop, live in cities and walled towns, and by so doing turn the salvation of others into the profit of your own soul. But if you desire to be in deed what you are in name—a monk, that is, one who lives alone, what have you to do with cities which are the homes not of solitaries but of crowds? Every mode of life has its own exponents. For instance, let Roman generals imitate men like Camillus, Fabricius, Regulus, and Scipio. Let philosophers take for models Pythagoras, Socrates, Plato, and Aristotle. Let poets strive to rival Homer, Virgil, Menander, and Terence. Let writers of history follow Thucydides, Sallust, Herodotus and Livy. Let orators find masters in Lysias, the Gracchi, Demosthenes, and Tully. And, to come to our own case, let bishops and presbyters take for their examples the apostles or their companions; and as they hold the rank which these once held, let them endeavour to exhibit the same excellence. And last of all let us monks take as the patterns which we are to follow the lives of Paul, of Antony, of Julian, of Hilarion, of the Macarii. And to go back to the authority of scripture, we have our masters in Elijah and Elisha, and our leaders in the sons of the prophets; who lived in fields and solitary places and made themselves tents by the waters of Jordan. The sons of Rechab too are of the number who drank neither wine nor strong drink and who abode in tents; men whom God's voice praises through Jeremiah, and to whom a promise is made that there shall never be wanting a man of their stock to stand before God. This is probably what is meant by the title of the seventy-first psalm: "of the sons of Jonadab and of those who were first led into captivity." The person intended is Jonadab the son of Rechab who is described in the book of Kings as having gone up into the chariot of Jehu. His sons having always lived in tents until at last (owing to the inroads made by the Chaldean army) they were forced to come into Jerusalem, are described as being the first to undergo captivity; because after the

freedom of their lonely life they found confinement in a city as bad as imprisonment.

6. Since you are not wholly independent but are bound to a wife who is your sister in the Lord, I entreat you—whether here or there—that you will avoid large gatherings, visits official and complimentary, and social parties, indulgences all of which tend to enchain the soul. Let your food be coarse—say cabbage and pulse—and do not take it until evening. Sometimes as a great delicacy you may have some small fish. He who longs for Christ and feeds upon the true bread cares little for dainties which must be transmuted into ordure. Food that you cannot taste when once it has passed your gullet might as well be—so far as you are concerned—bread and pulse. You have my books against Jovinian which speak yet more largely of despising the appetite and the palate. Let some holy volume be ever in your hand. Pray constantly, and bowing down your body lift up your mind to the Lord. Keep frequent vigils and sleep often on an empty stomach. Avoid tittle-tattle and all self-laudation. Flee from wheedling flatterers as from open enemies. Distribute with your own hand provisions to alleviate the miseries of the poor and of the brethren. With your own hands, I say, for good faith is rare among men. You do not believe what I say? Think of Judas and his bag. Seek not a lowly garb for a swelling soul. Avoid the society of men of the world, especially if they are in power. Why need you look again on things contempt for which has made you a monk? Above all let your sister hold aloof from married ladies. And, if women round her wear silk dresses and gems while she is meanly attired, let her neither fret nor congratulate herself. For by so doing she will either regret her resolution or sow the seeds of pride. If you are already famed as a faithful steward of your own substance, do not take other people's money to give away. You understand what I mean, for the Lord has given you understanding in all things. Be simple as a dove and lay snares for no man: but be cunning as a serpent and let no man lay snares for you. For a Christian who allows others to deceive him is almost at much at fault as one who tries to deceive others. If a man talks to you always or nearly always about money (except it be about alms-giving, a topic which is open to all) treat him as a broker rather than a monk. Besides food and clothing and things manifestly necessary give no man anything; for dogs must not eat the children's bread.

7. The true temple of Christ is the believer's soul; adorn this, clothe it, offer gifts to it, welcome Christ in it. What use are walls blazing with jewels when Christ in His poor is in danger of perishing from hunger? Your possessions are no longer your own but a stewardship is entrusted to you. Remember Ananias and Sapphira who from fear of the future kept what was their own, and be

careful for your part not rashly to squander what is Christ's. Do not, that is, by an error of judgment give the property of the poor to those who are not poor; lest, as a wise man has told us, charity prove the death of charity. Look not upon

Gay trappings or a Cato's empty name.

In the words of Persius, God says:—

I know thy thoughts and read thine inmost soul.

To be a Christian is the great thing, not merely to seem one. And somehow or other those please the world most who please Christ least. In speaking thus I am not like the sow lecturing Minerva; but, as a friend warns a friend, so I warn you before you embark on your new course. I would rather fail in ability than in will to serve you; for my wish is that where I have fallen you may keep your footing.

8. It is with much pleasure that I have read the book which you have sent to me containing your wise and eloquent defence of the emperor Theodosius; and your arrangement of the subject has particularly pleased me. While in the earlier chapters you surpass others, in the latter you surpass yourself. Your style is terse and neat; it has all the purity of Tully, and yet it is packed with meaning. For, as someone has said, that speech is a failure of which men only praise the diction. You have been successful in preserving both sequence of subjects and logical connexion. Whatever sentence one takes, it is always a conclusion to what goes before or an introduction to what follows. Theodosius is fortunate in having a Christian orator like you to plead his cause. You have made his purple illustrious and have consecrated for future ages his useful laws. Go on and prosper, for, if such be your first ventures in the field, what will you not do when you become a trained soldier? Oh! that it were mine to conduct a genius like you, not (as the poets sing) through the Aonian mountains and the peaks of Helicon but through Zion and Tabor and the high places of Sinai. If I might teach you what I have learned myself and might pass on to you the mystic rolls of the prophets, then might we give birth to something such as Greece with all her learning could not shew.

9. Hear me, therefore, my fellow-servant, my friend, my brother; give ear for a moment that I may tell you how you are to walk in the holy scriptures. All that we read in the divine books, while glistening and shining without, is yet far sweeter within. "He who desires to eat the kernel must first break the nut." "Open thou mine eyes," says David, "that I may behold wondrous things out of thy law." Now, if so great a prophet confesses that he is in the darkness of ignorance; how deep, think you, must be the night of misapprehension with which we, mere babes and unweaned infants, are enveloped! Now this veil rests

not only on the face of Moses, but on the evangelists and the apostles as well. To the multitudes the Saviour spoke only in parables and, to make it clear that His words had a mystical meaning, said:—"he that hath ears to hear, let him hear." Unless all things that are written are opened by Him "who hath the key of David, who openeth and no man shutteth, and shutteth and no man openeth," no one can undo the lock or set them before you. If only you had the foundation which He alone can give; nay, if even His fingers were but passed over your work; there would be nothing finer than your volumes, nothing more learned, nothing more attractive, nothing more Latin.

10. Tertullian is packed with meaning but his style is rugged and uncouth. The blessed Cyprian like a fountain of pure water flows softly and sweetly but, as he is taken up with exhortations to virtue and with the troubles consequent on persecution, he has nowhere discussed the divine scriptures. Victorinus, although he has the glory of a martyr's crown, yet cannot express what he knows. Lactantius has a flow of eloquence worthy of Tully: would that he had been as ready to teach our doctrines as he was to pull down those of others! Arnobius is lengthy and unequal, and often confused from not making a proper division of his subject. That reverend man Hilary gains in height from his Gallic buskin; yet, adorned as he is with the flowers of Greek rhetoric, he sometimes entangles himself in long periods and offers by no means easy reading to the less learned brethren. I say nothing of other writers whether dead or living; others will hereafter judge them both for good and for evil.

11. I will come to yourself, my fellow-mystic, my companion, and my friend; my friend, I say, though not yet personally known: and I will ask you not to suspect a flatterer in one so intimate. Better that you should think me mistaken or led astray by affection than that you should hold me capable of fawning on a friend. You have a great intellect and an inexhaustible store of language, your diction is fluent and pure, your fluency and purity are mingled with wisdom. Your head is clear and all your senses keen. Were you to add to this wisdom and eloquence a careful study and knowledge of scripture, I should soon see you holding our citadel against all comers; you would go up with Joab upon the roof of Zion, and sing upon the housetops what you had learned in the secret chambers. Gird up, I pray you, gird up your loins. As Horace says:—

Life hath no gifts for men except they toil.

Shew yourself as much a man of note in the church, as you were before in the senate. Provide for yourself riches which you may spend daily yet they will not fail. Provide them while you are still strong and while as yet your head has no gray hairs: before, in the words of Virgil,

Diseases creep on you, and gloomy age,
And pain, and cruel death's inclemency.

I am not content with mediocrity for you: I desire all that you do to be of the highest excellence.

How heartily I have welcomed the reverend presbyter Vigilantius, his own lips will tell you better than this letter. Why he has so soon left us and started afresh I cannot say; and, indeed, I do not wish to hurt anyone's feelings. Still, mere passer-by as he was, in haste to continue his journey, I managed to keep him back until I had given him a taste of my friendship for you. Thus you can learn from him what you want to know about me. Kindly salute your reverend sister and fellow-servant, who with you fights the good fight in the Lord.

LETTER LIX. TO MARCELLA

An answer to five questions put to Jerome by Marcella in a letter not preserved. The questions are as follows.

(1) What are the things which eye hath not seen nor ear heard (1 Cor. ii. 9)? Jerome answers that they are spiritual things which as such can only be spiritually discerned.

(2) Is it not a mistake to identify the sheep and the goats of Christ's parable (Matt. xxv. 31 sqq.) with Christians and heathens? Are they not rather the good and the bad? For an answer to this question Jerome refers Marcella to his treatise against Jovinian (II. S:S:18–23).

(3) Paul says that some shall be "alive and remain unto the coming of the Lord;" and that they shall be "caught up to meet the Lord in the air" (1 Thess. iv. 15, 17). Are we to suppose this assumption to be corporeal and that those assumed will escape death? Yes, Jerome answers, but their bodies will be glorified.

(4) How is John xx. 17, "touch me not," to be reconciled with Matt. xxviii. 9, "they came and held him by the feet"? In the one case, Jerome replies, Mary Magdalen failed to recognize the divinity of Jesus; in the other the women recognized it. Accordingly they were admitted to a privilege which was denied to her.

(5) Was the risen Christ before His ascension present only with the disciples, or was He in heaven and elsewhere as well? The latter according to Jerome is the true doctrine. "The Divine Nature," he writes, "exists everywhere in its entirety. Christ, therefore, was at one and the same time with the apostles and with the angels; in the Father and in the uttermost parts of the sea. So

afterwards he was with Thomas in India, with Peter at Rome, with Paul in Illyricum, with Titus in Crete, with Andrew in Achaia." The date of the letter is a.d. 395 or a.d. 396.

LETTER LX. TO HELIODORUS

One of Jerome's finest letters, written to console his old friend, Heliodorus, now Bp. of Altinum, for the loss of his nephew Nepotian who had died of fever a short time previously. Jerome tries to soothe his friend's grief (1) by contrasting pagan despair or resignation with Christian hope, (2) by an eulogy of the departed both as man and presbyter, and (3) by a review of the evils which then beset the Empire and from which, as he contended, Nepotian had been removed. The letter is marked throughout with deep and sincere feeling. Its date is 396 a.d.

1. Small wits cannot grapple large themes but venturing beyond their strength fail in the very attempt; and, the greater a subject is, the more completely is he overwhelmed who cannot find words to unfold its grandeur. Nepotian who was mine and yours and ours—or rather who was Christ's and because Christ's all the more ours—has forsaken us his elders so that we are smitten with pangs of regret and overcome with a grief which is past bearing. We supposed him our heir, yet now his corpse is all that is ours. For whom shall my intellect now labour? Whom shall my poor letters desire to please? Where is he, the impeller of my work, whose voice was sweeter than a swan's last song? My mind is dazed, my hand trembles, a mist covers my eyes, stammering seizes my tongue. Whatever my words, they seem as good as unspoken seeing that he no longer hears them. My very pen seems to feel his loss, my very wax tablet looks dull and sad; the one is covered with rust, the other with mould. As often as I try to express myself in words and to scatter the flowers of this encomium upon his tomb, my eyes fill with tears, my grief returns, and I can think of nothing but his death. It was a custom in former days for children over the dead bodies of their parents publicly to proclaim their praises and (as when pathetic songs are sung) to draw tears from the eyes and sighs from the breasts of those who heard them. But in our case, behold, the order of things is changed: to deal us this blow nature has forfeited her rights. For the respect which the young man should have paid to his elders, we his elders are paying to him.

2. What shall I do then? Shall I join my tears to yours? The apostle forbids me for he speaks of dead Christians as "them which are asleep." So too in the

gospel the Lord says, "the damsel is not dead but sleepeth," and Lazarus when he is raised from the dead is said to have been asleep. No, I will be glad and rejoice that "speedily he was taken away lest that wickedness should alter his understanding" for "his soul pleased the Lord." But though I am loth to give way and combat my feelings, tears flow down my cheeks, and in spite of the teachings of virtue and the hope of the resurrection a passion of regret crushes my too yielding mind. O death that dividest brothers knit together in love, how cruel, how ruthless thou art so to sunder them! "The Lord hath fetched a burning wind that cometh up from the wilderness: which hath dried thy veins and hath made thy well spring desolate." Thou didst swallow up our Jonah, but even in thy belly He still lived. Thou didst carry Him as one dead, that the world's storm might be stilled and our Nineveh saved by His preaching. He, yes He, conquered thee, He slew thee, that fugitive prophet who left His home, gave up His inheritance and surrendered his dear life into the hands of those who sought it. He it was who of old threatened thee in Hosea: "O death, I will be thy plagues; O grave, I will be thy destruction." By His death thou art dead; by His death we live. Thou hast swallowed up and thou art swallowed up. Whilst thou art smitten with a longing for the body assumed by Him, and whilst thy greedy jaws fancy it a prey, thy inward parts are wounded with hooked fangs.

3. To Thee, O Saviour Christ, do we Thy creatures offer thanks that, when Thou wast slain, Thou didst slay our mighty adversary. Before Thy coming was there any being more miserable than man who cowering at the dread prospect of eternal death did but receive life that he might perish! For "death reigned from Adam to Moses even over them that had not sinned after the similitude of Adam's transgression." If Abraham, Isaac, and Jacob be in hell, who can be in the kingdom of heaven? If Thy friends—even those who had not sinned themselves—were yet for the sins of another liable to the punishment of offending Adam, what must we think of those who have said in their hearts "There is no God;" who "are corrupt and abominable" in their self-will, and of whom it is said "they are gone out of the way, they are become unprofitable; there is none that doeth good, no not one"? Even if Lazarus is seen in Abraham's bosom and in a place of refreshment, still the lower regions cannot be compared with the kingdom of heaven. Before Christ's coming Abraham is in the lower regions: after Christ's coming the robber is in paradise. And therefore at His rising again "many bodies of the saints which slept arose, and were seen in the heavenly Jerusalem." Then was fulfilled the saying: "Awake thou that sleepest, and arise from the dead, and Christ shall give thee light." John the Baptist cries in the desert: "repent ye; for the kingdom of heaven is at

hand." For "from the days of John the Baptist the kingdom of heaven suffereth violence and the violent take it by force." The flaming sword that keeps the way of paradise and the cherubim that are stationed at its doors are alike quenched and unloosed by the blood of Christ. It is not surprising that this should be promised us in the resurrection: for as many of us as living in the flesh do not live after the flesh, have our citizenship in heaven, and while we are still here on earth we are told that "the kingdom of heaven is within us."

4. Moreover before the resurrection of Christ God was "known in Judah" only and "His name was great in Israel" alone. And they who knew Him were despite their knowledge dragged down to hell. Where in those days were the inhabitants of the globe from India to Britain, from the frozen zone of the North to the burning heat of the Atlantic ocean? Where were the countless peoples of the world? Where the great multitudes?

Unlike in tongue, unlike in dress and arms?

They were crushed like fishes and locusts, like flies and gnats. For apart from knowledge of his Creator every man is but a brute. But now the voices and writings of all nations proclaim the passion and the resurrection of Christ. I say nothing of the Jews, the Greeks, and the Romans, peoples which the Lord has dedicated to His faith by the title written on His cross. The immortality of the soul and its continuance after the dissolution of the body—truths of which Pythagoras dreamed, which Democritus refused to believe, and which Socrates discussed in prison to console himself for the sentence passed upon him—are now the familiar themes of Indian and of Persian, of Goth and of Egyptian. The fierce Bessians and the throng of skinclad savages who used to offer human sacrifices in honour of the dead have broken out of their harsh discord into the sweet music of the cross and Christ is the one cry of the whole world.

5. What can we do, my soul? Whither must we turn? What must we take up first? What must we pass over? Have you forgotten the precepts of the rhetoricians? Are you so preoccupied with grief, so overcome with tears, so hindered with sobs, that you forget all logical sequence? Where are the studies you have pursued from your childhood? Where is that saying of Anaxagoras and Telamon (which you have always commended) "I knew myself to have begotten a mortal"? I have read the books of Crantor which he wrote to soothe his grief and which Cicero has imitated. I have read the consolatory writings of Plato, Diogenes, Clitomachus, Carneades, Posidonius, who at different times strove by book or letter to lessen the grief of various persons. Consequently, were my own wit to dry up, it could be watered anew from the fountains which these have opened. They set before us examples without number; and particularly those of Pericles and of Socrates's pupil Xenophon. The former of

these after the loss of his two sons put on a garland and delivered a harangue; while the latter, on hearing when he was offering sacrifice that his son had been slain in war, is said to have laid down his garland; and then, on learning that he had fallen fighting bravely, is said to have put it on his head again. What shall I say of those Roman generals whose heroic virtues glitter like stars on the pages of Latin history? Pulvillus was dedicating the capitol when receiving the news of his son's sudden death, he gave orders that the funeral should take place without him. Lucius Paullus entered the city in triumph in the week which intervened between the funerals of his two sons. I pass over the Maximi, the Catos, the Galli, the Pisos, the Bruti, the Scaevolas, the Metelli, the Scauri, the Marii, the Crassi, the Marcelli, the Aufidii, men who shewed equal fortitude in sorrow and war, and whose bereavements Tully has set forth in his book Of consolation. I pass them over lest I should seem to have chosen the words and woes of others in preference to my own. Yet even these instances may suffice to ensure us mortification if our faith fails to surpass the achievements of unbelief.

6. Let me come then to my proper subject. I will not beat my breast with Jacob and with David for sons dying in the Law, but I will receive them rising again with Christ in the Gospel. The Jew's mourning is the Christian's joy. "Weeping may endure for a night but joy cometh in the morning." "The night is far spent, the day is at hand." Accordingly when Moses dies, mourning is made for him, but when Joshua is buried, it is without tears or funeral pomp. All that can be drawn from scripture on the subject of lamentation I have briefly set forth in the letter of consolation which I addressed to Paula at Rome. Now I must take another path to arrive at the same goal. Otherwise I shall seem to be walking anew in a track once beaten but now long disused.

7. We know indeed that our Nepotian is with Christ and that he has joined the choirs of the saints. What here with us he groped after on earth afar off and sought for to the best of his judgment, there he sees nigh at hand, so that he can say: "as we have heard so have we seen in the city of the Lord of hosts, in the city of our God." Still we cannot bear the feeling of his absence, and grieve, if not for him, for ourselves. The greater the happiness which he enjoys, the deeper the sorrow in which the loss of a blessing so great plunges us. The sisters of Lazarus could not help weeping for him, although they knew that he would rise again. And the Saviour himself—to shew that he possessed true human feeling—mourned for him whom He was about to raise. His apostle also, though he says: "I desire to depart and to be with Christ," and elsewhere "to me to live is Christ and to die is gain," thanks God that Epaphras (who had been "sick nigh unto death") has been given back to him that he might

not have sorrow upon sorrow. Words prompted not by the fear that springs of unbelief but by the passionate regret that comes of true affection. How much more deeply must you who were to Nepotian both uncle and bishop, (that is, a father both in the flesh and in the spirit), deplore the loss of one so dear, as though your heart were torn from you. Set a limit, I pray you, to your sorrow and remember the saying "in nothing overmuch." Bind up for a little while your wound and listen to the praises of one in whose virtue you have always delighted. Do not grieve that you have lost such a paragon: rejoice rather that he has once been yours. As on a small tablet men depict the configuration of the earth, so in this little scroll of mine you may see his virtues if not fully depicted at least sketched in outline. I beg that you will take the will for the performance.

8. The advice of the rhetoricians in such cases is that you should first search out the remote ancestors of the person to be eulogized and recount their exploits, and then come gradually to your hero; so as to make him more illustrious by the virtues of his forefathers, and to show either that he is a worthy successor of good men, or that he has conferred lustre upon a lineage in itself obscure. But as my duty is to sing the praises of the soul, I will not dwell upon those fleshly advantages which Nepotian for his part always despised. Nor will I boast of his family, that is of the good points belonging not to him but to others; for even those holy men Abraham and Isaac had for sons the sinners Ishmael and Esau. And on the other hand Jephthah who is reckoned by the apostle in the roll of the righteous is the son of a harlot. It is said "the soul that sinneth, it shall die." The soul therefore that has not sinned shall live. Neither the virtues nor the vices of parents are imputed to their children. God takes account of us only from the time when we are born anew in Christ. Paul, the persecutor of the church, who is in the morning the ravening wolf of Benjamin, in the evening "gave food," that is yields himself up to the sheep Ananias. Let us likewise reckon our Nepotian a crying babe and an untutored child who has been born to us in a moment fresh from the waters of Jordan.

9. Another would perhaps describe how for his salvation you left the east and the desert and how you soothed me your dearest comrade by holding out hopes of a return: and all this that you might save, if possible, both your sister, then a widow with one little child, or, should she reject your counsels, at any rate your sweet little nephew. It was of him that I once used the prophetic words: "though your little nephew cling to your neck." Another, I say, would relate how while Nepotian was still in the service of the court, beneath his uniform and his brilliantly white linen, his skin was chafed with sackcloth; how, while standing before the powers of this world, his lips were discoloured

with fasting; how still in the uniform of one master he served another; and how he wore the sword-belt only that he might succour widows and wards, the afflicted and the unhappy. For my part I dislike men to delay the complete dedication of themselves to God. When I read of the centurion Cornelius that he was a just man I immediately hear of his baptism.

10. Still we may approve these things as the swathing bands of an infant faith. He who has been a loyal soldier under a strange banner is sure to deserve the laurel when he comes to serve his own king. When Nepotian laid aside his baldrick and changed his dress, he bestowed upon the poor all the pay that he had received. For he had read the words: "if thou wilt be perfect, sell that thou hast, and give to the poor and follow me," and again: "ye cannot serve two masters, God and Mammon." He kept nothing for himself but a common tunic and cloak to cover him and to keep out the cold. Made in the fashion of his province his attire was not remarkable either for elegance or for squalor. He burned daily to make his way to the monasteries of Egypt, or to visit the communities of Mesopotamia, or at least to live a lonely life in the Dalmatian islands, separated from the mainland only by the strait of Altinum. But he had not the heart to forsake his episcopal uncle in whom he beheld a pattern of many virtues and from whom he could take lessons without going abroad. In one and the same person he both found a monk to imitate and a bishop to revere. What so often happens did not happen here. Constant intimacy did not produce familiarity, nor did familiarity breed contempt. He revered him as a father and every day admired him for some new virtue. To be brief, he became a clergyman, and after passing through the usual stages was ordained a presbyter. Good Jesus! how he sighed and groaned! how he fasted and fled the eyes of all! For the first and only time he was angry with his uncle, complaining that the burthen laid upon him was too heavy for him and that his youth unfitted him for the priesthood. But the more he struggled against it, the more he drew to himself the hearts of all: his refusal did but prove him worthy of an office which he was reluctant to assume, and all the more worthy because he declared himself unworthy. We too in our day have our Timothy; we too have seen that wisdom which is as good as gray hairs; our Moses has chosen an elder whom he has known to be an elder indeed. Nepotian regarded the clerical state less as an honour than a burthen. He made it his first care to silence envy by humility, and his next to give no cause for scandal that such as assailed his youth might marvel at his continence. He helped the poor, visited the sick, stirred men up to hospitality, soothed them with soft words, rejoiced with those who rejoiced and wept with those who wept. He was a staff to the blind, food to the hungry, hope to the dejected, consolation to the bereaved. Each

single virtue was as conspicuous in him as if he possessed no other. Among his fellow-presbyters while ever foremost in work, he was ever satisfied with the lowest place. Any good that he did he ascribed to his uncle: but if the result did not correspond to his expectations, he would say that his uncle knew nothing of it, that it was his own mistake. In public he recognized him as a bishop; at home he looked upon him as a father. The seriousness of his disposition was mitigated by a cheerful expression. But while his laughter was joyous it was never loud. Christ's virgins and widows he honoured as mothers and exhorted as sisters "with all purity." When he returned home he used to leave the clergyman outside and to give himself over to the hard rule of a monk. Frequent in supplication and watchful in prayer he would offer his tears not to man but to God. His fasts he regulated—as a driver does the pace of his horses—according to the weariness or vigour of his body. When at his uncle's table he would just taste what was set before him, so as to avoid superstition and yet to preserve self-control. In conversing at entertainments his habit was to propose some topic from scripture, to listen modestly, to answer diffidently, to support the right, to refute the wrong, but both without bitterness; to instruct his opponent rather than to vanquish him. Such was the ingenuous modesty which adorned his youth that he would frankly confess from what sources his several arguments came; and in this way, while disclaiming a reputation for learning, he came to be held most learned. This he would say is the opinion of Tertullian, that of Cyprian; this of Lactantius, that of Hilary; to this effect speaks Minucius Felix, thus Victorinus, after this manner Arnobius. Myself too he would sometimes quote, for he loved me because of my intimacy with his uncle. Indeed by constant reading and long-continued meditation he had made his breast a library of Christ.

11. How often in letters from beyond the sea he urged me to write something to him! How often he reminded me of the man in the gospel who sought help by night and of the widow who importuned the cruel judge! And when I silently ignored his request and made my petitioner blush by blushing to reply, he put forward his uncle to enforce his suit, knowing that as the boon was for another he would more readily ask it, and that as I held his episcopal office in respect he would more easily obtain it. Accordingly I did what he wished and in a brief essay dedicated our mutual friendship to everlasting remembrance. On receiving this Nepotian boasted that he was richer than Croesus and wealthier than Darius. He held it in his hands, devoured it with his eyes, kept it in his bosom, repeated it with his lips. And often when he unrolled it upon his couch, he fell asleep with the cherished page upon his breast. When a stranger came or a friend, he rejoiced to let them know my witness to him.

The deficiencies of my little book he made good by careful punctuation and varied emphasis, so that when it was read aloud it was always he not I who seemed to please or to displease. Whence came such zeal, if not from the love of God? Whence came such untiring study of Christ's law, if not from a yearning for Him who gave it? Let others add coin to coin till their purses are chock-full; let others demean themselves to sponge on married ladies; let them be richer as monks than they were as men of the world; let them possess wealth in the service of a poor Christ such as they never had in the service of a rich devil; let the church lose breath at the opulence of men who in the world were beggars. Our Nepotian spurns gold and begs only for written books. But while he despises himself in the flesh and walks abroad more splendid than ever in his poverty, he still seeks out everything that may adorn the church.

12. In comparison with what has gone before what I am now about to say may appear trivial, but even in trifles the same spirit makes itself manifest. For as we admire the Creator not only as the framer of heaven and earth, of sun and ocean, of elephants, camels, horses, oxen, pards, bears, and lions; but also as the maker of the most tiny creatures, ants, gnats, flies, worms, and the like, whose shapes we know better than their names, and as in all alike we revere the same creative skill; so the mind that is given to Christ shews the same earnestness in things of small as of great importance, knowing that it must render an account of every idle word. Nepotian took pains to keep the altar bright, the church walls free from soot and the pavement duly swept. He saw that the doorkeeper was constantly at his post, that the doorhangings were in their places, the sanctuary clean and the vessels shining. The careful reverence that he shewed to every rite led him to neglect no duty small or great. Whenever you looked for him in church you found him there.

In Quintus Fabius antiquity admired a nobleman and the author of a history of Rome, yet his paintings gained him more renown than his writings. Our own Bezaleel also and Hiram, the son of a Tyrian woman, are spoken of in scripture as filled with wisdom and the spirit of God because they framed, the one the furniture of the tabernacle, the other that of the temple. For, as it is with fertile tillage-fields and rich plough-lands which at times go out into redundant growths of stalk or ear, so is it with distinguished talents and a mind filled with virtue. They are sure to overflow into elegant and varied accomplishments. Accordingly among the Greeks we hear of a philosopher who used to boast that everything he wore down to his cloak and ring was made by himself. We may pass the same eulogy on our friend, for he adorned both the basilicas of the church and the halls of the martyrs with sketches of flowers, foliage, and vine-tendrils, so that everything attractive in the church, whether made so by its position or by its appearance, bore witness to the labour and zeal of the presbyter set over it.

13. Go on blessed in thy goodness! What kind of ending should we expect after such a beginning! Ah! hapless plight of mortal men and vanity of all life that is not lived in Christ! Why, O my words, do you shrink back? Why do you shift and turn? I fear to come to the end, as if I could put off his death or make his life longer. "All flesh is as grass and all the glory of man as the flower of grass." Where now are that handsome face and dignified figure with which as with a fair garment his beautiful soul was clothed? The lily began to wither, alas! when the south wind blew, and the purple violet slowly faded into paleness. Yet while he burned with fever and while the fire of sickness was drying up the fountains of his veins, gasping and weary he still tried to comfort his sorrowing uncle. His countenance shone with gladness, and while all around him wept he and he only smiled. He flung aside his cloak, put out his hand, saw what others failed to see, and even tried to rise that he might welcome new comers. You would have thought that he was starting on a journey instead of dying and that in place of leaving all his friends behind him he was merely passing from some to others. Tears roll down my cheeks and, however much I steel my mind, I cannot disguise the grief that I feel. Who could suppose that at such an hour he would remember his intimacy with me, and that while he struggled for life he would recall the sweetness of study? Yet grasping his uncle's hand he said to him: "Send this tunic that I wore in the service of Christ to my dear friend, my father in age, but my brother in office, and transfer the affection hitherto claimed by your nephew to one who is as dear to you as he is to me." With these words he passed away holding his uncle's hand and with my name upon his lips.

14. I know how unwilling you were to prove the affection of your people at such a cost, and that you would have preferred to win your countrymen's love while retaining your happiness. Such expressions of feeling, pleasant as they are when all goes well, are doubly welcome in time of sorrow. All Altinum, all Italy mourned Nepotian. The earth received his body; his soul was given back to Christ. You lost a nephew, the church a priest. He who should have followed you went before you. To the office which you held, he in the judgment of all deserved to succeed. And so one family has had the honour of producing two bishops, the first to be congratulated because he has held the office, the second to be lamented because he has been taken away too soon to hold it. Plato thinks that a wise man's whole life ought to be a meditation of death; and philosophers praise the sentiment and extol it to the skies. But much more full of power are the words of the apostle: "I die daily through your glory." For to

have an ideal is one thing, to realize it another. It is one thing to live so as to die, another to die so as to live. The sage and Christian must both of them die: but the one always dies out of his glory, the other into it. Therefore we also should consider beforehand the end which must one day overtake us and which, whether we wish it or not, cannot be very far distant. For though we should live nine hundred years or more, as men did before the deluge, and though the days of Methuselah should be granted us, yet that long space of time, when once it should have passed away and come to an end, would be as nothing. For to the man who has lived ten years and to him who has lived a thousand, when once the end of life comes and death's inexorable doom, all the past whether long or short is just the same; except that the older a man is, the heavier is the load of sin that he has to take with him.

First hapless mortals lose from out their life
The fairest days: disease and age come next;
And lastly cruel death doth claim his prey.

The poet Naevius too says that

Mortals must many woes perforce endure.

Accordingly antiquity has feigned that Niobe because of her much weeping was turned to stone and that other women were metamorphosed into beasts. Hesiod also bewails men's birthdays and rejoices in their deaths, and Ennius wisely says:

The mob has one advantage o'er its king:
For it may weep while tears for him are shame.

If a king may not weep, neither may a bishop; indeed a bishop has still less license than a king. For the king rules over unwilling subjects, the bishop over willing ones. The king compels submission by terror; the bishop exercises lordship by becoming a servant. The king guards men's bodies till they die; the bishop saves their souls for life eternal. The eyes of all are turned upon you. Your house is set on a watchtower; your life fixes for others the limits of their self-control. Whatever you do, all think that they may do the same. Do not so commit yourself that those who seek ground for cavil may be thought to have rightly assailed you, or that those who are eager to imitate you may be forced to do wrong. Overcome as much as you can—nay even more than you can—the sensitiveness of your mind and check the copious flow of your tears. Else your deep affection for your nephew may be construed by unbelievers as indicating despair of God. You must regretim not as dead but as absent. You must seem to be looking for him rather than have lost him.

15. But why do I try to heal a sorrow which has already, I suppose, been assuaged by time and reason? Why do I not rather unfold to you—they are not

far to seek—the miseries of our rulers and the calamities of our time? He who has lost the light of life is not so much to be pitied as he is to be congratulated who has escaped from such great evils. Constantius, the patron of the Arian heresy, was hurrying to do battle with his enemy when he died at the village of Mopsus and to his great vexation left the empire to his foe. Julian , the betrayer of his own soul, the murderer of a Christian army, felt in Media the hand of the Christ whom he had previously denied in Gaul. Desiring to annex new territories to Rome, he did but lose annexations previously made. Jovian had but just tasted the sweets of sovereignty when a coal-fire suffocated him: a good instance of the transitoriness of human power. Valentinian died of a broken blood vessel, the land of his birth laid waste, and his country unavenged. His brother Valens defeated in Thrace by the Goths, was buried where he died. Gratian, betrayed by his army and refused admittance by the cities on his line of march, became the laughing-stock of his foe; and your walls, Lyons, still bear the marks of that bloody hand. Valentinian was yet a youth—I may say, a mere boy—when, after flight and exile and the recovery of his power by bloodshed, he was put to death not far from the city which had witnessed his brother's end. And not only so but his lifeless body was gibbeted to do him shame. What shall I say of Procopius, of Maximus, of Eugenius, who while they held sovereign sway were a terror to the nations, yet stood one and all as prisoners in the presence of their conquerors, and—cruellest wound of all to the great and powerful—felt the pang of an ignominious slavery before they fell by the edge of the sword.

16. Some one may say: such is the lot of kings:
The lightning ever smites the mountain-tops.

I will come therefore to persons of private position, and in speaking of these I will not go farther back than the last two years. In fact I will content myself—omitting all others—with recounting the respective fates of three recent consulars. Abundantius is a beggared exile at Pityus. The head of Rufinus has been carried on a pike to Constantinople, and his severed hand has begged alms from door to door to shame his insatiable greed. Timasius, hurled suddenly from a position of the highest rank thinks it an escape that he is allowed to live in obscurity at Assa. I am describing not the misfortunes of an unhappy few but the thread upon which human fortunes as a whole depend. I shudder when I think of the catastrophes of our time. For twenty years and more the blood of Romans has been shed daily between Constantinople and the Julian Alps. Scythia, Thrace, Macedonia, Dardania, Dacia, Thessaly, Achaia, Epirus, Dalmatia, the Pannonias—each and all of these have been sacked and pillaged and plundered by Goths and Sarmatians, Quades and Alans, Huns and Vandals and Marchmen. How many of God's matrons and virgins, virtuous and noble ladies, have been made the sport of these brutes! Bishops have been made captive, priests and those in minor orders have been put to death. Churches have been overthrown, horses have been stalled by the altars of Christ, the relics of martyrs have been dug up.

Mourning and fear abound on every side
And death appears in countless shapes and forms.

The Roman world is falling: yet we hold up our heads instead of bowing them. What courage, think you, have the Corinthians now, or the Athenians or the Lacedaemonians or the Arcadians, or any of the Greeks over whom the barbarians bear sway? I have mentioned only a few cities, but these once the capitals of no mean states. The East, it is true, seemed to be safe from all such evils: and if men were panic-stricken here, it was only because of bad news from other parts. But lo! in the year just gone by the wolves (no longer of Arabia but of the whole North) were let loose upon us from the remotest fastnesses of Caucasus and in a short time overran these great provinces. What a number of monasteries they captured! What many rivers they caused to run red with blood! They laid siege to Antioch and invested other cities on the Halys, the Cydnus, the Orontes, and the Euphrates. They carried off troops of captives. Arabia, Phenicia, Palestine and Egypt, in their terror fancied themselves already enslaved.

Had I a hundred tongues, a hundred lips,
A throat of iron and a chest of brass,
I could not tell men's countless sufferings.

And indeed it is not my purpose to write a history: I only wish to shed a few tears over your sorrows and mine. For the rest, to treat such themes as they deserve, Thucydides and Sallust would be as good as dumb.

17. Nepotian is happy who neither sees these things nor hears them. We are unhappy, for either we suffer ourselves or we see our brethren suffer. Yet we desire to live, and regard those beyond the reach of these evils as miserable rather than blessed. We have long felt that God is angry, yet we do not try to appease Him. It is our sins which make the barbarians strong, it is our vices which vanquish Rome's soldiers: and, as if there were here too little material for carnage, civil wars have made almost greater havoc among us than the swords of foreign foes. Miserable must those Israelites have been compared with whom Nebuchadnezzar was called God's servant. Unhappy too are we who are so displeasing to God that He uses the fury of the barbarians to execute His wrath against us. Still when Hezekiah repented, one hundred and eighty-five thousand Assyrians were destroyed in one night by a single angel.

When Jehosaphat sang the praises of the Lord, the Lord gave His worshipper the victory. Again when Moses fought against Amalek, it was not with the sword but with prayer that he prevailed. Therefore, if we wish to be lifted up, we must first prostrate ourselves. Alas! for our shame and folly reaching even to unbelief! Rome's army, once victor and lord of the world, now trembles with terror at the sight of the foe and accepts defeat from men who cannot walk afoot and fancy themselves dead if once they are unhorsed. We do not understand the prophet's words: "One thousand shall flee at the rebuke of one." We do not cut away the causes of the disease, as we must do to remove the disease itself. Else we should soon see the enemies' arrows give way to our javelins, their caps to our helmets, their palfreys to our chargers.

18. But I have gone beyond the office of a consoler, and while forbidding you to weep for one dead man I have myself mourned the dead of the whole world. Xerxes the mighty king who rased mountains and filled up seas, looking from high ground upon the untold host, the countless army before him, is said to have wept at the thought that in a hundred years not one of those whom he then saw would be alive. Oh! if we could but get up into a watch-tower so high that from it we might behold the whole earth spread out under our feet, then I would shew you the wreck of a world, nation warring against nation and kingdom in collision with kingdom; some men tortured, others put to the sword, others swallowed up by the waves, some dragged away into slavery; here a wedding, there a funeral; men born here, men dying there; some living in affluence, others begging their bread; and not the army of Xerxes, great as that was, but all the inhabitants of the world alive now but destined soon to pass away. Language is inadequate to a theme so vast and all that I can say must fall short of the reality.

19. Let us return then to ourselves and coming down from the skies let us look for a few moments upon what more nearly concerns us. Are you conscious, I would ask, of the stages of your growth? Can you fix the time when you became a babe, a boy, a youth, an adult, an old man? Every day we are changing, every day we are dying, and yet we fancy ourselves eternal. The very moments that I spend in dictation, in writing, in reading over what I write, and in correcting it, are so much taken from my life. Every dot that my secretary makes is so much gone from my allotted time. We write letters and reply to those of others, our missives cross the sea, and, as the vessel ploughs its furrow through wave after wave, the moments which we have to live vanish one by one. Our only gain is that we are thus knit together in the love of Christ. "Charity suffereth long and is kind; charity envieth not; charity vaunteth not itself, is not puffed up; beareth all things, believeth all things,

hopeth all things, endureth all things. Charity never faileth." It lives always in the heart, and thus our Nepotian though absent is still present, and widely sundered though we are has a hand to offer to each. Yes, in him we have a hostage for mutual charity. Let us then be joined together in spirit, let us bind ourselves each to each in affection and let us who have lost a son shew the same fortitude with which the blessed pope Chromatius bore the loss of a brother. Let every page that we write echo his name, let all our letters ring with it. If we can no longer clasp him to our hearts, let us hold him fast in memory; and if we can no longer speak with him, let us never cease to speak of him.

LETTER LXI. TO VIGILANTIUS

Vigilantius on his return to the West after his visit to Jerusalem (whither he had gone as the bearer of letters from Paulinus of Nola—see Letter LVIII. S:11.) had openly accused Jerome of a leaning to the heresy of Origen. Jerome now writes to him in the most severe tone repudiating the charge of Origenism and fastening upon his opponent those of ignorance and blasphemy. He singles out for especial reprobation Vigilantius's explanation of the stone cut out without hands' in Daniel and urges him to repent of his sins in which case he will have as much chance of forgiveness as the devil has according to Origen! The letter is often referred to as showing Jerome's way of dealing with Origen's works. Jerome subsequently wrote a refutation of Vigilantius's work, of all his controversial writings the most violent and the least reasonable. See the translation of it in this volume. See also Letter CIX. The date of this letter is 396 a.d.

1. Since you have refused to believe your own ears, I might justly decline to satisfy you by a letter; for, if you have failed to credit the living voice, it is not likely that you will give way to a written paper. But, since Christ has shown us in Himself a pattern of perfect humility, bestowing a kiss upon His betrayer and receiving the robber's repentance upon the cross, I tell you now when absent as I have told you already when present, that I read and have read Origen only as I read Apollinaris, or other writers whose books in some things the Church does not receive. I by no means say that everything contained in such books is to be condemned, but I admit that there are things in them deserving of censure. Still, as it is my task and study by reading many authors to cull different flowers from as large a number as possible, not so much making it an object to prove all things as to choose what are good. I take up many writers that from the many I may learn many things; according to that which is

written "reading all things, holding fast those that are good." Hence I am much surprised that you have tried to fasten upon me the doctrines of Origen, of whose mistaken teaching on many points you are up to the present altogether unaware. Am I a heretic? Why pray then do heretics dislike me so? And are you orthodox, you who either against your convictions and the words of your own mouth signed unwillingly and are consequently a prevaricator, or else signed deliberately and are consequently a heretic? You have taken no account of Egypt; you have relinquished all those provinces where numbers plead freely and openly for your sect; and you have singled out me for assault, me who not only censure but publicly condemn all doctrines that are contrary to the church.

2. Origen is a heretic, true; but what does that take from me who do not deny that on very many points he is heretical? He has erred concerning the resurrection of the body, he has erred concerning the condition of souls, he has erred by supposing it possible that the devil may repent, and—an error more important than these—he has declared in his commentary upon Isaiah that the Seraphim mentioned by the prophet are the divine Son and the Holy Ghost. If I did not allow that he has erred or if I did not daily anathematize his errors I should be partaker of his fault. For while we receive what is good in his writings we must on no account bind ourselves to accept also what is evil. Still in many passages he has interpreted the scriptures well, has explained obscure places in the prophets, and has brought to light very great mysteries, both in the old and in the new testament. If then I have taken over what is good in him and have either cut away or altered or ignored what is evil, am I to be regarded as guilty on the score that through my agency those who read Latin receive the good in his writings without knowing anything of the bad? If this be a crime the confessor Hilary must be convicted; for he has rendered from Greek into Latin Origen's Explanation of the Psalms and his Homilies on Job. Eusebius of Vercellae, who witnessed a like confession, must also be held in fault; for he has translated into our tongue the Commentaries upon all the Psalms of his heretical namesake, omitting however the unsound portions and rendering only those parts which are profitable. I say nothing of Victorinus of Petavium and others who have merely followed and expanded Origen in their explanation of the scriptures. Were I to do so, I might seem less anxious to defend myself than to find for myself companions in guilt. I will come to your own case: Why do you keep copies of his treatises on Job? In these, while arguing against the devil and concerning the stars and heavens, he has said certain things which the Church does not receive. Is it for you alone, with that very wise head of yours, to pass sentence upon all writers Greek and Latin,

with a wave of your censor's wand to eject some from our libraries and to admit others, and as the whim takes you to pronounce me either a Catholic or a heretic? And am I to be forbidden to reject things which are wrong and to condemn what I have often condemned already? Read what I have written upon the epistle to the Ephesians, read my other works, particularly my commentary upon Ecclesiastes, and you will clearly see that from my youth up I have never been terrified by any man's influence into acquiescence in heretical pravity.

3. It is no small gain to know your own ignorance. It is a man's wisdom to know his own measure, that he may not be led away at the instigation of the devil to make the whole world a witness of his incapacity. You are bent, I suppose, on magnifying yourself and boast in your own country that I found myself unable to answer your eloquence and that I dreaded in you the sharp satire of a Chrysippus. Christian modesty holds me back and I do not wish to lay open the retirement of my poor cell with biting words. Otherwise I should soon shew up all your bravery and your parade of triumph. But these I leave to others either to talk of or to laugh at; while for my own part as a Christian speaking to a Christian I beseech you my brother not to pretend to know more than you do, lest your pen may proclaim your innocence and simplicity, or at any rate those qualities of which I say nothing but which, though you do not see them in yourself others see in you. For then you will give everyone reason to laugh at your folly. From your earliest childhood you have been taught other lessons and have been used to a different kind of schooling. One and the same person can hardly be a tester both of gold coins on the counter and also of the scriptures, or be a connoisseur of wines and an adept in expounding prophets or apostles. As for me, you tear me limb from limb, our reverend brother Oceanus you charge with heresy, you dislike the judgment of the presbyters Vincent and Paulinian, and our brother Eusebius also displeases you. You alone are to be our Cato, the most eloquent of the Roman race, and you wish us to accept what you say as the words of prudence herself. Pray call to mind the day when I preached on the resurrection and on the reality of the risen body, and when you jumped up beside me and clapped your hands and stamped your feet and applauded my orthodoxy. Now, however, that you have taken to sea travelling the stench of the bilge water has affected your head, and you have called me to mind only as a heretic. What can I do for you? I believed the letters of the reverend presbyter Paulinus, and it did not occur to me that his judgment concerning you could be wrong. And although, the moment that you handed me the letter, I noticed a certain incoherency in your language, yet I fancied this due to want of culture and knowledge in you and not to an

unsettled brain. I do not censure the reverend writer who preferred, no doubt, in writing to me to keep back what he knew rather than to accuse in his missive one who was both under his patronage and entrusted with his letter; but I find fault with myself that I have rested in another's judgment rather than my own, and that, while my eyes saw one thing, I believed on the evidence of a scrap of paper something else than what I saw.

4. Wherefore cease to worry me and to overwhelm me with your scrolls. Spare at least your money with which you hire secretaries and copyists, employing the same persons to write for you and to applaud you. Possibly their praise is due to the fact that they make a profit out of writing for you. If you wish to exercise your mind, hand yourself over to the teachers of grammar and rhetoric, learn logic, have yourself instructed in the schools of the philosophers; and when you have learned all these things you will perhaps begin to hold your tongue. And yet I am acting foolishly in seeking teachers for one who is competent to teach everyone, and in trying to limit the utterance of one who does not know how to speak yet cannot remain silent. The old Greek proverb is quite true "A lyre is of no use to an ass." For my part I imagine that even your name was given you out of contrariety. For your whole mind slumbers and you actually snore, so profound is the sleep—or rather the lethargy—in which you are plunged. In fact amongst the other blasphemies which with sacrilegious lips you have uttered you have dared to say that the mountain in Daniel out of which the stone was cut without hands is the devil, and that the stone is Christ, who having taken a body from Adam (whose sins had before connected him with the devil) is born of a virgin to separate mankind from the mountain, that is, from the devil. Your tongue deserves to be cut out and torn into fragments. Can any true Christian explain this image of the devil instead of referring it to God the Father Almighty, or defile the ears of the whole world with so frightful an enormity? If your explanation has ever been accepted by any—I will not say Catholic but—heretic or heathen, let your words be regarded as pious. If on the other hand the Church of Christ has never yet heard of such an impiety, and if yours has been the first mouth through which he who once said "I will be like the Most High" has declared that he is the mountain spoken of by Daniel, then repent, put on sackcloth and ashes, and with fast-flowing tears wash away your awful guilt; if so be that this impiety may be forgiven you, and, supposing Origen's heresy to be true, that you may obtain pardon when the devil himself shall obtain it, the devil who has never been convicted of greater blasphemy than that which he has uttered through you. Your insult offered to myself I bear with patience: your impiety towards God I cannot bear. Accordingly I may seem to have been somewhat more acrid in this latter

part of my letter than I declared I would be at the outset. Yet having once before repented and asked pardon of me, it is extremely foolish in you again to commit a sin for which you must anew do penance. May Christ give you grace to hear and to hold your peace, to understand and so to speak.

LETTER LXII. TO TRANQUILLINUS

Tranquillinus, one of Jerome's Roman friends, had written (1) to tell him of the stand that Oceanus was making against the Origenists at Rome, and (2) to ask whether any parts of Origen's works might be studied with safety and profit. Jerome welcomes the tidings about Oceanus and answers the question of Tranquillinus in the affirmative. He classes Origen with Tertullian, Apollinaris and others whose works continued to be read in spite of their heresies. Written in 396 or 397 a.d.

1. Though I formerly doubted the fact, I have now proved that the links which bind spirit to spirit are stronger than any physical bond. For you, my reverend friend, cling to me with all your soul, and I am united to you by the love of Christ. I speak simply and sincerely to your spotless heart: the very paper on which you write, the very letters which you have formed—voiceless though they are—inspire in me a sense of your affection.

2. You tell me that many have been deceived by the mistaken teaching of Origen, and that that saintly man, my son Oceanus, is doing battle with their madness. I grieve to think that simple folk have been thrown off their balance, but I am rejoiced to know that one so learned as Oceanus is doing his best to set them right again. Moreover you ask me, insignificant though I am, for an opinion as to the advisability of reading Origen's works. Are we, you say, to reject him altogether with our brother Faustinus, or are we, as others tell us, to read him in part? My opinion is that we should sometimes read him for his learning just as we read Tertullian, Novatus, Arnobius, Apollinarius and some other church writers both Greek and Latin, and that we should select what is good and avoid what is bad in their writings according to the words of the Apostle, "Prove all things: hold fast that which is good." Those, however, who are led by some perversity in their dispositions to conceive for him too much fondness or too much aversion seem to me to lie under the curse of the Prophet:—"Woe unto them that call evil good and good evil; that put bitter for sweet and sweet for bitter!" For while the ability of his teaching must not lead us to embrace his wrong opinions, the wrongness of his opinions should not cause us altogether to reject the useful commentaries which he has published

on the holy scriptures. But if his admirers and his detractors are bent on having a tug of war one against the other, and if, seeking no mean and observing no moderation, they must either approve or disapprove his works indiscriminately, I would choose rather to be a pious boor than a learned blasphemer. Our reverend brother, Tatian the deacon, heartily salutes you.

LETTER LXIII. TO THEOPHILUS

When the dispute arose between Jerome and Epiphanius on the one side and Rufinus and John of Jerusalem on the other (see Letter LI.), Theophilus bishop of Alexandria, being appealed to by the latter sent the presbyter Isidore to report to him on the matter. Isidore reported against Jerome and consequently Theophilus refused to answer several of his letters. Finally he wrote counselling him to obey the canons of the church. Jerome replies that to do this has always been his first object. He then remonstrates with Theophilus on his too great leniency towards the Origenists and declares it to be productive of the worst results. The date of the letter is probably 397 a.d.

Jerome to the most blessed pope Theophilus.

1. Your holiness will remember that at the time when you kept silence towards me, I never ceased to do my duty by writing to you, not taking so much into account what you in the exercise of your discretion were then doing as what it became me to do. And now that I have received a letter from your grace, I see that my reading of the gospel has not been without fruit. For if the frequent prayers of a woman changed the determination of an unyielding judge, how much more must my constant appeals have softened a fatherly heart like yours?

2. I thank you for your reminder concerning the canons of the Church. Truly, "whom the Lord loveth he chasteneth, and scourgeth every son whom he receiveth." Still I would assure you that nothing is more my aim than to maintain the rights of Christ, to keep to the lines laid down by the fathers, and always to remember the faith of Rome; that faith which is praised by the lips of an apostle, and of which the Alexandrian church boasts to be a sharer.

3. Many religious persons are displeased that you are so long-suffering in regard to that shocking heresy, and that you suppose yourself able by such lenity to amend those who are attacking the Church's vitals. They believe that, while you are waiting for the penitence of a few, your action is fostering the boldness of abandoned men and making their party stronger. Farewell in Christ.

LETTER LXIV. TO FABIOLA

Fabiola's visit to Bethlehem had been shortened by the threatened invasion of the Huns which compelled Jerome and his friends to take refuge for a time on the seaboard of Palestine. Fabiola here took leave of her companions and set sail for Italy, but not until Jerome had completed this letter for her use (S:22). It contains a mystical account of the vestments of the High Priest worked out with Jerome's usual ingenuity and learning. Similar treatises are ascribed to Tertullian and to Hosius bishop of Cordova, but these have long since perished. Its date is 396 or 397 a.d.

LETTER LXV. TO PRINCIPIA

A commentary on Ps. XLV. addressed to Marcella's friend and companion Principia (see Letter CXXVII.). Jerome prefaces what he has to say by a defence of his practice of writing for women, a practice which had exposed him to many foolish sneers. He deals with the same subject in his dedication of the Commentary of Sophronius. The date of the letter is 397 a.d.

LETTER LXVI. TO PAMMACHIUS

Pammachius a Roman senator, had lost his wife Paulina one of Paula's daughters, while she was still in the flower of her youth. It was not till two years had elapsed that Jerome ventured to write to him; and when he did so he dwelt but little on the life and virtues of Paulina. Probably there was but little to tell. The greater part of the letter is taken up with commendation of Pammachius himself who, in spite of his high rank and position, had become a monk and was now living a life of severe self-denial. Jerome speaks approvingly of the Hospice for Strangers which, in conjunction with Fabiola, Pammachius had set up at Portus, and describes his own somewhat similar institutions at Bethlehem. He also mentions Paula, Eustochium, and the dead Blaesilla, all in terms of the highest praise. The date of the letter is 397 a.d.

1. Supposing a wound to be healed and a scar to have been formed upon the skin, any course of treatment designed to remove the mark must in its effort to improve the appearance renew the smart of the original wound. After two years of inopportune silence my condolence now comes rather late; yet even so I am afraid that my present speech may be still more inopportune. I

fear lest in touching the sore spot in your heart I may by my words inflame afresh a wound which time and reflection have availed to cure. For who can have ears so dull or hearts so flinty as to hear the name of your Paulina without weeping? Even though reared on the milk of Hyrcanian tigresses they must still shed tears. Who can with dry eyes see thus untimely cut down and withered an opening rose, an undeveloped bud, which has not yet formed itself into a cup nor spread forth the proud display of its crimson petals? In her a most priceless pearl is broken. In her a vivid emerald is shattered. Sickness alone shews us the blessedness of health. We realize better what we have had when we cease to have it.

2. The good ground of which we read in the parable brought forth fruit, some an hundred-fold, some sixtyfold, and some thirtyfold. In this threefold yield I recognize an emblem of the three different rewards of Christ which have fallen to three women closely united in blood and moral excellence. Eustochium culls the flowers of virginity. Paula sweeps the toilsome threshing floor of widowhood. Paulina keeps the bed undefiled of marriage. A mother with such daughters wins for herself on earth all that Christ has promised to give in heaven. Then to complete the team—if I may so call it—of four saints turned out by a single family, and to match the women's virtues by those of a man, the three have a fit companion in Pammachius who is a cherub such as Ezekiel describes, brother-in-law to the first, son-in-law to the second, husband to the third. Husband did I say? Nay, rather a most devoted brother; for the language of marriage is inadequate to describe the holy bonds of the Spirit. Of this team Jesus holds the reins, and it is of steeds like these that Habakkuk sings: "ride upon thy horses and let thy riding be salvation." With like resolve if with unlike speed they strain after the victor's palm. Their colours are different; their object is the same. They are harnessed in one yoke, they obey one driver, not waiting for the lash but answering the call of his voice with fresh efforts.

3. Let me use for a moment the language of philosophy. According to the Stoics there are four virtues so closely related and mutually coherent that he who lacks one lacks all. They are prudence, justice, fortitude, and temperance. While all of you possess the four, yet each is remarkable for one. You have prudence, your mother has justice, your virgin sister has fortitude, your wedded wife has temperance. I speak of you as wise, for who can be wiser than one who, despising the folly of the world, has followed Christ "the power of God and the wisdom of God"? Or what better instance can there be of justice than your mother, who having divided her substance among her offspring has taught them by her own contempt of riches the true object on which to fix

their affections? Who has set a better example of courage than Eustochium, who by resolving to be a virgin has breached the gates of the nobility and broken down the pride of a consular house? The first of Roman ladies, she has brought under the yoke the first of Roman families. Has there ever been temperance greater than that of Paulina, who, reading the words of the apostle: "marriage is honourable in all and the bed undefiled," and not presuming to aspire to the happiness of her virgin sister or the continence of her widowed mother, has preferred to keep to the safe track of a lower path rather than treading on air to lose herself in the clouds? When once she had entered upon the married state, her one thought day and night was that, as soon as her union should be blessed with offspring, she would live thenceforth in the second degree of chastity, and

Though woman, foremost in the high emprise,

would induce her husband to follow a like course. She would not forsake him but looked for the day when he would become a companion in salvation. Finding by several miscarriages that her womb was not barren, she could not give up all hope of having children and had to allow her own reluctance to give way to the eagerness of her mother-in-law and the chagrin of her husband. Thus she suffered much as Rachel suffered, although instead of bringing forth like her a son of pangs and of the right hand, the heir she had longed for was no other than her husband. I have learned on good authority that her wish in submitting herself to her husband was not to take advantage of God's primitive command "Be faithful and multiply and replenish the earth" but that she only desired children that she might bring forth virgins to Christ.

4. We read that the wife of Phinehas the priest, on hearing that the ark of the Lord had been taken, was seized suddenly with the pains of travail and that she brought forth a son Ichabod and died a mother in the hands of the women who nursed her. Rachel's son is called Benjamin, that is son of excellence' or of the right hand'; but the son of the other, afterwards to be a distinguished priest of God, derives his name from the ark. The same thing has come to pass in our own day, for since Paulina fell asleep the Church has posthumously borne the monk Pammachius, a patrician by his parentage and marriage, rich in alms, and lofty in lowliness. The apostle writes to the Corinthians, "Ye see your calling, brethren, how that not many wise men, not many noble are called." The conditions of the nascent church required this to be so that the grain of mustard seed might grow up little by little into a tree, and that the leaven of the gospel might gradually raise more and more the whole lump of the church. In our day Rome possesses what the world in days gone by knew not of. Then few of the wise or mighty or noble were Christians; now many wise powerful

and noble are not Christians only but even monks. And among them all my Pammachius is the wisest, the mightiest, and the noblest; great among the great, a leader among leaders, he is the commander in chief of all monks. He and others like him are the offspring which Paulina desired to have in her life time and which she has given us in her death. "Sing, O barren, thou that didst not bear; break forth into singing and cry aloud, thou that didst not travail with child"; for in a moment thou hast brought forth as many sons as there are poor men in Rome.

5. The glowing gems which in old days adorned the neck and face of Paulina now purchase food for the needy. Her silk dresses and gold brocades are exchanged for soft woollen garments intended to keep out the cold and not to expose the body to vain admiration. All that formerly ministered to luxury is now at the service of virtue. That blind man holding out his hand, and often crying aloud when there is none to hear, is the heir of Paulina, is co-heir with Pammachius. That poor cripple who can scarcely drag himself along, owes his support to the help of a tender girl. Those doors which of old poured forth crowds of visitors, are now beset only by the wretched. One suffers from a dropsy, big with death; another mute and without the means of begging, begs the more appealingly because he cannot beg; another maimed from his childhood implores an alms which he may not himself enjoy. Still another has his limbs rotted with jaundice and lives on after his body has become a corpse. To use the language of Virgil:

Had I a hundred tongues, a hundred lips,
I could not tell men's countless sufferings.

Such is the bodyguard which accompanies Pammachius wherever he walks; in the persons of such he ministers to Christ Himself; and their squalor serves to whiten his soul. Thus he speeds on his way to heaven, beneficent as a giver of games to the poor, and kind as a provider of shows for the needy. Other husbands scatter on the graves of their wives violets, roses, lilies, and purple flowers; and assuage the grief of their hearts by fulfilling this tender duty. Our dear Pammachius also waters the holy ashes and the revered bones of Paulina, but it is with the balm of almsgiving. These are the confections and the perfumes with which he cherishes the dead embers of his wife knowing that it is written: "Water will quench a flaming fire; and alms maketh an atonement for sins." What great power compassion has and what high rewards it is destined to win, the blessed Cyprian sets forth in an extensive work. It is proved also by the counsel of Daniel who desired the most impious of kings—had he been willing to hear him—to be saved by shewing mercy to the poor. Paulina's mother may well be glad of Paulina's heir. She cannot regret that her daughter's wealth has passed into new hands when she sees it still spent upon the objects she had at heart. Nay, rather she must congratulate herself that without any exertion of her own her wishes are being carried out. The sum available for distribution is the same as before: only the distributor is changed.

6. Who can credit the fact that one, who is the glory of the Furian stock and whose grandfathers and great grandfathers have been consuls, moves amid the senators in their purple clothed in sombre garb, and that, so far from blushing when he meets the eyes of his companions, he actually derides those who deride him! "There is a shame that leadeth to death and there is a shame that leadeth to life." It is a monk's first virtue to despise the judgments of men and always to remember the apostle's words:—"If I yet pleased men, I should not be the servant of Christ." In the same sense the Lord says to the prophets that He has made their face a brazen city and a stone of adamant and an iron pillar, to the end that they shall not be afraid of the insults of the people but shall by the sternness of their looks discompose the effrontery of those who sneered at them. A finely strung mind is more readily overcome by contumely than by terror. And men whom no tortures can overawe are sometimes prevailed over by the fear of shame. Surely it is no small thing for a man of birth, eloquence, and wealth to avoid the company of the powerful in the streets, to mingle with the crowd, to cleave to the poor, to associate on equal terms with the untaught, to cease to be a leader and to become one of the people. The more he humbles himself, the more he is exalted.

7. A pearl will shine in the midst of squalor and a gem of the first water will sparkle in the mire. This is what the Lord promised when He said: "Them that honour me I will honour." Others may understand this of the future when sorrow shall be turned into joy and when, although the world shall pass away, the saints shall receive a crown which shall never pass. But I for my part see that the promises made to the saints are fulfilled even in this present life. Before he began to serve Christ with his whole heart, Pammachius was a well known person in the senate. Still there were many other senators who wore the badges of proconsular rank. The whole world is filled with similar decorations. He was in the first rank it is true, but there were others in it besides him. Whilst he took precedence of some, others took precedence of him. The most distinguished privilege loses its prestige when lavished on a crowd, and dignities themselves become less dignified in the eyes of good men when held by persons who have no dignity. Thus Tully finely says of Caesar, when he wished to advance some of his adherents, "he did not so much honour them as dishonour the honourable positions in which he placed them." To-day all the churches of Christ are talking of Pammachius. The whole world admires as a

poor man one whom heretofore it ignored as rich. Can anything be more splendid than the consulate? Yet the honour lasts only for a year and when another has succeeded to the post its former occupant gives way. Each man's laurels are lost in the crowd and sometimes triumphs themselves are marred by the shortcomings of those who celebrate them. An office which was once handed down from patrician to patrician, which only men of noble birth could hold, of which the consul Marius—victor though he was over Numidia and the Teutons and the Cimbri—was held unworthy on account of the obscurity of his family, and which Scipio won before his time as the reward of valour,—this great office is now obtained by merely belonging to the army; and the shining robe of victory now envelops men who a little while ago were country boors. Thus we have received more than we have given. The things we have renounced are small; the things we possess are great. All that Christ promises is duly performed and for what we have given up we have received an hundredfold. This was the ground in which Isaac sowed his seed, Isaac who in his readiness to die bore the cross of the Gospel before the Gospel came.

8. "If thou wilt be perfect," the Lord says, "go and sell that thou hast and give to the poor. . . . and come and follow me." If thou wilt be perfect. Great enterprises are always left to the free choice of those who hear of them. Thus the apostle refrains from making virginity a positive duty, because the Lord in speaking of eunuchs who had made themselves such for the kingdom of heaven's sake finally said: "He that is able to receive it, let him receive it." For, to quote the apostle, "it is not of him that willeth, nor of him that runneth, but of God that sheweth mercy." If thou wilt be perfect. There is no compulsion laid upon you: if you are to win the prize it must be by the exercise of your own free will. If therefore you will to be perfect and desire to be as the prophets, as the apostles, as Christ Himself, sell not a part of your substance (lest the fear of want become an occasion of unfaithfulness, and so you perish with Ananias and Sapphira) but all that you have. And when you have sold all, give the proceeds not to the wealthy or to the high-minded but to the poor. Give each man enough for his immediate need but do not give money to swell what a man has already. "Thou shalt not muzzle the mouth of the ox that treadeth out the corn," and "the labourer is worthy of his reward." Again "they which wait at the altar are partakers with the altar." Remember also these words: "having food and raiment let us be therewith content." Where you see smoking dishes, steaming pheasants, massive silver plate, spirited nags, long-haired boy-slaves, expensive clothing, and embroidered hangings, give nothing there. For he to whom you would give is richer than you the giver. It is moreover a kind of sacrilege to give what belongs to the poor to those who are not poor.

Yet to be a perfect and complete Christian it is not enough to despise wealth or to squander and fling away one's money, a thing which can be lost and found in a single moment. Crates the Theban did this, so did Antisthenes and several others, whose lives shew them to have had many faults. The disciple of Christ must do more for the attainment of spiritual glory than the philosopher of the world, than the venal slave of flying rumours and of the people's breath. It is not enough for you to despise wealth unless you follow Christ as well. And only he follows Christ who forsakes his sins and walks hand in hand with virtue. We know that Christ is wisdom. He is the treasure which in the scriptures a man finds in his field. He is the peerless gem which is bought by selling many pearls. But if you love a captive woman, that is, worldly wisdom, and if no beauty but hers attracts you, make her bald and cut off her alluring hair, that is to say, the graces of style, and pare away her dead nails. Wash her with the nitre of which the prophet speaks, and then take your ease with her and say "Her left hand is under my head, and her right hand doth embrace me." Then shall the captive bring to you many children; from a Moabitess she shall become an Israelitish woman. Christ is that sanctification without which no man shall see the face of God. Christ is our redemption, for He is at once our Redeemer and our Ransom. Christ is all, that he who has left all for Christ may find One in place of all, and may be able to proclaim freely, "The Lord is my portion."

9. I see clearly that you have a warm affection for divine learning and that far from trying—like some rash persons—to teach that of which you are yourself ignorant you make it your first object to learn what you are going to teach. Your letters in their simplicity are redolent of the prophets and savour strongly of the apostles. You do not affect a stilted eloquence, nor boylike balance shallow sentences in clauses neatly-turned. The quickly frothing foam disappears with equal quickness; and a tumour though it enlarges the size of the body is injurious to health. It is moreover a shrewd maxim, this of Cato, "Fast enough if well enough." Long ago it is true in the days of our youth we laughed outright at this dictum when the finished orator used it in his exordium. I fancy you remember the mistake shared by the speaker in our Athenaeum and how the whole room resounded with the cry taken up by the students "Fast enough if well enough." According to Fabius crafts would be sure to prosper if none but craftsmen were allowed to criticise them. No man can adequately estimate a poet unless he is competent himself to write verse. No man can comprehend philosophers, unless he is acquainted with the various theories that they have held. Material and visible products are best appraised by those who make them. To what a cruel lot we men of letters are exposed

you may gather from the fact that we are forced to rely on the judgment of the public; and many a man is in company a formidable opponent who would certainly be despised could he be seen alone. I have touched on this in passing to make you content, if possible, with the ear of the learned. Disregard the remarks which uneducated persons make concerning your ability; but day by day imbibe the marrow of the prophets, that you may know the mystery of Christ and share this mystery with the patriarchs.

10. Whether you read or write, whether you wake or sleep, let the herdsman's horn of Amos always ring in your ears. Let the sound of the clarion arouse your soul, let the divine love carry you out of yourself; and then seek upon your bed him whom your soul loveth, and boldly say: "I sleep, but my heart waketh." And when you have found him and taken hold of him, let him not go. And if you fall asleep for a moment and He escapes from your hands, do not forthwith despair. Go out into the streets and charge the daughters of Jerusalem: then shall you find him lying down in the noontide weary and drunk with passion, or wet with the dew of night by the flocks of his companions, or fragrant with many kinds of spices, amid the apples of the garden. There give to him your breasts, let him suck your learned bosom, let him rest in the midst of his heritage, his feathers as those of a dove overlaid with silver and his inward parts with the brightness of gold. This young child, this mere boy, who is fed on butter and honey, and who is reared among curdled mountains, quickly grows up to manhood, speedily spoils all that is opposed to him in you, and when the time is ripe plunders [the spiritual] Damascus and puts in chains the king of [the spiritual] Assyria.

11. I hear that you have erected a hospice for strangers at Portus and that you have planted a twig from the tree of Abraham upon the Ausonian shore. Like AEneas you are tracing the outlines of a new encampment; only that, whereas he, when he reached the waters of the Tiber, under pressure of want had to eat the square flat cakes which formed the tables spoken of by the oracle, you are able to build a house of bread to rival this little village of Bethlehem wherein I am staying; and here after their long privations you propose to satisfy travellers with sudden plenty. Well done. You have surpassed my poor beginning. You have reached the highest point. You have made your way from the root to the top of the tree. You are the first of monks in the first city of the world: you do right therefore to follow the first of the patriarchs. Let Lot, whose name means one who turns aside' choose the plain and let him follow the left and easy branch of the famous letter of Pythagoras. But do you make ready for yourself a monument like Sarah's on steep and rocky heights. Let the City of Books be near; and when you have destroyed the giants, the sons of

Anak, make over your heritage to joy and merriment. Abraham was rich in gold and silver and cattle, in substance and in raiment: his household was so large that on an emergency he could bring a picked body of young men into the field, and could pursue as far as Dan and then slay four kings who had already put five kings to flight. Frequently exercising hospitality and never turning any man away from his door, he was accounted worthy at last to entertain God himself. He was not satisfied with giving orders to his servants and hand-maids to attend to his guests, nor did he lessen the favour he conferred by leaving others to care for them; but as though he had found a prize, he and Sarah his wife gave themselves to the duties of hospitality. With his own hands he washed the feet of his guests, upon his own shoulders he brought home a fat calf from the herd. While the strangers dined he stood by to serve them, and set before them the dishes cooked by Sarah's hands—though meaning to fast himself.

12. The regard which I feel for you, my dear brother, makes me remind you of these things; for you must offer to Christ not only your money but yourself, to be a "living sacrifice, holy, acceptable unto God, which is your reasonable service," and you must imitate the son of man who "came not to be ministered unto but to minister." What the patriarch did for strangers that our Lord and Master did for His servants and disciples. "Skin for skin, yea, all that a man hath will he give for his life. But," says the devil, "touch his flesh and he will curse thee to thy face." The old enemy knows that the battle with impurity is a harder one than that with covetousness. It is easy to cast off what clings to us from without, but a war within our borders involves far greater peril. We have to unfasten things joined together, we have to sunder things firmly united. Zacchaeus was rich while the apostles were poor. He restored fourfold all that he had taken and gave to the poor the half of his remaining substance. He welcomed Christ as his guest, and salvation came unto his house. And yet because he was little of stature and could not reach the apostolic standard of height, he was not numbered with the twelve apostles. Now as regards wealth the apostles gave up nothing at all, but as regards will they one and all gave up the whole world. If we offer to Christ our souls as well as our riches, he will gladly receive our offering. But if we give to God only those things which are without while we give to the devil those things which are within, the division is not fair, and the divine voice says: "Hast thou not sinned in offering aright, and yet not dividing aright?"

13. That you, the leader of the patrician order, first set the example of turning monk should not be to you an occasion of boasting but rather one of humility, knowing as you do that the Son of God became the Son of man.

However low you may abase yourself, you cannot be more lowly than Christ. Even supposing that you walk barefooted, that you dress in sombre garb, that you rank yourself with the poor, that you condescend to enter the tenements of the needy, that you are eyes to the blind, hands to the weak, feet to the lame, that you carry water and hew wood and make fires—even supposing that you do all this, where are the chains, the buffets, the spittings, the scourgings, the gibbet, the death which the Lord endured? And even when you have done all the things I have mentioned, you are still surpassed by your sister Eustochium as well as by Paula: for considering the weakness of their sex they have done more work relatively if less absolutely, than you. I myself was not at Rome but in the desert—would that I had continued there—at the time when your father-in-law Toxotius was still alive and his daughters were still given up to the world. But I have heard that they were too dainty to walk in the muddy streets, that they were carried about in the arms of eunuchs, that they disliked crossing uneven ground, that they found a silk dress a burthen and felt sunshine too scorching. But now, squalid and sombre in their dress, they are positive heroines in comparison with what they used to be. They trim lamps, light fires, sweep floors, clean vegetables, put heads of cabbage in the pot to boil, lay tables, hand cups, help dishes and run to and fro to wait on others. And yet there is no lack of virgins under the same roof with them. Is it then that they have no servants upon whom they can lay these duties? Surely not. They are unwilling that others should surpass them in physical toil whom they themselves surpass in rigour of mind. I say all this not because I doubt your mental ardour but that I may quicken the pace at which you are running, and in the heat of battle may add warmth to your warmth.

14. I for my part am building in this province a monastery and a hospice close by; so that, if Joseph and Mary chance to come to Bethlehem, they may not fail to find shelter and welcome. Indeed, the number of monks who flock here from all quarters of the world is so overwhelming that I can neither desist from my enterprise nor bear so great a burthen. The warning of the gospel has been all but fulfilled in me, for I did not sufficiently count the cost of the tower I was about to build; accordingly I have been constrained to send my brother Paulinian to Italy to sell some ruinous villas which have escaped the hands of the barbarians, and also the property inherited from our common parents. For I am loth, now that I have begun it, to give up ministering to the saints, lest I incur the ridicule of carping and envious persons.

15. Now that I have come to the conclusion of my letter I recall my metaphor of the four-horse team, and recollect that Blaesilla would have made a fifth had she been spared to share your resolve. I had almost forgotten to

mention her, the first of you all to go to meet the Lord. You who once were five I now see to be two and three. Blaesilla and her sister Paulina rest in sweet sleep: you with the two others on either side of you will fly upward to Christ more easily.

LETTER LXVII. FROM AUGUSTINE

Jerome having written him a short letter (no longer extant) Augustine now replies. He speaks with approval of Jerome's treatise On Famous Men, incorrectly called the Epitaph (see Letter CXII. S:3). He also repeats his objections to Jerome's account of the quarrel between Paul and Peter at Antioch and then concludes with a request that he will draw up a short notice of the principal heresies condemned by the Church.

Like the preceding letter of Augustine (Letter LVI.) this also failed to reach Jerome. It was however published in the West, but without Augustine's knowledge and by degrees its contents found their way to Bethlehem where they caused much annoyance and pain. The date of the letter is 397 a.d. In Augustine's correspondence in this Library it is printed in full as Letter XL.

LETTER LXVIII. TO CASTRUTIUS

Castrutius, a blind man of Pannonia, had set out for Bethlehem to visit Jerome. However, on reaching Cissa (whether that in Thrace or that on the Adriatic is uncertain) he was induced by his friends to turn back. Jerome writes to thank him for his intention and to console him for his inability to carry it out. He then tries to comfort him in his blindness (1) by referring to Christ's words concerning the man born blind (Joh. ix. 3) and (2) by telling him the story of Antony and Didymus. The date of the letter is 397 a.d.

1. My reverend son Heraclius the deacon has reported to me that in your eagerness to see me you came as far as Cissa, and that, though a Pannonian and consequently a land animal, you did not quail before the surges of the Adriatic and the dangers of the AEgean and Ionian seas. He tells me that you would have actually accomplished your purpose, had not our brethren with affectionate care held you back. I thank you all the same and regard it as a kindness shewn. For in the case of friends one must accept the will for the deed. Enemies often give us the latter, but only sincere attachment can bring us the former. And now that I am writing to you I beseech you do not regard the bodily affliction which has befallen you as due to sin. When the Apostles

speculated concerning the man that was born blind from the womb and asked our Lord and Saviour: "Who did sin, this man or his parents, that he was born blind?" they were told "Neither hath this man sinned nor his parents, but that the works of God should be made manifest in him." Do we not see numbers of heathens, Jews, heretics and men of various opinions rolling in the mire of lust, bathed in blood, surpassing wolves in ferocity and kites in rapacity, and for all this the plague does not come nigh their dwellings? They are not smitten as other men, and accordingly they wax insolent against God and lift up their faces even to heaven. We know on the other hand that holy men are afflicted with sicknesses, miseries, and want, and perhaps they are tempted to say "Verily I have cleansed my heart in vain, and washed my hands in innocency." Yet immediately they go on to reprove themselves, "If I say, I will speak thus; behold I should offend against the generation of thy children." If you suppose that your blindness is caused by sin, and that a disease which physicians are often able to cure is an evidence of God's anger, you will think Isaac a sinner because he was so wholly sightless that he was deceived into blessing one whom he did not mean to bless. You will charge Jacob with sin, whose vision became so dim that he could not see Ephraim and Manasseh, although with the inner eye and the prophetic spirit he could foresee the distant future and the Christ that was to come of his royal line. Were any of the kings holier than Josiah? Yet he was slain by the sword of the Egyptians. Were there ever loftier saints than Peter and Paul? Yet their blood stained the blade of Nero. And to say no more of men, did not the Son of God endure the shame of the cross? And yet you fancy those blessed who enjoy in this world happiness and pleasure? God's hottest anger against sinners is when he shews no anger. Wherefore in Ezekiel he says to Jerusalem: "My jealousy will depart from thee and I will be quiet and will be no more angry." For "whom the Lord loveth He chasteneth, and scourgeth every son whom He receiveth." The father does not instruct his son unless he loves him. The master does not correct his disciple unless he sees in him signs of promise. When once the doctor gives over caring for the patient, it is a sign that he despairs. You should answer thus: "as Lazarus in his lifetime received evil things so will I now gladly suffer torments that future glory may be laid up for me." For "affliction shall not rise up the second time." If Job, a man holy and spotless and righteous in his generation, suffered terrible afflictions, his own book explains the reason why.

2. That I may not make myself tedious or exceed the due limits of a letter by repeating old stories, I will briefly relate to you an incident which happened in my childhood. The saintly Athanasius bishop of Alexandria had summoned the blessed Antony to that city to confute the heretics there. Hereupon Didy-

mus, a man of great learning who had lost his eyes, came to visit the hermit and, the conversation turning upon the holy scriptures, Antony could not help admiring his ability and eulogizing his insight. At last he said: You do not regret, do you, the loss of your eyes? At first Didymus was ashamed to answer, but when the question had been repeated a second time and a third, he frankly confessed that his blindness was a great grief to him. Whereupon Antony said: "I am surprised that a wise man should grieve at the loss of a faculty which he shares with ants and flies and gnats, and not rejoice rather in having one of which only saints and apostles have been thought worthy." From this story you may perceive how much better it is to have spiritual than carnal vision and to possess eyes into which the mote of sin cannot fall.

Though you have failed to come this year, I do not yet despair of your coming. If the reverend deacon who is the bearer of this letter is again caught in the toils of your affection, and if you come hither in his company I shall be delighted to welcome you and shall readily acknowledge that the delay in payment is made up for by the largeness of the interest.

LETTER LXIX. TO OCEANUS

Oceanus, a Roman nobleman zealous for the faith, had asked Jerome to back him in a protest against Carterius a Spanish bishop who contrary to the apostolic rule that a bishop is to be "the husband of one wife" had married a second time. Jerome refuses to take the line suggested on the ground that Carterius's first marriage having preceded his baptism cannot be taken into account. He therefore advises Oceanus to let the matter drop. The date of the letter is 397 a.d.

1. I never supposed, son Oceanus, that the clemency of the Emperor would be assailed by criminals, or that persons just released from prison would after their own experience of its filth and fetters complain of relaxations allowed to others. In the gospel he who envies another's salvation is thus addressed: "Friend, is thine eye evil because I am good?" "God hath concluded them all in sin that he might have mercy upon all." "When sin abounded grace did much more abound." The first born of Egypt are slain and not even a beast belonging to Israel is left behind in Egypt. The heresy of the Cainites rises before me and the once slain viper lifts up its shattered head, destroying not partially as most often hitherto but altogether the mystery of Christ. This heresy declares that there are some sins which Christ cannot cleanse with His blood, and that the scars left by old transgressions on the body and the soul are sometimes so

deep that they cannot be effaced by the remedy which He supplies. What else is this but to say that Christ has died in vain? He has indeed died in vain if there are any whom He cannot make alive. When John the Baptist points to Christ and says: "Behold the lamb of God which taketh away the sins of the world" he utters a falsehood if after all there are persons living whose sins Christ has not taken away. For either it must be shewn that they are not of the world whom the grace of Christ thus ignores: or, if it be admitted that they are of the world, we have to choose between the horns of a dilemma. Either they have been delivered from their sins, in which case the power of Christ to save all men is proved; or they remain undelivered and as it were still under the charge of misdoing, in which case Christ is proved to be powerless. But far be it from us to believe of the Almighty that He is powerless in aught. For "what things soever the Father doeth, these also doeth the Son likewise." To ascribe weakness to the Son is to ascribe it to the Father also. The shepherd carries the whole sheep and not only this or that part of it: all the epistles of the apostle speak continually of the grace of Christ. And, lest a single announcement of this grace might seem a little thing, Peter says: "Grace unto you and peace be multiplied." The Scripture promises abundance; yet we affirm scarcity.

2. To what does all this tend, you ask. I reply; you remember the question that you proposed. It was this. A Spanish bishop named Carterius, old in years and in the priesthood has married two wives, one before he was baptized, and, she having died, another since he has passed through the laver; and you are of opinion that he has violated the precept of the apostle, who in his list of episcopal qualifications commands that a bishop shall be "the husband of one wife." I am surprised that you have pilloried an individual when the whole world is filled with persons ordained in similar circumstances; I do not mean presbyters or clergy of lower rank, but speak only of bishops of whom if I were to enumerate them all one by one I should gather a sufficient number to surpass the crowd which attended the synod of Ariminum. Still it does not become me to defend one by incriminating many; nor if reason condemns a sin, to make the number of those who commit it an excuse for it. At Rome an eloquent pleader caught me, as the phrase goes, between the horns of a dilemma: whichever way I turned I was held fast. Is it sinful, said he, to marry a wife, or is it not sinful? I in my simplicity, not being wary enough to avoid the snare laid for me, replied that it was not sinful. Then he propounded another question: Is it good deeds which are done away with in baptism or is it evil? Here again my simplicity induced me to say that it was sins which were forgiven. At this point, just as I began to fancy myself secure, the horns of the dilemma commenced to close in on me from this side and from that and their

points hidden before began to shew themselves. If, said he, to marry a wife is not sinful, and if baptism forgives sins, all that is not done away with is held over. On the instant a dark mist rose before my eyes as though I had been struck by a strong boxer. Yet recalling the sophism attributed to Chrysippus: "Whether you lie or whether you speak the truth, in either case you lie," I came to myself again and turned upon my opponent with a dilemma of my own. Pray tell me, I said, does baptism make a new man or does it not? He grudgingly admitted that it did. I pursued my advantage by saying, Does it make him wholly new or only partially so? He replied, Wholly. Then I asked, Is there nothing then of the old man held over in baptism? He assented. Hereupon I propounded the argument; If baptism makes a man new and creates a wholly new being, and if there is nothing of the old man held over in the new, that which once was in the old cannot be imputed to the new. At first my thorny friend held his tongue; afterwards however, making Piso's mistake, though he had nothing to say he could not remain silent. Sweat stood upon his brow, his cheeks turned pale, his lips trembled, his tongue clove to his mouth, his throat became dry; and fear (not age) made him cower. At last he broke out in these words, Have you not read how the apostle permits none to be ordained priest save the husband of one wife, and that what he lays stress upon is the fact of the marriage and not the time at which it is contracted? Now as the fellow had challenged me with syllogisms, and as I saw that he was feeling his way towards some intricate and awkward questions, I proceeded to turn his own weapons against him. I said therefore, Whom did the apostle select for the episcopate, baptized persons or catechumens? He refused to reply. I however made a fresh onslaught repeating my question a second time and a third. You would have taken him for Niobe changed to stone by excessive weeping. I turned to the audience and said: It is all the same to me, good people, whether I bind my opponent awake or sleeping; but it is easier to fetter a man who offers no resistance. If those whom the apostle admits into the ranks of the clergy are not catechumens but the faithful, and if he who is ordained bishop is always one of the faithful, being one of the faithful he cannot have the faults of a catechumen imputed to him. Such were the darts I hurled at my paralysed opponent. Such the quivering spears I cast at him. At last his mouth opened and he vomited forth the contents of his mind. Certainly, he blurted out, that is the doctrine of the apostle Paul.

3. Accordingly I bring out two epistles of the apostle, the first to Timothy, and the second to Titus. In the first is the following passage: "If a man desire the office of a bishop he desireth a good work. A bishop then must be blameless, the husband of one wife, vigilant, sober, of good behaviour, given to

hospitality, apt to teach, not given to wine, no striker . . . but patient, not a brawler, not covetous; one that ruleth well his own house, having his children in subjection with all gravity. (For if a man know not how to rule his own house, how shall he take care of the church of God?) Not a novice lest being lifted up with pride he fall into the condemnation of the devil. Moreover he must have a good report of them which are without; lest he fall into reproach and the snare of the devil." While immediately at the commencement of the epistle to Titus the following behests are laid down: "For this cause left I thee in Crete that thou shouldest set in order the things that are wanting, and ordain elders in every city, as I had appointed thee: if any be blameless, the husband of one wife, having faithful children not accused of riot or unruly. For a bishop must be blameless as the steward of God; not self-willed, not soon angry, not given to wine, no striker, not given to filthy lucre; but a lover of hospitality, a lover of good men, sober, just, holy, temperate; holding fast the faithful word as he hath been taught, that he may be able by sound doctrine both to exhort and to convince the gainsayers." In both epistles commandment is given that only monogamists should be chosen for the clerical office whether as bishops or as presbyters. Indeed with the ancients these names were synonymous, one alluding to the office, the other to the age of the clergy. No one at any rate can doubt that the apostle is speaking only of those who have been baptized. If therefore it in no wise prejudices the case of one who is to be ordained bishop that before his baptism he has not possessed all the requisite qualifications (for it is asked what he is and not what he has been), why should a previous marriage—the one thing which is in itself not sinful—prove a hindrance to his ordination? You argue that as his marriage was not a sin it was not done away with at his baptism. This is news to me indeed, that what in itself was not a sin is to be reckoned as such. All fornication and contamination with open vice, impiety towards God, parricide and incest, the change of the natural use of the sexes into that which is against nature and all extraordinary lusts are washed away in the fountain of Christ. Can it be possible that the stains of marriage are indelible, and that harlotry is judged more leniently than honourable wedlock? I do not, Carterius might say, hold you to blame for the hosts of mistresses and the troops of favourites that you have kept; I do not charge you with your bloodshedding and sow-like wallowings in the mire of uncleanness: yet you are ready to drag from her grave for my confusion my poor wife, who has been dead long years, and whom I married that I might be kept from those sins into which you have fallen. Tell this to the heathen who form the church's harvest with which she stores her granaries; tell this to the catechumens who seek admission to the number of the faithful; tell them, I say, not to contract marriages before their baptism, not to enter upon honourable wedlock, but like the Scots and the Atacotti and the people of Plato's republic to have community of wives and no discrimination of children, nay more, to beware of any semblance even of matrimony; lest, after they have come to believe in Christ, He shall tell them that those whom they have had have not been concubines or mistresses but wedded wives.

4. Let every man examine his own conscience and let him deplore the violence he has done to it at every period of his life; and then when he has brought himself to deliver a true judgment on his own former misdeeds, let him give ear to the chiding of Jesus: "Thou hypocrite, first cast out the beam out of thine own eye; and then shalt thou see clearly to cast out the mote out of thy brother's eye." Truly like the scribes and pharisees we strain out the gnat and swallow the camel, we pay tithe of mint and anise, and we omit the just judgment which God requires. What parallel can be drawn between a wife and a prostitute? Is it fair to make a marriage now dissolved by death a ground of accusation, while dissolute living wins for itself a garland of praise? He, had his former wife lived, would not have married another; but as for you, how can you defend the bestial unions you indiscriminately make? Perhaps indeed you will say that you feared to contract marriage lest by so doing you might disqualify yourself for ordination. He took a wife that he might have children by her; you by taking a harlot have lost the hope of children. He withdrew into the privacy of his own chamber when he sought to obey nature and to win God's blessing: "Be fruitful and multiply and replenish the earth." You on the contrary outraged public decency in the hot eagerness of your lust. He covered a lawful indulgence beneath a veil of modesty; you pursued an unlawful one shamelessly before the eyes of all. For him it is written "Marriage is honourable and the bed undefiled," while to you the words are read, "but whoremongers and adulterers God wilt judge," and "if any man destroyeth the temple of God, him shall God destroy." All iniquities, we are told, are forgiven us at our baptism, and when once we have received God's mercy we need not afterwards dread from Him the severity of a judge. The apostle says:—"And such were some of you: but ye are washed, but ye are sanctified, but ye are justified in the name of the Lord Jesus, and by the Spirit of our God." All sins then are forgiven; it is an honest and faithful saying. But I ask you, how comes it that, while your uncleanness is washed away, my cleanness is made unclean? You reply, "No, it is not made unclean, it remains just what it was. Had it been uncleanness, it would have been washed away like mine." I want to know what you mean by this shuffling. Your remarks seem to have no more point in them than the round end of a pestle. Is a thing sin because it is not sin? or is a thing

unclean because it is not unclean? The Lord, you say, has not forgiven because He had nothing to forgive; yet because He has not forgiven, that which has not been forgiven still remains.

5. What the true effect of baptism is, and what is the real grace conveyed by water hallowed in Christ, I will presently tell you; meantime I will deal with this argument as it deserves. An ill knot,' says the common proverb, requires but an ill wedge to split it.' The text quoted by the objector, "a bishop must be the husband of one wife," admits of quite another explanation. The apostle came of the Jews and the primitive Christian church was gathered out of the remnants of Israel. Paul knew that the Law allowed men to have children by several wives, and was aware that the example of the patriarchs had made polygamy familiar to the people. Even the very priests might at their own discretion enjoy the same license. He gave commandment therefore that the priests of the church should not claim this liberty, that they should not take two wives or three together, but that they should each have but one wife at one time. Perhaps you may say that this explanation which I have given is disputed; in that case listen to another. You must not have a monopoly of bending the Law to suit your will instead of bending your will to suit the Law. Some by a strained interpretation say that wives are in this passage to be taken for churches and husbands for their bishops. A decree was made by the fathers assembled at the council of Nicaea that no bishop should be translated from one church to another, lest scorning the society of a poor yet virgin see he should seek the embraces of a wealthy and adulterous one. For as the word logismoi, that is, "disputings," refers to the fault and misdoing of sons in the faith, and as the precept concerning the management of a house refers to the right direction of body and of soul, so by the wives of the bishops we are to understand their churches. Concerning whom it is written in Isaiah, "Make haste ye women and come from the show, for it is a people of no understanding." And again "Rise up, ye women that are wealthy, and hear my voice." And in the Book of Proverbs, "Who can find a virtuous woman? for her price is far above rubies. The heart of her husband doth safely trust in her." In the same book too it is written, "Every wise woman buildeth her house: but the foolish plucketh it down with her hands." Nor does this, say they, derogate from the dignity of the episcopate; for the same figure is used in relation to God. Jeremiah writes: "As a wife treacherously departeth from her husband, so have ye dealt treacherously with me, O house of Israel." And the apostle employs the same comparison: "I have espoused you," he says to his converts, "to one husband, that I may present you as a chaste virgin to Christ." The word woman is in the Greek ambiguous and should in all these places be understood as meaning wife. You

will say that this interpretation is harsh and does violence to the sense. In that case give back to the scripture its simple meaning and save me from the necessity of fighting you on your own ground. I will ask you the following question, Can a man who before his baptism has kept a concubine, and after her death has received baptism and has taken a wife, become a clergyman or not? You will answer me that he can, because his first partner was a concubine and not a wife. What the apostle condemns then, it would seem, is not mere sexual intercourse but marriage contracts and conjugal rights. Many persons, we see, because of narrow circumstances refuse to take upon them the burthen of matrimony. Instead of taking wives they live with their maid-servants and bring up as their own the children which these bear to them. Thus, if through the bounty of the Emperor they gain for their mistresses the right of wearing a matron's robes, they will at once come beneath the yoke of the apostle and sorely against their will will have to receive their partners as their wedded wives. But, if their poverty prevents them from obtaining an imperial rescript such as I have mentioned, the decrees of the Church will vary with the laws of Rome. Be careful therefore not to interpret the words "the husband of one wife," that is, of one woman, as approving indiscriminate intercourse and condemning only contracts of marriage.

I bring forward all these explanations not for the purpose of resisting the true and simple sense of the words in question but to shew you that you must take the holy scriptures as they are written, and that you must not empty of its efficacy the baptismal rite ordained by the Saviour, or render vain the whole mystery of the cross.

6. Let me now fulfil the promise I made a little while ago and with all the skill of a rhetorician sing the praises of water and of baptism. In the beginning the earth was without form and void, there was no dazzling sun or pale moon, there were no glittering stars. There was nothing but matter inorganic and invisible, and even this was lost in abysmal depths and shrouded in a distorting gloom. The Spirit of God above moved, as a charioteer, over the face of the waters, and produced from them the infant world, a type of the Christian child that is drawn from the laver of baptism. A firmament is constructed between heaven and earth, and to this is allotted the name heaven,—in the Hebrew Shamayim or what comes out of the waters,'—and the waters which are above the heavens are parted from the others to the praise of God. Wherefore also in the vision of the prophet Ezekiel there is seen above the cherubim a crystal stretched forth, that is, the compressed and denser waters. The first living beings come out of the waters; and believers soar out of the laver with wings to heaven. Man is formed out of clay and God holds the mystic waters in the

hollow of his hand. In Eden a garden is planted, and a fountain in the midst of it parts into four heads. This is the same fountain which Ezekiel later on describes as issuing out of the temple and flowing towards the rising of the sun, until it heals the bitter waters and quickens those that are dead. When the world falls into sin nothing but a flood of waters can cleanse it again. But as soon as the foul bird of wickedness is driven away, the dove of the Holy Spirit comes to Noah as it came afterwards to Christ in the Jordan, and, carrying in its beak a branch betokening restoration and light, brings tidings of peace to the whole world. Pharaoh and his host, loth to allow God's people to leave Egypt, are overwhelmed in the Red Sea figuring thereby our baptism. His destruction is thus described in the book of Psalms: "Thou didst endow the sea with virtue through thy power: thou brakest the heads of the dragons in the waters: thou brakest the heads of leviathan in pieces." For this reason adders and scorpions haunt dry places and whenever they come near water behave as if rabid or insane. As wood sweetens Marah so that seventy palm-trees are watered by its streams, so the cross makes the waters of the law lifegiving to the seventy who are Christ's apostles. It is Abraham and Isaac who dig wells, the Philistines who try to prevent them. Beersheba too, the city of the oath, and [Gihon], the scene of Solomon's coronation, derive their names from springs. It is beside a well that Eliezer finds Rebekah. Rachel too is a drawer of water and wins a kiss thereby from the supplanter Jacob. When the daughters of the priests of Midian are in a strait to reach the well, Moses opens a way for them and delivers them from outrage. The Lord's forerunner at Salem (a name which means peace or perfection) makes ready the people for Christ with spring-water. The Saviour Himself does not preach the kingdom of heaven until by His baptismal immersion He has cleansed the Jordan. Water is the matter of His first miracle and it is from a well that the Samaritan woman is bidden to slake her thirst. To Nicodemus He secretly says:—"Except a man be born of water and of the Spirit, he cannot enter into the Kingdom of God." As His earthly course began with water, so it ended with it. His side is pierced by the spear, and blood and water flow forth, twin emblems of baptism and of martyrdom. After His resurrection also, when sending His apostles to the Gentiles, He commands them to baptize these in the mystery of the Trinity. The Jewish people repenting of their misdoing are sent forthwith by Peter to be baptized. Before Sion travails she brings forth children, and a nation is born at once. Paul the persecutor of the church, that ravening wolf out of Benjamin, bows his head before Ananias one of Christ's sheep, and only recovers his sight when he applies the remedy of baptism. By the reading of the prophet the eunuch of Candace the queen of Ethiopia is made ready for the baptism of

Christ. Though it is against nature the Ethiopian does change his skin and the leopard his spots. Those who have received only John's baptism and have no knowledge of the Holy Spirit are baptized again, lest any should suppose that water unsanctified thereby could suffice for the salvation of either Jew or Gentile. "The voice of the Lord is upon the waters . . . The Lord is upon many waters . . . the Lord maketh the flood to inhabit it." His "teeth are like a flock of sheep that are even shorn which came up from the washing; whereof every-one bear twins, and none is barren among them." If none is barren among them, all of them must have udders filled with milk and be able to say with the apostle: "Ye are my little children, of whom I travail in birth again until Christ be formed in you;" and "I have fed you with milk and not with meat." And it is to the grace of baptism that the prophecy of Micah refers: "He will turn again, he will have compassion upon us: he will subdue our iniquities, and will cast all our sins into the depths of the sea."

7. How then can you say that all sins are drowned in the baptismal laver if a man's wife is still to swim on the surface as evidence against him? The psalmist says:—"Blessed is he whose transgression is forgiven, whose sin is covered. Blessed is the man unto whom the Lord imputeth not iniquity." It would seem that we must add something to this song and say "Blessed is the man to whom the Lord imputeth not a wife." Let us hear also the declaration which Ezekiel the so called "son of man" makes concerning the virtue of him who is to be the true son of man, the Christian: "I will take you," he says, "from among the heathen . . . then will I sprinkle clean water upon you, and ye shall be clean from all your filthiness . . . a new heart also will I give you and a new spirit." "From all your filthiness" he says, "will I cleanse you." If all is taken away nothing can be left. If filthiness is cleansed, how much more is cleanness kept from defilement. "A new heart also will I give you and a new spirit." Yes, for "in Christ Jesus neither circumcision availeth anything nor uncircumcision but a new nature." Wherefore the song also which we sing is a new song, and putting off the old man we walk not in the oldness of the letter but in the newness of the spirit. This is the new stone wherein the new name is written, "which no man knoweth saving he that receiveth it." "Know ye not," says the apostle, "that so many of us as were baptized into Jesus Christ were baptized into his death? Therefore we are buried with him by baptism into death: that like as Christ was raised up from the dead by the glory of the Father, even so we also should walk in newness of life." Do we read so often of newness and of making new and yet can no renewing efface the stain which the word wife brings with it? We are buried with Christ by baptism and we have risen again by faith in the working of God who hath called Him from the dead. And

"when we were dead in our sins and in the uncircumcision of our flesh, God hath quickened us together with Him, having forgiven us all trespasses; blotting out the handwriting of ordinances that was against us, which was contrary to us, and took it out of the way nailing it to His cross." Can it be that when our whole being is dead with Christ and when all the sins noted down in the old "handwriting" are blotted out, the one word "wife" alone lives on? Time would fail me were I to try to lay before you in order all the passages in the Holy Scriptures which relate to the efficacy of baptism or to explain the mysterious doctrine of that second birth which though it is our second is yet our first in Christ.

8. Before I make an end of dictating (for I perceive that I have already exceeded the just limits of a letter) I wish to give a brief explanation of the previous verses of the epistle in which the apostle describes the life of him that is to be made a bishop. We shall thus recognize him as Doctor of the Nations not only for his praise of monogamy but also for all his precepts. At the same time I beg that no one will suppose that in what I write my design is to blacken the priests of the present day. My one object is to promote the interest of the church. Just as orators and philosophers in giving their notions of the perfect orator and the perfect philosopher do not detract from Demosthenes and Plato but merely set forth abstract ideals; so, when I describe a bishop and explain the qualifications laid down for the episcopate, I am but supplying a mirror for priests. Every man's conscience will tell him that it rests with himself what image he will see reflected there, whether one that will grieve him by its deformity or one that will gladden him by its beauty. I turn now to the passage in question. "If a man desire the office of a bishop, he desireth a good work." Work, you see, not rank; toil not pleasure; work that he may increase in lowliness, not grow proud by reason of elevation. "A bishop then must be blameless." The same thing that he says to Titus, "if any be blameless." All the virtues are comprehended in this one word; thus he seems to require an impossible perfection. For if every sin, even every idle word, is deserving of blame, who is there in this world that is sinless and blameless? Still he who is chosen to be shepherd of the church must be one compared with whom other men are rightly regarded as but a flock of sheep. Rhetoricians define an orator as a good man able to speak. To be worthy of so high an honour he must be blameless in life and lip. For a teacher loses all his influence whose words are rendered null by his deeds. "The husband of one wife." Concerning this requirement I have spoken above. I will now only warn you that if monogamy is insisted on before baptism the other conditions laid down must be insisted on before baptism too. For it is impossible to regard the remaining obligations as binding only on

the baptized and this alone as binding also on the unbaptized. "Vigilant (or "temperate" for nephalios means both), wise, of good behaviour, given to hospitality, apt to teach." The priests who minister in God's temple are forbidden to drink wine and strong drink, to keep their wits from being stupefied with drunkenness and to enable their understanding to do its duty in God's service. By the word wise' those are excluded who plead simplicity as an excuse for a priest's folly. For if the brain be not sound, all the members will be amiss. The phrase "of good behaviour" is an extension of the previous epithet "blameless." One who has no faults is called "blameless;" one who is rich in virtues is said to be "of good behaviour." Or the words may be differently explained in accord with Tully's maxim, the main thing is that what you do you should do gracefully.' For some persons are so ignorant of their own measure and so stupid and foolish that they make themselves laughing stocks to those who see them because of their gesture or gait or dress or conversation. Fancying that they knew what is and what is not good taste they deck themselves out with finery and bodily adornments and give banquets which profess to be elegant: but all such attempts at dress and display are nastier than a beggar's rags. As regards the obligation of priests to be teachers we bare have the precepts of the old Law and the fuller instructions given on the subject to Titus. For an innocent and unobtrusive conversation does as much harm by its silence as it does good by its example. If the ravening wolves are to be frightened away it must be by the barking of dogs and by the staff of the shepherd. "Not given to wine, no striker." With the virtues they are to aim at he contrasts the vices they are to avoid.

9. We have learned what we ought to be: let us now learn what priests ought not to be. Indulgence in wine is the fault of diners out and revellers. When the body is heated with drink it soon boils over with lust. Wine drinking means self-indulgence, self-indulgence means sensual gratification, sensual gratification means a breach of chastity. He that lives in pleasure is dead while he lives, and he that drinks himself drunk is not only dead but buried. One hour's debauch makes Noah uncover his nakedness which through sixty years of sobriety he had kept covered. Lot in a fit of intoxication unwittingly adds incest to incontinence, and wine overcomes the man whom Sodom failed to conquer. A bishop that is a striker is condemned by Him who gave His back to the smiters, and when He was reviled reviled not again. "But moderate"; one good thing is set over against two evil things. Drunkenness and passion are to be held in check by moderation. "Not a brawler, not covetous." Nothing is more overweening than the assurance of the ignorant who fancy that incessant chatter will carry conviction with it and are always ready for a dispute that they

may thunder with turgid eloquence against the flock committed to their charge. That a priest must avoid covetousness even Samuel teaches when he proves before all the people that he has taken nothing from any man. And the same lesson is taught by the poverty of the apostles who used to receive sustenance and refreshment from their brethren and to boast that they neither had nor wished to have anything besides food and raiment. What the epistle to Timothy calls covetousness, that to Titus openly censures as the desire for filthy lucre. "One that ruleth well his own house." Not by increasing riches, not by providing regal banquets, not by having a pile of finely-wrought plates, not by slowly steaming pheasants so that the heat may reach the bones without melting the flesh upon them; no, but by first requiring of his own household the conduct which he has to inculcate in others. "Having his children in subjection with all gravity." They must not, that is, follow the example of the sons of Eli who lay with the women in the vestibule of the Temple and, supposing religion to consist in plunder, diverted to the gratification of their own appetites all the best parts of the victims. "Not a novice lest being lifted up with pride he fall into the condemnation of the devil." I cannot sufficiently express my amazement at the great blindness which makes men discuss such questions as that of marriage before baptism and causes them to charge people with a transaction which is dead in baptism, nay even quickened into a new life with Christ, while no one regards a commandment so clear and unmistakable as this about bishops not being novices. One who was yesterday a catechumen is to-day a bishop ; one who was yesterday in the amphitheatre is to-day in the church; one who spent the evening in the circus stands in the morning at the altar: one who a little while ago was a patron of actors is now a dedicator of virgins. Was the apostle ignorant of our shifts and subterfuges? did he know nothing of our foolish arguments? He not only says that a bishop must be the husband of one wife, but he has given commandment that he must be blameless, vigilant, sober, of good behaviour, given to hospitality, apt to teach, moderate, not given to wine, no striker, not a brawler, not covetous, not a novice. Yet to all these requirements we shut our eyes and notice nothing but the wives of the aspirants. Who cannot give instances to shew the need of the warning: "lest being lifted up with pride he fall into the condemnation of the devil?" A priest who is made such in a moment knows nothing of the lowliness and meekness which mark the meanest of the faithful, he knows nothing of Christian courtesy, he is not wise enough to think little of himself. He passes from one dignity to another, yet he has not fasted, he has not wept, he has not taken himself to task for his life, he has not striven by constant meditation to amend it, he has not given his substance to the poor. Yet he is moved from one see to another, he passes, that is, from pride to pride. There can be no doubt that arrogance is what the Apostle means when he speaks of the condemnation and downfall of the devil. And all men fall into this who are in a moment made masters, actually before they are disciples. "Moreover he must have a good report of them which are without." The last requirement is like the first. One who is really "blameless" obtains the unanimous approval not only of his own household but of outsiders as well. By aliens and persons outside the church we are to understand Jews, heretics and Gentiles. A Christian bishop then must be such that they who cavil at his religion may not venture to cavil at his life. At present however we see but too many bishops who are willing, like the charioteers in the horse races, to bid money for the popular applause; while there are some so universally hated that they can wring no money from their people, a feat which clowns accomplish by means of a few gestures.

10. Such are the conditions, son Oceanus, which the master-teachers of the church ought with anxiety and fear to require of others and to observe themselves. Such too are the canons which they should follow in the choice of persons for the priesthood; for they must not interpret the law of Christ to suit private animosities and feuds or to gratify ill-feeling which is sure to recoil on the man who cherishes it. Consider how unimpeachable is the character of Carterius in whose life his ill-wishers can find nothing to censure except a marriage contracted before baptism. "He that said, Do not commit adultery, said also, Do not kill. If we commit no adultery yet if we kill, we are become transgressors of the law." "Whosoever shall keep the whole law and yet offend in one point, he is guilty of all." Accordingly when they cast in our teeth a marriage entered into before baptism, we must require of them compliance with all the precepts which are given to the baptized. For they pass over much that is not allowable while they censure much that is allowed.

LETTER LXX. TO MAGNUS AN ORATOR OF ROME

Jerome thanks Magnus, a Roman orator, for his services in bringing a young man named Sebesius to apologize to him for some fault that he had committed. He then replies to a criticism of Magnus on his fondness for making quotations from profane writers, a practice which he defends by the example of the fathers of the church and of the inspired penmen of scripture. He ends by hinting that the objection really comes not from Magnus himself but from

Rufinus (here nicknamed Calpurnius Lanarius). The date of the letter is 397 a.d.

1. That our friend Sebesius has profited by your advice I have learned less from your letter than from his own penitence. And strange to say the pleasure which he has given me since his rebuke is greater than the pain he caused me from his previous waywardness. There has been indeed a conflict between indulgence in the father, and affection in the son; while the former is anxious to forget the past, the latter is eager to promise dutiful behaviour in the future. Accordingly you and I must equally rejoice, you because you have successfully put a pupil to the test, I because I have received a son again.

2. You ask me at the close of your letter why it is that sometimes in my writings I quote examples from secular literature and thus defile the whiteness of the church with the foulness of heathenism. I will now briefly answer your question. You would never have asked it, had not your mind been wholly taken up with Tully; you would never have asked it had you made it a practice instead of studying Volcatius to read the holy scriptures and the commentators upon them. For who is there who does not know that both in Moses and in the prophets there are passages cited from Gentile books and that Solomon proposed questions to the philosophers of Tyre and answered others put to him by them. In the commencement of the book of Proverbs he charges us to understand prudent maxims and shrewd adages, parables and obscure discourse, the words of the wise and their dark sayings; all of which belong by right to the sphere of the dialectician and the philosopher. The Apostle Paul also, in writing to Titus, has used a line of the poet Epimenides: "The Cretians are always liars, evil beasts, slow bellies." Half of which line was afterwards adopted by Callimachus. It is not surprising that a literal rendering of the words into Latin should fail to preserve the metre, seeing that Homer when translated into the same language is scarcely intelligible even in prose. In another epistle Paul quotes a line of Menander: "Evil communications corrupt good manners." And when he is arguing with the Athenians upon the Areopagus he calls Aratus as a witness citing from him the words "For we are also his offspring;" in Greek tou gar kai genos esmen, the close of a heroic verse. And as if this were not enough, that leader of the Christian army, that unvanquished pleader for the cause of Christ, skilfully turns a chance inscription into a proof of the faith. For he had learned from the true David to wrench the sword of the enemy out of his hand and with his own blade to cut off the head of the arrogant Goliath. He had read in Deuteronomy the command given by the voice of the Lord that when a captive woman had had her head shaved, her eyebrows and all her hair cut off, and her nails pared, she might then be taken

to wife. Is it surprising that I too, admiring the fairness of her form and the grace of her eloquence, desire to make that secular wisdom which is my captive and my handmaid, a matron of the true Israel? Or that shaving off and cutting away all in her that is dead whether this be idolatry, pleasure, error, or lust, I take her to myself clean and pure and beget by her servants for the Lord of Sabaoth? My efforts promote the advantage of Christ's family, my so-called defilement with an alien increases the number of my fellow-servants. Hosea took a wife of whoredoms, Gomer the daughter of Diblaim, and this harlot bore him a son called Jezreel or the seed of God. Isaiah speaks of a sharp razor which shaves "the head of sinners and the hair of their feet;" and Ezekiel shaves his head as a type of that Jerusalem which has been an harlot, in sign that whatever in her is devoid of sense and life must be removed.

3. Cyprian, a man renowned both for his eloquence and for his martyr's death, was assailed—so Firmian tells us—for having used in his treatise against Demetrius passages from the Prophets and the Apostles which the latter declared to be fabricated and made up, instead of passages from the philosophers and poets whose authority he, as a heathen, could not well gainsay. Celsus and Porphyry have written against us and have been ably answered, the former by Origen, the latter by Methodius, Eusebius, and Apollinaris. Origen wrote a treatise in eight books, the work of Methodius extended to ten thousand lines while Eusebius and Apollinaris composed twenty-five and thirty volumes respectively. Read these and you will find that compared with them I am a mere tyro in learning, and that, as my wits have long lain fallow, I can barely recall as in a dream what I have learned as a boy. The emperor Julian found time during his Parthian campaign to vomit forth seven books against Christ and, as so often happens in poetic legends, only wounded himself with his own sword. Were I to try to confute him with the doctrines of philosophers and stoics you would doubtless forbid me to strike a mad dog with the club of Hercules. It is true that he presently felt in battle the hand of our Nazarene or, as he used to call him, the Galilaean, and that a spear-thrust in the vitals paid him due recompense for his foul calumnies. To prove the antiquity of the Jewish people Josephus has written two books against Appio a grammarian of Alexandria; and in these he brings forward so many quotations from secular writers as to make me marvel how a Hebrew brought up from his childhood to read the sacred scriptures could also have perused the whole library of the Greeks. Need I speak of Philo whom critics call the second or the Jewish Plato?

4. Let me now run through the list of our own writers. Did not Quadratus a disciple of the apostles and bishop of the Athenian church deliver to the Emperor Hadrian (on the occasion of his visit to the Eleusinian mysteries) a

treatise in defence of our religion. And so great was the admiration caused in everyone by his eminent ability that it stilled a most severe persecution. The philosopher Aristides, a man of great eloquence, presented to the same Emperor an apology for the Christians composed of extracts from philosophic writers. His example was afterwards followed by Justin another philosopher who delivered to Antoninus Pius and his sons and to the senate a treatise Against the Gentiles, in which he defended the ignominy of the cross and preached the resurrection of Christ with all freedom. Need I speak of Melito bishop of Sardis, of Apollinaris chief-priest of the Church of Hierapolis, of Dionysius bishop of the Corinthians, of Tatian, of Bardesanes, of Irenaeus successor to the martyr Pothinus; all of whom have in many volumes explained the uprisings of the several heresies and tracked them back, each to the philosophic source from which it flows. Pantaenus, a philosopher of the Stoic school, was on account of his great reputation for learning sent by Demetrius bishop of Alexandria to India, to preach Christ to the Brahmans and philosophers there. Clement, a presbyter of Alexandria, in my judgment the most learned of men, wrote eight books of Miscellanies and as many of Outline Sketches, a treatise against the Gentiles, and three volumes called the Pedagogue. Is there any want of learning in these, or are they not rather drawn from the very heart of philosophy? Imitating his example Origen wrote ten books of Miscellanies, in which he compares together the opinions held respectively by Christians and by philosophers, and confirms all the dogmas of our religion by quotations from Plato and Aristotle, from Numenius and Cornutus. Miltiades also wrote an excellent treatise against the Gentiles. Moreover Hippolytus and a Roman senator named Apollonius have each compiled apologetic works. The books of Julius Africanus who wrote a history of his own times are still extant, as also are those of Theodore who was afterwards called Gregory, a man endowed with apostolic miracles as well as with apostolic virtues. We still have the works of Dionysius bishop of Alexandria, of Anatolius chief priest of the church of Laodicea, of the presbyters Pamphilus, Pierius, Lucian, Malchion; of Eusebius bishop of Caesarea, Eustathius of Antioch and Athanasius of Alexandria; of Eusebius of Emisa, of Triphyllius of Cyprus, of Asterius of Scythopolis, of the confessor Serapion, of Titus bishop of Bostra; and of the Cappadocians Basil, Gregory, and Amphilochius. All these writers so frequently interweave in their books the doctrines and maxims of the philosophers that you might easily be at a loss which to admire most, their secular erudition or their knowledge of the scriptures.

5. I will pass on to Latin writers. Can anything be more learned or more pointed than the style of Tertullian? His Apology and his books Against the

Gentiles contain all the wisdom of the world. Minucius Felix a pleader in the Roman courts has ransacked all heathen literature to adorn the pages of his Octavius and of his treatise Against the astrologers (unless indeed this latter is falsely ascribed to him). Arnobius has published seven books against the Gentiles, and his pupil Lactantius as many, besides two volumes, one on Anger and the other on the creative activity of God. If you read any of these you will find in them an epitome of Cicero's dialogues. The Martyr Victorinus though as a writer deficient in learning is not deficient in the wish to use what learning he has. Then there is Cyprian. With what terseness, with what knowledge of all history, with what splendid rhetoric and argument has he touched the theme that idols are no Gods! Hilary too, a confessor and bishop of my own day, has imitated Quintilian's twelve books both in number and in style, and has also shewn his ability as a writer in his short treatise against Dioscorus the physician. In the reign of Constantine the presbyter Juvencus set forth in verse the story of our Lord and Saviour, and did not shrink from forcing into metre the majestic phrases of the Gospel. Of other writers dead and living I say nothing. Their aim and their ability are evident to all who read them.

6. You must not adopt the mistaken opinion, that while in dealing with the Gentiles one may appeal to their literature in all other discussions one ought to ignore it; for almost all the books of all these writers—except those who like Epicurus are no scholars—are extremely full of erudition and philosophy. I incline indeed to fancy—the thought comes into my head as I dictate—that you yourself know quite well what has always been the practice of the learned in this matter. I believe that in putting this question to me you are only the mouthpiece of another who by reason of his love for the histories of Sallust might well be called Calpurnius Lanarius. Please beg of him not to envy eaters their teeth because he is toothless himself, and not to make light of the eyes of gazelles because he is himself a mole. Here as you see there is abundant material for discussion, but I have already filled the limits at my disposal.

LETTER LXXI. TO LUCINIUS

Lucinius was a wealthy Spaniard of Baetica who in conformity with the ascetic ideas of his time had made a vow of continence with his wife Theodora. Being much interested in the study of scripture he proposed to visit Bethlehem, and in a.d. 397 sent several scribes thither to transcribe for him Jerome's principal writings. To these on their return home Jerome now entrusts the following letter. In it he encourages Lucinius to fulfil his purpose of coming to Bethlehem, describes the books which he is sending to him, and answers two questions relating to ecclesiastical usage. He also sends him some trifling presents.

Shortly after receiving the letter (written in 398 a.d.) Lucinius died and Jerome wrote to Theodora to console her for her loss (Letter LXXV).

1. Your letter which has suddenly arrived was not expected by me, and coming in an unlooked for way it has helped to rouse me from my torpor by the glad tidings which it conveys. I hasten to embrace with the arms of love one whom my eyes have never seen, and silently say to myself:—"oh that I had wings like a dove! for then would I flee away and be at rest."' Then would I find him "whom my soul loveth." In you the Lord's words are now truly fulfilled: "many shall come from the east and west and shall sit down with Abraham." In those days the faith of my Lucinius was foreshadowed in Cornelius, "centurion of the band called the Italian band." And when the apostle Paul writes to the Romans: "whensoever I take my journey into Spain I will come to you: for I trust to see you in my journey, and to be brought on my way thitherward by you;" he shews by the tale of his previous successes what he looked to gain from that province. Laying in a short time the foundation of the gospel "from Jerusalem and round about unto Illyricum," he enters Rome in bonds, that he may free those who are in the bonds of error and superstition. Two years he dwells in his own hired house that he may give to us the house eternal which is spoken of in both the testaments. The apostle, the fisher of men, has cast forth his net, and, among countless kinds of fish, has landed you like a magnificent gilt-bream. You have left behind you the bitter waves, the salt tides, the mountain-fissures; you have despised Leviathan who reigns in the waters. Your aim is to seek the wilderness with Jesus and to sing the prophet's song: "my soul thirsteth for thee, my flesh longeth for thee in a dry and thirsty land where no water is; to see thy power and thy glory, so as I have seen thee in the sanctuary," or, as he sings in another place, "lo, then would I wander far off and remain in the wilderness. I would hasten my escape from the windy storm and tempest." Since you have left Sodom and are hastening to the mountains, I beseech you with a father's affection not to look behind you. Your hands have grasped the handle of the plough, the hem of the Saviour's garment, and His locks wet with the dew of night; do not let them go. Do not come down from the housetop of virtue to seek for the clothes which you wore of old, nor return home from the field. Do not like Lot set your heart on the plain or upon the pleasant gardens; for these are watered not, as the holy land, from heaven but by Jordan's muddy stream made salt by contact with the Dead Sea.

2. Many begin but few persevere to the end. "They which run in a race run all, but one receiveth the crown." But of us on the other hand it is said: "So run that ye may obtain." Our master of the games is not grudging; he does not give the palm to one and disgrace another. His wish is that all his athletes may alike win garlands. My soul rejoices, yet the very greatness of my joy makes me feel sad. Like Ruth when I try to speak I burst into tears. Zacchaeus, the convert of an hour, is accounted worthy to receive the Saviour as his guest. Martha and Mary make ready a feast and then welcome the Lord to it. A harlot washes His feet with her tears and against His burial anoints His body with the ointment of good works. Simon the leper invites the Master with His disciples and is not refused. To Abraham it is said: "Get thee out of thy country and from thy kindred and from thy father's house, unto a land that I will shew thee." He leaves Chaldaea, he leaves Mesopotamia; he seeks what he knows not, not to lose Him whom he has found. He does not deem it possible to keep both his country and his Lord; even at that early day he is already fulfilling the prophet David's words: "I am a stranger with thee and a sojourner, as all my fathers were." He is called "a Hebrew," in Greek perates, a passer-over, for not content with present excellence but forgetting those things which are behind he reaches forth to that which is before. He makes his own the words of the psalmist: "they shall go from strength to strength." Thus his name has a mystic meaning and he has opened for you a way to seek not your own things but those of another. You too must leave your home as he did, and must take for your parents, brothers, and relations only those who are linked to you in Christ. "Whosoever," He says, "shall do the will of my father . . . the same is my brother and sister and mother."

3. You have with you one who was once your partner in the flesh but is now your partner in the spirit; once your wife but now your sister; once a woman but now a man; once an inferior but now an equal. Under the same yoke as you she hastens toward the same heavenly kingdom.

A too careful management of one's income, a too near calculation of one's expenses—these are habits not easily laid aside. Yet to escape the Egyptian woman Joseph had to leave his garment with her. And the young man who followed Jesus having a linen cloth cast about him, when he was assailed by the servants had to throw away his earthly covering and to flee naked. Elijah also when he was carried up in a chariot of fire to heaven left his mantle of sheepskin on earth. Elisha used for sacrifice the oxen and the yokes which hitherto he had employed in his work. We read in Ecclesiasticus: "he that toucheth pitch shall be defiled therewith." As long as we are occupied with the things of the world, as long as our soul is fettered with possessions and revenues, we cannot think freely of God. "For what fellowship hath righteousness with unrighteousness? And what communion hath light with darkness? And what concord hath Christ with Belial? Or what part hath he that believeth with an infidel?" "Ye cannot," the Lord says, "serve God and Mammon." Now the laying aside of money is for those who are beginners in the way, not for those who are made perfect. Heathens like Antisthenes and Crates the Theban have done as much before now. But to offer one's self to God, this is the mark of Christians and apostles. These like the widow out of their penury cast their two mites into the treasury, and giving all that they have to the Lord are counted worthy to hear his words: "ye also shall sit upon twelve thrones judging the twelve tribes of Israel."

4. You can see for yourself why I mention these things; without expressly saying it I am inviting you to take up your abode at the holy places. Your abundance has supported the want of many that some day their riches may abound to supply your want; you have made to yourself "friends of the mammon of unrighteousness that they may receive you into everlasting habitations." Such conduct deserves praise and merits to be compared with the virtue of apostolic times. Then, as you know, believers sold their possessions and brought the prices of them and laid them down at the apostles' feet: a symbolic act designed to shew that men must trample on covetousness. But the Lord yearns for believers' souls more than for their riches. We read in the Proverbs: "the ransom of a man's soul are his own riches." We may, indeed, take a man's own riches to be those which do not come from some one else, or from plunder; according to the precept: "honour God with thy just labours." But the sense is better if we understand a man's "own riches" to be those hidden treasures which no thief can steal and no robber wrest from him.

5. As for my poor works which from no merits of theirs but simply from your own kindness you say that you desire to have; I have given them to your servants to transcribe, I have seen the paper-copies made by them, and I have repeatedly ordered them to correct them by a diligent comparison with the originals. For so many are the pilgrims passing to and fro that I have been unable to read so many volumes. They have found me also troubled by a long illness from which this Lent I am slowly recovering as they are leaving me. If then you find errors or omissions which interfere with the sense, these you must impute not to me but to your own servants; they are due to the ignorance or carelessness of the copyists, who write down not what they find but what they take to be the meaning, and do but expose their own mistakes when they try to correct those of others. It is a false rumour which has reached you to the effect that I have translated the books of Josephus and the volumes of the holy

men Papias and Polycarp. I have neither the leisure nor the ability to preserve the charm of these masterpieces in another tongue. Of Origen and Didymus I have translated a few things, to set before my countrymen some specimens of Greek teaching. The canon of the Hebrew verity—except the octoteuch which I have at present in hand—I have placed at the disposal of your slaves and copyists. Doubtless you already possess the version from the septuagint which many years ago I diligently revised for the use of students. The new testament I have restored to the authoritative form of the Greek original. For as the true text of the old testament can only be tested by a reference to the Hebrew, so the true text of the new requires for its decision an appeal to the Greek.

6. You ask me whether you ought to fast on the Sabbath and to receive the eucharist daily according to the custom—as currently reported—of the churches of Rome and Spain. Both these points have been treated by the eloquent Hippolytus, and several writers have collected passages from different authors bearing upon them. The best advice that I can give you is this. Church-traditions—especially when they do not run counter to the faith—are to be observed in the form in which previous generations have handed them down; and the use of one church is not to be annulled because it is contrary to that of another. As regards fasting, I wish that we could practise it without intermission as—according to the Acts of the Apostles—Paul did and the believers with him even in the season of Pentecost and on the Lord's Day. They are not to be accused of manichaeism, for carnal food ought not to be preferred before spiritual. As regards the holy eucharist you may receive it at all times without qualm of conscience or disapproval from me. You may listen to the psalmist's words:—"O taste and see that the Lord is good;" you may sing as he does:—"my heart poureth forth a good word." But do not mistake my meaning. You are not to fast on feast-days, neither are you to abstain on the week days in Pentecost. In such matters each province may follow its own inclinations, and the traditions which have been handed down should be regarded as apostolic laws.

7. You send me two small cloaks and a sheepskin mantle from your wardrobe and ask me to wear them myself or to give them to the poor. In return I send to you and your sister in the Lord four small haircloths suitable to your religious profession and to your daily needs, for they are the mark of poverty and the outward witness of a continual penitence. To these I have added a manuscript containing Isaiah's ten most obscure visions which I have lately elucidated with a critical commentary. When you look upon these trifles call to mind the friend in whom you delight and hasten the voyage which you have for a time deferred. And because "the way of man is not in himself" but it is

the Lord that "directeth his steps;" if any hindrance should interfere—I hope none may—to prevent you from coming, I pray that distance may not sever those united in affection and that I may find my Lucinius present in absence through an interchange of letters.

LETTER LXXII. TO VITALIS

Vitalis had asked Jerome "Is Scripture credible when it tells us that Solomon and Ahaz became fathers at the age of eleven?" The difficulty had previously occurred to Jerome himself (Letter XXXVI. 10, whence perhaps Vitalis took it) and in this letter he suggests several ways in which it may be met. He is quite prepared, if necessary, to accept the alleged fact on the grounds that "there are many things in Scripture which sound incredible and yet are true" and that "nature cannot resist the Lord of nature" (S:2). He is disposed, however, to regard the question as trivial and of no importance. The date of the letter is 398 a.d.

LETTER LXXIII. TO EVANGELUS

Evangelus had sent Jerome an anonymous treatise in which Melchisedek was identified with the Holy Ghost, and had asked him what he thought of the theory. Jerome in his reply repudiates the idea as absurd and insists that Melchisedek was a real man, possibly, as the Jews said, Shem the eldest son of Noah. The date of the letter is 398 a.d.

LETTER LXXIV. TO RUFINUS OF ROME

Rufinus, a Roman Presbyter (to be carefully distinguished from Rufinus of Aquileia and Rufinus the Syrian), had written to Jerome for an explanation of the judgment of Solomon (1 Kings iii. 16–28). This Jerome gives at length, treating the narrative as a parable and making the false and true mothers types of the Synagogue and the Church. The date of the letter is 398 a.d.

LETTER LXXV. TO THEODORA

Theodora the wife of the learned Spaniard Lucinius (for whom see Letter LXXI.) had recently lost her husband, a bereavement which suggested the present letter. In it Jerome recounts the many virtues of Lucinius and especially his zeal in resisting the gnostic heresy of Marcus which during his life was prevalent in Spain. The date of the letter is 399 a.d.

1. So overpowered am I by the sad intelligence of the falling asleep of the holy and by me deeply revered Lucinius that I am scarcely able to dictate even a short letter. I do not, it is true, lament his fate, for I know that he has passed to better things: like Moses he can say: "I will now turn aside and see this great sight," but I am tormented with regret that I was not allowed to look upon the face of one, who was likely, as I believed, in a short time to come hither. True indeed is the prophetic warning concerning the doom of death that it divides brothers, and with harsh and cruel hand sunders those whose names are linked together in the bonds of love. But we have this consolation that it is slain by the word of the Lord. For it is said: "O death, I will be thy plagues; O grave, I will be thy destruction," and in the next verse: "An east wind shall come, the wind of the Lord shall come up from the wilderness, and his spring shall become dry, and his fountain shall be dried up." For, as Isaiah says, "there shall come forth a rod out of the stem of Jesse, and a branch shall grow out of his roots": and He says Himself in the Song of Songs, "I am the rose of Sharon and the lily of the valley." Our rose is the destruction of death, and died that death itself might die in His dying. But, when it is said that He is to be brought "from the wilderness," the virgin's womb is indicated, which without sexual intercourse or impregnation has given to us God in the form of an infant able to quench by the glow of the Holy Spirit the fountains of lust and to sing in the words of the psalm: "as in a dry and pathless and waterless land, so have I appeared unto thee in the sanctuary." Thus when we have to face the hard and cruel necessity of death, we are upheld by this consolation, that we shall shortly see again those whose absence we now mourn. For their end is not called death but a slumber and a falling asleep. Wherefore also the blessed apostle forbids us to sorrow concerning them which are asleep, telling us to believe that those whom we know to sleep now may hereafter be roused from their sleep, and when their slumber is ended may watch once more with the saints and sing with the angels:—"Glory to God in the highest and on earth peace among men of good will." In heaven where there is no sin, there is glory and perpetual praise and unwearied singing; but on earth where sedition reigns, and war and discord hold sway, peace must be gained by prayer, and it

is to be found not among all but only among men of good will, who pay heed to the apostolic salutation: "Grace to you and peace from God our Father and the Lord Jesus Christ." For "His abode is in peace and His dwelling place is in Zion," that is, on a watch-tower, on a height of doctrines and of virtues, in the soul of the believer; for the angel of this latter daily beholds the face of God, and contemplates with unveiled face the glory of God.

2. Wherefore, though you are already running in the way, I urge a willing horse, as the saying goes, and implore you, while you regret in your Lucinius a true brother, to rejoice as well that he now reigns with Christ. For, as it is written in the book of Wisdom, he was "taken away lest that wickedness should alter his understanding . . . for his soul pleased the Lord . . . and he . . . in a short time fulfilled a long time." We may with more right weep for ourselves that we stand daily in conflict with our sins, that we are stained with vices, that we receive wounds, and that we must give account for every idle word. Victorious now and free from care he looks down upon you from on high and supports you in your struggle, nay more, he prepares for you a place near to himself; for his love and affection towards you are still the same as when, disregarding his claim on you as a husband, he resolved to treat you even on earth as a sister, or indeed I may say as a brother, for difference of sex while essential to marriage is not so to a continent tie. And since even in the flesh, if we are born again in Christ, we are no longer Greek and Barbarian, bond and free, male and female, but are all one in Him, how much more true will this be when this corruptible has put on incorruption and when this mortal has put on immortality. "In the resurrection," the Lord tells us, "they neither marry nor are given in marriage but are as the angels . . . in heaven." Now when it is said that they neither marry nor are given in marriage but are as the angels in heaven, there is no taking away of a natural and real body but only an indication of the greatness of the glory to come. For the words are not "they shall be angels" but "they shall be as the angels": thus while likeness to the angels is promised identity with them is refused. "They shall be," Christ tells us, "as the angels," that is like the angels; therefore they will not cease to be human. Glorious indeed they shall be, and graced with angelic splendour, but they will still be human; the apostle Paul will still be Paul, Mary will still be Mary. Then shall confusion overtake that heresy which holds out great but vague promises only that it may take away hopes which are at once modest and certain.

3. And now that I have once mentioned the word "heresy," where can I find a trumpet loud enough to proclaim the eloquence of our dear Lucinius, who, when the filthy heresy of Basilides raged in Spain and like a pestilence

ravaged the provinces between the Pyrenees and the ocean, upheld in all its purity the faith of the church and altogether refused to embrace Armagil, Barbelon, Abraxas, Balsamum, and the absurd Leusibora. Such are the portentous names which, to excite the minds of unlearned men and weak women, they pretend to draw from Hebrew sources, terrifying the simple by barbarous combinations which they admire the more the less they understand them. The growth of this heresy is described for us by Irenaeus, bishop of the church of Lyons, a man of the apostolic times, who was a disciple of Papias the hearer of the evangelist John. He informs us that a certain Mark, of the stock of the gnostic Basilides, came in the first instance to Gaul, that he contaminated with his teaching those parts of the country which are watered by the Rhone and the Garonne, and that in particular he misled by his errors high-born women; to whom he promised certain secret mysteries and whose affection he enlisted by magic arts and hidden indulgence in unlawful intercourse. Irenaeus goes on to say that subsequently Mark crossed the Pyrenees and occupied Spain, making it his object to seek out the houses of the wealthy, and in these especially the women, concerning whom we are told that they are "led away with divers lusts, ever learning and never able to come to the knowledge of the truth." All this he wrote about three hundred years ago in the extremely learned and eloquent books which he composed under the title Against all heresies.

4. From these facts you in your wisdom will realize how worthy of praise our dear Lucinius shewed himself when he shut his ears that he might not have to hear the judgement passed upon blood shedders, and dispersed all his substance and gave to the poor that his righteousness might endure for ever. And not satisfied with bestowing his bounty upon his own country, he sent to the churches of Jerusalem and Alexandria gold enough to alleviate the want of large numbers. But while many will admire and extol in him this liberality, I for my part will rather praise him for his zeal and diligence in the study of the scriptures. With what eagerness he asked for my poor works! He actually sent six copyists (for in this province there is a dearth of scribes who understand Latin) to copy for him all that I have ever dictated from my youth until the present time. The honour was not of course paid to me who am but a little child, the least of all Christians, living in the rocks near Bethlehem because I know myself a sinner; but to Christ who is honoured in his servants and who makes this promise to them, "He that receiveth you receiveth me, and he that receiveth me receiveth him that sent me."

5. Therefore, my beloved daughter, regard this letter as the epitaph which love prompts me to write upon your husband, and if there is any spiritual work

of which you think me to be capable, boldly command me to undertake it: that so ages to come may know that He who says of Himself in Isaiah, "He hath made me a polished shaft; in his quiver hath he hid me," has with His sharp arrow so wounded two men severed by an immense interval of sea and land, that, although they know each other not in the flesh, they are knit together in love in the spirit.

May you be kept holy both in body and spirit by the Samaritan—that is, saviour and keeper—of whom it is said in the psalm, "He that keepeth Israel shall neither slumber nor sleep." May the watcher and the holy one who came down to Daniel come also to you, that you too may be able to say, "I sleep but my heart waketh."

LETTER LXXVI. TO ABIGAUS

Abigaus the recipient of this letter was a blind presbyter of Baetica in Spain. He had asked the help of Jerome's prayers in his struggles with evil and Jerome now writes to cheer and to console him. He concludes his remarks by commending to his especial care the widow Theodora. The letter should be compared with that addressed to Castrutius (LXVIII.). It was written at the same time with the preceding.

1. Although I am conscious of many sins and every day pray on bended knees, "Remember not the sins of my youth nor my transgressions, yet because I know that it has been said by the Apostle "let a man not be lifted up with pride lest he fall into the condemnation of the devil," and that it is written in another passage, "God resisteth the proud but giveth grace to the humble," there is nothing I have striven so much to avoid from my boyhood up as a swelling mind and a stiff neck, things which always provoke against themselves the wrath of God. For I know that my master and Lord and God has said in the lowliness of His flesh: "Learn of me; for I am meek and lowly in heart," and that before this He has sung by the mouth of David: "Lord, remember David and all his gentleness." Again we read in another passage, "Before destruction the heart of man is haughty; and before honour is humility." Do not, then, I implore you, suppose that I have received your letter and have passed it over in silence. Do not, I beseech you, lay to my charge the dishonesty and negligence of which others have been guilty. For why should I, when called on to respond to your kind advances, continue dumb and repel by my silence the friendship which you offer? I who am always forward to seek intimate relations with the good and even to thrust myself upon their affection.

"Two," we read, "are better than one. . . . for if they fall, the one will lift up his fellow. . . . a three fold cord is not quickly broken, and a brother that helps his brother shall be exalted." Write to me, therefore, boldly, and overcome the effect of absence by frequent colloquies.

2. You should not grieve that you are destitute of those bodily eyes which ants, flies, and creeping things have as well as men; rather you should rejoice that you possess that eye of which it is said in the Song of Songs, "Thou hast ravished my heart, my sister, my spouse; thou hast ravished my heart with one of thine eyes." This is the eye with which God is seen and to which Moses refers when he says:—"I will now turn aside and see this great sight." We even read of some philosophers of this world that they have plucked out their eyes in order to turn all their thoughts upon the pure depths of the mind. And a prophet has said "Death has entered through your windows." Our Lord too tells the Apostles: "Whosoever looketh upon a woman to lust after her hath committed adultery with her already in his heart." Consequently they are commanded to lift up their eyes and to look on the fields, for these are white and ready for harvest.

3. You request me by my exhortations to slay in you Nebuchadnezzar and Rabshakeh and Nebuzar-adan and Holofernes. Were they alive in you, you would never have sought my aid. No, they are dead within you, and you have begun to build up the ruins of Jerusalem with the help of Zerubbabel and of Joshua the son of Josedech the high priest, of Ezra and of Nehemiah. You do not put your wages into a bag with holes, but you lay up for yourselves treasures in heaven, and if you seek my friendship, it is because you believe me to be a servant of Christ.

I commend to you—although she needs no commendation but her own—my holy daughter Theodora, formerly the wife or rather the sister of Lucinius of blessed memory. Tell her that she must not grow weary of the path upon which she has entered, and that she can only reach the Holy Land by toiling through the wilderness. Warn her against supposing that the work of virtue is perfected when she has made her exodus from Egypt. Remind her that she must pass through snares innumerable to arrive at mount Nebo and the River Jordan, that she must receive circumcision anew at Gilgal, that Jericho must fall before her, overthrown by the blasts of priestly trumpets, that Adoni-zedec must be slain, that Ai and Hazor, once fairest of cities, must both fall.

The brothers who are with me in the monastery salute you, and I through you earnestly salute those reverend persons who deign to bestow upon me their regard.

LETTER LXXVII. TO OCEANUS

The eulogy of Fabiola whose restless life had come to an end in 399 a.d. Jerome tells the story of her sin and of her penitence (for which see Letter LV.), of the hospital established by her at Portus, of her visit to Bethlehem, and of her earnestness in the study of scripture. He relates how he wrote for her his account of the vestments of the high priest (Letter LXIV.) and how at the time of her death he was at her request engaged upon a commentary on the forty-two halting-places of the Israelites in the wilderness (Letter LXXIX.). This last he now sends along with this letter to Oceanus. Jerome also bestows praise upon Pammachius as the companion of all Fabiola's labours. The date of the letter is 399 a.d.

1. Several years since I consoled the venerated Paula, whilst her affliction was still recent for the falling asleep of Blaesilla. Four summers ago I wrote for the bishop Heliodorus the epitaph of Nepotian, and expended what ability I possessed in giving expression to my grief at his loss. Only two years have elapsed since I sent a brief letter to my dear Pammachius on the sudden flitting of his Paulina. I blushed to say more to one so learned or to give him back his own thoughts: lest I should seem less the consoler of a friend than the officious instructor of one already perfect. But now, Oceanus my son, the duty that you lay upon me is one that I gladly accept and would even seek unasked. For when new virtues have to be dealt with, an old subject itself becomes new. In previous cases I have had to soften and restrain a mother's affection, an uncle's grief, and a husband's yearning; according to the different requirements of each I have had to apply from scripture different remedies.

2. To-day you give me as my theme Fabiola, the praise of the Christians, the marvel of the gentiles, the sorrow of the poor, and the consolation of the monks. Whatever point in her character I choose to treat of first, pales into insignificance compared with those which follow after. Shall I praise her fasts? Her alms are greater still. Shall I commend her lowliness? The glow of her faith is yet brighter. Shall I mention her studied plainness in dress, her voluntary choice of plebeian costume and the garb of a slave that she might put to shame silken robes? To change one's disposition is a greater achievement than to change one's dress. It is harder for us to part with arrogance than with gold and gems. For, even though we throw away these, we plume ourselves sometimes on a meanness that is really ostentatious, and we make a bid with a saleable poverty for the popular applause. But a virtue that seeks concealment and is cherished in the inner consciousness appeals to no judgement but that of God. Thus the eulogies which I have to bestow upon Fabiola will be altogether

new: I must neglect the order of the rhetoricians and begin all I have to say only from the cradle of her conversion and of her penitence. Another writer, mindful of the school, would perhaps bring forward Quintus Maximus, "the man who by delaying rescued Rome," and the whole Fabian family; he would describe their struggles and battles and would exult that Fabiola had come to us through a line so noble, shewing that qualities not apparent in the branch still existed in the root. But as I am a lover of the inn at Bethlehem and of the Lord's stable in which the virgin travailed with and gave birth to an infant God, I shall deduce the lineage of Christ's handmaid not from a stock famous in history but from the lowliness of the church.

3. And because at the very outset there is a rock in the path and she is overwhelmed by a storm of censure, for having forsaken her first husband and having taken a second, I will not praise her for her conversion till I have first cleared her of this charge. So terrible then were the faults imputed to her former husband that not even a prostitute or a common slave could have put up with them. If I were to recount them, I should undo the heroism of the wife who chose to bear the blame of a separation rather than to blacken the character and expose the stains of him who was one body with her. I will only urge this one plea which is sufficient to exonerate a chaste matron and a Christian woman. The Lord has given commandment that a wife must not be put away "except it be for fornication, and that, if put away, she must remain unmarried." Now a commandment which is given to men logically applies to women also. For it cannot be that, while an adulterous wife is to be put away, an incontinent husband is to be retained. The apostle says: "he which is joined to an harlot is one body." Therefore she also who is joined to a whoremonger and unchaste person is made one body with him. The laws of Caesar are different, it is true, from the laws of Christ: Papinianus commands one thing; our own Paul another. Earthly laws give a free rein to the unchastity of men, merely condemning seduction and adultery; lust is allowed to range unrestrained among brothels and slave girls, as if the guilt were constituted by the rank of the person assailed and not by the purpose of the assailant. But with us Christians what is unlawful for women is equally unlawful for men, and as both serve the same God both are bound by the same obligations. Fabiola then has put away—they are quite right—a husband that was a sinner, guilty of this and that crime, sins—I have almost mentioned their names—with which the whole neighbourhood resounded but which the wife alone refused to disclose. If however it is made a charge against her that after repudiating her husband she did not continue unmarried, I readily admit this to have been a fault, but at the same time declare that it may have been a case of necessity. "It is better,"

the apostle tells us, "to marry than to burn." She was quite a young woman, she was not able to continue in widowhood. In the words of the apostle she saw another law in her members warring against the law of her mind; she felt herself dragged in chains as a captive towards the indulgences of wedlock. Therefore she thought it better openly to confess her weakness and to accept the semblance of an unhappy marriage than, with the name of a monogamist, to ply the trade of a courtesan. The same apostle wills that the younger widows should marry, bear children, and give no occasion to the adversary to speak reproachfully. And he at once goes on to explain his wish: "for some are already turned aside after Satan." Fabiola therefore was fully persuaded in her own mind: she thought she had acted legitimately in putting away her husband, and that when she had done so she was free to marry again. She did not know that the rigour of the gospel takes away from women all pretexts for remarriage so long as their former husbands are alive; and not knowing this, though she contrived to evade other assaults of the devil, she at this point unwittingly exposed herself to a wound from him.

4. But why do I linger over old and forgotten matters, seeking to excuse a fault for which Fabiola has herself confessed her penitence? Who would believe that, after the death of her second husband at a time when most widows, having shaken off the yoke of servitude, grow careless and allow themselves more liberty than ever, frequenting the baths, flitting through the streets, shewing their harlot faces everywhere; that at this time Fabiola came to herself? Yet it was then that she put on sackcloth to make public confession of her error. It was then that in the presence of all Rome (in the basilica which formerly belonged to that Lateranus who perished by the sword of Caesar) she stood in the ranks of the penitents and exposed before bishop, presbyters, and people—all of whom wept when they saw her weep—her dishevelled hair, pale features, soiled hands and unwashed neck. What sins would such a penance fail to purge away? What ingrained stains would such tears be unable to wash out? By a threefold confession Peter blotted out his threefold denial. If Aaron committed sacrilege by fashioning molten gold into the head of a calf, his brother's prayers made amends for his transgressions. If holy David, meekest of men, committed the double sin of murder and adultery, he atoned for it by a fast of seven days. He lay upon the earth, he rolled in the ashes, he forgot his royal power, he sought for light in the darkness. And then, turning his eyes to that God whom he had so deeply offended, he cried with a lamentable voice: "Against thee, thee only, have I sinned, and done this evil in thy sight," and "Restore unto me the joy of thy salvation and uphold me with thy free spirit." He who by his virtues teaches me how to stand and not to fall, by his peni-

tence teaches me how, if I fall, I may rise again. Among the kings do we read of any so wicked as Ahab, of whom the scripture says: "there was none like unto Ahab which did sell himself to work wickedness in the sight of the Lord"? For shedding Naboth's blood Elijah rebuked him, and the prophet denounced God's wrath against him: "Hast thou killed and also taken possession? . . . behold I will bring evil upon thee and will take away thy posterity" and so on. Yet when Ahab heard these words "he rent his clothes, and put sackcloth upon his flesh, and fasted . . . in sackcloth, and went softly." Then came the word of God to Elijah the Tishbite saying: "Seest thou how Ahab humbleth himself before me? Because he humbleth himself before me, I will not bring the evil in his days." O happy penitence which has drawn down upon itself the eyes of God, and which has by confessing its error changed the sentence of God's anger! The same conduct is in the Chronicles attributed to Manasseh, and in the book of the prophet Jonah to Nineveh, and in the gospel to the publican. The first of these not only was allowed to obtain forgiveness but also recovered his kingdom, the second broke the force of God's impending wrath, while the third, smiting his breast with his hands, "would not lift up so much as his eyes to heaven." Yet for all that the publican with his humble confession of his faults went back justified far more than the Pharisee with his arrogant boasting of his virtues. This is not however the place to preach penitence, neither am I writing against Montanus and Novatus. Else would I say of it that it is "a sacrifice . . . well pleasing to God," I would cite the words of the psalmist: "the sacrifices of God are a broken spirit," and those of Ezekiel "I prefer the repentance of a sinner rather than his death," and those of Baruch, "Arise, arise, O Jerusalem," and many other proclamations made by the trumpets of the prophets.

5. But this one thing I will say, for it is at once useful to my readers and pertinent to my present theme. As Fabiola was not ashamed of the Lord on earth, so He shall not be ashamed of her in heaven. She laid bare her wound to the gaze of all, and Rome beheld with tears the disfiguring scar which marred her beauty. She uncovered her limbs, bared her head, and closed her mouth. She no longer entered the church of God but, like Miriam the sister of Moses, she sat apart without the camp, till the priest who had cast her out should himself call her back. She came down like the daughter of Babylon from the throne of her daintiness, she took the millstones and ground meal, she passed barefooted through rivers of tears. She sat upon the coals of fire, and these became her aid. That face by which she had once pleased her second husband she now smote with blows; she hated jewels, shunned ornaments and could not bear to look upon fine linen. In fact she bewailed the sin she had commit-

ted as bitterly as if it had been adultery, and went to the expense of many remedies in her eagerness to cure her one wound.

6. Having found myself aground in the shallows of Fabiola's sin, I have dwelt thus long upon her penitence in order that I might open up a larger and quite unimpeded space for the description of her praises. Restored to communion before the eyes of the whole church, what did she do? In the day of prosperity she was not forgetful of affliction; and, having once suffered shipwreck she was unwilling again to face the risks of the sea. Instead therefore of re-embarking on her old life, she broke up and sold all that she could lay hands on of her property (it was large and suitable to her rank), and turning it into money she laid out this for the benefit of the poor. She was the first person to found a hospital, into which she might gather sufferers out of the streets, and where she might nurse the unfortunate victims of sickness and want. Need I now recount the various ailments of human beings? Need I speak of noses slit, eyes put out, feet half burnt, hands covered with sores? Or of limbs dropsical and atrophied? Or of diseased flesh alive with worms? Often did she carry on her own shoulders persons infected with jaundice or with filth. Often too did she wash away the matter discharged from wounds which others, even though men, could not bear to look at. She gave food to her patients with her own hand, and moistened the scarce breathing lips of the dying with sips of liquid. I know of many wealthy and devout persons who, unable to overcome their natural repugnance to such sights, perform this work of mercy by the agency of others, giving money instead of personal aid. I do not blame them and am far from construing their weakness of resolution into a want of faith. While however I pardon such squeamishness, I extol to the skies the enthusiastic zeal of a mind that is above it. A great faith makes little of such trifles. But I know how terrible was the retribution which fell upon the proud mind of the rich man clothed in purple for not having helped Lazarus. The poor wretch whom we despise, whom we cannot so much as look at, and the very sight of whom turns our stomachs, is human like ourselves, is made of the same clay as we are, is formed out of the same elements. All that he suffers we too may suffer. Let us then regard his wounds as though they were our own, and then all our insensibility to another's suffering will give way before our pity for ourselves.

Not with a hundred tongues or throat of bronze
Could I exhaust the forms of fell disease

which Fabiola so wonderfully alleviated in the suffering poor that many of the healthy fell to envying the sick. However she showed the same liberality towards the clergy and monks and virgins. Was there a monastery which was not supported by Fabiola's wealth? Was there a naked or bedridden person who was not clothed with garments supplied by her? Were there ever any in want to whom she failed to give a quick and unhesitating supply? Even Rome was not wide enough for her pity. Either in her own person or else through the agency of reverend and trustworthy men she went from island to island and carried her bounty not only round the Etruscan Sea, but throughout the district of the Volscians, as it stands along those secluded and winding shores where communities of monks are to be found.

7. Suddenly she made up her mind, against the advice of all her friends, to take ship and to come to Jerusalem. Here she was welcomed by a large concourse of people and for a short time took advantage of my hospitality. Indeed, when I call to mind our meeting, I seem to see her here now instead of in the past. Blessed Jesus, what zeal, what earnestness she bestowed upon the sacred volumes! In her eagerness to satisfy what was a veritable craving she would run through Prophets, Gospels, and Psalms: she would suggest questions and treasure up the answers in the desk of her own bosom. And yet this eagerness to hear did not bring with it any feeling of satiety: increasing her knowledge she also increased her sorrow, and by casting oil upon the flame she did but supply fuel for a still more burning zeal. One day we had before us the book of Numbers written by Moses, and she modestly questioned me as to the meaning of the great mass of names there to be found. Why was it, she inquired, that single tribes were differently associated in this passage and in that, how came it that the soothsayer Balaam in prophesying of the future mysteries of Christ spoke more plainly of Him than almost any other prophet? I replied as best I could and tried to satisfy her enquiries. Then unrolling the book still farther she came to the passage in which is given the list of all the halting-places by which the people after leaving Egypt made its way to the waters of Jordan. And when she asked me the meaning and reason of each of these, I spoke doubtfully about some, dealt with others in a tone of assurance, and in several instances simply confessed my ignorance. Hereupon she began to press me harder still, expostulating with me as though it were a thing unallowable that I should be ignorant of what I did not know, yet at the same time affirming her own unworthiness to understand mysteries so deep. In a word I was ashamed to refuse her request and allowed her to extort from me a promise that I would devote a special work to this subject for her use. Till the present time I have had to defer the fulfilment of my promise: as I now perceive, by the Will of God in order that it should be consecrated to her memory. As in a previous work I clothed her with the priestly vestments, so in the pages of the present she may rejoice that she has passed through the wilderness of this world and has come at last to the land of promise.

8. But let me continue the task which I have begun. Whilst I was in search of a suitable dwelling for so great a lady, whose only conception of the solitary life included a place of resort like Mary's inn; suddenly messengers flew this way and that and the whole East was terror-struck. For news came that the hordes of the Huns had poured forth all the way from Maeotis (they had their haunts between the icy Tanais and the rude Massagetae where the gates of Alexander keep back the wild peoples behind the Caucasus); and that, speeding hither and thither on their nimble-footed horses, they were filling all the world with panic and bloodshed. The Roman army was absent at the time, being detained in Italy on account of the civil wars. Of these Huns Herodotus tells us that under Darius King of the Medes they held the East in bondage for twenty years and that from the Egyptians and Ethiopians they exacted a yearly tribute. May Jesus avert from the Roman world the farther assaults of these wild beasts! Everywhere their approach was unexpected, they outstripped rumour in speed, and, when they came, they spared neither religion nor rank nor age, even for wailing infants they had no pity. Children were forced to die before it could be said that they had begun to live; and little ones not realizing their miserable fate might be seen smiling in the hands and at the weapons of their enemies. It was generally agreed that the goal of the invaders was Jerusalem and that it was their excessive desire for gold which made them hasten to this particular city. Its walls uncared for in time of peace were accordingly put in repair. Antioch was in a state of siege. Tyre, desirous of cutting itself off from the land, sought once more its ancient island. We too were compelled to man our ships and to lie off the shore as a precaution against the arrival of our foes. No matter how hard the winds might blow, we could not but dread the barbarians more than shipwreck. It was not, however, so much for our own safety that we were anxious as for the chastity of the virgins who were with us. Just at that time also there was dissension among us, and our intestine struggles threw into the shade our battle with the barbarians. I myself clung to my long-settled abode in the East and gave way to my deep-seated love for the holy places. Fabiola, used as she was to moving from city to city and having no other property but what her baggage contained, returned to her native land; to live in poverty where she had once been rich, to lodge in the house of another, she who in old days had lodged many guests in her own, and—not unduly to prolong my account—to bestow upon the poor before the eyes of Rome the proceeds of that property which Rome knew her to have sold.

9. This only do I lament that in her the holy places lost a necklace of the loveliest. Rome recovered what it had previously parted with, and the wanton and slanderous tongues of the heathen were confuted by the testimony of their

own eyes. Others may commend her pity, her humility, her faith: I will rather praise her ardour of soul. The letter in which as a young man I once urged Heliodorus to the life of a hermit she knew by heart, and whenever she looked upon the walls of Rome she complained that she was in a prison. Forgetful of her sex, unmindful of her frailty, and only desiring to be alone she was in fact there where her soul lingered. The counsels of her friends could not hold her back; so eager was she to burst from the city as from a place of bondage. Nor did she leave the distribution of her alms to others; she distributed them herself. Her wish was that, after equitably dispensing her money to the poor, she might herself find support from others for the sake of Christ. In such haste was she and so impatient of delay that you would fancy her on the eve of her departure. As she was always ready, death could not find her unprepared.

10. As I pen her praises, my dear Pammachius seems suddenly to rise before me. His wife Paulina sleeps that he may keep vigil; she has gone before her husband that he remaining behind may be Christ's servant. Although he was his wife's heir, others—I mean the poor—are now in possession of his inheritance. He and Fabiola contended for the privilege of setting up a tent like that of Abraham at Portus. The contest which arose between them was for the supremacy in shewing kindness. Each conquered and each was overcome. Both admitted themselves to be at once victors and vanquished for what each had desired to effect alone both accomplished together. They united their resources and combined their plans that harmony might forward what rivalry must have brought to nought. No sooner was the scheme broached than it was carried out. A house was purchased to serve as a shelter, and a crowd flocked into it. "There was no more travail in Jacob nor distress in Israel." The seas carried voyagers to find a welcome here on landing. Travellers left Rome in haste to take advantage of the mild coast before setting sail. What Publius once did in the island of Malta for one apostle and—not to leave room for gainsaying—for a single ship's crew, Fabiola and Pammachius have done over and over again for large numbers; and not only have they supplied the wants of the destitute, but so universal has been their munificence that they have provided additional means for those who have something already. The whole world knows that a home for strangers has been established at Portus; and Britain has learned in the summer what Egypt and Parthia knew in the spring.

11. In the death of this noble lady we have seen a fulfilment of the apostle's words:—"All things work together for good to them that fear God." Having a presentiment of what would happen, she had written to several monks to come and release her from the burthen under which she laboured; for she wished to make to herself friends of the mammon of unrighteousness that they might

receive her into everlasting habitations. They came to her and she made them her friends; she fell asleep in the way that she had wished, and having at last laid aside her burthen she soared more lightly up to heaven. How great a marvel Fabiola had been to Rome while she lived came out in the behaviour of the people now that she was dead. Hardly had she breathed her last breath, hardly had she given back her soul to Christ whose it was when

Flying Rumour heralding the woe

gathered the entire city to attend her obsequies. Psalms were chaunted and the gilded ceilings of the temples were shaken with uplifted shouts of Alleluia.

The choirs of young and old extolled her deeds
And sang the praises of her holy soul.

Her triumph was more glorious far than those won by Furius over the Gauls, by Papirius over the Samnites, by Scipio over Numantia, by Pompey over Pontus. They had conquered physical force, she had mastered spiritual iniquities. I seem to hear even now the squadrons which led the van of the procession, and the sound of the feet of the multitude which thronged in thousands to attend her funeral. The streets, porches, and roofs from which a view could be obtained were inadequate to accommodate the spectators. On that day Rome saw all her peoples gathered together in one, and each person present flattered himself that he had some part in the glory of her penitence. No wonder indeed that men should thus exult in the salvation of one at whose conversion there was joy among the angels in heaven.

12. I give you this, Fabiola, the best gift of my aged powers, to be as it were a funeral offering. Oftentimes have I praised virgins and widows and married women who have kept their garments always white and who follow the Lamb whithersoever He goeth. Happy indeed is she in her encomium who throughout her life has been stained by no defilement. But let envy depart and censoriousness be silent. If the father of the house is good why should our eye be evil? The soul which fell among thieves has been carried home upon the shoulders of Christ. In our father's house are many mansions. Where sin hath abounded, grace hath much more abounded. To whom more is forgiven the same loveth more.

LETTER LXXVIII. TO FABIOLA

A treatise on the Forty-two Mansions or Halting-places of the Israelites, originally intended for Fabiola but not completed until after her death. Sent to Oceanus along with the preceding letter. These Mansions are made an emblem of the Christian's pilgrimage, the true Hebrew hastening to pass from earth to heaven.

LETTER LXXIX. TO SALVINA

A letter of consolation addressed by Jerome to Salvina (a lady of the imperial court) on the death of her husband Nebridius. After excusing his temerity in addressing a complete stranger Jerome eulogizes the virtues of Nebridius, particularly his chastity and his bounty to the poor. He next warns Salvina (in no courtier-like terms) of the dangers that will beset her as a widow and recommends her to devote all her energies to the careful training of the son and daughter who are now her principal charge. The tone of the letter is somewhat arrogant and it can hardly be regarded as one of Jerome's happiest efforts. Salvina, however, consecrated her life to deeds of piety, and became one of Chrysostom's deaconesses. Its date is 400 a.d.

1. My desire to do my duty may, I fear, expose me to a charge of self-seeking; and although I do but follow the example of Him who said: "learn of me for I am meek and lowly of heart," the course that I am taking may be attributed to a desire for notoriety. Men may say that I am not so much trying to console a widow in affliction as endeavouring to creep into the imperial court; and that, while I make a pretext of offering comfort, I am really seeking the friendship of the great. Clearly this will not be the opinion of any one who knows the commandment: "thou shalt not respect the person of the poor," a precept given lest under pretext of shewing pity we should judge unjust judgment. For each individual is to be judged not by his personal importance but by the merits of his case. His wealth need not stand in the way of the rich man, if he makes a good use of it; and poverty can be no recommendation to the poor if in the midst of squalor and want he fails to keep clear of wrong doing. Proofs of these things are not wanting either in scriptural times or our own; for Abraham, in spite of his immense wealth, was "the friend of God" and poor men are daily arrested and punished for their crimes by law. She whom I now address is both rich and poor so that she cannot say what she actually has. For it is not of her purse that I am speaking but of the purity of her soul. I do not know her face but I am well acquainted with her virtues; for report speaks well of her and her youth makes her chastity all the more commendable. By her grief for her young husband she has set an example to all wives; and by her resignation she has proved that she believes him not lost but gone before. The greatness of her bereavement has brought out the reality of her religion. For

while she forgets her lost Nebridius, she knows that in Christ he is with her still.

But why do I write to one who is a stranger to me? For three reasons. First, because (as a priest is bound to do) I love all Christians as my children and find my glory in promoting their welfare. Secondly because the father of Nebridius was bound to me by the closest ties. Lastly—and this is a stronger reason than the others—because I have failed to say no to my son Avitus. With an importunacy surpassing that of the widow towards the unjust judge he wrote to me so frequently and put before me so many instances in which I had previously dealt with a similar theme, that he overcame my modest reluctance and made the resolve to do not what would best become me but what would most nearly meet his wishes.

2. As the mother of Nebridius was sister to the empress and as he was brought up in the bosom of his aunt, another might perhaps praise him for having so much endeared himself to the unvanquished emperor. Theodosius, indeed, procured him from Africa a wife of the highest rank, who, as her native land at this time was distracted by civil wars, became a kind of hostage for its loyalty. I ought to say at the very outset that Nebridius seems to have had a presentiment that he would die early. For amid the splendour of the palace and in the high positions to which his rank and not his years entitled him he lived always as one who believed that he must soon go to meet Christ. Of Cornelius, the centurion of the Italian band, the sacred narrative tells us that God so fully accepted him as to send to him an angel; and that this angel told him that to his merit was due the mystery whereby Peter from the narrow limits of the circumcision was conveyed to the wide field of the uncircumcision. He was the first Gentile baptized by the apostle, and in him the Gentiles were set apart to salvation. Now of this man it is written: "there was a certain man in Caesarea called Cornelius, a centurion of the band called the Italian band, a devout man and one that feared God with all his house, which gave much alms to the people, and prayed to God alway." All this that is said of him I claim—with a change of name only—for my dear Nebridius. So "devout" was this latter and so enamoured of chastity that at his marriage he was still pure. So truly did he "fear God with all his house" that forgetting his high position he spent all his time with monks and clergymen. So profuse were the alms which he gave to the people that his doors were continually beset with swarms of sick and poor. And assuredly he "prayed to God alway" that what was for the best might happen to him. Therefore "speedily was he taken away lest that wickedness should alter his understanding . . . for his soul pleased the Lord." Thus I may truthfully apply to him the apostle's words: "Of a truth I perceive that God is

no respecter of persons: but in every nation he that feareth Him and worketh righteousness, is accepted with Him." As a soldier Nebridius took no harm from his cloak and sword-belt and troops of orderlies; for while he wore the uniform of the emperor he was enlisted in the service of God. On the other hand nothing is gained by men who while they affect coarse mantles, sombre tunics, dirt, and poverty, belie by their deeds their lofty pretensions. Of another centurion we find in the gospel this testimony from our Lord:—"I have not found so great faith, no not in Israel." And, to go back to earlier times, we read of Joseph who gave proof of his integrity both when he was in want and when he was rich, and who inculcated freedom of soul both as slave and as lord. He was made next to Pharaoh and invested with the emblems of royalty; yet so dear was he to God that, alone of all the patriarchs, he became the father of two tribes. Daniel and the three children were set over the affairs of Babylon and were numbered among the princes of the state; yet although they wore the dress of Nebuchadnezzar, in their hearts they served God. Mordecai also and Esther amid purple and silk and jewels overcame pride with humility; and although captives were so highly esteemed as to be able to impose commands upon their conquerors.

3. These remarks are intended to shew that the youth of whom I speak used his kinship to the royal family, his abundant wealth, and the outward tokens of power, as helps to virtue. For, as the preacher says, "wisdom is a defence and money is a defence" also. We must not hastily conclude that this statement conflicts with that of the Lord: "verily I say unto you that a rich man shall hardly enter into the kingdom of heaven; and again I say unto you, It is easier for a camel to go through the eye of a needle than for a rich man to enter into the kingdom of heaven." Were it so, the salvation of Zacchaeus the publican, described in scripture as a man of great wealth, would contradict the Lord's declaration. But that what is impossible with men is possible with God we are taught by the counsel of the apostle who thus writes to Timothy:—"charge them that are rich in this world that they be not highminded, nor trust in uncertain riches, but in the living God who giveth us richly all things to enjoy, that they do good, that they be rich in good works, ready to distribute. willing to communicate, laying up in store for themselves a good foundation against the time to come that they may lay hold on the true life." We have learned how a camel can pass through a needle's eye, how an animal with a hump on its back, when it has laid down its packs, can take to itself the wings of a dove and rest in the branches of the tree which has grown from a grain of mustard seed. In Isaiah we read of camels, the dromedaries of Midian and Ephah and Sheba, which carry gold and incense to the city of the Lord. On like typical

camels the Ishmaelitish merchantmen bring down to the Egyptians perfume and incense and balm (of the kind that grows in Gilead good for the healing of wounds); and so fortunate are they that in the purchase and sale of Joseph they have for their merchandise the Saviour of the world. And AEsop's fable tells us of a mouse which after eating its fill can no longer creep out as before it crept in.

4. Daily did my dear Nebridius revolve the words: "they that will be rich fall into temptation and a snare" of the devil "and into many lusts." All the money that the Emperor's bounty gave him or that his badges of office procured him he laid out for the benefit of the poor. For he knew the commandment of the Lord: "If thou wilt be perfect go and sell that thou hast, and give to the poor, and come and follow me." And because he could not literally fulfil these directions, having a wife and little children and a large household, he made to himself friends of the mammon of unrighteousness that they might receive him into everlasting habitations. He did not once for all cast away his brethren, as did the apostles who forsook father and nets and ship, but by an equality he ministered to the want of others out of his own abundance that afterwards their wealth might be a supply for his own want. The lady to whom this letter is addressed knows that what I narrate is only known to me by hearsay, but she is aware also that I am no Greek writer repaying with flattery some benefit conferred upon me. Far be such an imputation from all Christians. Having food and raiment we are therewith content. Where there is cheap cabbage and household bread, a sufficiency to eat and a sufficiency to drink, these riches are superfluous and no place is left for flattery with its sordid calculations. You may conclude therefore that, where there is no motive to tell a falsehood, the testimony given is true.

5. It must not, however, be supposed that I praise Nebridius only for his liberality in alms-giving, although we are taught the great importance of this in the words: "water will quench a flaming fire; and alms maketh an atonement for sins." I will pass on now to his other virtues each one of which is to be found but in few men. Who ever entered the furnace of the King of Babylon without being burned? Was there ever a young man whose garment his Egyptian mistress did not seize? Was there ever a eunuch's wife contented with a childless marriage bed? Is there any man who is not appalled by the struggle of which the apostle says: "I see another law in my members warring against the law of my mind, and bringing me into captivity to the law of sin which is in my members?" But wonderful to say Nebridius, though bred up in a palace as a companion and fellow pupil of the Augusti (whose table is supplied by the whole world and ministered to by land and sea); Nebridius, I say, though in

the midst of abundance and in the flower of his age, shewed himself more modest than a girl and never gave occasion, even the slightest, for scandalous rumours. Again though he was the friend, companion, and cousin of princes and had been educated along with them—a thing which makes even strangers intimate—he did not allow pride to inflate him or frown with contempt upon others who were less fortunate than he: no, he was kind to all, and while he loved the princes as brothers he revered them as sovereigns. He used to avow that his own health and safety were dependent upon theirs. Their attendants and all those officers of the palace who by their numbers add to the grandeur of the imperial court he had so well conciliated by shewing his regard for them, that men who were in reality inferior to him were led by his attention to believe themselves his peers. It is no easy task to throw one's rank into the shade by one's virtue, or to gain the affection of men who are forced to yield you precedence. What widow was not supported by his help? What ward did not find in him a father? To him the bishops of the entire East used to bring the prayers of the unfortunate and the petitions of the distressed. Whenever he asked the Emperor for a boon, he sought either alms for the poor or ransom for captives or clemency for the afflicted. Accordingly the princes also used gladly to accede to his requests, for they knew well that their bounty would benefit not one man but many.

6. Why do I farther postpone the end? "All flesh is grass and all the goodliness thereof is as the flower of the field." The dust has returned to the dust. He has fallen asleep in the Lord and has been laid with his fathers, full of days and of light and fostered in a good old age. For "wisdom is the grey hair unto men." "In a short time he" has "fulfilled a long time." In his place we now have his charming children. His wife is the heir of his chastity. To those who miss his father the tiny Nebridius shews him once more, for

Such were the eyes and hands and looks he bore.

A spark of the parent's excellence shines in the son: the child's face betrays like a mirror a resemblance in character.

That narrow frame contains a hero's heart.

And with him there is his sister, a basket of roses and lilies, a mixture of ivory and purple. Her face though it takes after that of her father inclines to be still more attractive; and, while her complexion is that of her mother, she is so like both her parents that the lineaments of each are reflected in her features. So sweet and honied is she that she is the pride of all her kinsfolk. The Emperor does not disdain to hold her in his arms, and the Empress likes nothing better than to nurse her on her lap. Everyone runs to be the first to catch her up. Now she clings to the neck of one, and now she is fondled in the arms of another. She prattles and stammers, and is all the sweeter for her faltering tongue.

7. You have, therefore, Salvina, those to nurse who may well represent to you your absent husband: "Lo, children are an heritage of the Lord; and the fruit of the womb is his reward." In the place of one husband you have received two children, and thus your affection has more objects than before. All that was due to him you can give to them. Temper grief with love, for if he is gone they are still with you. It is no small merit in God's eyes to bring up children well. Hear the apostle's counsel: "Let not a widow be taken into the number under threescore years old, having been the wife of one man, well reported of for good works; if she have brought up children, if she have lodged strangers, if she have washed the saints' feet, if she have relieved the afflicted, if she have diligently followed every good work." Here you learn the roll of the virtues which God requires of you, what is due to the name of widow which you bear, and by what good deeds you can attain to that second degree of chastity which is still open to you. Do not be disturbed because the apostle allows none to be chosen as a widow under threescore years old, neither suppose that he intends to reject those who are still young. Believe that you are indeed chosen by him who said to his disciple, "Let no man despise thy youth," your want of age that is, not your want of continence. If this be not his meaning, all who become widows under threescore years will have to take husbands. He is training a church still untaught in Christ, and making provision for people of all stations but especially for the poor, the charge of whom had been committed to himself and Barnabas. Thus he wishes only those to be supported by the exertions of the church who cannot labour with their own hands, and who are widows indeed, approved by their years and by their lives. The faults of his children made Eli the priest an offence to God. On the other hand He is appeased by the virtues of such as "continue in faith and charity and holiness with chastity." "O Timothy," cries the apostle, "keep thyself pure." Far be it from me to suspect you capable of doing anything wrong; still it is only a kindness to admonish one whose youth and opulence lead her into temptation. You must take what I am going to say as addressed not to you but to your girlish years. A widow "that liveth in pleasure is dead while she liveth." So speaks the "chosen vessel" and the words are brought out from his treasure who could boldly say: "Do ye seek a proof of Christ speaking in me?" Yet they are the words of one who in his own person admitted the weakness of the human body, saying: "The good that I would I do not: but the evil which I would not that I do." And again: Therefore "I keep under my body and bring it into subjection lest that by any means when I have preached to others I

myself should be a castaway." If Paul is afraid, which of us can venture to be confident? If David the friend of God and Solomon who loved God were overcome like other men, if their fall is meant to warn us and their penitence to lead us to salvation, who in this slippery life can be sure of not falling? Never let pheasants be seen upon your table, or plump turtledoves or black cock from Ionia, or any of those birds so expensive that they fly away with the largest properties. And do not fancy that you eschew meat diet when you reject pork, hare, and venison and the savoury flesh of other quadrupeds. It is not the number of feet that makes the difference but delicacy of flavour. I know that the apostle has said: "every creature of God is good and nothing to be refused if it be received with thanksgiving." But the same apostle says: "it is good neither to eat flesh nor to drink wine," and in another place: "be not drunk with wine wherein is excess." "Every creature of God is good"—the precept is intended for those who are careful how they may please their husbands. Let those feed on flesh who serve the flesh, whose bodies boil with desire, who are tied to husbands, and who set their hearts on having offspring. Let those whose wombs are burthened cram their stomachs with flesh. But you have buried every indulgence in your husband's tomb: over his bier you have cleansed with tears a face stained with rouge and whitelead; you have exchanged a white robe and gilded buskins for a sombre tunic and black shoes; and only one thing more is needed, perseverance in fasting. Let paleness and squalor be henceforth your jewels. Do not pamper your youthful limbs with a bed of down or kindle your young blood with hot baths. Hear what words a heathen poet puts into the mouth of a chaste widow:

He, my first spouse, has robbed me of my loves.
So be it: let him keep them in the tomb.

If common glass is worth so much, what must be the value of a pearl of price? If in deference to a law of nature a Gentile widow can condemn all sensual indulgence, what must we expect from a Christian widow who owes her chastity not to one who is dead but to one with whom she shall reign in heaven?

8. Do not, I pray you, regard these general remarks—applying as they do to all young women—as intended to insult you or to take you to task. I write in a spirit of apprehension, yet pray that you may never know the nature of my fears. A woman's reputation is a tender plant; it is like a fair flower which withers at the slightest blast and fades away at the first breath of wind. Especially is this so when she is of an age to fall into temptation and the authority of a husband is wanting to her. For the very shadow of a husband is a wife's safeguard. What has a widow to do with a large household or with troops of

retainers? As servants, it is true, she must not despise them, but as men she ought to blush before them. If a grand establishment requires such domestics, let her at least set over them an old man of spotless morals whose dignity may guard the honour of his mistress. I know of many widows who, although they live with closed doors, have not escaped the imputation of too great intimacy with their servants. These latter become objects of suspicion when they dress above their degree, or when they are stout and sleek, or when they are of an age inclined to passion, or when knowledge of the favour in which they are secretly held betrays itself in a too confident demeanour. For such pride, however carefully concealed, is sure to break out in a contempt for fellow-servants as servants. I make these seemingly superfluous remarks that you may keep your heart with all diligence and guard against every scandal that may be broached concerning you.

9. Take no well-curled steward to walk with you, no effeminate actor, no devilish singer of poisoned sweetness, no spruce and smooth-shorn youth. Let no theatrical compliments, no obsequious adulation be associated with you. Keep with you bands of widows and virgins; and let your consolers be of your own sex. The character of the mistress is judged by that of the maid. So long as you have with you a holy mother, so long as an aunt vowed to virginity is at your side, you ought not to neglect them and at your own risk to seek the company of strangers. Let the divine scripture be always in your hands, and give yourself so frequently to prayer that such shafts of evil thoughts as ever assail the young may thereby find a shield to repel them. It is difficult, nay more it is impossible, to escape the beginnings of those internal motions which the Greeks with much significance call propatheiai that is predispositions to passion.' The fact is that suggestions of sin tickle all our minds, and the decision rests with our own hearts either to admit or to reject the thoughts which come. The Lord of nature Himself says in the gospel:—"out of the heart proceed evil thoughts, murders, adulteries, fornications, thefts, false witness, blasphemies." It is clear from the testimony of another book that "the imagination of man's heart is evil from his youth," and that the soul wavers between the works of the flesh and of the spirit enumerated by the apostle, desiring now the former and now the latter. For

From faults no mortal man is wholly free;
The best is he who has but few of them.

And, to quote the same poet,

At moles men cavil when they mark fair skins.

To the same effect in different words the prophet says:—"I am so troubled that I cannot speak," and in the same book, "Be ye angry and sin not." So

Archytas of Tarentum once said to a careless steward: "I should have flogged you to death had I not been in a passion." For "the wrath of man worketh not the righteousness of God." Now what is here said of one form of perturbation may be applied to all. Just as anger is human and the repression of it Christian, so it is with other passions. The flesh always lusts after the things of the flesh, and by its allurements draws the soul to partake of deadly pleasures; but it is for us Christians to restrain the desire for sensual indulgence by an intenser love for Christ. It is for us to break in the mettlesome brute within us by fasting, in order that it may desire not lust but food and amble easily and steadily forward having for its rider the Holy Spirit.

10. Why do I write thus? To shew you that you are but human and subject, unless you guard against them, to human passions. We are all of us made of the same clay and formed of the same elements. Whether we wear silk or rags we are all at the mercy of the same desire. It does not fear the royal purple; it does not disdain the squalor of the mendicant. It is better then to suffer in stomach than in soul, to rule the body than to serve it, to lose one's balance than to lose one's chastity. Let us not lull ourselves with the delusion that we can always fall back on penitence. For this is at best but a remedy for misery. Let us shrink from incurring a wound which must be painful to cure. For it is one thing to enter the haven of salvation with ship safe and merchandise uninjured, and another to cling naked to a plank and, as the waves toss you this way and that, to be dashed again and again on the sharp rocks. A widow should be ignorant that second marriage is permitted; she should know nothing of the apostle's words:—"It is better to marry than to burn." Remove what is said to be worse, the risk of burning, and marriage will cease to be regarded as good. Of course I repudiate the slanders of the heretics; I know that "marriage is honourable . . . and the bed undefiled." Yet Adam even after he was expelled from paradise had but one wife. The accursed and blood-stained Lamech, descended from the stock of Cain, was the first to make out of one rib two wives; and the seedling of digamy then planted was altogether destroyed by the doom of the deluge. It is true that in writing to Timothy the apostle from fear of fornication is forced to countenance second marriage. His words are these:—"I will therefore that the younger women marry, bear children, guide the house, give none occasion to the adversary to speak reproachfully." But he immediately adds as a reason for this concession; "for some are already turned aside after Satan." Thus we see that he is offering not a crown to those who stand but a helping hand to those who are down. What must a second marriage be if it is looked on merely as an alternative to the brothel! "For some," he writes, "are already turned aside after Satan." The upshot of the

whole matter is that, if a young widow cannot or will not contain herself, she had better take a husband to her bed than the devil.

A noble alternative truly which is only to be embraced in preference to Satan! In old days even Jerusalem went a-whoring and opened her feet to every one that passed by. It was in Egypt that she was first deflowered and there that her teats were bruised. And afterwards when she had come to the wilderness and, impatient of the delays of her leader Moses, had said when maddened by the stings of lust: "these be thy gods, O Israel, which brought thee up out of the land of Egypt," she received statutes that were not good and commandments that were altogether evil whereby she should not live but should be punished through them. Is it surprising then that when the apostle had said in another place of young widows: "when they have begun to wax wanton against Christ they will marry, having damnation because they have cast off their first faith," he granted to such as should wax wanton statutes of digamy that were not good and commandments that were altogether evil? For the reason which he gives for allowing a second husband would justify a woman in marrying a third or even, if she liked, a twentieth. He evidently wished to shew them that he was not so much anxious that they should take husbands as that they should avoid paramours. These things, dearest daughter in Christ, I impress upon you and frequently repeat, that you may forget those things which are behind and reach forth unto those things which are before. You have widows like yourself worthy to be your models, Judith renowned in Hebrew story and Anna the daughter of Phanuel famous in the gospel. Both these lived day and night in the temple and preserved the treasure of their chastity by prayer and by fasting. One was a type of the Church which cuts off the head of the devil and the other first received in her arms the saviour of the world and had revealed to her the holy mysteries which were to come. In conclusion I beg you to attribute the shortness of my letter not to want of language or scarcity of matter but to a deep sense of modesty which makes me fear to force myself too long upon the ears of a stranger, and causes me to dread the secret verdict of those who read my words.

LETTER LXXX. FROM RUFINUS TO MACARIUS

Rufinus on his return from Bethlehem to Rome published a Latin version of Origen's treatise peri 'Archon, On First Principles. To this he prefixed the preface which is here printed among Jerome's letters. Professing to take as his model Jerome's own translations of Origen's commentaries which he greatly praises, he declares that, following his example, he has paraphrased the obscure passages of the treatise and has paraphrased the obscure passages of the treatise and has omitted as due to interpolators such parts as seem heretical. This preface with its insincere praise of Jerome (whose name, however, is not mentioned) and its avowed manipulation of Origen's text caused much perplexity at Rome (see Letters LXXXI., LXXXIII., and LXXXIV.), and gave rise to the controversy between Rufinus and Jerome described in the Prolegomena, and given at length in vol. iii. of this Series. The date is 398 a.d.

1. Large numbers of the brethren have, I know, in their zeal for the knowledge of the scriptures begged learned men skilled in Greek literature to make Origen a Roman by bringing home his teaching to Latin ears. One of these scholars, a dear brother and associate, at the request of bishop Damasus translated from Greek into Latin his two homilies on the Song of Songs and prefaced the work with an eloquent and eulogistic introduction such as could not fail to arouse in all an ardent desire to read and to study Origen. To the soul of that just man—so he declared—the words of the Song were applicable: "the king hath brought me into his chambers;" and he went on to speak thus: "while in his other books Origen surpasses all former writers, in dealing with the Song of Songs he surpasses himself." In his preface he pledges himself to give to Roman ears these homilies of Origen and as many of his other works as he can. His style is certainly attractive but I can see that he aims at a more ambitious task than that of a mere translator. Not content with rendering the words of Origen he desires to be himself the teacher. I for my part do but follow up an enterprise which he has sanctioned and commenced, but I lack his vigorous eloquence with which to adorn the sayings of this great man. I am even afraid lest my deficiencies and inadequate command of Latin may detract seriously from the reputation of one whom this writer has deservedly termed second only to the apostles as a teacher of the Church in knowledge and in wisdom.

2. Often turning this over in my mind I held my peace and refused to listen to the brethren when—as frequently happened—they urged me to undertake the work. But your persistence, most faithful brother Macarius, is so great that even want of ability cannot resist it. Thus, to escape the constant importunings to which you subject me, I have given way contrary to my resolution; yet only on these terms that, so far as is possible, I am to be free to follow the rules of translation laid down by my predecessors, and particularly those acted upon by the writer whom I have just mentioned. He has rendered into Latin more than seventy of Origen's homiletical treatises and a few also of his commentaries upon the apostle; and in these wherever the Greek text presents a stumbling

block, he has smoothed it down in his version and has so emended the language used that a Latin writer can find no word that is at variance with our faith. In his steps, therefore, I propose to walk, if not displaying the same vigorous eloquence at least observing the same rules. I shall not reproduce passages in Origen's books which disagree with or contradict his own statements elsewhere. The reason of these inconsistencies I have put more fully before you in the defence of Origen's writings composed by Pamphilianus which I have supplemented by a short treatise of my own. I have given what I consider plain proofs that his books have been corrupted in numbers of places by heretics and ill-disposed persons, and particularly those which you now urge me to translate. The books peri 'Archon, that is of Principles or of Powers, are in fact in other respects extremely obscure and difficult. For they treat of subjects on which the philosophers have spent all their days and yet have been able to discover nothing. In dealing with these themes Origen has done his best to make belief in a Creator and a rational account of things created subservient to religion and not, as with the philosophers, to irreligion. Wherever then in his books I have found a statement concerning the Trinity contrary to those which in other places he has faithfully made on the same subject, I have either omitted the passage as garbled and misleading or have substituted that view of the matter which I find him to have frequently asserted. Again, wherever—in haste to get on with his theme—he is brief or obscure relying on the skill and intelligence of his readers, I, to make the passage clearer, have sought to explain it by adding any plainer statements that I have read on the point in his other books. But I have added nothing of my own. The words used may be found in other parts of his writings: they are his, not mine. I mention this here to take from cavillers all pretext for once more finding fault. But let such perverse and contentious persons look well to what they are themselves doing.

3. Meantime I have taken up this great task—if so be that God will grant your prayers—not to stop the mouths of slanderers (an impossible feat except perhaps to God) but to give to those who desire it the means of making progress in knowledge.

In the sight of God, the Father, the Son, and the Holy Ghost, I adjure and require everyone who shall either read or copy these books of mine, by his belief in a kingdom to come, by the mystery of the resurrection from the dead, by the eternal fire which is "prepared for the devil and his angels;" as he hopes not to inherit eternally that place where "there is weeping and gnashing of teeth," and where "their worm dieth not and the fire is not quenched," let him add nothing to what is written, let him subtract nothing, let him insert nothing, let him alter nothing, but let him compare his transcript with the copies from which it is made, let him correct it to the letter, and let him punctuate it aright. Every manuscript that is not properly corrected and punctuated he must reject: for otherwise the difficulties in the text arising from the want of punctuation will make obscure arguments still more obscure to those who read them.

LETTER LXXXI. TO RUFINUS

A friendly letter of remonstrance written by Jerome to Rufinus on receipt of his version of the peri 'Archon see the preceding letter). Being sent in the first instance to Pammachius this latter treacherously suppressed it and thus put an end to all hope of the reconciliation of the two friends. The date of the letter is 399 a.d.

1. That you have lingered some time at Rome your own language shews. Yet I feel sure that a yearning to see your spiritual parents would have drawn you to your native country, had not grief for your mother deterred you lest a sorrow scarce bearable away might have proved unbearable at home.

As to your complaint that men listen only to the dictates of passion and refuse to acquiesce in your judgement and mine; the Lord is witness to my conscience that since our reconciliation I have harboured no rancour in my breast to injure anyone; on the contrary I have taken the utmost pains to prevent any chance occurrence being set down to ill-will. But what can I do so long as everyone supposes that he has a right to do as he does and thinks that in publishing a slander he is requiting not originating a calumny? True friendship ought never to conceal what it thinks.

The short preface to the books peri 'Archon which has been sent to me I recognize as yours by the style. You know best with what intention it was written; but even a fool can see how it must necessarily be understood. Covertly or rather openly I am the person aimed at. I have often myself feigned a controversy to practise declamation. Thus I might now recall this well-worn artifice and praise you in your own method. But far be it from me to imitate what I blame in you. In fact I have so far restrained my feelings that I make no charge against you, and, although injured, decline for my part to injure a friend. But another time, if you wish to follow any one, pray be satisfied with your own judgement. The objects which we seek are either good or bad. If they are good, they need no help from another; and if they are bad, the fact that many sin together is no excuse. I prefer thus to expostulate with you as a friend rather than to give public vent to my indignation at the wrong I have suffered. I want you to see that when I am reconciled to anyone I become his sincere friend and do not—to borrow a figure from Plautus—while offering him bread with one hand, hold a stone in the other.

2. My brother Paulinian has not yet returned from home and I fancy that you will see him at Aquileia at the house of the reverend pope Chromatius. I am also sending the reverend presbyter Rufinus on business to Milan by way of Rome, and have requested him to communicate to you my feelings and respects. I am sending the same message to the rest of my friends; lest, as the apostle says, ye bite and devour one another, ye be consumed one of another. It only remains for you and your friends to shew your moderation by giving no offence to those who are disinclined to put up with it. For you will hardly find everyone like me. There are few who can be pleased with pretended eulogies.

LETTER LXXXII. TO THEOPHILUS BISHOP OF ALEXANDRIA

Two years after his former attempt (see Letter LXIII.) Theophilus again wrote to Jerome urging him to be reconciled with John of Jerusalem. Jerome replies that there is nothing he desires more earnestly than peace but that this must be real and not a hollow truce. He speaks very bitterly of John who has, he alleges, intrigued to procure his banishment from Palestine. He also deals with the ordination of his brother Paulinian (for which see Letter LI.) and defends himself for having translated Origen's commentaries by adducing the example of Hilary of Poitiers. This letter should be compared with the Treatise "Against John of Jerusalem" in this volume. Its date is 399 a.d.

1. Your letter shews you to possess that heritage of the Lord of which when going to the Father he said to the apostles, "peace I leave with you, my peace I give unto you," and to own the happiness described in the words, "blessed are the peace-makers." You coax as a father, you teach as a master, you enjoin as a bishop. You come to me not with a rod and severity but in a spirit of kindness, gentleness, and meekness. Your opening words echo the humility of Christ who saved men not with thunder and lightning but as a wailing babe in the manger and as a silent sufferer upon the cross. You have read the prediction made in one who was a type of Him, "Lord, remember David and all his meekness," and you know how it was fulfilled afterwards in Himself. "Learn of me," He said, "for I am meek and lowly in heart." You have quoted many passages from the sacred books in praise of peace, you have flitted like a bee over the flowery fields of scripture, you have culled with cunning eloquence all that is sweet and conducive to concord. I was already running after peace, but

you have made me quicken my pace: my sails were set for the voyage but your exhortation has filled them with a stronger breeze. I drink in the sweet streams of peace not reluctantly and with aversion but eagerly and with open mouth.

2. But what can I do, I who can only wish for peace and have no power to bring it about? Even though the wish may win its recompense with God, its futility must still sadden him who cherishes it. When the apostle said, "as much as lieth in you, live peaceably with all men," he knew quite well that the realisation of peace depends upon the consent of two parties. The prophet truly cries "They say Peace, peace: and yet there is no peace." To overthrow peace by actions while professing it in words is not hard. To point out its advantages is one thing and to strive for it another. Men's speeches may be all for unity but their actions may enforce bondage. I wish for peace as much as others; and not only do I wish for it, I ask for it. But the peace which I want is the peace of Christ; a true peace, a peace without rancour, a peace which does not involve war, a peace which will not reduce opponents but will unite friends. How can I term domination peace? I must call things by their right names. Where there is hatred there let men talk of feuds; and where there is mutual esteem, there only let peace be spoken of. For my part I neither rend the church nor separate myself from the communion of the fathers. From my very cradle, I may say, I have been reared on Catholic milk; and no one can be a better churchman than one who has never been a heretic. But I know nothing of a peace that is without love or of a communion that is without peace. In the gospel I read:—"if thou bring thy gift to the altar and there rememberest that thy brother hath aught against thee; leave there thy gift before the altar and go thy way; first be reconciled to thy brother, and then come and offer thy gift." If then we may not offer gifts that are our own unless we are at peace with our brothers; how much less can we receive the body of Christ if we cherish enmity in our hearts? How can I conscientiously approach Christ's eucharist and answer the Amen if I doubt the charity of him who ministers it?

3. Hear me, I beg you with patience and do not take truthfulness for flattery. Is any man reluctant to communicate with you? Does any turn his face away when you hold out your hand? Does any at the holy banquet offer you the kiss of Judas? At your approach the monks instead of trembling rejoice. They race to meet you and leaving their dens in the desert are fain to master you by their humility. What compels them to come forth? Is it not their love for you? What draws together the scattered dwellers in the desert? Is it not the esteem in which they hold you? A parent ought to love his children; and not only a parent but a bishop ought to be loved by his children. Neither ought to be feared. There is an old saying: "whom a man fears he hates; and whom he

hates, he would fain see dead." Accordingly, while for the young the holy scripture makes fear the beginning of knowledge, it also tells us that "perfect love casteth out fear." You exact no obedience from them; therefore the monks obey you. You offer them a kiss; therefore they bow the neck. You shew yourself a common soldier; therefore they make you their general. Thus from being one among many you become one above many. Freedom is easily roused if attempts are made to crush it. No one gets more from a free man than he who does not force him to be a slave. I know the canons of the church; I know what rank her ministers hold; and from men and books I have daily up to the present learned and gathered many things. The kingdom of the mild David was quickly dismembered by one who chastised his people with scorpions and fancied that his fingers were thicker than his father's loins. The Roman people refused to brook insolence even in a king. Moses was leader of the host of Israel; he brought ten plagues upon Egypt; sky, earth, and sea alike obeyed his commands: yet he is spoken of as "very meek above all the men which were" at that time "upon the face of the earth." He maintained his forty-years' supremacy because he tempered the insolence of office with gentleness and meekness. When he was being stoned by the people he made intercession for them; nay more he wished to be blotted out of God's book sooner than that the flock committed to him should perish. He sought to imitate the Shepherd who would, he knew, carry on his shoulders even the wandering sheep. "The good Shepherd"—they are the Lord's own words—"layeth down his life for the sheep." One of his disciples can wish to be anathema from Christ for his brethren's sake, his kinsmen according to the flesh who were Israelites. If then Paul can desire to perish that the lost may not be lost, how much should good parents not provoke their children to wrath or by too great severity embitter those who are naturally mild.

4. The limits of a letter compel me to restrain myself; otherwise, indignation would make me diffuse. In an epistle which its writer regards as conciliatory but which to me appears full of malice my opponent admits that I have never calumniated him or accused him of heresy. Why then does he calumniate me by spreading a rumour that I am infected with that awful malady and am in revolt against the Church? Why is he so ready to spare his real assailants and so eager to injure me who have done nothing to injure him? Before my brother's ordination he said nothing of any dogmatic difference between himself and pope Epiphanius. What then can have "forced" him—I use his own word—publicly to argue a point which no one had yet raised? One so full of wisdom as you knows well the danger of such discussions and that silence is in such cases the safest course; except, indeed, on some occasion which renders

it imperative to deal with great matters. What ability and eloquence it must have needed to compress into a single sermon—as he boasts to have done—all the topics which the most learned writers have treated in detail in voluminous treatises! But this is nothing to me: it is for the hearers of the sermon to notice and for the writer of the letter to realize. But as for me he ought of his own accord to acquit me of bringing the charge against him. I was not present and did not hear the sermon. I was only one of the many, indeed hardly one of them; for while others were crying out I held my peace. Let us confront the accused and the accuser, and let us give credit to him whose services, life, and doctrine are seen to be the best.

5. You see, do you not, that I shut my eyes to many things and touch upon others only in the most cursory manner, hinting at what I suppose rather than saying out what I think.

I understand and approve your manoeuvres; how in the interests of the peace of the Church you stop your ears when you come within range of the Sirens. Moreover, trained as you have been from childhood in sacred studies, you know exactly what is meant by each expression which you use. You knowingly employ ambiguous terms and carefully balanced sentences so as not to condemn others or repudiate us. But it is not a pure faith and a frank confession which look for quibbles or circumlocutions. What is simply believed must be professed with equal simplicity. For my part I could cry out—though it were amid the swords and fires of Babylon, "why does the answer evade the question? why is there no frank, straightforward declaration?" From beginning to end all is shrinking, compromise, ambiguity: as though he were trying to walk on spikes of corn. His blood boils with eagerness for peace; yet he will not give a straightforward answer! others are free to insult him; for, when he is insulted, he does not venture to retaliate. I meantime hold my peace: for the present I shall let it be thought that I am too busy, or ignorant, or afraid; for how would he treat me were I to accuse him, if when I praise him—as he admits himself that I do—he secretly traduces me?

6. His whole letter is less an exposition of his faith than a mass of calumnies aimed at myself. Without any of those mutual courtesies which men may use towards each other without flattery, he takes up my name again and again, flouts it, and bandies it about as though I were blotted out of the book of the living. He thinks that he has beaten me black and blue with his letter; and that I live for the trifles at which he aims, I who from my boyhood have been shut up in a monastic cell, and have always made it my aim to be rather than to seem a good man. Some of us, it is true, he mentions with respect, but only that he may afterwards wound us more deeply. As if, forsooth, we too have no

open secrets to reveal! One of his charges is that we have allowed a slave to be ordained. Yet he himself has clergymen of the same class, and he must have read of Onesimus who, being made regenerate by Paul in prison, from a slave became a deacon. Then he throws out that the slave in question was a common informer; and, lest he should be compelled to prove the charge, declares he has it from hearsay only! Why, if I had chosen to repeat the talk of the crowd and to listen to scandal-mongers, he would have learned before now that I too know what all the world knows and have heard the same stories as other people. He declares farther that ordination has been given to this slave as a reward for a slander spread abroad by him. Does not such cunning and subtlety appal one? And is there any answer to eloquence so overwhelming? Which is best, to spread a calumny or to suffer from one? To accuse a man whose love you may afterwards wish for, or to pardon a sinner? And is it more tolerable that a common informer should be made a consul than that he should be made an aedile? He knows what I pass over in silence and what I say; what I myself have heard and what—from the fear of Christ—I perhaps refuse to believe.

7. He charges me with having translated Origen into Latin. In this I do not stand alone for the confessor Hilary has done the same, and we are both at one in this that while we have rendered all that is useful, we have cut away all that was harmful. Let him read our versions for himself, if he knows how (and as he constantly converses and daily associates with Italians, I think he cannot be ignorant of Latin); or else, if he cannot quite take it in, let him use his interpreters and then he will come to know that I deserve nothing but praise for the work on which he grounds a charge against me. For, while I have always allowed to Origen his great merit as an interpreter and critic of the scriptures, I have invariably denied the truth of his doctrines. Is it I then that let him loose upon the crowd? Is it I that act sponsor to other preachers like him? No, for I know that a difference must be made between the apostles and all other preachers. The former always speak the truth; but the latter being men sometimes go astray. It would be a strange defence of Origen surely to admit his faults and then to excuse them by saying that other men have been guilty of similar ones! As if, when you cannot venture to defend a man openly, you may hope to shield him by imputing his mistake to a number of others! As for the six thousand volumes of Origen of which he speaks, it is impossible that any one should have read books which have never been written: and I for my part find it easier to suppose that this falsehood is due to the man who professes to have heard it rather than to him who is said to have told it.

8. Again he avers that my brother is the cause of the disagreement which has arisen, a man who is content to stay in a monastic cell and who regards the clerical office as onerous rather than honourable. And although up to this very day he has spoon-fed us with insincere protestations of peace, he has caused commotion in the minds of the western bishops by telling them that a mere youth, hardly more than a boy, has been ordained presbyter of Bethlehem in his own diocese. If this is the truth, all the bishops of Palestine must be aware of it. For the monastery of the reverend pope Epiphanius—called the old monastery—where my brother was ordained presbyter is situated in the district of Eleutheropolis and not in that of AElia. Furthermore his age is well known to your Holiness; and as he has now attained to thirty years I apprehend that no blame can attach to him on that score. Indeed this particular age is stamped as full and complete by the mystery of Christ's assumed manhood. Let him call to mind the ancient law, and he will see that after his twenty-fifth year a Levite might be chosen to the priesthood; or if in this passage he prefers to follow the Hebrew he will find that candidates for the priesthood must be thirty years old. And that he may not venture to say that "old things are passed away; and, behold, all things are become new," let him hear the apostle's words to Timothy, "Let no man despise thy youth." Certainly when my opponent was himself ordained bishop, he was not much older than my brother is now. And if he argues that youth is no hindrance to a bishop but that it is to a presbyter because a young elder is a contradiction in terms, I ask him this question: Why has he himself ordained a presbyter of this age or younger still, and that too to minister in another man's church? But if he cannot be at peace with my brother unless he consents to submit and to renounce the bishop who has ordained him, he shews plainly that his object is not peace but revenge, and that he will not rest satisfied with the quietude of repose and peace unless he is able to inflict to the full every penalty that he now threatens. Had he himself ordained my brother, it would have made no difference to this latter. So dearly does he love seclusion that he would even then have continued to live quietly and would not have exercised his office. And should the bishop have seen fit to rend the church on that score, he would then have owed him nothing save the respect which is due to all who offer sacrifice.

9. So much for his prolix defence of himself or I should rather say his attack on me. In this letter I have only answered him briefly and cursorily that from what I have said he may perceive what I do not say, and may know that as I am a human being I am a rational animal and well able to understand his shrewdness, and that I am not so obtuse or brutish as to catch only the sound of his words and not their meaning. I now ask of you to pardon my chagrin and to

allow that if it is arrogant to answer back, it is yet more arrogant to bring baseless charges. Yet my answer has indicated what I might have said rather than has actually said it. Why do men look for peace at a distance? and why do they wish to have it enforced by word of command? Let them shew themselves peacemakers, and peace will follow at once. Why do they use the name of your holiness to terrorize us, when your letter—strange contrast to their harsh and menacing words—breathes only peace and meekness? For that the letter which Isidore the presbyter has brought for me from you does make for peace and harmony I know by this, that these insincere professors of a wish for peace have refused to deliver it to me. Let them choose whichever alternative they please. Either I am a good man or I am a bad one. If I am a good one let them leave me in quiet: if I am a bad one, why do they desire to be in bad company? Surely my opponent has learnt by experience the value of humility. He who now tears asunder things which, formerly separate, he of his own will put together, proves that in severing now what he then joined, he is acting at the instigation of another.

10. Recently he sought and obtained a decree of exile against me, and I only wish that he had been able to carry it out, so that, as the will is imputed to him for the deed, so I too not in will only but in deed might wear the crown of exile. The church of Christ has been founded by shedding its own blood not that of others, by enduring outrage not by inflicting it. Persecutions have made it grow; martyrdoms have crowned it. Or if the Christians among whom I live are unique in their love of severity and know only how to persecute and not how to undergo persecution, there are Jews here, there are heretics professing various false doctrines, and in particular the foulest of all, I mean, Manichaeism. Why is it that they do not venture to say a word against them? Why am I the only person they wish to drive into exile? Am I who communicate with the church the only person of whom it can be said that he rends the church? I put it to you, is it not a fair demand either that they should expel these others as well as myself, or that, if they keep them, they should keep me too? All the same they honour men by sending them into exile, for by so doing they separate them from the company of heretics. It is a monk, shame to say, who menaces monks and obtains decrees of exile against them; and that too a monk who boasts that he holds an apostolic chair. But the monastic tribe does not succumb to terrorism: it prefers to expose its neck to the impending sword rather than to allow its hands to be tied. Is not every monk an exile from his country? Is he not an exile from the whole world? Where is the need for the public authority, the cost of a rescript, the journeyings up and down the earth to obtain one? Let him but touch me with his little finger, and I will go into

exile of myself. "The earth is the Lord's and the fulness thereof." Christ is not shut up in any one spot.

11. Moreover when he writes that, though I seem to be separated from communion with him, I in reality hold communion with him through you and through the church of Rome: he need not go so far afield, for I am connected with him in the same way also here in Palestine. And lest even this should appear distant, in this village of Bethlehem I hold communion with his presbyters as much as I can. Thus it is clear that a private chagrin is not to be taken for the cause of the church, and that one man's choler, or even that of several stirred up by him, ought not to be styled the displeasure of the church. Accordingly I now repeat what I said at the beginning of my letter that I for my part am desirous of Christ's peace, that I pray for harmony, and that I request you to admonish him not to exact peace but to purpose it. Let him be satisfied with the pain which he has caused by the insults that he has inflicted upon me in the past. Let him efface old wounds by a little new charity. Let him shew himself what he was before, when of his own choice he bestowed upon me his esteem. Let his words no longer be tinged with a gall that flows from the heart of another. Let him do what he wishes himself, and not what others force him to wish. Either as a pontiff, let him exercise authority over all alike, or as a follower of the apostle, let him serve all for the salvation of all. If he will shew himself such, I am ready freely to yield and to hold out my arms; he will find me a friend and a kinsman, and will perceive that in Christ I am submissive to him as to all the saints. "Charity," writes the apostle, "suffereth long and is kind; charity envieth not; . . . is not puffed up . . . beareth all things, believeth all things." Charity is the mother of all virtues, and the apostle's words about faith, hope and charity are like that threefold cord which is not quickly broken. We believe, we hope, and through our faith and hope we are joined together in the bond of charity. It is for these virtues that I and others have left our homes, it is for these that we would live peaceably without any contention in the fields and alone; paying all due veneration to Christ's pontiffs—so long as they preach the right faith—not because we fear them as lords but because we honour them as fathers deferring also to bishops as bishops, but refusing to serve under compulsion, beneath the shadow of episcopal authority, men whom we do not choose to obey. I am not so much puffed up in mind as not to know what is due to the priests of Christ. For he who receives them, receives not them but Him, whose bishops they are. But let them be content with the honour which is theirs. Let them know that they are fathers and not lords, especially in relation to those who scorn the ambitions of the world and count peace and repose the best of all things. And may Christ

who is Almighty God grant to your prayers that I and my opponent may be united not in a feigned and hollow peace but in true and sincere mutual esteem, lest biting and devouring one another we be consumed one of another.

LETTER LXXXIII. FROM PAMMACHIUS AND OCEANUS

A letter from Pammachius and Oceanus in which they express the perplexity into which they have been thrown by Rufinus's version of Origen's treatise, On First Principles (see Letter LXXX.) and request Jerome to make for them a literal translation of the work. Written in 399 or 400 a.d.

1. Pammachius and Oceanus to the presbyter Jerome, health.

A reverend brother has brought to us sheets containing a certain person's translation into Latin of a treatise by Origen—entitled peri archon. These contain many things which disturb our poor wits and which appear to us to be uncatholic. We suspect also that with a view of clearing the author many passages of his books have been removed which had they been left would have plainly proved the irreligious character of his teaching. We therefore request your excellency to be so good as to bestow upon this particular matter an attention which will benefit not only ourselves but all who reside in the city; we ask you to publish in your own language the abovementioned book of Origen exactly as it was brought out by the author himself; and we desire you to make evident the interpolations which his defender has introduced. You will also confute and overthrow all statements in the sheets which we have sent to your holiness that are ignorantly made or contradict the Catholic faith. The writer in the preface to his work has, with much subtlety but without mentioning your holiness's name, implied that he has done no more than complete a work which you had yourself promised, thus indirectly suggesting that you agree with him. Remove then the suspicions men cannot help feeling and confute your assailant; for, if you ignore his implications, people will say that you admit their truth.

LETTER LXXXIV. TO PAMMACHIUS AND OCEANUS

A calm letter in which Jerome defines and justifies his own attitude towards Origen, but unduly minimizes his early enthusiasm for him. He admires him in the same way that Cyprian admired Tertullian but does not in any way adopt his errors. He then describes his own studies and recounts his obligations to Apollinaris, Didymus, and a Jew named Bar-anina. The rest of the letter deals with the errors of Origen, the state of the text of his writings, and the eulogy of him composed by the martyr Pamphilus (the authenticity of which Jerome assails without any sufficient reason). The date of the letter is 400 a.d.

Jerome to the brothers Pammachius and Oceanus, with all good wishes.

1. The sheets that you send me cover me at once with compliments and confusion; for, while they praise my ability, they take away my sincerity in the faith. But as both at Alexandria and at Rome and, I may say, throughout the whole world good men have made it a habit to take the same liberties with my name, esteeming me only so far that they cannot bear to be heretics without having me of the number, I will leave aside personalities and only answer specific charges. For it is of no benefit to a cause to encounter railing with railing and to retaliate for attacks upon oneself by attacks upon one's opponents. We are commanded not to return evil for evil but to overcome evil with good, to take our fill of insults, and to turn the other cheek to the smiter.

2. It is charged against me that I have sometimes praised Origen. If I am not mistaken I have only done so in two places, in the short preface (addressed to Damasus) to his homilies on the Song of Songs and in the prologue to my book of Hebrew Names. In these passages do the dogmas of the church come into question? Is anything said of the Father, the Son, and the Holy Ghost? or of the resurrection of the flesh? or of the condition and material of the soul? I have merely praised the simplicity of his rendering and commentary and neither the faith nor the dogmas of the Church come in at all. Ethics only are dealt with and the mist of allegory is dispelled by a clear explanation. I have praised the commentator but not the theologian, the man of intellect but not the believer, the philosopher but not the apostle. But if men wish to know my real judgement upon Origen; let them read my commentaries upon Ecclesiastes, let them go through my three books upon the epistle to the Ephesians: they will then see that I have always opposed his doctrines. How foolish it would be to eulogize a system so far as to endorse its blasphemy! The blessed Cyprian takes Tertullian for his master, as his writings prove; yet, delighted as he is with the ability of this learned and zealous writer he does not join him in following Montanus and Maximilla. Apollinaris is the author of a most weighty book against Porphyry, and Eusebius has composed a fine history of the Church; yet of these the former has mutilated Christ's incarnate humanity, while the latter is the most open champion of the Arian impiety. "Woe," says Isaiah, "unto them that call evil good and good evil; that put bitter for sweet and sweet for bitter." We must not detract from the virtues of our opponents—if they have any praiseworthy qualities—but neither must we praise the

defects of our friends. Each several case must be judged on its own merits and not by a reference to the persons concerned. While Lucilius is rightly assailed by Horace for the unevenness of his verses, he is equally rightly praised for his wit and his charming style.

3. In my younger days I was carried away with a great passion for learning, yet I was not like some presumptuous enough to teach myself. At Antioch I frequently listened to Apollinaris of Laodicea, and attended his lectures; yet, although he instructed me in the holy scriptures, I never embraced his disputable doctrine as to their meaning. At length my head became sprinkled with gray hairs so that I looked more like a master than a disciple. Yet I went on to Alexandria and heard Didymus. And I have much to thank him for: for what I did not know I learned from him, and what I knew already I did not forget. So excellent was his teaching. Men fancied that I had now made an end of learning. Yet once more I came to Jerusalem and to Bethlehem. What trouble and expense it cost me to get Baraninas to teach me under cover of night. For by his fear of the Jews he presented to me in his own person a second edition of Nicodemus. Of all of these I have frequently made mention in my works. The doctrines of Apollinaris and of Didymus are mutually contradictory. The squadrons of the two leaders must drag me in different directions, for I acknowledge both as my masters. If it is expedient to hate any men and to loath any race, I have a strange dislike to those of the circumcision. For up to the present day they persecute our Lord Jesus Christ in the synagogues of Satan. Yet can anyone find fault with me for having had a Jew as a teacher? Does a certain person dare to bring forward against me the letter I wrote to Didymus calling him my master? It is a great crime, it would seem, for me a disciple to give to one both old and learned the name of master. And yet when I ask leave to look at the letter which has been held over so long to discredit me at last, there is nothing in it but courteous language and a few words of greeting. Such charges are both foolish and frivolous. It would be more to the point to exhibit a passage in which I have defended heresy or praised some wicked doctrine of Origen. In the portion of Isaiah which describes the crying of the two seraphim he explains these to be the Son and the Holy Ghost; but have not I altered this hateful explanation into a reference to the two testaments? I have the book in my hand as it was published twenty years ago. In numbers of my works and especially in my commentaries I have, as occasion has offered, mangled this heathen school. And if my opponents allege that I have done more than anyone else to form a collection of Origen's books, I answer that I only wish I could have the works of all theological writers that by diligent study of them, I might make up for the slowness of my own wits. I have made

a collection of his books, I admit; but because I know everything that he has written I do not follow his errors. I speak as a Christian to Christians: believe one who has tried him. His doctrines are poisonous, they are unknown to the Holy Scriptures, nay more, they do them violence. I have read Origen, I repeat, I have read him; and if it is a crime to read him, I admit my guilt: indeed, these Alexandrian writings have emptied my purse. If you will believe me, I have never been an Origenist: if you will not believe me, I have now ceased to be one. But if even this fails to convince you, you will compel me in self-defence to write against your favourite, so that, if you will not believe me when I disclaim him, you will have to believe me when I attack him. But I find readier credence when I go wrong than when I shew amendment. And this is not surprising, for my would-be friends suppose me a fellow-disciple with them in the arcana of their system. I am loath, they fancy, to profess esoteric doctrines before persons who according to them are brute-like and made of clay. For it is an axiom with them that pearls ought not to be lightly cast before swine, nor that which is holy given to the dogs. They agree with David when he says: "Thy word have I hid in mine heart that I might not sin against thee;" and when in another place he describes the righteous man as one "who speaketh truth with his neighbour," that is with those who "are of the household of faith." From these passages they conclude that those of us who as yet are uninitiated ought to be told falsehoods, lest, being still unweaned babes, we should be choked by too solid food. Now that perjury and lying enter into their mysteries and form a bond between them appears most clearly from the sixth book of Origen's Miscellanies, in which he harmonizes the Christian doctrine with the conceptions of Plato.

4. What must I do then? deny that I am of Origen's opinion? They will not believe me. Swear that I am not? They will laugh and say that I deal in lies. I will do the one thing which they dread. I will bring forward their sacred rites and mysteries, and will expose the cunning whereby they delude simple folk like myself. Perhaps, although they refuse credence to my voice when I deny, they may believe my pen when I accuse. Of one thing they are particularly apprehensive, and that is that their writings may some day be taken as evidence against their master. They are ready to make statements on oath and to disclaim them afterwards with an oath as false as the first. When asked for their signatures they use shifts and seek excuses. One says: "I cannot condemn what no one else has condemned." Another says: "No decision was arrived at on the point by the Fathers." It is thus that they appeal to the judgment of the world to put off the necessity of assenting to a condemnation. Another says with yet more assurance: "how am I to condemn men whom the council of Nicaea has

left untouched? For the council which condemned Arius would surely have condemned Origen too, had it disapproved of his doctrines." They were bound in other words to cure all the diseases of the church at once and with one remedy; and by parity of reasoning we must deny the majesty of the Holy Ghost because nothing was said of his nature in that council. But the question was of Arius, not of Origen; of the Son, not of the Holy Ghost. The bishops at the council proclaimed their adherence to a dogma which was at the time denied; they said nothing about a difficulty which no one had raised. And yet they covertly struck at Origen as the source of the Arian heresy: for, in condemning those who deny the Son to be of the substance of the Father, they have condemned Origen as much as Arius. On the ground taken by these persons we have no right to condemn Valentine, Marcion, or the Cataphrygians, or Manichaeus, none of whom are named by the council of Nicaea, and yet there is no doubt that in time they were prior to it. But when they find themselves pressed either to subscribe or to leave the Church, you may see some strange twisting. They qualify their words, they arrange them anew, they use vague expressions; so as, if possible, to hold both our confession and that of our opponents, to be called indifferently heretics and Catholics. As if it were not in the same spirit that the Delphian Apollo (or, as he is sometimes called, Loxias) gave his oracles to Croesus and to Pyrrhus; cheating with a similar device two men widely separated in time. To make my meaning clear I will give a few examples.

5. We believe, say they, in the resurrection of the body. This confession, if only it be sincere, is free from objection. But as there are bodies celestial and bodies terrestrial and as thin air and the aether are both according to their natures called bodies, they use the word body instead of the word flesh in order that an orthodox person hearing them say body may take them to mean flesh while a heretic will understand that they mean spirit. This is their first piece of craft, and if this is found out, they devise fresh wiles, and, pretending innocence themselves, accuse us of malice. As though they were frank believers they say, "We believe in the resurrection of the flesh." Now when they have said this, the ignorant crowd thinks it ought to be satisfied, particularly because these exact words are found in the creed. If you go on to question them farther, a buzz of disapproval is heard in the ring and their backers cry out: "You have heard them say that they believe in the resurrection of the flesh; what more do you want?" the popular favour is transferred from our side to theirs, and while they are called honest, we are looked on as false accusers. But if you set your face steadily and keeping a firm hold of their admission about the flesh, proceed to press them as to whether they assert the resurrection of that

flesh which is visible and tangible, which walks and speaks, they first laugh and then signify their assent. And when we inquire whether the resurrection will exhibit anew the hair and the teeth, the chest and the stomach, the hands and the feet, and all the other members of the body, then no longer able to contain their mirth they burst out laughing and tell us that in that case we shall need barbers, and cakes, and doctors, and cobblers. Do we, they ask us in turn, believe that after the resurrection men's cheeks will still be rough and those of women smooth, and that sex will differentiate their bodies as it does at present? Then if we admit this, they at once deduce from our admission conclusions involving the grossest materialism. Thus, while they maintain the resurrection of the body as a whole, they deny the resurrection of its separate members.

6. The present is not a time to speak rhetorically against a perverse doctrine. Neither the rich vocabulary of Cicero nor the fervid eloquence of Demosthenes could adequately convey the warmth of my feeling, were I to attempt to expose the quibbles by which these heretics, while verbally professing a belief in the resurrection, in their hearts deny it. For their women finger their breasts, slap their chests, pinch their legs and arms, and say, "What will a resurrection profit us if these frail bodies are to rise again? No, if we are to be like angels, we shall have the bodies of angels." That is to say they scorn to rise again with the flesh and bones wherewith even Christ rose. Now suppose for a moment that in my youth I went astray and that, trained as I was in the schools of heathen philosophy, I was ignorant, in the beginning of my faith, of the dogmas of Christianity, and fancied that what I had read in Pythagoras and Plato and Empedocles was also contained in the writings of the apostle: Supposing, I say, that I believed all this, why do you yet follow the error of a mere babe and sucking child in Christ? Why do you learn irreligion of one who as yet knew not religion? After shipwreck one has still a plank to cling to; and one may atone for sin by a frank confession. You have followed me when I have gone astray; follow me also now that I have been brought back. In youth we have wandered; now that we are old let us mend our ways. Let us unite our tears and our groans; let us weep together, and return to the Lord our Maker. Let us not wait for the repentance of the devil; for this is a vain anticipation and one that will drag us into the deep of hell. Life must be sought or lost here. If I have never followed Origen, it is in vain that you seek to discredit me: if I have been his disciple, imitate my penitence. You have believed my confession; credit also my denial.

7. But it will be said, "If you knew these things, why did you praise him in your works?" I should praise him today but that you and men like you praise his errors. I should still find his talent attractive, but that some people have

been attracted by his impiety. "Read all things," says the apostle, "hold fast that which is good." Lactantius in his books and particularly in his letters to Demetrian altogether denies the subsistence of the Holy Spirit, and following the error of the Jews says that the passages in which he is spoken of refer to the Father or to the Son and that the words holy spirit' merely prove the holiness of these two persons in the Godhead. But who can forbid me to read his Institutes—in which he has written against the Gentiles with much ability—simply because this opinion of his is to be abhorred? Apollinaris has written excellent treatises against Porphyry, and I approve of his labours, although I despise his doctrine in many points because of its foolishness. If you too for your parts will but admit that Origen errs in certain things I will not say another syllable. Acknowledge that he thought amiss concerning the Son, and still more amiss concerning the Holy Spirit, point out the impiety of which he has been guilty in speaking of men's souls as having fallen from heaven, and shew that, while in word he asserts the resurrection of the flesh, he destroys the force of this language by other assertions. As, for instance, that, after many ages and one "restitution of all things," it will be the same for Gabriel as for the devil, for Paul as for Caiaphas, for virgins as for prostitutes. When once you have rejected these misstatements and have parted them with your censor's wand from the faith of the Church, I may read what is left with safety, and having first taken the antidote need no longer dread the poison. For instance it will do me no harm to say as I have said, "Whereas in his other books Origen has surpassed all other writers, in commenting on the Song of Songs he has surpassed himself"; nor will I fear to face the words with which formerly in my younger days I spoke of him as a doctor of the churches. Will it be pretended, that I was bound to accuse a man whose works I was translating by special request? that I was bound to say in my preface, "This writer whose books I translate is a heretic: beware of him, reader, read him not, flee from the viper: or, if you are bent on reading him, know that the treatises which I have translated have been garbled by heretics and wicked men; yet you need not fear, for I have corrected all the places which they have corrupted," that in other words I ought to have said: "the writer that I translate is a heretic, but I, his translator, am a Catholic." The fact is that you and your party in your anxiety to be straightforward, ingenuous, and honest, have paid too little regard to the precepts of rhetoric and to the devices of oratory. For in admitting that his books On First Principles are heretical and in trying to lay the blame of this upon others, you raise difficulties for your readers; you induce them to examine the whole life of the author and to form a judgment on the question from the remainder of his writings. I on the other hand have been wise enough to emend silently what I wished to emend: thus by ignoring the crime I have averted prejudice from the criminal. Doctors tell us that serious maladies ought not to be subjected to treatment, but should be left to nature, lest the remedies applied should intensify the disease. It is now almost one hundred and fifty years since Origen died at Tyre. Yet what Latin writer has ever ventured to translate his books On the Resurrection and On First Principles, his Miscellanies and his Commentaries or as he himself calls them his Tomes? Who has ever cared by so infamous a work to cover himself with infamy? I am not more eloquent than Hilary or truer to the faith than Victorinus who both have rendered his Homilies not in exact versions but in independent paraphrases. Recently also Ambrose appropriated his Six Days' Work, but in such a way that it expressed the views of Hippolytus and Basil rather than of Origen. You profess to take me for your model, and blind as moles in relation to others you scan me with the eyes of gazelles. Well, had I been ill-disposed towards Origen, I might have translated these very books so as to make his worst writings known to Latin readers; but this I have never done; and, though many have asked me, I have always refused. For it has never been my habit to crow over the mistakes of men whose talents I admire. Origen himself, were he still alive, would soon fall out with you his would-be patrons and would say with Jacob: "Ye have troubled me to make me to stink among the inhabitants of the land."

8. Does any one wish to praise Origen? Let him praise him as I do. From his childhood he was a great man, and truly a martyr's son. At Alexandria he presided over the school of the church, succeeding a man of great learning the presbyter Clement. So greatly did he abhor sensuality that, out of a zeal for God but yet one not according to knowledge, he castrated himself with a knife. Covetousness he trampled under foot. He knew the scriptures by heart and laboured hard day and night to explain their meaning. He delivered in church more than a thousand sermons, and published innumerable commentaries which he called tomes. These I now pass over, for it is not my purpose to catalogue his writings. Which of us can read all that he has written? and who can fail to admire his enthusiasm for the scriptures? If some one in the spirit of Judas the Zealot brings up to me his mistakes, he shall have his answer in the words of Horace:

'Tis true that sometimes Homer sleeps, but then
He's not without excuse:
The fault is venial, for his work is long.

Let us not imitate the faults of one whose virtues we cannot equal. Other men have erred concerning the faith, both Greeks and Latins, but I must not mention their names lest I should be supposed to defend Origen not by his own merits but by the errors of others. This, you will say, is to accuse them and not to excuse him. You would be right, if I had declared him not to have erred, or if I had professed a belief that the apostle Paul or an angel from heaven ought to be listened to in a depravation of the faith. But as it is seeing I frankly admit him to be wrong, I may read him on the same terms as I read others, because if he is wrong so also are they. But you may say, If error is common to many, why do you assail him alone? I answer, because he alone is praised by you as an apostle. Take away your exaggerated love for him, and I am ready to take away the greatness of my dislike. While you gather other men's faulty statements out of their books merely to defend Origen in his error, you extol this latter to the sky and will not allow that he has erred at all. Whosoever you are who are thus preaching new doctrines, I beseech you, spare the ears of the Romans, spare the faith of a church which an apostle has praised. Why after four hundred years do you try to teach us Romans doctrines of which until now we have known nothing? Why do you publicly proclaim opinions which Peter and Paul refused to profess? Until now no such teaching has been heard of, and yet the world has become christian. For my part I will hold fast in my old age the faith wherein I was born again in my boyhood. They speak of us as claytowners, made out of dirt, brutish and carnal, because, say they, we refuse to receive the things of the spirit; but of course they themselves are citizens of Jerusalem and their mother is in heaven. I do not despise the flesh in which Christ was born and rose again, or scorn the mud which, baked into a clean vessel, reigns in heaven. And yet I wonder why they who detract from the flesh live after the flesh, and cherish and delicately nurture that which is their enemy. Perhaps indeed they wish to fulfil the words of scripture: "love your enemies and bless them that persecute you." I love the flesh, but I love it only when it is chaste, when it is virginal, when it is mortified by fasting: I love not its works but itself, that flesh which knows that it must be judged, and therefore dies as a martyr for Christ, which is scourged and torn asunder and burned with fire.

9. The folly also of their contention that certain heretics and ill-disposed persons have tampered with Origen's writings may be shewn thus. Could any person be more wise, more learned, or more eloquent than were Eusebius and Didymus, Origen's supporters? Of these the former in the six volumes of his Apology asserts that Origen is of the same mind with himself; while the latter, though he tries to excuse his errors, admits that he has made them. Not being able to deny what he finds written, he endeavours to explain it away. It is one thing to say that additions have been made by heretics, but another to maintain that heretical statements are commendable. Origen's case would be unique

if his writings were falsified all over the world and if in one day by an edict like that of Mithridates all the truth were shorn from his volumes. Even supposing that some one treatise of his has been tampered with, can it be possible that all his works, published as they were at different times and places, have been corrupted? Origen himself in a letter written to Fabian, bishop of Rome, expresses penitence for having made erroneous statements, and charges Ambrose with over haste in making public what was meant only for private circulation. And yet to this day his disciples search for shifts to prove that all that excites disapprobation in his writings is due not to him but to others.

10. Moreover, when they speak of Pamphilus as one who praised Origen, I am personally much obliged to them for accounting me worthy to be calumniated with that martyr. For if, sirs, you tell me that Origen's books have been tampered with by his enemies to bring them into discredit; why may not I in my turn allege that his friends and followers have attributed to Pamphilus a volume composed by themselves to vindicate their master from disrepute by the testimony of a martyr? Lo and behold, you yourselves correct in Origen's books passages which (according to you) he never wrote: and yet you are surprised if a man is said to have published a book which as a matter of fact he did not publish. But while your statements can easily be brought to the test by an appeal to Origen's published works; as Pamphilus has published nothing else, it is easier for calumny to fix a book upon him. For shew me any other work of Pamphilus; you will nowhere find any, this is his only one. How then can I know that it is by Pamphilus? You will tell me, that the style and tone ought to inform me. Well, I shall never believe that a man so learned has dedicated the first fruits of his talent to defend doubtful and discredited positions. The very name of an apology which the treatise bears implies a previous charge made; for nothing is defended that is not first attacked. I will now bring forward but a single argument, one, however, the force of which only folly and effrontery can deny. The treatise attributed to Pamphilus contains nearly the first thousand lines of Eusebius's sixth book in defence of Origen. Yet in the remaining parts of his work the writer brings forward passages by which he seeks to prove that Origen was a Catholic. Now Eusebius and Pamphilus were in such thorough harmony with each other that they seemed to have but one soul between them, and one even went so far as to adopt the other's name. How then could they have disagreed so fundamentally on this point, Eusebius in all his works proving Origen to be an Arian, and Pamphilus describing him as a supporter of the Nicene council, which had not yet been held? It is evident from this consideration that the book belongs not to Pamphilus but to Didymus or somebody else, who having cut off the head of Eusebius's sixth book

supplied the other members himself. But I am willing to be generous and to allow that the book is written by Pamphilus, only by Pamphilus not yet a martyr. For he must have written the book before he underwent martyrdom. And why, you will say, was he accounted worthy of martyrdom? Surely that he might efface his error by a martyr's death, and wash away his one fault by shedding his blood. How many martyrs there have been all the world over who before their deaths have been the slaves of sins! Are we then to palliate the sins because those who committed them have afterwards become martyrs?

11. This reply to your letter, my most loving brothers, I have dictated in all haste; and, overcoming my scruples, I have taken up my pen against a man whose ability I once eulogized. I would sooner, indeed, risk my reputation than my faith. My friends have placed me in the awkward dilemma that if I say nothing I shall be held guilty, and if I offer a defence I shall be accounted an enemy. Both alternatives are hard; but of the two I will choose that which is the least so. A quarrel can be made up, but blasphemy can find no forgiveness. I leave to your judgment to discover how much labour I have expended in translating the books On First Principles; for on the one hand if one alters anything from the Greek the work becomes less a version than a perversion; and on the other hand a literal adherence to the original by no means tends to preserve the charm of its eloquence.

LETTER LXXXV. TO PAULINUS

Paulinus had asked Jerome two questions, (1) how can certain passages of scripture (Exod. vii. 13; Rom. ix. 16) be reconciled with Free Will? and (2) Why are the children of believers said to be holy (1 Cor. vii. 14) apart from baptismal grace? For the first of these questions Jerome refers Paulinus to his version (newly made) of Origen's treatise, On First Principles. For the second he quotes the explanation of Tertullian. Written in 400 a.d.

1. Your words urge me to write to you but your eloquence deters me from doing so. For as a letter-writer you are almost as good as Tully. You complain that my letters are short and unpolished: this is not due to carelessness but to fear of you, lest writing to you at greater length I should but send you more sentences to find fault with. Moreover, to make a clean breast of it to a good man like you, just about the time the vessels sail for the west, so many letters are demanded of me at once that, if I were to reply to all my correspondents, I should be unable to accomplish my task. Hence it happens that, neglecting the niceties of composition and not revising the work of my secretaries, I dictate

whatever first comes into my head. Thus when I write to you I regard you as a friend and not as a critic.

2. Your letter propounds two questions, the first, why God hardened Pharaoh's heart, and why the apostle said: "So then it is not of him that willeth, nor of him that runneth, but of God that sheweth mercy;" and other things which appear to do away with free will: the second, how those are holy who are born of believing, that is, of baptized parents, seeing that without the gift of grace afterwards received and kept they cannot be saved.

3. Your first question is most ably answered by Origen in his treatise on First Principles which, at the request of my friend Pammachius, I have recently translated. This task has occupied me so fully that I am unable to keep my word with you and must again postpone the sending my commentary on Daniel. Indeed, distinguished and devoted to me as Pammachius is, had he been alone in his request, I should have deferred it to another time, but, as it was, almost all our brothers at Rome urged the same demand declaring that many persons were in danger, and that some even accepted Origen's heretical teaching. I have found myself forced therefore to translate a book in which there is more of bad than of good, and to keep to this rule that I should neither add nor subtract but should preserve in Latin in its integrity the true sense of the Greek. You will be able to borrow a copy of my version from the aforesaid brother, though in your case the Greek will serve quite as well; neither should you, who can drink from the fountain head, turn to the muddy streamlets supplied by my poor wits.

4. Moreover, as I am speaking to an educated man, well versed both in the sacred scriptures and in secular literature, I desire to give your excellency this note of warning. Do not suppose that I am a clumsy buffoon who condemn everything that Origen has written,—as his injudicious friends falsely assert—or that I have changed my mind as suddenly as the philosopher Dionysius. The fact is that I repudiate merely his objectionable dogmas. For I know that one curse hangs over those who call evil good and over those who call good evil, over those who put bitter for sweet, and over those who put sweet for bitter. Who would go so far in praise of another man's teaching as to acquiesce in blasphemy?

5. Your second question is discussed by Tertullian in his books on Monogamy where he declares that the children of believers are called holy because they are as it were candidates for the faith and have suffered no pollution from idolatry. Consider also that the vessels of which we read in the tabernacle are called holy and everything else required for the ceremonial worship: although in strictness of speech there can be nothing holy except creatures which know

of and worship God. But it is a scriptural usage sometimes to give the name of holy to those who are clean, or who have been purified, or who have made expiation. For instance, it is written of Bathsheba that she was made holy from her uncleanness, and the temple itself is called the holy place.

6. I beg that you will not silently in your mind accuse me either of vanity or of insincerity. God bears me witness in my conscience that the unavoidable circumstances mentioned above drew me back when I was just going to grapple with my commentary; and you know that what is done when the mind is pre-occupied is never well done. I gladly accept the cap that you have sent me, a mark, though small, of no small affection and just the thing to keep an old man's head warm. I am delighted alike with the gift and with the giver.

LETTER LXXXVI. TO THEOPHILUS

Jerome congratulates Theophilus on the success of his crusade against Origenism, and speaks of the good work done in Palestine by his emissaries Priscus and Eubulus. He then (by a singular change in his sentiments) asks Theophilus to forgive John of Jerusalem for having unwittingly received an excommunicated Egyptian. The date of the Letter is 400 a.d.

Jerome to the most blessed Pope Theophilus. I have recently received despatches from your blessedness setting right your long silence and summoning me to return to my duty. So, though the reverend brothers Priscus and Eubulus have been slow in bringing me your letters, yet, as they are now hastening in the ardour of faith from end to end of Palestine and scattering and driving into their holes the basilisks of heresy, I write a few lines to congratulate you on your success. The whole world glories in your victories. An exultant crowd of all nations gazes on the standard of the cross raised by you at Alexandria and upon the shining trophies which mark your triumph over heresy. Blessings on your courage! blessings on your zeal! You have shewn that your long silence has been due to policy and not to inclination. I speak quite openly to your reverence. I grieved to find you too forbearing, and, knowing nothing of the course shaped by the pilot, I yearned for the destruction of those abandoned men. But, as I now see, you have had your hand raised and, if you have delayed to strike, it has only been that you might strike harder. As regards the welcome given to a certain person, you have no reason to be vexed with the prelate of this city; for as you gave no instructions on the point in your letter, it would have been rash in him to decide a case of which he knew nothing. Still I think that he would neither wish nor venture to annoy you in any way.

LETTER LXXXVII. FROM THEOPHILUS TO JEROME

Theophilus informs Jerome that he has expelled the Origenists from the monasteries of Nitria, and urges him to shew his zeal for the faith by writing against the prevalent heresy. The date of the letter is 400 a.d.

Theophilus, bishop, to the well-beloved and most loving brother, the presbyter Jerome. The reverend bishop Agatho with the well-beloved deacon Athanasius is accredited to you with tidings relating to the church. When you learn their import I feel no doubt but that you will approve my resolution and will exult in the church's victory. For we have cut down with the prophet's sickle certain wicked fanatics who were eager to sow broadcast in the monasteries of Nitria the heresy of Origen. We have remembered the warning words of the apostle, "rebuke with all authority." Do you therefore on your part, as you hope to receive a share in this reward, make haste to bring back with scriptural discourses those who have been deceived. It is our desire, if possible, to guard in our days not only the Catholic faith and the rules of the church, but the people committed to our charge, and to give a quietus to all strange doctrines.

LETTER LXXXVIII. TO THEOPHILUS

Replying to the preceding letter Jerome again congratulates Theophilus on the success of his efforts to put down Origenism, and informs him that they have already borne fruit as far west as Italy. He then asks him for the decrees of his council (held recently at Alexandria). The date of the letter is 400 a.d.

Jerome to the most blessed pope Theophilus. The letter of your holiness has given me a twofold pleasure, partly because it has had for its bearers those reverend and estimable men, the bishop Agatho and the deacon Athanasius, and partly because it has shewn your zeal for the faith against a most wicked heresy. The voice of your holiness has rung throughout the world, and to the joy of all Christ's churches the poisonous suggestions of the devil have been silenced. The old serpent hisses no longer, but, writhing and disembowelled, lurks in dark caverns unable to bear the shining of the sun. I have already, before the writing of your letter, sent missives to the West pointing out to those of my own language some of the quibbles employed by the heretics. I hold it due to the special providence of God that you should have written to the pope Anastasius at the same time as myself, and should thus without knowing it have been the means of confirming my testimony. Now that you have directly urged me to do so, I shall shew myself more zealous than ever to recall from their error simple souls both near and far. Nor shall I hesitate, if needful, to incur odium with some, for we ought to please God rather than men: although indeed they have been much more forward to defend their heresy than I and others have been to attack it. At the same time I beg that if you have any synodical decrees bearing upon the subject you will forward them to me, that, strengthened with the authority of so great a prelate, I may open my mouth for Christ with more freedom and confidence. The presbyter Vincent has arrived from Rome two days ago and humbly salutes you. He tells me again and again that Rome and almost the whole of Italy owe their deliverance after Christ to your letters. Shew diligence therefore, most loving and most blessed pope, and whenever opportunity offers write to the bishops of the West not to hesitate—in your own words—to cut down with a sharp sickle the sprouts of evil.

LETTER LXXXIX. FROM THEOPHILUS TO JEROME

This letter (probably earlier in date than the three preceding) commends to Jerome the monk Theodore, who, having come from Rome to declare the condemnation of Origenism by the church there, had visited the monasteries of Nitria now purged of heresy, and wished before returning to the West to see the Holy Places as well. The date of the letter is 400 a.d.

Theophilus, bishop, to the well-beloved lord and most loving brother the presbyter Jerome. I have learned the project of the monk Theodore—which will be known also to your holiness—and I approve of it. Having to leave us on a voyage for Rome, he has been unwilling to set out without first visiting and embracing as his own flesh and blood you and the reverend brothers who are with you in the monastery. You will, I am sure, rejoice in the news with which he will meet your welcome, that quiet has been restored to the church here. He has seen all the monasteries of Nitria and can tell you of the continence and meekness of the monks in them; as also how the Origenists have been put down and scattered, how peace has been restored to the church, and how the discipline of the Lord is being upheld. How gladly would I see the mask of hypocrisy laid aside by those also who near you are said to be undermining the truth. I feel obliged to write thus because the brothers in your neighbourhood are mistaken concerning them. Wherefore take heed to yourselves and shun men of this type; even as it is written:—"if any man bring not to you the faith of the church, bid him not God speed." It may, indeed, be superfluous to write thus to you who can recall the erring from their error, yet no harm is done when those careful for the faith admonish even the wise and learned. Kindly salute in my name all the brothers who are with you.

LETTER XC. FROM THEOPHILUS TO EPIPHANIUS

Theophilus writes to Epiphanius to convoke a council in Cyprus for the condemnation of Origenism and asks him to transmit to Constantinople by a trustworthy messenger a copy of its decrees together with the synodical letter of Theophilus himself. His anxiety about this last point is caused by the news that certain of the excommunicated monks have set sail for Constantinople to lay their case before the bishop, John Chrysostom. The date of the letter is 400 a.d.

Theophilus to his well-beloved lord, brother, and fellow-bishop Epiphanius.

The Lord has said to his prophet "See, I have this day set thee over the nations and over the kingdoms to root out and to pull down and to destroy and . . . to build and to plant." In every age he bestows the same grace upon his church, that His Body may be preserved intact and that the poison of heretical opinions may nowhere prevail over it. And now also do we see the words fulfilled. For the church of Christ "not having spot or wrinkle or any such thing" has with the sword of the gospel cut down the Origenist serpents crawling out of their caves, and has delivered from their deadly contagion the fruitful host of the monks of Nitria. I have compressed a short account of my proceedings (it was all that time would allow) into the general letter which I have addressed indiscriminately to all. As your excellency has often fought in contests of the kind before me, it is your present duty to strengthen the hands of those who are in the field and to gather together to this end the bishops of your entire island. A synodical letter should be sent to myself and the bishop of Constantinople and to any others whom you think fit; that by universal consent Origen himself may be expressly condemned and also the infamous heresy of which he was the author. I have learned that certain calumniators of the true faith, named Ammonius, Eusebius, and Euthymius, filled with a fresh access of enthusiasm in behalf of the heresy, have taken ship for Constantinople, to ensnare with their deceits as many new converts as they can and to confer anew with the old companions of their impiety. Let it be your care, therefore, to set forth the course of the matter to all the bishops throughout Isauria and Pamphylia and the rest of the neighbouring provinces: moreover, if you think fit, you can add my letter, so that all of us gathered together in one spirit with the power of our Lord Jesus Christ may deliver these men unto Satan for the destruction of the impiety which possesses them. And to ensure the speedy arrival of my despatches at Constantinople, send a diligent messenger, one of the clergy (as I send fathers from the monasteries of Nitria with others also of the monks, learned men and continent) that when they arrive they may be able themselves to relate what has been done. Above all I beg of you to offer up earnest prayers to the Lord that we may be able in this contest also to gain the victory; for no small joy has filled the hearts of the people both in Alexandria and throughout all Egypt, because a few men have been expelled from the Church that the body of it might be kept pure. Salute the brothers who are with you. The people with us salute you in the Lord.

LETTER XCI. FROM EPIPHANIUS TO JEROME

An exultant letter from Epiphanius in which he describes the success of his council (convened at the suggestion of Theophilus), sends Jerome a copy of its synodical letter. and urges him to go on with his work of translating into Latin documents bearing on the Origenistic controversy. Written in 400 a.d.

To his most loving lord, son, and brother, the presbyter Jerome, Epiphanius sends greeting in the Lord. The general epistle written to all Catholics belongs particularly to you; for you, having a zeal for the faith against all heresies, particularly oppose the disciples of Origen and of Apollinaris whose poisoned roots and deeply planted impiety almighty God has dragged forth into our midst, that having been unearthed at Alexandria they might wither throughout the world. For know, my beloved son, that Amalek has been destroyed root and branch and that the trophy of the cross has been set up on the hill of Rephidim. For as when the hands of Moses were held up on high Israel prevailed, so the Lord has strengthened His servant Theophilus to plant His standard against Origen on the altar of the church of Alexandria; that in him might be fulfilled the words: "Write this for a memorial, for I will utterly put out Origen's heresy from under heaven together with that Amalek himself." And that I may not appear to be repeating the same things over and over and thus to be making my letter tedious, I send you the actual missive written to me that you may know what Theophilus has said to me, and what a great blessing the Lord has granted to my last days in approving the principles which I have always proclaimed by the testimony of so great a prelate. I fancy that by this time you also have published something and that, as I suggested in my former letter to you on this subject, you have elaborated a treatise for readers of your own language. For I hear that certain of those who have made shipwreck have come also to the West, and that, not content with their own destruction, they desire to involve others in death with them; as if they thought that the multitude of sinners lessens the guilt of sin and the flames of Gehenna do not grow in size in proportion as more logs are heaped upon them. With you and by you we send our best greetings to the reverend brothers who are with you in the monastery serving God.

LETTER XCII. THE SYNODICAL LETTER OF THEOPHILUS TO THE BISHOPS OF PALESTINE AND OF CYPRUS

The synodical letter of the council held at Alexandria in 400 a.d. to condemn Origenism. Written originally in Greek it was translated into Latin by Jerome.

This letter has been sent in identical terms to the Bishops of Palestine and to those of Cyprus. We reproduce the headings of both copies. That to the Bishops of Palestine commences thus: To the well-beloved lords, brothers, and fellow-bishops, Eulogius, John, Zebianus, Auxentius, Dionysius, Gennadius, Zeno, Theodosius, Dicterius, Porphyry, Saturninus, Alan, Paul, Ammonius, Helianus, Eusebius, the other Paul, and to all the Catholic bishops gathered together at the dedication festival of AElid, Theophilus [sends] greeting in the Lord.

The Cyprians he addresses thus: To the well-beloved lords, brothers, and fellow-bishops, Epiphanius, Marcianus, Agapetus, Boethius, Helpidius, Entasius, Norbanus, Macedonius. Aristo, Zeno, Asiaticus, Heraclides, the other Zeno, Cyriacus, and Aphroditus, Theophilus [sends] greeting in the Lord.

The scope of the letter is as follows:

We have personally visited the monasteries of Nitria and find that the Origenistic heresy has made great ravages among them. It is accompanied by a strange fanaticism: men even maim themselves or cut out their tongues to show how they despise the body. I find that some men of this kind have gone from Egypt into Syria and other countries where they speak against us and the truth.

The books of Origen have been read before a council of bishops and unanimously condemned. The following are his chief errors, mainly found in the peri 'Archon.

1. The Son compared with us is truth, but compared with the Father he is falsehood.

2. Christ's kingdom will one day come to an end.

3. We ought to pray to the Father alone, not to the Son.

4. Our bodies after the resurrection will be corruptible and mortal.

5. There is nothing perfect even in heaven; the angels themselves are faulty, and some of them feed on the Jewish sacrifices.

6. The stars are conscious of their own movements, and the demons know the future by their courses.

7. Magic, if real, is not evil.

8. Christ suffered once for men; he will suffer again for the demons.

The Origenists have tried to coerce me; they have even stirred up the heathen by denouncing the destruction of the Serapeum; and have sought to withdraw from the ecclesiastical jurisdiction two persons accused of grave crimes. One of these is the woman who was wrongly placed on the list of widows by Isidore, the other Isidore himself. He is the standard-bearer of the heretical faction, and his wealth supplies them with unbounded resources for their violent enterprises. They have tried to murder me; they seized the monastery church at Nitria, and for a time prevented the bishops from entering and the offices from being performed. Now, like Zebul (Beelzebub) they go to and fro on the earth.

I have done them no harm; I have even protected them. But I would not let an old friendship (with Isidore) impair our faith and discipline. I implore you to oppose them wherever they come, and to prevent them from unsettling the brethren committed to you.

LETTER XCIII. FROM THE BISHOPS OF PALESTINE TO THEOPHILUS

The synodical letter of the council of Jerusalem sent to Theophilus in reply to the preceding. The translation as before is due to Jerome.

The following is an epitome: We have done all that you wished, and Palestine is almost wholly free from the taint of heresy. We wish that not only the Origenists, but Jews, Samaritans and heathen also, could be put down. Origenism does not exist among us. The doctrines you describe are never heard here. We anathematize those who hold such doctrines, and also those of Apollinaris, and shall not receive anyone whom you excommunicate.

LETTER XCIV. FROM DIONYSIUS TO THEOPHILUS

In this letter (translated into Latin by Jerome) Dionysius, bishop of Lydda, praises Theophilus for his signal victories over Origenism and urges him to continue his efforts against that heresy. Written in 400 a.d.

LETTER XCV. FROM POPE ANASTASIUS TO SIMPLICIANUS

At the request of Theophilus Anastasius, bishop of Rome, writes to Simplicianus, bishop of Milan, to inform him that he, like Theophilus, has condemned Origen whose blasphemies have been brought under his notice by Eusebius of Cremona. This latter had shown him a copy of the version by Rufinus of the treatise On First Principles. The date of the letter is 400 a.d.

To his lord and brother Simplicianus, Anastasius.

1. It is felt right that a shepherd should bestow great care and watchfulness upon his flock. In like manner too from his lofty tower the careful watchman keeps a lookout day and night on behalf of the city. So also in the hour of tempest when the sea is dangerous the shipmaster suffers keen anxiety lest the gale and the violence of the waves shall dash his vessel upon the rocks. It is with similar feelings that the reverend and honourable Theophilus our brother and fellow-bishop, ceases not to watch over the things that make for salvation, that God's people in the different churches may not by reading Origen run into awful blasphemies.

2. Being informed, then, by a letter of the aforesaid bishop, we inform your holiness that we in like manner who are set in the city of Rome in which the prince of the apostles, the glorious Peter, first founded the church and then by his faith strengthened it; to the end that no man may contrary to the commandment read these books which we have mentioned, have condemned the same; and have with earnest prayers urged the strict observance of the precepts which God and Christ have inspired the evangelists to teach. We have charged men to remember the words of the venerable apostle Paul, prophetic and full of warning:—"if any than preach any other gospel unto you than that which we have preached unto you, let him be accursed." Holding fast, therefore, this precept, we have intimated that everything written in days gone by Origen that is contrary to our faith is even by us rejected and condemned.

3. I send this letter to your holiness by the hand of the presbyter Eusebius, a man filled with a glowing faith and love for the Lord. He has shewn to me some blasphemous chapters which made me shudder as I passed judgement on

them. If Origen has put forth any other writings, you are to know that they and their author are alike condemned by me. The Lord have you in safe keeping, my lord and brother deservedly held in honour.

LETTER XCVI. FROM THEOPHILUS

A translation by Jerome of Theophilus's paschal letter for the year 401 a.d. In it Theophilus refutes at length the heresies of Apollinaris and Origen.

LETTER XCVII. TO PAMMACHIUS AND MARCELLA

With this letter Jerome sends to Pammachius and Marcella a translation of the paschal letter issued by Theophilus for the year 402 a.d. together with the Greek original. He takes the precaution of sending this latter because in the preceding year complaints have been made that his translation was not accurate. Written in 402 a.d.

1. Once more with the return of spring I enrich you with the wares of the east and send the treasures of Alexandria to Rome: as it is written, "God shall come from the south and the Holy One from Mount Paran, even a thick shadow." (Hence in the Song of Songs the joyous cry of the bride: "I sat down under his shadow with great delight and his fruit was sweet to my taste.") Now truly is Isaiah's prophecy fulfilled: "In that day shall there be an altar to the Lord in the land of Egypt." "Where sin hath abounded, grace doth much more abound." They who fostered the infant Christ now with glowing faith defend Him in His manhood; and they who once saved Him from the hands of Herod are ready to save Him again from this blasphemer and heretic. Demetrius expelled Origen from the city of Alexander; but he is now thanks to Theophilus outlawed from the whole world. Like him to whom Luke has dedicated the Acts of the Apostles this bishop derives his name from his love to God. Where now is the wriggling serpent? In what plight does the venomous viper find himself? His is

A human face with wolfish body joined.

Where now is that heresy which crawled hissing through the world and boasted that both the bishop Theophilus and I were partisans of its errors? Where now is the yelping of those shameless hounds who, to win over the simple minded, falsely proclaimed our adherence to their cause? Crushed by the authority and eloquence of Theophilus they are now like demon-spirits only able to mutter and that from out of the earth. For they know nothing of Him who, as He comes from above, speaks only of the things that are above.

2. Would that this generation of vipers would either honestly accept our doctrines, or else consistently defend its own; that we might know whom we are to esteem and whom we are to shun. As it is they have invented a new kind of penitence, hating us as enemies though they dare not deny our faith. What, I ask, is this chagrin of theirs which neither time nor reason seems able to cure? When swords flash in battle and men fall and blood flows in streams, hostile hands are often clasped in amity and the fury of war is exchanged for an unexpected peace. The partisans of this heresy alone can make no terms with churchmen; for they repudiate mentally the verbal assent that is extorted from them. When their open blasphemy is made plain to the public ear, and when they perceive their hearers clamouring against them; then they assume an air of simplicity, declaring that they hear such doctrines for the first time and that they have no previous knowledge of them as taught by their master. And when you hold their writings in your hand, they deny with their lips what their hands have written. Why, sirs, need you beset the Propontis, shift your abode, wander through different countries, and rend with foaming mouths a distinguished prelate of Christ and his followers? If your recantations are sincere, you should replace your former zeal for error with an equal zeal for the faith. Why do you patch together from this quarter and from that these rags of cursing? And why do you rail at the lives of men whose faith you cannot resist? Do you cease to be heretics because according to you sundry persons believe us to be sinners? And does impiety cease to disfigure your lips because you can point to scars on our ears? So long as you have a leopard's spots and an Ethiopian's skin, how can it help your perfidy to know that I too am marked by moles? See, Pope Theophilus is freely allowed to prove Origen a heretic; and the disciples do not defend the master's words. They merely pretend that they have been altered by heretics and tampered with, like the works of many other writers. Thus they seek to maintain his cause not by their own belief but by other people's errors. So much I would say against heretics who in the fury of their unjust hostility to us betray the secret feelings of their minds and prove the incurable nature of the wound that rankles in their breasts.

3. But you are Christians and the lights of the senate: accept therefore from me the letter which I append. This year I send it both in Greek and Latin that the heretics may not again lyingly assert that I have made many changes in and additions to the original. I have laboured hard, I must confess, to preserve the charm of the diction by a like elegance in my version: and keeping within fixed lines and never allowing myself to deviate from these I have done my best to

maintain the smooth flow of the writer's eloquence and to render his remarks in the tone in which they are made. Whether I have succeeded in these two objects or not I must leave to your judgement to determine. As for the letter itself you are to know that it is divided into four parts. In the first Theophilus exhorts believers to celebrate the Lord's passover; in the second he slays Apollinarius; in the third he demolishes Origen; while in the fourth and last he exhorts the heretics to penitence. If the polemic against Origen should seem to you to be inadequate, you are to remember that Origenism was fully treated in last year's letter; and that this which I have just translated, as it aims at brevity, was not bound to dwell farther upon the subject. Besides, its terse and clear confession of faith directed against Apollinarius is not lacking in dialectical subtlety. Theophilus first wrests the dagger from his opponent's hand, and then stabs him to the heart.

4. Entreat the Lord, therefore, that a composition which has won favour in Greek may not fail to win it also in Latin, and that what the whole East admires and praises Rome may gladly take to her heart. And may the chair of the apostle Peter by its preaching confirm the preaching of the chair of the evangelist Mark. Popular rumour, indeed, has it that the blessed pope Anastasius is of like zeal and spirit with Theophilus and that he has pursued the heretics even to the dens in which they lurk. Moreover his own letters inform us that he condemns in the West what is already condemned in the East. May he live for many years so that the reviving sprouts of heresy may in course of time by his efforts be made to wither and to die.

LETTER XCVIII. FROM THEOPHILUS

A translation by Jerome of Theophilus's paschal letter for the year 402 a.d. Like that of the previous year (Letter XCVI.) it deals mainly with the heresies of Apollinarius and Origen.

LETTER XCIX. TO THEOPHILUS

Jerome forwards to Theophilus a translation of the latter's paschal letter for 404 a.d. and apologizes for his delay in sending it, on the ground that ill-health and grief for the death of Paula have prevented him from doing literary work. The date of the letter is 404 a.d.

To the most blessed pope Theophilus, Jerome.

1. From the time that I received the letters of your holiness together with the paschal treatise until the present day I have been so harassed with sorrow and mourning, with anxiety, and with the different reports which have come from all quarters concerning the condition of the church, that I have hardly been able to turn your volume into Latin. You know the truth of the old saying, grief chokes utterance; and it is more than ever true when to sickness of the mind is added sickness of the body. I have now been five days in bed in a burning fever: consequently it is only by using the greatest haste that I can dictate this very letter. But I wish to shew your holiness in a few words what pains I have taken, in translating your treatise, to transfer the charm of diction which marks every sentence in the original, and to make the style of the Latin correspond in some degree with that of the Greek.

2. At the outset you use the language of philosophy; and, without appearing to particularize, you slay one while you instruct all. In the remaining sections—a task most difficult of accomplishment—you combine philosophy and rhetoric and draw together for us Demosthenes and Plato. What diatribes you have launched against self-indulgence! What eulogies you have bestowed upon the virtue of continence! With what secret stores of wisdom you have spoken of the interchange of day and night, the course of the moon, the laws of the sun, the nature of our world; always appealing to the authority of scripture lest in a paschal treatise you should appear to have borrowed anything from secular sources! To be brief, I am afraid to praise you for these things lest I should be charged with offering flattery. The book is excellent both in the philosophical portions and where, without making personal attacks, you plead the cause which you have espoused. Wherefore, I beseech you, pardon me my backwardness: I have been so completely overcome by the falling asleep of the holy and venerable Paula that except my translation of this book I have hitherto written nothing bearing on sacred subjects. As you yourself know, I have suddenly lost the comforter whom I have led about with me, not—the Lord is my witness—to minister to my own needs, but for the relief and refreshment of the saints upon whom she has waited with all diligence. Your holy and estimable daughter Eustochium (who refuses to be comforted for the loss of her mother), and with her all the brotherhood humbly salute you. Kindly send me the books which you say that you have lately written that I may translate them or, if not that, at least read them. Farewell in Christ.

LETTER C. FROM THEOPHILUS

A translation by Jerome of Theophilus's paschal letter for 404 a.d. In it Theophilus inculcates penitence for sinners, recommends the practice of fasting and condemns the errors of Origen.

LETTER CI. FROM AUGUSTINE

A letter from Augustine in which he denies that he has written a book against Jerome and sent it to Rome but confesses that he has criticized him although without giving details. Written in 402 a.d. This and the following letters are to be found in the First Volume of the First Series of this Library. Letter LXVII.

LETTER CII. TO AUGUSTINE

Jerome's reply to the foregoing in which, it has been said, friendship struggles with suspicion and resentment. He warns Augustine not to provoke him, lest old as he is he may prove a dangerous opponent; and encloses part of his reply to the apology of Rufinus. Written in 402 a.d. See Augustine, vol. i., Letter XXXIX.

LETTER CIII. TO AUGUSTINE

A letter of introduction in which Jerome commends the deacon Praesidius to the kind offices of Augustine. Written in 403 a.d. See Augustine, vol. i., Letter XXXIX.

LETTER CIV. FROM AUGUSTINE

In this letter Augustine (1) commends to Jerome the deacon Cyprian, (2) explains how it is that his first letter (Letter LVI.) has miscarried, and (3) urges Jerome to base his scriptural labours not on the Hebrew text but on the version of the LXX. The date of the letter is 403 a.d. See Augustine, vol. i., Letter LXXI.

LETTER CV. TO AUGUSTINE

Jerome's answer to the foregoing. He complains that even now he has not received Augustine's letter and asks him to send him a copy of it. Popular rumour, he declares, credits Augustine with a deliberate suppression of the letter in order that he may seem to win an easy victory over his opponent. Jerome next deals with Augustine's denial of having made a written attack upon him and concludes by refusing for the present all discussion of points of criticism. The date of the letter is 403 a.d. See Augustine, vol. i., Letter LXXII.

LETTER CVI. TO SUNNIAS AND FRETELA

A long letter in which Jerome answers a number of questions put to him by two sojourners in Getica, Sunnias and Fretela. Diligent students of scripture, these men were at a loss to understand the frequent differences between Jerome's Latin psalter of 383 a.d. (the so-called Roman psalter) and the LXX, and accordingly sent him a long list of passages with a request for explanation. Jerome in his reply deals fully with all these and points out to his correspondents that they have been misled by their edition of the LXX. (the "common" edition) which differs widely from the critical text of Origen as given in the Hexapla and used by himself. He also expresses his joy to find that even among the Getae the scriptures are now diligently studied. The date of the letter is about 403 a.d.

LETTER CVII. TO LAETA

Laeta, the daughter-in-law of Paula, having written from Rome to ask Jerome how she ought to bring up her infant daughter (also called Paula) as a virgin consecrated to Christ, Jerome now instructs her in detail as to the child's training and education. Feeling some doubt, however, as to whether the scheme proposed by him will be practicable at Rome, he advises Laeta in case of difficulty to send Paula to Bethlehem where she will be under the care of her grandmother and aunt, the elder Paula and Eustochium. Laeta subsequently accepted Jerome's advice and sent the child to Bethlehem where she eventually succeeded Eustochium as head of the nunnery founded by her grandmother. The date of the letter is 403 a.d.

1. The apostle Paul writing to the Corinthians and instructing in sacred discipline a church still untaught in Christ has among other commandments laid down also this: "The woman which hath an husband that believeth not, and if he be pleased to dwell with her, let her not leave him. For the unbelieving husband is sanctified by the believing wife, and the unbelieving wife is sanctified by the believing husband; else were your children unclean but now are they holy." Should any person have supposed hitherto that the bonds of discipline are too far relaxed and that too great indulgence is conceded by the teacher, let him look at the house of your father, a man of the highest distinction and learning, but one still walking in darkness; and he will perceive as the result of the apostle's counsel sweet fruit growing from a bitter stock and precious balsams exhaled from common canes. You yourself are the offspring of a mixed marriage; but the parents of Paula—you and my friend Toxotius—are both Christians. Who could have believed that to the heathen pontiff Albinus should be born—in answer to a mother's vows—a Christian granddaughter; that a delighted grandfather should hear from the little one's faltering lips Christ's Alleluia, and that in his old age he should nurse in his bosom one of God's own virgins? Our expectations have been fully gratified. The one unbeliever is sanctified by his holy and believing family. For, when a man is surrounded by a believing crowd of children and grandchildren, he is as good as a candidate for the faith. I for my part think that, had he possessed so many Christian kinsfolk when he was a young man, he might then have been brought to believe in Christ. For though he may spit upon my letter and laugh at it, and though he may call me a fool or a madman, his son-in-law did the same before he came to believe. Christians are not born but made. For all its gilding the Capitol is beginning to look dingy. Every temple in Rome is covered with soot and cobwebs. The city is stirred to its depths and the people pour past their half-ruined shrines to visit the tombs of the martyrs. The belief which has not been accorded to conviction may come to be extorted by very shame.

2. I speak thus to you, Laeta my most devout daughter in Christ, to teach you not to despair of your father's salvation. My hope is that the same faith which has gained you your daughter may win your father too, and that so you may be able to rejoice over blessings bestowed upon your entire family. You know the Lord's promise: "The things which are impossible with men are possible with God." It is never too late to mend. The robber passed even from the cross to paradise. Nebuchadnezzar also, the king of Babylon, recovered his reason, even after he had been made like the beasts in body and in heart and had been compelled to live with the brutes in the wilderness. And to pass over

such old stories which to unbelievers may well seem incredible, did not your own kinsman Gracchus whose name betokens his patrician origin, when a few years back he held the prefecture of the City, overthrow, break in pieces, and shake to pieces the grotto of Mithras and all the dreadful images therein? Those I mean by which the worshippers were initiated as Raven, Bridegroom, Soldier, Lion, Perseus, Sun, Crab, and Father? Did he not, I repeat, destroy these and then, sending them before him as hostages, obtain for himself Christian baptism?

Even in Rome itself paganism is left in solitude. They who once were the gods of the nations remain under their lonely roofs with horned-owls and birds of night. The standards of the military are emblazoned with the sign of the Cross. The emperor's robes of purple and his diadem sparkling with jewels are ornamented with representations of the shameful yet saving gibbet. Already the Egyptian Serapis has been made a Christian; while at Gaza Marnas mourns in confinement and every moment expects to see his temple overturned. From India, from Persia, from Ethiopia we daily welcome monks in crowds. The Armenian bowman has laid aside his quiver, the Huns learn the psalter, the chilly Scythians are warmed with the glow of the faith. The Getae, ruddy and yellow-haired, carry tent-churches about with their armies: and perhaps their success in fighting against us may be due to the fact that they believe in the same religion.

3. I have nearly wandered into a new subject, and while I have kept my wheel going, my hands have been moulding a flagon when it has been my object to frame an ewer. For, in answer to your prayers and those of the saintly Marcella, I wish to address you as a mother and to instruct you how to bring up our dear Paula, who has been consecrated to Christ before her birth and vowed to His service before her conception. Thus in our own day we have seen repeated the story told us in the Prophets, of Hannah, who though at first barren afterwards became fruitful. You have exchanged a fertility bound up with sorrow for offspring which shall never die. For I am confident that having given to the Lord your first-born you will be the mother of sons. It is the first-born that is offered under the Law. Samuel and Samson are both instances of this, as is also John the Baptist who when Mary came in leaped for joy. For he heard the Lord speaking by the mouth of the Virgin and desired to break from his mother's womb to meet Him. As then Paula has been born in answer to a promise, her parents should give her a training suitable to her birth. Samuel, as you know, was nurtured in the Temple, and John was trained in the wilderness. The first as a Nazarite wore his hair long, drank neither wine nor strong drink, and even in his childhood talked with God. The second shunned cities,

wore a leathern girdle, and had for his meat locusts and wild honey. Moreover, to typify that penitence which he was to preach, he was clothed in the spoils of the hump-backed camel.

4. Thus must a soul be educated which is to be a temple of God. It must learn to hear nothing and to say nothing but what belongs to the fear of God. It must have no understanding of unclean words, and no knowledge of the world's songs. Its tongue must be steeped while still tender in the sweetness of the psalms. Boys with their wanton thoughts must be kept from Paula: even her maids and female attendants must be separated from worldly associates. For if they have learned some mischief they may teach more. Get for her a set of letters made of boxwood or of ivory and called each by its proper name. Let her play with these, so that even her play may teach her something. And not only make her grasp the right order of the letters and see that she forms their names into a rhyme, but constantly disarrange their order and put the last letters in the middle and the middle ones at the beginning that she may know them all by sight as well as by sound. Moreover, so soon as she begins to use the style upon the wax, and her hand is still faltering, either guide her soft fingers by laying your hand upon hers, or else have simple copies cut upon a tablet; so that her efforts confined within these limits may keep to the lines traced out for her and not stray outside of these. Offer prizes for good spelling and draw her onwards with little gifts such as children of her age delight in. And let her have companions in her lessons to excite emulation in her, that she may be stimulated when she sees them praised. You must not scold her if she is slow to learn but must employ praise to excite her mind, so that she may be glad when she excels others and sorry when she is excelled by them. Above all you must take care not to make her lessons distasteful to her lest a dislike for them conceived in childhood may continue into her maturer years. The very words which she tries bit by bit to put together and to pronounce ought not to be chance ones, but names specially fixed upon and heaped together for the purpose, those for example of the prophets or the apostles or the list of patriarchs from Adam downwards as it is given by Matthew and Luke. In this way while her tongue will be well-trained, her memory will be likewise developed. Again, you must choose for her a master of approved years, life, and learning. A man of culture will not, I think, blush to do for a kinswoman or a highborn virgin what Aristotle did for Philip's son when, descending to the level of an usher, he consented to teach him his letters. Things must not be despised as of small account in the absence of which great results cannot be achieved. The very rudiments and first beginnings of knowledge sound differently in the mouth of an educated man and of an uneducated. Accordingly you must see

that the child is not led away by the silly coaxing of women to form a habit of shortening long words or of decking herself with gold and purple. Of these habits one will spoil her conversation and the other her character. She must not therefore learn as a child what afterwards she will have to unlearn. The eloquence of the Gracchi is said to have been largely due to the way in which from their earliest years their mother spoke to them. Hortensius became an orator while still on his father's lap. Early impressions are hard to eradicate from the mind. When once wool has been dyed purple who can restore it to its previous whiteness? An unused jar long retains the taste and smell of that with which it is first filled. Grecian history tells us that the imperious Alexander who was lord of the whole world could not rid himself of the tricks of manner and gait which in his childhood he had caught from his governor Leonides. We are always ready to imitate what is evil; and faults are quickly copied where virtues appear inattainable. Paula's nurse must not be intemperate, or loose, or given to gossip. Her bearer must be respectable, and her foster-father of grave demeanour. When she sees her grandfather, she must leap upon his breast, put her arms round his neck, and, whether he likes it or not, sing Alleluia in his ears. She may be fondled by her grandmother, may smile at her father to shew that she recognizes him, and may so endear herself to everyone, as to make the whole family rejoice in the possession of such a rosebud. She should be told at once whom she has for her other grandmother and whom for her aunt; and she ought also to learn in what army it is that she is enrolled as a recruit, and what Captain it is under whose banner she is called to serve. Let her long to be with the absent ones and encourage her to make playful threats of leaving you for them.

5. Let her very dress and garb remind her to Whom she is promised. Do not pierce her ears or paint her face consecrated to Christ with white lead or rouge. Do not hang gold or pearls about her neck or load her head with jewels, or by reddening her hair make it suggest the fires of gehenna. Let her pearls be of another kind and such that she may sell them hereafter and buy in their place the pearl that is "of great price." In days gone by a lady of rank, Praetextata by name, at the bidding of her husband Hymettius, the uncle of Eustochium, altered that virgin's dress and appearance and arranged her neglected hair after the manner of the world, desiring to overcome the resolution of the virgin herself and the expressed wishes of her mother. But lo in the same night it befell her that an angel came to her in her dreams. With terrible looks he menaced punishment and broke silence with these words, Have you presumed to put your husband's commands before those of Christ? Have you presumed to lay sacrilegious hands upon the head of one who is God's virgin? Those

hands shall forthwith wither that you may know by torment what you have done, and at the end of five months you shall be carried off to hell. And farther, if you persist still in your wickedness, you shall be bereaved both of your husband and of your children.' All of which came to pass in due time, a speedy death marking the penitence too long delayed of the unhappy woman. So terribly does Christ punish those who violate His temple, and so jealously does He defend His precious jewels. I have related this story here not from any desire to exult over the misfortunes of the unhappy, but to warn you that you must with much fear and carefulness keep the vow which you have made to God.

6. We read of Eli the priest that he became displeasing to God on account of the sins of his children; and we are told that a man may not be made a bishop if his sons are loose and disorderly. On the other hand it is written of the woman that "she shall be saved in childbearing, if they continue in faith and charity and holiness with chastity." If then parents are responsible for their children when these are of ripe age and independent; how much more must they be responsible for them when, still unweaned and weak, they cannot, in the Lord's words, "discern between their right hand and their left:"—when, that is to say, they cannot yet distinguish good from evil? If you take precautions to save your daughter from the bite of a viper, why are you not equally careful to shield her from "the hammer of the whole earth"? to prevent her from drinking of the golden cup of Babylon? to keep her from going out with Dinah to see the daughters of a strange land? to save her from the tripping dance and from the trailing robe? No one administers drugs till he has rubbed the rim of the cup with honey; so, the better to deceive us, vice puts on the mien and the semblance of virtue. Why then, you will say, do we read:—"the son shall not bear the iniquity of the father, neither shall the father bear the iniquity of the son," but "the soul that sinneth it shall die"? The passage, I answer, refers to those who have discretion, such as he of whom his parents said in the gospel:—"he is of age . . . he shall speak for himself." While the son is a child and thinks as a child and until he comes to years of discretion to choose between the two roads to which the letter of Pythagoras points, his parents are responsible for his actions whether these be good or bad. But perhaps you imagine that, if they are not baptized, the children of Christians are liable for their own sins; and that no guilt attaches to parents who withhold from baptism those who by reason of their tender age can offer no objection to it. The truth is that, as baptism ensures the salvation of the child, this in turn brings advantage to the parents. Whether you would offer your child or not lay within your choice, but now that you have offered her, you neglect her at your

peril. I speak generally for in your case you have no discretion, having offered your child even before her conception. He who offers a victim that is lame or maimed or marked with any blemish is held guilty of sacrilege. How much more then shall she be punished who makes ready for the embraces of the king a portion of her own body and the purity of a stainless soul, and then proves negligent of this her offering?

7. When Paula comes to be a little older and to increase like her Spouse in wisdom and stature and in favour with God and man, let her go with her parents to the temple of her true Father but let her not come out of the temple with them. Let them seek her upon the world's highway amid the crowds and the throng of their kinsfolk, and let them find her nowhere but in the shrine of the scriptures, questioning the prophets and the apostles on the meaning of that spiritual marriage to which she is vowed. Let her imitate the retirement of Mary whom Gabriel found alone in her chamber and who was frightened, it would appear, by seeing a man there. Let the child emulate her of whom it is written that "the king's daughter is all glorious within." Wounded with love's arrow let her say to her beloved, "the king hath brought me into his chambers." At no time let her go abroad, lest the watchmen find her that go about the city, and lest they smite and wound her and take away from her the veil of her chastity, and leave her naked in her blood. Nay rather when one knocketh at her door let her say: "I am a wall and my breasts like towers. I have washed my feet; how shall I defile them?"

8. Let her not take her food with others, that is, at her parents' table; lest she see dishes she may long for. Some, I know, hold it a greater virtue to disdain a pleasure which is actually before them, but I think it a safer self-restraint to shun what must needs attract you. Once as a boy at school I met the words: It is ill blaming what you allow to become a habit.' Let her learn even now not to drink wine "wherein is excess." But as, before children come to a robust age, abstinence is dangerous and trying to their tender frames, let her have baths if she require them, and let her take a little wine for her stomach's sake. Let her also be supported on a flesh diet, lest her feet fail her before they commence to run their course. But I say this by way of concession not by way of command; because I fear to weaken her, not because I wish to teach her self-indulgence. Besides why should not a Christian virgin do wholly what others do in part? The superstitious Jews reject certain animals and products as articles of food, while among the Indians the Brahmans and among the Egyptians the Gymnosophists subsist altogether on porridge, rice, and apples. If mere glass repays so much labour, must not a pearl be worth more labour still? Paula has been born in response to a vow. Let her life be as the lives of those

who were born under the same conditions. If the grace accorded is in both cases the same, the pains bestowed ought to be so too. Let her be deaf to the sound of the organ, and not know even the uses of the pipe, the lyre, and the cithern.

9. And let it be her task daily to bring to you the flowers which she has culled from scripture. Let her learn by heart so many verses in the Greek, but let her be instructed in the Latin also. For, if the tender lips are not from the first shaped to this, the tongue is spoiled by a foreign accent and its native speech debased by alien elements. You must yourself be her mistress, a model on which she may form her childish conduct. Never either in you nor in her father let her see what she cannot imitate without sin. Remember both of you that you are the parents of a consecrated virgin, and that your example will teach her more than your precepts. Flowers are quick to fade and a baleful wind soon withers the violet, the lily, and the crocus. Let her never appear in public unless accompanied by you. Let her never visit a church or a martyr's shrine unless with her mother. Let no young man greet her with smiles; no dandy with curled hair pay compliments to her. If our little virgin goes to keep solemn eves and all-night vigils, let her not stir a hair's breadth from her mother's side. She must not single out one of her maids to make her a special favourite or a confidante. What she says to one all ought to know. Let her choose for a companion not a handsome well-dressed girl, able to warble a song with liquid notes but one pale and serious, sombrely attired and with the hue of melancholy. Let her take as her model some aged virgin of approved faith, character, and chastity, apt to instruct her by word and by example. She ought to rise at night to recite prayers and psalms; to sing hymns in the morning; at the third, sixth, and ninth hours to take her place in the line to do battle for Christ; and, lastly, to kindle her lamp and to offer her evening sacrifice. In these occupations let her pass the day, and when night comes let it find her still engaged in them. Let reading follow prayer with her, and prayer again succeed to reading. Time will seem short when employed on tasks so many and so varied.

10. Let her learn too how to spin wool, to hold the distaff, to put the basket in her lap, to turn the spinning wheel and to shape the yarn with her thumb. Let her put away with disdain silken fabrics, Chinese fleeces, and gold brocades: the clothing which she makes for herself should keep out the cold and not expose the body which it professes to cover. Let her food be herbs and wheaten bread with now and then one or two small fishes. And that I may not waste more time in giving precepts for the regulation of appetite (a subject I have treated more at length elsewhere) let her meals always leave her hungry

and able on the moment to begin reading or chanting. I strongly disapprove—especially for those of tender years—of long and immoderate fasts in which week is added to week and even oil and apples are forbidden as food. I have learned by experience that the ass toiling along the high way makes for an inn when it is weary. Our abstinence may turn to glutting, like that of the worshippers of Isis and of Cybele who gobble up pheasants and turtle-doves piping hot that their teeth may not violate the gifts of Ceres. If perpetual fasting is allowed, it must be so regulated that those who have a long journey before them may hold out all through; and we must take care that we do not, after starting well, fall halfway. However in Lent, as I have written before now, those who practise self-denial should spread every stitch of canvas, and the charioteer should for once slacken the reins and increase the speed of his horses. Yet there will be one rule for those who live in the world and another for virgins and monks. The layman in Lent consumes the coats of his stomach, and living like a snail on his own juices makes ready a paunch for rich foods and feasting to come. But with the virgin and the monk the case is different; for, when these give the rein to their steeds, they have to remember that for them the race knows of no intermission. An effort made only for a limited time may well be severe, but one that has no such limit must be more moderate. For whereas in the first case we can recover our breath when the race is over, in the last we have to go on continually and without stopping.

11. When you go a short way into the country, do not leave your daughter behind you. Leave her no power or capacity of living without you, and let her feel frightened when she is left to herself. Let her not converse with people of the world or associate with virgins indifferent to their vows. Let her not be present at the weddings of your slaves and let her take no part in the noisy games of the household. As regards the use of the bath, I know that some are content with saying that a Christian virgin should not bathe along with eunuchs or with married women, with the former because they are still men, at all events in mind, and with the latter because women with child offer a revolting spectacle. For myself, however, I wholly disapprove of baths for a virgin of full age. Such an one should blush and feel overcome at the idea of seeing herself undressed. By vigils and fasts she mortifies her body and brings it into subjection. By a cold chastity she seeks to put out the flame of lust and to quench the hot desires of youth. And by a deliberate squalor she makes haste to spoil her natural good looks. Why, then, should she add fuel to a sleeping fire by taking baths?

12. Let her treasures be not silks or gems but manuscripts of the holy scriptures; and in these let her think less of gilding, and Babylonian parchment, and

arabesque patterns, than of correctness and accurate punctuation. Let her begin by learning the psalter, and then let her gather rules of life out of the proverbs of Solomon. From the Preacher let her gain the habit of despising the world and its vanities. Let her follow the example set in Job of virtue and of patience. Then let her pass on to the gospels never to be laid aside when once they have been taken in hand. Let her also drink in with a willing heart the Acts of the Apostles and the Epistles. As soon as she has enriched the storehouse of her mind with these treasures, let her commit to memory the prophets, the heptateuch, the books of Kings and of Chronicles, the rolls also of Ezra and Esther. When she has done all these she may safely read the Song of Songs but not before: for, were she to read it at the beginning, she would fail to perceive that, though it is written in fleshly words, it is a marriage song of a spiritual bridal. And not understanding this she would suffer hurt from it. Let her avoid all apocryphal writings, and if she is led to read such not by the truth of the doctrines which they contain but out of respect for the miracles contained in them; let her understand that they are not really written by those to whom they are ascribed, that many faulty elements have been introduced into them, and that it requires infinite discretion to look for gold in the midst of dirt. Cyprian's writings let her have always in her hands. The letters of Athanasius and the treatises of Hilary she may go through without fear of stumbling. Let her take pleasure in the works and wits of all in whose books a due regard for the faith is not neglected. But if she reads the works of others let it be rather to judge them than to follow them.

13. You will answer, How shall I, a woman of the world, living at Rome, surrounded by a crowd, be able to observe all these injunctions?' In that case do not undertake a burthen to which you are not equal. When you have weaned Paula as Isaac was weaned and when you have clothed her as Samuel was clothed, send her to her grandmother and aunt; give up this most precious of gems, to be placed in Mary's chamber and to rest in the cradle where the infant Jesus cried. Let her be brought up in a monastery, let her be one amid companies of virgins, let her learn to avoid swearing, let her regard lying as sacrilege, let her be ignorant of the world, let her live the angelic life, while in the flesh let her be without the flesh, and let her suppose that all human beings are like herself. To say nothing of its other advantages this course will free you from the difficult task of minding her, and from the responsibility of guardianship. It is better to regret her absence than to be for ever trembling for her. For you cannot but tremble as you watch what she says and to whom she says it, to whom she bows and whom she likes best to see. Hand her over to Eustochium while she is still but an infant and her every cry is a prayer for you. She will

thus become her companion in holiness now as well as her successor hereafter. Let her gaze upon and love, let her "from her earliest years admire" one whose language and gait and dress are an education in virtue. Let her sit in the lap of her grandmother, and let this latter repeat to her granddaughter the lessons that she once bestowed upon her own child. Long experience has shewn Paula how to rear, to preserve, and to instruct virgins; and daily inwoven in her crown is the mystic century which betokens the highest chastity. O happy virgin! happy Paula, daughter of Toxotius, who through the virtues of her grandmother and aunt is nobler in holiness than she is in lineage! Yes, Laeta: were it possible for you with your own eyes to see your mother-in-law and your sister, and to realize the mighty souls which animate their small bodies; such is your innate thirst for chastity that I cannot doubt but that you would go to them even before your daughter, and would emancipate yourself from God's first decree of the Law to put yourself under His second dispensation of the Gospel. You would count as nothing your desire for other offspring and would offer up yourself to the service of God. But because "there is a time to embrace, and a time to refrain from embracing," and because "the wife hath not power of her own body," and because the apostle says "Let every man abide in the same calling wherein he was called" in the Lord, and because he that is under the yoke ought so to run as not to leave his companion in the mire, I counsel you to pay back to the full in your offspring what meantime you defer paying in your own person. When Hannah had once offered in the tabernacle the son whom she had vowed to God she never took him back; for she thought it unbecoming that one who was to be a prophet should grow up in the same house with her who still desired to have other children. Accordingly after she had conceived him and given him birth, she did not venture to come to the temple alone or to appear before the Lord empty, but first paid to Him what she owed; and then, when she had offered up that great sacrifice, she returned home and because she had borne her firstborn for God, she was given five children for herself. Do you marvel at the happiness of that holy woman? Imitate her faith. Moreover, if you will only send Paula, I promise to be myself both a tutor and a foster father to her. Old as I am I will carry her on my shoulders and train her stammering lips; and my charge will be a far grander one than that of the worldly philosopher; for while he only taught a King of Macedon who was one day to die of Babylonian poison, I shall instruct the handmaid and spouse of Christ who must one day be offered to her Lord in heaven.

LETTER CVIII. TO EUSTOCHIUM

This, one of the longest of Jerome's letters, was written to console Eustochium for the loss of her mother who had recently died. Jerome relates the story of Paula in detail; speaking first of her high birth, marriage, and social success at Rome, and then narrating her conversion and subsequent life as a Christian ascetic. Much space is devoted to an account of her journey to the East which included a visit to Egypt and to the monasteries of Nitria as well as a tour of the most sacred spots in the Holy Land. The remainder of the letter describes her daily routine and studies at Bethlehem, and recounts the many virtues for which she was distinguished. It then concludes with a touching description of her death and burial and gives the epitaph placed upon her grave. The date of the letter is 404 a.d.

1. If all the members of my body were to be converted into tongues, and if each of my limbs were to be gifted with a human voice, I could still do no justice to the virtues of the holy and venerable Paula. Noble in family, she was nobler still in holiness; rich formerly in this world's goods, she is now more distinguished by the poverty that she has embraced for Christ. Of the stock of the Gracchi and descended from the Scipios, the heir and representative of that Paulus whose name she bore, the true and legitimate daughter of that Martia Papyria who was mother to Africanus, she yet preferred Bethlehem to Rome, and left her palace glittering with gold to dwell in a mud cabin. We do not grieve that we have lost this perfect woman; rather we thank God that we have had her, nay that we have her still. For "all live unto" God, and they who return unto the Lord are still to be reckoned members of his family. We have lost her, it is true, but the heavenly mansions have gained her; for as long as she was in the body she was absent from the Lord and would constantly complain with tears:—"Woe is me that I sojourn in Mesech, that I dwell in the tents of Kedar; my soul hath been this long time a pilgrim." It was no wonder that she sobbed out that even she was in darkness (for this is the meaning of the word Kedar) seeing that, according to the apostle, "the world lieth in the evil one;" and that, "as its darkness is, so is its light;" and that "the light shineth in darkness and the darkness comprehended it not." She would frequently exclaim: "I am a stranger with thee and a sojourner as all my fathers were," and again, I desire "to depart and to be with Christ." As often too as she was troubled with bodily weakness (brought on by incredible abstinence and by redoubled fastings), she would be heard to say: "I keep under my body and bring it into subjection; lest that by any means, when I have preached to others, I myself should be a castaway;" and "It is good neither to eat flesh nor

to drink wine;" and "I humbled my soul with fasting;" and "thou wilt make all" my "bed in" my "sickness;" and "Thy hand was heavy upon me: my moisture is turned into the drought of summer." And when the pain which she bore with such wonderful patience darted through her, as if she saw the heavens opened she would say "Oh that I had wings like a dove! for then would I fly away and be at rest."

2. I call Jesus and his saints, yes and the particular angel who was the guardian and the companion of this admirable woman to bear witness that these are no words of adulation and flattery but sworn testimony every one of them borne to her character. They are, indeed, inadequate to the virtues of one whose praises are sung by the whole world, who is admired by bishops, regretted by bands of virgins, and wept for by crowds of monks and poor. Would you know all her virtues, reader, in short? She has left those dependent on her poor, but not so poor as she was herself. In dealing thus with her relatives and the men and women of her small household—her brothers and sisters rather than her servants—she has done nothing strange; for she has left her daughter Eustochium—a virgin consecrated to Christ for whose comfort this sketch is made—far from her noble family and rich only in faith and grace.

3. Let me then begin my narrative. Others may go back a long way even to Paula's cradle and, if I may say so, to her swaddling-clothes, and may speak of her mother Blaesilla and her father Rogatus. Of these the former was a descendant of the Scipios and the Gracchi; whilst the latter came of a line distinguished in Greece down to the present day. He was said, indeed, to have in his veins the blood of Agamemnon who destroyed Troy after a ten years siege. But I shall praise only what belongs to herself, what wells forth from the pure spring of her holy mind. When in the gospel the apostles ask their Lord and Saviour what He will give to those who have left all for His sake, He tells them that they shall receive an hundredfold now in this time and in the world to come eternal life. From which we see that it is not the possession of riches that is praiseworthy but the rejection of them for Christ's sake; that, instead of glorying in our privileges, we should make them of small account as compared with God's faith. Truly the Saviour has now in this present time made good His promise to His servants and handmaidens. For one who despised the glory of a single city is to-day famous throughout the world; and one who while she lived at Rome was known by no one outside it has by hiding herself at Bethlehem become the admiration of all lands Roman and barbarian. For what race of men is there which does not send pilgrims to the holy places? And who could there find a greater marvel than Paula? As among many jewels the most precious shines most brightly, and as the sun with its beams obscures and puts

out the paler fires of the stars; so by her lowliness she surpassed all others in virtue and influence and, while she was least among all, was greater than all. The more she cast herself down, the more she was lifted up by Christ. She was hidden and yet she was not hidden. By shunning glory she earned glory; for glory follows virtue as its shadow; and deserting those who seek it, it seeks those who despise it. But I must not neglect to proceed with my narrative or dwell too long on a single point forgetful of the rules of writing.

4. Being then of such parentage, Paula married Toxotius in whose veins ran the noble blood of AEneas and the Julii. Accordingly his daughter, Christ's virgin Eustochium, is called Julia, as he Julius.

A name from great Iulus handed down.

I speak of these things not as of importance to those who have them, but as worthy of remark in those who despise them. Men of the world look up to persons who are rich in such privileges. We on the other hand praise those who for the Saviour's sake despise them; and strangely depreciating all who keep them, we eulogize those who are unwilling to do so. Thus nobly born, Paula through her fruitfulness and her chastity won approval from all, from her husband first, then from her relatives, and lastly from the whole city. She bore five children; Blaesilla, for whose death I consoled her while at Rome; Paulina, who has left the reverend and admirable Pammachius to inherit both her vows and property, to whom also I addressed a little book on her death; Eustochium, who is now in the holy places, a precious necklace of virginity and of the church; Rufina, whose untimely end overcame the affectionate heart of her mother; and Toxotius, after whom she had no more children. You can thus see that it was not her wish to fulfil a wife's duty, but that she only complied with her husband's longing to have male offspring.

5. When he died, her grief was so great that she nearly died herself: yet so completely did she then give herself to the service of the Lord, that it might have seemed that she had desired his death.

In what terms shall I speak of her distinguished, and noble, and formerly wealthy house; all the riches of which she spent upon the poor? How can I describe the great consideration she shewed to all and her far reaching kindness even to those whom she had never seen? What poor man, as he lay dying, was not wrapped in blankets given by her? What bedridden person was not supported with money from her purse? She would seek out such with the greatest diligence throughout the city, and would think it a misfortune were any hungry or sick person to be supported by another's food. So lavish was her charity that she robbed her children; and, when her relatives remonstrated with her for doing so, she declared that she was leaving to them a better inheritance in the mercy of Christ.

6. Nor was she long able to endure the visits and crowded receptions, which her high position in the world and her exalted family entailed upon her. She received the homage paid to her sadly, and made all the speed she could to shun and to escape those who wished to pay her compliments. It so happened that at that time the bishops of the East and West had been summoned to Rome by letter from the emperors to deal with certain dissensions between the churches, and in this way she saw two most admirable men and Christian prelates, Paulinus bishop of Antioch and Epiphanius, bishop of Salamis or, as it is now called, Constantia, in Cyprus. Epiphanius, indeed, she received as her guest; and, although Paulinus was staying in another person's house, in the warmth of her heart she treated him as if he too were lodged with her. Inflamed by their virtues she thought more and more each moment of forsaking her home. Disregarding her house, her children, her servants, her property, and in a word everything connected with the world, she was eager—alone and unaccompanied (if ever it could be said that she was so)—to go to the desert made famous by its Pauls and by its Antonies. And at last when the winter was over and the sea was open, and when the bishops were returning to their churches, she also sailed with them in her prayers and desires. Not to prolong the story, she went down to Portus accompanied by her brother, her kinsfolk and above all her own children eager by their demonstrations of affection to overcome their loving mother. At last the sails were set and the strokes of the rowers carried the vessel into the deep. On the shore the little Toxotius stretched forth his hands in entreaty, while Rufina, now grown up, with silent sobs besought her mother to wait till she should be married. But still Paula's eyes were dry as she turned them heavenwards; and she overcame her love for her children by her love for God. She knew herself no more as a mother, that she might approve herself a handmaid of Christ. Yet her heart was rent within her, and she wrestled with her grief, as though she were being forcibly separated from parts of herself. The greatness of the affection she had to overcome made all admire her victory the more. Among the cruel hardships which attend prisoners of war in the hands of their enemies, there is none severer than the separation of parents from their children. Though it is against the laws of nature, she endured this trial with unabated faith; nay more she sought it with a joyful heart: and overcoming her love for her children by her greater love for God, she concentrated herself quietly upon Eustochium alone, the partner alike of her vows and of her voyage. Meantime the vessel ploughed onwards and all her fellow-passengers looked back to the shore. But she turned away her

eyes that she might not see what she could not behold without agony. No mother, it must be confessed, ever loved her children so dearly. Before setting out she gave them all that she had, disinheriting herself upon earth that she might find an inheritance in heaven.

7. The vessel touched at the island of Pontia ennobled long since as the place of exile of the illustrious lady Flavia Domitilla who under the Emperor Domitian was banished because she confessed herself a Christian; and Paula, when she saw the cells in which this lady passed the period of her long martyrdom, taking to herself the wings of faith, more than ever desired to see Jerusalem and the holy places. The strongest winds seemed weak and the greatest speed slow. After passing between Scylla and Charybdis she committed herself to the Adriatic sea and had a calm passage to Methone. Stopping here for a short time to recruit her wearied frame

She stretched her dripping limbs upon the shore:
Then sailed past Malea and Cythera's isle,
The scattered Cyclades, and all the lands
That narrow in the seas on every side.

Then leaving Rhodes and Lycia behind her, she at last came in sight of Cyprus, where falling at the feet of the holy and venerable Epiphanius, she was by him detained ten days; though this was not, as he supposed, to restore her strength but, as the facts prove, that she might do God's work. For she visited all the monasteries in the island, and left, so far as her means allowed, substantial relief for the brothers in them whom love of the holy man had brought thither from all parts of the world. Then crossing the narrow sea she landed at Seleucia, and going up thence to Antioch allowed herself to be detained for a little time by the affection of the reverend confessor Paulinus. Then, such was the ardour of her faith that she, a noble lady who had always previously been carried by eunuchs, went her way—and that in midwinter—riding upon an ass.

8. I say nothing of her journey through Coele-Syria and Phoenicia (for it is not my purpose to give you a complete itinerary of her wanderings); I shall only name such places as are mentioned in the sacred books. After leaving the Roman colony of Berytus and the ancient city of Zidon she entered Elijah's town on the shore at Zarephath and therein adored her Lord and Saviour. Next passing over the sands of Tyre on which Paul had once knelt she came to Acco or, as it is now called, Ptolemais, rode over the plains of Megiddo which had once witnessed the slaying of Josiah, and entered the land of the Philistines. Here she could not fail to admire the ruins of Dor, once a most powerful city; and Strato's Tower, which though at one time insignificant was rebuilt by

Herod king of Judaea and named Caesarea in honour of Caesar Augustus. Here she saw the house of Cornelius now turned into a Christian church; and the humble abode of Philip; and the chambers of his daughters the four virgins "which did prophesy." She arrived next at Antipatris, a small town half in ruins, named by Herod after his father Antipater, and at Lydda, now become Diospolis, a place made famous by the raising again of Dorcas and the restoration to health of AEneas. Not far from this are Arimathaea, the village of Joseph who buried the Lord, and Nob, once a city of priests but now the tomb in which their slain bodies rest. Joppa too is hard by, the port of Jonah's flight; which also—if I may introduce a poetic fable—saw Andromeda bound to the rock. Again resuming her journey, she came to Nicopolis, once called Emmaus, where the Lord became known in the breaking of bread; an action by which He dedicated the house of Cleopas as a church. Starting thence she made her way up lower and higher Beth-horon, cities founded by Solomon but subsequently destroyed by several devastating wars; seeing on her right Ajalon and Gibeon where Joshua the son of Nun when fighting against the five kings gave commandments to the sun and moon, where also he condemned the Gibeonites (who by a crafty stratagem had obtained a treaty) to be hewers of wood and drawers of water. At Gibeah also, now a complete ruin, she stopped for a little while remembering its sin, and the cutting of the concubine into pieces, and how in spite of all this three hundred men of the tribe of Benjamin were saved that in after days Paul might be called a Benjamite.

9. To make a long story short, leaving on her left the mausoleum of Helena queen of Adiabene who in time of famine had sent corn to the Jewish people, Paula entered Jerusalem, Jebus, or Salem, that city of three names which after it had sunk to ashes and decay was by AElius Hadrianus restored once more as AElia. And although the proconsul of Palestine, who was an intimate friend of her house, sent forward his apparitors and gave orders to have his official residence placed at her disposal, she chose a humble cell in preference to it. Moreover, in visiting the holy places so great was the passion and the enthusiasm she exhibited for each, that she could never have torn herself away from one had she not been eager to visit the rest. Before the Cross she threw herself down in adoration as though she beheld the Lord hanging upon it: and when she entered the tomb which was the scene of the Resurrection she kissed the stone which the angel had rolled away from the door of the sepulchre. Indeed so ardent was her faith that she even licked with her mouth the very spot on which the Lord's body had lain, like one athirst for the river which he has longed for. What tears she shed there, what groans she uttered, and what grief she poured forth, all Jerusalem knows; the Lord also to whom she prayed

knows. Going out thence she made the ascent of Zion; a name which signifies either "citadel" or "watch-tower." This formed the city which David formerly stormed and afterwards rebuilt. Of its storming it is written, "Woe to Ariel, to Ariel"—that is, God's lion, (and indeed in those days it was extremely strong)—"the city which David stormed:" and of its rebuilding it is said, "His foundation is in the holy mountains: the Lord loveth the gates of Zion more than all the dwellings of Jacob." He does not mean the gates which we see to-day in dust and ashes; the gates he means are those against which hell prevails not and through which the multitude of those who believe in Christ enter in. There was shewn to her upholding the portico of a church the bloodstained column to which our Lord is said to have been bound when He suffered His scourging. There was shewn to her also the spot where the Holy Spirit came down upon the souls of the one hundred and twenty believers, thus fulfilling the prophecy of Joel.

10. Then, after distributing money to the poor and her fellow-servants so far as her means allowed, she proceeded to Bethlehem stopping only on the right side of the road to visit Rachel's tomb. (Here it was that she gave birth to her son destined to be not what his dying mother called him, Benoni, that is the "Son of my pangs" but as his father in the spirit prophetically named him Benjamin, that is "the Son of the right hand)." After this she came to Bethlehem and entered into the cave where the Saviour was born. Here, when she looked upon the inn made sacred by the virgin and the stall where the ox knew his owner and the ass his master's crib, and where the words of the same prophet had been fulfilled "Blessed is he that soweth beside the waters where the ox and the ass trample the seed under their feet:" when she looked upon these things I say, she protested in my hearing that she could behold with the eyes of faith the infant Lord wrapped in swaddling clothes and crying in the manger, the wise men worshipping Him, the star shining overhead, the virgin mother, the attentive foster-father, the shepherds coming by night to see "the word that was come to pass" and thus even then to consecrate those opening phrases of the evangelist John "In the beginning was the word" and "the word was made flesh." She declared that she could see the slaughtered innocents, the raging Herod, Joseph and Mary fleeing into Egypt; and with a mixture of tears and joy she cried: Hail Bethlehem, house of bread, wherein was born that Bread that came down from heaven. Hail Ephratah, land of fruitfulness and of fertility, whose fruit is the Lord Himself. Concerning thee has Micah prophesied of old, "Thou Bethlehem Ephratah art not the least among the thousands of Judah, for out of thee shall he come forth unto me that is to be ruler in Israel; whose goings forth have been from of old, from everlasting. Therefore

wilt thou give them up, until the time that she which travaileth hath brought forth: then the remnant of his brethren shall return unto the children of Israel." For in thee was born the prince begotten before Lucifer. Whose birth from the Father is before all time: and the cradle of David's race continued in thee, until the virgin brought forth her son and the remnant of the people that believed in Christ returned unto the children of Israel and preached freely to them in words like these: "It was necessary that the word of God should first have been spoken to you; but seeing ye put it from you and judge yourselves unworthy of everlasting life, lo, we turn to the Gentiles." For the Lord hath said: "I am not sent but unto the lost sheep of the house of Israel." At that time also the words of Jacob were fulfilled concerning Him, "A prince shall not depart from Judah nor a lawgiver from between his feet, until He come for whom it is laid up, and He shall be for the expectation of the nations." Well did David swear, well did he make a vow saying: "Surely I will not come into the tabernacle of my house nor go up into my bed: I will not give sleep to mine eyes, or slumber to my eyelids, or rest to the temples of my head, until I find out a place for the Lord, an habitation for the . . . God of Jacob." And immediately he explained the object of his desire, seeing with prophetic eyes that He would come whom we now believe to have come. "Lo we heard of Him at Ephratah: we found Him in the fields of the wood." The Hebrew word Zo as have learned from your lessons means not her, that is Mary the Lord's mother, but him that is the Lord Himself. Therefore he says boldly: "We will go into His tabernacle: we will worship at His footstool." I too, miserable sinner though I am, have been accounted worthy to kiss the manger in which the Lord cried as a babe, and to pray in the cave in which the travailing virgin gave birth to the infant Lord. "This is my rest" for it is my Lord's native place; "here will I dwell" for this spot has my Saviour chosen. "I have prepared a lamp for my Christ." "My soul shall live unto Him and my seed shall serve Him."

After this Paula went a short distance down the hill to the tower of Edar, that is of the flock,' near which Jacob fed his flocks, and where the shepherds keeping watch by night were privileged to hear the words: "Glory to God in the highest and on earth peace, goodwill toward men." While they were keeping their sheep they found the Lamb of God; whose fleece bright and clean was made wet with the dew of heaven when it was dry upon all the earth beside, and whose blood when sprinkled on the doorposts drove off the destroyer of Egypt and took away the sins of the world.

11. Then immediately quickening her pace she began to move along the old road which leads to Gaza, that is to the power' or wealth' of God, silently

meditating on that type of the Gentiles, the Ethiopian eunuch, who in spite of the prophet changed his skin and whilst he read the old testament found the fountain of the gospel. Next turning to the right she passed from Bethzur to Eshcol which means "a cluster of grapes." It was hence that the spies brought back that marvellous cluster which was the proof of the fertility of the land and a type of Him who says of Himself: "I have trodden the wine press alone; and of the people there was none with me." Shortly afterwards she entered the home of Sarah and beheld the birthplace of Isaac and the traces of Abraham's oak under which he saw Christ's day and was glad. And rising up from thence she went up to Hebron, that is Kirjath-Arba, or the City of the Four Men. These are Abraham, Isaac, Jacob, and the great Adam whom the Hebrews suppose (from the book of Joshua the son of Nun) to be buried there. But many are of opinion that Caleb is the fourth and a monument at one side is pointed out as his. After seeing these places she did not care to go on to Kirjath-sepher, that is "the village of letters;" because despising the letter that killeth she had found the spirit that giveth life. She admired more the upper springs and the nether springs which Othniel the son of Kenaz the son of Jephunneh received in place of a south land and a waterless possession, and by the conducting of which he watered the dry fields of the old covenant. For thus did he typify the redemption which the sinner finds for his old sins in the waters of baptism. On the next day soon after sunrise she stood upon the brow of Capharbarucha, that is, "the house of blessing," the point to which Abraham pursued the Lord when he made intercession with Him. And here, as she looked down upon the wide solitude and upon the country once belonging to Sodom and Gomorrah, to Admah and Zeboim, she beheld the balsam vines of Engedi and Zoar. By Zoar I mean that "heifer of three years old" which was formerly called Bela and in Syriac is rendered Zoar that is little.' She called to mind the cave in which Lot found refuge, and with tears in her eyes warned the virgins her companions to beware of "wine wherein is excess;" for it was to this that the Moabites and Ammonites owe their origin.

12. I linger long in the land of the midday sun for it was there and then that the spouse found her bridegroom at rest and Joseph drank wine with his brothers once more. I will return to Jerusalem and, passing through Tekoa the home of Amos, I will look upon the glistening cross of Mount Olivet from which the Saviour made His ascension to the Father. Here year by year a red heifer was burned as a holocaust to the Lord and its ashes were used to purify the children of Israel. Here also according to Ezekiel the Cherubim after leaving the temple founded the church of the Lord.

After this Paula visited the tomb of Lazarus and beheld the hospitable roof of Mary and Martha, as well as Bethphage, the town of the priestly jaws.' Here it was that a restive foal typical of the Gentiles received the bridle of God, and covered with the garments of the apostles offered its lowly back for Him to sit on. From this she went straight on down the hill to Jericho thinking of the wounded man in the gospel, of the savagery of the priests and Levites who passed him by, and of the kindness of the Samaritan, that is, the guardian, who placed the half-dead man upon his own beast and brought him down to the inn of the church. She noticed the place called Adomim or the Place of Blood, so-called because much blood was shed there in the frequent incursions of marauders. She beheld also the sycamore tree of Zacchaeus, by which is signified the good works of repentance whereby he trod under foot his former sins of bloodshed and rapine, and from which he saw the Most High as from a pinnacle of virtue. She was shewn too the spot by the wayside where the blind men sat who, receiving their sight from the Lord, became types of the two peoples who should believe upon Him. Then entering Jericho she saw the city which Hiel founded in Abiram his firstborn and of which he set up the gates in his youngest son Segub. She looked upon the camp of Gilgal and the hill of the foreskins suggestive of the mystery of the second circumcision: and she gazed at the twelve stones brought thither out of the bed of Jordan to be symbols of those twelve foundations on which are written the names of the twelve apostles. She saw also that fountain of the Law most bitter and barren which the true Elisha healed by his wisdom changing it into a well sweet and fertilising. Scarcely had the night passed away when burning with eagerness she hastened to the Jordan, stood by the brink of the river, and as the sun rose recalled to mind the rising of the sun of righteousness; how the priest's feet stood firm in the middle of the river-bed; how afterwards at the command of Elijah and Elisha the waters were divided hither and thither and made way for them to pass; and again how the Lord had cleansed by His baptism waters which the deluge had polluted and the destruction of mankind had defiled.

13. It would be tedious were I tell of the valley of Achor, that is, of trouble and crowds,' where theft and covetousness were condemned; and of Bethel, the house of God,' where Jacob poor and destitute slept upon the bare ground. Here it was that, having set beneath his head a stone which in Zechariah is described as having seven eyes and in Isaiah is spoken of as a corner-stone, he beheld a ladder reaching up to heaven; yes, and the Lord standing high above it holding out His hand to such as were ascending and hurling from on high such as were careless. Also when she was in Mount Ephraim she made pilgrimages to the tombs of Joshua the son of Nun and of Eleazar the son of Aaron

the priest, exactly opposite the one to the other; that of Joshua being built at Timnath-serah "on the north side of the hill of Gaash," and that of Eleazar "in a hill that pertained to Phinehas his son." She was somewhat surprised to find that he who had had the distribution of the land in his own hands had selected for himself portions uneven and rocky. What shall I say about Shiloh where a ruined altar is still shewn to-day, and where the tribe of Benjamin anticipated Romulus in the rape of the Sabine women? Passing by Shechem (not Sychar as many wrongly read) or as it is now called Neapolis, she entered the church built upon the side of Mount Gerizim around Jacob's well; that well where the Lord was sitting when hungry and thirsty He was refreshed by the faith of the woman of Samaria. Forsaking her five husbands by whom are intended the five books of Moses, and that sixth not a husband of whom she boasted, to wit the false teacher Dositheus, she found the true Messiah and the true Saviour. Turning away thence Paula saw the tombs of the twelve patriarchs, and Samaria which in honour of Augustus Herod renamed Augusta or in Greek Sebaste. There lie the prophets Elisha and Obadiah and John the Baptist than whom there is not a greater among those that are born of women. And here she was filled with terror by the marvels she beheld; for she saw demons screaming under different tortures before the tombs of the saints, and men howling like wolves, baying like dogs, roaring like lions, hissing like serpents and bellowing like bulls. They twisted their heads and bent them backwards until they touched the ground; women too were suspended head downward and their clothes did not fall off. Paula pitied them all, and shedding tears over them prayed Christ to have mercy on them. And weak as she was she climbed the mountain on foot; for in two of its caves Obadiah in a time of persecution and famine had fed a hundred prophets with bread and water. Then she passed quickly through Nazareth the nursery of the Lord; Cana and Capernaum familiar with the signs wrought by Him; the lake of Tiberias sanctified by His voyages upon it; the wilderness where countless Gentiles were satisfied with a few loaves while the twelve baskets of the tribes of Israel were filled with the fragments left by them that had eaten. She made the ascent of mount Tabor whereon the Lord was transfigured. In the distance she beheld the range of Hermon; and the wide stretching plains of Galilee where Sisera and all his host had once been overcome by Barak; and the torrent Kishon separating the level ground into two parts. Hard by also the town of Nain was pointed out to her, where the widow's son was raised. Time would fail me sooner than speech were I to recount all the places to which the revered Paula was carried by her incredible faith.

14. I will now pass on to Egypt, pausing for a while on the way at Socoh, and at Samson's well which he clave in the hollow place that was in the jaw. Here I will lave my parched lips and refresh myself before visiting Moresheth; in old days famed for the tomb of the prophet Micah, and now for its church. Then skirting the country of the Horites and Gittites, Mareshah, Edom, and Lachish, and traversing the lonely wastes of the desert where the tracks of the traveller are lost in the yielding sand, I will come to the river of Egypt called Sihor, that is "the muddy river," and go through the five cities of Egypt which speak the language of Canaan, and through the land of Goshen and the plains of Zoan on which God wrought his marvellous works. And I will visit the city of No, which has since become Alexandria; and Nitria, the town of the Lord, where day by day the filth of multitudes is washed away with the pure nitre of virtue. No sooner did Paula come in sight of it than there came to meet her the reverend and estimable bishop, the confessor Isidore, accompanied by countless multitudes of monks many of whom were of priestly or of Levitical rank. On seeing these Paula rejoiced to behold the Lord's glory manifested in them; but protested that she had no claim to be received with such honour. Need I speak of the Macarii, Arsenius, Serapion, or other pillars of Christ! Was there any cell that she did not enter? Or any man at whose feet she did not throw herself? In each of His saints she believed that she saw Christ Himself; and whatever she bestowed upon them she rejoiced to feel that she had bestowed it upon the Lord. Her enthusiasm was wonderful and her endurance scarcely credible in a woman. Forgetful of her sex and of her weakness she even desired to make her abode, together with the girls who accompanied her, among these thousands of monks. And, as they were all willing to welcome her, she might perhaps have sought and obtained permission to do so; had she not been drawn away by a still greater passion for the holy places. Coming by sea from Pelusium to Maioma on account of the great heat, she returned so rapidly that you would have thought her a bird. Not long afterwards, making up her mind to dwell permanently in holy Bethlehem, she took up her abode for three years in a miserable hostelry; till she could build the requisite cells and monastic buildings, to say nothing of a guest house for passing travellers where they might find the welcome which Mary and Joseph had missed. At this point I conclude my narrative of the journeys that she made accompanied by Eustochium and many other virgins.

15. I am now free to describe at greater length the virtue which was her peculiar charm; and in setting forth this I call God to witness that I am no flatterer. I add nothing. I exaggerate nothing. On the contrary I tone down much that I may not appear to relate incredibilities. My carping critics must not

insinuate that I am drawing on my imagination or decking Paula, like AEsop's crow, with the fine feathers of other birds. Humility is the first of Christian graces, and hers was so pronounced that one who had never seen her, and who on account of her celebrity had desired to see her, would have believed that he saw not her but the lowest of her maids. When she was surrounded by companies of virgins she was always the least remarkable in dress, in speech, in gesture, and in gait. From the time that her husband died until she fell asleep herself she never sat at meat with a man, even though she might know him to stand upon the pinnacle of the episcopate. She never entered a bath except when dangerously ill. Even in the severest fever she rested not on an ordinary bed but on the hard ground covered only with a mat of goat's hair; if that can be called rest which made day and night alike a time of almost unbroken prayer. Well did she fulfil the words of the psalter: "All the night make I my bed to swim; I water my couch with my tears"! Her tears welled forth as it were from fountains, and she lamented her slightest faults as if they were sins of the deepest dye. Constantly did I warn her to spare her eyes and to keep them for the reading of the gospel; but she only said: I must disfigure that face which contrary to God's commandment I have painted with rouge, white lead, and antimony. I must mortify that body which has been given up to many pleasures. I must make up for my long laughter by constant weeping. I must exchange my soft linen and costly silks for rough goat's hair. I who have pleased my husband and the world in the past, desire now to please Christ.' Were I among her great and signal virtues to select her chastity as a subject of praise, my words would seem superfluous; for, even when she was still in the world, she set an example to all the matrons of Rome, and bore herself so admirably that the most slanderous never ventured to couple scandal with her name. No mind could be more considerate than hers, or none kinder towards the lowly. She did not court the powerful; at the same time, if the proud and the vainglorious sought her, she did not turn from them with disdain. If she saw a poor man, she supported him: and if she saw a rich one, she urged him to do good. Her liberality alone knew no bounds. Indeed, so anxious was she to turn no needy person away that she borrowed money at interest and often contracted new loans to pay off old ones. I was wrong, I admit; but when I saw her so profuse in giving, I reproved her alleging the apostle's words: "I mean not that other men be eased and ye burthened; but by an equality that now at this time your abundance may be a supply for their want, that their abundance also may be a supply for your want." I quoted from the gospel the Saviour's words: "he that hath two coats, let him impart one of them to him that hath none"; and I warned her that she might not always have means to do as she would wish.

Other arguments I adduced to the same purpose; but with admirable modesty and brevity she overruled them all. "God is my witness," she said, "that what I do I do for His sake. My prayer is that I may die a beggar not leaving a penny to my daughter and indebted to strangers for my winding sheet." She then concluded with these words: "I, if I beg, shall find many to give to me; but if this beggar does not obtain help from me who by borrowing can give it to him, he will die; and if he dies, of whom will his soul be required?" I wished her to be more careful in managing her concerns, but she with a faith more glowing than mine clave to the Saviour with her whole heart and poor in spirit followed the Lord in His poverty, giving back to Him what she had received and becoming poor for His sake. She obtained her wish at last and died leaving her daughter overwhelmed with a mass of debt. This Eustochium still owes and indeed cannot hope to pay off by her own exertions; only the mercy of Christ can free her from it.

16. Many married ladies make it a habit to confer gifts upon their own trumpeters, and while they are extremely profuse to a few, withhold all help from the many. From this fault Paula was altogether free. She gave her money to each according as each had need, not ministering to self-indulgence but relieving want. No poor person went away from her empty handed. And all this she was enabled to do not by the greatness of her wealth but by her careful management of it. She constantly had on her lips such phrases as these: "Blessed are the merciful for they shall obtain mercy:" and "water will quench a flaming fire; and alms maketh an atonement for sins;" and "make to yourselves friends of the mammon of unrighteousness that . . . they may receive you into everlasting habitations;" and "give alms . . . and behold all things are clean unto you;" and Daniel's words to King Nebuchadnezzar in which he admonished him to redeem his sins by almsgiving. She wished to spend her money not upon these stones, that shall pass away with the earth and the world, but upon those living stones, which roll over the earth; of which in the apocalypse of John the city of the great king is built; of which also the scripture tells us that they shall be changed into sapphire and emerald and jasper and other gems.

17. But these qualities she may well share with a few others and the devil knows that it is not in these that the highest virtue consists. For, when Job has lost his substance and when his house and children have been destroyed, Satan says to the Lord: "Skin for skin, yea all that a man hath, will he give for his life. But put forth thine hand now and touch his bone and his flesh, and he will curse thee to thy face." We know that many persons while they have given alms have yet given nothing which touches their bodily comfort; and while

they have held out a helping hand to those in need are themselves overcome with sensual indulgences; they whitewash the outside but within they are "full of dead men's bones." Paula was not one of these. Her self-restraint was so great as to be almost immoderate; and her fasts and labours were so severe as almost to weaken her constitution. Except on feast days she would scarcely ever take oil with her food; a fact from which may be judged what she thought of wine, sauce, fish, honey, milk, eggs, and other things agreeable to the palate. Some persons believe that in taking these they are extremely frugal; and, even if they surfeit themselves with them, they still fancy their chastity safe.

18. Envy always follows in the track of virtue: as Horace says, it is ever the mountain top that is smitten by the lightning. It is not surprising that I declare this of men and women, when the jealousy of the Pharisees succeeded in crucifying our Lord Himself. All the saints have had illwishers, and even Paradise was not free from the serpent through whose malice death came into the world. So the Lord stirred up against Paula Hadad the Edomite to buffet her that she might not be exalted, and warned her frequently by the thorn in her flesh not to be elated by the greatness of her own virtues or to fancy that, compared with other women, she had attained the summit of perfection. For my part I used to say that it was best to give in to rancour and to retire before passion. So Jacob dealt with his brother Esau; so David met the unrelenting persecution of Saul. I reminded her how the first of these fled into Mesopotamia; and how the second surrendered himself to the Philistines, and chose to submit to foreign foes rather than to enemies at home. She however replied as follows:—Your suggestion would be a wise one if the devil did not everywhere fight against God's servants and handmaidens, and did he not always precede the fugitives to their chosen refuges. Moreover, I am deterred from accepting it by my love for the holy places; and I cannot find another Bethlehem elsewhere. Why may I not by my patience conquer this ill will? Why may I not by my humility break down this pride, and when I am smitten on the one cheek offer to the smiter the other? Surely the apostle Paul says "Overcome evil with good." Did not the apostles glory when they suffered reproach for the Lord's sake? Did not even the Saviour humble Himself, taking the form of a servant and being made obedient to the Father unto death, even the death of the cross, that He might save us by His passion? If Job had not fought the battle and won the victory, he would never have received the crown of righteousness, or have heard the Lord say: "Thinkest thou that I have spoken unto thee for aught else than this, that thou mightest appear righteous." In the gospel those only are said to be blessed who suffer persecution for righteousness' sake. My conscience is at rest, and I know that it is not from any fault of mine that I am

suffering; moreover affliction in this world is a ground for expecting a reward hereafter.' When the enemy was more than usually forward and ventured to reproach her to her face, she used to chant the words of the psalter: "While the wicked was before me, I was dumb with silence; I held my peace even from good:" and again, "I as a deaf man heard not; and I was as a dumb man that openeth not his mouth:" and "I was as a man that heareth not, and in whose mouth are no reproofs." When she felt herself tempted, she dwelt upon the words in Deuteronomy: "The Lord your God proveth you, to know whether ye love the Lord your God with all your heart and with all your soul." In tribulations and afflictions she turned to the splendid language of Isaiah: "Ye that are weaned from the milk and drawn from the breasts, look for tribulation upon tribulation, for hope also upon hope: yet a little while must these things be by reason of the malice of the lips and by reason of a spiteful tongue." This passage of scripture she explained for her own consolation as meaning that the weaned, that is, those who have come to full age, must endure tribulation upon tribulation that they may be accounted worthy to receive hope upon hope. She recalled to mind also the words of the apostle, "we glory in tribulations also: knowing that tribulation worketh patience, and patience experience, and experience hope: and hope maketh not ashamed" and "though our outward man perish, yet the inward man is renewed day by day": and "our light affliction which is but for a moment worketh in us an eternal weight of glory; while we look not at the things which are seen but at the things which are not seen: for the things which are seen are temporal but the things which are not seen are eternal." She used to say that, although to human impatience the time might seem slow in coming, yet that it would not be long but that presently help would come from God who says: "In an acceptable time have I heard thee, and in a day of salvation have I helped thee." We ought not, she declared, to dread the deceitful lips and tongues of the wicked, for we rejoice in the aid of the Lord who warns us by His prophet: "fear ye not the reproach of men, neither be ye afraid of their revilings; for the moth shall eat them up like a garment, and the worm shall eat them like wool": and she quoted His own words, "In your patience ye shall win your souls": as well as those of the apostle, "the sufferings of this present time are not worthy to be compared with the glory which shall be revealed in us": and in another place, "we are to suffer affliction" that we may be patient in all things that befall us, for "he that is slow to wrath is of great understanding: but he that is hasty of spirit exalteth folly."

19. In her frequent sicknesses and infirmities she used to say, "when I am weak, then am I strong:" "we have our treasure in earthen vessels" until "this

corruptible shall have put on incorruption and this mortal shall have put on immortality" and again "as the sufferings of Christ abound in us, so our consolation also aboundeth by Christ:" and then as ye are partakers of the sufferings, so shall ye be also of the consolation. In sorrow she used to sing: "Why art thou cast down, O my soul? and why art thou disquieted within me? hope thou in God for I shall yet praise him who is the health of my countenance and my God." In the hour of danger she used to say: "If any man will come after me, let him deny himself and take up his cross and follow me:" and again "whosoever will save his life shall lose it," and "whosoever will lose his life for my sake the same shall save it." When the exhaustion of her substance and the ruin of her property were announced to her she only said: "What is a man profited, if he shall gain the whole world and lose his own soul? or what shall a man give in exchange for his soul:" and "naked came I out of my mother's womb, and naked shall I return thither. The Lord gave, and the Lord hath taken away: blessed be the name of the Lord:" and Saint John's words, "Love not the world neither the things that are in the world. For all that is in the world, the lust of the flesh, and the lust of the eyes and the pride of life, is not of the Father but is of the world. And the world passeth away and the lust thereof." I know that when word was sent to her of the serious illnesses of her children and particularly of Toxotius whom she dearly loved, she first by her self-control fulfilled the saying: "I was troubled and I did not speak," and then cried out in the words of scripture, "He that loveth son or daughter more than me is not worthy of me." And she prayed to the Lord and said: Lord "preserve thou the children of those that are appointed to die," that is, of those who for thy sake every day die bodily. I am aware that a talebearer—a class of persons who do a great deal of harm—once told her as a kindness that owing to her great fervour in virtue some people thought her mad and declared that something should be done for her head. She replied in the words of the apostle, "we are made a spectacle unto the world and to angels and to men," and "we are fools for Christ's sake" but "the foolishness of God is wiser than men." It is for this reason she said that even the Saviour says to the Father, "Thou knowest my foolishness," and again "I am as a wonder unto many, but thou art my strong refuge." "I was as a beast before thee; nevertheless I am continually with thee." In the gospel we read that even His kinsfolk desired to bind Him as one of weak mind. His opponents also reviled him saying "thou art a Samaritan and hast a devil," and another time "he casteth out devils through Beelzebub the chief of the devils." But let us, she continued, listen to the exhortation of the apostle, "Our rejoicing is this, the testimony of our conscience that in simplicity and sincerity . . . by the grace of God we have had our conversation in the world." And let us hear the Lord when He says to His apostles, "If ye were of the world the world would love his own; but because ye are not of the world . . . therefore the world hateth you." And then she turned to the Lord Himself, saying, "Thou knowest the secrets of the heart," and "all this is come upon us; yet have we not forgotten thee, neither have we dealt falsely in thy covenant; our heart is not turned back." "Yea for thy sake are we killed all the day long; we are counted as sheep for the slaughter." But "the Lord is on my side: I will not fear what man doeth unto me." She had read the words of Solomon, "My son, honour the Lord and thou shalt be made strong; and beside the Lord fear thou no man." These passages and others like them she used as God's armour against the assaults of wickedness, and particularly to defend herself against the furious onslaughts of envy; and thus by patiently enduring wrongs she soothed the violence of the most savage breasts. Down to the very day of her death two things were conspicuous in her life, one her great patience and the other the jealousy which was manifested towards her. Now jealousy gnaws the heart of him who harbours it: and while it strives to injure its rival raves with all the force of its fury against itself.

20. I shall now describe the order of her monastery and the method by which she turned the continence of saintly souls to her own profit. She sowed carnal things that she might reap spiritual things; she gave earthly things that she might receive heavenly things; she forewent things temporal that she might in their stead obtain things eternal. Besides establishing a monastery for men, the charge of which she left to men, she divided into three companies and monasteries the numerous virgins whom she had gathered out of different provinces, some of whom are of noble birth while others belonged to the middle or lower classes. But, although they worked and had their meals separately from each other, these three companies met together for psalm-singing and prayer. After the chanting of the Alleluia—the signal by which they were summoned to the Collect—no one was permitted to remain behind. But either first or among the first Paula used to await the arrival of the rest, urging them to diligence rather by her own modest example than by motives of fear. At dawn, at the third, sixth, and ninth hours, at evening, and at midnight they recited the psalter each in turn. No sister was allowed to be ignorant of the psalms, and all had every day to learn a certain portion of the holy scriptures. On the Lord's day only they proceeded to the church beside which they lived, each company following its own mother-superior. Returning home in the same order, they then devoted themselves to their allotted tasks, and made garments either for themselves or else for others. If a virgin was of noble birth, she was not allowed to have an attendant belonging to her own household lest her

maid having her mind full of the doings of old days and of the license of childhood might by constant converse open old wounds and renew former errors. All the sisters were clothed alike. Linen was not used except for drying the hands. So strictly did Paula separate them from men that she would not allow even eunuchs to approach them; lest she should give occasion to slanderous tongues (always ready to cavil at the religious) to console themselves for their own misdoing. When a sister was backward in coming to the recitation of the psalms or shewed herself remiss in her work, Paula used to approach her in different ways. Was she quick-tempered? Paula coaxed her. Was she phlegmatic? Paula chid her, copying the example of the apostle who said: "What will ye? Shall I come to you with a rod or in love and in the spirit of meekness?" Apart from food and raiment she allowed no one to have anything she could call her own, for Paul had said, "Having food and raiment let us be therewith content." She was afraid lest the custom of having more should breed covetousness in them; an appetite which no wealth can satisfy, for the more it has the more it requires, and neither opulence nor indigence is able to diminish it. When the sisters quarrelled one with another she reconciled them with soothing words. If the younger ones were troubled with fleshly desires, she broke their force by imposing redoubled fasts; for she wished her virgins to be ill in body rather than to suffer in soul. If she chanced to notice any sister too attentive to her dress, she reproved her for her error with knitted brows and severe looks, saying; "a clean body and a clean dress mean an unclean soul. A virgin's lips should never utter an improper or an impure word, for such indicate a lascivious mind and by the outward man the faults of the inward are made manifest." When she saw a sister verbose and talkative or forward and taking pleasure in quarrels, and when she found after frequent admonitions that the offender shewed no signs of improvement; she placed her among the lowest of the sisters and outside their society, ordering her to pray at the door of the refectory instead of with the rest, and commanding her to take her food by herself, in the hope that where rebuke had failed shame might bring about a reformation. The sin of theft she loathed as if it were sacrilege; and that which among men of the world is counted little or nothing she declared to be in a monastery a crime of the deepest dye. How shall I describe her kindness and attention towards the sick or the wonderful care and devotion with which she nursed them? Yet, although when others were sick she freely gave them every indulgence, and even allowed them to eat meat; when she fell ill herself, she made no concessions to her own weakness, and seemed unfairly to change in her own case to harshness the kindness which she was always ready to shew to others.

21. No young girl of sound and vigorous constitution could have delivered herself up to a regimen so rigid as that imposed upon herself by Paula whose physical powers age had impaired and enfeebled. I admit that in this she was too determined, refusing to spare herself or to listen to advice. I will relate what I know to be a fact. In the extreme heat of the month of July she was once attacked by a violent fever and we despaired of her life. However by God's mercy she rallied, and the doctors urged upon her the necessity of taking a little light wine to accelerate her recovery; saying that if she continued to drink water they feared that she might become dropsical. I on my side secretly appealed to the blessed pope Epiphanius to admonish, nay even to compel her, to take the wine. But she with her usual sagacity and quickness at once perceived the stratagem, and with a smile let him see that the advice he was giving her was after all not his but mine. Not to waste more words, the blessed prelate after many exhortations left her chamber; and, when I asked him what he had accomplished, replied, "Only this that old as I am I have been almost persuaded to drink no more wine." I relate this story not because I approve of persons rashly taking upon themselves burthens beyond their strength (for does not the scripture say: "Burden not thyself above thy power"?) but because I wish from this quality of perseverance in her to shew the passion of her mind and the yearning of her believing soul; both of which made her sing in David's words, "My soul thirsteth for thee, my flesh longeth after thee." Difficult as it is always to avoid extremes, the philosophers are quite right in their opinion that virtue is a mean and vice an excess, or as we may express it in one short sentence "In nothing too much." While thus unyielding in her contempt for food Paula was easily moved to sorrow and felt crushed by the deaths of her kinsfolk, especially those of her children. When one after another her husband and her daughters fell asleep, on each occasion the shock of their loss endangered her life. And although she signed her mouth and her breast with the sign of the cross, and endeavoured thus to alleviate a mother's grief; her feelings overpowered her and her maternal instincts were too much for her confiding mind. Thus while her intellect retained its mastery she was overcome by sheer physical weakness. On one occasion a sickness seized her and clung to her so long that it brought anxiety to us and danger to herself. Yet even then she was full of joy and repeated every moment the apostle's words: "O wretched man that I am! who shall deliver me from the body of this death?"

The careful reader may say that my words are an invective rather than an eulogy. I call that Jesus whom she served and whom I desire to serve to be my witness that so far from unduly eulogizing her or depreciating her I tell the truth about her as one Christian writing of another; that I am writing a memoir and not a panegyric, and that what were faults in her might well be virtues in others less saintly. I speak thus of her faults to satisfy my own feelings and the passionate regret of us her brothers and sisters, who all of us love her still and all of us deplore her loss.

22. However, she has finished her course, she has kept the faith, and now she enjoys the crown of righteousness. She follows the Lamb whithersoever he goes. She is filled now because once she was hungry. With joy does she sing: "as we have heard, so have we seen in the city of the Lord of hosts, in the city of our God." O blessed change! Once she wept but now laughs for evermore. Once she despised the broken cisterns of which the prophet speaks; but now she has found in the Lord a fountain of life. Once she wore haircloth but now she is clothed in white raiment, and can say: "thou hast put off my sackcloth, and girded me with gladness." Once she ate ashes like bread and mingled her drink with weeping; saying "my tears have been my meat day and night;" but now for all time she eats the bread of angels and sings: "O taste and see that the Lord is good;" and "my heart is overflowing with a goodly matter; I speak the things which I have made touching the king." She now sees fulfilled Isaiah's words, or rather those of the Lord speaking through Isaiah: "Behold, my servants shall eat but ye shall be hungry: behold, my servants shall drink but ye shall be thirsty: behold, my servants shall rejoice, but ye shall be ashamed: behold, my servants shall sing for joy of heart, but ye shall cry for sorrow of heart, and shall howl for vexation of spirit." I have said that she always shunned the broken cisterns: she did so that she might find in the Lord a fountain of life, and that she might rejoice and sing: "as the hart panteth after the waterbrooks, so panteth my soul after Thee, O God. When shall I come and appear before God?"

23. I must briefly mention the manner in which she avoided the foul cisterns of the heretics whom she regarded as no better than heathen. A certain cunning knave, in his own estimation both learned and clever, began without my knowledge to put to her such questions as these: What sin has an infant committed that it should be seized by the devil? Shall we be young or old when we rise again? If we die young and rise young, we shall after the resurrection require to have nurses. If however we die young and rise old, the dead will not rise again at all: they will be transformed into new beings. Will there be a distinction of sexes in the next world? Or will there be no such distinction? If the distinction continues, there will be wedlock and sexual intercourse and procreation of children. If however it does not continue, the bodies that rise again will not be the same. For, he argued, "the earthy tabernacle weigheth down the mind that museth upon many things," but the bodies that we shall

have in heaven will be subtle and spiritual according to the words of the apostle: "it is sown a natural body: it is raised a spiritual body." From all of which considerations he sought to prove that rational creatures have been for their faults and previous sins subjected to bodily conditions; and that according to the nature and guilt of their transgression they are born in this or that state of life. Some, he said, rejoice in sound bodies and wealthy and noble parents; others have for their portion diseased frames and poverty stricken homes; and by imprisonment in the present world and in bodies pay the penalty of their former sins. Paula listened and reported what she heard to me, at the same time pointing out the man. Thus upon me was laid the task of opposing this most noxious viper and deadly pest. It is of such that the Psalmist speaks when he writes: "deliver not the soul of thy turtle dove unto the wild beast," and "Rebuke the wild beast of the reeds;" creatures who write iniquity and speak lies against the Lord and lift up their mouths against the Most High. As the fellow had tried to deceive Paula, I at her request went to him, and by asking him a few questions involved him in a dilemma. Do you believe, said I, that there will be a resurrection of the dead or do you disbelieve? He replied, I believe. I went on: Will the bodies that rise again be the same or different? He said, The same. Then I asked: What of their sex? Will that remain unaltered or will it be changed? At this question he became silent and swayed his head this way and that as a serpent does to avoid being struck. Accordingly I continued, As you have nothing to say I will answer for you and will draw the conclusion from your premises. If the woman shall not rise again as a woman nor the man as a man, there will be no resurrection of the dead. For the body is made up of sex and members. But if there shall be no sex and no members what will become of the resurrection of the body, which cannot exist without sex and members? And if there shall be no resurrection of the body, there can be no resurrection of the dead. But as to your objection taken from marriage, that, if the members shall remain the same, marriage must inevitably be allowed; it is disposed of by the Saviour's words: "ye do err not knowing the scriptures nor the power of God. For in the resurrection they neither marry nor are given in marriage but are as the angels." When it is said that they neither marry nor are given in marriage, the distinction of sex is shewn to persist. For no one says of things which have no capacity for marriage such as a stick or a stone that they neither marry nor are given in marriage; but this may well be said of those who while they can marry yet abstain from doing so by their own virtue and by the grace of Christ. But if you cavil at this and say, how shall we in that case be like the angels with whom there is neither male nor female, hear my answer in brief as follows. What the Lord promises to us is not the nature of angels but their mode of life and their bliss. And therefore John the Baptist is called an angel even before he is beheaded, and all God's holy men and virgins manifest in themselves even in this world the life of angels. When it is said "ye shall be like the angels," likeness only is promised and not a change of nature.

24. And now do you in your turn answer me these questions. How do you explain the fact that Thomas felt the hands of the risen Lord and beheld His side pierced by the spear? And the fact that Peter saw the Lord standing on the shore and eating a piece of a roasted fish and a honeycomb. If He stood, He must certainly have had feet. If He pointed to His wounded side He must have also had chest and belly for to these the sides are attached and without them they cannot be. If He spoke, He must have used a tongue and palate and teeth. For as the bow strikes the strings, so to produce vocal sound does the tongue come in contact with the teeth. If His hands were felt, it follows that He must have had arms as well. Since therefore it is admitted that He had all the members which go to make up the body, He must have also had the whole body formed of them, and that not a woman's but a man's; that is to say, He rose again in the sex in which He died. And if you cavil farther and say: We shall eat then, I suppose, after the resurrection; or How can a solid and material body enter in contrary to its nature through closed doors? you shall receive from me this reply. Do not for this matter of food find fault with belief in the resurrection: for our Lord after raising the daughter of the ruler of the synagogue commanded food to be given her. And Lazarus who had been dead four days is described as sitting at meat with Him, the object in both cases being to shew that the resurrection was real and not merely apparent. And if from our Lord's entering in through closed doors you strive to prove that His body was spiritual and aerial, He must have had this spiritual body even before He suffered; since—contrary to the nature of heavy bodies—He was able to walk upon the sea. The apostle Peter also must be believed to have had a spiritual body for he also walked upon the waters with buoyant step. The true explanation is that when anything is done against nature, it is a manifestation of God's might and power. And to shew plainly that in these great signs our attention is asked not to a change in nature but to the almighty power of God, he who by faith had walked on water began to sink for the want of it and would have done so had not the Lord lifted him up with the reproving words, "O thou of little faith wherefore didst thou doubt?" I wonder that you can display such effrontery when the Lord Himself said, "reach hither thy finger, and behold my hands; and reach hither thy hand and thrust it into my side: and be not faithless but believing," and in another place, "behold my hands and my feet that it is I myself: handle me and see; for a spirit hath not flesh and bones as ye

see me have. And when he had thus spoken he shewed them his hands and his feet." You hear Him speak of bones and flesh, of feet and hands; and yet you want to palm off on me the bubbles and airy nothings of which the stoics rave!

25. Moreover, if you ask how it is that a mere infant which has never sinned is seized by the devil, or at what age we shall rise again seeing that we die at different ages; my only answer—an unwelcome one, I fancy—will be in the words of scripture: "The judgments of God are a great deep," and "O the depth of the riches both of the wisdom and knowledge of God! how unsearchable are his judgments, and his ways past finding out! For who hath known the mind of the Lord? or who hath been his counsellor?" No difference of age can affect the reality of the body. Although our frames are in a perpetual flux and lose or gain daily, these changes do not make us different individuals. I was not one person at ten years old, another at thirty and another at fifty; nor am I another now when all my head is gray. According to the traditions of the church and the teaching of the apostle Paul, the answer must be this; that we shall rise as perfect men in the measure of the stature of the fulness of Christ. At this age the Jews suppose Adam to have been created and at this age we read that the Lord and Saviour rose again. Many other arguments did I adduce from both testaments to stifle the outcry of this heretic.

26. From that day forward so profoundly did Paula commence to loathe the man—and all who agreed with him in his doctrines—that she publicly proclaimed them as enemies of the Lord. I have related this incident less with the design of confuting in a few words a heresy which would require volumes to confute it, than with the object of shewing the great faith of this saintly woman who preferred to subject herself to perpetual hostility from men rather than by friendships hurtful to herself to provoke or to offend God.

27. To revert then to that description of her character which I began a little time ago; no mind was ever more docile than was hers. She was slow to speak and swift to hear, remembering the precept, "Keep silence and hearken, O Israel." The holy scriptures she knew by heart, and said of the history contained in them that it was the foundation of the truth; but, though she loved even this, she still preferred to seek for the underlying spiritual meaning and made this the keystone of the spiritual building raised within her soul. She asked leave that she and her daughter might read over the old and new testaments under my guidance. Out of modesty I at first refused compliance, but as she persisted in her demand and frequently urged me to consent to it, I at last did so and taught her what I had learned not from myself—for self-confidence is the worst of teachers—but from the church's most famous writers. Wherever I stuck fast and honestly confessed myself at fault she would by no means rest

content but would force me by fresh questions to point out to her which of many different solutions seemed to me the most probable. I will mention here another fact which to those who are envious may well seem incredible. While I myself beginning as a young man have with much toil and effort partially acquired the Hebrew tongue and study it now unceasingly lest if I leave it, it also may leave me; Paula, on making up her mind that she too would learn it, succeeded so well that she could chant the psalms in Hebrew and could speak the language without a trace of the pronunciation peculiar to Latin. The same accomplishment can be seen to this day in her daughter Eustochium, who always kept close to her mother's side, obeyed all her commands, never slept apart from her, never walked abroad or took a meal without her, never had a penny that she could call her own, rejoiced when her mother gave to the poor her little patrimony, and fully believed that in filial affection she had the best heritage and the truest riches. I must not pass over in silence the joy which Paula felt when she heard her little granddaughter and namesake, the child of Laeta and Toxotius—who was born and I may even say conceived in answer to a vow of her parents dedicating her to virginity—when, I say, she heard the little one in her cradle sing "alleluia" and falter out the words "grandmother" and "aunt." One wish alone made her long to see her native land again; that she might know her son and his wife and child to have renounced the world and to be serving Christ. And it has been granted to her in part. For while her granddaughter is destined to take the veil, her daughter-in-law has vowed herself to perpetual chastity, and by faith and alms emulates the example that her mother has set her. She strives to exhibit at Rome the virtues which Paula set forth in all their fulness at Jerusalem.

28. What ails thee, my soul? Why dost thou shudder to approach her death? I have made my letter longer than it should be already; dreading to come to the end and vainly supposing that by saying nothing of it and by occupying myself with her praises I could postpone the evil day. Hitherto the wind has been all in my favour and my keel has smoothly ploughed through the heaving waves. But now my speech is running upon the rocks, the billows are mountains high, and imminent shipwreck awaits both you and me. We must needs cry out: "Master; save us we perish:" and "awake, why sleepest thou, O Lord?" For who could tell the tale of Paula's dying with dry eyes? She fell into a most serious illness and thus gained what she most desired, power to leave us and to be joined more fully to the Lord. Eustochium's affection for her mother, always true and tried, in this time of sickness approved itself still more to all. She sat by Paula's bedside, she fanned her, she supported her head, she arranged her pillows, she chafed her feet, she rubbed her stomach, she

smoothed down the bedclothes, she heated hot water, she brought towels. In fact she anticipated the servants in all their duties, and when one of them did anything she regarded it as so much taken away from her own gain. How unceasingly she prayed, how copiously she wept, how constantly she ran to and fro between her prostrate mother and the cave of the Lord! imploring God that she might not be deprived of a companion so dear, that if Paula was to die she might herself no longer live, and that one bier might carry to burial her and her mother. Alas for the frailty and perishableness of human nature! Except that our belief in Christ raises us up to heaven and promises eternity to our souls, the physical conditions of life are the same for us as for the brutes. "There is one event to the righteous and to the wicked; to the good and to the evil; to the clean and to the unclean; to him that sacrificeth and to him that sacrificeth not: as is the good so is the sinner; and he that sweareth as he that feareth an oath." Man and beast alike are dissolved into dust and ashes.

29. Why do I still linger, and prolong my suffering by postponing it? Paula's intelligence shewed her that her death was near. Her body and limbs grew cold and only in her holy breast did the warm beat of the living soul continue. Yet, as though she were leaving strangers to go home to her own people, she whispered the verses of the psalmist: "Lord, I have loved the habitation of thy house and the place where thine honour dwelleth," and "How amiable are thy tabernacles, O Lord of hosts! My soul longeth yea even fainteth for the courts of the Lord," and "I had rather be an outcast in the house of my God than to dwell in the tents of wickedness." When I asked her why she remained silent refusing to answer my call, and whether she was in pain, she replied in Greek that she had no suffering and that all things were to her eyes calm and tranquil. After this she said no more but closed her eyes as though she already despised all mortal things, and kept repeating the verses just quoted down to the moment in which she breathed out her soul, but in a tone so low that we could scarcely hear what she said. Raising her finger also to her mouth she made the sign of the cross upon her lips. Then her breath failed her and she gasped for death; yet even when her soul was eager to break free, she turned the death-rattle (which comes at last to all) into the praise of the Lord. The bishop of Jerusalem and some from other cities were present, also a great number of the inferior clergy, both priests and levites. The entire monastery was filled with bodies of virgins and monks. As soon as Paula heard the bridegroom saying: "Rise up my love my fair one, my dove, and come away: for, lo, the winter is past, the rain is over and gone," she answered joyfully "the flowers appear on the earth; the time to cut them has come" and "I believe that I shall see the good things of the Lord in the land of the living."

30. No weeping or lamentation followed her death, such as are the custom of the world; but all present united in chanting the psalms in their several tongues. The bishops lifted up the dead woman with their own hands, placed her upon a bier, and carrying her on their shoulders to the church in the cave of the Saviour, laid her down in the centre of it. Other bishops meantime carried torches and tapers in the procession, and yet others led the singing of the choirs. The whole population of the cities of Palestine came to her funeral. Not a single monk lurked in the desert or lingered in his cell. Not a single virgin remained shut up in the seclusion of her chamber. To each and all it would have seemed sacrilege to have withheld the last tokens of respect from a woman so saintly. As in the case of Dorcas, the widows and the poor shewed the garments Paula had given them; while the destitute cried aloud that they had lost in her a mother and a nurse. Strange to say, the paleness of death had not altered her expression; only a certain solemnity and seriousness had overspread her features. You would have thought her not dead but asleep.

One after another they chanted the psalms, now in Greek, now in Latin, now in Syriac; and this not merely for the three days which elapsed before she was buried beneath the church and close to the cave of the Lord, but throughout the remainder of the week. All who were assembled felt that it was their own funeral at which they were assisting, and shed tears as if they themselves had died. Paula's daughter, the revered virgin Eustochium, "as a child that is weaned of his mother," could not be torn away from her parent. She kissed her eyes, pressed her lips upon her brow, embraced her frame, and wished for nothing better than to be buried with her.

31. Jesus is witness that Paula has left not a single penny to her daughter but, as I said before, on the contrary a large mass of debt; and, worse even than this, a crowd of brothers and sisters whom it is hard for her to support but whom it would be undutiful to cast off. Could there be a more splendid instance of self-renunciation than that of this noble lady who in the fervour of her faith gave away so much of her wealth that she reduced herself to the last degree of poverty? Others may boast, if they will, of money spent in charity, of large sums heaped up in God's treasury, of votive offerings hung up with cords of gold. None of them has given more to the poor than Paula, for Paula has kept nothing for herself. But now she enjoys the true riches and those good things which eye hath not seen nor ear heard, neither have they entered into the heart of man. If we mourn, it is for ourselves and not for her; yet even so, if we persist in weeping for one who reigns with Christ, we shall seem to envy her her glory.

32. Be not fearful, Eustochium: you are endowed with a splendid heritage. The Lord is your portion; and, to increase your joy, your mother has now after a long martyrdom won her crown. It is not only the shedding of blood that is accounted a confession: the spotless service of a devout mind is itself a daily martyrdom. Both alike are crowned; with roses and violets in the one case, with lilies in the other. Thus in the Song of Songs it is written: "my beloved is white and ruddy;" for, whether the victory be won in peace or in war, God gives the same guerdon to those who win it. Like Abraham your mother heard the words: "get thee out of thy country, and from thy kindred, unto a land that I will shew thee;" and not only that but the Lord's command given through Jeremiah: "flee out of the midst of Babylon, and deliver every man his soul." To the day of her death she never returned to Chaldaea, or regretted the fleshpots of Egypt or its strong-smelling meats. Accompanied by her virgin bands she became a fellow-citizen of the Saviour; and now that she has ascended from her little Bethlehem to the heavenly realms she can say to the true Naomi: "thy people shall be my people and thy God my God."

33. I have spent the labour of two nights in dictating for you this treatise; and in doing so I have felt a grief as deep as your own. I say in dictating' for I have not been able to write it myself. As often as I have taken up my pen and have tried to fulfil my promise; my fingers have stiffened, my hand has fallen, and my power over it has vanished. The rudeness of the diction, devoid as it is of all elegance or charm, bears witness to the feeling of the writer.

34. And now, Paula, farewell, and aid with your prayers the old age of your votary. Your faith and your works unite you to Christ; thus standing in His presence you will the more readily gain what you ask. In this letter "I have built" to your memory "a monument more lasting than bronze," which no lapse of time will be able to destroy. And I have cut an inscription on your tomb, which I here subjoin; that, wherever my narrative may go, the reader may learn that you are buried at Bethlehem and not uncommemorated there.

The Inscription on Paula's Tomb.

Within this tomb a child of Scipio lies,
A daughter of the farfamed Pauline house,
A scion of the Gracchi, of the stock
Of Agamemnon's self, illustrious:
Here rests the lady Paula, well-beloved
Of both her parents, with Eustochium
For daughter; she the first of Roman dames
Who hardship chose and Bethlehem for Christ.

In front of the cavern there is another inscription as follows:—

Seest thou here hollowed in the rock a grave,
'Tis Paula's tomb; high heaven has her soul.
Who Rome and friends, riches and home forsook
Here in this lonely spot to find her rest.
For here Christ's manger was, and here the kings
To Him, both God and man, their offerings made.

35. The holy and blessed Paula fell asleep on the seventh day before the Kalends of February, on the third day of the week, after the sun had set. She was buried on the fifth day before the same Kalends, in the sixth consulship of the Emperor Honorius and the first of Aristaenetus. She lived in the vows of religion five years at Rome and twenty years at Bethlehem. The whole duration of her life was fifty-six years eight months and twenty-one days.

LETTER CIX. TO RIPARIUS

Riparius, a presbyter of Aquitaine had written to inform Jerome that Vigilantius (for whom see Letter LXI.) was preaching in southern Gaul against the worship of relics and the keeping of night vigils; and this apparently with the consent of his bishop. Jerome now replies in a letter more noteworthy for its bitterness than for its logic. Nevertheless he offers to write a full confutation of Vigilantius if Riparius will send him the book containing his heresies. This Riparius subsequently did and then Jerome wrote his treatise Against Vigilantius, the most extreme and least convincing of all his works.

The date of the letter is 404 a.d.

1. Now that I have received a letter from you, if I do not answer it I shall be guilty of pride, and if I do I shall be guilty of rashness. For the matters concerning which you ask my opinion are such that they cannot either be spoken of or listened to without profanity. You tell me that Vigilantius (whose very name Wakeful is a contradiction: he ought rather to be described as Sleepy) has again opened his fetid lips and is pouring forth a torrent of filthy venom upon the relics of the holy martyrs; and that he calls us who cherish them ashmongers and idolaters who pay homage to dead men's bones. Unhappy wretch! to be wept over by all Christian men, who sees not that in speaking thus he makes himself one with the Samaritans and the Jews who hold dead bodies unclean and regard as defiled even vessels which have been in the same house with them, following the letter that killeth and not the spirit that giveth life. We, it is true, refuse to worship or adore, I say not the relics of the martyrs, but even the sun and moon, the angels and archangels, the Cherubim and

Seraphim and "every name that is named, not only in this world but also in that which is to come." For we may not serve the creature rather than the Creator, who is blessed for ever. Still we honour the relics of the martyrs, that we may adore Him whose martyrs they are. We honour the servants that their honour may be reflected upon their Lord who Himself says:—"he that receiveth you receiveth me." I ask Vigilantius, Are the relics of Peter and of Paul unclean? Was the body of Moses unclean, of which we are told (according to the correct Hebrew text) that it was buried by the Lord Himself? And do we, every time that we enter the basilicas of apostles and prophets and martyrs, pay homage to the shrines of idols? Are the tapers which burn before their tombs only the tokens of idolatry? I will go farther still and ask a question which will make this theory recoil upon the head of its inventor and which will either kill or cure that frenzied brain of his, so that simple souls shall be no more subverted by his sacrilegious reasonings. Let him answer me this, Was the Lord's body unclean when it was placed in the sepulchre? And did the angels clothed in white raiment merely watch over a corpse dead and defiled, that ages afterwards this sleepy fellow might indulge in dreams and vomit forth his filthy surfeit, so as, like the persecutor Julian, either to destroy the basilicas of the saints or to convert them into heathen temples?

2. I am surprised that the reverend bishop in whose diocese he is said to be a presbyter acquiesces in this his mad preaching, and that he does not rather with apostolic rod, nay with a rod of iron, shatter this useless vessel and deliver him for the destruction of the flesh that the spirit may be saved. He should remember the words that are said: "When thou sawest a thief, then thou consentedst unto him; and hast been partaker with adulterers;" and in another place, "I will early destroy all the wicked of the land; that I may cut off all wicked doers from the city of the Lord;" and again "Do not I hate them, O Lord, that hate thee? and am not I grieved with those that rise up against thee? I hate them with perfect hatred." If the relics of the martyrs are not worthy of honour, how comes it that we read "Precious in the sight of the Lord is the death of his saints?" If dead men's bones defile those that touch them, how came it that the dead Elisha raised another man also dead, and that life came to this latter from the body of the prophet which according to Vigilantius must have been unclean? In that case every encampment of the host of Israel and the people of God was unclean; for they carried the bodies of Joseph and of the patriarchs with them in the wilderness, and carried their unclean ashes even into the holy land. In that case Joseph, who was a type of our Lord and Saviour, was a wicked man; for he carried up Jacob's bones with great pomp to Hebron merely to put his unclean father beside his unclean grandfather and

great grandfather, that is, one dead body along with others. The wretch's tongue should be cut out, or he should be put under treatment for insanity. As he does not know how to speak, he should learn to be silent. I have myself before now seen the monster, and have done my best to bind the maniac with texts of scripture, as Hippocrates binds his patients with chains; but "he went away, he departed, he escaped, he broke out," and taking refuge between the Adriatic and the Alps of King Cotius declaimed in his turn against me. For all that a fool says must be regarded as mere noise and mouthing.

3. You may perhaps in your secret thoughts find fault with me for thus assailing a man behind his back. I will frankly admit that my indignation overpowers me; I cannot listen with patience to such sacrilegious opinions. I have read of the javelin of Phinehas, of the harshness of Elijah, of the jealous anger of Simon the zealot, of the severity of Peter in putting to death Ananias and Sapphira, and of the firmness of Paul who, when Elymas the sorcerer withstood the ways of the Lord, doomed him to lifelong blindness. There is no cruelty in regard for God's honour. Wherefore also in the Law it is said: "If thy brother or thy friend or the wife of thy bosom entice thee from the truth, thine hand shall be upon them and thou shalt shed their blood, and so shalt thou put the evil away from the midst of Israel." Once more I ask, Are the relics of the martyrs unclean? If so, why did the apostles allow themselves to walk in that funeral procession before the body—the unclean body—of Stephen? Why did they make great lamentation over him, that their grief might be turned into our joy?

You tell me farther that Vigilantius execrates vigils. In this surely he goes contrary to his name. The Wakeful one wishes to sleep and will not hearken to the Saviour's words, "What, could ye not watch with me one hour? Watch and pray that ye enter not into temptation: the spirit indeed is willing but the flesh is weak." And in another place a prophet sings: "At midnight I will rise to give thanks unto thee because of thy righteous judgments." We read also in the gospel how the Lord spent whole nights in prayer and how the apostles when they were shut up in prison kept vigil all night long, singing their psalms until the earth quaked, and the keeper of the prison believed, and the magistrates and citizens were filled with terror. Paul says: "continue in prayer and watch in the same," and in another place he speaks of himself as "in watchings often." Vigilantius may sleep if he pleases and may choke in his sleep, destroyed by the destroyer of Egypt and of the Egyptians. But let us say with David: "Behold, he that keepeth Israel shall neither slumber nor sleep." So will the Holy One and the Watcher come to us. And if ever by reason of our sins He fall asleep, let us say to Him: "Awake, why sleepest thou, O Lord;" and when our ship is tossed by the waves let us rouse Him and say, "Master, save us: we perish."

4. I would dictate more were it not that the limits of a letter impose upon me a modest silence. I might have gone on, had you sent me the books which contain this man's rhapsodies, for in that case I should have known what points I had to refute. As it is I am only beating the air and revealing not so much his infidelity—for this is patent to all—as my own faith. But if you wish me to write against him at greater length, send me those wretched dronings of his and in my answer he shall hear an echo of John the Baptist's words "Now also the axe is laid unto the root of the trees; therefore every tree which bringeth not forth good fruit is hewn down and cast into the fire."

LETTER CX. FROM AUGUSTINE

Augustine's answer to Letter CII. He now tries to soothe Jerome's wounded feelings, begs him to overlook the offence that he has committed, and implores him not to break off the friendly relations hitherto maintained between them. He touches on the quarrel between Jerome and Rufinus and sincerely hopes that no such breach may ever separate Jerome from himself. The tone of the letter is throughout conciliatory and is marked in places with deep feeling. More than once Augustine dwells on Jerome's words ("would that I could embrace you and that by mutual converse we might learn one from the other," Letter CII. S:2) and speaks of the comfort which they have brought to him.

The date of the letter is 404 a.d.

LETTER CXI. FROM AUGUSTINE TO PRAESIDIUS

Augustine asks Praesidius to forward the preceding letter to Jerome and also to write himself to urge him to forgive Augustine.

LETTER CXII. TO AUGUSTINE

On receiving Letter CIV. together with duly authenticated copies of Letters LVI. and LXVII. Jerome in three days completes an exhaustive reply to all the questions which Augustine had raised. He explains what is the true title of his book On Illustrious Men, deals at great length with the dispute between Paul and Peter, expounds his views with regard to the Septuagint, and shews by the story of "the gourd" how close and accurate his translations are. His language throughout is kind but rather patronising: indeed in this whole correspondence Jerome seldom sufficiently recognizes the greatness of Augustine. The date of the letter is 404 a.d.

LETTER CXIII. FROM THEOPHILUS TO JEROME

Theophilus, bishop of Alexandria, had compiled an invective against John Chrysostom, bishop of Constantinople who was nosy (largely through his efforts) an exile from his see. This he now sends to Jerome with a request that the latter will render it into Latin for dissemination in the West. The invective (of which only a few fragments remain) is of the most violent kind. Nevertheless Jerome translated it along with this letter, the date of which is 405 a.d. The latter part of the letter has perished.

To the well-beloved and most loving brother Jerome, Theophilus sends greeting in the Lord.

1. At the outset the verdict which is in accordance with the truth satisfies but few. But the Lord speaking by the prophet says: "my judgment goeth forth as the light:" and they who are surrounded with a horror of darkness and do not with clear comprehension perceive the nature of things, are covered with eternal shame and know by the issues of their acts that their efforts have been in vain. Wherefore we also have always desired for John who has for a time ruled the church of Constantinople grace that he might please God, and we have been slow to attribute to him the rash acts which have caused his downfall. But, not to speak of his other misdeeds, he has taken the Origenists into his confidence, has advanced many of them to the priesthood, and by committing this crime has saddened with no slight grief that man of God, Epiphanius of blessed memory, who has shone throughout all the world a bright star among bishops. And therefore he has rightly come to hear the words of doom: "Babylon is fallen, is fallen."

2. Knowing then that the Saviour has said: "judge not according to the appearance but judge righteous judgment." . . .

LETTER CXIV. TO THEOPHILUS

Jerome writes to Theophilus to apologize for his delay in sending Latin versions of the latter's letter (CXIII.) and invective against John Chrysostom. Possibly, however, the allusion may be not to these but to some other work of

Theophilus (e.g. a paschal letter.) This delay he attributes to the disturbed state of Palestine, the severity of the winter, the prevalent famine, and his own ill-health. He now sends the translations that he has made and, while he deprecates criticism on his own work, praises that of Theophilus, quoting with particular approval the directions given by this latter for the reverent care of the vessels used in celebrating the holy communion. The date of the letter is 405 a.d.

To the most blessed pope Theophilus, Jerome.

1. My delay in sending back to your holiness your treatise translated into Latin is accounted for by the many interruptions and obstacles that I have met with. There has been a sudden raid of the Isaurians; Phoenicia and Galilee have been laid waste; Palestine has been panic-stricken, and particularly Jerusalem; we have all been engaged in making not books but walls. There has also been a severe winter and an almost unbearable famine; and these have told heavily upon me who have the charge of many brothers. Amid these difficulties the work of translation went on by night, as I could save or snatch time to give to it. At last I got it done and by Lent nothing remained but to collate the fair copy with the original. However, just then a severe illness seized me and I was brought to the threshold of death, from which I have only been saved by God's mercy and your prayers; perhaps for this very purpose that I might fulfil your behest and render with its writer's elegance the charming volume which you have adorned with the scripture's fairest flowers. But bodily weakness and sorrow of heart have, I need hardly say, dulled the edge of my intellect and obstructed the free flow of my language.

2. I admire in your work its practical aim, designed as it is to instruct by the authority of scripture ignorant persons in all the churches concerning the reverence with which they must handle holy things and minister at Christ's altar; and to impress upon them that the sacred chalices, veils, and other accessories used in the celebration of the Lord's passion are not mere lifeless and senseless objects devoid of holiness, but that rather, from their association with the body and blood of the Lord, they are to be venerated with the same awe as the body and the blood themselves.

3. Take back then your book, nay mine or better still ours; for when you flatter me you will but flatter yourself. It is for you that my brain has toiled; it is for you that I have striven with the poor resources of the Latin tongue to find an equivalent for the eloquence of the Greek. I have not indeed given a word-for-word rendering, as skilled translators do, nor have I counted out the money you have given to me coin by coin; but I have given you full weight. Some words may be missing but none of the sense is lost. Moreover I have

translated into Latin and prefixed to this volume the letter that you sent to me, so that all who read it may know that I have acted under the commands of your holiness, and have not rashly and over-confidently undertaken a task that is beyond my powers. Whether I have succeeded in it I must leave to your judgment. Even though you may blame my weakness, you will at least give me credit for my good intention.

LETTER CXV. TO AUGUSTINE

A short but most friendly letter in which Jerome excuses himself for the freedom with which he has dealt with Augustine's questions (the allusion is to Letter CXII.) and hopes that henceforth they may be able to avoid controversy and to labour like brothers in the field of scripture.

Written probably in 405 a.d.

LETTER CXVI. FROM AUGUSTINE

A long letter in which Augustine for the third time (see Letters LVI., LXVII.) restates his opinion about Jerome's theory of the dispute between Peter and Paul at Antioch. In doing so, however, he disclaims all desire to hurt Jerome's feelings, apologizes for the tone of his previous letters, and again explains that it is not his fault that they have failed so long to reach Jerome.

Written shortly after the preceding.

LETTER CXVII. TO A MOTHER AND DAUGHTER LIVING IN GAUL

A monk of Gaul had during a visit to Bethlehem asked Jerome for advice under the following circumstances. His mother was a church-widow and his sister a religious virgin but the two could not agree. They were accordingly living apart but neither by herself. For each had taken into her house a monk ostensibly to act as steward but really to be a paramour. At the request of his visitor Jerome now writes to both mother and daughter urging them to dismiss their companions; or at any rate to live together: and pointing out the grave scandal that must otherwise be caused.

From the treatise against Vigilantius (S:3) we learn that ill-natured critics maintained that the persons and circumstances described in the letter were alike fictitious and that Jerome in writing it was but exercising his ingenuity on a congenial theme.

The date is a.d. 405.

Introduction.

1. A certain brother from Gaul has told me that his virgin-sister and widowed mother, though living in the same city, have separate abodes and have taken to themselves clerical protectors either as guests or stewards; and that by thus associating with strangers they have caused more scandal than by living apart. When I groaned and expressed what I felt more by silence than words; "I beseech you," said he, "rebuke them in a letter and recall them to mutual harmony; make them once more mother and daughter." To whom I replied, "a nice task this that you lay upon me, for me a stranger to reconcile two women whom you, a son and brother, have failed to influence. You speak as though I occupied the chair of a bishop instead of being shut up in a monastic cell where, far removed from the world's turmoil, I lament the sins of the past and try to avoid the temptations of the present. Moreover, it is surely inconsistent, while one buries oneself out of sight, to allow one's tongue free course through the world." "You are too fearful," he replied; "where is that old hardihood of yours which made you scour the world with copious salt,' as Horace says of Lucilius?" "It is this," I rejoined, "that makes me shy and forbids me to open my lips. For through accusing crime I have been myself made out a criminal. Men have disputed and denied my assertions until, as the proverb goes, I hardly know whether I have ears or feeling left. The very walls have resounded with curses levelled at me, and I was the song of drunkards.' Under the compulsion of an unhappy experience I have learned to be silent, thinking it better to set a watch before my mouth and to keep the door of my lips than to incline my heart to any evil thing, or, while censuring the faults of others, myself to fall into that of detraction." In answer to this he said: "Speaking the truth is not detraction. Nor will you lecture the world by administering a particular rebuke; for there are few persons, if any, open to this special charge. I beg of you, therefore, as I have put myself to the trouble of this long journey, that you will not suffer me to have come for nothing. The Lord knows that, after the sight of the holy places, my principal object in coming has been to heal by a letter from you the division between my sister and my mother." "Well," I replied, "I will do as you wish, for after all the letters will be to persons beyond the sea and words written with reference to definite persons can seldom offend other people. But I must ask you to keep what I say secret. You will take my advice with you to encourage you by the way; if it is listened

to, I will rejoice as much as you; while if, as I rather think, it is rejected, I shall have wasted my words and you will have made a long journey for nothing."

The Letter.

2. In the first place my sister and my daughter, I wish you to know that I am not writing to you because I suspect anything evil of you. On the contrary I implore you to live in harmony, so as to give no ground for any such suspicions. Moreover had I supposed you fast bound in sin—far be this from you—I should never have written, for I should have known that my words would be addressed to deaf ears. Again, if I write to you somewhat sharply, I beg of you to ascribe this not to any harshness on my part but to the nature of the ailment which I attempt to treat. Cautery and the knife are the only remedies when mortification has once set in; poison is the only antidote known for poison; great pain can only be relieved by inflicting greater pain. Lastly I must say this that even if your own consciences acquit you of misdoing, yet the very rumour of such brings disgrace upon you. Mother and daughter are names of affection; they imply natural ties and reciprocal duties; they form the closest of human relations after that which binds the soul to God. If you love each other, your conduct calls for no praise: but if you hate each other, you have committed a crime. The Lord Jesus was subject to His parents. He reverenced that mother of whom He was Himself the parent; He respected the foster-father whom He had Himself fostered; for He remembered that He had been carried in the womb of the one and in the arms of the other. Wherefore also when He hung upon the cross He commended to His disciple the mother whom He had never before His passion parted from Himself.

3. Well, I shall say no more to the mother, for perhaps age, weakness, and loneliness make sufficient excuses for her; but to you the daughter I say: "Is a mother's house too small for you whose womb was not too small? When you have lived with her for ten months in the one, can you not bear to live with her for one day in the other? or are you unable to meet her gaze? Can it be that one who has borne you and reared you, who has brought you up and knows you, is dreaded by you as a witness of your home-life? If you are a true virgin, why do you fear her careful guardianship; and, if you have fallen, why do you not openly marry? Wedlock is like a plank offered to a shipwrecked man and by its means you may remedy what previously you have done amiss. I do not mean that you are not to repent of your sin or that you are to continue in evil courses; but, when a tie of the kind has been formed, I despair of breaking it altogether. However, a return to your mother will make it easier for you to bewail the virginity which you have lost through leaving her. Or if you are still unspotted and have not lost your chastity, be careful of it for you may lose it.

Why must you live in a house where you must daily struggle for life and death? Can any one sleep soundly with a viper near him? No; for, though it may not attack him it is sure to frighten him. It is better to be where there is no danger, than to be in danger and to escape. In the one case we have a calm; in the other careful steering is necessary. In the one case we are filled with joy; in the other we do but avoid sorrow.

4. But you will perhaps reply: "my mother is not well-behaved, she desires the things of the world, she loves riches, she disregards fasting, she stains her eyes with antimony, she likes to walk abroad in gay attire, she hinders me from the monastic vow, and so I cannot live with her." But first of all, even though she is as you say, you will have the greater reward for refusing to forsake her with all her faults. She has carried you in her womb, she has reared you; with gentle affection she has borne with the troublesome ways of your childhood. She has washed your linen, she has tended you when sick, and the sickness of maternity was not only borne for you but caused by you. She has brought you up to womanhood, she has taught you to love Christ. You ought not to be displeased with the behaviour of a mother who has consecrated you as a virgin to the service of your spouse. Still if you cannot put up with her dainty ways and feel obliged to shun them, and if your mother really is, as people so often say, a woman of the world, you have others, virgins like yourself, the holy company of chastity. Why, when you forsake your mother, do you choose for companion a man who perhaps has left behind him a sister and mother of his own? You tell me that she is hard to get on with and that he is easy; that she is quarrelsome and that he is amiable. I will ask you one question: Did you go straight from your home to the man, or did you fall in with him afterwards? If you went straight to him, the reason why you left your mother is plain. If you fell in with him afterwards, you shew by your choice what you missed under your mother's roof. The pain that I inflict is severe and I feel the knife as much as you. "He that walketh uprightly walketh surely." Only that my conscience would smite me, I should keep silence and be slow to blame others where I am not guiltless myself. Having a beam in my own eye I should be reluctant to see the mote in my neighbour's. But as it is I live far away among Christian brothers; my life with them is honourable as eyewitnesses of it can testify; I rarely see, or am seen by, others. It is most shameless, therefore, in you to refuse to copy me in respect of self-restraint, when you profess to take me as your model. If you say: "my conscience is enough for me too. God is my judge who is witness of my life. I care not what men may say;" let me urge upon you the apostle's words: "provide things honest" not only in the sight of God but also "in the sight of all men." If any one carps at you for being a Christian and a

virgin, mind it not; you have left your mother it may be said to live in a monastery among virgins, but censure on this score is your glory. When men blame a maid of God not for self-indulgence but only for insensibility to affection, what they condemn as callous disregard of a parent is really a lively devotion towards God. For you prefer to your mother Him whom you are bidden to prefer to your own soul. And if the day ever comes that she also shall so prefer Him, she will find in you not a daughter only but a sister as well.

5. "What then?" you will say, "is it a crime to have a man of religion in the house with me?" You seize me by the collar and drag me into court either to sanction what I disapprove or else to incur the dislike of many. A man of religion never separates a daughter from her mother. He welcomes both and respects both. A daughter may be as religious as she pleases; still a mother who is a widow is a guaranty for her chastity. If this person whoever he is is of the same age with yourself, he should honour your mother as though she were his own; and, if he is older, he should love you as a daughter and subject you to a mother's discipline. It is not good either for your reputation or for his that he should like you more than your mother; for his affection might appear to be less for you than for your youth. This is what I should say if a monk were not your brother and if you had no relatives able to protect you. But what excuse has a stranger for thrusting himself in where there are both a mother and a brother, the one a widow and the other a monk? It is good for you to feel that you are a daughter and a sister. However, if you cannot manage both, and if your mother is too hard a morsel to swallow, your brother at any rate should satisfy you. Or, if he is too harsh, she that bore you may prove more gentle. Why do you turn pale? Why do you get excited? Why do you blush, and with trembling lips betray the restlessness of your mind? One thing only can surpass a woman's love for her mother and brother; and that is her passion for her husband.

6. I am told, moreover, that you frequent suburban villas and their pleasant gardens in the company of relatives and intimate friends. I have no doubt that it is some female cousin or connexion who for her own satisfaction carries you about with her as a novel kind of attendant. Far be it from me to suspect that you would desire men's society; even though they should be those of your own family. But pray, maiden, answer me this; do you appear alone in your kinsfolk's society? or do you bring your favourite with you? Shameless as you may be, you will hardly venture to flaunt him in the eyes of the world. If you ever do so, your whole circle will cry out about both you and him; every one's finger will be pointed at you; and your cousins who in your presence to please you call him a monk and a man of religion, will laugh at you behind your back

for having such an unnatural husband. If on the other hand you go out alone—which I rather suppose to be the case—you will find yourself clothed in sober garb among slave youths, women married or soon to be so, wanton girls, and dandies with long hair and tight-fitting vests. Some bearded fop will offer you his hand, he will hold you up if you feel tired, and the pressure of his fingers will either be a temptation to you, or will shew that you are a temptation to him. Again when you sit down to table with married men and women, you will have to see kisses in which you have no part, and dishes partaken of which are not for you. Moreover it cannot but do you harm to see other women attired in silk dresses and gold brocades. At table also whether you like it or not, you will be forced to eat flesh and that of different kinds. To make you drink wine they will praise it as a creature of God. To induce you to take baths they will speak of dirt with disgust; and, when on second thoughts you do as you are bid, they will with one voice salute you as spotless and open, a thorough lady. Meantime some singer will give to the company a selection of softly flowing airs; and as he will not venture to look at other men's wives, he will constantly fix his eyes on you who have no protector. He will speak by nods and convey by his tone what he is afraid to put into words. Amid inducements to sensuality so marked as these, even iron wills are apt to be overcome with desire; an appetite which is the more imperious in virgins because they suppose that sweetest of which they have no experience. Heathen legends tell us that sailors actually ran their ships on the rocks that they might listen to the songs of the Sirens; and that the lyre of Orpheus had power to draw to itself trees and animals and to soften flints. In the banquet-hall chastity is hard to keep. A shining skin shews a sin-stained soul.

7. As a schoolboy I have read of one—and have seen his effigy true to the life in the streets—who continued to cherish an unlawful passion even when his flesh scarcely clung to his bones, and whose malady remained uncured until death cured it. What then will become of you a young girl physically sound, dainty, stout, and ruddy, if you allow yourself free range among flesh-dishes, wines, and baths, not to mention married men and bachelors? Even if when solicited you refuse to consent, you will take the fact of your being asked as evidence that you are considered handsome. A sensual mind pursues dishonourable objects with greater zest than honourable ones; and when a thing is forbidden hankers after it with greater pleasure. Your very dress, cheap and sombre as it is, is an index of your secret feelings. For it has no creases and trails along the ground to make you appear taller than you are. Your vest is purposely ripped asunder to shew what is beneath and while hiding what is repulsive, to reveal what is fair. As you walk, the very creaking of your black

and shiny shoes attracts the notice of the young men. You wear stays to keep your breasts in place, and a heaving girdle closely confines your chest. Your hair covers either your forehead or your ears. Sometimes too you let your shawl drop so as to lay bare your white shoulders; and, as if unwilling that they should be seen, you quickly conceal what you have purposely disclosed. And when in public you for modesty's sake cover your face, like a practised harlot you only shew what is likely to please.

8. You will exclaim "How do you know what I am like, or how, when you are so far away, can you see what I am doing?" Your own brother's tears and sobs have told me, his frequent and scarcely endurable bursts of grief. Would that he had lied or that his words had been words of apprehension only and not of accusation. But, believe me, liars do not shed tears. He is indignant that you prefer to himself a young man, not it is true clothed in silk or wearing his hair long but muscular and dainty in the midst of his squalor; and that this fellow holds the purse-strings, looks after the weaving, allots the servants their tasks, rules the household, and buys from the market all that is needed. He is at once steward and master, and, as he anticipates the slaves in their duties, he is carped at by all the domestics. Everything that their mistress has not given them they declare that he has stolen from them. Servants as a class are full of complaints; and no matter what you give them, it is always too little. For they do not consider how much you have but only how much you give; and they make up for their chagrin in the only way they can, that is, by grumbling. One calls him a parasite, another an impostor, another a money-seeker, another by some novel appellation that hits his fancy. They noise it abroad that he is constantly at your bed-side, that when you are sick he runs to fetch nurses, that he holds basins, airs sheets, and folds bandages for you. The world is only too ready to believe scandal, and stories invented at home soon get afloat abroad. Nor need you be surprised if your servantmen and servantmaids get up such tales about you, when even your mother and your brother complain of your conduct.

9. Do, therefore, what I advise you and entreat you to do: if possible, be reconciled with your mother; or, if this may not be, at least come to terms with your brother. Or if you are filled with an implacable hatred of relationships usually so dear, separate at all events from the man, whom you are said to prefer to your own flesh and blood, and, if even this is impossible for you, (for, if you could leave him, you would certainly return to your own) pay more regard to appearances in harbouring him as your companion. Live in a separate building and take your meals apart; for if you remain under one roof with him slanderers will say that you share with him your bed. You may thus easily get

help from him when you feel you need it, and yet to a considerable degree escape public discredit. Yet you must take care not to contract the stain of which Jeremiah tells us that no nitre or fuller's soap can wash it out. When you wish him to come to see you, always have witnesses present; either friends, or freedmen, or slaves. A good conscience is afraid of no man's eyes. Let him come in unembarrassed and go out at his ease. Let his silent looks, his unspoken words and his whole carriage, though at times they may imply embarrassment, yet indicate peace of mind. Pray, open your ears and listen to the outcry of the whole city. You have already both of you lost your own names and are known each by that of the other. You are spoken of as his, and he is said to be yours. Your mother and your brother have heard this and are ready to take you in between them. They implore you to consent to this arrangement, so that the scandal of your intimacy with this man which is confined to yourself may give place to a glory common to all. You can live with your mother and he with your brother. You can more boldly shew your regard for one who is your brother's comrade; and your mother will more properly esteem one who is the friend of her son and not of her daughter. But if you frown and refuse to accept my advice, this letter will openly expostulate with you. Why,' it will say, do you beset another man's servant? Why do you make Christ's minister your slave? Look at the people and scan each face as it comes under your view. When he reads in the church all eyes are fixed upon you; and you, using the licence of a wife, glory in your shame. Secret infamy no longer contents you; you call boldness freedom; "you have a whore's forehead and refuse to be ashamed."

10. Once more you exclaim that I am over-suspicious, a thinker of evil, too ready to follow rumours. What? I suspicious? I ill-natured? I, who as I said in the beginning have taken up my pen because I have no suspicions? Or is it you that are careless, loose, disdainful? You who at the age of twenty-five have netted in your embrace a youth whose beard has scarcely grown? An excellent instructor he must be, able no doubt by his severe looks both to warn and frighten you! No age is safe from lust, yet gray hairs are some security for decent conduct. A day will surely come (for time glides by imperceptibly) when your handsome young favourite will find a wealthier or more youthful mistress. For women soon age and particularly if they live with men. You will be sorry for your decision and regret your obstinacy in a day when your means and reputation shall be alike gone, and when this unhappy intimacy shall be happily broken off. But perhaps you feel sure of your ground and see no reason to fear a breach where affection has had so long a time to develop and grow.

11. To you also, her mother, I must say a word. Your years put you beyond the reach of scandal; do not take advantage of this to indulge in sin. It is more fitting that your daughter should learn from you how to part from a companion than that you should learn from her how to give up a paramour. You have a son, a daughter, and a son-in-law, or at least one who is your daughter's partner. Why then should you seek other society than theirs, or wish to kindle anew expiring flames? It would be more becoming in you to screen your daughter's fault than to make it an excuse for your own misdoing. Your son is a monk, and, if he were to live with you, he would strengthen you in your religious profession and in your vow of widowhood. Why should you take in a complete stranger, especially in a house not large enough to hold a son and a daughter? You are old enough to have grand-children. Invite the pair home then. Your daughter went away by herself; let her return with this man. I say man' and not husband' that none may cavil. The word describes his sex and not his relation to her. Or if she blushes to accept your offer or finds the house in which she was born too narrow for her, then move both of you to her abode. However limited may be its accommodation, it can take in a mother and a brother better than a stranger. In fact, if she lives in the same house and occupies the same room with a man, she cannot long preserve her chastity. It is different when two women and two men live together. If the third person concerned—he, I mean, who fosters your old age—will not make one of the party and causes only dissension and confusion, the pair of you can do without him. But if the three of you remain together, then your brother and son will offer him a sister and a mother. Others may speak of the two strangers as step-father and son-in-law; but your son must speak of them as his foster-father and his brother.

Note.

12. Working quickly I have completed this letter in a single night anxious alike to gratify a friend and to try my hand on a rhetorical theme. Then early in the morning he has knocked at my door on the point of starting. I wish also to shew my detractors that like them I too can say the first thing that comes into my head. I have, therefore, introduced few quotations from the scriptures and have not, as in most of my books, interwoven its flowers in my discourse. The letter has been, in fact, dictated off-hand and poured forth by lamp-light so fast that my tongue has outstripped my secretaries' pens and that my volubility has baffled the expedients of shorthand. I have said this much that those who make no allowances for want of ability may make some for want of time.

LETTER CXVIII. TO JULIAN

Jerome writes to Julian, a wealthy nobleman apparently of Dalmatia (S:5), to console him for the loss of his wife and two daughters all of whom had recently died. He reminds Julian of the trials of Job and recommends him to imitate the patience of the patriarch. He also urges him to follow the example set by Pammachius and Paulinus, that is, to give up his riches and to become a monk for the sake of Christ. The date of the letter is 406 a.d.

1. At the very instant of his departure Ausonius, a son to me as he is a brother to you, gave me a late glimpse of himself but quickly hurried away again, saying good-morning and good-bye together. Yet he thought that he would return empty-handed unless he could bring you some trifle from me however hastily written. Clothed in scarlet as befitted his rank, he had already strapped on his sword-belt and sent down a requisition to have a stage-horse saddled. Still he made me send for my secretary and dictate a letter to him. This I did with such rapidity that his nimble hand could hardly keep pace with my words or manage to put down my hurried sentences. Thus hasty dictation has taken the place of careful writing; and, if I break my long silence, it is but to offer you an expression of good will. This is an impromptu letter without logical order or charm of style. You must look on me for once as a friend only; you will find, I assure you, nothing of the orator here. Bear in mind that it has been dashed off on the spur of the moment and given as a provision for the way to one in a hurry to depart.

Holy scripture says: "a tale out of season is as musick in mourning." Accordingly I have disdained the graces of rhetoric and those charms of eloquence which boys find so captivating, and have fallen back on the serious tone of the sacred writings. For in these are to be found true medicines for wounds and sure remedies for sorrow. In these a mother receives back her only son even on the bier. In these a crowd of mourners hears the words: "the maid is not dead but sleepeth." In these one that is four days dead comes forth bound at the call of the Lord.

2. I hear that in a short space of time you have suffered several bereavements, that you have buried in quick succession two young unmarried daughters, and that Faustina, most chaste and loyal of wives, your sister in the fervour of her faith and your one comfort in the loss of your children, has suddenly fallen asleep and been taken from you. You have been like a shipwrecked man, who has no sooner reached the shore than he falls into the hands of brigands, or in the eloquent language of the prophet like one "who did flee from a lion, and a bear met him; or went into the house, and leaned his hand

on the wall, and a serpent bit him." Pecuniary losses have followed your bereavements; the entire province has been overrun by a barbarian enemy, and in the general devastation your private property has been destroyed, your flocks and herds have been driven off, and your poor slaves either made prisoners or else slain. To crown all, your only daughter, made all the more dear to you by the loss of the others, has for her husband a young nobleman who, to say nothing worse of him, has given you more occasion for sorrow than for rejoicing. Such is the list of the trials that have been laid upon you; such is the conflict waged by the old enemy against Julian a raw recruit to Christ's standard. If you look only to yourself your troubles are indeed great but if you look to the strong Warrior, they are but child's play and the conflict is only the semblance of one. After untold trials a wicked wife was still left to the blessed Job, the devil hoping that he might learn from her to blaspheme God. You on the other hand have been deprived of an excellent one that you might learn to go without consolation in the hour of misfortune. Yet it is far harder to put up with a wife whom you dislike than it is to mourn for one whom you dearly love. Moreover when Job's children died they found a common tomb beneath the ruins of his house, and all he could do to shew his parental affection was to rend his garments, to fall upon the ground and to worship, saying: "Naked came I out of my mother's womb, and naked shall I return thither: the Lord gave and the Lord hath taken away: it has been as the Lord pleased: blessed be the name of the Lord." But you, to put the matter briefly, have been allowed to perform the obsequies of your dear ones; and those obsequies have been attended by many respectful kinsmen and comforting friends. Again Job lost all his wealth at once; and, as, one after another, the messengers of woe unfolded new calamities, he flinched as little as the sage of whom Horace writes:—

Shatter the world to atoms if you will.
Fearless will be the man on whom it falls.

But with you the case is different. The greater part of your substance has been left to you, and your trials have not been greater than you can bear. For you have not yet attained to such perfection that the devil has to marshal all his forces against you.

3. Long ago this wealthy proprietor and still wealthier father was made by a sudden stroke destitute and bereaved. But as, in spite of all that befel him, he had not sinned before God or spoken foolishly, the Lord—exulting in the victory of his servant and regarding Job's patience as His own triumph—said to the devil: "Hast thou considered my servant Job, that there is none like him in the earth, a perfect and an upright man, one that feareth God and escheweth evil? and still he holdeth fast his integrity?" He finely adds the last

clause because it is difficult for innocence to refrain from murmuring when it is overborne by misfortune; and to avoid making a shipwreck of faith when it sees that its sufferings are unjustly inflicted. The devil answered the Lord and said: "Skin for skin, yea, all that a man hath will he give for his life. But put forth thine hand now, and touch his bone and his flesh, and he will curse thee to thy face." See how crafty the adversary is, and how hardened in sin his evil days have made him! He knows the difference between things external and internal. He knows that even the philosophers of the world call the former adiaphora, that is indifferent, and that the perfection of virtue does not consist in losing or disdaining them. It is the latter, those that are internal and objects of preference, the loss of which inevitably causes chagrin. Wherefore he boldly contradicts what God has said and declares that Job deserves no praise at all; since he has yielded up no part of himself but only what is outside himself, since he has given for his own skin the skins of his children, and since he has but laid down his purse to secure the health of his body. From this your sagacity may perceive that your trials have so far only reached the point at which you give hide for hide, skin for skin, and are ready to give all that you have for your life. The Lord has not yet stretched forth His hand upon you, or touched your flesh, or broken your bones. Yet it is when such afflictions as these are laid upon you that it is hard not to groan and not to bless' God to His face, that is to curse Him. The word bless' is used in the same way in the books of Kings where it is said of Naboth that he blessed' God and the king and was therefore stoned by the people. But the Lord knew His champion and felt sure that this great hero would even in this last and severest conflict prove unconquerable. Therefore He said: "Behold he is in thine hand; but save his life." The holy man's flesh is placed at the devil's disposal, but his vital powers are withheld. For if the devil had smitten that on which sensation and mental judgment depend, the guilt arising from a misuse of these faculties I would have lain at the door not of him who committed the sin but of him who had overthrown the balance of his mind.

4. Others may praise you if they will, and celebrate your victories over the devil. They may eulogize you for the smiling face with which you bore the loss of your daughters, or for the resolution with which, forty days after they fell asleep, you exchanged your mourning for a white robe to attend the dedication of a martyr's bones; unconcerned for a bereavement which was the concern of the whole city, and anxious only to share in a martyr's triumph. Nay, say they, when you bore your wife to burial, it was not as one dead but as one setting forth on a journey. But I shall not deceive you with flattering words or take the ground from under your feet with slippery praises. Rather will I say what it is

good for you to hear: "My son, if thou come to serve the Lord, prepare thy soul for temptation," and "when thou shalt have done all those things which are commanded thee, say, I am an unprofitable servant; I have done that which was my duty to do." Say to God: "the children that thou hast taken from me were Thine own gift. The hand-maiden that Thou hast taken to Thyself Thou also didst lend to me for a season to be my solace. I am not aggrieved that Thou hast taken her back, but thankful rather that Thou hast previously given her to me."

Once upon a time a rich young man boasted that he had fulfilled all the requirements of the law, but the Lord said to him (as we read in the gospel): "One thing thou lackest: if thou wilt be perfect, go thy way, sell whatsoever thou hast, and give to the poor; and come and follow me." He who declared that he had done all things gave way at the first onset to the power of riches. Wherefore they who are rich find it hard to enter the kingdom of heaven, a kingdom which desires for its citizens souls that soar aloft free from all ties and hindrances. "Go thy way," the Lord says, "and sell" not a part of thy substance but "all that thou hast, and give to the poor;" not to thy friends or kinsfolk or relatives, not to thy wife or to thy children. I will even go farther and say: keep back nothing for yourself because you fear to be some day poor, lest by so doing you share the condemnation of Ananias and Sapphira; but give everything to the poor and make to yourself friends of the mammon of unrighteousness that they may receive you into everlasting habitations. Obey the Master's injunction "follow me," and take the Lord of the world for your possession; that you may be able to sing with the prophet, "The Lord is my portion," and like a true Levite may possess no earthly inheritance. I cannot but advise you thus if you wish to be perfect, if you desire to attain the pinnacle of the apostles' glory, if you wish to take up your cross and to follow Christ. When once you have put your hand to the plough you must not look back; when once you stand on the housetop you must think no more of your clothes within; to escape your Egyptian mistress you must abandon the cloak that belongs to this world. Even Elijah, in his quick translation to heaven could not take his mantle with him, but left in the world the garments of the world. Such conduct, you will object, is for him who would emulate the apostles, for the man who aspires to be perfect. But why should not you aspire to be perfect? Why should not you who hold a foremost place in the world hold a foremost place also in Christ's household? Is it because you have been married? Peter was married too, but when he forsook his ship and his nets he forsook his wife also. The Lord who wills that all men shall be saved and prefers the repentance of a sinner to his death has, in His almighty providence, removed from you this excuse. Your wife can no longer draw you earthwards, but you can follow her as she draws you heavenwards. Provide good things for your children who have gone home before you to the Lord. Do not let their portions go to swell their sister's fortune, but use them to ransom your own soul and to give sustenance to the needy. These are the necklaces your daughters expect from you; these are the jewels they wish to see sparkle on their foreheads. The money which they would have wasted in buying silks may well be considered saved when it provides cheap clothing for the poor. They ask you for their portions. Now that they are united to their spouse they are loth to appear poor and undistinguished: they desire to have the ornaments that befit their rank.

5. Nor may you excuse yourself on the score of your noble station and the responsibilities of wealth. Look at Pammachius and at Paulinus that presbyter of glowing faith both of whom have offered to the Lord not only their riches but themselves. In spite of the devil and his shuffling they have by no means given skin for skin, but have consecrated their own flesh and bones, yea and their very souls unto the Lord. Surely these may lead you to higher things both by their example and by their preaching, that is, by their deeds and words. You are of noble birth, so are they: but in Christ they are made nobler still. You are rich and held in repute, so once were they: but now instead of being rich and held in repute they are poor and obscure, yet, because it is for Christ's sake, they are really richer and more famous than ever. You too, it is true, shew yourself beneficent, you are said to minister to the wants of the saints, to entertain monks, and to present large sums of money to churches. This however is only the a b c of your soldiership. You despise money; the world's philosophers have done the same. One of these—to say nothing of the rest—cast the price of many possessions into the sea, saying as he did so "To the bottom with you, ye provokers of evil lusts. I shall drown you in the sea that you may never drown me in sin." If then a philosopher—a creature of vanity whom popular applause can buy and sell—laid down all his burthen at once, how can you think that you have reached virtue's crowning height when you have yielded up but a portion of yours? It is you yourself that the Lord wishes for, "a living sacrifice . . . acceptable unto God." Yourself, I say, and not what you have. And therefore, as he trained Israel by subjecting it to many plagues and afflictions, so does He now admonish you by sending you trials of different kinds. "For whom the Lord loveth he chasteneth, and scourgeth every son whom he receiveth." The poor widow did but cast two mites into the treasury; yet because she cast in all that she had it is said of her that she surpassed all the rich in offering gifts to God. Such gifts are valued not by their weight but by the good-will with which they are made. You may have spent your substance

upon numbers of people, and a portion of your fellows may have reason to rejoice in your bounty; yet those who have received nothing at your hands are still more numerous. Neither the wealth of Darius nor the riches of Croesus would suffice to satisfy the wants of the world's poor. But if you once give yourself to the Lord and resolve to follow the Saviour in the perfection of apostolic virtue, then you will come to see what your place has hitherto been, and how you have lagged in the rear of Christ's army. Hardly had you begun to mourn for your dead daughters when the fear of Christ dried the tears of paternal affection upon your cheeks. It was a great triumph of faith, true. But how much greater was that won by Abraham who was content to slay his only son, of whom he had been told that he was to inherit the world, yet did not cease to hope that after death Isaac would live again. Jephthah too offered up his virgin daughter, and for this is placed by the apostle in the roll of the saints. I would not therefore have you offer to the Lord only what a thief may steal from you or an enemy fall upon, or a proscription confiscate, what is liable to fluctuations in value now going up and now down, what belongs to a succession of masters who follow each other as fast as in the sea wave follows wave, and—to say everything in a word—what, whether you like it or not, you must leave behind you when you die. Rather offer to God that which no enemy can carry off and no tyrant take from you, which will go down with you into the grave, nay on to the kingdom of heaven and the enchantments of paradise. You already build monasteries and support in the various islands of Dalmatia a large number of holy men. But you would do better still if you were to live among these holy men as a holy man yourself. "Be ye holy, saith the Lord, for I am holy." The apostles boasted that they had left all things and had followed the Saviour. We do not read that they left anything except their ship and their nets; yet they were crowned with the approval of Him who was to be their judge. Why? Because in offering up themselves they had indeed left all that they had.

6. I say all this not in disparagement of your good works or because I wish to under-rate your generosity in almsgiving, but because I do not wish you to be a monk among men of the world and a man of the world among monks. I shall require every sacrifice of you for I hear that your mind is devoted to the service of God. If some friend, or follower, or kinsman tries to combat this counsel of mine and to recall you to the pleasures of a handsome table, be sure that he is thinking less of your soul than of his own belly, and remember that death in a moment terminates both elegant entertainments and all other pleasures provided by wealth. Within the short space of twenty days you have lost two daughters, the one eight years old and the other six; and do you

suppose that one so old as you are yourself can live much longer? David tells you how long a time you can look for: "the days of our years are threescore years and ten; and if by reason of strength they be fourscore years, yet is their strength labour and sorrow." Happy is he and to be held worthy of the highest bliss whom old age shall find a servant of Christ and whom the last day shall discover fighting for the Saviour's cause. "He shall not be ashamed when he speaketh with his enemies in the gate." On his entrance into paradise it shall be said to him: "thou in thy lifetime receivedst evil things but nowhere thou art comforted." The Lord will not avenge the same sin twice. Lazarus, formerly poor and full of ulcers, whose sores the dogs licked and who barely managed to live, poor wretch, on the crumbs that fell from the rich man's table, is now welcomed into Abraham's bosom and has the joy of finding a father in the great patriarch. It is difficult nay impossible for a man to enjoy both the good things of the present and those of the future, to satisfy his belly here and his mind yonder, to pass from the pleasures of this life to the pleasures of that, to be first in both worlds, and to be held in honour both on earth and in heaven.

7. And if in your secret thoughts you are troubled because I who give you this advice am not myself what I desire you to be, and because you have seen some after beginning well fall midway on their journey; I shall briefly plead in reply that the words which I speak are not mine but those of the Lord and Saviour, and that I urge upon you not the standard which is possible to myself but the ideal which every true servant of Christ must wish for and realize. Athletes as a rule are stronger than their backers; yet the weaker presses the stronger to put forth all his efforts. Look not upon Judas denying his Lord but upon Paul confessing Him. Jacob's father was a man of great wealth; yet, when Jacob went to Mesopotamia, he went alone and destitute leaning upon his staff. When he felt weary he had to lie down by the wayside and, delicately nurtured as he had been by his mother Rebekah, was forced to content himself with a stone for a pillow. Yet it was then that he saw the ladder set up from earth to heaven, and the angels ascending and descending on it, and the Lord above it holding out a helping hand to such as fall and encouraging the climbers to fresh efforts by the vision of Himself. Therefore is the spot called Bethel or the house of God; for there day by day there is ascending and descending. When they are careless, even holy men lose their footing; and sinners, if they wash away their stains with tears regain their place. I say this not that those coming down may frighten you but that those going up may stimulate you. For evil can never supply a model and even in worldly affairs incentives to virtue come always from the brighter side.

But I have forgotten my purpose and the limits set to my letter. I should have liked to say a great deal more. Indeed all that I can say is inadequate alike to satisfy the seriousness of the subject and the claims of your rank. But here is our Ausonius beginning to be impatient for the sheets, hurrying the secretaries, and in his impatience at the neighing of his horse, accusing my poor wits of slowness. Remember me, then, and prosper in Christ. And one thing more; follow the example set you at home by the holy Vera, who like a true follower of Christ does not fear to endure the hardships of pilgrimage. Find in a woman your leader in this high emprise.'

LETTER CXIX. TO MINERVIUS AND ALEXANDER

Minervius and Alexander two monks of Toulouse had written to Jerome asking him to explain for them a large number of passages in scripture. Jerome in his reply postpones most of these to a future time but deals with two in detail viz. (1) "we shall not all sleep but we shall all be changed," 1 Cor. xv. 51; and (2) "we shall be caught up in the clouds," 1 Thes. iv. 17. With regard to (1) Jerome prefers the reading "we shall all sleep but we shall not all be changed," and with regard to (2) he looks upon the language as metaphorical and interprets it to mean that believers will be assumed' into the company of the apostles and prophets. The date of the letter is 406 a.d.

LETTER CXX. TO HEDIBIA

At the request of Hedibia, a lady of Gaul much interested in the study of scripture, Jerome deals with the following twelve questions. It will be noticed that several of them belong to the historical criticism of our own day.

(1) How can anyone be perfect? and How ought a widow without children to live to God?

(2) What is the meaning of Matt. xxvi. 29?

(3) How are the discrepancies in the evangelical narratives to be accounted for? How can Matt. xxviii. 1 be reconciled with Mark xvi. 1, 2.

(4) How can Matt. xxviii. 9 (Saturday evening) be reconciled with John xx. 1–18 (Sunday morning)?

(5) How can Matt. xxviii. 9 be reconciled with John xx. 17?

(6) How was it that, if there was a guard of soldiers at the sepulchre, Peter and John were allowed to go in freely? (Matt. xxvii. 66; John xx. 1–8.)

(7) How is the statement of Matthew and Mark that the apostles were ordered to go into Galilee to see Jesus there to be reconciled with that of Luke and John who make Him appear to them in Jerusalem?

(8) What is the meaning of Matt. xxvii. 50, 51?

(9) How is the statement of John xx. 22 that Jesus breathed on his apostles the Holy Ghost to be reconciled with that of Luke (Luke xxiv. 49: Acts i. 4) that He would send it to them after His ascension?

(10) What is the meaning of the passage, Rom. ix. 14–29?

(11) What is the meaning of 2 Cor. ii. 16?

(12) What is the meaning of 1 Thes. v. 23?

The date of the letter is 406 or 407 a.d.

LETTER CXXI. TO ALGASIA

Jerome writes to a lady of Gaul named Algasia to answer eleven questions which she had submitted to him. They were as follows:—

(1) How is Luke vii. 18, 19, to be reconciled with John i. 36?

(2) What is the meaning of Matt. xii. 20?

(3) And of Matt. xvi. 24?

(4) And of Matt. xxiv. 19, 20?

(5) And of Luke ix. 53?

(6) What is the meaning of the parable of the unjust steward?

(7) What is the meaning of Rom. v. 7?

(8) And of Rom. vii. 8?

(9) And of Rom. ix. 3?

(10) And of Col. ii. 18?

(11) And of 2 Thes. ii. 3?

The date of the letter is 406 a.d.

LETTER CXXII. TO RUSTICUS

Rusticus and Artemia his wife having made a vow of continence broke it. Artemia proceeded to Palestine to do penance for her sin and Rusticus promised to follow her. However he failed to do so, and Jerome was asked to write this letter in the hope that it might induce him to fulfil his promise. The date is about 408 a.d.

1. I am induced to write to you, a stranger to a stranger, by the entreaties of that holy servant of Christ Hedibia and of my daughter in the faith Artemia,

once your wife but now no longer your wife but your sister and fellow-servant. Not content with assuring her own salvation she has sought yours also, in former days at home and now in the holy places. She is anxious to emulate the thoughtfulness of the apostles Andrew and Philip; who after Christ had found them, desired in their turn to find, the one his brother Simon and the other his friend Nathanael. To the former of these it was said "Thou art Simon, the son of Jona: thou shalt be called Cephas which is by interpretation a stone;" while the latter, whose name Nathanael means the gift of God, was comforted by Christ's witness to him: "behold an Israelite indeed in whom is no guile." So of old Lot desired to rescue his wife as well as his two daughters, and refusing to leave blazing Sodom and Gomorrah until he was himself half-on-fire, tried to lead forth one who was tied and bound by her past sins. But in her despair she lost her composure, and looking back became a monument of an unbelieving soul. Yet, as if to make up for the loss of a single woman, Lot's glowing faith set free the whole city of Zoar. In fact when he left the dark valleys in which Sodom lay and came to the mountains, the sun rose upon him as he entered Zoar or the little City; so-called because the little faith that Lot possessed, though unable to save greater places, was at least able to preserve smaller ones. For one who had gone so far astray as to live in Gomorrah could not all at once reach the noonland where Abraham, the friend of God, entertained God and His angels. (For it was in Egypt that Joseph fed his brothers, and when the bride speaks to the Bridegroom her cry is: "tell me where thou feedest, where thou makest thy flock to rest at noon.") Good men have always sorrowed for the sins of others. Samuel of old lamented for Saul because he neglected to treat the ulcers of pride with the balm of penitence. And Paul wept for the Corinthians who refused to wash out with their tears the stains of fornication. For the same reason Ezekiel swallowed the book where were written within and without song, and lamentation and woe; the song in praise of the righteous, the lamentation over the penitent, and the woe for those of whom it is written, "When the wicked man falleth into the depths of evil, then is he filled with scorn." It is to these that Isaiah alludes when he says: "in that day did the Lord God of hosts call to weeping and to mourning and to baldness and to girding with sackcloth: and behold joy and gladness, slaying oxen; and killing sheep, eating flesh" and saying, "let us eat and drink, for tomorrow we die." Yet of such persons Ezekiel is bidden to speak thus: "O thou son of man, speak unto the house of Israel; Thus ye speak, saying, If our transgressions and our sins be upon us, and we pine away in them, how should we then live? Say unto them, As I live, saith the Lord God, I have no pleasure in the death of the wicked; but that the wicked turn from his way and live," and again, "turn ye, turn ye from your evil ways; for why will ye die, O house of Israel?" Nothing makes God so angry as when men from despair of better things cleave to those which are worse; and indeed this despair in itself is a sign of unbelief. One who despairs of salvation can have no expectation of a judgment to come. For if he dreaded such, he would by doing good works prepare to meet his Judge. Let us hear what God says through Jeremiah, "withhold thy foot from a rough way and thy throat from thirst" and again "shall they fall, and not arise? Shall he turn away, and not return?" Let us hear also what God says by Isaiah: "When thou shalt turn and bewail thyself, then shalt thou be saved, and then shalt thou know where thou hast hitherto been." We do not realize the miseries of sickness till returning health reveals them to us. So sins serve as a foil to the blessedness of virtue; and light shines more brightly when it is relieved against darkness. Ezekiel uses language like that of the other prophets because he is animated by a similar spirit. "Repent," he cries, "and turn yourselves from all your transgressions; so iniquity shall not be your ruin. Cast away from you all your transgressions whereby ye have transgressed; and make you a new heart and a new spirit: for why will ye die, O house of Israel? For I have no pleasure in the death of him that dieth, saith the Lord." Wherefore in a subsequent passage he says: "As I live, saith the Lord God, I have no pleasure in the death of the wicked: but that the wicked turn from his way and live." These words shew us that the mind must not through disbelief in the promised blessings give way to despair; and that the soul once marked out for perdition must not refuse to apply remedies on the ground that its wounds are past curing. Ezekiel describes God as swearing, that if we refuse to believe His promise in regard to our salvation we may at least believe His oath. It is with full confidence that the righteous man prays and says, "Turn us, O God of our salvation, and cause thine anger toward us to cease," and again, "Lord, by thy favour thou hast made my mountain to stand strong: thou didst hide thy face and I was troubled." He means to say, "when I forsook the foulness of my faults for the beauty of virtue, God strengthened my weakness with His grace." Lo, I hear His promise: "I will pursue mine enemies and overtake them: neither will I turn again till they are consumed," so that I who was once thine enemy and a fugitive from thee, shall be laid hold of by thine hand. Cease not from pursuing me till my wickedness is consumed, and I return to my old husband who will give me my wool and my flax, my oil and my fine flour and will feed me with the richest foods. He it was who hedged up and enclosed my evil ways that I might find Him the true way who says in the gospel, "I am the way, the truth, and the life." Hear the words of the prophet: "they that sow in tears shall reap in joy. He that goeth forth and weepeth, bearing precious seed, shall doubtless come again with rejoicing, bringing his sheaves with him." Say also with him: "All the night make I my bed to swim; I water my couch with my tears" : and again, "As the hart panteth after the water brooks, so panteth my soul after thee, O God. My soul thirsteth for God, for the living God: when shall I come and appear before God? My tears have been my meat day and night," and in another place, "O God, thou art my God; early will I seek thee: my soul thirsteth for thee, my flesh longeth for thee in a dry and weary land where no water is. So have I looked upon thee in the sanctuary." For although my soul has thirsted after thee, yet much more have I sought thee by the labour of my flesh and have not been able to look upon thee in thy sanctuary; not at any rate till I have first dwelt in a land barren of sin, where the weary wayfarer is no more assailed by the adversary, and where there are no pools or rivers of lust.

The Saviour also wept over the city of Jerusalem because its inhabitants had not repented; and Peter washed out his triple denial with bitter tears, thus fulfilling the words of the prophet: "rivers of waters run down mine eyes." Jeremiah too laments over his impenitent people, saying: "Oh that my head were waters and mine eyes a fountain of tears, that I might weep day and night for . . . my people!" And farther on he gives a reason for his lamentation: "weep ye not for the dead," he writes, "neither bemoan him: but weep sore for him that goeth away: for he shall return no more." The Jew and the Gentile therefore are not to be bemoaned, for they have never been in the Church and have died once for all (it is of these that the Saviour says: "let the dead bury their dead"); weep rather for those who by reason of their crimes and sins go away from the Church, and who suffering condemnation for their faults shall no more return to it. It is in this sense that the prophet speaks to ministers of the Church, calling them its walls and towers, and saying to each in turn, "O wall, let tears run down." In this way, it is prophetically implied, you will fulfil the apostolic precept: "rejoice with them that do rejoice and weep with them that weep," and by your tears you will melt the hard hearts of sinners till they too weep; whereas, if they persist in evil doing they will find these words applied to them, "I . . . planted thee a noble vine, wholly a right seed: how then art thou turned into the degenerate plant of a strange vine unto me?" and again "saying to a stock, Thou art my father; and to a stone, Thou hast brought me forth: for they have turned their back unto me, and not their face." He means, they would not turn towards God in penitence; but in the hardness of their hearts turned their backs upon Him to insult Him. Wherefore also the Lord says to Jeremiah: "hast thou seen that which backsliding Israel hath done? She is gone up upon every high mountain and under every green tree, and there hath played the harlot. And I said after she" had played the harlot and "had done all these things, Turn thou unto me. But she returned not."

2. How hard hearted we are and how merciful God is! who even after our many sins urges us to seek salvation. Yet not even so are we willing to turn to better things. Hear the words of the Lord: "If a man put away his wife, and she go from him, and become another man's and shall afterwards desire to return to him, will he at all receive her? Will he not loathe her rather? But thou hast played the harlot with many lovers: yet return again to me, saith the Lord." In place of the last clause the true Hebrew text (which is not preserved in the Greek and Latin versions) gives the following: "thou hast forsaken me, yet return, and I will receive thee, saith the Lord." Isaiah also speaking in the same sense uses almost the same words: "Return," he cries, "O children of Israel, ye who think deep counsel and wicked. Return thou unto me and I will redeem thee. I am God, and there is no God else beside me; a just God and a Saviour; there is none beside me. Look unto me, and be ye saved, all the ends of the earth. Remember this and shew yourselves men: bring it again to mind, O ye transgressors. Return in heart and remember the former things of old: for I am God and there is none else." Joel also writes: "turn ye even to me with all your heart, and with fasting and with weeping and with mourning: and rend your heart and not your garments and turn unto the Lord your God; for he is gracious and merciful . . . and repenteth him of the evil." How great His mercy is and how excessive—if I may so say—and unspeakable is His pitifulness, the prophet Hosea tells us when he speaks in the Lord's name: "how shall I give thee up, Ephraim? how shall I deliver thee, Israel? how shall I make thee as Admah? How shall I set thee as Zeboim? Mine heart is turned within me, my repentings are kindled together. I will not execute the fierceness of mine anger." David also says in a psalm: "in death there is no remembrance of thee; in the grave who shall give thee thanks?" and in another place: "I acknowledged my sin unto thee, and mine iniquity have I not hid. I said, I will confess my transgressions unto the Lord; and thou forgavest the iniquity of my sin. For this shall every one that is godly pray unto thee in a time when thou mayest be found: surely in the floods of great waters they shall not come nigh unto him."

3. Think how great that weeping must be which deserves to be compared to a flood of waters. Whosoever so weeps and says with the prophet Jeremiah "let not the apple of mine eye cease" shall straightway find the words fulfilled of him: "mercy and truth are met together: righteousness and peace have kissed

each other;" so that, if righteousness and truth terrify him, mercy and peace may encourage him to seek salvation.

The whole repentance of a sinner is exhibited to us in the fifty-first psalm written by David after he had gone in unto Bathsheba the wife of Uriah the Hittite, and when, to the rebuke of the prophet Nathan he had replied, "I have sinned." Immediately that he confessed his fault he was comforted by the words: "the Lord also hath put away thy sin." He had added murder to adultery; yet bursting into tears he says: "Have mercy upon me, O God, according to thy loving kindness: according unto the multitude of thy tender mercies blot out my transgressions." A sin so great needed to find great mercy. Accordingly he goes on to say: "Wash me thoroughly from mine iniquity, and cleanse me from my sin. For I acknowledge my transgressions: and my sin is ever before me. Against thee, thee only have I sinned"—as a king he had no one to fear but God—"and done this evil in thy sight; that thou mightest be justified when thou speakest and be clear when thou judgest." For "God hath concluded all in unbelief, that he might have mercy upon all." And such was the progress that David made that he who had once been a sinner and a penitent afterwards became a master able to say: "I will teach transgressors thy ways; and sinners shall be converted unto thee." For as "confession and beauty are before God," so a sinner who confesses his sins and says: "my wounds stink and are corrupt because of my foolishness" loses his foul wounds and is made whole and clean. But "he that covereth his sins shall not prosper."

The ungodly king Ahab, who shed the blood of Naboth to gain his vineyard, was with Jezebel, the partner less of his bed than of his cruelty, severely rebuked by Elijah. "Thus saith the Lord, hast thou killed and also taken possession?" and again, "in the place where dogs licked the blood of Naboth, shall dogs lick thy blood, even thine;" and "the dogs shall eat Jezebel by the wall of Jezreel." "And it came to pass"—the passage goes on—"when Ahab heard those words that he rent his clothes, and put sackcloth upon his flesh, and fasted, and lay in sackcloth . . . and the word of the Lord came to Elijah saying, Because Ahab humbleth himself before me, I will not bring the evil in his days." Ahab's sin and Jezebel's were the same; yet because Ahab repented, his punishment was postponed so as to fall upon his sons, while Jezebel persisting in her wickedness met her doom then and there.

Moreover the Lord tells us in the gospel, "the men of Nineveh shall rise in judgment with this generation and shall condemn it: because they repented at the preaching of Jonas;" and again He says "I am not come to call the righteous but sinners to repentance." The lost piece of silver is sought for until it is found in the mire. So also the ninety and nine sheep are left in the wilderness, while the shepherd carries home on his shoulders the one sheep which has gone astray. Wherefore also "there is joy in the presence of the angels over one sinner that repenteth." What a blessed thought it is that heavenly beings rejoice in our salvation! For it is of us that the words are said: "Repent ye: for the kingdom of heaven is at hand." Death and life are contrary the one to the other; there is no middle term. Yet penitence can knit death to life. The prodigal son, we are told, wasted all his substance, and in the far country away from his father "would fain have filled his belly with the husks that the swine did eat." Yet, when he comes back to his father, the fatted calf is killed, a robe and a ring are given to him. That is to say, he receives again Christ's robe which he had before defiled, and hears to his comfort the injunction: "let thy garments be always white." He receives the signet of God and cries to the Lord: "Father, I have sinned against heaven and before thee;" and receiving the kiss of reconciliation, he says to Him: "Now is the light of thy countenance sealed upon us, O Lord."

Hear the words of Ezekiel: "as for the wickedness of the wicked, he shall not fall thereby in the day that he turneth from his wickedness; neither shall the righteous be able to live for his righteousness in the day that he sinneth." The Lord judges every man according as he finds him. It is not the past that He looks upon but the present. Bygone sins there may be, but renewal and conversion remove them. "A just man," we read "falleth seven times and riseth up again." If he falls, how is he just? and if he is just, how does he fall? The answer is that a sinner does not lose the name of just if he always repents of his sins and rises again. If a sinner repents, his sins are forgiven him not only till seven times but till seventy times seven. To whom much is forgiven, the same loveth much. The harlot washed with her tears the Saviour's feet and wiped them with her hair; and to her, as a type of the Church gathered from the nations, was the declaration made: "Thy sins are forgiven." The self-righteous Pharisee perished in his pride, while the humble publican was saved by his confession.

God makes asseveration by the mouth of the prophet Jeremiah: "At what instant I shall speak concerning a nation and concerning a kingdom, to pluck up, to pull down and to destroy it: if that nation, against whom I have pronounced, turn from their evil, I will repent of the evil that I thought to do unto them. And at what instant I shall speak concerning a nation, and concerning a kingdom to build and to plant it; if it do evil in my sight, that it obey not my voice, then I will repent of the good wherewith I said I would benefit them." And immediately he adds: "Behold, I frame evil against you, and devise a device against you: return ye now every one from his evil way, and make your ways and your doings good. And they said, there is no hope: but we will walk after our own devices, and we will every one do the imagination of his evil heart." The righteous Simeon says in the gospel: "Behold, this child is set for the fall and rising again of many," for the fall, that is, of sinners and for the rising again of the penitent. So the apostle writes to the Corinthians: "it is reported commonly that there is fornication among you, and such fornication as is not so much as named among the Gentiles, that one should have his father's wife. And ye are puffed up and have not rather mourned that he that hath done this deed might be taken away from among you." And in his second epistle to the same, "lest such a one should be swallowed up with overmuch sorrow," he calls him back, and begs them to confirm their love towards him, so that he who had been destroyed by incest might be saved by penitence.

"There is no man clean from sin; even though he has lived but for one day." And the years of man's life are many in number. "The stars are not pure in his sight, and his angels he charged with folly." If there is sin in heaven, how much more must there be sin on earth? If they are stained with guilt who have no bodily temptations, how much more must we be, enveloped as we are in frail flesh and forced to cry each one of us with the apostle: "O wretched man that I am! who shall deliver me from the body of this death? For in my flesh there dwelleth no good thing." For we do not what we would but what we would not; the soul desires to do one thing, the flesh is compelled to do another. If any persons are called righteous in scripture, and not only righteous but righteous in the sight of God, they are called righteous according to that righteousness mentioned in the passage I have quoted: "A just man falleth seven times and riseth up again," and on the principle laid down that the wickedness of the wicked shall not hurt him in the day that he turns to repentance. In fact Zachariah the father of John who is described as a righteous man sinned in disbelieving the message sent to him and was at once punished with dumbness. Even Job, who at the outset of his history is spoken of as perfect and upright and uncomplaining, is afterwards proved to be a sinner both by God's words and by his own confession. If Abraham, Isaac, and Jacob, the prophets also and the apostles were by no means free from sin and if the finest wheat had chaff mixed with it, what can be said of us of whom it is written: "What is the chaff to the wheat, saith the Lord?" Yet the chaff is reserved for future burning; as also are the tares which at present are mingled with the growing corn. For one shall come whose fan is in His hand, and shall purge His floor, and shall gather His wheat into the garner, and shall burn the chaff in the fire of hell.

4. Roaming thus through the fairest fields of scripture I have culled its loveliest flowers to weave for your brows a garland of penitence; for my aim is that, flying on the wings of a dove, you may find rest and make your peace with the Father of mercy. Your former wife, who is now your sister and fellow-servant, has told me that, acting on the apostolic precept, you and she lived apart by consent that you might give yourselves to prayer; but that after a time your feet sank beneath you as if resting on water and indeed—to speak plainly—gave way altogether. For her part she heard the Lord saying to her as to Moses: "as for thee stand thou here by me;" and with the psalmist she said of Him: "He hath set my feet upon a rock." But your house—she went on—having no sure foundation of faith fell before a whirlwind of the devil. Hers however still stands in the Lord, and does not refuse its shelter to you; you can still be joined in spirit to her to whom you were once joined in body. For, as the apostle says, "he that is joined unto the Lord is one spirit" with him. Moreover, when the fury of the barbarians and the risk of captivity separated you again, you promised with a solemn oath that, if she made her way to the holy places, you would follow her either immediately or later, and that you would try to save your soul now that by your carelessness you had seemed to lose it. Perform, now, the vow which you then made in the presence of God. Human life is uncertain. Therefore, lest you may be snatched away before you have fulfilled your promise, imitate her whose teacher you ought to have been. For shame! the weaker vessel overcomes the world, and yet the stronger is overcome by it!

A woman leadeth in the high emprise;^

and yet you will not follow her when her salvation leads you to the threshold of the faith! Perhaps, however, you desire to save the remnants of your property and to see the last of your friends and fellow-citizens and of their cities and villas. If so, amid the horrors of captivity, in the presence of exulting foes, and in the shipwreck of the province, at least hold fast to the plank of penitence; and remember your fellow-servant who daily sighs for your salvation and never despairs of it. While you are wandering about your own country (though, indeed, you no longer have a country; that which you once had, you have lost) she is interceding for you in the venerable spots which witnessed the nativity, crucifixion and resurrection of our Lord and Saviour, and in the first of which He uttered His infant-cry. She draws you to her by her prayers that you may be saved, if not by your own exertions, at any rate by her faith. Of old one lay upon his bed sick of the palsy, so powerless in all his joints that he could neither move his feet to walk nor his hands to pray; yet when he was carried to our Lord by others, he was by Him so completely restored to health as to carry the bed which a little before had carried him. You too—absent in the body but present to her faith—your fellow-servant offers to her Lord and Saviour; and with the Canaanite woman she says of you: "my daughter is grievously vexed with a devil." Souls are of no sex; therefore I may fairly call your soul the daughter of hers. For as a mother coaxes her unweaned child which is as yet unable to take solid food; so does she call you to the milk suitable for babes and offer to you the sustenance that a nursing mother gives. Thus shall you be able to say with the prophet: "I have gone astray like a lost sheep; seek thy servant; for I do not forget thy commandments."

LETTER CXXIII. TO AGERUCHIA

An appeal to the widow Ageruchia, highborn lady of Gaul, not to marry again. It should be compared with the letters to Furia (LIV.) and to Salvina (LXXIX.) The allusion to Stilicho's treaty with Alaric fixes the date to 409 a.d.

1. I must look for a new track on the old road and devise a natural treatment, the same yet not the same, for a hackneyed and well-worn theme. It is true that there is but one road; yet one can often reach one's goal by striking across country. I have several times written letters to widows in which for their instruction I have sought out examples from scripture, weaving its varied flowers into a single garland of chastity. On the present occasion I address myself to Ageruchia; whose very name (allotted to her by the divine guidance) has proved a prophecy of her after-life. Around her stand her grandmother, her mother, and her aunt; a noble band of tried Christian women. Her grandmother, Metronia, now a widow for forty years, reminds us of Anna the daughter of Phanuel in the gospel. Her mother, Benigna, now in the fourteenth year of her widowhood, is surrounded by virgins whose chastity bears fruit a hundredfold. The sister of Celerinus, Ageruchia's father, has nursed her niece from infancy and indeed took her into her lap the moment that she was born. Deprived of the solace of her husband she has for twenty years trained her brother's child, teaching her the lessons which she has learned from her own mother.

2. I make these brief remarks to shew my young friend that in resolving not to marry again she does but perform a duty to her family; and that, while she will deserve no praise for fulfilling it, she will be justly blamed if she fails to do so. The more so that she has a posthumous son named after his father Simplicius and thus cannot plead loneliness or the want of an heir. For the lust of many shelters itself under such excuses as though the promptings of inconti-

nence were only a desire for offspring. But why do I speak as to one who wavers when I hear that Ageruchia seeks the church's protection against the many suitors whom she meets in the palace? For the devil inflames men to vie with one another in proving the chastity of our beloved widow; and rank and beauty, youth and riches cause her to be sought after by all. But the greater the assaults that are made upon her continence, the greater will be the rewards that will follow her victory.

3. But no sooner do I clear the harbour than I find my way to the sea barred by a rock. I am confronted with the authority of the apostle Paul who in writing to Timothy thus speaks concerning widows: "I will therefore that the younger women marry, bear children, guide the house, give none occasion to the adversary to speak reproachfully. For some are already turned aside after Satan." I must accordingly begin by considering the meaning of this pronouncement and examining the context of the whole passage. I must then plant my feet in the steps of the apostle and, as the saying goes, not deviate a hair's breadth from them either to this side or to that. He had previously described his ideal widow as one who had been the wife of one man, who had brought up children, who was well reported of for good works, who had relieved the afflicted with her substance, whose trust had been in God, and who had continued in prayer day and night. With her he contrasted her opposite, saying: "She that liveth in pleasure is dead while she liveth." And that he might warn his disciple Timothy with all needful admonition, he immediately added these words: "the younger widows refuse: for when they have begun to wax wanton against Christ they will marry; having damnation because they have cast off their first faith." It is then for these who have outraged Christ their Spouse by committing fornication against Him (for this is the sense of the Greek word katastreniasosi)—it is for these that the apostle wishes a second marriage, thinking digamy preferable to fornication; but this second marriage is a concession and not a command.

4. We must also take the passage clause by clause. "I will," he says, "that the younger women marry." Why, pray? because I would not have young women commit fornication. "That they bear children;" for what reason? That they may not be induced by fear of the consequences to kill children whom they have conceived in adultery. "That they be the heads of households." Wherefore, pray? Because it is much more tolerable that a woman should marry again than that she should be a prostitute, and better that she should have a second husband than several paramours. The first alternative brings relief in a miserable plight, but the second involves a sin and its punishment. He continues: "that they give none occasion to the adversary to speak reproachfully," a brief

and comprehensive precept in which many admonitions are summed up. As for instance these: that a woman must not bring discredit upon her profession of widowhood by too great attention to her dress, that she must not draw troops of young men after her by gay smiles or expressive glances, that she must not profess one thing by her words and another by her behaviour, that she must give no ground for the application to herself of the well known line:

She gave a meaning look and slyly smiled.

Lastly, that Paul may compress into a few words all the reasons for such marriages, he shews the motive of his command by saying: "for some are already turned aside after Satan." Thus he allows to the incontinent a second marriage, or in case of need a third, simply that he may rescue them from Satan, preferring that a woman should be joined to the worst of husbands rather than to the devil. To the Corinthians he uses somewhat similar language: "I say therefore to the unmarried and widows, It is good for them if they abide even as I. But if they cannot contain, let them marry: for it is better to marry than to burn." Why, O apostle, is it better to marry? He answers immediately: because it is worse to burn.

5. Apart from these considerations, that which is absolutely good and not merely relatively so is to be as the apostle, that is loose, not bound; free, not enslaved; caring for the things of God, not for the things of a wife. Immediately afterwards he adds: "The wife is bound by the law to her husband as long as her husband liveth, but if her husband be fallen asleep, she is at liberty to be married to whom she will; only in the Lord. But she is happier if she so abide, after my judgment: and I think also that I have the spirit of God." This passage corresponds with the former in meaning, because the spirit of the two is the same. For though the epistles are different, they are the work of one author. While her husband lives the woman is bound, and when he is dead, she is loosed. Marriage then is a bond, and widowhood is the loosing of it. The wife is bound to the husband and the husband to the wife; and so close is the tie that they have no power over their own bodies, but each stands indebted to the other. They who are under the yoke of wedlock have not the option of choosing continence. When the apostle adds the words "only in the Lord," he excludes heathen marriages of which he had spoken in another place thus: "be ye not unequally yoked together with unbelievers: for what fellowship hath righteousness with unrighteousness? and what communion hath light with darkness? and what concord hath Christ with Belial? or what part hath he that believeth with an infidel? and what agreement hath the temple of God with idols?" We must not plough with an ox and an ass together; nor weave our wedding garment of different colours. He at once takes back the concession he

made, and, as if repenting of his opinion, withdraws it by saying: "She is happier if she so abide," that is, unmarried; and declares that in his judgment this course is preferable. And that this may not be made light of as a merely human utterance, he claims for it the authority of the Holy Spirit, so that we are listening not to a fellowman making concessions to the weakness of the flesh but to the Holy Spirit using the apostle for his mouthpiece.

6. Again, no widow of youthful age must quiet her qualms of conscience by the plea that he gives commandment that no widow is to be taken into the number under three-score years old. He does not by this arrangement urge unmarried girls or youthful widows to marry, seeing that even of the married he says: "the time is short: it remaineth that they that have wives be as though they had none." No, he is speaking of widows who have relations able to support them, who have sons and grandsons to be responsible for their maintenance. The apostle commands these latter to shew piety at home, and to requite their parents and to relieve them adequately; that the church may not be charged, but may be free to relieve those that are widows indeed. "Honour widows," he writes, "that are widows indeed," that is, such as are desolate and have no relations to help them, who cannot labour with their hands, who are weakened by poverty and overcome by years, whose trust is in God and their only work prayer. From which it is easy to infer that the younger widows, unless they are excused by ill health, are either left to their own exertions or else are consigned to the care of their children or relations. The word honour' in this passage implies either alms or a gift, as also in the verse immediately following: "Let the elders . . . be counted worthy of double honour, especially they who labour in the word and doctrine." So also in the gospel when the Lord discusses that commandment of the Law which says: "Honour thy father and thy mother," He declares that it is to be interpreted not of mere words which while offering an empty shew of regard may still leave a parent's wants unrelieved, but of the actual provision of the necessaries of life. The Lord commanded that poor parents should be supported by their children and that these should pay them back when old those benefits which they had themselves received in their childhood. The scribes and pharisees on the other hand taught the children to answer their parents by saying: "It is Corban, that is to say, a gift which I have promised to the altar and engaged to present to the temple: it will relieve you as much there, as if I were to give it you directly to buy food." So it frequently happened that while father and mother were destitute their children were offering sacrifices for the priests and scribes to consume. If then the apostle compels poor widows—yet only those who are young and not broken down by sickness—to labour with their hands that the

church, not charged with their maintenance, may be able to support such widows as are old, what plea can be urged by one who has abundance of this world's goods, both for her own wants and those of others, and who can make to herself friends of the mammon of unrighteousness able to receive her into everlasting habitations?

Consider too that no one is to be elected a widow, except she has been the wife of one husband. We sometimes fancy it to be the distinctive mark of the priesthood that none but monogamists shall be admitted to the altar. But not only are the twice-married excluded from the priestly office, they are debarred from receiving the alms of the church. A woman who has resorted to a second marriage is held unworthy to be supported by the faithful. And even the layman is bound by the law of the priest, for his conduct must be such as to admit of his election to the priesthood. If he has been twice married, he cannot be so elected. Therefore, as priests are chosen from the ranks of laymen, the layman also is bound by the commandment, fulfilment of which is indispensable for the attainment of the priesthood.

7. We must distinguish between what the apostle himself desires and what he is compelled to acquiesce in. If he allows me to marry again, this is due to my own incontinence and not to his wish. For he wishes all men to be as he is, and to think the things of God, and when once they are loosed no more to seek to be bound. But when he sees unstable men in danger through their incontinence of falling into the abyss of lust, he extends to them the offer of a second marriage; that, if they must wallow in the mire, it may be with one and not with many. The husband of a second wife must not consider this a harsh saying or one that conflicts with the rule laid down by the apostle. The apostle is of two minds: first, he proclaims a command, "I say therefore to the unmarried and widows, It is good for them if they abide even as I." Next. he makes a concession, "But if they cannot contain, let them marry: for it is better to marry than to burn." He first shews what he himself desires, then that in which he is forced to acquiesce. He wishes us—after one marriage—to abide even as he, that is, unmarried, and sets before us in his own apostolic example an instance of the blessedness of which he speaks. If however he finds that we are unwilling to do as he wishes, he makes a concession to our incontinence. Which then of the two alternatives do we choose for ourselves? The one which he prefers and which is in itself good? Or the one which in comparison with evil is tolerable, yet as it is only a substitute for evil is not altogether good? Suppose that we choose that course which the apostle does not wish but to which he only consents against his will, allowing those who seek lower ends to have their own way; in this case we carry out not the apostle's wish but our

own. We read in the old testament that the daughters of the priests who have been married once and have become widows are to eat of the priests' food and that when they die they are to be buried with the same ceremonies as their father and mother. If on the other hand they take other husbands they are to be kept apart both from their father and from the sacrifices and are to be counted as strangers.

8. These restraints on marriage are observed even among the heathen; and it is our condemnation if the true faith cannot do for Christ what false ones do for the devil, who has substituted for the saving chastity of the gospel a damning chastity of his own. The Athenian hierophant disowns his manhood and weakens his passions by a perpetual restraint. The holy office of the flamen is limited to those who have been once married, and the attendants of the flamens' wives must also have had but one husband. Only monogamists are allowed to share in the sacred rites connected with the Egyptian bull. I need say nothing of the vestal virgins and those of Apollo, the Achivan Juno, Diana, and Minerva, all of whom waste away in the perpetual virginity required by their vocation. I will just glance at the queen of Carthage who was willing to burn herself rather than marry king Iarbas; at the wife of Hasdrubal who taking her two children one in each hand cast, herself into the flames beneath her rather than surrender her honour; and at Lucretia who having lost the prize of her chastity refused to survive the defilement of her soul. I will not lengthen my letter by quoting the many instances of the like virtue which you can read to your profit in my first book against Jovinian. I will merely relate one which took place in your own country and which will shew you that chastity is held in high honour even among wild and barbarous and cruel peoples. Once the Teutons who came from the remote shores of the German Ocean overran all parts of Gaul, and it was only when they had cut to pieces several Roman armies that Marius at last defeated them in an encounter at Aquae Sextiae. By the conditions of the surrender three hundred of their married women were to be handed over to the Romans. When the Teuton matrons heard of this stipulation they first begged the consul that they might be set apart to minister in the temples of Ceres and Venus; and then when they failed to obtain their request and were removed by the lictors, they slew their little children and next morning were all found dead in each other's arms having strangled themselves in the night.

9. Shall then a highborn lady do what these barbarian women refused to do even as prisoners of war? After losing a first husband, good or bad as the case may be, shall she make trial of a second, and thus run counter to the judgment of God? And in case that she immediately loses this second, shall she take a

third? And if he too is called to his rest, shall she go on to a fourth and a fifth, and by so doing identify herself with the harlots? No, a widow must take every precaution not to overstep by an inch the bounds of chastity. For if she once oversteps them and breaks through the modesty which becomes a matron, she will soon riot in every kind of excess; so much so that the prophet's words shall be true of her "Thou hast a whore's forehead, thou refusest to be ashamed."

What then? do I condemn second marriages? not at all; but I commend first ones. Do I expel twice-married persons from the church? Far from it; but I urge those who have been once married to lives of continence. The Ark of Noah contained unclean animals as well as clean. It contained both creeping things and human beings. In a great house there are vessels of different kinds, some to honour and some to dishonour. In the gospel parable the seed sown in the good ground brings forth fruit, some an hundredfold, some sixtyfold, some thirtyfold. The hundredfold which comes first betokens the crown of virginity; the sixtyfold which comes next refers to the work of widows; while the thirty-fold—indicated by joining together the points of the thumb and forefinger—denotes the marriage-tie. What room is left for double marriages? None. They are not counted. Such weeds do not grow in good ground but among briers and thorns, the favourite haunts of those foxes to whom the Lord compares the impious Herod. A woman who marries more than once fancies herself worthy of praise because she is not so bad as the prostitutes, because she compares favourably with these victims of indiscriminate lust by surrendering herself to one alone and not to a number.

10. The story which I am about to relate is an incredible one; yet it is vouched for by many witnesses. A great many years ago when I was helping Damasus bishop of Rome with his ecclesiastical correspondence, and writing his answers to the questions referred to him by the councils of the east and west, I saw a married couple, both of whom were sprung from the very dregs of the people. The man had already buried twenty wives, and the woman had had twenty-two husbands. Now they were united to each other as each believed for the last time. The greatest curiosity prevailed both among men and women to see which of these two veterans would live to bury the other. The husband triumphed and walked before the bier of his often-married wife, amid a great concourse of people from all quarters, with garland and palm-branch, scattering spelt as he went along among an approving crowd. What shall we say to such a woman as that? Surely just what the Lord said to the woman of Samaria: "Thou hast had twenty-two husbands, and he by whom you are now buried is not your husband."

11. I beseech you therefore, my devout daughter in Christ, not to dwell on those passages which offer succour to the incontinent and the unhappy but rather to read those in which chastity is crowned. It is enough for you that you have lost the first and highest kind, that of virginity, and that you have passed through the third to the second; that is to say, having formerly fulfilled the obligations of a wife, that you now live in continence as a widow. Think not of the lowest grade, nay of that which does not count at all, I mean, second marriage; and do not seek for far fetched precedents to justify you in marrying again. You cannot too closely imitate your grandmother, your mother, and your aunt; whose teaching and advice as to life will form for you a rule of virtue. For if many wives in the lifetime of their husbands come to realize the truth of the apostle's words: "all things are lawful unto me but all things are not expedient," and make eunuchs of themselves for the kingdom of heaven's sake either by consent after their regeneration through the baptismal laver, or else in the ardour of their faith immediately after their marriage; why should not a widow, who by God's decree has ceased to have a husband, joyfully cry again and again with Job: "the Lord gave, and the Lord hath taken away," and seize the opportunity offered to her of having power over her own body instead of again becoming the servant of a man. Assuredly it is much harder to abstain from enjoying what you have than it is to regret what you have lost. Virginity is the easier because virgins know nothing of the promptings of the flesh, and widowhood is the harder because widows cannot help thinking of the license they have enjoyed in the past. And it is harder still if they suppose their husbands to be lost and not gone before; for while the former alternative brings pain, the latter causes joy.

12. The creation of the first man should teach us to reject more marriages than one. There was but one Adam and but one Eve; in fact the woman was fashioned from a rib of Adam. Thus divided they were subsequently joined together in marriage; in the words of scripture "the twain shall be one flesh," not two or three. "Therefore shall a man leave his father and his mother, and shall cleave unto his wife." Certainly it is not said "to his wives." Paul in explaining the passage refers it to Christ and the church; making the first Adam a monogamist in the flesh and the second a monogamist in the spirit. As there is one Eve who is "the mother of all living," so is there one church which is the parent of all Christians. And as the accursed Lamech made of the first Eve two separate wives, so also the heretics sever the second into several churches which, according to the apocalypse of John, ought rather to be called synagogues of the devil than congregations of Christ. In the Book of Songs we read as follows:—"there are threescore queens, and fourscore concubines, and

virgins without number. My dove, my undefiled is but one; she is the only one of her mother, she is the choice one of her that bare her." It is to this choice one that the same John addresses an epistle in these words, "the elder unto the elect lady and her children." So too in the case of the ark which the apostle Peter interprets as a type of the church, Noah brings in for his three sons one wife apiece and not two. Likewise of the unclean animals pairs only are taken, male and female, to shew that digamy has no place even among brutes, creeping things, crocodiles and lizards. And if of the clean animals there are seven taken of each kind, that is, an uneven number; this points to the palm which awaits virginal chastity. For on leaving the ark Noah sacrificed victims to God not of course of the animals taken by twos for these were kept to multiply their species, but of those taken by sevens some of which had been set apart for sacrifice.

13. It is true that the patriarchs had each of them more wives than one and that they had numerous concubines besides. And as if their example was not enough, David had many wives and Solomon a countless number. Judah went in to Tamar thinking her to be a harlot; and according to the letter that killeth the prophet Hosea married not only a whore but an adulteress. If these instances are to justify us let us neigh after every woman that we meet; like the people of Sodom and Gomorrah let us be found by the last day buying and selling, marrying and giving in marriage; and let us only end our marrying with the close of our lives. And if both before and after the deluge the maxim held good: "be fruitful and multiply and replenish the earth:" what has that to do with us upon whom the ends of the ages are come, unto whom it is said, "the time is short," and "now the axe is laid unto the root of the trees;" that is to say, the forests of marriage and of the law must be cut down by the chastity of the gospel. There is "a time to embrace, and a time to refrain from embracing." Owing to the near approach of the captivity Jeremiah is forbidden to take a wife. In Babylon Ezekiel says: "my wife is dead and my mouth is opened." Neither he who wished to marry nor he who had married could in wedlock prophesy freely. In days gone by men rejoiced to hear it said of them: "thy children shall be like olive plants round about thy table," and "thou shalt see thy children's children." But now it is said of those who live in continence: "he that is joined unto the Lord is one spirit;" and "my soul followeth hard after thee: thy right hand upholdeth me." Then it was said "an eye for an eye;" now the commandment is "whosoever shall smite thee on thy right cheek, turn to him the other also." In those days men said to the warrior: "gird thy sword upon thy thigh, O most mighty;" now it is said to Peter: "put up again thy

sword into his place: for all they that take the sword shall perish with the sword."

In speaking thus I do not mean to sever the law from the gospel, as Marcion falsely does. No, I receive one and the same God in both who, as the time and the object vary, is both the Beginning and the End, who sows that He may reap, who plants that He may have somewhat to cut down, and who lays the foundation that in the fulness of time He may crown the edifice. Besides, if we are to deal with symbols and types of things to come, we must judge of them not by our own opinions but in the light of the apostle's explanations. Hagar and Sarah, or Sinai and Zion, are typical of the two testaments. Leah who was tender-eyed and Rachel whom Jacob loved signify the synagogue and the church. So likewise do Hannah and Peninnah of whom the former, at first barren, afterwards exceeded the latter in fruitfulness. In Isaac and Rebekah we see an early example of monogamy: it was only to Rebekah that the Lord revealed Himself in the hour of childbirth and she alone went of herself to enquire of the Lord. What shall I say of Tamar who bore twin sons, Pharez and Zarah? At their birth was broken down that middle wall of partition which typified the division existing between the two peoples; while the binding of Zarah's hand with the scarlet thread even then marked the conscience of the Jews with the stain of Christ's blood. And how shall I speak of the whore married by the prophet who is a figure either of the church as gathered in from the Gentiles or—an interpretation which better suits the passage—of the synagogue? First adopted from among the idolaters by Abraham and Moses, this has now denied the Saviour and proved unfaithful to Him. Therefore it has long been deprived of its altar, priests, and prophets and has to abide many days for its first husband. For when the fulness of the Gentiles shall have come in, all Israel shall be saved.

14. I have tried to compress a great deal into a limited space as a draughtsman does when he delineates a large country in a small map. For I wish to deal with other questions, the first of which I shall give in Anna's words to her sister Dido:

Why waste your youth alone in ceaseless grief
Unblest with offspring, sweetest gift of love?
Think you the buried dead require this?
To whom the sufferer thus briefly replies:
'Twas you, my sister, you, who were the first
To plunge my frenzied soul into this woe.
Why could I not have lived a virgin life
Like some wild creature innocent of care?

Alas! I pledged my soul unto the dead:
I vowed a vow and I have broken it.

You set before me the joys of wedlock. I for my part will remind you of Dido's sword and pyre and funeral flames. In marriage there is not so much good to be hoped for as there is evil which may happen and must be feared. Passion when indulged always brings repentance with it; it is never satisfied, and once quenched it is soon kindled anew. Its growth or decay is a matter of habit; led like a captive by impulse it refuses to obey reason. But you will argue, the management of wealth and property requires the superintendence of a husband.' Do you mean to say that the affairs of those who live single are ruined; and that, unless you make yourself as much a slave as your own servants, you will not be able to govern your household? Do not your grandmother, your mother and your aunt enjoy even more than their old influence and respect, looked up to as they are by the whole province and by the leaders of the churches? Do not soldiers and travellers manage their domestic affairs and give entertainments to one another with no wives to help them? Why can you not have grave and elderly servants or freed-men, such as those who have nursed you in your childhood, to preside over your house, to answer public calls, to pay taxes; men who will look up to you as a patroness, who will love you as a nursling, who will revere you as a saint? "Seek first the kingdom of God, and all these things shall be added unto you." If you are careful for raiment the gospel bids you "consider the lilies;" and, if for food, to go back to the fowls which "sow not neither do they reap; yet your heavenly father feedeth them." How many virgins and widows there are who have looked after their property for themselves without thereby incurring any stain of scandal!

15. Do not associate with young women or cleave to them, for it is on account of such that the apostle makes his concession of second marriage, and so you may be shipwrecked in what appears to be calm water. If Paul can say to Timothy, "the younger widows refuse," and again "love the elder women as mothers; the younger as sisters, with all purity," what plea can you urge for refusing to hear my admonitions? Avoid all persons to whom a suspicion of evil living may attach itself, and do not content yourself with the trite answer, my own conscience is enough for me; I do not care what people say of me.' That was not the principle on which the apostle acted. He provided things honest not only in the sight of God but in the sight of all men; that the name of God might not be blasphemed among the Gentiles. Though he had power to lead about a sister, a wife, he would not do so, for he did not wish to be judged by an unbeliever's conscience. And, though he might have lived by the gospel, he laboured day and night with his own hands, that he might not be

burdensome to the believers. "If meat," he says, "make my brother to offend. I will eat no flesh while the world standeth." Let us then say, if a sister or a brother causes not one or two but the whole church to offend, I will not see that sister or that brother.' It is better to lose a portion of one's substance than to imperil the salvation of one's soul. It is better to lose that which some day, whether we like it or not, must be lost to us and to give it up freely, than to lose that for which we should sacrifice all that we have. Which of us can add—I will not say a cubit for that would be an immense addition—but the tenth part of a single inch to his stature? Why are we careful what we shall eat or what we shall drink? Let us "take no thought for the morrow: sufficient unto the day is the evil thereof."

Jacob in his flight from his brother left behind in his father's house great riches and made his way with nothing into Mesopotamia. Moreover, to prove to us his powers of endurance, he took a stone for his pillow. Yet as he lay there he beheld a ladder set up on the earth reaching to heaven and behold the Lord stood above it, and the angels ascended and descended on it; the lesson being thus taught that the sinner must not despair of salvation nor the righteous man rest secure in his virtue. To pass over much of the story (for there is no time to explain all the points in the narrative) after twenty years he who before had passed over Jordan with his staff returned into his native land with three droves of cattle, rich in flocks and herds and richer still in children. The apostles likewise travelled throughout the world without either money in their purses, or staves in their hands, or shoes on their feet; and yet they could speak of themselves as "having nothing and yet possessing all things." "Silver and gold," say they, "have we none, but such as we have give we thee: in the name of Jesus Christ of Nazareth rise up and walk." For they were not weighed down with the burthen of riches. Therefore they could stand, as Elijah, in the crevice of the rock, they could pass through the needle's eye, and behold the back parts of the Lord.

But as for us we burn with covetousness and, even while we declaim against the love of money, we hold out our skirts to catch gold and never have enough. There is a common saying about the Megarians which may rightly be applied to all who suffer from this passion: "They build as if they are to live forever; they live as if they are to die to-morrow." We do the same, for we do not believe the Lord's words. When we attain the age which all desire we forget the nearness of that death which as human beings we owe to nature and with futile hope promise to ourselves a long length of years. No old man is so weak and decrepit as to suppose that he will not live for one year more. A forgetfulness of his true condition gradually creeps upon him; so that—earthly creature that he is and close to dissolution as he stands—he is lifted up into pride, and in imagination seats himself in heaven.

16. But what am I doing? Whilst I talk about the cargo, the vessel itself founders. He that letteth is taken out of the way, and yet we do not realize that Antichrist is near. Yes, Antichrist is near whom the Lord Jesus Christ "shall consume with the spirit of his mouth." "Woe unto them," he cries, "that are with child, and to them that give suck in those days." Now these things are both the fruits of marriage.

I shall now say a few words of our present miseries. A few of us have hitherto survived them, but this is due not to anything we have done ourselves but to the mercy of the Lord. Savage tribes in countless numbers have overrun all parts of Gaul. The whole country between the Alps and the Pyrenees, between the Rhine and the Ocean, has been laid waste by hordes of Quadi, Vandals, Sarmatians, Alans, Gepids, Herules, Saxons, Burgundians, Allemanni and—alas! for the commonweal!—even Pannonians. For "Assur also is joined with them." The once noble city of Moguntiacum has been captured and destroyed. In its church many thousands have been massacred. The people of Vangium after standing a long siege have been extirpated. The powerful city of Rheims, the Ambiani, the Altrebatae, the Belgians on the skirts of the world, Tournay, Spires, and Strasburg have fallen to Germany: while the provinces of Aquitaine and of the Nine Nations, of Lyons and of Narbonne are with the exception of a few cities one universal scene of desolation. And those which the sword spares without, famine ravages within. I cannot speak without tears of Toulouse which has been kept from falling hitherto by the merits of its reverend bishop Exuperius. Even the Spains are on the brink of ruin and tremble daily as they recall the invasion of the Cymry; and, while others suffer misfortunes once in actual fact, they suffer them continually in anticipation.

17. I say nothing of other places that I may not seem to despair of God's mercy. All that is ours now from the Pontic Sea to the Julian Alps in days gone by once ceased to be ours. For thirty years the barbarians burst the barrier of the Danube and fought in the heart of the Roman Empire. Long use dried our tears. For all but a few old people had been born either in captivity or during a blockade, and consequently they did not miss a liberty which they had never known. Yet who will hereafter credit the fact or what histories will seriously discuss it, that Rome has to fight within her own borders not for glory but for bare life; and that she does not even fight but buys the right to exist by giving gold and sacrificing all her substance? This humiliation has been brought upon her not by the fault of her Emperors who are both most religious men, but by the crime of a half-barbarian traitor who with our money has armed our foes

against us. Of old the Roman Empire was branded with eternal shame because after ravaging the country and routing the Romans at the Allia, Brennus with his Gauls entered Rome itself. Nor could this ancient stain be wiped out until Gaul, the birth-place of the Gauls, and Gaulish Greece, wherein they had settled after triumphing over East and West, were subjugated to her sway. Even Hannibal who swept like a devastating storm from Spain into Italy, although he came within sight of the city, did not dare to lay siege to it. Even Pyrrhus was so completely bound by the spell of the Roman name that destroying everything that came in his way, he yet withdrew from its vicinity and, victor though he was, did not presume to gaze upon what he had learned to be a city of kings. Yet in return for such insults—not to say such haughty pride—as theirs which ended thus happily for Rome, one banished from all the world found death at last by poison in Bithynia; while the other returning to his native land was slain in his own dominions. The countries of both became tributary to the Roman people. But now, even if complete success attends our arms, we can wrest nothing from our vanquished foes but what we have already lost to them. The poet Lucan describing the power of the city in a glowing passage says:

If Rome be weak, where shall we look for strength?

we may vary his words and say:

If Rome be lost, where shall we look for help?

or quote the language of Virgil:

Had I a hundred tongues and throat of bronze
The woes of captives I could not relate
Or ev'n recount the names of all the slain.

Even what I have said is fraught with danger both to me who say it and to all who hear it; for we are no longer free even to lament our fate, and are unwilling, nay, I may even say, afraid to weep for our sufferings.

Dearest daughter in Christ, answer me this question: will you marry amid such scenes as these? Tell me, what kind of husband will you take? One that will run or one that will fight? In either case you know what the result will be. Instead of the Fescennine song, the hoarse blare of the terrible trumpet will deafen your ears and your very brideswomen may be turned into mourners. In what pleasures can you hope to revel now that you have lost the proceeds of all your possessions, now that you see your small retinue under close blockade and a prey to the inroads of pestilence and famine? But far be it from me to think so meanly of you or to harbour any suspicions of one who has dedicated her soul to the Lord. Though nominally addressed to you my words are really meant for others such as are idle, inquisitive and given to gossip. These wander from house to house and from one married lady to another, their god is their belly and their glory is in their shame, of the scriptures they know nothing except the texts which favour second marriages, but they love to quote the example of others to justify their own self-indulgence, and flatter themselves that they are no worse than their fellow-sinners. When you have confounded the shameless proposals of such women by explaining the true drift of the apostle's meaning; then to show you by what mode of life you can best preserve your widowhood, you may read with advantage what I have written. I mean my treatise on the preservation of virginity addressed to Eustochium and my two letters to Furia and Salvina. Of these two latter you may like to know that the first is daughter-in-law to Probus some time consul, and the second daughter to Gildo formerly governour of Africa. This tract on monogamy I shall call by your name.

LETTER CXXIV. TO AVITUS

Avitus to whom this letter is addressed is probably the same person who induced Jerome to write to Salvina (see Letter LXXIX., S:I, ante). The occasion of writing is as follows. Ten years previously (that is to say in a.d. 399 or 400) Pammachius had asked Jerome to supply him with a correct version of Origen's First Principles to enable him to detect the variations introduced by Rufinus into his rendering. This Jerome willingly did (see Letters LXXXIII. and LXXXIV.) but when the work in its integrity was perused by Pammachius he thought it so erroneous in doctrine that he determined not to circulate it. However, "a certain brother" induced him to lend the ms. to him for a short time; and then, when he had got it into his hands, had a hasty and incorrect transcript made, which he forthwith published much to the chagrin of Pammachius. Falling into the hands of Avitus a copy of this much perplexed him and he seems to have appealed to Jerome for an explanation. This the latter now gives forwarding at the same time an authentic edition of his version of the First Principles. The date of the letter is a.d. 409 or 410.

1. About ten years ago that saintly man Pammachius sent me a copy of a certain person's rendering, or rather misrendering, of Origen's First Principles; with a request that in a Latin version I should give the true sense of the Greek and should set down the writer's words for good or for evil without bias in either direction. When I did as he wished and sent him the book, he was shocked to read it and locked it up in his desk lest being circulated it might wound the souls of many. However, a certain brother, who had "a zeal for God

but not according to knowledge," asked for a loan of the manuscript that he might read it; and, as he promised to return it without delay, Pammachius, thinking no harm could happen in so short a time, unsuspectingly consented. Hereupon he who had borrowed the book to read, with the aid of scribes copied the whole of it and gave it back much sooner than he had promised. Then with the same rashness or—to use a less severe term—thoughtlessness he made bad worse by confiding to others what he had thus stolen. Moreover, since a bulky treatise on an abstruse subject is difficult to reproduce with accuracy, especially if it has to be taken down surreptitiously and in a hurry, order and sense were sacrificed in several passages. Whence it comes, my dear Avitus, that you ask me to send you a copy of my version as made for Pammachius and not for the public, a garbled edition of which has been published by the aforesaid brother.

2. Take then what you have asked for; but know that there are countless things in the book to be abhorred, and that, as the Lord says, you will have to walk among scorpions and serpents. It begins by saying that Christ was made God's son not born; that God the Father, as He is by nature invisible, is invisible even to the Son; that the Son, who is the likeness of the invisible Father, compared with the Father is not the truth but compared with us who cannot receive the truth of the almighty Father seems a figure of the truth so that we perceive the majesty and magnitude of the greater in the less, the Father's glory limited in the Son; that God the Father is a light incomprehensible and that Christ compared with him is but a minute brightness, although by reason of our incapacity to us he appears a great one. The Father and the Son are compared to two statues, a larger one and a small; the first filling the world and being somehow invisible through its size, the second cognisable by the eyes of men. God the Father omnipotent the writer terms good and of perfect goodness; but of the Son he says: "He is not good but an emanation and likeness of goodness; not good absolutely but only with a qualification, as the good shepherd' and the like." The Holy Spirit he places after the Father and the Son as third in dignity and honour. And while he declares that he does not know whether the Holy Spirit is created or uncreated, he has later on given his own opinion that except God the Father alone there is nothing uncreated. "The Son," he states, "is inferior to the Father, inasmuch as He is second and the Father first; and the Holy Spirit which dwells in all the saints is inferior to the Son. In the same way the power of the Father is greater than that of the Son and of the Holy Spirit. Likewise the power of the Son is greater than that of the Holy Spirit, and as a consequence the Holy Spirit in its turn has greater virtue than other things called holy."

3. Then, when he comes to deal with rational creatures and to describe their lapse into earthly bodies as due to their own negligence, he goes on to say: "Surely it argues great negligence and sloth for a soul so far to empty itself as to fall into sin and allow itself to be tied to the material body of an unreasoning brute;" and in a subsequent passage: "These reasonings induce me to suppose that it is by their own free act that some are numbered with God's saints and servants, and that it was through their own fault that others fell from holiness into such negligence that they were changed into forces of an opposite kind." He maintains that after every end a fresh beginning springs forth and an end from each beginning, and that wholesale variation is possible; so that one who is now a human being may in another world become a demon, while one who by reason of his negligence is now a demon may hereafter be placed in a more material body and thus become a human being. So far does he carry this transforming process that on his theory an archangel may become the devil and the devil in turn be changed back into an archangel. "Such as have wavered or faltered but have not altogether fallen shall be made subject, for rule and government and guidance, to better things—to principalities and powers, to thrones and dominations"; and of these perhaps another human race will be formed, when in the words of Isaiah there shall be "new heavens and a new earth.' But such as have not deserved to return through humanity to their former estate shall become the devil and his angels, demons of the worst sort; and according to what they have done shall have special duties assigned to them in particular worlds." Moreover, the very demons and rulers of darkness in any world or worlds, if they are willing to turn to better things, may become human beings and so come back to their first beginning. That is to say, after they have borne the discipline of punishment and torture for a longer or a shorter time in human bodies, they may again reach the angelic pinnacles from which they have fallen. Hence it may be shewn that we men may change into any other reasonable beings, and that not once only or on emergency but time after time; we and angels shall become demons if we neglect our duty; and demons, if they will take to themselves virtues, may attain to the rank of angels.

4. Bodily substances too are to pass away utterly or else at the end of all things will become highly rarified like the sky and aether and other subtle bodies. It is clear that these principles must affect the writer's view of the resurrection. The sun also and the moon and the rest of the constellations are alive. Nay more; as we men by reason of our sins are enveloped in bodies material and sluggish; so the lights of heaven have for like reasons received bodies more or less luminous, and demons have been for more serious faults

clothed with starry frames. This, he argues, is the view of the apostle who writes:—"the creation has been subjected to vanity and shall be delivered for the revealing of the sons of God." That it may not be supposed that I am imputing to him ideas of my own I shall give his actual words. "At the end and consummation of the world," he writes, "when souls and beings endowed with reason shall be released from prison by the Lord, they will move slowly or fly quickly according as they have previously been slothful or energetic. And as all of them have free will and are free to choose virtue or vice, those who choose the latter will be much worse off than they now are. But those who choose the former will improve their condition. Their movements and decisions in this direction or in that will determine their various futures; whether, that is, angels are to become men or demons, and whether demons are to become men or angels." Then after adducing various arguments in support of his thesis and maintaining that while not incapable of virtue the devil has yet not chosen to be virtuous, he has finally reasoned with much diffuseness that an angel, a human soul, and a demon—all according to him of one nature but of different wills—may in punishment for great negligence or folly be transformed into brutes. Moreover, to avoid the agony of punishment and the burning flame the more sensitive may choose to become low organisms, to dwell in water, to assume the shape of this or that animal; so that we have reason to fear a metamorphosis not only into four-footed things but even into fishes. Then, lest he should be held guilty of maintaining with Pythagoras the transmigration of souls, he winds up the wicked reasoning with which he has wounded his reader by saying: "I must not be taken to make dogmas of these things; they are only thrown out as conjectures to shew that they are not altogether overlooked."

5. In his second book he maintains a plurality of worlds; not, however, as Epicurus taught, many like ones existing at once, but a new one beginning each time that the old comes to an end. There was a world before this world of ours, and after it there will be first one and then another and so on in regular succession. He is in doubt whether one world shall be so completely similar to another as to leave no room for any difference between them, or whether one world shall never wholly be indistinguishable from another. And again a little farther on he writes: "if, as the course of the discussion makes necessary, all things can live without body, all bodily existence shall be swallowed up and that which once has been made out of nothing shall again be reduced to nothing. And yet a time will come when its use will be once more necessary." And in the same context: "but if, as reason and the authority of scripture shew, this corruptible shall put on incorruption and this mortal shall put on immortality, death shall be swallowed up in victory and corruption in incorruption. And it

may be that all bodily existence shall be removed, for it is only in this that death can operate." And a little farther on: "if these things are not contrary to the faith, it may be that we shall some day live in a disembodied state. Moreover, if only he is fully subject to Christ who is disembodied, and if all must be made subject to Him, we too shall lose our bodies when we become fully subject to Him." And in the same passage: "if all are to be made subject to God, all shall lay aside their bodies; and then all bodily existence shall be brought to nought. But if through the fall of reasonable beings it is a second time required it will reappear. For God has left souls to strive and struggle, to teach them that full and complete victory is to be attained not by their own efforts but by His grace. And so to my mind worlds vary with the sins which cause them, and those are exploded theories which maintain that all worlds are alike." And again: "three conjectures occur to me with regard to the end; it is for the reader to determine which is nearest to the truth. For either we shall be bodiless when being made subject to Christ we shall be made subject to God and He shall be all in all; or as things made subject to Christ shall be with Christ Himself made subject to God and brought under one law, so all substance shall be refined into its most perfect form and rarified into aether which is a pure and uncompounded essence; or else the sphere which I have called motionless and all that it contains will be dissolved into nothing, and the sphere in which the antizone itself is contained shall be called good ground,' and that other sphere which in its revolution surrounds the earth and goes by the name of heaven shall be reserved for the abode of the saints."

6. In speaking thus does he not most clearly follow the error of the heathen and foist upon the simple faith of Christians the ravings of philosophy? In the same book he writes: "it remains that God is invisible. But if He is by nature invisible, He must be so even to the Saviour." And lower down: "no soul which has descended into a human body has borne upon it so true an impress of its previous character as Christ's soul of which He says: no man taketh it from me, but I lay it down of myself.'" And in another place: "we must carefully consider whether souls, when they have won salvation and have attained to the blessed life, may not cease to be souls. For as the Lord and Saviour came to seek and to save that which was lost that it might cease to be lost; so the lost soul which the Lord came to save, when saved, will cease to be a soul. We must ask ourselves whether, as the lost was not lost once and again will not be, the soul likewise may have been and again may be not a soul." And after a good many remarks upon the soul he brings in the following, "nous or" intelligence by falling becomes a soul; and by acquiring virtue this will become intelligence again. This at least is a fair inference from the case of Esau who for his old sins

is condemned to lead a lower life. And concerning the heavenly bodies we must make a similar acknowledgment. The soul of the sun—or whatever else you like to call it—does not date its existence from the creation of the world; it already existed before it entered its shining and glowing body. So also with the moon and stars. From antecedent causes they have been made subject to vanity not willingly but for future reward, and are forced to do not their own will but the creator's who has assigned to them their several spheres."

7. Hellfire, moreover, and the torments with which holy scripture threatens sinners he explains not as external punishments but as the pangs of guilty consciences when by God's power the memory of our transgressions is set before our eyes. "The whole crop of our sins grows up afresh from seeds which remain in the soul, and all our dishonourable and undutiful acts are again pictured before our gaze. Thus it is the fire of conscience and the stings of remorse which torture the mind as it looks back on former self-indulgence." And again: "but perhaps this coarse and earthly body ought to be described as mist and darkness; for at the end of this world and when it becomes necessary to pass into another, the like darkness will lead to the like physical birth." In speaking thus he clearly pleads for the transmigration of souls as taught by Pythagoras and Plato. And at the end of the second book in dealing with our perfection he has said: "when we shall have made such progress as not only to cease to be flesh or body but perhaps also to cease to be souls our perfect intelligence and perception, undimmed with any mist of passion, will discern reasonable and intelligible substances face to face.

8. In the third book the following faulty statements are contained. "If we once admit that, when one vessel is made to honour and another to dishonour, this is due to antecedent causes; why may we not revert to the mystery of the soul and allow that it is loved in one and hated in another because of its past actions, before in Jacob it becomes a supplanter and before in Esau it is supplanted?" And again: "the fact that souls are made some to honour and some to dishonour is to be explained by their previous history." And in the same place: "on this hypothesis of mine a vessel made to honour which fails to fulfil its object will in another world become a vessel made to dishonour; and contrariwise a vessel which has from a previous fault been condemned to dishonour will, if it accepts correction in this present life, become in the new creation a vessel sanctified and meet for the Master's use and prepared unto every good work.'" And he immediately goes on to say: "I believe that men who begin with small faults may become so hardened in wickedness that, if they do not repent and turn to better things, they must become inhuman energies; and contrariwise that hostile and demonic beings may in course of time so far heal

their wounds and check the current of their former sins that they may attain to the abode of the perfect. As I have often said, in those countless and unceasing worlds in which the soul lives and has its being some grow worse and worse until they reach the lowest depths of degradation; while others in those lowest depths grow better and better until they reach the perfection of virtue." Thus he tries to shew that men, or rather their souls, may become demons; and that demons in turn may be restored to the rank of angels. In the same book he writes: "this too must be considered; why the human soul is diversely acted upon now by influences of one kind and now by influences of another." And he surmises that this is due to conduct which has preceded birth. It is for this, he argues, that John leaps in his mother's womb when at Mary's salutation Elizabeth declares herself unworthy of her notice. And he immediately subjoins: "on the other hand infants that are hardly weaned are possessed with evil spirits and become diviners and soothsayers; indeed, some are indwelt from their earliest years with the spirit of a python. Now as they have done nothing to bring upon themselves these visitations, one who holds that nothing happens without God's permission, and that all things are governed by His justice, cannot suppose that God's providence has abandoned them without good reason."

9. Again, of the world he writes thus: "The belief commends itself to me that there was a world before this world and that after it there will be another. Do you wish to know that after the decay of this world there will be a new one? Hear the words of Isaiah: the new heavens and the new earth which I will make shall remain before me.' Do you wish to know that before the making of this world there have previously been others? Listen to the Preacher who says: the thing which hath been, it is that which shall be; and that which is done is that which shall be done: and there is no new thing under the sun. Is there anything whereof it may be said, See, this is new? it hath been already of old time, which was before us.' A passage which proves not only that other worlds have been but that other worlds shall be; not, however, simultaneously and side by side but one after another." And he immediately adds: "I hold that heaven is the abode of the deity, the true place of rest; and that it was there that reasonable creatures enjoyed their ancient bliss, before coming down to a lower plane and exchanging the invisible for the visible, they fell to the earth and came to need material bodies. Now that they have fallen, God the creator has made for them bodies suitable to their surroundings; and has fashioned this visible world, and has sent into it ministers to ensure the salvation and correction of the fallen. Of these ministers some have held assigned positions and have been subject to the world's necessary laws; while others have intelli-

gently performed duties laid upon them in times and seasons determined by God's plan. To the former class belong the sun, moon, and stars called by the apostle the creation;' and these have had allotted to them the heights of heaven. Now the creation is subjected to vanity because it is encased in material bodies and visible to the eye. And yet it is made subject to vanity not willingly but by reason of him who hath subjected the same in hope.' Others again of the second class, at particular places and times known to their Maker only, we believe to be His angels sent to steer the world." A little farther on he says: "the affairs of the world are so ordered by Providence that while some angels fall from heaven others freely glide down to earth. The former are hurled down against their will; the latter descend from choice alone. The former are forced to continue in a distasteful service for a fixed period; the latter spontaneously embrace the task of lending a hand to those who fall." Again he writes: "whence it follows that these different movements result in the creation of different worlds; and that this world of ours will be succeeded by one quite unlike it. Now, as regards this falling and rising, this rewarding of virtue and punishment of vice, whether they take place in the past, present, or future, God, the creator, can alone apportion desert and make all things converge to one end. For He only knows why He allows some to follow their own inclination and to descend from the higher planes to the lowest; and why He visits others and giving them His hand draws them back to their former state and places them once more in heaven."

10. In discussing the end of the world he has made use of the following language. "Since, as I have often said, a new beginning springs from the end, it may be asked whether bodies will then continue to exist, or whether, when they have been annihilated, we shall live without bodies and be incorporeal as we know God to be. Now there can be no doubt but that, if bodies or, as the apostle calls them, visible things, belong only to our sensible world, the life of the disembodied will be incorporeal." And a little farther on: "when the apostle writes, the creation shall be delivered from the bondage of corruption into the liberty of the glory of the children of God,' I explain his words thus. Reasonable and incorporeal beings are the highest of God's creatures, for not being clothed with bodies they are not the slaves of corruption. Since where there are bodies, there corruption is sure to be found. But hereafter the creation shall be delivered from the bondage of corruption,' and then men shall receive the glory of the children of God and God shall be all in all." And in the same passage he writes: "that the final state will be an incorporeal one is rendered credible by the words of our Saviour's prayer: as thou, Father, art in me and I in thee, that they also may be one in us.' For we ought to realize what God is

and what the Saviour will finally be, and how the likeness to the Father and the Son here promised to the Saints consists in this that as They are one in Themselves so we shall be one in Them. For if in the end the life of the Saints is to be assimilated to the life of God, we must either admit that the Lord of the universe is clothed with a body and that he is enveloped in matter as we are in flesh; or, if it is unbecoming to suppose this, especially in persons who have but small clues from which to infer God's majesty and to guess at the glory of His innate and transcendent nature, we are reduced to the following dilemma. Either we shall always have bodies and in that case must despair of ever being like God; or, if the blessedness of the life of God is really promised to us, the conditions of His life must be the conditions of ours."

11. These passages prove what his view is regarding the resurrection. For he evidently maintains that all bodies will perish and that we shall be incorporeal as according to him we were before we received our present bodies. Again when he comes to argue for a variety of worlds and to maintain that angels will become demons, demons either angels or men, and men in their turn demons; in a word that everything will be turned into something else, he thus sums up his own opinion: "no doubt, after an interval matter will exist afresh and bodies will be formed and a different world will be created to meet the varying wills of reasonable beings who, having forfeited the perfect bliss which continues to the end, have gradually fallen into so great wickedness as to change their nature and refuse to keep their first estate of unalloyed blessedness. Many reasonable beings, it is right to say, keep it until a second, a third, and a fourth world, and give God no ground for changing their condition. Others deteriorate so little that they seem to have lost hardly anything, and others again have to be hurled headlong into the abyss. God who orders all things alone knows how to use each class according to its deserts in a suitable sphere; for He only understands opportunities and motives and the course in which the world must be steered. Thus one who has borne away the palm for wickedness and has sunk into the lowest degradation will in the world which is hereafter to be fashioned be made a devil, a kind of first fruits of the Lord's handiwork, to be a laughing stock to the angels who have lost their first virtue." What is this but to argue that the sinful men of this world may become a devil and demons in another; and contrariwise that those who are now demons may hereafter become either men or angels? And after a lengthy discussion in which he maintains that all corporeal creatures must exchange their material for subtle and spiritual bodies and that all substance must become one pure and inconceivably bright body, of which the human mind can at present form no conception, he winds up thus:—"God shall be all in all;' that is to say, all bodily

existence shall be made as perfect as possible; it shall be brought into the divine essence, than which there is none better."

12. In the fourth and last book of his work the following passages deserve the church's condemnation. "It may be that as, when men die in this world by the separation of soul and body, they are allotted different positions in hell according to the difference in their works; so when angels die, out of the system of the heavenly Jerusalem, they come down to this world as a hell and are placed on earth according to their deserts." And again: "as we have compared the souls which pass from this world to hell with those which as they come from heaven to us are in a manner dead; so we must carefully inquire whether this is true of all souls without exception. For in that case souls born on earth when they desire better things rise out of hell and assume human bodies or when they desire worse things come down to us from better worlds; and in the firmament above us likewise there are souls on their way from our world to higher ones, and others who, while they have fallen from heaven, have not sinned so grievously as to be thrust down to earth." He thus tries to prove that the firmament, that is the sky, is hell compared with heaven; and that this earth is hell compared with the firmament; and again that our world is heaven to hell. Or in other words what is hell to some is heaven to others. And not content with saying this he goes on: "at the end of all things when we shall return to the heavenly Jerusalem the hostile powers shall declare war against the people of God to breathe and exercise their valour and strengthen their resolve. For this they cannot have until they have faced and foiled their foes; of whom we read in the book of Numbers that they are overcome by reason, discipline, and tactical skill."

13. After saying that according to the apocalypse of John "the everlasting gospel" which shall be revealed in heaven as much surpasses our gospel as Christ's preaching does the sacraments of the ancient law, he has asserted what it is sacrilegious even to think; that Christ will once more suffer in the sky for the salvation of demons. And although he has not expressly said it, it is yet implied in his words that as for men God became man to set men free, so for the salvation of demons when He comes to deliver them He will become a demon. To shew that this is no gloss of mine, I must give his own words: "As Christ," he writes, "has fulfilled the shadow of the law by the shadow of the gospel, and as all law is a pattern and shadow of things done in heaven, we must inquire whether we are justified in supposing that even the heavenly law and the rites of the celestial worship are still incomplete and need the true gospel which in the apocalypse of John is called everlasting to distinguish it from ours which is only temporal, set forth in a world that shall pass away.

Now if we extend our inquiry to the passion of our Lord and Saviour, it may indeed be overbold to suppose that He will suffer in heaven; yet if there is spiritual wickedness in heavenly places and if we confess without a blush that the Lord has once been crucified to destroy those things which He has destroyed by His passion; why need we fear to imagine a like occurrence in the upper world in the fulness of time, so that the nations of all realms shall be saved by a passion of Christ?"

14. Here is another blasphemy which he has spoken of the Son. "Assuming that the Son knows the Father, it would seem that by this knowledge He can comprehend Him as much as a craftsman can comprehend the rules of his art. And, doubtless, if the Father is in the Son, He is also comprehended by Him in whom He is. But if we mean by comprehension not merely that the knower takes a thing in by perception and insight but that he contains it within himself by virtue of a special faculty; in this sense we cannot say that the Son comprehends the Father. For the Father comprehends all things, and of these the Son is one; therefore, He comprehends the Son." And to shew us reasons why, while the Father comprehends the Son, the Son cannot comprehend the Father, he adds: "the curious reader may inquire whether the Father knows Himself in the same way that the Son knows Him. But if he recalls the words: the Father who sent me is greater than I,' he will allow that they must be universally true and will admit that, in knowledge as in everything else, the Father is greater than the Son, and knows Himself more perfectly and immediately than the Son can do."

15. The following passage is a convincing proof that he holds the transmigration of souls and annihilation of bodies. "If it can be shewn that an incorporeal and reasonable being has life in itself independently of the body and that it is worse off in the body than out of it; then beyond a doubt bodies are only of secondary importance and arise from time to time to meet the varying conditions of reasonable creatures. Those who require bodies are clothed with them, and contrariwise, when fallen souls have lifted themselves up to better things, their bodies are once more annihilated. They are thus ever vanishing and ever reappearing." And to prevent us from minimizing the impiety of his previous utterances he ends his work by maintaining that all reasonable beings, that is, the Father, the Son, and the Holy Ghost, angels, powers, dominations, and virtues, and even man by right of his soul's dignity, are of one and the same essence. "God," he writes, "and His only-begotten Son and the Holy Spirit are conscious of an intellectual and reasonable nature. But so also are the angels, the powers, and the virtues, as well as the inward man who is created in the image and after the likeness of God. From which I conclude that God and

they are in some sort of one essence." He adds "in some sort" to escape the charge of blasphemy; and while in another place he will not allow the Son and the Holy Spirit to be of one substance with the Father lest by so doing he should appear to make the divine essence divisible, he here bestows the nature of God almighty upon angels and men.

16. This being the nature of Origen's book, is it anything short of madness to change a few blasphemous passages regarding the Son and the Holy Spirit and then to publish the rest unchanged with an unprincipled eulogy when the parts unaltered as well as the parts altered flow from the same fountain head of gross impiety? This is not the time to confute all the statements made in detail; and indeed those who have written against Arius, Eunomius, Manichaeus, and various other heretics must be supposed to have answered these blasphemies as well. If anyone, therefore, wishes to read the work let him walk with his feet shod towards the land of promise; let him guard against the jaws of the serpent and the crooked jaws of the scorpion; let him read this treatise first and before he enters upon the path let him know the dangers which he will have to avoid.

LETTER CXXV. TO RUSTICUS

Rusticus, a young monk of Toulouse, (to be carefully distinguished from the recipient of Letter CXXII.) is advised by Jerome not to become an anchorite but to continue in a community. Rules are suggested for the monastic life and a vivid picture is drawn of the difference between a good monk and a bad. Incidentally Jerome indulges his spleen against his dead opponent Rufinus (S:18). The date of the letter is 411 a.d.

1. No man is happier than the Christian, for to him is promised the kingdom of heaven. No man struggles harder than he, for he goes daily in danger of his life. No man is stronger, for he overcomes the Devil. No man is weaker, for he is overcome by the flesh. Both pairs of statements can be proved by many examples. For instance, the robber believes upon the cross and immediately hears the assuring words: "verily I say unto thee, To-day shalt thou be with me in paradise:" while Judas falls from the pinnacle of the apostolate into the abyss of perdition. Neither the close intercourse of the banquet nor the dipping of the sop nor the Lord's gracious kiss can save him from betraying as man Him whom he had known as the Son of God. Could any one have been viler than the woman of Samaria? Yet not only did she herself believe, and after her six husbands find one Lord, not only did she recognize that Messiah by the well, whom the Jews failed to recognize in the temple; she brought salvation to

many and, while the apostles were away buying food, refreshed the Saviour's hunger and relieved His weariness. Was ever man wiser than Solomon? Yet love for women made even him foolish. Salt is good, and every offering must be sprinkled with it. Wherefore also the apostle has given commandment: "let your speech be alway with grace, seasoned with salt." But "if the salt have lost his savour," it is cast out. And so utterly does it lose its value that it is not even fit for the dunghill, whence believers fetch manure to enrich the barren soil of their souls.

I begin thus, Rusticus my son, to teach you the greatness of your enterprise and the loftiness of your ideal; and to shew you that only by trampling under foot youthful lusts can you hope to climb the heights of true maturity. For the path along which you walk is a slippery one and the glory of success is less than the shame of failure.

2. I need not now conduct the stream of my discourse through the meadows of virtue, nor exert myself to shew to you the beauty of its several flowers. I need not dilate on the purity of the lily, the modest blush of the rose, the royal purple of the violet, or the promise of glowing gems which their various colours hold out. For through the mercy of God you have already put your hand to the plough; you have already gone up upon the housetop like the apostle Peter. Who when he became hungry among the Jews had his hunger satisfied by the faith of Cornelius, and stilled the craving caused by their unbelief through the conversion of the centurion and other Gentiles. By the vessel let down from heaven to earth, the four corners of which typified the four gospels, he was taught that all men can be saved. Once more, this fair white sheet which in his vision was taken up again was a symbol of the church which carries believers from earth to heaven, an assurance that the Lord's promise should be fulfilled: "blessed are the pure in heart, for they shall see God."

All this means that I take you by the hand and do my best to impress certain facts upon your mind; that, like a skilled sailor who has been through many shipwrecks, I am anxious to caution an inexperienced passenger of the risks before him. For on one side is the Charybdis of covetousness, "the root of all evil;" and on the other lurks the Scylla of detraction girt with the railing hounds of which the apostle says: "if ye bite and devour one another, take heed that ye be not consumed one of another." Sometimes, you must know, the quicksands of vice suck us down as we sail at ease through the calm water; and the desert of this world is not untenanted by venomous reptiles.

3. Those who navigate the Red Sea—where we must pray that the true Pharaoh may be drowned with all his host—have to encounter many difficul-

ties and dangers before they reach the city of Auxuma. Nomad savages and ferocious wild beasts haunt the shores on either side. Thus travellers must be always armed and on the alert, and they must carry with them a whole year's provisions. Moreover, so full are the waters of hidden reefs and impassable shoals that a look-out has constantly to be kept from the masthead to direct the helmsman how to shape his course. They may count themselves fortunate if after six months they make the port of the above-mentioned city. At this point the ocean begins, to cross which a whole year hardly suffices. Then India is reached and the river Ganges—called in holy scripture Pison—"which compasseth the whole land of Havilah" and is said to carry down with it—from its source in paradise—various dyes and pigments. Here are found rubies and emeralds, glowing pearls and gems of the first water, such as high born ladies passionately desire. There are also mountains of gold which however men cannot approach by reason of the griffins, dragons, and huge monsters which haunt them; for such are the guardians which avarice needs for its treasures.

4. What, you ask, is the drift of all this? Surely it is clear enough. For if the merchants of the world undergo such hardships to win a doubtful and passing gain, and if after seeking it through many dangers they only keep it at risk of their lives; what should Christ's merchant do who "selleth all that he hath" that he may acquire the "one pearl of great price;" who with his whole substance buys a field that he may find therein a treasure which neither thief can dig up nor robber carry away?

5. I know that I must offend large numbers who will be angry with my criticisms as aimed at their own deficiencies. Yet such anger does but shew an uneasy conscience and they will pass a far severer sentence on themselves than on me. For I shall not mention names; or copy the licence of the old comedy which criticized individuals. Wise men and wise women will try to hide or rather to correct whatever they perceive to be amiss in them; they will be more angry with themselves than with me, and will not be disposed to heap curses upon the head of their monitor. For he, although he is liable to the same charges, is certainly superior in this that he is discontented with his own faults.

6. I am told that your mother is a religious woman, a widow of many years' standing; and that when you were a child she reared and taught you herself. Afterwards when you had spent some time in the flourishing schools of Gaul she sent you to Rome, sparing no expense and consoling herself for your absence by the thought of the future that lay before you. She hoped to see the exuberance and glitter of your Gallic eloquence toned down by Roman sobriety, for she saw that you required the rein more than the spur. So we are told of

the greatest orators of Greece that they seasoned the bombast of Asia with the salt of Athens and pruned their vines when they grew too fast. For they wished to fill the wine-press of eloquence not with the tendrils of mere words but with the rich grape-juice of good sense. Your mother has done the same thing for you; you should, therefore, look up to her as a parent, love her as a tender nurse, and venerate her as a saint. You must not imitate those who leave their own relations and pay court to strange women. Their infamy is apparent to all, for what they aim at under the pretence of pure affection is simply illicit intercourse. I know some women of riper years, indeed a good many, who, finding pleasure in their young freedmen, make them their spiritual children and thus, pretending to be mothers to them, gradually overcome their own sense of shame and allow themselves in the licence of marriage. Other women desert their maiden sisters and unite themselves to strange widows. There are some who hate their parents and have no affection for their kin. Their state of mind is indicated by a restlessness which disdains excuses; they rend the veil of chastity and put it aside like a cobweb. Such are the ways of women; not, indeed, that men are any better. For there are persons to be seen who (for all their girded loins, sombre garb, and long beards) are inseparable from women, live under one roof with them, dine in their company, have young girls to wait upon them, and, save that they do not claim to be called husbands, are as good as married. Still it is no fault of Christianity that a hypocrite falls into sin; rather, it is the confusion of the Gentiles that the churches condemn what is condemned by all good men.

7. But if for your part you desire to be a monk and not merely to seem one, be more careful of your soul than of your property; for in adopting a religious profession you have renounced this once for all. Let your garments be squalid to shew that your mind is white; and your tunic coarse to prove that you despise the world. But give not way to pride lest your dress and language be found at variance. Baths stimulate the senses and must, therefore, be avoided; for to quench natural heat is the aim of chilling fasts. Yet even these must be moderate, for, if they are carried to excess, they weaken the stomach and by making more food necessary to it promote indigestion, that fruitful parent of unclean desires. A frugal and temperate diet is good for both body and soul.

See your mother as often as you please but not with other women, for their faces may dwell in your thoughts and so

A secret wound may fester in your breast.

The maidservants who attend upon her you must regard as so many snares laid to entrap you; for the lower their condition is the more easy is it for you to effect their ruin. John the Baptist had a religious mother and his father was a priest. Yet neither his mother's affection nor his father's wealth could induce him to live in his parents' house at the risk of his chastity. He lived in the desert, and seeking Christ with his eyes refused to look at anything else. His rough garb, his girdle made of skins, his diet of locusts and wild honey were all alike designed to encourage virtue and continence. The sons of the prophets, who were the monks of the Old Testament, built for themselves huts by the waters of Jordan and forsaking the crowded cities lived in these on pottage and wild herbs. As long as you are at home make your cell your paradise, gather there the varied fruits of scripture, let this be your favourite companion, and take its precepts to your heart. If your eye offend you or your foot or your hand, cast them from you. To spare your soul spare nothing else. The Lord says: "whosoever looketh on a woman to lust after her hath committed adultery with her already in his heart." "Who can say," writes the wise man, "I have made my heart clean?" The stars are not pure in the Lord's sight; how much less men whose whole life is one long temptation. Woe be to us who commit fornication every time that we cherish lust. "My sword," God says, "hath drunk its fill in heaven;" much more then upon the earth with its crop of thorns and thistles. The chosen vessel who had Christ's name ever on his lips kept under his body and brought it into subjection. Yet even he was hindered by carnal desire and had to do what he would not. As one suffering violence he cries: "O wretched man that I am! who shall deliver me from the body of this death?" Is it likely then that you can pass without fall or wound, unless you keep your heart with all diligence, and say with the Saviour: "my mother and my brethren are these which hear the word of God and do it." This may seem cruelty, but it is really affection. What greater proof, indeed, can there be of affection than to guard for a holy mother a holy son? She too desired your eternal welfare and is content to forego seeing you for a time that she may see you for ever with Christ. She is like Hannah who brought forth Samuel not for her own solace but for the service of the tabernacle.

The sons of Jonadab, we are told, drank neither wine nor strong drink and dwelt in tents pitched wherever night overtook them. According to the psalter they were the first to undergo captivity; for, when the Chaldaeans began to ravage Judah they were compelled to take refuge in cities.

8. Others may think what they like and follow each his own bent. But to me a town is a prison and solitude paradise. Why do we long for the bustle of cities, we whose very name speaks of loneliness? To fit him for the leadership of the Jewish people Moses was trained for forty years in the wilderness; and it was not till after these that the shepherd of sheep became a shepherd of men. The apostles were fishers on lake Gennesaret before they became "fishers of

men." But at the Lord's call they forsook all that they had, father, net, and ship, and bore their cross daily without so much as a rod in their hands.

I say these things that, in case you desire to enter the ranks of the clergy, you may learn what you must afterwards teach, that you may offer a reasonable sacrifice to Christ, that you may not think yourself a finished soldier while still a raw recruit, or suppose yourself a master while you are as yet only a learner. It does not become one of my humble abilities to pass judgment upon the clergy or to speak to the discredit of those who are ministers in the churches. They have their own rank and station and must keep it. If ever you become one of them my published letter to Nepotian will teach you the mode of life suitable to you in that vocation. At present I am dealing with the forming and training of a monk; of one too who has put the yoke of Christ upon his neck after receiving a liberal education in his younger days.

9. The first point to be considered is whether you ought to live by yourself or in a monastery with others. For my part I should like you to have the society of holy men so as not to be thrown altogether on your resources. For if you set out upon a road that is new to you without a guide, you are sure to turn aside immediately either to the right or to the left, to lay yourself open to the assaults of error, to go too far or else not far enough, to weary yourself with running too fast or to loiter by the way and to fall asleep. In loneliness pride quickly creeps upon a man: if he has fasted for a little while and has seen no one, he fancies himself a person of some note; forgetting who he is, whence he comes, and whither he goes, he lets his thoughts riot within and outwardly indulges in rash speech. Contrary to the apostle's wish he judges another man's servants, puts forth his hand to grasp whatever his appetite desires, sleeps as long he pleases, fears nobody, does what he likes, fancies everyone inferior to himself, spends more of his time in cities than in his cell, and, while with the brothers he affects to be retiring, rubs shoulders with the crowd in the streets. What then, you will say? Do I condemn a solitary life? By no means: in fact I have often commended it. But I wish to see the monastic schools turn out soldiers who have no fear of the rough training of the desert, who have exhibited the spectacle of a holy life for a considerable time, who have made themselves last that they might be first, who have not been overcome by hunger or satiety, whose joy is in poverty, who teach virtue by their garb and mien, and who are too conscientious to invent—as some silly men do—monstrous stories of struggles with demons, designed to magnify their heroes in the eyes of the crowd and before all to extort money from it.

10. Quite recently we have seen to our sorrow a fortune worthy of Croesus brought to light by a monk's death, and a city's alms, collected for the poor,

left by will to his sons and successors. After sinking to the bottom the iron has once more floated upon the surface, and men have again seen among the palm-trees the bitter waters of Marah. In this there is, however, nothing strange, for the man had for his companion and teacher one who turned the hunger of the needy into a source of wealth for himself and kept back sums left to the miserable to his own subsequent misery. Yet their cry came up to heaven and entering God's ears overcame His patience. Wherefore, He sent an angel of woe to say to this new Carmelite, this second Nabal, "Thou fool, this night thy soul shall be required of thee: then whose shall those things be which thou hast provided?"

11. If I wish you then not to live with your mother, it is for the reasons given above, and above all for the two following. If she offers you delicacies to eat, you will grieve her by refusing them; and if you take them, you will add fuel to the flame that already burns within you. Again in a house where there are so many girls you will see in the daytime sights that will tempt you at night. Never take your hand or your eyes off your book; learn the psalms word for word, pray without ceasing, be always on the alert, and let no vain thoughts lay hold upon you. Direct both body and mind to the Lord, overcome wrath by patience, love the knowledge of scripture, and you will no longer love the sins of the flesh. Do not let your mind become a prey to excitement, for if this effects a lodgment in your breast it will have dominion over you and will lead you into the great transgression. Always have some work on hand, that the devil may find you busy. If apostles who had the right to live of the Gospel laboured with their own hands that they might be chargeable to no man, and bestowed relief upon others whose carnal things they had a claim to reap as having sown unto them spiritual things; why do you not provide a supply to meet your needs? Make creels of reeds or weave baskets out of pliant osiers. Hoe your ground; mark out your garden into even plots; and when you have sown your cabbages or set your plants convey water to them in conduits; that you may see with your own eyes the lovely vision of the poet:

Art draws fresh water from the hilltop near
Till the stream plashing down among the rocks
Cools the parched meadows and allays their thirst.

Graft unfruitful stocks with buds and slips that you may shortly be rewarded for your toil by plucking sweet apples from them. Construct also hives for bees, for to these the proverbs of Solomon send you, and you may learn from the tiny creatures how to order a monastery and to discipline a kingdom. Twist lines too for catching fish, and copy books; that your hand may earn your food and your mind may be satisfied with reading. For "every one that is idle is a prey to vain desires." In Egypt the monasteries make it a rule to receive none who are not willing to work; for they regard labour as necessary not only for the support of the body but also for the salvation of the soul. Do not let your mind stray into harmful thoughts, or, like Jerusalem in her whoredoms, open its feet to every chance comer.

12. In my youth when the desert walled me in with its solitude I was still unable to endure the promptings of sin and the natural heat of my blood; and, although I tried by frequent fasts to break the force of both, my mind still surged with [evil] thoughts. To subdue its turbulence I betook myself to a brother who before his conversion had been a Jew and asked him to teach me Hebrew. Thus, after having familiarised myself with the pointedness of Quintilian, the fluency of Cicero, the seriousness of Fronto and the gentleness of Pliny, I began to learn my letters anew and to study to pronounce words both harsh and guttural. What labour I spent upon this task, what difficulties I went through, how often I despaired, how often I gave over and then in my eagerness to learn commenced again, can be attested both by myself the subject of this misery and by those who then lived with me. But I thank the Lord that from this seed of learning sown in bitterness I now cull sweet fruits.

13. I will recount also another thing that I saw in Egypt. There was in a community a young Greek the flame of whose desire neither continual fasting nor the severest labour could avail to quench. He was in great danger of falling, when the father of the monastery saved him by the following device. He gave orders to one of the older brothers to pursue him with objurgations and reproaches, and then after having thus wronged him to be beforehand with him in laying a complaint against him. When witnesses were called they spoke always on behalf of the aggressor. On hearing such falsehoods he used to weep that no one gave credit to the truth; the father alone used cleverly to put in a word for him that he might not be "swallowed up with overmuch sorrow." To make the story short, a year passed in this way and at the expiration of it the young man was asked concerning his former evil thoughts and whether they still troubled him. "Good gracious," he replied, "how can I find pleasure in fornication when I am not allowed so much as to live?" Had he been a solitary hermit, by whose aid could he have overcome the temptations that assailed him?

14. The world's philosophers drive out an old passion by instilling a new one; they hammer out one nail by hammering in another. It was on this principle that the seven princes of Persia acted towards king Ahasuerus, for they subdued his regret for queen Vashti by inducing him to love other maidens. But whereas they cured one fault by another fault and one sin by another

sin, we must overcome our faults by learning to love the opposite virtues. "Depart from evil," says the psalmist, "and do good; seek peace and pursue it." For if we do not hate evil we cannot love good. Nay more, we must do good if we are to depart from evil. We must seek peace if we are to avoid war. And it is not enough merely to seek it; when we have found it and when it flees before us we must pursue it with all our energies. For "it passeth all understanding;" it is the habitation of God. As the psalmist says, "in peace also is his habitation." The pursuing of peace is a fine metaphor and may be compared with the apostle's words, "pursuing hospitality." It is not enough, he means, for us to invite guests with our lips; we should be as eager to detain them as though they were robbers carrying off our savings.

15. No art is ever learned without a master. Even dumb animals and wild herds follow leaders of their own. Bees have princes, and cranes fly after one of their number in the shape of a Y. There is but one emperor and each province has but one judge. Rome was founded by two brothers, but, as it could not have two kings at once, was inaugurated by an act of fratricide. So too Esau and Jacob strove in Rebekah's womb. Each church has a single bishop, a single archpresbyter, a single archdeacon; and every ecclesiastical order is subjected to its own rulers. A ship has but one pilot, a house but one master, and the largest army moves at the command of one man. That I may not tire you by heaping up instances, my drift is simply this. Do not rely on your own discretion, but live in a monastery. For there, while you will be under the control of one father, you will have many companions; and these will teach you, one humility, another patience, a third silence, and a fourth meekness. You will do as others wish; you will eat what you are told to eat; you will wear what clothes are given you; you will perform the task allotted to you; you will obey one whom you do not like, you will come to bed tired out; you will go to sleep on your feet and you will be forced to rise before you have had sufficient rest. When your turn comes, you will recite the psalms, a task which requires not a well modulated voice but genuine emotion. The apostle says: "I will pray with the spirit and I will pray with the understanding also," and to the Ephesians, "make melody in your hearts to the Lord." For he had read the precept of the psalmist: "Sing ye praises with understanding." You will serve the brothers, you will wash the guests' feet; if you suffer wrong you will bear it in silence; the superior of the community you will fear as a master and love as a father. Whatever he may order you to do you will believe to be wholesome for you. You will not pass judgment upon those who are placed over you, for your duty will be to obey them and to do what you are told, according to the words spoken by Moses: "keep silence and hearken, O Israel." You will have so many tasks to

occupy you that you will have no time for [evil] thoughts; and while you pass from one thing to another and fresh work follows work done, you will only be able to think of what you have it in charge at the moment to do.

16. But I myself have seen monks of quite a different stamp from this, men whose renunciation of the world has consisted in a change of clothes and a verbal profession, while their real life and their former habits have remained unchanged. Their property has increased rather than diminished. They still have the same servants and keep the same table. Out of cheap glasses and common earthenware they swallow gold. With servants about them in swarms they claim for themselves the name of hermits. Others who though poor think themselves discerning, walk as solemnly as pageants through the streets and do nothing but snarl at every one whom they meet. Others shrug their shoulders and croak out what is best known to themselves. While they keep their eyes fixed upon the earth, they balance swelling words upon their tongues. Only a crier is wanted to persuade you that it is his excellency the prefect who is coming along. Some too there are who from the dampness of their cells and from the severity of their fasts, from their weariness of solitude and from excessive study have a singing in their ears day and night and turn melancholy mad so as to need the poultices of Hippocrates more than exhortations from me. Great numbers are unable to break free from the crafts and trades they have previously practised. They no longer call themselves dealers but they carry on the same traffic as before; seeking for themselves not "food and raiment" as the apostle directs, but money-profits and these greater than are looked for by men of the world. In former days the greed of sellers was kept within bounds by the action of the AEdiles or as the Greeks call them market-inspectors, and men could not then cheat with impunity. But now persons who profess religion are not ashamed to seek unjust profits and the good name of Christianity is more often a cloak for fraud than a victim to it. I am ashamed to say it, yet it must be said—we are at least bound to blush for our infamy—while in public we hold out our hands for alms we conceal gold beneath our rags; and to the amazement of every one after living as poor men we die rich and with our purses well-filled.

But you, since you will not be alone but one of a community, will have no temptation to act thus. Things at first compulsory will become habitual. You will set to work unbidden and will find pleasure in your toil. You will forget things which are behind and will reach forth to those which are before. You will think less of the evil that others do than of the good you ought to do.

17. Be not led by the multitude of those who sin, neither let the host of those who perish tempt you to say secretly: "What? must all be lost who live in

cities? Behold, they continue to enjoy their property, they serve churches, they frequent baths, they do not disdain cosmetics, and yet they are universally well-spoken of." To this kind of remark I have before replied and now shortly reply again that the object of this little work is not to discuss the clergy but to lay down rules for a monk. The clergy are holy men and their lives are always worthy of praise. Rouse yourself then and so live in your monastery that you may deserve to be a clergyman, that you may preserve your youth from defilement, that you may go to Christ's altar as a virgin out of her chamber. See that you are well-reported of without and that women are familiar with your reputation but not with your appearance. When you come to mature years, if, that is, you live so long, and when you have been chosen into the ranks of the clergy either by the people of the city or by its bishop, act in a way that befits a clergyman, and choose for your models the best of your brothers. For in every rank and condition of life the bad are mingled with the good.

18. Do not be carried away by some mad caprice and rush into authorship. Learn long and carefully what you propose to teach. Do not credit all that flatterers say to you, or, I should rather say, do not lend too ready an ear to those who mean to mock you. They will fawn upon you with fulsome praise and do their best to blind your judgment; yet if you suddenly look behind you, you will find that they are making gestures of derision with their hands, either a stork's neck or the flapping ears of a donkey or a thirsty dog's protruding tongue.

Never speak evil of anyone or suppose that you make yourself better by assailing the reputations of others. The charges we bring against them often come home to ourselves; we inveigh against faults which are as much ours as theirs; and so our eloquence ends by telling against ourselves. It is as though dumb persons were to criticize orators. When the grunter wished to speak he used to come forward at a snail's pace and to utter a word now and again with such long pauses between that he seemed less making a speech than gasping for breath. Then, when he had placed his table and arranged on it his pile of books, he used to knit his brow, to draw in his nostrils, to wrinkle his forehead and to snap his fingers, signs meant to engage the attention of his pupils. Then he would pour forth a torrent of nonsense and declaim so vehemently against every one that you would take him for a critic like Longinus or fancy him a second Cato the Censor passing judgment on Roman eloquence and excluding whom he pleased from the senate of the learned. As he had plenty of money he made himself still more popular by giving entertainments. Numbers of persons shared in his hospitality; and thus it was not surprising that when he went out he was surrounded always by a buzzing throng. At home he was a monster like

Nero, abroad a paragon like Cato. Made up of different and opposing natures, as a whole he baffled description. You would say that he was formed of jarring elements like that unnatural and unheard of monster of which the poet tells us that it was in front a lion, behind a dragon, in the middle the goat whose name it bears.'

19. Men such as these you must never look at or associate with. Nor must you turn aside your heart unto words of evil lest the psalmist say to you: "Thou sittest and speakest against thy brother; thou slanderest thine own mother's son," and lest you become as "the sons of men whose teeth are spears and arrows," and as the man whose "words were softer than oil yet were they drawn swords." The Preacher expresses this more clearly still when he says: "Surely the serpent will bite where there is no enchantment, and the slanderer is no better." But you will say, I am not given to detraction, but how can I check others who are?' If we put forward such a plea as this it can only be that we may "practise wicked works with men that work iniquity." Yet Christ is not deceived by this device. It is not I but an apostle who says: "Be not deceived; God is not mocked." "Man looketh upon the outward appearance but the Lord looketh upon the heart." And in the proverbs Solomon tells us that as "the north wind driveth away rain, so doth an angry countenance a backbiting tongue." It sometimes happens that an arrow when it is aimed at a hard object rebounds upon the bowman, wounding the would-be wounder, and thus, the words are fulfilled, "they were turned aside like a deceitful bow," and in another passage: "whoso casteth a stone on high casteth it on his own head." So when a slanderer sees anger in the countenance of his hearer who will not hear him but stops his ears that he may not hear of blood, he becomes silent on the moment, his face turns pale, his lips stick fast, his mouth becomes parched. Wherefore the same wise man says: "meddle not with them that are given to detraction: for their calamity shall rise suddenly; and who knoweth the ruin of them both?" of him who speaks, that is, and of him who hears. Truth does not love corners or seek whisperers. To Timothy it is said, "Against an elder receive not an accusation suddenly; but him that sinneth rebuke before all, that others also may fear." When a man is advanced in years you must not be too ready to believe evil of him; his past life is itself a defence, and so also is his rank as an elder. Still, since we are but human and sometimes in spite of the ripeness of our years fall into the sins of youth, if I do wrong and you wish to correct me, accuse me openly of my fault: do not backbite me secretly. "Let the righteous smite me, it shall be a kindness, and let him reprove me; but let not the oil of the sinner enrich my head." For what says the apostle? "Whom the Lord loveth, he chasteneth, and scourgeth every son whom he receiveth." By the

mouth of Isaiah the Lord speaks thus: "O my people, they who call you happy cause you to err and destroy the way of your paths." How do you help me by telling my misdeeds to others? You may, without my knowing of it, wound some one else by the narration of my sins or rather of those which you slanderously attribute to me; and while you are eager to spread the news in all quarters, you may pretend to confide in each individual as though you had spoken to no one else. Such a course has for its object not my correction but the indulgence of your own failing. The Lord gives commandment that those who sin against us are to be arraigned privately or else in the presence of a witness, and that if they refuse to hear reason, the matter is to be laid before the church, and those who persist in their wickedness are to be regarded as heathen men and publicans.

20. I lay great emphasis on these points that I may deliver a young man who is dear to me from the itching both of the tongue and of the ears: that, since he has been born again in Christ, I may present him without spot or wrinkle as a chaste virgin, chaste in mind as well as in body; that the virginity of which he boasts may be more than nominal and that he may not be shut out by the bridegroom because being unprovided with the oil of good works his lamp has gone out. In Proculus you have a reverend and most learned prelate, able by the sound of his voice to do more for you than I with my written sheets and sure to direct you on your path by daily homilies. He will not suffer you to turn to the right hand or to the left or to leave the king's highway; for to this Israel pledges itself to keep in its hasty passage to the land of promise. May God hear the voice of the church's supplication. "Lord, ordain peace for us, for thou hast also wrought all our works for us." May our renunciation of the world be made freely and not under compulsion! May we seek poverty gladly to win its glory and not suffer anguish because others lay it upon us! For the rest amid our present miseries with the sword making havoc around us, he is rich enough who has bread sufficient for his need, and he is abundantly powerful who is not reduced to be a slave. Exuperius the reverend bishop of Toulouse, imitating the widow of Zarephath, feeds others though hungry himself. His face is pale with fasting, yet it is the cravings of others that torment him most. In fact he has bestowed his whole substance to meet the needs of Christ's poor. Yet none is richer than he, for his wicker basket contains the body of the Lord, and his plain glass-cup the precious blood. Like his Master he has banished greed out of the temple; and without either scourge of cords or words of chiding he has overthrown the chairs of them that sell doves, that is, the gifts of the Holy Spirit. He has upset the tables of Mammon and has scattered the money of the money-changers; zealous that the house of God may be called a

house of prayer and not a den of robbers. In his steps follow closely and in those of others like him in virtue, whom the priesthood makes poor men and more than ever humble. Or if you will be perfect, go out with Abraham from your country and from your kindred, and go whither you know not. If you have substance, sell it and give to the poor. If you have none, then are you free from a great burthen. Destitute yourself, follow a destitute Christ. The task is a hard one, it is great and difficult; but the reward is also great.

LETTER CXXVI. TO MARCELLINUS AND ANAPSYCHIA

Marcellinus, a Roman official of high rank, and Anapsychia his wife had written to Jerome from Africa to ask him his opinion on the vexed question of the origin of the soul. Jerome in his reply briefly enumerates the several views that have been held on the subject. For fuller information he refers his questioners to his treatise against Rufinus and also to their bishop Augustin who will, he says, explain the matter to them by word of mouth. Although it hardly appears in this letter Jerome is a decided creationist (see his Comm. on Eccles. xii. 7). But, though he vehemently condemns Rufinus (Ap. ii. 10) for professing ignorance on the subject, he assents (Letter CXXXIV.) to Augustin (Letter CXXXI.) who similarly professes ignorance but seems to lean to traducianism. The date of writing is a.d. 412.

To his truly holy lord and lady, his children worthy of the highest respect and affection, Marcellinus and Anapsychia, Jerome sends greeting.

1. I have at last received from Africa your joint letter and no longer regret the effrontery which led me, in spite of your silence to ply you both with so many missives. I hoped, indeed, by so doing to gain a reply and to learn of your welfare not indirectly from others but directly from yourselves. I well remember your little problem about the nature of the soul; although I ought not to call it little, seeing that it is one of the greatest with which the church has to deal. You ask whether it has fallen from heaven, as Pythagoras, all Platonists, and Origen suppose; or whether it is part of God's essence as the Stoics, Manes, and the Spanish Priscillianists hint. Whether souls created long since are kept in God's storehouse as some ecclesiastical writers foolishly imagine; or whether they are formed by God and introduced into bodies day by day according to that saying in the Gospel: "my Father worketh hitherto and I work;" or whether, lastly, they are transmitted by propagation. This is the view of Tertullian, Apollinaris, and most western writers who hold that soul is derived from soul as body is from body and that the conditions of life

are the same for men and brutes. I have given my opinion on the matter in my reply to the treatise which Rufinus presented to Anastasius, bishop of Rome, of holy memory. He strives in this by an evasive and crafty but sufficiently foolish confession to play with the simplicity of his hearers, but only succeeds in playing with his own faith or rather want of it. My book, which has been published a good while, contains an answer to the calumnies which in his various writings Rufinus has directed against me. Your reverend father Oceanus has, I think, a copy of it. But if you cannot procure it your bishop Augustine is both learned and holy. He will teach you by word of mouth and will give you his opinion, or rather mine, in his own words.

2. I have long wished to attack the prophecies of Ezekiel and to make good the promises which I have so often given to curious readers. When, however, I began to dictate I was so confounded by the havoc wrought in the West and above all by the sack of Rome that, as the common saying has it, I forgot even my own name. Long did I remain silent knowing that it was a time to weep. This year I began again and had written three books of commentary when a sudden incursion of those barbarians of whom your Virgil speaks as the "far-wandering men of Barce" (and to whom may be applied what holy scripture says of Ishmael: "he shall dwell over against all his brethren") overran the borders of Egypt, Palestine, Phenicia, and Syria, and like a raging torrent carried everything before them. It was with difficulty and only through Christ's mercy that we were able to escape from their hands. But if, as the great orator says, "amid the clash of arms law ceases to be heard;" how much more truly may it be said that war puts an end to the study of holy scripture. For this requires plenty of books and silence and careful copyists and above all freedom from alarm and a sense of security. I have accordingly only been able to complete two books and these I have sent to my daughter, Fabiola, from whom you can if you like borrow them. For want of time I have not been able as yet to transcribe the rest. But when you have read these you will have seen the ante-chamber and will easily form from this a notion of the whole edifice. I trust in God's mercy and believe that, as he has helped me in the difficult opening chapters of the prophecy, so he will help me in the chapters towards the close. These describe the wars of Gog and Magog, and set forth the mode of building, the plan, and the dimensions of the holy and mysterious temple.

3. Our reverend brother Oceanus to whom you desire an introduction is a great and good man and so learned in the law of the Lord that no words of mine are needed to make him able and willing to instruct you both and to explain to you in conformity with the rules which govern our common studies, my opinion and his on all questions arising out of the scriptures. In conclu-

sion, my truly holy lord and lady, may Christ our God by his almighty power have you in his safekeeping and cause you to live long and happily.

LETTER CXXVII. TO PRINCIPIA

This letter is really a memoir of Marcella (for whom see note on Letter XXIII.) addressed to her greatest friend. After describing her history, character, and favourite studies, Jerome goes on to recount her eminent services in the cause of orthodoxy at a time when, through the efforts of Rufinus, it seemed likely that Origenism would prevail at Rome (S:S:9, 10). He briefly relates the fall of the city and the horrors consequent upon it (S:S:12, 13) which appear to have been the immediate cause of Marcella's death (S:14). The date of the letter is 412 a.d.

1. You have besought me often and earnestly, Principia, virgin of Christ, to dedicate a letter to the memory of that holy woman Marcella, and to set forth the goodness long enjoyed by us for others to know and to imitate. I am so anxious myself to do justice to her merits that it grieves me that you should spur me on and fancy that your entreaties are needed when I do not yield even to you in love of her. In putting upon record her signal virtues I shall receive far more benefit myself than I can possibly confer upon others. If I have hitherto remained silent and have allowed two years to go over without making any sign, this has not been owing to a wish to ignore her as you wrongly suppose, but to an incredible sorrow which so overcame my mind that I judged it better to remain silent for a while than to praise her virtues in inadequate language. Neither will I now follow the rules of rhetoric in eulogizing one so dear to both of us and to all the saints, Marcella the glory of her native Rome. I will not set forth her illustrious family and lofty lineage, nor will I trace her pedigree through a line of consuls and praetorian prefects. I will praise her for nothing but the virtue which is her own and which is the more noble, because forsaking both wealth and rank she has sought the true nobility of poverty and lowliness.

2. Her father's death left her an orphan, and she had been married less than seven months when her husband was taken from her. Then as she was young, and highborn, as well as distinguished for her beauty—always an attraction to men—and her self-control, an illustrious consular named Cerealis paid court to her with great assiduity. Being an old man he offered to make over to her his fortune so that she might consider herself less his wife than his daughter. Her mother Albina went out of her way to secure for the young widow so

exalted a protector. But Marcella answered: "had I a wish to marry and not rather to dedicate myself to perpetual chastity, I should look for a husband and not for an inheritance;" and when her suitor argued that sometimes old men live long while young men die early, she cleverly retorted: "a young man may indeed die early, but an old man cannot live long." This decided rejection of Cerealis convinced others that they had no hope of winning her hand.

In the gospel according to Luke we read the following passage: "there was one Anna, a prophetess, the daughter of Phanuel, of the tribe of Aser: she was of great age, and had lived with an husband seven years from her virginity; and she was a widow of about fourscore and four years, which departed not from the temple but served God with fastings and prayers night and day." It was no marvel that she won the vision of the Saviour, whom she sought so earnestly. Let us then compare her case with that of Marcella and we shall see that the latter has every way the advantage. Anna lived with her husband seven years; Marcella seven months. Anna only hoped for Christ; Marcella held Him fast. Anna confessed him at His birth; Marcella believed in Him crucified. Anna did not deny the Child; Marcella rejoiced in the Man as king. I do not wish to draw distinctions between holy women on the score of their merits, as some persons have made it a custom to do as regards holy men and leaders of churches; the conclusion at which I aim is that, as both have one task, so both have one reward.

3. In a slander-loving community such as Rome, filled as it formerly was with people from all parts and bearing the palm for wickedness of all kinds, detraction assailed the upright and strove to defile even the pure and the clean. In such an atmosphere it is hard to escape from the breath of calumny. A stainless reputation is difficult nay almost impossible to attain; the prophet yearns for it but hardly hopes to win it: "Blessed," he says, "are the undefiled in the way who walk in the law of the Lord." The undefiled in the way of this world are those whose fair fame no breath of scandal has ever sullied, and who have earned no reproach at the hands of their neighbours. It is this which makes the Saviour say in the gospel: "agree with," or be complaisant to, "thine adversary whilst thou art in the way with him." Who ever heard a slander of Marcella that deserved the least credit? Or who ever credited such without making himself guilty of malice and defamation? No; she put the Gentiles to confusion by shewing them the nature of that Christian widowhood which her conscience and mien alike set forth. For women of the world are wont to paint their faces with rouge and white-lead, to wear robes of shining silk, to adorn themselves with jewels, to put gold chains round their necks, to pierce their ears and hang in them the costliest pearls of the Red Sea, and to scent them-

selves with musk. While they mourn for the husbands they have lost they rejoice at their own deliverance and freedom to choose fresh partners—not, as God wills, to obey these but to rule over them.

With this object in view they select for their partners poor men who contented with the mere name of husbands are the more ready to put up with rivals as they know that, if they so much as murmur, they will be cast off at once. Our widow's clothing was meant to keep out the cold and not to shew her figure. Of gold she would not wear so much as a seal-ring, choosing to store her money in the stomachs of the poor rather than to keep it at her own disposal. She went nowhere without her mother, and would never see without witnesses such monks and clergy as the needs of a large house required her to interview. Her train was always composed of virgins and widows, and these women serious and staid; for, as she well knew, the levity of the maids speaks ill for the mistress and a woman's character is shewn by her choice of companions.

4. Her delight in the divine scriptures was incredible. She was for ever singing, "Thy words have I hid in mine heart that I might not sin against thee," as well as the words which describe the perfect man, "his delight is in the law of the Lord; and in his law doth he meditate day and night." This meditation in the law she understood not of a review of the written words as among the Jews the Pharisees think, but of action according to that saying of the apostle, "whether, therefore, ye eat or drink or what soever ye do, do all to the glory of God." She remembered also the prophet's words, "through thy precepts I get understanding," and felt sure that only when she had fulfilled these would she be permitted to understand the scriptures. In this sense we read elsewhere that "Jesus began both to do and teach." For teaching is put to the blush when a man's conscience rebukes him; and it is in vain that his tongue preaches poverty or teaches alms-giving if he is rolling in the riches of Croesus and if, in spite of his threadbare cloak, he has silken robes at home to save from the moth.

Marcella practised fasting, but in moderation. She abstained from eating flesh, and she knew rather the scent of wine than its taste; touching it only for her stomach's sake and for her often infirmities. She seldom appeared in public and took care to avoid the houses of great ladies, that she might not be forced to look upon what she had once for all renounced. She frequented the basilicas of apostles and martyrs that she might escape from the throng and give herself to private prayer. So obedient was she to her mother that for her sake she did things of which she herself disapproved. For example, when her mother, careless of her own offspring, was for transferring all her property from her children and grandchildren to her brother's family, Marcella wished the money to be given to the poor instead, and yet could not bring herself to thwart her parent. Therefore she made over her ornaments and other effects to persons already rich, content to throw away her money rather than to sadden her mother's heart.

5. In those days no highborn lady at Rome had made profession of the monastic life, or had ventured—so strange and ignominious and degrading did it then seem—publicly to call herself a nun. It was from some priests of Alexandria, and from pope Athanasius, and subsequently from Peter, who, to escape the persecution of the Arian heretics, had all fled for refuge to Rome as the safest haven in which they could find communion—it was from these that Marcella heard of the life of the blessed Antony, then still alive, and of the monasteries in the Thebaid founded by Pachomius, and of the discipline laid down for virgins and for widows. Nor was she ashamed to profess a life which she had thus learned to be pleasing to Christ. Many years after her example was followed first by Sophronia and then by others, of whom it may be well said in the words of Ennius:

Would that ne'er in Pelion's woods
Had the axe these pinetrees felled.

My revered friend Paula was blessed with Marcella's friendship, and it was in Marcella's cell that Eustochium, that paragon of virgins, was gradually trained. Thus it is easy to see of what type the mistress was who found such pupils.

The unbelieving reader may perhaps laugh at me for dwelling so long on the praises of mere women; yet if he will but remember how holy women followed our Lord and Saviour and ministered to Him of their substance, and how the three Marys stood before the cross and especially how Mary Magdalen—called the tower from the earnestness and glow of her faith—was privileged to see the rising Christ first of all before the very apostles, he will convict himself of pride sooner than me of folly. For we judge of people's virtue not by their sex but by their character, and hold those to be worthy of the highest glory who have renounced both rank and wealth. It was for this reason that Jesus loved the evangelist John more than the other disciples. For John was of noble birth and known to the high priest, yet was so little appalled by the plottings of the Jews that he introduced Peter into his court, and was the only one of the apostles bold enough to take his stand before the cross. For it was he who took the Saviour's parent to his own home; it was the virgin son who received the virgin mother as a legacy from the Lord.

6. Marcella then lived the ascetic life for many years, and found herself old before she bethought herself that she had once been young. She often quoted with approval Plato's saying that philosophy consists in meditating on death. A truth which our own apostle indorses when he says: "for your salvation I die daily." Indeed according to the old copies our Lord himself says: "whosoever doth not bear His cross daily and come after me cannot be my disciple." Ages before, the Holy Spirit had said by the prophet: "for thy sake are we killed all the day long: we are counted as sheep for the slaughter." Many generations afterwards the words were spoken: "remember the end and thou shalt never do amiss," as well as that precept of the eloquent satirist: "live with death in your mind; time flies; this say of mine is so much taken from it." Well then, as I was saying, she passed her days and lived always in the thought that she must die. Her very clothing was such as to remind her of the tomb, and she presented herself as a living sacrifice, reasonable and acceptable, unto God.

7. When the needs of the Church at length brought me to Rome in company with the reverend pontiffs, Paulinus and Epiphanius—the first of whom ruled the church of the Syrian Antioch while the second presided over that of Salamis in Cyprus,—I in my modesty was for avoiding the eyes of highborn ladies, yet she pleaded so earnestly, "both in season and out of season" as the apostle says, that at last her perseverance overcame my reluctance. And, as in those days my name was held in some renown as that of a student of the scriptures, she never came to see me that she did not ask me some question concerning them, nor would she at once acquiesce in my explanations but on the contrary would dispute them; not, however, for argument's sake but to learn the answers to those objections which might, as she saw, be made to my statements. How much virtue and ability, how much holiness and purity I found in her I am afraid to say; both lest I may exceed the bounds of men's belief and lest I may increase your sorrow by reminding you of the blessings that you have lost. This much only will I say, that whatever in me was the fruit of long study and as such made by constant meditation a part of my nature, this she tasted, this she learned and made her own. Consequently after my departure from Rome, in case of a dispute arising as to the testimony of scripture on any subject, recourse was had to her to settle it. And so wise was she and so well did she understand what philosophers call to prepon, that is, the becoming, in what she did, that when she answered questions she gave her own opinion not as her own but as from me or some one else, thus admitting that what she taught she had herself learned from others. For she knew that the apostle had said: "I suffer not a woman to teach," and she would not seem to

inflict a wrong upon the male sex many of whom (including sometimes priests) questioned her concerning obscure and doubtful points.

8. I am told that my place with her was immediately taken by you, that you attached yourself to her, and that, as the saying goes, you never let even a hair's-breadth come between her and you. You both lived in the same house and occupied the same room so that every one in the city knew for certain that you had found a mother in her and she a daughter in you. In the suburbs you found for yourselves a monastic seclusion, and chose the country instead of the town because of its loneliness. For a long time you lived together, and as many ladies shaped their conduct by your examples, I had the joy of seeing Rome transformed into another Jerusalem. Monastic establishments for virgins became numerous, and of hermits there were countless numbers. In fact so many were the servants of God that monasticism which had before been a term of reproach became subsequently one of honour. Meantime we consoled each other for our separation by words of mutual encouragement, and discharged in the spirit the debt which in the flesh we could not pay. We always went to meet each other's letters, tried to outdo each other in attentions, and anticipated each other in courteous inquiries. Not much was lost by a separation thus effectually bridged by a constant correspondence.

9. While Marcella was thus serving the Lord in holy tranquillity, there arose in these provinces a tornado of heresy which threw everything into confusion; indeed so great was the fury into which it lashed itself that it spared neither itself nor anything that was good. And as if it were too little to have disturbed everything here, it introduced a ship freighted with blasphemies into the port of Rome itself. The dish soon found itself a cover; and the muddy feet of heretics fouled the clear waters of the faith of Rome. No wonder that in the streets and in the market places a soothsayer can strike fools on the back or, catching up his cudgel, shatter the teeth of such as carp at him; when such venomous and filthy teaching as this has found at Rome dupes whom it can lead astray. Next came the scandalous version of Origen's book On First Principles, and that fortunate' disciple who would have been indeed fortunate had he never fallen in with such a master. Next followed the confutation set forth by my supporters, which destroyed the case of the Pharisees and threw them into confusion. It was then that the holy Marcella, who had long held back lest she should be thought to act from party motives, threw herself into the breach. Conscious that the faith of Rome—once praised by an apostle—was now in danger, and that this new heresy was drawing to itself not only priests and monks but also many of the laity besides imposing on the bishop

who fancied others as guileless as he was himself, she publicly withstood its teachers choosing to please God rather than men.

10. In the gospel the Saviour commends the unjust steward because, although he defrauded his master, he acted wisely for his own interests. The heretics in this instance pursued the same course; for, seeing how great a matter a little fire had kindled, and that the flames applied by them to the foundations had by this time reached the housetops, and that the deception practised on many could no longer be hid, they asked for and obtained letters of commendation from the church, so that it might appear that till the day of their departure they had continued in full communion with it. Shortly afterwards the distinguished Anastasius succeeded to the pontificate; but he was soon taken away, for it was not fitting that the head of the world should be struck off during the episcopate of one so great. He was removed, no doubt, that he might not seek to turn away by his prayers the sentence of God passed once for all. For the words of the Lord to Jeremiah concerning Israel applied equally to Rome: "pray not for this people for their good. When they fast I will not hear their cry; and when they offer burnt-offering and oblation, I will not accept them; but I will consume them by the sword and by the famine and by the pestilence." You will say, what has this to do with the praises of Marcella? I reply, She it was who originated the condemnation of the heretics. She it was who furnished witnesses first taught by them and then carried away by their heretical teaching. She it was who showed how large a number they had deceived and who brought up against them the impious books On First Principles, books which were passing from hand to hand after being improved' by the hand of the scorpion. She it was lastly who called on the heretics in letter after letter to appear in their own defence. They did not indeed venture to come, for they were so conscience-stricken that they let the case go against them by default rather than face their accusers and be convicted by them. This glorious victory originated with Marcella, she was the source and cause of this great blessing. You who shared the honour with her know that I speak the truth. You know too that out of many incidents I only mention a few, not to tire out the reader by a wearisome recapitulation. Were I to say more, ill natured persons might fancy me, under pretext of commending a woman's virtues, to be giving vent to my own rancour. I will pass now to the remainder of my story.

11. The whirlwind passed from the West into the East and threatened in its passage to shipwreck many a noble craft. Then were the words of Jesus fulfilled: "when the son of man cometh, shall he find faith on the earth?" The love of many waxed cold. Yet the few who still loved the true faith rallied to

my side. Men openly sought to take their lives and every expedient was employed against them. So hotly indeed did the persecution rage that "Barnabas also was carried away with their dissimulation;" nay more he committed murder, if not in actual violence at least in will. Then behold God blew and the tempest passed away; so that the prediction of the prophet was fulfilled, "thou takest away their breath, they die, and return to their dust. In that very day his thoughts perish," as also the gospel-saying, "Thou fool, this night thy soul shall be required of thee: then whose shall those things be, which thou hast provided?"

12. Whilst these things were happening in Jebus a dreadful rumour came from the West. Rome had been besieged and its citizens had been forced to buy their lives with gold. Then thus despoiled they had been besieged again so as to lose not their substance only but their lives. My voice sticks in my throat; and, as I dictate, sobs choke my utterance. The City which had taken the whole world was itself taken; nay more famine was beforehand with the sword and but few citizens were left to be made captives. In their frenzy the starving people had recourse to hideous food; and tore each other limb from limb that they might have flesh to eat. Even the mother did not spare the babe at her breast. In the night was Moab taken, in the night did her wall fall down. "O God, the heathen have come into thine inheritance; thy holy temple have they defiled; they have made Jerusalem an orchard. The dead bodies of thy servants have they given to be meat unto the fowls of the heaven, the flesh of thy saints unto the beasts of the earth. Their blood have they shed like water round about Jerusalem; and there was none to bury them."

Who can set forth the carnage of that night?
What tears are equal to its agony?
Of ancient date a sovran city falls;
And lifeless in its streets and houses lie
Unnumbered bodies of its citizens.
In many a ghastly shape doth death appear.

13. Meantime, as was natural in a scene of such confusion, one of the bloodstained victors found his way into Marcella's house. Now be it mine to say what I have heard, to relate what holy men have seen; for there were some such present and they say that you too were with her in the hour of danger. When the soldiers entered she is said to have received them without any look of alarm; and when they asked her for gold she pointed to her coarse dress to shew them that she had no buried treasure. However they would not believe in her self-chosen poverty, but scourged her and beat her with cudgels. She is said to have felt no pain but to have thrown herself at their feet and to have pleaded

with tears for you, that you might not be taken from her, or owing to your youth have to endure what she as an old woman had no occasion to fear. Christ softened their hard hearts and even among bloodstained swords natural affection asserted its rights. The barbarians conveyed both you and her to the basilica of the apostle Paul, that you might find there either a place of safety or, if not that, at least a tomb. Hereupon Marcella is said to have burst into great joy and to have thanked God for having kept you unharmed in answer to her prayer. She said she was thankful too that the taking of the city had found her poor, not made her so, that she was now in want of daily bread, that Christ satisfied her needs so that she no longer felt hunger, that she was able to say in word and in deed: "naked came I out of my mother's womb, and naked shall I return thither: the Lord gave and the Lord hath taken away; blessed be the name of the Lord."

14. After a few days she fell asleep in the Lord; but to the last her powers remained unimpaired. You she made the heir of her poverty, or rather the poor through you. When she closed her eyes, it was in your arms; when she breathed her last breath, your lips received it; you shed tears but she smiled conscious of having led a good life and hoping for her reward hereafter.

In one short night I have dictated this letter in honour of you, revered Marcella, and of you, my daughter Principia; not to shew off my own eloquence but to express my heartfelt gratitude to you both; my one desire has been to please both God and my readers.

LETTER CXXVIII. TO GAUDENTIUS

Gaudentius had written from Rome to ask Jerome's advice as to the bringing up of his infant daughter; whom after the religious fashion of the day he had dedicated to a life of virginity. Jerome's reply may be compared with his advice to Laeta (Letter CVII.) which it closely resembles. It is noticeable also for the vivid account which it gives of the sack of Rome by Alaric in a.d. 410. The date of the letter is a.d. 413.

1. It is hard to write to a little girl who cannot understand what you say, of whose mind you know nothing, and of whose inclinations it would be rash to prophesy. In the words of a famous orator "she is to be praised more for what she will be than for what she is." For how can you speak of self-control to a child who is eager for cakes, who babbles on her mother's knee, and to whom honey is sweeter than any words? Will she hear the deep things of the apostle when all her delight is in nursery tales? Will she heed the dark sayings of the

prophets when her nurse can frighten her by a frowning face? Or will she comprehend the majesty of the gospel, when its splendour dazzles the keenest intellect? Shall I urge her to obey her parents when with her chubby hand she beats her smiling mother? For such reasons as these my dear Pacatula must read some other time the letter that I send her now. Meanwhile let her learn the alphabet, spelling, grammar, and syntax. To induce her to repeat her lessons with her little shrill voice, hold out to her as rewards cakes and mead and sweetmeats. She will make haste to perform her task if she hopes afterwards to get some bright bunch of flowers, some glittering bauble, some enchanting doll. She must also learn to spin, shaping the yarn with her tender thumb; for, even if she constantly breaks the threads, a day will come when she will no longer break them. Then when she has finished her lessons she ought to have some recreation. At such times she may hang round her mother's neck, or snatch kisses from her relations. Reward her for singing psalms that she may love what she has to learn. Her task will then become a pleasure to her and no compulsion will be necessary.

2. Some mothers when they have vowed a daughter to virginity clothe her in sombre garments, wrap her up in a dark cloak, and let her have neither linen nor gold ornaments. They wisely refuse to accustom her to what she will afterwards have to lay aside. Others act on the opposite principle. "What is the use," say they, "of keeping such things from her? Will she not see them with others? Women are fond of finery and many whose chastity is beyond question dress not for men but for themselves. Give her what she asks for, but shew her that those are most praised who ask for nothing. It is better that she should enjoy things to the full and so learn to despise them than that from not having them she should wish to have them." "This," they continue, "was the plan which the Lord adopted with the children of Israel. When they longed for the fleshpots of Egypt He sent them flights of quails and allowed them to gorge themselves until they were sick. Those who have once lived worldly lives more readily forego the pleasures of sense than such as from their youth up have known nothing of desire." For while the former—so they argue—trample on what they know, the latter are attracted by what is to them unknown. While the former penitently shun the insidious advances which pleasure makes, the latter coquet with the allurements of sense and fancying them to be as sweet as honey find them to be deadly poison. They quote the passage which says that "the lips of a strange woman drop as an honeycomb;" which is sweet indeed in the eater's mouth but is afterwards found more bitter than gall. This they argue, is the reason that neither honey nor wax is offered in the sacrifices of the Lord, and that oil the product of the bitter olive is burned in His temple.

Moreover it is with bitter herbs that the passover is eaten, and "with the unleavened bread of sincerity and truth." He that receives these shall suffer persecution in the world. Wherefore the prophet symbolically sings: "I sat alone because I was filled with bitterness."

3. What then, I reply? Is youth to run riot that self-indulgence may afterwards be more resolutely rejected? Far from it, they rejoin: "let every man, wherein he is called, therein abide. Is any called being circumcised,"—that is, as a virgin?—"let him not become uncircumcised"—that is, let him not seek the coat of marriage given to Adam on his expulsion from the paradise of virginity. "Is any called in uncircumcision,"—that is, having a wife and enveloped in the skin of matrimony? let him not seek the nakedness of virginity and of that eternal chastity which he has lost once for all. No, let him "possess his vessel in sanctification and honour," let him drink of his own wells not out of the dissolute cisterns of the harlots which cannot hold within them the pure waters of chastity. The same Paul also in the same chapter, when discussing the subjects of virginity and marriage, calls those who are married slaves of the flesh, but those not under the yoke of wedlock freemen who serve the Lord in all freedom.

What I say I do not say as universally applicable; my treatment of the subject is only partial. I speak of some only, not of all. However my words are addressed to those of both sexes, and not only to "the weaker vessel." Are you a virgin? Why then do you find pleasure in the society of a woman? Why do you commit to the high seas your frail patched boat, why do you so confidently face the great peril of a dangerous voyage? You know not what you desire, and yet you cling to her as though you had either desired her before or, to put it as leniently as possible, as though you would hereafter desire her. Women, you will say, make better servants than men. In that case choose a misshapen old woman, choose one whose continence is approved in the Lord. Why should you find pleasure in a young girl, pretty, and voluptuous? You frequent the baths, walk abroad sleek and ruddy, eat flesh, abound in riches, and wear the most expensive clothes; and yet you fancy that you can sleep safely beside a death-dealing serpent. You tell me perhaps that you do not live in the same house with her. This is only true at night. But you spend whole days in conversing with her. Why do you sit alone with her? Why do you dispense with witnesses? By so doing if you do not actually sin you appear to do so, and (so important is your influence) you embolden unhappy men by your example to do what is wrong. You too, whether virgin or widow, why do you allow a man to detain you in conversation so long? Why are you not afraid to be left alone with him? At least go out of doors to satisfy the wants of nature, and for this at any rate leave the man with whom you have given yourself more liberty than you would with your brother, and have behaved more immodestly than you would with your husband. You have some question, you say, to ask concerning the holy scriptures. If so, ask it publicly; let your maids and your attendants hear it. "Everything that is made manifest is light." He who says only what he ought does not look for a corner to say it in; he is glad to have hearers for he likes to be praised. He must be a fine teacher, on the other hand, who thinks little of men, does not care for the brothers, and labours in secret merely to instruct just one weak woman!

3a. I have wandered for a little from my immediate subject to discuss the procedure of others in such a case as yours; and while it is my object to train, nay rather to nurse, the infant Pacatula, I have in a moment drawn upon myself the hostility of many women who are by no means daughters of peace. But I shall now return to my proper theme.

A girl should associate only with girls, she should know nothing of boys and should dread even playing with them. She should never hear an unclean word, and if amid the bustle of the household she should chance to hear one, she should not understand it. Her mother's nod should be to her as much a command as a spoken injunction. She should love her as her parent, obey her as her mistress, and reverence her as her teacher. She is now a child without teeth and without ideas, but, as soon as she is seven years old, a blushing girl knowing what she ought not to say and hesitating as to what she ought, she should until she is grown up commit to memory the psalter and the books of Solomon; the gospels, the apostles and the prophets should be the treasure of her heart. She should not appear in public too freely or too frequently attend crowded churches. All her pleasure should be in her chamber. She must never look at young men or turn her eyes upon curled fops; and the wanton songs of sweet voiced girls which wound the soul through the ears must be kept from her. The more freedom of access such persons possess, the harder is it to avoid them when they come; and what they have once learned themselves they will secretly teach her and will thus contaminate our secluded Danae by the talk of the crowd. Give her for guardian and companion a mistress and a governess, one not given to much wine or in the apostle's words idle and a tattler, but sober, grave, industrious in spinning wool and one whose words will form her childish mind to the practice of virtue. For, as water follows a finger drawn through the sand, so one of soft and tender years is pliable for good or evil; she can be drawn in whatever direction you choose to guide her. Moreover spruce and gay young men often seek access for themselves by paying court to nurses or dependants or even by bribing them, and when they have thus gently effected their approach they blow up the first spark of passion until it bursts into flame and little by little advance to the most shameless requests. And it is quite impossible to check them then, for the verse is proved true in their case: "It is ill rebuking what you have once allowed to become ingrained." I am ashamed to say it and yet I must; high born ladies who have rejected more high born suitors cohabit with men of the lowest grade and even with slaves. Sometimes in the name of religion and under the cloak of a desire for celibacy they actually desert their husbands in favour of such paramours. You may often see a Helen following her Paris without the smallest dread of Menelaus. Such persons we see and mourn for but we cannot punish, for the multitude of sinners procures tolerance for the sin.

4. The world sinks into ruin: yes! but shameful to say our sins still live and flourish. The renowned city, the capital of the Roman Empire, is swallowed up in one tremendous fire; and there is no part of the earth where Romans are not in exile. Churches once held sacred are now but heaps of dust and ashes; and yet we have our minds set on the desire of gain. We live as though we are going to die tomorrow; yet we build as though we are going to live always in this world. Our walls shine with gold, our ceilings also and the capitals of our pillars; yet Christ dies before our doors naked and hungry in the persons of His poor. The pontiff Aaron, we read, faced the raging flames, and by putting fire in his censer checked the wrath of God. The High Priest stood between the dead and the living, and the fire dared not pass his feet. On another occasion God said to Moses, "Let me alone. . . . that I may consume this people," shewing by the words "let me alone" that he can be withheld from doing what he threatens. The prayers of His servant hindered His power. Who, think you, is there now under heaven able to stay God's wrath, to face the flame of His judgment, and to say with the apostle, "I could wish that I myself were accursed for my brethren"? Flocks and shepherds perish together, because as it is with the people, so is it with the priest. Of old it was not so. Then Moses spoke in a passion of pity, "yet now if thou wilt forgive their sin—; and if not, blot me, I pray thee, out of thy book." He is not satisfied to secure his own salvation, he desires to perish with those that perish. And he is right, for "in the multitude of people is the king's honour."

Such are the times in which our little Pacatula is born. Such are the swaddling clothes in which she draws her first breath; she is destined to know of tears before laughter and to feel sorrow sooner than joy. And hardly does she come upon the stage when she is called on to make her exit. Let her then suppose that the world has always been what it is now. Let her know nothing of the past, let her shun the present, and let her long for the future.

These thoughts of mine are but hastily mustered. For my grief for lost friends has known no intermission and only recently have I recovered sufficient composure to write an old man's letter to a little child. My affection for you, brother Gaudentius, has induced me to make the attempt and I have thought it better to say a few words than to say nothing at all. The grief that paralyses my will will excuse my brevity; whereas, were I to say nothing, the sincerity of my friendship might well be doubted.

LETTER CXXIX. TO DARDANUS

In answer to a question put by Dardanus, prefect of Gaul, Jerome writes concerning the Promised Land which he identifies not with Canaan but with heaven. He then points out that the present sufferings of the Jews are due altogether to the crime of which they have been guilty in the crucifixion of Christ. The date of the letter is 414 a.d.

LETTER CXXX. TO DEMETRIAS

Jerome writes to Demetrias, a highborn lady of Rome who had recently embraced the vocation of a virgin. After narrating her life's history first at Rome and then in Africa, he goes on to lay down rules and principles to guide her in her new life. These which cover the whole field of ascetic practice and include the duties of study, of prayer, of fasting, of obedience, of giving up money for Christ, and of constant industry, are in substance similar to those which thirty years before Jerome had suggested to Eustochium (Letter XXII.). The tone of the letter is however milder and less fanatical; the asceticism recommended is not so severe; there is less of rhapsody and more of common sense. This letter should also be compared with the letter addressed to Demetrias by Pelagius, which is given in Vol. xi. of Jerome's works (Migne's Patr. Lat. xxx. ed.). The date is 414 a.d.

1. Of all the subjects that I have treated from my youth up until now, either with my own pen or that of my secretaries I have dealt with none more difficult than that which now occupies me. I am going to write to Demetrias a virgin of Christ and a lady whose birth and riches make her second to none in the Roman world. If, therefore, I employ language adequate to describe her virtue, I shall be thought to flatter her; and if I suppress some details on the score that they might appear incredible, my reserve will not do justice to her undoubted merits. What am I to do then? I am unequal to the task before me,

yet I cannot venture to decline it. Her grandmother and her mother are both women of mark, and they have alike authority to command, faith to seek and perseverance to obtain that which they require. It is not indeed anything very new or special that they ask of me; my wits have often been exercised upon similar themes. What they wish for is that I should raise my voice and bear witness as strongly as I can to the virtues of one who—in the words of the famous orator—is to be praised less for what she is than for what she gives promise of being. Yet, girl though she is, she has a glowing faith beyond her years, and has started from a point at which others think it a mark of signal virtue to leave off.

2. Let detraction stand aloof and envy give way; let no charge of self seeking be brought against me. I write as a stranger to a stranger, at least so far as the personal appearance is concerned. For the inner man finds itself well known by that knowledge whereby the apostle Paul knew the Colossians and many other believers whom he had never seen. How high an esteem I entertain for this virgin, nay more what a miracle of virtue I think her, you may judge by the fact that being occupied in the explanation of Ezekiel's description of the temple—the hardest piece in the whole range of scripture—and finding myself in that part of the sacred edifice wherein is the Holy of Holies and the altar of incense, I have chosen by way of a brief rest to pass from that altar to this, that upon it I might consecrate to eternal chastity a living offering acceptable to God and free from all stain. I am aware that the bishop has with words of prayer covered her holy head with the virgin's bridal-veil, reciting the while the solemn sentence of the apostle: "I wish to present you all as a chaste virgin to Christ." She stood as a queen at his right hand, her clothing of wrought gold and her raiment of needlework. Such was the coat of many colours, that is, formed of many different virtues, which Joseph wore; and similar ones were of old the ordinary dress of king's daughters. Thereupon the bride herself rejoices and says: "the king hath brought me into his chambers," and the choir of her companions responds: "the king's daughter is all glorious within." Thus she is a professed virgin. Still these words of mine will not be without their use. The speed of racehorses is quickened by the applause of spectators; prize fighters are urged to greater efforts by the cries of their backers; and when armies are drawn up for battle and swords are drawn, the general's speech does much to fire his soldiers' valour. So also is it on the present occasion. The grandmother and the mother have planted, but it is I that water and the Lord that giveth the increase.

3. It is the practice of the rhetoricians to exalt him who is the subject of their praises by referring to his forefathers and the past nobility of his race, so

that a fertile root may make up for barren branches and that you may admire in the stem what you have not got in the fruit. Thus I ought now to recall the distinguished names of the Probi and of the Olybrii, and that illustrious Anician house, the representatives of which have seldom or never been unworthy of the consulship. Or I ought to bring forward Olybrius our virgin's father, whose untimely loss Rome has had to mourn. I fear to say more of him, lest I should intensify the pain of your saintly mother, and lest the commemoration of his virtues should become a renewing of her grief. He was a dutiful son, a loveable husband, a kind master, a popular citizen. He was made consul while still a boy; but the goodness of his character made him more illustrious as a senator. He was happy in his death for it saved him from seeing the ruin of his country; and happier still in his offspring, for the distinguished name of his great grandmother Demetrias has become yet more distinguished now that his daughter Demetrias has vowed herself to perpetual chastity.

4. But what am I doing? Forgetful of my purpose and filled with admiration for this young man, I have spoken in terms of praise of mere worldly advantages; whereas I should rather have commended our virgin for having rejected all these, and for having determined to regard herself not as a wealthy or a high born lady, but simply as a woman like other women. Her strength of mind almost passes belief. Though she had silks and jewels freely at her disposal, and though she was surrounded by crowds of eunuchs and serving-women, a bustling household of flattering and attentive domestics, and though the daintiest feasts that the abundance of a large house could supply were daily set before her; she preferred to all these severe fasting, rough clothing, and frugal living. For she had read the words of the Lord: "they that wear soft clothing are in kings' houses." She was filled with admiration for the manner of life followed by Elijah and by John the Baptist; both of whom confined and mortified their loins with girdles of skin, while the second of them is said to have come in the spirit and power of Elijah as the forerunner of the Lord. As such he prophesied while still in his mother's womb, and before the day of judgment won the commendation of the Judge. She admired also the zeal of Anna the daughter of Phanuel, who continued even to extreme old age to serve the Lord in the temple with prayers and fastings. When she thought of the four virgins who were the daughters of Philip, she longed to join their band and to be numbered with those who by their virginal purity have attained the grace of prophecy. With these and similar meditations she fed her mind, dreading nothing so much as to offend her grandmother and her mother. Although she was encouraged by their example, she was discouraged by their expressed wish and desire; not indeed that they disapproved of her holy purpose, but that the

prize was so great that they did not venture to hope for it, or to aspire to it. Thus this poor novice in Christ's service was sorely perplexed. She came to hate all her fine apparel and cried like Esther to the Lord: "Thou knowest that I abhor the sign of my high estate"—that is to say, the diadem which she wore as queen—"and that I abhor it as a menstruous rag." Among the holy and highborn ladies who have seen and known her some have been driven by the tempest which has swept over Africa, from the shores of Gaul to a refuge in the holy places. These tell me that secretly night after night, though no one knew of it but the virgins dedicated to God in her mother's and grandmother's retinue, Demetrias, refusing sheets of linen and beds of down, spread a rug of goat's hair upon the ground and watered her face with ceaseless tears. Night after night she cast herself in thought at the Saviour's knees and implored him to accept her choice, to fulfil her aspiration, and to soften the hearts of her grandmother and of her mother.

5. Why do I still delay to relate the sequel? When her wedding day was now close at hand and when a marriage chamber was being got ready for the bride and bridegroom; secretly without any witnesses and with only the night to comfort her, she is said to have nerved herself with such considerations as these: "What ails you, Demetrias? Why are you so fearful of defending your chastity? What you need is freedom and courage. If you are so panic-stricken in time of peace, what would you do if you were called on to undergo martyrdom? If you cannot bear so much as a frown from your own, how would you steel yourself to face the tribunals of persecutors? If men's examples leave you unmoved, at least gather courage and confidence from the blessed martyr Agnes who vanquished the temptations both of youth and of a despot and by her martyrdom hallowed the very name of chastity. Unhappy girl! you know not, you know not to whom your virginity is due. It is not long since you have trembled in the hands of the barbarians and clung to your grandmother and your mother cowering under their cloaks for safety. You have seen yourself a prisoner and your chastity not in your own power. You have shuddered at the fierce looks of your enemies; you have seen with secret agony the virgins of God ravished. Your city, once the capital of the world, is now the grave of the Roman people; and will you on the shores of Libya, yourself an exile, accept an exile for a husband? Where will you find a matron to be present at your bridal? Whom will you get to escort you home? No tongue but a harsh Punic one will sing for you the wanton Fescennine verses. Away with all hesitations! Perfect love' of God casteth out fear.' Take to yourself the shield of faith, the breastplate of righteousness, the helmet of salvation, and sally forth to battle. The preservation of your chastity involves a martyrdom of its own. Why do you

fear your grandmother? Why do you dread your mother? Perhaps they may themselves wish for you a course which they do not think you wish for yourself." When by these and other arguments she had wrought herself to the necessary pitch of resolution, she cast from her as so many hindrances all her ornaments and worldly attire. Her precious necklaces, costly pearls, and glowing gems she put back in their cases. Then dressing herself in a coarse tunic and throwing over herself a still courser cloak she came in at an unlooked for moment, threw herself down suddenly at her grandmother's knees, and with tears and sobs shewed her what she really was. That staid and holy woman was amazed when she beheld her granddaughter in so strange a dress. Her mother was completely overcome for joy. Both women could hardly believe that true which they had longed to be true. Their voices stuck in their throats, and, what with blushing and turning pale, with fright and with joy, they were a prey to many conflicting emotions.

6. I must needs give way here and not attempt to describe what defies description. In the effort to explain the greatness of that joy past all belief, the flow of Tully's eloquence would run dry and the bolts poised and hurled by Demosthenes would become spent and fall short. Whatever mind can conceive or speech can interpret of human gladness was seen then. Mother and child, grandmother and granddaughter kissed each other again and again. The two elder women wept copiously for joy, they raised the prostrate girl, they embraced her trembling form. In her purpose they recognized their own mind, and congratulated each other that now a virgin was to make a noble house more noble still by her virginity. She had found they said, a way to benefit her family and to lessen the calamity of the ruin of Rome. Good Jesus! What exultation there was all through the house! Many virgins sprouted out at once as shoots from a fruitful stem, and the example set by their patroness and lady was followed by a host both of clients and servants. Virginity was warmly espoused in every house and although those who made profession of it were as regards the flesh of lower rank than Demetrias they sought one reward with her, the reward of chastity. My words are too weak. Every church in Africa danced for joy. The news reached not only the cities, towns, and villages but even the scattered huts. Every island between Africa and Italy was full of it, the glad tidings ran far and wide, disliked by none. Then Italy put off her mourning and the ruined walls of Rome resumed in part their olden splendour; for they believed the full conversion of their fosterchild to be a sign of God's favour towards them. You would fancy that the Goths had been annihilated and that that concourse of deserters and slaves had fallen by a thunderbolt from the Lord on high. There was less elation in Rome when Marcellus won

his first success at Nola after thousands of Romans had fallen at the Trebia, Lake Thrasymenus, and Cannae. There was less joy among the nobles cooped up in the capitol, on whom the future of Rome depended, when after buying their lives with gold they heard that the Gauls had at length been routed. The news penetrated to the coasts of the East, and this triumph of Christian glory was heard of in the remote cities of the interior. What Christian virgin was not proud to have Demetrias as a companion? What mother did not call Juliana's womb blessed? Unbelievers may scoff at the doubtfulness of rewards to come. Meantime, in becoming a virgin you have gained more than you have sacrificed. Had you become a man's bride but one province would have known of you; while as a Christian virgin you are known to the whole world. Mothers who have but little faith in Christ are unhappily wont to dedicate to virginity only deformed and crippled daughters for whom they can find no suitable husbands. Glass beads, as the saying goes, are thought equal to pearls. Men who pride themselves on their religion give to their virgin daughters sums scarcely sufficient for their maintenance, and bestow the bulk of their property upon sons and daughters living in the world. Quite recently in this city a rich presbyter left two of his daughters who were professed virgins with a mere pittance, while he provided his other children with ample means for self-indulgence and pleasure. The same thing has been done, I am sorry to say, by many women who have adopted the ascetic life. Would that such instances were rare, but unfortunately they are not. Yet the more frequent they are the more blessed are those who refuse to follow an example which is set them by so many.

7. All Christians are loud in their praises of Christ's holy yokefellows, because they gave to Demetrias when she professed herself a virgin the money which had been set apart as a dowry for her marriage. They would not wrong her heavenly bridegroom; in fact they wished her to come to Him with all her previous riches, that these might not be wasted on the things of the world, but might relieve the distress of God's servants.

Who would believe it? That Proba, who of all persons of high rank and birth in the Roman world bears the most illustrious name, whose holy life and universal charity have won for her esteem even among the barbarians, who has made nothing of the regular consulships enjoyed by her three sons, Probinus, Olybrius, and Probus,—that Proba, I say, now that Rome has been taken and its contents burned or carried off, is said to be selling what property she has and to be making for herself friends of the mammon of unrighteousness, that these may receive her into everlasting habitations! Well may the church's ministers, whatever their degree, and those monks who are only monks in name, blush for shame that they are buying estates, when this noble lady is selling them.

Hardly had she escaped from the hands of the barbarians, hardly had she ceased weeping for the virgins whom they had torn from her arms, when she was overwhelmed by a sudden and unbearable bereavement, one too which she had had no cause to fear, the death of her loving son. Yet as one who was to be grandmother to a Christian virgin, she bore up against this death-dealing stroke, strong in hope of the future and proving true of herself the words of the lyric:

"Should the round world in fragments burst, its fall
May strike the just, may slay, but not appal."

We read in the book of Job how, while the first messenger of evil was yet speaking, there came also another; and in the same book it is written: "is there not a temptation"—or as the Hebrew better gives it—"a warfare to man upon earth?" It is for this end that we labour, it is for this end that we risk our lives in the warfare of this world, that we may be crowned in the world to come. That we should believe this to be true of men is nothing wonderful, for even the Lord Himself was tempted, and of Abraham the scripture bears witness that God tempted him. It is for this reason also that the apostle says: "we glory in tribulations. . . . knowing that tribulation worketh patience; and patience experience; and experience hope; and hope maketh not ashamed;" and in another passage: "Who shall separate us from the love of Christ? Shall tribulation or distress or persecution or famine or nakedness or peril or sword? As it is written, For thy sake we are killed all the day long; we are accounted as sheep for the slaughter." The prophet Isaiah comforts those in like case in these words: "ye that are weaned from the milk, ye that are drawn from the breasts, look for tribulation upon tribulation, but also for hope upon hope." For, as the apostle puts it "the sufferings of this present time are not worthy to be compared with the glory which shall be revealed in us." Why I have here brought together all these passages the sequel will make plain.

Proba who had seen from the sea the smoke of her native city and had committed her own safety and that of those dear to her to a fragile boat, found the shores of Africa even more cruel than those which she had left. For one lay in wait for her of whom it would be hard to say whether he was more covetous or heartless, one who cared for nothing but wine and money, one who under pretence of serving the mildest of emperors stood forth as the most savage of all despots. If I may be allowed to quote a fable of the poets, he was like Orcus in Tartarus. Like him too he had with him a Cerberus, not three headed but many headed, ready to seize and rend everything within his reach. He tore betrothed daughters from their mothers' arms and sold high-born maidens in marriage to those greediest of men, the merchants of Syria. No plea of poverty induced him to spare either ward or widow or virgin dedicated to Christ. Indeed he looked more at the hands than at the faces of those who appealed to him. Such was the dread Charybdis and such the hound-girt Scylla which this lady encountered in fleeing from the barbarians; monsters who neither spared the shipwrecked nor heeded the cry of those made captive. Cruel wretch! at least imitate the enemy of the Roman Empire. The Brennus of our day took only what he found, but you seek what you cannot find.

Virtue, indeed, is always exposed to envy, and cavillers may marvel at the secret agreement by which Proba purchased the chastity of her numerous companions. They may allege that the count who could have taken all would not have been satisfied with a part; and that she could not have questioned his claim since in spite of her rank she was but a slave in his despotic hands. I perceive also that I am laying myself open to the attacks of enemies and that I may seem to be flattering a lady of the highest birth and distinction. Yet these men will not be able to accuse me when they learn that hitherto I have said nothing about her. I have never either in the lifetime of her husband or since his decease praised her for the antiquity of her family or for the extent of her wealth and power, subjects which others might perhaps have improved in mercenary speeches. My purpose is to praise the grandmother of my virgin in a style befitting the church, and to thank her for having aided with her goodwill the desire which Demetrias has formed. For the rest my cell, my food and clothing, my advanced years, and my narrow circumstances sufficiently refute the charge of flattery. In what remains of my letter I shall direct all my words to Demetrias herself, whose holiness ennobles her as much as her rank, and of whom it may be said that the higher she climbs the more terrible will be her fall.

For the rest
This one thing, child of God, I lay on thee;
Yea before all, and urge it many times:

Love to occupy your mind with the reading of scripture. Do not in the good ground of your breast gather only a crop of darnel and wild oats. Do not let an enemy sow tares among the wheat when the householder is asleep (that is when the mind which ever cleaves to God is off its guard); but say always with the bride in the song of songs: "By night I sought him whom my soul loveth. Tell me where thou feedest, where thou makest thy flock to rest at noon;" and with the psalmist: "my soul followeth hard after thee: thy right hand upholdeth me;" and with Jeremiah: "I have not found it hard. . . . to follow thee," for "there is no grief in Jacob neither is there travail in Israel." When you were in the world you loved the things of the world. You rubbed your cheeks with rouge and used whitelead to improve your complexion. You dressed your hair and built up a tower on your head with tresses not your own. I shall say nothing of your costly earrings, your glistening pearls from the depths of the Red Sea, your bright green emeralds, your flashing onyxes, your liquid sapphires,—tones which turn the heads of matrons, and make them eager to possess the like. For you have relinquished the world and besides your baptismal vow have taken a new one; you have entered into a compact with your adversary and have said: "I renounce thee, O devil, and thy world and thy pomp and thy works." Observe, therefore, the treaty that you have made, and keep terms with your adversary while you are in the way of this world. Otherwise he may some day deliver you to the judge and prove that you have taken what is his; and then the judge will deliver you to the officer—at once your foe and your avenger—and you will be cast into prison; into that outer darkness which surrounds us with the greater horror as it severs us from Christ the one true light. And you shall by no means come out thence till you have paid the uttermost farthing, that is, till you have expiated your most trifling sins; for we shall give account of every idle word in the day of judgment.

8. In speaking thus I do not wish to utter an ill-omened prophecy against you but only to warn you as an apprehensive and prudent monitor who in your case fears even what is safe. What says the scripture? "If the spirit of the ruler rise up against thee, leave not thy place." We must always stand under arms and in battle array, ready to engage the foe. When he tries to dislodge us from our position and to make us fall back, we must plant our feet firmly down, and say with the psalmist, "he hath set my feet upon a rock" and "the rocks are a refuge for the conies." In this latter passage for conies' many read hedgehogs.' Now the hedgehog is a small animal, very shy, and covered over with thorny bristles. When Jesus was crowned with thorns and bore our sins and suffered for us, it was to make the roses of virginity and the lilies of chastity grow for us out of the brambles and briers which have formed the lot of women since the day when it was said to Eve, "in sorrow thou shalt bring forth children; and thy desire shall be to thy husband and he shall rule over thee." We are told that the bridegroom feeds among the lilies, that is, among those who have not defiled their garments, for they have remained virgins and have hearkened to the precept of the Preacher: "let thy garments be always white." As the author and prince of virginity He says boldly of Himself: "I am the rose of Sharon and the lily of the valleys." "The rocks" then "are a refuge for the conies" who when they are persecuted in one city flee into another and have no

fear that the prophetic words "refuge failed me" will be fulfilled in their case. "The high hills are a refuge for the wild goats," and their food are the serpents which a little child draws out of their holes. Meanwhile the leopard lies down with the kid and the lion eats straw like the ox; not of course that the ox may learn ferocity from the lion but that the lion may learn docility from the ox.

But let us turn back to the passage first quoted, "If the spirit of the ruler rise up against thee, leave not thy place," a sentence which is followed by these words: "for yielding pacifieth great offences." The meaning is, that if the serpent finds his way into your thoughts you must "keep your heart with all diligence" and sing with David, "cleanse thou me from secret faults: keep back thy servant also from presumptuous sins," and come not to "the great transgression" which is sin in act. Rather slay the allurements to vice while they are still only thoughts; and dash the little ones of the daughter of Babylon against the stones where the serpent can leave no trail. Be wary and vow a vow unto the Lord: "let them not have dominion over me: then shall I be upright and I shall be innocent from the great transgression." For elsewhere also the scripture testifies, "I will visit the iniquity of the fathers upon the children unto the third and fourth generation." That is to say, God will not punish us at once for our thoughts and resolves but will send retribution upon their offspring, that is, upon the evil deeds and habits of sin which arise out of them. As He says by the mouth of Amos: "for three transgressions of such and such a city and for four I will not turn away the punishment thereof."

9. I cull these few flowers in passing from the fair field of the holy scriptures. They will suffice to warn you that you must shut the door of your breast and fortify your brow by often making the sign of the cross. Thus alone will the destroyer of Egypt find no place to attack you; thus alone will the first-born of your soul escape the fate of the first-born of the Egyptians; thus alone will you be able with the prophet to say: "my heart is fixed, O God, my heart is fixed; I will sing and give praise. Awake up, my glory; awake, psaltery and harp." For, sin stricken as she is, even Tyre is bidden to take up her harp and to do penance; like Peter she is told to wash away the stains of her former foulness with bitter tears. Howbeit, let us know nothing of penitence, lest the thought of it lead us into sin. It is a plank for those who have had the misfortune to be shipwrecked; but an inviolate virgin may hope to save the ship itself. For it is one thing to look for what you have cast away, and another to keep what you have never lost. Even the apostle kept under his body and brought it into subjection, lest having preached to others he might himself become a castaway. Heated with the violence of sensual passion he made himself the spokesman of the human race: "O wretched man that I am! who shall deliver

me from the body of this death?" and again, "I know that in me, that is in my flesh, dwelleth no good thing: for to will is present with me; but how to perform that which is good, I find not. For the good that I would, I do not: but the evil which I would not, that I do;" and once more: "they that are in the flesh cannot please God. But ye are not in the flesh, but in the spirit, if so be that the spirit of God dwell in you."

10. After you have paid the most careful attention to your thoughts, you must then put on the armour of fasting and sing with David: "I chastened my soul with fasting," and "I have eaten ashes like bread," and "as for me when they troubled me my clothing was sackcloth." Eve was expelled from paradise because she had eaten of the forbidden fruit. Elijah on the other hand after forty days of fasting was carried in a fiery chariot into heaven. For forty days and forty nights Moses lived by the intimate converse which he had with God, thus proving in his own case the complete truth of the saying, "man doth not live by bread only but by every word that proceedeth out of the mouth of the Lord." The Saviour of the world, who in His virtues and His mode of life has left us an example to follow, was, immediately after His baptism, taken up by the spirit that He might contend with the devil, and after crushing him and overthrowing him might deliver him to his disciples to trample under foot. For what says the apostle? "God shall bruise Satan under your feet shortly." And yet after the Saviour had fasted forty days, it was through food that the old enemy laid a snare for him, saying, "If thou be the Son of God, command that these stones be made bread." Under the law, in the seventh month after the blowing of trumpets and on the tenth day of the month, a fast was proclaimed for the whole Jewish people, and that soul was cut off from among his people which on that day preferred self-indulgence to self-denial. In Job it is written of behemoth that "his strength is in his loins, and his force is in the navel of his belly." Our foe uses the heat of youthful passion to tempt young men and maidens and "sets on fire the wheel of our birth." He thus fulfils the words of Hosea, "they are all adulterers, their heart is like an oven;" an oven which only God's mercy and severe fasting can extinguish. These are "the fiery darts" with which the devil wounds men and sets them on fire, and it was these which the king of Babylon used against the three children. But when he made his fire forty-nine cubits high he did but turn to his own ruin the seven weeks which the Lord had appointed for a time of salvation. And as then a fourth bearing a form like the son of God slackened the terrible heat and cooled the flames of the blazing fiery furnace, until, menacing as they looked, they became quite harmless, so is it now with the virgin soul. The dew of heaven and severe fasting quench in a girl the flame of passion and enable her soul even in its

earthly tenement to live the angelic life. Therefore the chosen vessel declares that concerning virgins he has no commandment of the Lord. For you must act against nature or rather above nature if you are to forswear your natural function, to cut off your own root, to cull no fruit but that of virginity, to abjure the marriage-bed, to shun intercourse with men, and while in the body to live as though out of it.

11. I do not, however, lay on you as an obligation any extreme fasting or abnormal abstinence from food. Such practices soon break down weak constitutions and cause bodily sickness before they lay the foundations of a holy life. It is a maxim of the philosophers that virtues are means, and that all extremes are of the nature of vice; and it is in this sense that one of the seven wise men propounds the famous saw quoted in the comedy, "In nothing too much." You must not go on fasting until your heart begins to throb and your breath to fail and you have to be supported or carried by others. No; while curbing the desires of the flesh, you must keep sufficient strength to read scripture, to sing psalms, and to observe vigils. For fasting is not a complete virtue in itself but only a foundation on which other virtues may be built. The same may be said of sanctification and of that chastity without which no man shall see the Lord. Each of these is a step on the upward way, yet none of them by itself will avail to win the virgin's crown. The gospel teaches us this in the parable of the wise and foolish virgins; the former of whom enter into the bridechamber of the bridegroom, while the latter are shut out from it because not having the oil of good works they allow their lamps to fail. This subject of fasting opens up a wide field in which I have often wandered myself, and many writers have devoted treatises to the subject. I must refer you to these if you wish to learn the advantages of self-restraint and on the other hand the evils of over-feeding.

12. Follow the example of your Spouse: be subject to your grandmother and to your mother. Never look upon a man, especially upon a young man, except in their company. Never know a man whom they do not know. It is a maxim of the world that the only sure friendship is one based on an identity of likes and dislikes. You have been taught by their example as well as instructed by the holy life of your home to aspire to virginity, to recognize the commandments of Christ, to know what is expedient for you and what course you ought to choose. But do not regard what is your own as absolutely your own. Remember that part of it belongs to those who have communicated their chastity to you and from whose honourable marriages and beds undefiled you have sprung up like a choice flower. For you are destined to produce perfect fruit if only you will humble yourself under the mighty hand of God, always remembering that it is written: "God resisteth the proud and giveth grace to

the humble." Now where there is grace, this is not given in return for works but is the free gift of the giver, so that the apostles' words are fulfilled: "it is not of him that willeth nor of him that runneth, but of God that sheweth mercy." And yet it is ours to will and not to will; and all the while the very liberty that is ours is only ours by the mercy of God.

13. Again in selecting for yourself eunuchs and maids and servingmen look rather to their characters than to their good looks; for, whatever their age or sex, and even if mutilation ensures in them a compulsory chastity, you must take account of their dispositions, for these cannot be operated on save by the fear of Christ. When you are present buffoonery and loose talk must find no place. You should never hear an improper word; if you do hear one, you must not be carried away by it. Abandoned men often make use of a single light expression to try the gates of chastity. Leave to worldlings the privileges of laughing and being laughed at. One who is in your position ought to be serious. Cato the Censor, in old time a leading man in your city, (the same who in his last days turned his attention to Greek literature without either blushing for himself as censor or despairing of success on account of his age) is said by Lucilius to have laughed only once in his life, and the same remark is made about Marcus Crassus. These men may have affected this austere mien to gain for themselves reputation and notoriety. For so long as we dwell in the tabernacle of this body and are enveloped with this fragile flesh, we can but restrain and regulate our affections and passions; we cannot wholly extirpate them. Knowing this the psalmist says: "be ye angry and sin not;" which the apostle explains thus: "let not the sun go down upon your wrath." For, if to be angry is human, to put an end to one's anger is Christian.

14. I think it unnecessary to warn you against covetousness since it is the way of your family both to have riches and to despise them. The apostle too tells us that covetousness is idolatry, and to one who asked the Lord the question: "Good Master what good thing shall I do that I may have eternal life?" He thus replied: "If thou wilt be perfect, go and sell that thou hast and give to the poor, and thou shalt have treasure in heaven; and come and follow me." Such is the climax of complete and apostolic virtue—to sell all that one has and to distribute to the poor, and thus freed from all earthly encumbrance to fly up to the heavenly realms with Christ. To us, or I should rather say to you, a careful stewardship is entrusted, although in such matters full freedom of choice is left to every individual, whether old or young. Christ's words are "if thou wilt be perfect." I do not compel you, He seems to say, I do not command you, but I set the palm before you, I shew you the prize; it is for you to choose whether you will enter the arena and win the crown. Let us consider

how wisely Wisdom has spoken. "Sell that thou hast." To whom is the command given? Why, to him to whom it was said, "if thou wilt be perfect." Sell not a part of thy goods but "all that thou hast." And when you have sold them, what then? "Give to the poor." Not to the rich, not to your kinsfolk, not to minister to self indulgence; but to relieve need. It does not matter whether a man is a priest or a relation or a connexion, you must think of nothing but his poverty. Let your praises come from the stomachs of the hungry and not from the rich banquets of the overfed. We read in the Acts of the Apostles how, while the blood of the Lord was still warm and believers were in the fervour of their first faith, they all sold their possessions and laid the price of them at the apostles' feet (to shew that money ought to be trampled underfoot) and "distribution was made unto every man according as he had need." But Ananias and Sapphira proved timid stewards, and what is more, deceitful ones; therefore they brought on themselves condemnation. For having made a vow they offered their money to God as if it were their own and not His to whom they had vowed it; and keeping back for their own use a part of that which belonged to another, through fear of famine which true faith never fears, they drew down on themselves suddenly the avenging stroke, which was meant not in cruelty towards them but as a warning to others. In fact the apostle Peter by no means called down death upon them as Porphyry foolishly says. He merely announced God's judgment by the spirit of prophecy, that the doom of two persons might be a lesson to many. From the time of your dedication to perpetual virginity your property is yours no longer; or rather is now first truly yours because it has come to be Christ's. Yet while your grandmother and mother are living you must deal with it according to their wishes. If, however, they die and rest in the sleep of the saints (and I know that they desire that you should survive them); when your years are riper, and your will steadier, and your resolution stronger, you will do with your money what seems best to you, or rather what the Lord shall command, knowing as you will that hereafter you will have nothing save that which you have here spent on good works. Others may build churches, may adorn their walls when built with marbles, may procure massive columns, may deck the unconscious capitals with gold and precious ornaments, may cover church doors with silver and adorn the altars with gold and gems. I do not blame those who do these things; I do not repudiate them. Everyone must follow his own judgment. And it is better to spend one's money thus than to hoard it up and brood over it. However your duty is of a different kind. It is yours to clothe Christ in the poor, to visit Him in the sick, to feed Him in the hungry, to shelter Him in the homeless, particularly such as are of the household of faith, to support communities of virgins, to take care of God's servants, of those who are poor in spirit, who serve the same Lord as you day and night, who while they are on earth live the angelic life and speak only of the praises of God. Having food and raiment they rejoice and count themselves rich. They seek for nothing more, contented if only they can persevere in their design. For as soon as they begin to seek more they are shewn to be undeserving even of those things that are needful.

The preceding counsels have been addressed to a virgin who is wealthy and a lady of rank.

15. But what I am now going to say will be addressed to the virgin alone. I shall take into consideration, that is, not your circumstances but yourself. In addition to the rule of psalmody and prayer which you must always observe at the third, sixth, and ninth hours, at evening, at midnight, and at dawn, you should determine how much time you will bind yourself to give to the learning and reading of scripture, aiming to please and instruct the soul rather than to lay a burthen upon it. When you have spent your allotted time in these studies, often kneeling down to pray as care for your soul will impel you to do; have some wool always at hand, shape the threads into yarn with your thumb, attach them to the shuttle, and then throw this to weave a web, or roll up the yarn which others have spun or lay it out for the weavers. Examine their work when it is done, find fault with its defects, and arrange how much they are to do. If you busy yourself with these numerous occupations, you will never find your days long; however late the summer sun may be in setting, a day will always seem too short on which something remains undone. By observing such rules as these you will save yourself and others, you will set a good example as a mistress, and you will place to your credit the chastity of many. For the scripture says: "the soul of every idler is filled with desires." Nor may you excuse yourself from toil on the plea that God's bounty has left you in want of nothing. No; you must labour with the rest, that being always busy you may think only of the service of the Lord. I shall speak quite plainly. Even supposing that you give all your property to the poor, Christ will value nothing more highly than what you have wrought with your own hands. You may work for yourself or to set an example to your virgins; or you may make presents to your mother and grandmother to draw from them larger sums for the relief of the poor.

16. I have all but passed over the most important point of all. While you were still quite small, bishop Anastasius of holy and blessed memory ruled the Roman church. In his days a terrible storm of heresy came from the East and strove first to corrupt and then to undermine that simple faith which an apostle has praised. However the bishop, rich in poverty and as careful of his flock as an apostle, at once smote the noxious thing on the head, and stayed

the hydra's hissing. Now I have reason to fear—in fact a report has reached me to this effect—that the poisonous germs of this heresy still live and sprout in the minds of some to this day. I think, therefore, that I ought to warn you, in all kindness and affection, to hold fast the faith of the saintly Innocent, the spiritual son of Anastasius and his successor in the apostolic see; and not to receive any foreign doctrine, however wise and discerning you may take yourself to be. Men of this type whisper in corners and pretend to inquire into the justice of God. Why, they ask, was a particular soul born in a particular province? What is the reason that some are born of Christian parents, others among wild beasts and savage tribes who have no knowledge of God? Wherever they can strike the simple with their scorpion-sting and form an ulcer fitted to their purpose, there they diffuse their venom. "Is it for nothing, think you,"—thus they argue—"that a little child scarcely able to recognize its mother by a laugh or a look of joy, which has done nothing either good or evil, is seized by a devil or overwhelmed with jaundice or doomed to bear afflictions which godless men escape, while God's servants have to bear them?" Now if God's judgments, they say, are "true and righteous altogether," and if "there is no unrighteousness in Him," we are compelled by reason to believe that our souls have pre-existed in heaven, that they are condemned to and, if I may so say, buried in human bodies because of some ancient sins, and that we are punished in this valley of weeping for old misdeeds. This according to them is the prophet's reason for saying: "Before I was afflicted I went astray," and again, "Bring my soul out of prison." They explain in the same way the question of the disciples in the gospel: "Who did sin, this man or his parents, that he was born blind?" and other similar passages.

This godless and wicked teaching was formerly ripe in Egypt and the East; and now it lurks secretly like a viper in its hole among many persons in those parts, defiling the purity of the faith and gradually creeping on like an inherited disease till it assails a large number. But I am sure that if you hear it you will not accept it. For you have preceptresses under God whose faith is a rule of sound doctrine. You will understand what I mean, for God will give you understanding in all things. You must not ask me on the spot to give you a refutation of this dreadful heresy and of others worse still; for were I to do so I should "criticize where I ought to forbid," and my present object is not to refute heretics but to instruct a virgin. However, I have defeated their wiles and counterworked their efforts to undermine the truth in a treatise which by God's help I have written; and if you desire to have this, I shall send it to you promptly and with pleasure. I say, if you desire to have it, for as the proverb says, wares proffered unasked are little esteemed, and a plentiful supply brings down prices, which are always highest where scarcity prevails.

17. Men often discuss the comparative merits of life in solitude and life in a community; and the preference is usually given to the first over the second. Still even for men there is always the risk that, being withdrawn from the society of their fellows, they may become exposed to unclean and godless imaginations, and in the fulness of their arrogance and disdain may look down upon everyone but themselves, and may arm their tongues to detract from the clergy or from those who like themselves are bound by the vows of a solitary life. Of such it is well said by the psalmist, "as for the children of men their teeth are spears and arrows and their tongue a sharp sword." Now if all this is true of men, how much more does it apply to women whose fickle and vacillating minds, if left to their own devices, soon degenerate. I am myself acquainted with anchorites of both sexes who by excessive fasting have so impaired their faculties that they do not know what to do or where to turn, when to speak or when to be silent. Most frequently those who have been so affected have lived in solitary cells, cold and damp. Moreover if persons untrained in secular learning read the works of able church writers, they only acquire from them a wordy fluency and not, as they might do, a fuller knowledge of the scriptures. The old saying is found true of them, although they have not the wit to speak, they cannot remain silent. They teach to others the scriptures that they do not understand themselves; and if they are fortunate enough to convince them, they take upon themselves airs as men of learning. In fact, they set up as instructors of the ignorant before they have gone to school themselves. It is a good thing therefore to defer to one's betters, to obey those set over one, to learn not only from the scriptures but from the example of others how one ought to order one's life, and not to follow that worst of teachers, one's own self-confidence. Of women who are thus presumptuous the apostle says that they "are carried about with every wind of doctrine, ever learning and never able to come to the knowledge of the truth."

18. Avoid the company of married women who are devoted to their husbands and to the world, that your mind may not become unsettled by hearing what a husband says to his wife, or a wife to her husband. Such conversations are filled with deadly venom. To express his condemnation of them the apostle has taken a verse of a profane writer and has pressed it into the service of the church. It may be literally rendered at the expense of the metre: "evil communications corrupt good manners." No; you should choose for your companions staid and serious women, particularly widows and virgins, persons of approved conversation, of few words, and of a holy modesty. Shun gay and thoughtless

girls, who deck their heads and wear their hair in fringes, who use cosmetics to improve their skins and affect tight sleeves, dresses without a crease, and dainty buskins; and by pretending to be virgins more easily sell themselves into destruction. Moreover, the character and tastes of a mistress are often inferred from the behaviour of her attendants. Regard as fair and lovable and a fitting companion one who is unconscious of her good looks and careless of her appearance; who does not expose her breast out of doors or throw back her cloak to reveal her neck; who veils all of her face except her eyes, and only uses these to find her way.

19. I hesitate about what I am going to say but, as often happens, whether I like it or not, it must be said; not that I have reason to fear anything of the kind in your case, for probably you know nothing of such things and have never even heard of them, but that in advising you I may warn others. A virgin should avoid as so many plagues and banes of chastity all ringletted youths who curl their hair and scent themselves with musk; to whom may well be applied the words of Petronius Arbiter, "too much perfume makes an ill perfume." I need not speak of those who by their pertinacious visits to virgins bring discredit both on themselves and on these; for, even if nothing wrong is done by them, no wrong can be imagined greater than to find oneself exposed to the calumnies and attacks of the heathen. I do not here speak of all, but only of those whom the church itself rebukes, whom sometimes it expels, and against whom the censure of bishops and presbyters is not seldom directed. For, as it is, it is almost more dangerous for giddy girls to shew themselves in the abodes of religion than even to walk abroad. Virgins who live in communities and of whom large numbers are assembled together, should never go out by themselves or unaccompanied by their mother. A hawk often singles out one of a flight of doves, pounces on it and tears it open till it is gorged with its flesh and blood. Sick sheep stray from the flock and fall into the jaws of wolves. I know some saintly virgins who on holy days keep at home to avoid the crowds and refuse to go out when they must either take a strong escort, or altogether avoid all public places.

It is about thirty years since I published a treatise on the preservation of virginity, in which I felt constrained to oppose certain vices and to lay bare the wiles of the devil for the instruction of the virgin to whom it was addressed. My language then gave offence to a great many, for everyone applied what I said to himself and instead of welcoming my admonitions turned away from me as an accuser of his deeds. Was it any use, do you ask, thus to arm a host of remonstrants and to show by my complaints the wounds which my conscience received? Yes, I answer, for, while they have passed away, my book still remains. I have also written short exhortations to several virgins and widows, and in these smaller works I have gathered together all that there is to be said on the subject. So that I am reduced to the alternative of repeating exhortations which seem superfluous or of omitting them to the serious injury of this treatise. The blessed Cyprian has left a noble work on virginity; and many other writers, both Greek and Latin, have done the same. Indeed the virginal life has been praised both with tongue and pen among all nations and particularly among the churches. Most, however, of those who have written on the subject have addressed themselves to such as have not yet chosen virginity, and who need help to enable them to choose aright. But I and those to whom I write have made our choice; and our one object is to remain constant to it. Therefore, as our way lies among scorpions and adders, among snares and banes, let us go forward staff in hand, our loins girded and our feet shod; that so we may come to the sweet waters of the true Jordan, and enter the land of promise and go up to the house of God. Then shall we sing with the prophet: "Lord, I have loved the habitation of thy house and the place where thine honour dwelleth;" and again: "one thing have I desired of the Lord, that will I seek after; that I may dwell in the house of the Lord all the days of my life."

Happy is the soul, happy is the virgin in whose heart there is room for no other love than the love of Christ. For in Himself He is wisdom and chastity, patience and justice and every other virtue. Happy too is she who can recall a man's face without the least sigh of regret, and who has no desire to set eyes on one whom, after she has seen him, she may find herself unwilling to give up. Some there are, however, who by their ill-behaviour bring discredit on the holy profession of virginity and upon the glory of the heavenly and angelic company who have made it. These must be frankly told either to marry if they cannot contain, or to contain if they will not marry. It is also a matter for laughter or rather for tears, that when mistresses walk abroad they are preceded by maids better dressed than themselves; indeed so usual has this become that, if of two women you see one less neat than the other, you take her for the mistress as a matter of course. And yet these maids are professed virgins. Again not a few virgins choose sequestered dwellings where they will not be under the eyes of others, in order that they may live more freely than they otherwise could do. They take baths, do what they please, and try as much as they can to escape notice. We see these things and yet we put up with them; in fact, if we catch sight of the glitter of gold, we are ready to account of them as good works.

20. I end as I began, not content to have given you but a single warning. Love the holy scriptures, and wisdom will love you. Love wisdom, and it will keep you safe. Honour wisdom, and it will embrace you round about. Let the

jewels on your breast and in your ears be the gems of wisdom. Let your tongue know no theme but Christ, let no sound pass your lips that is not holy, and let your words always reproduce that sweetness of which your grandmother and your mother set you the example. Imitate them, for they are models of virtue.

LETTER CXXXI. FROM AUGUSTINE

At the suggestion of Jerome, Marcellinus (for whom see Letter CXXVI.) had consulted Augustine on the difficult question of the origin of the soul but had failed to get any definite opinion from this latter. Augustine now writes to Jerome confessing his inability to decide the question and asking for advice upon it. He begins by reciting—and justifying—his own belief that the soul is immortal and incorporeal and that its fall into sin is due not to God but to its own free choice. He then goes on to say that he is quite ready to accept creationism as a solution of the difficulty if Jerome will shew him how this theory is reconcilable with the church's condemnation of Pelagius and its assertion of the doctrine of original sin. The damnation of unbaptized infants is assumed throughout.

The date of the letter is 415 a.d. Its number in the Letters of Augustine is CLXVI.

LETTER CXXXII. FROM AUGUSTINE

In this letter Augustine deals with the statement of James ii. 10 ("whosoever shall keep the whole law and yet offend in one point, he is guilty of all") and explains it by saying that every breach of the law is a breach of love. He also takes occasion to criticise two doctrines of the schools then prevalent, (1) that all sins are equal and (2) that he who has one virtue has all and that all virtues are wanting to him who lacks one.

The date of the letter is 415 a.d. Its number in the Letters of Augustine is CLXVII.

LETTER CXXXIII. TO CTESIPHON

Ctesiphon had written to Jerome for his opinion on two points in the teaching of Pelagius, (1) his quietism and (2) his denial of original sin. Jerome now refutes these two doctrines and points out that Pelagius has drawn them partly from the philosophers and partly from the heretics. He censures Rufinus, who had died 5 years before, for attributing to Sixtus bishop of Rome a book which is really the work of Xystus a Pythagorean, and for passing off as the composition of the martyr Pamphilus a panegyric of Origen really due to his friend Eusebius. In both these assertions, however, Jerome is more wrong than right. (See Prolegomena to the works of Rufinus.) The letter concludes with a promise to deal more fully with the heresy of Pelagius at some future time, a promise afterwards redeemed by the publication of a dialogue against the Pelagians.' The date of the letter is 415 a.d.

1. In acquainting me with the new controversy which has taken the place of the old you are wrong in thinking that you have acted rashly, for your conduct has been prompted by zeal and friendship. Already before the arrival of your letter many in the East have been deceived into a pride which apes humility and have said with the devil: "I will ascend into heaven, I will exalt my throne above the stars of God; I will be like the Most High." Can there be greater presumption than to claim not likeness to God but equality with Him, and so to compress into a few words the poisonous doctrines of all the heretics which in their turn flow from the statements of the philosophers, particularly of Pythagoras and Zeno the founder of the Stoic school? For those states of feeling which the Greeks call pathe and which we may describe as "passions," relating to the present or the future such as vexation and gladness, hope and fear,—these, they tell us, it is possible to root out of our minds; in fact all vice may be destroyed root and branch in man by meditation on virtue and constant practice of it. The position which they thus take up is vehemently assailed by the Peripatetics who trace themselves to Aristotle, and by the new Academics of whom Cicero is a disciple; and these overthrow not the facts of their opponents—for they have no facts—but the shadows and wishes which do duty for them. To maintain such a doctrine is to take man's nature from him, to forget that he is constituted of body as well as soul, to substitute mere wishes for sound teaching. For the apostle says:—"O wretched man that I am! who shall deliver me from the body of this death?" But as I cannot say all that I wish in a short letter I will briefly touch on the points that you must avoid. Virgil writes:—

Thus mortals fear and hope, rejoice and grieve,
And shut in darkness have no sight of heaven.

For who can escape these feelings? Must we not all clap our hands when we are joyful, and shrink at the approach of sorrow? Must not hope always animate us and fear put us in terror? So in one of his Satires the poet Horace, whose words are so weighty, writes:

From faults no mortal is completely free;
He that has fewest is the perfect man.

2. Well does one of our own writers say: "the philosophers are the patriarchs of the heretics." It is they who have stained with their perverse doctrine the spotlessness of the Church, not knowing that of human weakness it is said: "Why is earth and ashes proud?" So likewise the apostle: "I see another law in my members warring against the law of my mind and bringing me into captivity"; and again, "The good that I would I do not: but the evil which I would not that I do." Now if Paul does what he wills not, what becomes of the assertion that a man may be without sin if he will? Given the will, how is it to have its way when the apostle tells us that he has no power to do what he wishes? Moreover if we ask them who the persons are whom they regard as sinless they seek to veil the truth by a new subterfuge. They do not, they say, profess that men are or have been without sin; all that they maintain is that it is possible for them to be so. Remarkable teachers truly, who maintain that a thing may be which on their own shewing, never has been; whereas the scripture says:—"The thing which shall be, it is that which hath been already of old time."

I need not go through the lives of the saints or call attention to the moles and spots which mark the fairest skins. Many of our writers, it is true, unwisely, take this course; however, a few sentences of scripture will dispose alike of the heretics and the philosophers. What says the chosen vessel? "God had concluded all in unbelief that he might have mercy upon all;" and in another place, "all have sinned and come short of the glory of God." The preacher also who is the mouthpiece of the Divine Wisdom freely protests and says: "there is not a just man upon earth, that doeth good and sinneth not:" and again, "if thy people sin against thee, for there is no man that sinneth not:" and "who can say, I have made my heart clean?" and "none is clean from stain, not even if his life on earth has been but for one day." David insists on the same thing when he says: "Behold, I was shapen in iniquity and in sin did my mother conceive me;" and in another psalm, "in thy sight shall no man living be justified." This last passage they try to explain away from motives of reverence, arguing that the meaning is that no man is perfect in comparison with God. Yet the scripture does not say: "in comparison with thee shall no man living be justified" but "in thy sight shall no man living be justified." And when it says "in thy sight" it means that those who seem holy to men to God in his fuller knowledge are by no means holy. For "man looketh on the outward appearance, but the Lord looketh on the heart." But if in the sight of God who sees all things and to whom the secrets of the heart lie open no man is just; then these heretics instead of adding to man's dignity, clearly take away from God's power. I might bring together many other passages of scripture of the same import; but were I to do so, I should exceed the limits I will not say of a letter but of a volume.

3. It is with no new doctrines that in their self-applauding perfidy they deceive the simple and untaught. They cannot, however, deceive theologians who meditate in the law of the Lord day and night. Let those blush then for their leaders and companions who say that a man may be "without sin" if he will, or, as the Greeks term it anamartetos , "sinless." As such a statement sounds intolerable to the Eastern churches, they profess indeed only to say that a man may be "without sin" and do not presume to allege that he may be "sinless" as well. As if, forsooth, "sinless" and "without sin" had different meanings; whereas the only difference between them is that Latin requires two words to express what Greek gives in one. If you adopt "without sin" and reject "sinless," then condemn the preachers of sinlessness. But this you cannot do. You know very well what it is that you teach your pupils in private; and that while you say one thing with your lips you engrave another on your heart. To us, ignorant outsiders you speak in parables; but to your own followers you avow your secret meaning. And for this you claim the authority of scripture which says: "to the multitudes Jesus spake in parables;" but to his own disciples He said: "it is given unto you to know the mysteries of the kingdom of heaven, but to them it is not given."

But to return; I will shortly set forth the names of your leaders and companions to shew you who those are of whose fellowship you make your boast. Manichaeus says of his elect—whom he places among Plato's orbits in heaven—that they are free from all sin, and cannot sin even if they will. To so great heights have they attained in virtue that they laugh at the works of the flesh. Then there is Priscillian in Spain whose infamy makes him as bad as Manichaeus, and whose disciples profess a high esteem for you. These are rash enough to claim for themselves the twofold credit of perfection and wisdom. Yet they shut themselves up alone with women and justify their sinful embraces by quoting the lines:

The almighty father takes the earth to wife;
Pouring upon her fertilizing rain,
That from her womb new harvest he may reap.

These heretics have affinities with Gnosticism which may be traced to the impious teaching of Basilides. It is from him that you derive the assertion that without knowledge of the law it is impossible to avoid sin. But why do I speak of Priscillian who has been condemned by the whole world and put to death by the secular sword? Evagrius of Ibera in Pontus who sends letters to virgins and monks and among others to her whose name bears witness to the blackness of her perfidy, has published a book of maxims on apathy, or, as we should say, impassivity or imperturbability; a state in which the mind ceases to be agitated and—to speak simply—becomes either a stone or a God. His work is widely read, in the East in Greek and in the West in a Latin translation made by his disciple Rufinus. He has also written a book which professes to be about monks and includes in it many not monks at all whom he declares to have been Origenists, and who have certainly been condemned by the bishops. I mean Ammonius, Eusebius, Euthymius, Evagrius himself, Horus, Isidorus, and many others whom it would be tedious to enumerate. He is careful, however, to do as the physicians, of whom Lucretius says:

To children bitter wormwood still they give
In cups with juice of sweetest honey smeared.

That is to say, he has set in the forefront of his book John, an undoubted Catholic and saint, by his means to introduce to the church the heretics mentioned farther on. But who can adequately characterize the rashness or madness which has led him to ascribe a book of the Pythagorean philosopher Xystus, a heathen who knew nothing of Christ, to Sixtus a martyr and bishop of the Roman church? In this work the subject of perfection is discussed at length in the light of the Pythagorean doctrine which makes man equal with God and of one substance with Him. Thus many not knowing that its author was a philosopher and supposing that they are reading the words of a martyr, drink of the golden cup of Babylon. Moreover in its pages there is no mention of prophets, patriarchs, apostles, or of Christ; so that according to Rufinus there has been a bishop and a martyr who had nothing to do with Christ. Such is the book from which you and your followers quote passages against the church. In the same way he played fast and loose with the name of the holy martyr Pamphilus ascribing to him the first of the six books in defence of Origen written by Eusebius of Caesarea who is admitted by every body to have been an Arian. His object in doing so was of course to commend to Latin ears Origen's four wonderful books about First Principles.

Would you have me name another of your masters in heresy? Much of your teaching is traceable to Origen. For, to give one instance only, when he comments on the psalmist's words: "My reins also instruct me in the night season," he maintains that when a holy man like yourself has reached perfection, he is free even at night from human infirmity and is not tempted by evil thoughts. You need not blush to avow yourself a follower of these men; it is of no use to disclaim their names when you adopt their blasphemies. Moreover, your teaching corresponds to Jovinian's second position. You must, therefore, take the answer which I have given to him as equally applicable to yourself. Where men's opinions are the same their destinies can hardly be different.

4. Such being the state of the case, what object is served by "silly women laden with sins, carried about with every wind of doctrine, ever learning and never able to come to the knowledge of the truth?" Or how is the cause helped by the men who dance attendance upon these, men with itching ears who know neither how to hear nor how to speak? They confound old mire with new cement and, as Ezekiel says, daub a wall with untempered mortar; so that, when the truth comes in a shower, they are brought to nought. It was with the help of the harlot Helena that Simon Magus founded his sect. Bands of women accompanied Nicolas of Antioch that deviser of all uncleanness. Marcion sent a woman before him to Rome to prepare men's minds to fall into his snares. Apelles possessed in Philumena an associate in his false doctrines. Montanus, that mouthpiece of an unclean spirit, used two rich and high born ladies Prisca and Maximilla first to bribe and then to pervert many churches. Leaving ancient history I will pass to times nearer to our own. Arius intent on leading the world astray began by misleading the Emperor's sister. The resources of Lucilla helped Donatus to defile with his polluting baptism many unhappy persons throughout Africa. In Spain the blind woman Agape led the blind man Elpidius into the ditch. He was followed by Priscillian, an enthusiastic votary of Zoroaster and a magian before he became a bishop. A woman named Galla seconded his efforts and left a gadabout sister to perpetuate a second heresy of a kindred form. Now also the mystery of iniquity is working. Men and women in turn lay snares for each other till we cannot but recall the prophet's words: "the partridge hath cried aloud, she hath gathered young which she hath not brought forth, she getteth riches and not by right; in the midst of her days she shall leave them, and at her end she shall be a fool."

5. The better to deceive men they have added to the maxim given above the saving clause "but not without the grace of God;" and this may at the first blush take in some readers. However, when it is carefully sifted and considered, it can deceive nobody. For while they acknowledge the grace of God, they tell us that our acts do not depend upon His help. Rather, they understand by the grace of God free will and the commandments of the Law. They quote Isaiah's words: "God hath given the law to aid men," and say that we ought to thank Him for having created us such that of our own free will we can choose the good and avoid the evil. Nor do they see that in alleging this the devil uses their lips to hiss out an intolerable blasphemy. For if God's grace is limited to this that He has formed us with wills of our own, and if we are to rest content

with free will, not seeking the divine aid lest this should be impaired, we should cease to pray; for we cannot entreat God's mercy to give us daily what is already in our hands having been given to us once for all. Those who think thus make prayer impossible and boast that free will makes them not merely controllers of themselves but as powerful as God. For they need no external help. Away with fasting, away with every form of self-restraint! For why need I strive to win by toil what has once for all been placed within my reach? The argument that I am using is not mine; it is that put forward by a disciple of Pelagius, or rather one who is the teacher and commander of his whole army. This man, who is the opposite of Paul for he is a vessel of perdition, roams through thickets—not, as his partisans say, of syllogisms, but of solecisms, and theorizes thus: "If I do nothing without the help of God and if all that I do is His act, I cease to labour and the crown that I shall win will belong not to me but to the grace of God. It is idle for Him to have given me the power of choice if I cannot use it without His constant help. For will that requires external support ceases to be will. God has given me freedom of choice, but what becomes of this if I cannot do as I wish?" Accordingly he propounds the following dilemma: "Either once for all I use the power which is given to me, and so preserve the freedom of my will; or I need the help of another, in which case the freedom of my will is wholly abrogated."

6. Surely the man who says this is no ordinary blasphemer; the poison of his heresy is no common poison. Since our wills are free, they argue, we are no longer dependent upon God; and they forget the Apostle's words "what hast thou that thou didst not receive? Now if thou didst receive it why dost thou glory as if thou hadst not received it?" A nice return, truly, does a man make to God when to assert the freedom of his will he rebels against Him! For our parts we gladly embrace this freedom, but we never forget to thank the Giver; knowing that we are powerless unless He continually preserves in us His own gift. As the apostle says, "it is not of him that willeth, nor of him that runneth, but of God that sheweth mercy." To will and to run are mine, but they will cease to be mine unless God brings me His continual aid. For the same apostle says "it is God which worketh in you both to will and to do." And in the Gospel the Saviour says: "my Father worketh hitherto and I work." He is always a giver, always a bestower. It is not enough for me that he has given me grace once; He must give it me always. I seek that I may obtain, and when I have obtained I seek again. I am covetous of God's bounty; and as He is never slack in giving, so I am never weary in receiving. The more I drink, the more I thirst. For I have read the song of the psalmist: "O taste and see that the Lord is good." Every good thing that we have is a tasting of the Lord. When I fancy

myself to have finished the book of virtue, I shall then only be at the beginning. For "the fear of the Lord is the beginning of wisdom," and this fear is in its turn cast out by love. Men are only perfect so far as they know themselves to be imperfect. "So likewise ye," Christ says, "when ye shall have done all those things which are commanded you, say, We are unprofitable servants: we have done that which was our duty to do." If he is unprofitable who has done all, what must we say of him who has failed to do so? This is why the Apostle declares that he has attained in part and apprehended in part, that he is not yet perfect, and that forgetting those things which are behind he reaches forth unto those things which are before. Now he who always forgets the past and longs for the future shews that he is not content with the present.

They are for ever objecting to us that we destroy free will. Nay, we reply, it is you who destroy it; for you use it amiss and disown the bounty of its Giver. Which really destroys freedom? the man who thanks God always and traces back his own tiny rill to its source in Him? or the man who says: "come not near to me, for I am holy; I have no need of Thee. Thou hast given me once for all freedom of choice to do as I wish. Why then dost Thou interfere again to prevent me from doing anything unless Thou Thyself first makest Thy gifts effective in me?" To such an one I would say: "your profession of belief in God's grace is insincere. For you explain this of the state in which man has been created and you do not look for God to help him in his actions. To do this, you argue, would be to surrender human freedom. Thus disdaining the aid of God you have to look to men for help."

7. Listen, only listen, to the blasphemer. "Suppose," he avers, "that I want to bend my finger or to move my hand, to sit, to stand, to walk, to run to and fro, to spit or to blow my nose, to perform the offices of nature; must the help of God be always indispensable to me?" Thankless, nay blasphemous wretch, hear the apostle's declaration: "whether therefore ye eat or drink, or whatsoever ye do, do all to the glory of God." Hear also the words of James: "go to now, ye that say, To-day or to-morrow we will go into such a city and continue there a year, and buy, and sell, and get gain. Whereas ye know not what shall be on the morrow: for what is your life? It is even a vapour that appeareth for a little time, and then vanisheth away. For that ye ought to say, If the Lord will, we shall live, and do this or that. But now ye rejoice in your boastings; all such rejoicing is evil." You fancy that a wrong is inflicted on you and your freedom of choice is destroyed if you are forced to fall back on God as the moving cause of all your actions, if you are made dependent on His Will, and if you have to echo the psalmist's words: "mine eyes are ever toward the Lord: for it is he that shall pluck my feet out of the net." And so you presume rashly to maintain

that each individual is governed by his own choice. But if he is governed by his own choice, what becomes of God's help? If he does not need Christ to rule him, why does Jeremiah write: "the way of man is not in himself" and "the Lord directeth his steps."

You say that the commandments of God are easy, and yet you cannot produce any one who has fulfilled them all. Answer me this: are they easy or are they difficult? If they are easy, then produce some one who has fulfilled them all. Explain also the words of the psalmist: "thou dost cause toil by thy law," and "because of the words of thy lips I have kept hard ways." And make plain our Lord's sayings in the gospel: "enter ye in at the strait gate;" and "love your enemies;" and "pray for them which persecute you." If on the other hand the commandments are difficult and if no man has kept them all, how have you presumed to say that they are easy? Do not you see that you contradict yourself? For either they are easy and countless numbers have kept them; or they are difficult and you have been too hasty in calling them easy.

8. It is a common argument with your party to say that God's commandments are either possible or impossible. So far as they are the former you admit that they are rightly laid upon us; but so far as they are the latter you allege that blame attaches not to us who have received them but to God who has imposed them on us. What! has God commanded me to be what He is, to put no difference between myself and my creator, to be greater than the greatest of the angels, to have a power which no angels possess? Sinlessness is made a characteristic of Christ, "who did no sin neither was guile found in his mouth." But if I am sinless as well as He, how is sinlessness any longer His distinguishing mark? for if this distinction exists, your theory becomes fatal to itself.

You assert that a man may be without sin if he will; and then, as though awakening from a deep sleep, you try to deceive the unwary by adding the saving clause "yet not without the grace of God." For if by his own efforts a man can keep himself without sin, what need has he of God's grace? If on the other hand he can do nothing without this, what is the use of saying that he can do what he cannot do? It is argued that a man may be without sin and perfect if he only wills it. What Christian is there who does not wish to be sinless or who would reject perfection if, as you say, it is to be had for the wishing, and if the will is sure to be followed by the power? There is no Christian who does not wish to be sinless; wishing to be so, therefore, they all will be so. Whether you like it or not you will be caught in this dilemma, that you can produce nobody or hardly anybody who is without sin, yet have to admit that everybody may be sinless if he likes. God's commandments, it is argued, are possible to keep. Who denies it? But how this truth is to be understood the chosen vessel thus most clearly explains: "what the law could not do in that it was weak through the flesh, God, sending his own Son in the likeness of sinful flesh and for sin, condemned sin in the flesh;" and again: "by the deeds of the law there shall no flesh be justified." And to shew that it is not only the law of Moses that is meant or all those precepts which collectively are termed the law, the same apostle writes: "I delight in the law of God after the inward man. But I see another law in my members, warring against the law of my mind, and bringing me into captivity to the law of sin which is in my members. O wretched man that I am: who shall deliver me from the body of this death? The grace of God through Jesus Christ our Lord." Other words of his further explain his meaning: "we know that the law is spiritual: but I am carnal, sold under sin. For that which I do I know not: for what I would that do I not, but what I hate that do I. If then I do that which I would not, I consent unto the law that it is good. Now then it is no more I that do it: but sin that dwelleth in me. For I know that in me (that is, in my flesh) dwelleth no good thing. For to will is present with me: but how to perform that which is good I find not. For the good that I would, I do not: but the evil which I would not, that I do. Now if I do that I would not, it is no more I that do it, but sin that dwelleth in me."

9. But you will demur to this and say that I follow the teaching of the Manichaeans and others who make war against the church's doctrine in the interest of their belief that there are two natures diverse from one another and that there is an evil nature which can in no wise be changed. But it is not against me that you must make this imputation but against the apostle who knows well that God is one thing and man another, that the flesh is weak and the spirit strong. "The flesh lusteth against the spirit and the spirit against the flesh: and these are contrary the one to the other: so that ye cannot do the things that ye would." But from me you will never hear that any nature is essentially evil. Let us learn then from him who tells us so in what sense the flesh is weak. Ask him why he has said: "the good that I would, I do not; the evil which I would not, that I do." What necessity fetters his will? What compulsion commands him to do what he dislikes? And why must he do not what he wishes but what he dislikes and does not wish? He will answer you thus: "nay, but, O man, who art thou that repliest against God? Shall the thing formed say unto him that formed it, Why hast thou made me thus? Hath not the potter power over the clay, of the same lump to make one vessel unto honour and another unto dishonour?" Bring a yet graver charge against God and ask Him why, when Esau and Jacob were still in the womb, He said:

"Jacob have I loved, but Esau have I hated." Accuse Him of injustice because, when Achan the son of Carmi stole part of the spoil of Jericho, He butchered so many thousands for the fault of one. Ask Him why for the sin of the sons of Eli the people were well-nigh annihilated and the ark captured. And why, when David sinned by numbering the people, so many thousands lost their lives. Or lastly make your own the favorite cavil of your associate Porphyry, and ask how God can be described as pitiful and of great mercy when from Adam to Moses and from Moses to the coming of Christ He has suffered all nations to die in ignorance of the Law and of His commandments. For Britain, that province so fertile in despots, the Scottish tribes, and all the barbarians round about as far as the ocean were alike without knowledge of Moses and the prophets. Why should Christ's coming have been delayed to the last times? Why should He not have come before so vast a number had perished? Of this last question the blessed apostle in writing to the Romans most wisely disposes by admitting that he does not know and that only God does. Do you too, then, condescend to remain ignorant of that into which you inquire. Leave to God His power over what is His own; He does not need you to justify His actions. I am the hapless being against whom you ought to direct your insults, I who am for ever reading the words: "by grace ye are saved," and "blessed is he whose transgression is forgiven, whose sin is covered." Yet, to lay bare my own weakness, I know that I wish to do many things which I ought to do and yet cannot. For while my spirit is strong and leads me to life my flesh is weak and draws me to death. And I have the warning of the Lord in my ears: "watch and pray that ye enter not into temptation. The spirit indeed is willing, but the flesh is weak."

10. It is in vain that you misrepresent me and try to convince the ignorant that I condemn free will. Let him who condemns it be himself condemned. We have been created endowed with free will; still it is not this which distinguishes us from the brutes. For human free will, as I have said before, depends upon the help of God and needs His aid moment by moment, a thing which you and yours do not choose to admit. Your position is that, if a man once has free will, he no longer needs the help of God. It is true that freedom of the will brings with it freedom of decision. Still man does not act immediately on his free will, but requires God's aid who Himself needs no aid. You yourself boast that a man's righteousness may be perfect and equal to God's; yet you confess that you are a sinner. Answer me this, then; do you or do you not wish to be free from sin? If you do, why on your principle do you not carry out your desire? And if you do not, do you not prove yourself a despiser of God's commandments? If you are a despiser, then you are a sinner. And if you are a

sinner, then the scripture says: "unto the wicked God saith, what hast thou to do to declare my statutes, or that thou shouldest take my covenant in thy mouth? seeing thou hatest instruction and castest my words behind thee." So long as you are unwilling to do what God commands, so long do you cast His words behind you. And yet like a new apostle you lay down for the world what to do and what not to do. However, your words and your thoughts by no means correspond. For when you say that you are a sinner—yet that a man may be without sin if he will, you wish it to be understood that you are a saint and free from all sin. It is only out of humility that you call yourself a sinner; to give you a chance of praising others while you depreciate yourself.

11. Another of your arguments is also intolerable, one which runs thus: "To be sinless is one thing, to be able to be so is another. The first is not in our power, the second generally is. For though none ever has been sinless, yet, if a man wills to be so, he can be so." What sort of reasoning, I ask, is this? that a man can be what a man never has been! that a thing is possible which according to your own admission, no man has yet achieved! You are predicating of man a quality which, for aught you know, he may never possess! and you are assigning to any chance person a grace which you cannot shew to have marked patriarchs, prophets, or apostles. Listen to the Church's words, plain as they may seem to you or crude or ignorant. And speak what you think; preach publicly what secretly you tell your disciples. You profess to have freedom of choice; why do you not speak your thoughts freely? Your secret chambers hear one doctrine, the crowd around the platform hear another. The uneducated throng, I suppose, is not able to digest your esoteric teaching. Satisfied with the milk-diet of an infant it cannot take solid food.

I have written nothing yet, and still you menace me with the thunders of a reply; hoping, I suppose, that I may be scared by your terrors and may not venture to open my mouth. You fail to see that my purpose in writing is to force you to answer and to commit yourself plainly to doctrines which at present you maintain or ignore, as time, place, and person require. One kind of freedom I must deny to you, the freedom to deny what you have once written. An open avowal on your part of the opinions that you hold will be a victory for the church. For either the language of your reply will correspond to mine, in which case I shall count you no longer as opponents but as friends; or else you will gainsay my doctrine, in which case the making known of your opinion to all the churches will be a triumph for me. To have brought your tenets to light is to have overcome them. Blasphemy is written on the face of them, and a doctrine, which in its very statement is blasphemous, needs no refutation. You threaten me with a reply, but this nobody can escape except the man who does not write at all. How do you know what I am going to say that you talk of a reply? Perhaps I shall take your view and then you will have sharpened your wits to no purpose. Eunomians, Arians, Macedonians—all these, unlike in name, alike in impiety, give me no trouble. For they say what they think. Yours is the only heresy which blushes openly to maintain what secretly it does not fear to teach. But the frenzy of the disciples exposes the silence of the masters; for what they have heard from them in the closet they preach upon the housetop. If their auditors like what they say, their masters get the credit; and if they dislike it, only the disciples are blamed, the masters go free. In this way your heresy has grown and you have deceived many; especially those who cleave to women and are assured that they cannot sin. You are always teaching, you are always denying; you deserve to have the prophet's words applied to you: "give to them glory, O Lord, when they are in travail and in the throes of labour. Give them, O Lord; what wilt thou give? Give them a miscarrying womb and dry breasts." My temper rises and I cannot check my words. The limits of a letter do not admit of a lengthy discussion. I assail nobody by name here. It is only against the teacher of perverse doctrine that I have spoken. If resentment shall induce him to reply, he will but betray himself like a mouse which always leaves traces of its presence; and, when it comes to blows in earnest, will receive more serious wounds.

12. From my youth up until now I have spent many years in writing various works and have always tried to teach my hearers the doctrine that I have been taught publicly in church. I have not followed the philosophers in their discussions but have preferred to acquiesce in the plain words of the apostles. For I have known that it is written: "I will destroy the wisdom of the wise, and will bring to nothing the understanding of the prudent," and "the foolishness of God is wiser than men." This being the case, I challenge my opponents thoroughly to sift all my past writings and, if they can find anything that is faulty in them, to bring it to light. One of two things must happen. Either my works will be found edifying and I shall confute the false charges brought against me; or they will be found blameworthy and I shall confess my error. For I would sooner correct an error than persevere in an opinion proved to be wrong. And as for you, illustrious doctor, go you and do likewise: either defend the statements that you have made, and support your clever theories with corresponding eloquence, and do not when the whim takes you disown your own words; or if, as a man may do, you have made a mistake, confess it frankly and restore harmony where there has been disagreement. Recall to mind how even the soldiers did not rend the coat of the Saviour. When you see brothers at strife you laugh; and are glad that some are called by your name and others

by that of Christ. Better would it be to imitate Jonah and say: "If it is for my sake that this great tempest is upon you, take me up and cast me forth into the sea." He in his humility was thrown into the deep that he might rise again in glory to be a type of the Lord. But you are lifted up in your pride to the stars, only that of you too Jesus may say: "I beheld Satan as lightning fall from heaven."

13. It is true that in the holy scriptures many are called righteous, as Zacharias and Elizabeth, Job, Jehosaphat, Josiah, and many others who are mentioned in the sacred writings. Of this fact I shall, if God gives me grace, give a full explanation in the work which I have promised ; in this letter it must suffice to say that they are called righteous, not because they are faultless but because their faults are eclipsed by their virtues. In fact Zacharias is punished with dumbness, Job is condemned out of his own mouth, and Jehoshaphat and Josiah who are beyond a doubt described as righteous are narrated to have done things displeasing to the Lord. The first leagued himself with the ungodly Ahab and brought upon himself the rebuke of Micaiah; and the second—though forbidden by the word of the Lord spoken by Jeremiah—went against Pharaoh-Nechoh, king of Egypt, and was slain by him. Yet they are both called righteous. Of the rest this is not the time to write; for you have asked me not for a treatise but for a letter. For a complete refutation I require leisure and then I hope to destroy all their cavils by the help of Christ. For this purpose I shall rely on the holy scriptures in which God every day speaks to those who believe. And this is the warning which I would give through you to all who are assembled within your holy and illustrious house, that they should not allow one or at the most three mannikins to taint them with the dregs of so many heresies and with the infamy—to say the least—attaching to them. A place once famous for virtue and holiness must not be defiled by the presumption of the devil and by unclean associations. And let those who supply money to such men know that they are adding to the ranks of the heretics, raising up enemies to Christ and fostering his avowed opponents. It is idle for them to profess one thing with their lips when by their actions they are proved to think another.

LETTER CXXXIV. TO AUGUSTINE

Jerome acknowledges the receipt of Letters CXXXI. and CXXXII. and excuses himself from answering the questions raised in them on the twofold ground (1) that the times are evil and (2) that it is inexpedient that he should be supposed to differ from Augustine. He prays for the speedy extinction of

Pelagianism, regrets that he cannot send Augustine a critical Latin text of the O.T., and concludes with a number of salutations from himself and those with him. The date of the letter is 416 a.d. Its number in Augustine's Letters is CLXXII.

LETTER CXXXV. FROM POPE INNOCENT TO AURELIUS

Shortly after the synod of Diospolis the Pelagians exulting in their success made an attack upon Jerome's monasteries at Bethlehem which they pillaged and partially burned. This gained for him the sympathy of Innocent who now (a.d. 417) asks Aurelius to transmit to him the letter which follows this.

Innocent to his most esteemed friend and brother Aurelius.

Our fellow-presbyter Jerome has informed us of your most dutiful desire to come to see us. We suffer with him as with a member of our own flock. We have been swift also to take such measures as have appeared to us expedient and practicable. As you count yourself one of us, most dear brother, make haste to transmit the following letter to the aforesaid Jerome.

LETTER CXXXVI. FROM POPE INNOCENT TO JEROME

Innocent expresses his sympathy with Jerome and promises to take strong measures to punish his opponents if he will bring specific charges against them. The date of the letter is a.d. 417.

Innocent to his most esteemed son, the presbyter Jerome.

The apostle bears witness that contention has never done good in the church; and for this reason he gives direction that heretics should be admonished once or twice in the beginning of their heresy and not subjected to a long series of rebukes. Where this rule is negligently observed, the evil to be guarded against so far from being evaded is rather intensified.

Your grief and lamentation have so affected us that we can neither act nor advise.

To begin however, we commend you for the constancy of your faith. To quote your own words spoken many times in the ears of many, a man will gladly face misrepresentation or even personal danger on behalf of the truth; if he is looking for the blessedness that is to come. We remind you of what you have yourself preached although we are sure that you need no reminder. The spectacle of these terrible evils has so thoroughly roused us that we have hastened to put forth the authority of the apostolic see to repress the plague in all its manifestations; but as your letters name no individuals and bring no specific charges, there is no one at present against whom we can proceed. But we do all that we can; we sympathize deeply with you. And if you will lay a clear and unambiguous accusation against any persons in particular we will appoint suitable judges to try their cases; or if you, our highly esteemed son, think that it is needful for us to take yet graver and more urgent action, we shall not be slow to do so. Meantime we have written to our brother bishop John advising him to act more considerately, so that nothing may occur in the church committed to him which it is his duty to foresee and to prevent, and that nothing may happen which may subsequently prove a source of trouble to him.

LETTER CXXXVII. FROM POPE INNOCENT TO JOHN, BISHOP OF JERUSALEM

Innocent censures John for having allowed the Pelagians to effuse the disturbance at Bethlehem mentioned in the two preceding letters and exhorts him to be more watchful over his diocese in future. The date of the letter is a.d. 417. This was the year of the death of both John and Innocent, and it is probable that John never received the letter.

Innocent to his most highly esteemed brother John.

The holy virgins Eustochium and Paula have deplored to me the ravages, murders, fires and outrages of all kinds, which they say that the devil has perpetrated in the district belonging to their church; for with wonderful clemency and generosity they have left untold the name and motive of his human agent. Now although there can be no doubt as to who is the guilty person; yet you, my brother, ought to have taken precautions and to have been more careful of your flock so that no disturbance of the kind might arise; for others suffer by your negligence, and you encourage men by it to make havoc of the Lord's flock till His tender lambs, fleeced and weakened by fire, sword and persecution, their relations murdered and dead, are, as we are informed, themselves scarce alive. Does it not touch your sacred responsibility as a priest that the devil has shewn himself so powerful against you and yours? Against you, I say; for surely it speaks ill of your capacity as a priest that a crime so terrible should have been committed in the pale of your church. Where were your precautions? Where, after the blow had been struck, were your attempts at relief? Where too were your words of comfort? These ladies tell me that up to the present they have been in a state of too great apprehension to complain of what they have already suffered. I should judge more gravely of the matter had they spoken to me concerning it more freely than they have. Beware then, brother, of the wiles of the old enemy, and in the spirit of a good ruler be vigilant either to correct or to repress such evils. For they have reached my ears in the shape of rumours rather than as specific accusations. If nothing is done, the law of the Church on the subject of injuries may compel the person who has failed to defend his flock to shew cause for his negligence.

LETTER CXXXVIII. TO RIPARIUS

Jerome praises Riparius for his zeal on behalf of the Catholic faith and for his efforts to put down the Pelagians. He then describes the attack made by these heretics upon the monasteries of Bethlehem. Now, he is glad to say, they have at last been driven from Palestine. Most of them, that is, for some still linger at Joppa including one of their chief leaders. The date is a.d. 417.

That you fight Christ's battles against the enemies of the Catholic Faith your own letters have informed me as well as the reports of many persons, but I am told that you find the winds contrary and that those who ought to have been the world's champions have backed the cause of perdition to each other's ruin. You are to know that in this part of the world, without any human help and merely by the decree of Christ, Catiline has been driven not only from the capital but from the borders of Palestine. Lentulus, however, and many of his fellow-conspirators still linger to our sorrow in Joppa. I myself have thought it better to change my abode than to surrender the true faith; and have chosen to leave my pleasant home rather than to suffer contamination from heresy. For I could not communicate with men who would either have insisted on my instant submission or would else have summoned me to support my opinions by the sword. A good many, I dare say, have told you the story of my sufferings and of the vengeance which Christ's uplifted hand has on my behalf taken upon my enemies. I would beg of you, therefore, to complete the task which you have taken up and not, while you are in it, to leave Christ's church without a defender. Every one knows the weapons that must be used in this warfare; and you, I feel sure will ask for no others. You must contend with all your might against the foe; but it must be not with physical force but with that spiritual charity which is never overcome. The reverend brothers who are with me, unworthy as I am, salute you warmly. The reverend brother, the deacon Alentius, is sure to give you, my worshipful friend, a faithful narrative of all the facts. May Christ our Lord, of His almighty power, keep you safe and mindful of me, truly reverend sir and esteemed brother.

LETTER CXXXIX. TO APRONIUS

Of Apronius nothing is known; but from the mention of Innocent (for whom see Letter CXLIII.) it seems a fair inference that he lived in the West. Jerome here congratulates him on his steadfastness in the faith and exhorts him to come to Bethlehem. He then touches on the mischief done by Pelagius and complains that his own monastery has been destroyed by him or by his partisans. The date of the letter is a.d. 417.

I know not by what wiles of the devil it has come to pass that all your toil and the efforts of the reverend presbyter Innocent and my own prayers and wishes seem for the moment to produce no effect. God be thanked that you are well and that the fire of faith glows in you even when you are in the midst of the devil's wiles. My greatest joy is to hear that my spiritual sons are fighting in the cause of Christ; and assuredly He in whom we believe will so quicken this zeal of ours that we shall be glad freely to shed our blood in defence of His faith.

I grieve to hear that a noble family has been subverted, for what reason I cannot learn; for the bearer of the letter could give me no information. We may well grieve over the loss of our common friends and ask Christ the only potentate and Lord to have mercy upon them. At the same time we have deserved to receive punishment at God's hand for we have harboured the enemies of the Lord.

The best course you can take is to leave everything and to come to the East, before all to the holy places; for everything is now quiet here. The heretics have not, it is true, purged the venom from their breasts, but they do not venture to open their impious mouths. They are "like the deaf adder that stoppeth her ear." Salute your reverend brothers on my behalf.

As for our house, so far as fleshly wealth is concerned, it has been completely destroyed by the onslaughts of the heretics; but by the mercy of Christ it is still filled with spiritual riches. To live on bread is better than to lose the faith.

LETTER CXL. TO CYPRIAN THE PRESBYTER

Cyprian had visited Jerome at Bethlehem and had asked him to write an exposition of Psalm XC. in simple language such as might be readily understood. With this request Jerome now complies, giving a very full account of the psalm, verse by verse, and bringing the treasures of his learning and especially his knowledge of Hebrew to bear upon it. He asserts its Mosaic authorship but is careful to add that "the man of God" may have spoken not for himself but in the name of the Jewish people. He speaks of the five books into which the psalter is divisible and says that it is a mistake to ascribe all the psalms to David. An allusion to the doctrine of Pelagius shows that the letter must belong to Jerome's last years, and Vallarsi is probably right in assigning it to a.d. 418.

LETTER CXLI. TO AUGUSTINE

A short note in which Jerome praises Augustine for the determined stand which he has made against heresy and speaks of him as "the restorer of the ancient faith." The allusion seems to be to his action in the Pelagian controversy. If so, the date is probably 418 a.d. This letter is among those of Augustine, number 195.

LETTER CXLII. TO AUGUSTINE

There is good ground for supposing this to form part of the previous letter. If so, Jerome speaks in a figure of the success gained by Pelagianism in Palestine. "Jerusalem," he says, "is in the hands of Nebuchadnezzar and will not heed the voice of Jeremiah," that is, as the context shews, Jerome himself. This letter is among those of Augustine, number 123.

LETTER CXLIII. TO ALYPIUS AND AUGUSTINE

In this letter Jerome congratulates Alypius and Augustine on their success in strangling the heresy of Caelestius, the co-adjutor of Pelagius, and states that, if he can find time and secretaries, he hopes to write a refutation of the absurd errors of the Pelagian pseudodeacon Annianus. The date is 419 a.d. This letter is among those of Augustine, number 202.

LETTER CXLIV. FROM AUGUSTINE TO OPTATUS

Augustine writes to Optatus, bishop of Milevis, to say that he cannot send him a copy of his letter to Jerome on the origin of the soul (Letter CXXXI.) as it is incomplete without Jerome's reply which he has not yet received. He then criticises the arguments with which Optatus combats traducianism and points out that his reasoning is inconclusive. The date of the letter is a.d. 420. The letter has been somewhat compressed in translation: the involved sentences of the original have been simplified and its redundancies curtailed.

To the blessed lord and brother, sincerely loved and longed-for, his fellow-bishop Optatus, Augustine [sends] greeting in the Lord.

1. By the hand of the reverend presbyter Saturninus I have received a letter from you, venerable sir, in which you earnestly ask me for what I have not yet got. You thus shew clearly your belief that I have already had a reply to my question on the subject. Would that I had! Knowing the eagerness of your expectation, I should never have dreamed of keeping back from you your share in the gift; but if you will believe me, dear brother, it is not so. Although five years have elapsed since I despatched to the East my letter (which was one of inquiry, not of assertion), I have so far received no reply, and am consequently unable to untie the knot as you wish me to do. Had I had both letters, I should gladly have sent you both; but I think it better not to circulate mine by itself lest he to whom it is addressed and who may still answer me as I desire should prove displeased. If I were to publish so elaborate a treatise as mine without his reply to it, he might be justly indignant, and suppose me more intent on displaying my talents than on promoting some useful end. It would look as if I were bent on starting problems too hard for him to solve. It is better to wait for the answer which he probably means to send. For I am well aware that he has other subjects to occupy him which are more serious and urgent than this question of mine. Your holiness will readily understand this if you read what he wrote to me a year later when my messenger was returning. The following is an extract from his letter:

"A most trying time has come upon us in which I have found it better to hold my peace than to speak. Consequently my studies have ceased, that I may not give occasion to what Appius calls the eloquence of dogs.' For this reason I have not been able to send any answer to your two learned and brilliant letters. Not, indeed, that I think anything in them needs correction, but that I recall the Apostle's words: One judges in this way, another in that; let every man give full expression to his own opinion.' All that a lofty intellect can draw from the well of holy scripture has been drawn by you. So much your reverence must allow me to say in praise of your ability. But though in any discussion between us our joint object is the advancement of learning, our rivals and especially the heretics will ascribe any difference of opinion between us to mutual jealousy. For my part, however, I am resolved to love you, to look up to you, to reverence and admire you, and to defend your opinions as my own. I have also in a dialogue which I have recently brought out made allusion to your holiness in suitable terms. Let us, rather, then, strain every nerve to banish from the churches that most pernicious heresy, which feigns repentance that it may have liberty to teach in our churches. For were it to come out into the light of day, it would be expelled and die."

2. You can see, worshipful brother, from this reply that my friend does not refuse to answer my inquiry; he postpones it because he is condemned to give his time to more urgent matters. Moreover, that he is well disposed towards me is clear from his friendly warning that a controversy between us begun in all charity and in the interests of learning may be misconstrued by jealous and heretical persons as due to mutual illfeeling. No; it will be better for the public to have both together, his explanation as well as my inquiry. For, as I shall have to thank him for instructing me if he is able to explain the matter, the discussion will be of no small advantage when it comes to the knowledge of the world. Those who come after us will not only know what view they ought to take of a subject thus fully argued but will also learn how under the divine mercy brothers in affection may dispute a difficult question and yet preserve each other's esteem.

3. On the other hand, if I were to publish the letter in which I raise this obscure point without the reply in which it may be set at rest, it might circulate widely and reach men who "comparing themselves," as the Apostle says, "with themselves," would misconstrue a motive which they could not understand, and would explain my feeling towards one whom I love and esteem for his immense services not as it would appear to them (for it would be invisible to them) but as their own fancy and malice would dictate. Now this is a danger which, so far as in me lies, I am bound to guard against. But if a document which I am unwilling to publish is published without my consent and placed in hands from which I would withhold it, then I shall have to resign myself to the will of God. Indeed, had I wished to keep my words permanently undivulged I should never have sent them to any one. For if (though I hope it may not be so) chance or necessity shall prevent any reply being ever given me, my letter of inquiry is still bound sooner or later to come to light. Nor will it be useless to those who read it; for, although they will nor find what they seek, they will learn how much better it is, when one is uninformed, to put questions than to make assertions; and in the meantime those whom they consult will work out the points raised by me, laying aside contention and in the interests of learning and charity trying to obtain sound opinions about them. Thus they will either arrive at the solutions they desire, or their faculties will be quickened and they will learn from the investigation that farther inquiry is

useless. At present, however, as I have no reason to despair of an answer from my friend I have decided not to publish the letter I have sent him, and I trust, my dear comrade, that this decision may commend itself to you. It should do so, for you have not asked for my letter so much as for the answer to it; and this I would gladly send you if I had it to send. It is true that in your epistle you speak of "the lucid demonstration of my wisdom which in virtue of my life the Giver of light has bestowed upon me"; and if by this you mean not the way in which I have stated the problem but a solution which I have obtained of the point in question, I should like to gratify your wish. But I must admit that I have so far failed to discover how the soul can derive its sin from Adam (a truth which it is unlawful to question) and yet not itself be derived from Adam. At present I think it better to sift the matter farther than to dogmatize rashly.

4. Your letter speaks of "many old men and persons educated by learned priests whom you have failed to recall to your modest way of thinking, and to a statement of the case which is truth itself." You do not, however, explain what this mode of expression is. If your old men hold fast what they have received from learned priests, how comes it that you are troubled by a boorish mob of unlettered clerics? On the other hand, if the old men and the unlettered clerics have wickedly departed from the priests' teachings, surely these latter are the persons to correct them and restrain them from controversial excesses. Again when you say that "you as a new-fledged and inexperienced teacher have been afraid to tamper with the doctrines handed down by great and famous bishops, and that you have been loth to draw men into a better path lest you should cast discredit on the dead," do you not imply that in refusing to agree with you the objects of your solicitude are but preferring the tradition of great and famous bishops to the views of a new-fledged and inexperienced teacher? Of their conduct in the matter I say nothing, but I am most anxious to learn that "mode of expression which is truth itself," not the thing expressed, but the mode of expression.

5. For you have made it sufficiently plain to me that you disapprove of those who assert that men's souls are derived from that of the protoplast and propagated from one generation to another; but as your letter does not inform me, I have no means of knowing on what grounds and from what passages of scripture you have shewn this view to be false. What does commend itself to you is not clear either from your letter to the brothers at Caesarea or from that which you have lately addressed to me. Only I see that you believe and write that "God has been, is, and will be the maker of men, and that there is nothing either in heaven or on earth which does not owe its existence wholly to Him."

This is of course a truism which nobody can call in question. But as you affirm that souls are not propagated, you ought to explain out of what God makes them. Is it out of some pre-existing material, or is it out of nothing? For it is impossible that you should hold the opinion of Origen, Priscillian, and other heretics that it is for deeds done in a former life that souls are confined in earthly and mortal bodies. This opinion is, indeed, flatly contradicted by the apostle who says of Jacob and Esau that before they were born they had done neither good nor evil. Your view of the matter, then, is known to me though only partially, but of your reasons for supposing it to be true I know nothing. This was why in a former letter I asked you to send me your confession of faith, the one which you were vexed to find that one of your presbyters had signed dishonestly. I now again ask you for this, as well as for any passages of scripture which you have brought to bear on the question. For you say in your letter to the brothers at Caesarea that you "have resolved to have all definitions of dogma reviewed by lay judges, sitting by general invitation, and investigating all points touching the faith." And you continue: "the divine mercy has made it possible for them to put forward their views in a positive and definite form, which your modest ability has reinforced with a great weight of evidence." Now it is this "great weight of evidence" which I am so anxious to obtain. For, so far as I can see, your one aim has been to refute your opponents when they deny that our souls are the handiwork of God. If they hold such a view, you are right in thinking that it should be condemned. Were they to say the same thing of our bodies, they would be forced to retract it, or else be held up to execration. For what Christian can deny that every single human body is the work of God? Yet when we admit that they are of divine origin we do not mean to deny that they are humanly engendered. When therefore it is asserted that our souls are procreated from a kind of immaterial seed, and that they, like our bodies, come to us from our parents, yet are made souls by the working of God, it is not by human guesses that the assertion is to be refuted, but by the witness of divine scripture. Numbers of passages may indeed be quoted from the sacred books which have canonical authority, to prove that our souls are God's handiwork. But such passages only refute those who deny that each several human soul is made by God; not at all those who while they admit this contend that, like our bodies, they are formed by divine agency through the instrumentality of parents. To refute these you must look for unmistakable texts; or, if you have already discovered such, shew your affection by communicating them to me. For though I seek them most diligently I fail to find them.

As stated shortly by yourself (at the end of your letter to the brothers at Caesarea) your dilemma is as follows: "inasmuch as I am your son and disciple and have but recently by God's help come to consider these mysteries, I beg you with your priestly wisdom to teach me which of two opposite views I ought to hold. Am I to maintain that souls are transmitted by generation, and that they are derived in some mysterious way from Adam our first-formed father? Or am I with your brothers and the priests who are here to hold that God has been, is, and will be the author and maker of all things and all men?"

6. Of the two alternatives which you thus put forward you wish to be urged to choose one or other; and this would be the course of wisdom if your alternatives were so contrary that the choice of one would involve the rejection of the other. But as it is, instead of selecting one of them a man may say that they are both true. He may maintain that the souls of all mankind are derived from Adam our first-formed father, and yet believe and assert that God has been, is, and will be the author and maker of all things and all men. How on your principles is such a man to be confuted? Shall we say: "If they are transmitted by generation God is not their author, for He does not make them?" In that case he will reply: "Bodies too are engendered and not made by God; on your shewing, then He is not their author." Will any one maintain that God is the maker of no bodies but Adam's which He made out of the dust and Eve's which He formed out of Adam's side; and that other bodies are not made by Him because they are engendered by human parents?

7. If your opponents go so far in maintaining the derivation of souls as to deny that they are made and formed by God, you may use this argument as a weapon to confute them so far as God's help enables you. But if, while they assert that the soul's beginnings come from Adam first and then from a man's parents, they at the same time hold that the soul in every man is created and formed by God the author of all things, they can only be confuted out of scripture. Search therefore till you find a passage that is neither obscure nor capable of a double meaning; or if you have already found one, hand it on to me as I have begged you to do. But if, like myself, you have so far failed to discover any such passage, you must still strain every nerve to confute those who say that souls are in no sense God's handiwork. This seems to be your opponents position, for in your first letter you write that "they have secretly whispered scandalous doctrines and have forsaken your communion and the obedience of the church on account of this foolish, nay impious opinion." Against such men defend and uphold by every possible expedient the doctrine you have laid down in the same letter, that God has been, is, and will be the maker of souls; and that everything in heaven and on earth owes its existence

wholly to Him. For this is true of every creature; and as such is to be believed, asserted, defended, and proved. God has been, is, and will be the author and maker of all things and all men as you have told your fellow-bishops of the province of Caesarea, exhorting them to adopt the doctrine by the example of your brothers and fellow-priests. But there are two quite distinct dilemmas: (1) Is God the author and maker of all souls and bodies (the true view), or is there something in nature which He has not made (a view which is wholly erroneous)? (2) If souls are undoubtedly God's handiwork, does He make them directly, or indirectly by propagation? It is in dealing with this second dilemma that I would have you to be sober and vigilant. Else in refuting the propagation-theory you may fall incautiously into the heresy of Pelagius. Everybody knows that human bodies are propagated by generation; yet if we are right in saying that all human souls—and not only those of Adam and Eve—are created by God, it is clear that to assert their transmission by generation is not to deny their divine origin. For in this view God makes the soul as He makes the body, indirectly by a process of generation. If the truth condemns this as an error, some fresh argument must be sought to confute it. No persons could better advise you on the point (if only they were within reach) than those dead worthies whom you feared to discredit by drawing men away from them into a better path. They were, you said, great and famous bishops while you were a new-fledged and inexperienced teacher; thus you were loth to tamper with their doctrines. Would that I could know on what passages these great men rested their opinion that souls are transmitted! For in your letter to the brothers at Caesarea, you speak of their view with a total disregard of their authority, as a new invention, an unheard-of doctrine; though we all know that, error as it may be, it is no novelty but old and of ancient date.

8. Now when we have reason to be doubtful about a point, we need not doubt that we are right in doubting. There is no doubt but that we ought to doubt things that are doubtful. For instance, the Apostle has no doubt about doubting whether he was in the body or out of the body when he was carried up into the third heaven. Whether it was thus or thus, he says, I know not; God knows. Why may not I, then, so long as I have no light, doubt whether my soul comes to me by generation or unengendered? Why may I not be doubtful about this, so long as I do not doubt that in either case it is the work of God most high? Why may I not say; "I know that my soul owes its existence to God and is altogether His handiwork; but whether it comes by generation, as the body does, or unengendered, as was Adam's soul, I know not; God knows." You wish me to assert positively one view or the other. I might do so if I knew which was right. You may have some light on the point, and if so you

will find me keener to learn what I know not than to teach what I know. But if, like myself, you are in the dark, you should pray, as I do, that either through one of His servants, or with His own lips, He would teach us who said to His disciples: "Be not ye called masters; for one is your master, even Christ." Yet such knowledge is only expedient for us when He knows it to be expedient who knows both what He has to teach and what we ought to learn. Nevertheless, to you, my dear friend, I confess my eagerness. Still much as I desire to know this after which you seek, I would sooner know when the desire of all nations shall come and when the kingdom of the saints will be set up, than how my soul has come to its earthly abode. But when His disciples (who are our apostles) put this question to the all-knowing Christ, they were told: "It is not yours to know the times or the seasons which the Father hath put in His own power." What if Christ, who knows what is expedient for us, knows this knowledge not to be expedient? Through Him I know that it is not ours to know the times which God has placed in His own power; but concerning the origin of souls, I am ignorant whether it is or is not ours to know. If I could be sure that such knowledge is not for us, I should cease not only to dogmatize, but even to inquire. As it is, though the subject is so deep and dark that my fear of becoming a rash teacher is almost greater than my eagerness to learn the truth, I still wish to know it if I can do so. It may be that the knowledge for which the psalmist prays: "Lord, make me to know mine end," is much more necessary; yet I would that my beginning also might be revealed to me.

9. But even as touching this I must not be ungrateful to my Master. I know that the human soul is spiritual not corporeal, that it is endowed with reason and intelligence, and that it is not of God's essence but a thing created. It is both mortal and immortal: the first because it is subject to corruption and separable from the life of God in which it is alone blessed, the second because its consciousness must ever continue and form the source of its happiness or woe. It does not, it is true, owe its immersion in the flesh to acts done before the flesh; yet in man it is never without sin, not even when "its life has been but for one day." Of those engendered of the seed of Adam no man is born without sin, and it is necessary even for babes to be born anew in Christ by the grace of regeneration. All this I know concerning the soul, and it is much; the greater part of it, indeed, is not only knowledge but matter of faith as well. I rejoice to have learned it all and I can truly say that I know it. If there are things of which I am still ignorant (as whether God creates souls by generation or apart from it—for that He does create them I have no doubt) I would sooner know the truth than be ignorant of it. But so long as I cannot know it I

had rather suspend my judgment than assert what is plainly contrary to an indisputable truth.

10. You, my brother, ask me to decide for you whether men's souls as made by the Creator come like their bodies by generation from Adam, or whether like his soul they are made without generation and separately for each individual. For in one way or the other we both admit that they are God's handiwork. Suffer me then in turn to ask you a question. Can a soul derive original sin from a source from which it is not itself derived? For unless we are to fall into the detestable heresy of Pelagius, we must both of us allow that all souls do derive original sin from Adam. And if you cannot answer my question, pray give me leave to confess my ignorance alike of your question and of my own. But if you already know what I ask, teach me and then I will teach you what you wish to know. Pray do not be displeased with me for taking this line, for though I have given you no positive answer to your question, I have shewn you how you ought to put it. When once you are clear about that, you may be quite positive where you have been doubtful.

This much I have thought it right to write to your holiness seeing that you are so sure that the transmission of souls is a doctrine to be rejected. Had I been writing to maintainers of the doctrine I might perhaps have shewn how ignorant they are of what they fancy they know and how cautious they should be not to make rash assertions.

It may perhaps perplex you that in my friend's answer as I have quoted it in this letter he mentions two letters of mine to which he has no time to reply. Only one of these deals with the problem of the soul; in the other I have asked light on another difficulty. Again when he urges me to take more pains for the removal from the church of a most pernicious heresy, he alludes to the error of the Pelagians which I earnestly beg you, my brother, at all hazards to avoid. In speculating or arguing on the origin of the soul you must never give place to this heresy with its insidious suggestions. For there is no soul, save that of the one Mediator, which does not derive original sin from Adam. Original sin is that which is fastened on the soul at its birth and from which it can only be freed by being born again.

LETTER CXLV. TO EXUPERANTIUS

Jerome advises Exuperantius, a Roman soldier, to come to Bethlehem and with his brother Quintilian to become a monk. According to Palladius (H. L. c.

lxxx.) Exuperantius came to Jerome but went away again unable to endure his violence and ill-will.' The date of the letter is unknown.

Among all the favours that my friendship with the reverend brother Quintilian has conferred upon me the greatest is this that he has introduced me in the spirit to you whom I do not know personally. Who can fail to love a man who, while he wears the cloak and uniform of a soldier does the work of a prophet, and while his outer man gives promise of quite a different character, overcomes this by the inner man which is formed after the image of the creator. I come forward therefore to challenge you to an interchange of letters and beg that you will often give me occasion to reply to you that I may for the future feel less constraint in writing.

For the present I will content myself by suggesting to your discretion that you should bear in mind the apostle's words: "Art thou bound unto a wife? Seek not to be loosed. Art thou loosed from a wife? Seek not a wife;" that is, seek not that binding which is contrary to loosing. He who has contracted the obligations of marriage, is bound, and he who is bound is a slave; on the other hand he who is loosed is free. Since therefore you rejoice in the freedom of Christ, since your life is better than your profession, since you are all but on the housetop of which the Saviour speaks; you ought not to come down to take your clothes, you ought not to look behind you, you ought not having put your hand to the plough, then to let it go. Rather, if you can, imitate Joseph and leave your garment in the hand of your Egyptian mistress, that naked you may follow your Lord and Saviour. For in the gospel He says: "Whosoever doth not leave all that he hath and bear his cross and come after me cannot be my disciple." Cast from you the burthen of the things of this world, and seek not those riches which in the gospel are compared to the humps of camels. Naked and unencumbered fly up to heaven; masses of gold will but impede the wings of your virtue. I do not speak thus because I know you to be covetous, but because I have a notion that your object in remaining so long in the army is to fill that purse which the Lord has commanded you to empty. For they who have possessions and riches are bidden to sell all that they have and to give to the poor and then to follow the Saviour. Thus if your worship is rich already you ought to fulfil the command and sell your riches; or if you are still poor you ought not to amass what you will have to pay away. Christ accepts the sacrifices made for him according as he who makes them has a willing mind. Never were any men poorer than the apostles; yet never any left more for the Lord than they. The poor widow in the gospel who cast but two mites into the treasury was set before all the men of wealth because she gave all that she had. So it should be with you. Seek not for wealth which you will have to pay away; but rather give up that which you have already acquired that Christ may know his new recruit to be brave and resolute, and then when you are a great way off His Father will run with joy to meet you. He will give you a robe, will put a ring upon your finger, and will kill for you the fatted calf. Then when you are freed from all encumbrances God will soon make a way for you to cross the sea to me with your reverend brother Quintilian. I have now knocked at the door of friendship: if you open it to me you will find me a frequent visitor.

LETTER CXLVI. TO EVANGELUS

Jerome refutes the opinion of those who make deacons equal to presbyters, but in doing so himself makes presbyters equal to bishops.

The date of the letter is unknown.

1. We read in Isaiah the words, "the fool will speak folly," and I am told that some one has been mad enough to put deacons before presbyters, that is, before bishops. For when the apostle clearly teaches that presbyters are the same as bishops, must not a mere server of tables and of widows be insane to set himself up arrogantly over men through whose prayers the body and blood of Christ are produced? Do you ask for proof of what I say? Listen to this passage: "Paul and Timotheus, the servants of Jesus Christ, to all the saints in Christ Jesus which are at Philippi with the bishops and deacons." Do you wish for another instance? In the Acts of the Apostles Paul thus speaks to the priests of a single church: "Take heed unto yourselves and to all the flock, in the which the Holy Ghost hath made you bishops, to feed the church of God which He purchased with His own blood." And lest any should in a spirit of contention argue that there must then have been more bishops than one in a single church, there is the following passage which clearly proves a bishop and a presbyter to be the same. Writing to Titus the apostle says: "For this cause left I thee in Crete, that thou shouldest set in order the things that are wanting, and ordain presbyters in every city, as I had appointed thee: if any be blameless, the husband of one wife, having faithful children not accused of riot or unruly. For a bishop must be blameless as the steward of God." And to Timothy he says: "Neglect not the gift that is in thee, which was given thee by prophecy, with the laying on of the hands of the presbytery." Peter also says in his first epistle: "The presbyters which are among you I exhort, who am your fellow-presbyter and a witness of the sufferings of Christ and also a partaker of the glory that shall be revealed: feed the flock of Christ . . . taking the oversight

thereof not by constraint but willingly, according unto God." In the Greek the meaning is still plainer, for the word used is episkopountes , that is to say, overseeing, and this is the origin of the name overseer or bishop. But perhaps the testimony of these great men seems to you insufficient. If so, then listen to the blast of the gospel trumpet, that son of thunder, the disciple whom Jesus loved and who reclining on the Saviour's breast drank in the waters of sound doctrine. One of his letters begins thus: "The presbyter unto the elect lady and her children whom I love in the truth;" and another thus: "The presbyter unto the well-beloved Gaius whom I love in the truth." When subsequently one presbyter was chosen to preside over the rest, this was done to remedy schism and to prevent each individual from rending the church of Christ by drawing it to himself. For even at Alexandria from the time of Mark the Evangelist until the episcopates of Heraclas and Dionysius the presbyters always named as bishop one of their own number chosen by themselves and set in a more exalted position, just as an army elects a general, or as deacons appoint one of themselves whom they know to be diligent and call him archdeacon. For what function, excepting ordination, belongs to a bishop that does not also belong to a presbyter? It is not the case that there is one church at Rome and another in all the world beside. Gaul and Britain, Africa and Persia, India and the East worship one Christ and observe one rule of truth. If you ask for authority, the world outweighs its capital. Wherever there is a bishop, whether it be at Rome or at Engubium, whether it be at Constantinople or at Rhegium, whether it be at Alexandria or at Zoan, his dignity is one and his priesthood is one. Neither the command of wealth nor the lowliness of poverty makes him more a bishop or less a bishop. All alike are successors of the apostles.

2. But you will say, how comes it then that at Rome a presbyter is only ordained on the recommendation of a deacon? To which I reply as follows. Why do you bring forward a custom which exists in one city only? Why do you oppose to the laws of the Church a paltry exception which has given rise to arrogance and pride? The rarer anything is the more it is sought after. In India pennyroyal is more costly than pepper. Their fewness makes deacons persons of consequence while presbyters are less thought of owing to their great numbers. But even in the church of Rome the deacons stand while the presbyters seat themselves, although bad habits have by degrees so far crept in that I have seen a deacon, in the absence of the bishop, seat himself among the presbyters and at social gatherings give his blessing to them. Those who act thus must learn that they are wrong and must give heed to the apostles words: "it is not reason that we should leave the word of God and serve tables." They must consider the reasons which led to the appointment of deacons at the begin-

ning. They must read the Acts of the Apostles and bear in mind their true position.

Of the names presbyter and bishop the first denotes age, the second rank. In writing both to Titus and to Timothy the apostle speaks of the ordination of bishops and of deacons, but says not a word of the ordination of presbyters; for the fact is that the word bishops includes presbyters also. Again when a man is promoted it is from a lower place to a higher. Either then a presbyter should be ordained a deacon, from the lesser office, that is, to the more important, to prove that a presbyter is inferior to a deacon; or if on the other hand it is the deacon that is ordained presbyter, this latter should recognize that, although he may be less highly paid than a deacon, he is superior to him in virtue of his priesthood. In fact as if to tell us that the traditions handed down by the apostles were taken by them from the old testament, bishops, presbyters and deacons occupy in the church the same positions as those which were occupied by Aaron, his sons, and the Levites in the temple.

LETTER CXLVII. TO SABINIANUS

Jerome writes in severe but moderate language to Sabinianus, a deacon, calling on him to repent of his sins. Of these he recounts at length the two most serious, an act of adultery at Rome and an attempt to seduce a nun at Bethlehem. The date of the letter is uncertain.

1. Of old, when it had repented the Lord that he had anointed Saul to be king over Israel, we are told that Samuel mourned for him; and again, when Paul heard that there was fornication among the Corinthians and such fornication as was not so much as named among the gentiles, he besought them to repent with these tearful words: "lest, when I come again, my God will humble me among you and that I shall bewail many which have sinned already and have not repented of the uncleanness and fornication and lasciviousness which they have committed." If an apostle or a prophet, themselves immaculate, could speak thus with a clemency embracing all, how much more earnestly should a sinner like me plead with a sinner like you. You have fallen and refuse to rise; you do not so much as lift your eyes to heaven; having wasted your father's substance you take pleasure in the husks that the swine eat; and climbing the precipice of pride you fall headlong into the deep. You make your belly your God instead of Christ; you are a slave to lust; your glory is in your shame; you fatten yourself like a victim for the slaughter, and imitate the lives of the wicked, careless of their doom. "Thou knowest not that the goodness of God

leadeth thee to repentance. But after thy hardness and impenitent heart thou treasurest up unto thyself wrath against the day of wrath." Or is it that your heart is hardened, as Pharaoh's was, because your punishment is deferred and you are not smitten at the moment? The ten plagues were sent upon Pharaoh not as by an angry God but as by a warning father, and his day of grace was prolonged until he repented of his repentance. Yet doom overtook him when he pursued through the wilderness the people whom he had previously let go and presumed to enter the very sea in the eagerness of his pursuit. For only in this one way could he learn the lesson that He is to be dreaded whom even the elements obey. He had said: "I know not the Lord, neither will I let Israel go;" and you imitate him when you say: "The vision that he seeth is for many days to come, and he prophesieth of the times that are far off." Yet the same prophet confutes you with these words: "Thus saith the Lord God, There shall none of my words be prolonged any more, but the word which I have spoken shall be done." David too says of the godless (and of godlessness you have proved yourself not a slight but an eminent example), that in this world they rejoice in good fortune and say: "How doth God know? And is there knowledge in the Most High? Behold these are the ungodly who prosper in the world; they increase in riches." Then almost losing his footing and staggering where he stands he complains, saying "Verily I have cleansed my heart in vain, and washed my hands in innocency." For he had previously said: "I was envious at the foolish, when I saw the prosperity of the wicked. For they have no regard for death, but their strength is firm. They are not in trouble as other men are; neither are they plagued like other men. Therefore pride compasseth them about as a chain; violence covereth them as a garment. Their eyes stand out with fatness: they have more than heart could wish. They are corrupt, and speak wickedly concerning oppression: they speak loftily. They set their mouth against the heavens, and their tongue walketh through the earth."

2. Does not this whole psalm seem to you to be written of yourself? Certainly you are hale and strong; and like a new apostle of Antichrist, when you are found out in one city, you pass to another. You are in no need of money, no crushing blow strikes you down, neither are you plagued as other men who are not like you mere brute beasts. Therefore you are lifted up into pride, and lust covers you as a garment. Out of your fat and bloated carcass you breathe out words fraught with death. You never consider that you must some day die, nor feel the slightest repentance when you have satisfied your lust. You have more than heart can wish; and, not to be alone in your wrongdoing, you invent scandals concerning those who are God's servants. Though you know it not, it is against the most High that you are speaking iniquity and against the

heavens that you are setting your mouth. It is no wonder that God's servants small and great are blasphemed by you, when your fathers did not scruple to call even the master of the house Beelzebub. "The disciple is not above his master nor the servant above his lord." If they did this with the green tree, what will you do with me, the dry? Much in the same way also the offended believers in the book of Malachi gave expression to feelings like yours; for they said, "It is vain to serve God: and what profit is it that we have kept his ordinance, and that we have walked mournfully before the Lord of Hosts? And now we call the proud happy; yea, they that work wickedness are set up; yea, they that tempt God are even delivered." Yet the Lord afterwards threatens them with a day of judgment; and announcing beforehand the distinction that shall then be made between the righteous and the unrighteous, speaks to them thus: "Return ye, and discern between the righteous and the wicked, between him that serveth God and him that serveth him not."

3. All this may perhaps seem to you matter for jesting, seeing that you take so much pleasure in comedies and lyrics and mimes like those of Lentulus; although so blunted is your wit that I am not disposed to allow that you can understand even language so simple. You may treat the words of prophets with contempt, but Amos will still make answer to you: "Thus saith the Lord, For three transgressions and for four shall I not turn away from him?" For inasmuch as Damascus, Gaza, Tyre, Edom, the Ammonites and the Moabites, the Jews also and the children of Israel, although God had often prophesied to them to turn and to repent, had refused to hear His voice, the Lord wishing to shew that He had most just cause for the wrath that he was going to bring upon them used the words already quoted, "For three transgressions and for four shall I not turn away from them?" It is wicked, God says, to harbour evil thoughts; yet I have allowed them to do so. It is still more wicked to carry them out; yet in My mercy and kindness I have permitted even this. But should the sinful thought have become the sinful deed? Should men in their pride have trampled thus on my tenderness? Nevertheless "I have no pleasure in the death of the wicked, but that the wicked turn from his way and live;" and as it is not they that are whole who need a physician but they that are sick, even after his sin I hold out a hand to the prostrate sinner and exhort him, polluted as he is in his own blood, to wash away his stains with tears of penitence. But if even then he shews himself unwilling to repent, and if, after he has suffered shipwreck, he refuses to clutch the plank which alone can save him, I am compelled at last to say: "Thus saith the Lord, For three transgressions and for four shall I not turn away from him?" For this "turning away" God accounts a punishment, inasmuch as the sinner is left to his own devices.

It is thus that he visits the sins of the fathers upon the children unto the third and fourth generation; not punishing those who sin immediately but pardoning their first offences and only passing sentence on them for their last. For if it were otherwise and if God were to stand forth on the moment as the avenger of iniquity, the church would lose many of its saints; and certainly would be deprived of the apostle Paul. The prophet Ezekiel, from whom we have quoted above, repeating God's words spoken to himself speaks thus: "Open thy mouth and eat what I shall give thee. And behold," he says, "an hand was sent unto me; and, lo, a roll of a book was therein; and he spread it before me; and it was written within and without: and there was written therein lamentations, and a song, and woe." The first of these three belongs to you if you prove willing, as a sinner, to repent of your sins. The second belongs to those who are holy, who are called upon to sing praises to God; for praise does not become a sinner's mouth. And the third belongs to persons like you who in despair have given themselves over to uncleanness, to fornication, to the belly, and to the lowest lusts; men who suppose that death ends all and that there is nothing beyond it; who say: "When the overflowing scourge shall pass through it shall not come unto us." The book which the prophet eats is the whole series of the Scriptures, which in turn bewail the penitent, celebrate the righteous, and curse the desperate. For nothing is so displeasing to God as an impenitent heart. Impenitence is the one sin for which there is no forgiveness. For if one who ceases to sin is pardoned even after he has sinned, and if prayer has power to bend the judge; it follows that every impenitent sinner must provoke his judge to wrath. Thus despair is the one sin for which there is no remedy. By obstinate rejection of God's grace men turn His mercy into sternness and severity. Yet, that you may know that God does every day call sinners to repentance, hear Isaiah's words: "In that day," he says, "did the Lord God of Hosts call to weeping and to mourning and to baldness and to girding with sackcloth: and behold joy and gladness, slaying oxen, and killing sheep, eating flesh, and drinking wine; let us eat and drink, for to-morrow we shall die." After these words filled with the recklessness of despair the Scripture goes on to say: "And it was revealed in my ears by the Lord of Hosts, Surely this iniquity shall not be purged from you till ye die." Only when they become dead to sin, will their sin be forgiven them. For, so long as they live in sin, it cannot be put away.

4. Have mercy I beseech you upon your soul. Consider that God's judgment will one day overtake you. Remember by what a bishop you were ordained. The holy man was mistaken in his choice; but this he might well be. For even God repented that he had anointed Saul to be king. Even among the

twelve apostles Judas was found a traitor. And Nicolas of Antioch—a deacon like yourself—disseminated the Nicolaitan heresy and all manner of uncleanness. I do not now bring up to you the many virgins whom you are said to have seduced, or the noble matrons who have suffered death because violated by you, or the greedy profligacy with which you have hied through dens of sin. For grave and serious as such sins are in themselves, they are trivial indeed when compared with those which I have now to narrate. How great must be the sin beside which seduction and adultery are insignificant? Miserable wretch that you are! when you enter the cave wherein the Son of God was born, where truth sprang out of the earth and the land did yield her increase, it is to make an assignation. Have you no fear that the babe will cry from the manger, that the newly delivered virgin will see you, that the mother of the Lord will behold you? The angels cry aloud, the shepherds run, the star shines down from heaven, the wise men worship, Herod is terrified, Jerusalem is in confusion, and meantime you creep into a virgin's cell to seduce the virgin to whom it belongs. I am filled with consternation and a shiver runs through me, soul and body, when I try to set before your eyes the deed that you have done. The whole church was keeping vigil by night and proclaiming Christ as its Lord; in one spirit though in different tongues the praises of God were being sung. Yet you were squeezing your love-notes into the openings of what is now the altar, as it was once the manger, of the Lord, choosing this place in order that your unhappy victim might find and read them when she came to kneel and worship there. Then you took your place among the singers, and with impudent nods communicated your passion to her.

5. Oh! crying shame! I can go no farther. For sobs anticipate my words, and indignation and grief choke me in the act of utterance. Oh! for the sea of Tully's eloquence! Oh! for the impetuous current of the invective of Demosthenes! Yet in this case I am sure you would both be dumb; your eloquence would fail you. A deed has been disclosed which no rhetoric can explain; a crime has been discovered which no mime can represent, nor jester play, nor comedian describe.

It is usual in the monasteries of Egypt and Syria for virgins and widows who have vowed themselves to God and have renounced the world and have trodden under foot its pleasures, to ask the mothers of their communities to cut their hair; not that afterwards they go about with heads uncovered in defiance of the apostle's command, for they wear a close-fitting cap and a veil. No one knows of this in any single case except the shearers and the shorn, but as the practice is universal, it is almost universally known. The custom has in fact become a second nature. It is designed to save those who take no baths and whose heads and faces are strangers to all unguents, from accumulated dirt and from the tiny creatures which are sometimes generated about the roots of the hair.

6. Let us see then, my good friend, how you acted in these surroundings. You promised to marry your unhappy victim; and then in that venerable cave you took from her, either as securities for her fidelity or as a pledge of the engagement, some locks of hair, some handkerchiefs, and a girdle, swearing at the same time that you would never love another as you loved her. Then you ran to the place where the shepherds were watching their flocks when they heard the angels singing over head, and there again you plighted your troth. I say no more; I do not accuse you of kissing her or of embracing her. Although I believe that there is nothing of which you are not capable, still the sacred character of stable and field forbids me to suppose you guilty except in will and determination. Unhappy man! When you first stood beside the virgin in the cave, surely a mist must have dimmed your eyes, your tongue must have been paralysed, your arms must have fallen to your sides, your chest must have heaved, your gait must have become unsteady. She had assumed the bridal-veil of Christ in the basilica of the apostle Peter and had vowed to live henceforth in the monastery, in the spots consecrated by the Lord's Cross, His Resurrection, and His Ascension; and yet after all this you dared to accept that hair, which at Christ's command she had cut off in the cave of His birth, as a token of her readiness to sleep with you. Again you used to sit beneath her window from the evening till the morning; and because owing to its height you could not come to close quarters with her, you conveyed things to her and she in her turn to you by the aid of a cord. How careful the lady superior must have been is shewn by the fact that you never saw the virgin except in church; and that, although both of you had the same inclination, you could find no means of conversing with each other except at a window under cover of night. As I was afterwards told you used to be quite sorry when the sun rose. Your face looked bloodless, shrunken, and pale; and to remove all suspicion, you used to be for ever reading Christ's gospel as if you were a deacon indeed. I and others used to attribute your paleness to fasting, and to admire your bloodless lips—so unlike the brilliant colour which they generally shewed—in the belief that they were caused by frequent vigils. You were already preparing ladders to fetch the unhappy virgin from her cell; you had already arranged your route, ordered vessels, settled a day, and thought out the details of your flight, when, behold, the angel who kept the door of Mary's chamber, who watched over the cradle of the Lord and who bore in his arms the infant Christ, in whose presence you had committed these great sins, himself and none other, betrayed you.

7. Oh! my unlucky eyes! Oh! day worthy of the most solemn curse, on which with utter consternation I read your letters, the contents of which I am forced to remember still! What obscenities they contained! What blandishments! What exultant triumph in the prospect of the virgin's dishonour. A deacon should not have even known such things, much less should he have spoken of them. Unhappy man! where can you have learned them, you who used to boast that you had been reared in the church. It is true, however, that in these letters you swear that you have never led a chaste life and that you are not really a deacon. If you try to disown them your own handwriting will convict you, and the very letters will cry out against you. But meantime you may make what you can of your sin, for what you have written is so foul that I cannot bring it up as evidence against you.

8. You threw yourself down at my knees, you prostrated yourself, you begged me—I use your own words—to spare "your half-pint of blood." Oh! miserable wretch! you thought nothing of God's judgment, and feared no vengeance but mine. I forgave you, I admit; what else being a Christian could I do? I urged you to repent, to wear sackcloth, to roll in ashes, to seek seclusion, to live in a monastery, to implore God's mercy with constant tears. You however showed yourself a pillar of confidence, and excited as you were by the viper's sting you became to me a deceitful bow; you shot at me arrows of reviling. I am become your enemy because I tell you the truth. I do not complain of your calumnies; everyone knows that you only praise men as infamous as yourself. What I lament is that you do not lament yourself, that you do not realize that you are dead, that, like a gladiator ready for Libitina, you deck yourself out for your own funeral. You wear not sackcloth but linen, you load your fingers with rings, you use toothpowder for your teeth, you arrange the stray hairs on your brown skull to the best advantage. Your bull's neck bulges out with fat and droops no whit because it has given way to lust. Moreover you are redolent of perfume, you go from one bath to another, you wage war against the hair that grows in spite of you, you walk through the forum and the streets a spruce and smooth-faced rake. Your face has become the face of a harlot: you know not how to blush. Return, unhappy man, to the Lord, and He will return to you. Repent, and He will repent of the evil that He has purposed to bring upon you.

9. Why is it that you disregard your own scars and try to defame others? Why is it that when I give you the best advice you attack me like a madman? It may be that I am as infamous as you publicly proclaim; in that case you can at least repent as heartily as I do. It may be that I am as great a sinner as you make me out; if so, you can at least imitate a sinner's tears. Are my sins your

virtues? Or does it alleviate your misery that many are in the same plight as yourself? Let a few tears fall on the silk and fine linen which make you so resplendent. Realize that you are naked, torn, unclean, a beggar. It is never too late to repent. You may have gone down from Jerusalem and may have been wounded on the way; yet the Samaritan will set you upon his beast, and will bring you to the inn and will take care of you. Even if you are lying in your grave, the Lord will raise you though your flesh may stink. At least imitate those blind men for whose sake the Saviour left His home and heritage and came to Jericho. They were sitting in darkness and in the shadow of death when the light shone upon them. For when they learned that it was the Lord who was passing by they began to cry out saying: "Thou Son of David, have mercy on us." You too will have your sight restored; if you cry to Him, and cast away your filthy garments at His call. "When thou shalt turn and bewail thyself then shalt thou be saved, and then shalt thou know where thou hast hitherto been." Let Him but touch your scars and pass his hands over your eyeballs; and although you may have been born blind from the womb and although your mother may have conceived you in sin, he will purge you with hyssop and you shall be clean, he will wash you and you shall be whiter than snow. Why is it that you are bowed together and bent down to the ground, why is it that you are still prostrate in the mire? She whom Satan had bound for eighteen years came to the Saviour; and being cured by Him was made straight so that she could once more look up towards heaven. God says to you what He said to Cain: "Thou hast sinned: hold thy peace." Why do you flee from the face of God and dwell in the land of Nod? Why do you struggle in the waves when you can plant your feet upon the rock? See to it that Phinehas does not thrust you through with his spear while you are committing fornication with the Midianitish woman. Amnon did not spare Tamar, and you her brother and kinsman in the faith have had no mercy upon this virgin. But why is it that when you have defiled her you change into an Absalom and desire to kill a David who mourns over your rebellion and spiritual death? The blood of Naboth cries out against you. The vineyard also of Jezreel, that is, of God's seed, demands due vengeance upon you, seeing that you have turned it into a garden of pleasures and made it a seed-bed of lust. God sends you an Elijah to tell you of torment and of death. Bow yourself down therefore and put on sackcloth for a little while; then perhaps the Lord will say of you what He said of Ahab: "Seest thou how Ahab humbleth himself before me? Because he humbleth himself before me, I will not bring the evil in his days."

10. But possibly you flatter yourself that since the bishop who has made you a deacon is a holy man, his merits will atone for your transgressions. I have

already told you that the father is not punished for the son nor the son for the father. "The soul that sinneth it shall die." Samuel too had sons who forsook the fear of the Lord and "turned aside after lucre" and iniquity. Eli also was a holy priest, but he had sons of whom we read in the Hebrew that they lay with the women that assembled at the door of the tabernacle of God, and that like you they shamelessly claimed for themselves the right to minister in His sanctuary. Wherefore the tabernacle itself was overthrown and the holy place made desolate by reason of the sins of those who were God's priests. And even Eli himself offended God by shewing too great leniency to his sons; therefore, so far from the righteousness of your bishop being able to deliver you, it is rather to be feared that your wickedness may hurl him from his seat and that falling on his back like Eli he may perish irretrievably. If the Levite Uzzah was smitten merely because he tried to hold up from falling the ark which it was his special province to carry; what punishment, think you, will be inflicted upon you who have tried to overthrow the Lord's ark when standing firm? The more estimable the bishop is who ordained you, the more detestable are you who have disappointed the expectations of so good a man. His long ignorance of your misdoings is indeed easy to account for; as it generally happens that we are the last to know the scandals which affect our homes, and are ignorant of the sins of our children and wives even when our neighbors talk of nothing else. At all events all Italy was aware of your evil life; and it was everywhere a subject of lamentation that you should still stand before the altar of Christ. For you had neither the cunning nor the forethought to conceal your vices. So hot were you, so lecherous, and so wanton, so entirely under the sway of this and that caprice of self-indulgence, that, not content with satisfying your passions, you gloried in each intrigue as a triumph and emerged from it bearing palms of victory.

11. Once more the fire of unchastity seized you, this time among savage swords and in the quarters of a married barbarian of great influence and power. You were not afraid to commit adultery in a house where the injured husband might have punished you without calling in a judge's aid. You found yourself attracted and drawn to suburban parks and gardens; and, in the husband's absence behaved as boldly and madly as if you supposed your companion to be not your paramour but your wife. She was at last captured, but you escaped through an underground passage and secretly made your way to Rome. There you hid yourself among some Samnite robbers; and on the first hint that the aggrieved husband was coming down from the Alps like a new Hannibal in search of you, you did not think yourself safe till you had taken refuge on shipboard. So hasty indeed was your flight that you chose to face a tempest at

sea rather than take the consequences of remaining on shore. Somehow or other you reached Syria, and on arriving there professed a wish to go on to Jerusalem and there to serve the Lord. Who could refuse to welcome one who declared himself to be a monk; especially if he were ignorant of your tragical career and had read the letters of commendation which your bishop had addressed to other prelates? Unhappy man! you transformed yourself into an angel of light; and while you were in reality a minister of Satan, you pretended to be a minister of righteousness. You were only a wolf in sheep's clothing; and having played the adulterer once towards the wife of a man, you desired now to play the adulterer to the spouse of Christ.

12. My design in recounting these events has been to sketch for you the picture of your evil life and to set your misdeeds plainly before your eyes. I have wished to prevent you from making God's mercy and His abundant tenderness an excuse for committing new sins and to save you from crucifying to yourself the son of God afresh and putting Him to an open shame. For you may do these things if you do not read the words which follow the passage to which I have alluded. They are these: "The earth which drinketh in the rain that cometh oft upon it, and bringeth forth herbs meet for them by whom it is dressed, receiveth blessings from God: but that which beareth thorns and briers is rejected and is nigh unto cursing; whose end is to be burned."

LETTER CXLVIII. TO THE MATRON CELANTIA

This is an interesting letter addressed to a lady of rank, on the principles and methods of a holy life. It is not, however, the work of Jerome, of whose style it shews few traces. It has been ascribed in turn to Paulinus of Nola and Sulpicius Severus.

LETTER CXLIX. ON THE JEWISH FESTIVALS

The theme of this letter is the abrogation of the Jewish festivals by the evangelical law. It has no claim to be considered a work of Jerome.

LETTER CL. FROM PROCOPIUS TO JEROME

This letter is extant also among those of Procopius of Gaza, to whose works it properly belongs. As this Procopius flourished a century later than Jerome, the letter cannot be addressed to him.

Printed in Great Britain
by Amazon

38795649R00284